HASKALAH AND HISTORY

THE LITTMAN LIBRARY OF
JEWISH CIVILIZATION

MANAGING EDITOR
Connie Webber

Dedicated to the memory of
LOUIS THOMAS SIDNEY LITTMAN
who founded the Littman Library
for the love of God
and in memory of his father
JOSEPH AARON LITTMAN
יהא זכרם ברוך

'*Get wisdom, get understanding:*
Forsake her not and she shall preserve thee'
PROV. 4: 5

The Littman Library of Jewish Civilization is a registered UK charity
Registered charity no. 1000784

HASKALAH AND HISTORY

◆

*The Emergence of a Modern
Jewish Historical Consciousness*

◆

SHMUEL FEINER

Translated by
CHAYA NAOR AND SONDRA SILVERSTON

Oxford · Portland, Oregon
The Littman Library of Jewish Civilization

The Littman Library of Jewish Civilization
Chief Executive Officer: Ludo Craddock

PO Box 645, Oxford OX2 0UJ, UK

Published in the United States and Canada by
The Littman Library of Jewish Civilization
c/o ISBS, 920 N.E. 58th Avenue, Suite 300
Portland, Oregon 97213-3786

First published 2002
First issued in paperback 2004

A catalogue record for this book is available from the British Library

The Library of Congress catalogued the hardback edition as follows:
Feiner Shmuel.
[Haskalah ve-historyah. English]
Haskalah and history : the emergence of a modern Jewish historical consciousness /
Shmuel Feiner; translated by Chaya Naor and Sondra Silverston.
p. cm.
1. Jews—Historiography.   2. Haskalah—History   3. Jewish learning and
scholarship—History—19th century.   I. Title.
DS115.5 F4513 2001   909'.04924'0072—dc21   2001041
ISBN 1-904113-10-9

Publishing co-ordinator: Janet Moth
Design: Pete Russell, Faringdon, Oxon.
Copy-editing: Lindsey Taylor-Guthartz
Index: Bonnie Blackburn
Production manager: John Saunders
Typeset by Footnote Graphics, Warminster, Wilts.
Printed in Great Britain on acid-free paper by
Biddles Ltd., Kings Lynn. www.biddles.co.uk

Preface

THE Enlightenment made a greater contribution than any other movement in intellectual history to the multifaceted and often discordant modernization of the Jews. It provided seventeenth- and eighteenth-century European thinkers with critical and secular tools, which were employed by some to formulate a doctrine of religious tolerance that paved the way for the Jewish exodus from the ghetto. Yet, paradoxically, other thinkers used the teachings of the Enlightenment to marshal secular rationalist arguments justifying the vilification of the Jews and Judaism and the denial of their political and civil rights. In the Jewish world, the Enlightenment ethos of criticism and freedom of thought created a compelling atmosphere of challenge that produced new forms of literature and thought, as well as new social and cultural utopias. At the same time, however, this ethos was perceived as a threat and was resisted by the advocates of tradition with a defensive Orthodox stance.

The Jewish version of the Enlightenment served as an impetus for the formation of circles of maskilim, members of the new Jewish intellectual élite that emerged during the eighteenth century. Judged on the basis of their acculturation, openness to European society, and adoption of new lifestyles, the maskilim were not the first modern Jews in Europe. They were, however, unquestionably the first who were conscious of being modern Jews, and the first to advocate a modernist, transformational ideology. These maskilim, the first to discover the 'modern age' and to make it a hallmark of their historical consciousness, are the heroes of this book. Its subject is the encounter between Clio, muse of history, and Minerva, goddess of wisdom and the symbol of enlightenment, and its plot re-creates the shifts in historical consciousness that underpin the ideology of the Haskalah.

As a historian who was born and bred in the State of Israel and is sensitive to the conflicts that pervade its society and culture, in particular to the clash of cultures currently raging within it, I have been particularly intrigued by the issue of enlightenment and by complex and contradictory attitudes towards the past. In the rhetoric and self-consciousness of the Israeli cultural conflict, the words 'enlightenment' and 'Haskalah' are regarded as derogatory terms by the Orthodox and anti-modernist camp, while they represent the bedrock of universal, secular openness to the liberals. In recent years, interest in the collective Jewish and Israeli historical memory has been deepening. The linchpins of traditional historical consciousness, as well as national and Zionist myths, are being re-examined in lively public debates that extend far beyond the ivory tower of scholarly research. The topical and political significance of these controversies has taken them outside the exclusive province of professional historians. The question of the legacy of the Haskalah is particularly crucial in the post-modern cultural climate, on one hand, and in the face of the growing strength of the fundamentalist position, on the other. Concepts and values such as rationalism, progress, freedom, equality, tolerance, moral education, and universal humanism—basic products of the culture of enlightenment—are being increasingly portrayed in a sceptical light and stripped of their validity. This is being done either in the name of relativism, which deconstructs absolute values, and the collapse of the great ideologies, or by means of the categorization of these concepts as ostensibly contrary to religious values.

My purpose here is to contribute to an understanding of the period that witnessed the emergence of a modernist mentality, the adoption of the ethos of enlightenment, and the formation of a new historical consciousness. It was in the 1780s that the highly optimistic maskilim first discovered the emerging light of the 'modern age', inspiring them to formulate the ethos of modernity, which they projected back into universal and Jewish history in order to invent an alternative Jewish tradition that promised a glowing future. From that moment the foundations were laid for a diversity of historical interpretations in the reviving Jewish culture. How and for what purpose was history recruited? How did the struggle against hasidism influence the development of rationalist maskilic history? What characterized the 'secondary', more popular track in historiography and its dissemination among the general population represented by the maskilim (a large historiographical corpus which has hitherto been ignored by scholars)? What transformations did maskilic historical consciousness undergo from the era of Mendelssohn in Germany to the birth of modern nationalism in eastern Europe in the final third of the nineteenth century? These are a few of the questions examined in this book, which focuses on one extremely influential instance of an ideological interpretation of history by Jews, and through it attempts to illuminate the Haskalah movement from a novel perspective.

*

The Hebrew edition of this book was published by the Zalman Shazar Centre in Jerusalem in 1995. Many changes and additions were made in preparing the English edition, and much effort has been invested to make the book accessible to the general reader as well as to specialists.

Although most of the book was written in the resonant silence of the reading room of the National Library in Jerusalem and drew upon that library's vast and invaluable treasures, no book is really written in splendid intellectual isolation. Many teachers, colleagues, and friends in Israel, the United States, and Europe played a part in it, and I should like to express my appreciation to them. My teachers in the 1980s at the Hebrew University, including Immanuel Etkes, Israel

Bartal, the late Shmuel Ettinger, the late Jacob Talmon, Joshua Arieli, Michael Graetz, and Michael Heyd are also the spiritual fathers of *Haskalah and History*. For many years members of the community of Haskalah scholars, in particular Shmuel Werses of the Hebrew University, Michael Meyer of Hebrew Union College in Cincinnati, and David Sorkin of Madison, Wisconsin, have been engaged in continuous debate with me, and their various comments and insights, as well as their encouragement, have greatly helped to improve the book. Throughout the last decade the Department of Jewish History at Bar-Ilan University has been the home providing me with the conditions and intellectual atmosphere essential to my historical research. The favourable reviews of the Hebrew edition by Zohar Shavit of Tel Aviv University, Michael Brenner of Munich University, and Michael Stanislawski of Columbia University encouraged me to embark on the lengthy process of publishing an English translation. Zevi Yekutieli, director of the Zalman Shazar publishing house, encouraged me to persevere, as did the evaluations by Joseph Kaplan, Isaiah Gafni, and Jonathan Frankel, who found my book worthy of the Hebrew University's Arnold Wiznitzer Prize for the best book on Jewish history published in 1995. I owe special thanks to Ya'akov Shavit of Tel Aviv University, both as a friend and as a historian; he made me aware of the importance of translation and kindly put me in touch with the Littman Library of Jewish Civilization. Without his unflagging interest and involvement this project would certainly not have reached a successful conclusion.

I should also like to thank the staff of the Littman Library for having chosen to publish this book, and for their devoted work. I am particularly grateful to Connie Webber, managing editor, for having personally followed up all the stages of the book's preparation over several years, with much dedication and warmth; to Ludo Craddock, director of marketing and administration, and to the copy-editor, Lindsey Taylor-Guthartz, all of whom worked tirelessly to publish the book, adhering to the Littman Library's high standards, with no compromises or short cuts. I greatly appreciate the painstaking and meticulous work of the translators, Chaya Naor and Sondra Silverston, who spent much time on a particularly difficult book, and succeeded in solving some rather complex problems, especially in the translation of eighteenth- and nineteenth-century maskilic texts in Hebrew, very few of which had ever been translated into another language. My research assistant Sarit Marmorstein was very helpful in preparing the bibliography and the notes. My thanks to all of them!

I received generous grants for the preparation of the book from the Samuel Braun Chair for History of the Jews in Prussia, Bar-Ilan University, directed by Zevi Bacharach; from the Bar-Ilan University Research Authority at the recommendation of the rector, Yehuda Friedlander; from the Institute for the Study of Polish Jewry, Hebrew University of Jerusalem, under the direction of Israel Bartal; and from the Koret Jewish Publication Program, in the United States, and its

deputy director, Sandra J. Edwards. I am indebted to them all; without their
assistance, the publication of this book would not have been possible.

I should like to dedicate this book with love to my wife, Rivka-Sharon, and to
our five beloved children, Merav-Hadas, Avital-Batya, Adi-Tamar, Noam-Yoel,
and Michal-Alona.

Jerusalem   S.F.
2000

Contents

Note on Transliteration and Conventions Used in the Text

THE transliteration of Hebrew in this book reflects a consideration of the type of book it is, in terms of its content, purpose, and readership. The system adopted therefore reflects a broad approach to transcription, rather than the narrower approaches found in the *Encyclopaedia Judaica* or other systems developed for text-based or linguistic studies. The aim has been to reflect the pronunciation prescribed for modern Hebrew, rather than the spelling or Hebrew word structure, and to do so using conventions that are generally familiar to the English-speaking Jewish reader,

In accordance with this approach, no attempt is made to indicate the distinctions between *alef* and *ayin*, *tet* and *taf*, *kaf* and *kuf*, *sin* and *samekh*, since these are not relevant to pronunciation; likewise, the *dagesh* is not indicated except where it affects pronunciation. Following the principle of using conventions familiar to the majority of readers, however, transcriptions that are well established have been retained even when they are not fully consistent with the transliteration system adopted. On similar grounds, the *tsadi* is rendered by 'tz' in such familiar words as barmitzvah, mitzvot, and so on. Likewise, the distinction between *het* and *khaf* has been retained, using *h* for the former and *kh* for the latter; the associated forms are generally familiar to readers, even if the distinction is not actually borne out in pronunciation, and for the same reason the final *heh* is indicated too. As in Hebrew, no capital letters are used, except that an initial capital has been retained in transliterating titles of published works (for example, *Shulhan arukh*).

Since no distinction is made between *alef* and *ayin*, they are indicated by an apostrophe only in intervocalic positions where a failure to do so could lead an English-speaking reader to pronounce the vowel-cluster as a diphthong—as, for example, in *ha'ir*—or otherwise mispronounce the word.

The *sheva na* in indicated by an *e*—*perikat ol*, *reshut*—except, again, when established convention dictates otherwise.

The *yod* is represented by an *i* when it occurs as a vowel (*bereshit*), by a *y* when it occurs as a consonant (*yesodot*), and by *yi* when it occurs as both (*yisra'el*).

Names have generally been left in their familiar forms, even when this is inconsistent with the overall system, and *het* has been represented by an ordinary 'h' in proper names of people and institutions appearing in the text.

Thanks are due to Jonathan Webber of the Oxford Centre for Hebrew and Jewish Studies for his help in elucidating the principles to be adopted.

INTRODUCTION

'Haskalah' and 'History'

> What man with a heart in his breast does not sigh over the lowly status of our people? . . . so that we may know what we are capable of doing, we will turn our eyes to the chronicles of the ancients to learn the course of time and the actions of the men who lived then, their ways, and their qualities . . . through this observation we will be shown the path we must take, after comparing era to era and man to man and class to class.
>
> J. S. BICK, 'El maskilei benei ami'

EVERY social, cultural, and political trend that has developed in modern Jewish history has been accompanied by a distinctive sense of the past, which supports the collective identity, ideology, and activity of its advocates and justifies them to themselves, contemporary Jewish society, and history. Nearly every new ideology seems to have been formulated as a historical schema, combing the past in order to select figures worthy of serving as heroes and to construct a range of supportive historical myths. However, each movement's picture of history attests less to the past *per se* than to the character, aspirations, and wishes of those who created and employed it. The test case chosen for this book is the Jewish Haskalah of the eighteenth and nineteenth centuries—the first modern ideology in Jewish history, which appeared at the threshold of the modern era and was promulgated by the maskilim—the first Jews who were conscious of being modern, and who concluded that the modern age called for a comprehensive programme of change in both the cultural and the practical life of Jewish society. What was the nature of the 'history' that the maskilim created, what tactics did they use, and what were the objectives for which they recruited this 'history'? These are a few of the questions that emerge from this encounter between 'Haskalah' and 'history'.

The modernization of Europe was accompanied by an upsurge of interest in the past and an ideological and scholarly preoccupation with history. Signs of the modern sense of history include changes in the attitude towards the past and its re-evaluation; a critical approach to the sources, which had hitherto been regarded as incontrovertibly authoritative; the secularization of history; the break with traditional theological modes of historical thought; and the use of history to serve modern social and political ideologies.[1] It is no longer possible to assert

---

[1] See, among others, Kelly, *Foundations of Modern History*; Burke, *The Renaissance Sense of the Past*; Hay, *Annalists and Historians*; Funkenstein, 'Continuity and Renewal', 105–31; C. Becker, *The Heavenly City*; Talmon, *Political Messianism*, 9–10; Rotenstreich, *Jewish Philosophy*, 9–20; id., *Jewish Existence*.

that the flowering of history can be entirely credited to the nineteenth century—during which, it used to be claimed, the historical world was discovered, scientific historiography was crystallized and institutionalized in academic settings, the concept of history was shaped, and the idealistic philosophy of history was formulated. Study of the annals of European historiography has shown that this was a gradual process that began with the 'historical revolution' of the fifteenth and sixteenth centuries, and has also demonstrated that the image of the eighteenth-century philosophers as ahistorical or anti-historical needs to be corrected. Nowadays the contribution of the European Enlightenment to the new historiography and to modern historical thought is no longer open to doubt.

Scholars studying the development of European historiography have investigated the historical writings of Voltaire, Montesquieu, Hume, Gibbon, Herder, Schlözer, Gatterer, and others.[2] H. Butterfield has pointed to the philological and historical achievements of historians from the University of Göttingen in northern Germany, and to their importance in providing the basis and groundwork for Ranke's school of history.[3] P. Reill has devoted a detailed study to proving the link between the Enlightenment and the study of history in eighteenth-century Germany, and the rise of historicism in that century.[4] These and other studies have revealed the innovations in the historiography of the Enlightenment, which offered a new interpretation of universal history, new historical explanations, a new division of history into periods, and a broader historical spectrum, opening the way for the description of spheres of human creativity beyond politics and biography, as well as new geographical vistas.[5] J. B. Bury, Ernst Cassirer, Isaiah Berlin, K. Löwith, and Yirmiyahu Yovel have studied the philosophical thinking of intellectuals such as Lessing, Herder, and Kant on history, while Carl Becker and Peter Gay place particular stress on the Enlightenment's picture of the past and the ways in which its scholars exploited the historical past.[6] Yehoshua Arieli's recent studies have emphasized the revolutionary character of the Enlightenment's perception of the past and its secularizing tendency.[7] Nearly every definitive work on the history of the European Enlightenment, such as those of N. Hampson or of H. Möller, contains a lengthy chapter devoted to the Enlightenment's attitude to history.[8] An article by J. Kocka emphasizes that one of the most definite conclusions of contemporary research is that history was central to the eighteenth-century German Enlightenment.[9]

[2] Thompson, *A History of Historical Writing*, vol. i; Stromberg, 'History in the Eighteenth Century', 295–304; Bury, *The Idea of Progress*; Iggers, *New Directions*, 3–20.

[3] Butterfield, *Man on his Past*, 32–61.

[4] Reill, *The German Enlightenment and the Rise of Historicism*.   [5] Arieli, 'New Horizons', 145–68.

[6] Cassirer, *The Philosophy of the Enlightenment*; Löwith, *Meaning in History*; Gay, *The Enlightenment*, vol. i; Yovel, *Kant and the Philosophy of History*; I. Berlin, *Vico and Herder*.

[7] Arieli, 'The Modern Age and the Problem of Secularization', 165–216; Chadwick, *The Secularization of the European Mind*, 189–228.

[8] Hampson, *The Enlightenment*, 232–50; Möller, *Vernunft und Kritik*, 144–89.

[9] Kocka, *Geschichte und Aufklärung*, 140–59.

On the other hand, for years historians of the Haskalah movement have almost completely ignored the attitude of the maskilim to history. The absence of any outstanding historians or comprehensive and well-formulated historiographical works until the third decade of the nineteenth century, when the works of Marcus Jost appeared, unquestionably contributed to the assertion that the maskilim had no interest in the historical past. Many scholars have quoted Moses Mendelssohn's remark 'I always yawn when I have to read something historical' as irrefutable evidence of the maskilim's lack of interest in history. It was used by Perez Smolenskin, a prominent maskil in the 1860s and 1870s, in his attack on Mendelssohn and the Berlin Haskalah, as proof that they were cut off from Jewish national roots; and it was quoted on numerous other occasions as proof of the maskilim's indifference to the Jewish past.[10] Simon Dubnow, the Russian Jewish historian, noted the first awakening of a 'historical feeling' among modern Jewry in the Wissenschaft des Judentums movement in western Europe from the 1820s onwards. He regarded Leopold Zunz, Solomon Judah Rapoport (Shir), Adolf Jellinek, Marcus Jost, and Samuel David Luzzato as the pioneers of the new historiography. In his view, no real interest in uncovering the secrets of Jewish history awoke until the end of the nineteenth century: 'We were like the blacks, like savages in the wilderness who have no history at all, like gypsies whose entire lives are in the present, without any future and past';[11] and Simon Bernfeld, in one of the first surveys of the development of Jewish historiography, thought it obvious that the eighteenth-century maskilim were incapable of reviving Jewish historical writing:

It is self-evident that this generation, which found its satisfaction in Hebrew imitations of the poetry of Gessner and the like, would not have been capable of rebuilding the structure of Jewish history; and, moreover, no historical research ever emanated from the school of Mendelssohn. On the contrary, he denigrated its importance and never found anything [of value] in it. And consequently his 'disciples' . . . were given no guidance in this regard, and the knowledge of history vanished from our people until the revival of Jewish sciences in the early twenties of the present century.[12]

Later historians, like Ben-Zion Dinur, claimed that the emphasis on critical reason in the Haskalah's world-view made it impossible to develop a historical approach, since there was no concept of historical continuity. The Haskalah actually drew its strength from a revolt against the past: 'It was anti-historical in its attitude towards the past but believed in the future and in progress, and the more critical it became towards the past, the greater was its faith in the future.'[13] Raphael Mahler cited the element of cosmopolitanism inherent in the Haskalah

---

[10] Mendelssohn, *Gesammelte Schriften*, 342–3; Wiener, *Jüdische Religion*, 70–3; Berney, 'Historical and Political Conceptions', 99–111, 248–70; Smolenskin, 'Et lata'at', 221–2.

[11] Dubnow, 'Nahpesah venahkorah', 226.   [12] Bernfeld, 'Dorshei reshumot', 203.

[13] Dinur, *At the Turn of the Generations*, 231–354. See also H. H. Ben-Sasson, *Continuity and Variety*, 35–6.

as an explanation for its ahistorical view: the movement tried to perform an impossible leap from feudalism to cosmopolitan rationalism, it 'betrayed' national historical continuity, and like every European stream of rationalism, it lacked a historical sense. Mahler combined the approach that denies the maskilim a historical sense, owing to their over-zealous rationalism, with an approach that regarded the Haskalah and its values as a departure from Jewish nationalism in favour of universal ideals.[14]

Most historians of modern Hebrew literature, who until recently took the lead in the study of the Haskalah, hold similar views. Pinhas Lachower, for example, has emphasized the Haskalah's deviation from the continuum of historical Judaism, although he does ascribe this radical trend solely to the Berlin maskilim, while in the Galician Haskalah 'historical criticism' had already begun to flourish in the early nineteenth century. Only then did the Jewish people regain a 'special history', which, in his view, the Berlin maskilim tried to gloss over.[15] Israel Zinberg has been even harsher in his criticism of the maskilim. He has accused them of deliberately cutting themselves off from the Jewish past and regards them as members of a typically anti-historical period, lacking any historical perspective or 'sense of historical evolution'. In his view, the new world of the Haskalah was dominated by abstract concepts; man was not conceived in his real condition as someone living in 'a certain defined social-historical environment . . . but rather the abstract concept of man, without a past, without tradition, without any inherited superstitions, outside place and time'.[16]

However, the attraction felt by many maskilim to the biblical past of the Jewish people has not been overlooked by scholars, who have found evidence of this trend in the works of Naphtali Herz Wessely (*Shirei tiferet*, Songs of Glory), Shalom Hacohen (*Nir david*, The Splendour of David), Joseph Ha'efrati (*Melukhat sha'ul*, The Kingdom of Saul), and of course of Abraham Mapu (*Ahavat tsiyon*, The Love of Zion; *Ashmat shomron*, The Guilt of Samaria). It has also been noted and stressed by those studying the roots of biblical criticism, who tend to view the biblical commentary written by Moses Mendelssohn and his colleagues as its starting-point. On the basis of these views, the maskilim's attitude towards the historical past (if they had one at all) has been regarded as having only one dimension: the tendency to glorify the biblical past, which has often been anachronistically interpreted as an expression of nationalistic trends.[17] The one exception is Shmuel Werses's comprehensive study of the Haskalah's atti-

---

[14] Mahler, *History of the Jewish People*, i. 81–2.

[15] Lahover, *History of Modern Hebrew Literature*, i. 52, ii. 4–5.

[16] Zinberg, *A History of Jewish Literature*, v. 40–1, 58–61, 84–5.

[17] On the tendency of Haskalah literature to draw on the biblical past, see J. Klausner, *History of Modern Hebrew Literature*, vol. i; Zinberg, *A History of Jewish Literature*, vol. v; Sha'anan, *The New Hebrew Literature*, chs. 1–2; T. Cohen, *From Dream to Reality*; Sandler, *Mendelssohn's Edition*; Shelly, *The Study of the Bible*; Almog, *Zionism and History*, 13; Kleinman, *Figures and Ages*, 31; Barzilay, 'National and Anti-National Trends', 165–92; id., 'The Ideology of the Berlin Haskalah', 1–37.

tude towards kabbalah, Shabbateanism, and Frankism, which he investigated as an important historical and literary issue in its own right.[18]

Reuven Michael made the first attempt to integrate the works of some maskilim into the mainstream of a new Jewish historiography. He strove to pinpoint the beginnings of historical writing and stated that, although this could not be placed before Jost's work, the first buds had already appeared in *Hame'asef*, in the Prague circle of maskilim, and in the periodical *Shulamit*, albeit at a relatively immature level. In any case, the stress in Michael's study was on the maskilic contribution to historiography, and he concluded that, as a rule, the maskilim's awareness of history was relegated to the sidelines and that 'the intellectual efforts of the maskilim were not directed towards the domain of historiography'.[19]

New surveys of the history of Jewish historical writing and thought continue to minimize the contribution of the maskilim to this field, and repeat the claim that the Haskalah had but a vague sense of the importance of historical knowledge: 'The Haskalah itself did not develop a concept of history fundamentally different from those that had prevailed earlier.' The Haskalah's approach is regarded as as apologetic as that of the sixteenth century, and the role of expropriating Jewish historiography from the hands of Christian historians such as Jacques Basnage, the French Huguenot, has been attributed not to maskilim but to the scholars of the Wissenschaft des Judentums in the early nineteenth century.[20]

In this book I am not concerned with assessing the achievements of the maskilim in writing history, and I definitely have no intention of judging the Haskalah as a 'historical', 'anti-historical', or 'ahistorical' movement. In my opinion, 'criticism of the past', which Dinur and others have cited as evidence of the lack of a historical approach, was in fact one of the important characteristics of the maskilic sense of the past, and thus merits study and analysis. It seems that those who have applied strict historicist criteria to the Haskalah's attitude to history, choosing to ignore 'low' manifestations of historical writing; those who have tended to view the return to historiography in Jewish history as a monopoly of the modern national trend; and those who believe one cannot speak of a new sense of the past in the absence of the development of a professional historiographical science have also found it difficult to recognize the distinguishing features of the maskilic sense of the past.

I have examined a range of sources from the 100-year period of the Haskalah (1782–1881), which show not only that the maskilim displayed a great interest

[18] Werses, *Haskalah and Shabbateanism*. The 'practical past' and the 'historical repertoire' of the maskilim was also recently discussed, focusing on the cultural encounter between Judaism and Hellenism, in Y. Shavit, *Athens in Jerusalem*.

[19] Michael, 'The Renewal of Interest', 1–19. Michael's *Jewish Historiography* has recently been published; it contains a comprehensive and detailed survey of the history of Jewish historiography, including a chapter devoted to the Haskalah period (pp. 90–159). See also Tsamriyon, 'The Promotion of Culture and Education', 5–50.

[20] Kochan, *The Jew and his History*, 64; Yerushalmi, *Zakhor*, 81–3.

in history, but also that their attitude to the past was significant both for the Haskalah's ideology and for the development of Jewish historical consciousness. This conclusion gave rise to three fundamental questions, which lie at the centre of this book:

1. What are the elements, principles, and concepts relating to 'history' that appear in the works created by the Haskalah in its formative stages (the German Haskalah and its branches at the end of the eighteenth century); and to what extent were the maskilim who adhered to them alienated from the traditional sense of the past even before the emergence of the Wissenschaft des Judentums?

2. How was the historical past used in the historical framework of the Haskalah movement, and what objectives did it serve? This question removes the discussion of the sense of the past from the ideological plane, connects it to the entire socio-cultural fabric of the Haskalah—its struggles, values, controversies, its searches for direction, and its transformations—and examines how 'history' actually functioned in the world of the Haskalah and what purposes it served.

3. How was the sense of the past of the maskilim in eastern Europe (Galicia and Russia) shaped and crystallized? This enquiry includes such factors as links to the formative stage of the Haskalah; the mixed reception, enthusiastic and critical by turns, of the mainly German Wissenschaft des Judentums movement; constant attentiveness to contemporary political and cultural changes; and the varied nature of the circles of maskilim themselves throughout the nineteenth century.

A study attempting to answer these questions calls for several preliminary considerations. First, a 'sense of the past', as I employ the term here, has a very broad meaning. Dinur's definition seemed a useful one; according to him, all historical knowledge entails historical awareness, and everything recorded about the past throughout the ages—whether in critical historiography, in historical legends and myths, or in historical interpretation—can serve as a source from which we can learn about a sense of the past.[21] 'Our interest', Dinur wrote, 'lies not in the "past" in and of itself, but in the knowledge of it, in the memory retained of it, in the image shaped by the generations, in the records of the past, and in the memory of the generations to come, which in their very essence are the "sense of the past" in the consciousness of the people.'[22] Everything written about history within the framework of the Haskalah movement can serve as a source from which we can reconstruct and analyse the maskilic sense of the past: translations and adaptations of history books, historical stories and poems, historical biographies, historical explanations, and examples from the past combined with journalistic essays, and, of course, original historical studies.

[21] Dinur, 'The Awareness of the Past', 9–24.   [22] Ibid. 11.

I have also been influenced by Peter Gay, who, in his exhaustive work on the eighteenth-century European Enlightenment, found that its attitude towards history provides a major key to understanding the movement's world-view. The historians of the Enlightenment, Gay wrote, looked into the past as into a mirror, drawing from history a past they could use. In this sense, the value of their historical research is indeed limited, but their attitude towards history is invaluable in giving us an understanding of the Enlightenment itself: 'it permits us to look over the philosophers' shoulders to discover in their historical portraits a portrait of themselves'.[23] In the Haskalah the sense of the past functioned as a 'topical field of polemic between the generations' and was employed for ideological, propaganda, apologetic, and other purposes. Thus even historical fiction written by the maskilim is valuable.[24] I propose to examine the ways in which history was used by the maskilim as they viewed the present through the past and introduced an active 'presence' of the past in the present.

I have no intention of concentrating on a discussion of prominent historians, nor of collecting ideas that add up to a philosophy of history. Rather, I propose to discuss the collective sense of the past of the maskilic circles, which, in my view, was one of the most important elements in their collective social and cultural character.

To a certain extent, I have tried to adopt several of Robert Darnton's suggestions and apply them to my study of the Haskalah, from the vantage-point of the social history of ideas. In particular, I found them useful in turning aside from the classical and prominent maskilim in order to look at a 'lower' culture, namely, writers of the second or third level and popular sources.[25] By shining the spotlight of research not only on Mendelssohn, Wessely, Rapoport, and Nahman Krochmal (Ranak), but also on secondary and even unknown maskilim (such as Shimon Baraz, Samuel Resser, Yehoshua Levinsohn, Mikhel Gordon, and others who served as agents and sub-agents of Haskalah propaganda), as well as considering second- and third-hand translated and adapted historical literature (such as the works of Mordecai Aaron Guenzburg, Kalman Schulman, and others) and scores of historical articles in contemporary journals, I believe we can discern the outlines of a secondary, more popular Jewish sense of the past. The contrast between this sense of the past and the achievements of scholars affiliated with the Wissenschaft des Judentums in the same period is particularly striking. I shall also try to trace attempts at popularization by maskilim, made in order to introduce the Haskalah's sense of the past to lower social groups, which were far from identifying with the maskilim.

[23] Gay, *The Enlightenment*, i. 32.

[24] Rotenstreich, *Jewish Existence*, 30. Cf. C. Becker, *The Heavenly City*, 21; Funkenstein, *Perceptions of Jewish History*, 3–21.

[25] Darnton, 'In Search of the Enlightenment', 113–32; Scott (ed.), *Enlightened Absolutism*, 1–15; Porter, *The Enlightenment*, 42–50; Jacob, *Living the Enlightenment*, 215–24.

I shall use the term 'maskilic history' in this book to mean the historical consciousness of the Jews affiliated with the Haskalah. 'Maskilic history', as I will
try to show, was distinct from the 'traditional' or pre-modern history that preceded it, moved on a separate path alongside the Wissenschaft des Judentums
(alternately absorbed and criticized by the maskilim) in the nineteenth century,
and differed from the 'nationalistic history' that emerged at the end of the nineteenth century. 'Maskilic history' encompassed several variations, but its link to
the maskilic group it served was always preserved. It is worth noting that 'maskilic
history' also endured in the nineteenth century well beyond the time of the
European Enlightenment, thanks to the continuation of the Haskalah movement
in eastern Europe at least until the 1890s.

Thus 'maskilic history', an abstract concept which is a product of the historian's
retrospective view, becomes a living historical entity whose development the historian attempts to reconstruct. This entity was in fact an exclusively ideological
product, usually a fictional one, of maskilic beliefs, maskilic mentality, and hopes
and images of the future, but it also possessed a historical life of its own and may
be traced from its birth, through its adolescence, its shifts in various directions,
and up to its demise. This book thus attempts to unfold the annals of 'maskilic
history' and the story of the earliest modern Jewish sense of the past, beginning
in the 1780s with the formation of the first circles of maskilim and carrying on
until the end of the 1870s, when the Haskalah began to relinquish its place to
other social movements and ideological trends.

ONE

From Traditional History to Maskilic History in Late Eighteenth-Century Germany

AN ENLIGHTENED AVANT-GARDE

A MODERN historical consciousness awoke among the Jews in Germany even before the new Jewish historiography crystallized in the nineteenth century, and before the Wissenschaft des Judentums movement formulated and shaped its concepts of scientific study. In terms of the history of ideas, this early break with the traditional sense of the past means that the focus must be shifted somewhat from the era of nineteenth-century historicism, idealism, and romanticism to the eighteenth-century era of rationalism and enlightenment. In terms of Jewish social and cultural history, the focus shifts from the circle of young intellectuals and academics who laid the foundations for the Wissenschaft des Judentums in the second and third decades of the nineteenth century to the circles of Jewish maskilim in Germany in the 1780s and 1790s.[1]

The maskilim were a very small group. The central core of maskilim (taking into account only the creative activists, not those who merely supported or identified with them) never numbered more than 200 throughout Germany and outside it. These were young Jewish intellectuals, most of them in their thirties, who had a two-layered culture. One was the Jewish Torah-oriented culture, which they acquired mainly through traditional education; the other was the European culture of the Enlightenment, which most of the maskilim acquired by studying on their own. They were employed in relatively marginal occupations, as tutors and clerks, and were almost wholly dependent on their employers—wealthy men from the Jewish economic élite. It was they who ensured the maskilim's legal right to residence and served as patrons of their literary activities. The group was concentrated mainly in Königsberg, Breslau, and Berlin, in the Kingdom of Prussia, and centred on a number of focal points: Moses Mendelssohn's 'court' in Berlin;

[1] On the beginnings of Wissenschaft des Judentums, see Glatzer, 'The Beginnings of Modern Jewish Studies', 135–49; Schorsch, 'The Emergence of Historical Consciousness', 413–37; Meyer, 'The Emergence of Modern Jewish Historiography', 160–75; Mendes-Flohr (ed.), *Modern Jewish Studies*.

the Hinukh Ne'arim (Freischule) school and its Hebrew printing-house there, the Orientalische Buchdruckerei; the journal *Hame'asef*; and the reading society Hevrat Dorshei Leshon Ever (Promoters of the Hebrew Language), founded in Königsberg.[2] In 1787 a supra-community organizational framework, Hevrat Shoharei Hatov Vehatushiyah (Seekers of Good and Wisdom), was set up to serve as an umbrella organization for the local groups of maskilim in Germany and outside it. By organizing societies, the maskilim were able to hold intellectual gatherings, exchange ideas, and read and discuss literary works, as well as to identify and define themselves through membership in an organization that set them apart from the general Jewish community, from which voices hostile to the Haskalah had already been heard.[3] 'How wonderful it is for wisdom-loving friends to sit together! How sweet and pleasant is their company; each man will aid his brother, and they will laugh at fear!'[4] In these sentences, taken from a song of praise written on the second anniversary of the establishment of the Hevrat Dorshei Leshon Ever in Königsberg, Shimon Baraz, one of its first members, gave expression to the sense of brotherhood and rapport which bolstered the maskilim's confidence and endowed them with an illusory sense of social power.

The maskilim were first and foremost writers who produced literary works of various genres, particularly in Hebrew, and considered themselves the bearers of a social and cultural mission. They regarded themselves as an avant-garde in Jewish society, adopting a critical approach to their surroundings and aspiring to shape a new Jewish ideal consistent with the future they envisaged. One of their most prominent members, Naphtali Herz Wessely, proposed a dualism of *torat ha'adam* (literally, 'the wisdom of man', i.e. universal human knowledge) and *torat hashem* ('the wisdom of God', i.e. Judaism), based on the German ideal of *Bildung*, and it was in the spirit of this twofold ideal that the maskilim strove to achieve social and cultural transformation. They believed this change would give rise to a new, advanced, and perfect Jewish society that would be benevolent, ethical, and appropriate to an era of religious tolerance, enlightened absolutism, rational thought, and European culture.[5] The maskilim believed that the changes they proposed could be realized fairly quickly, and conceived of themselves as the 'moral physicians' who knew how to cure society of its ills and extricate it from its state of ignorance, prejudice, and false concepts, primarily through a new type of Jewish education. Underpinning their view of the present and the future were utopian elements that fired them with enthusiasm and optimism,

---

[2] On the history and character of the Berlin Haskalah, see Altmann, *Moses Mendelssohn*; J. Katz, *Tradition and Crisis*, 245–74; Sorkin, *The Transformation of German Jewry*; id., 'From Context to Comparison', 23–58; Mahler, *History of the Jewish People*, i. 57–83, 133–60; Meyer, *The Origins of the Modern Jew*, 57–84; Lowenstein, *The Berlin Jewish Community*; Sorkin, *The Berlin Haskalah*.

[3] On the groups of maskilim, see Feiner, 'Isaac Euchel', 427–69; J. Katz, *Tradition and Crisis*, 263–4.   [4] Baraz, *Ma'arkhei lev*.

[5] Gilon, 'Hebrew Satire', 213–17; Ettinger, 'Jews in the Enlightenment', 48–61; Pelli, *The Age of Haskalah*.

and induced them to act: 'Now has come the age of science for all people . . . and why should we rest idle and unenterprising? Brethren, let us arise and revive stones from heaps of dust. Men of truth shall illuminate the path, until from above a sun of justice shall shine upon us and become the light of the world.'[6] This was the call sent forth by the maskilim in the manifesto of Hevrat Dorshei Leshon Ever in 1783. They believed that if they mustered strength and succeeded in overcoming their opponents, they would be able to disseminate the message of Enlightenment 'for the public good': 'Only the good shall we pursue . . . to teach the misguided understanding and the impetuous intelligence and wisdom, and the whole earth will be full of knowledge.'[7]

From the outset the maskilim saw as their objective the correction of the patterns and values of the 'old', traditional society. However, as a result of an accelerated process of acculturation in the communities of Berlin and Königsberg—the centres of the Haskalah—that led to assimilation, religious indifference, conversion, and deism, towards the end of the eighteenth century the maskilim also depicted themselves as soldiers in a rearguard action, with the aim of proposing a middle road between tradition and the abandonment of Jewish culture and society.[8] The maskilic utopia, their awareness of their social mission, their formation as a Jewish intellectual élite, the influence of the European Enlightenment, their criticism of traditional society, and their rationalistic and moralistic concepts led the maskilim to believe that they possessed the correct keys to the interpretation of historical trends, the identification of present and future challenges, and the transformation of Jewish society and culture. These were the factors that shaped the maskilic picture of the past, and they underpinned the new attitude to history which is defined here as maskilic history.

THE LEGITIMIZATION OF TRADITIONAL HISTORY

'Maskilic history' was largely detached from the patterns of the traditional sense of the past and offered an alternative to 'traditional history'. By 'traditional history', I mean the entire Jewish historical literature that had been created and had influenced Jewish society's sense of the past in the Middle Ages, in the early modern era, and in the seventeenth and eighteenth centuries; from the book of Josippon through Maimonides' introduction to his commentary on the Mishnah, *Sefer hakabalah* (The Book of Tradition), *Shalshelet hakabalah* (The Chain of Tradition), *Shevet yehudah* (The Staff of Judah), *Sefer yuhasin* (Book of Genealogy), and *Tsemah david* (Offspring of David), and up to *She'erit yisra'el* (The Remnant of Israel) and *Seder hadorot* (Order of the Generations). This historical literature was also available in the eighteenth century, thanks to frequent reprintings, which testify to these works' continued relevance to the traditional sense of the past.

---

[6] Hevrat Dorshei Leshon Ever, 'Nahal habesor' (1783). [7] Baraz, *Ma'arkhei lev.*
[8] Meyer, *The Origins of the Modern Jew*, 115–21; Feiner, 'Isaac Euchel', 459–69.

The chronicles and folk-tales from the Jewish past with the addition of episodes from general history, the chain of transmission of the Oral Law, and the line of succession of the Sages satisfied members of traditional society, and they felt no need for a new history.[9] For example, when Jehiel Heilprin of Minsk (1660–1746) began to write his chronicle *Seder hadorot* in the mid-eighteenth century, he had to apologize and reply to those who protested that there was no need to write new books since the older ones were perfectly adequate. Heilprin made it clear that his book was not a new work, but rather consisted of comments on and corrections of chronicles such as *Shalshelet hakabalah* or *Tsemaḥ david*.[10] In a similar fashion, Menahem Amelander of Amsterdam (d. *c.*1767), the author of *She'erit yisra'el* (1743), presented his popular book as the second half of the well-known medieval Book of Josippon. Early in the nineteenth century Abraham Triebesch of Moravia (b. 1760) updated *She'erit yisra'el*, and continued the chain of traditional chronicles with the addition of the events that had occurred up to the time of writing.[11]

A characteristic feature of 'traditional history' was its almost total delegitimization of any preoccupation with the historical past that was not harnessed to theological aims transcending history itself. Maskilim who began to take a renewed interest in the past were confronted by a Jewish tradition that regarded history as an external sphere of knowledge, requiring special legitimization. An apologetic approach, emphasizing the importance of history, and the search for some benefit that could be derived from it were conventions of classical historiography; they were expressed in the introductions of Greek and Roman historians and were passed down to Christian thinkers and chroniclers. As in the Christian concept formulated by St Augustine, religious considerations were the traditional Jewish criterion for permitting or disqualifying any preoccupation with history.[12] The Sages' relative indifference to historical questions involving a precise clarification of the true facts, expressed in the phrase 'Let bygones be bygones' (*mai dehava hava*), as well as the prohibition laid down by the writers of the Tosafot (twelfth to fourteenth centuries) against reading on the Sabbath of 'those wars written about in foreign tongues', naturally did not serve as an incentive for historical study.[13] The reader of the classic commentary on the Mishnah by Rabbi Obadiah of Bertinoro (*c.*1450–before 1516), finds that the words of Rabbi Akiva, which exclude anyone reading 'external' books from those meriting a share in the next world, also refer to the reader of 'the chronicles of the kings of

---

[9] On 'traditional history', see Kochan, *The Jew and his History*, and Yerushalmi, *Zakhor*. For a new appraisal of Jewish historiography during the Renaissance and Baroque periods, see Bonfil, 'How Golden was the Age of Renaissance?', 78–102.   [10] Heilprin, *Seder hadorot*, 1.

[11] Amelander, *She'erit yisra'el*, 49–53; Triebesch, *Korot ha'itim*, introd. See also Sedinova, 'Hebrew Historiography in Moravia', 51–61.

[12] Markus, *Saeculum*; Löwith, *Meaning in History*, 160–73.

[13] Herr, 'Conception of History', 129–42; Yerushalmi, *Zakhor*, 5–27; for the words of the Tosafists in the Babylonian Talmud, see *Shabat*, 116.

idol-worshippers . . . which contain neither wisdom nor benefit but are merely a waste of time' (*Sanhedrin* 10: 1). Rabbi Obadiah's words are almost an exact repetition of what Maimonides had written in his commentary on the Mishnah, in which he expresses the view that historiography *per se*—and certainly that concerned with general history—is a futile occupation: 'the external books . . . contain no wisdom and serve no useful purpose but rather are a waste of time in foolishness, such as the books of the Arabs that recount the annals and the legends of kings, the genealogies of the Arabs, the books of songs, and the like, books which contain no wisdom or real benefit but only waste time'.[14] However, one cannot conclude from this attitude that Maimonides completely excluded the historical past from his thought. Although he does unequivocally reject empirical research and historiography, historical thinking is legitimate once it is integrated in frames of reference charged with theological meaning. Maimonides assigns religious significance to the chain of tradition, which proves the unbroken sequence of the transmission of the Oral Torah. The historical stories recounted in the Torah have an essential value: they affirm the fundamental principles of the Torah and prevent sin and wickedness. The historical memory of the Jewish people is useful in strengthening their faith in the Almighty and His providence and in providing confidence and comfort to a people enduring the sorrows of exile. All historical events can be fitted into historical–philosophical systems that demonstrate the divine plan and guidance, and which mark out the destined path of the Jewish people, as all eyes are constantly raised to the messianic future. Maimonides' concept of history, which endured throughout centuries of 'traditional history', does not encourage Jewish historiography; nonetheless it does incorporate a trend that raises the events of the past to a level that allows them to become endowed with religious purpose and meaning.[15]

In the historical writing and thinking of the sixteenth century, which was concentrated mainly in the Sephardi community of Italy, a major apologetic effort was made for the purpose of defending this very preoccupation with this external domain. In the various, though largely repetitive, arguments, from Abraham Zacuto's *Sefer yuḥasin* to David Gans's *Tsemaḥ david* at the end of the century, a clear distinction was made between the benefit to be gained by studying Jewish history and that to be gained from the study of general history. Jewish history is given a mainly religious legitimization: it serves to strengthen faith in the Torah given at Sinai, to help halakhists make decisions as the later rabbinic authorities did, to validate principles of faith such as belief in reward and punishment, to

---

[14] Maimonides, *Commentary on the Mishnah*, introd. to the chapter 'Ḥelek' in *Sanhedrin*. Cf. his interpretation of *Pirkei avot*, 1: 17. See also Baron, *History and Jewish Historians*, 109–63, 'The Historical Outlook of Maimonides'.

[15] See Funkenstein, *Perceptions of Jewish History*, 131–55, 'The Political and Messianic Concept of Maimonides'; Twersky, *Introduction to the Code of Maimonides*, 220–8; Y. Ben-Sasson, 'Maimonides' Historical Thesis', 543–630.

enhance confidence in the Almighty's providential care for His people, to awaken readers' repentance through hagiographical stories about the martyrs who sanctified the Lord's name, and to reinforce the hope of redemption.[16] This last benefit reflects the traditional Jewish world-view, succinctly and coherently presented by Rabbi Judah Aryeh Modena in 1593:

Paying heed to these three things: how great is the good we had in the past, and the many troubles we find ourselves in today, and the great joy of living and the blessing that the future will restore—the memory of these three will guide us to our desired destiny. What I mean to say is that the past will sadden us, the present will distress us, and it is the future that we anticipate with hope.[17]

The writings of the sixteenth-century commentator and philosopher Obadiah Sforno (*c*.1470–*c*.1550) display a certain resemblance to a concept of history typical of the Renaissance historiography based on classical historical concepts—history as providing models for life. However, Sforno also emphasizes the religious moral in his work. In an attempt to explain the purpose of the narrative chapters in the Bible, he writes:

[The purpose is] to teach through the experience of the ancients a virtuous way of life to the wise man by teaching the ways of the righteous men of the generations and details of their actions, in which they found favour in the eyes of the Almighty, may His name be blessed, so that men will follow them; and also to teach a little of the actions of the evil men of the generations who deviated from the way directed by the Almighty; and in contrast to show their iniquities as hateful, so that the reader will distance himself from their ways and take the virtuous path.[18]

Though the chroniclers and philosophers succeeded in finding legitimization, supported by tradition, for engaging in the study of Jewish history, the problem was undoubtedly far more difficult when it came to writing universal history. There could be no doubt about the fundamental difference between the two types of history. Whereas sanctity and total credibility were attributed to the annals of the Jews, which had originated in the Bible, general history was regarded as devoid of any sanctity and suspected of being unreliable. This distinction is reflected in the structure of David Gans's book, which he divided into two parts: Jewish history and general history. The arguments offered to justify the study and writing of general history, unredeemed by any sanctity, usually included four main points: the history of other nations sheds light on important events in Jewish history; history has a practical use since it is a source of arguments and evidence that are helpful in religious debates with Christians; the hand of Providence, which

---

[16] A list of the 'benefits of history' appears in nearly all introductions to the writings: Zacuto, *Sefer yuhasin*, author's introd.; Gans, *Tsemah david*, introd. to pt. I; Ibn Verga, *Shevet yehudah*, 19, 115, 163–4; J. Hacohen, *Emek habakhah*, 10, 144.

[17] Modena, *Leket ketavim*, 119–21. See also his sermons on Hanukah (pp. 126–9) and on Passover (pp. 129–32).   [18] Sforno, *Be'ur al hatorah*, 371–89, 'Kavanot hatorah'.

'destroys a nation and raises up a nation', is also manifested in general history; and a comparison of the historical destiny of the nations of the world with the fate of the Jewish people strengthens faith in the continued existence and eternal mission of the Jews, when compared to the disappearance of other peoples.

The emphasis was still on religious values and the focus was still the Jewish people, but other 'benefits' were added: history provides the reader with pleasure for its own sake, in addition to a pragmatic benefit, 'for he will become more precise, hone his intelligence, and learn the affairs of the world, be they its [commercial] negotiations and its guiles and manipulations, the conduct of wars and the necessary stratagems, or how to speak to people in a fitting manner'.[19] In any case, the halakhic ruling, as expressed in the *Shulḥan arukh*, forbade the reading of 'books of war' on the Sabbath, adding that even on weekdays they should not be read because the readers would be distracted from their main preoccupation—study of the sacred texts.

David Gans (1541–1613), the author of *Tsemaḥ david*, who was aware of the halakhic problem and apprehensive about the fate of his book, marshalled the ruling of Moses Isserles (1530?–72), which tempered the prohibition of the *Shulḥan arukh*, limiting its applicability to books written in foreign languages. Moreover, Gans stated in the introduction to his book that the affairs of history are neutral from the standpoint of halakhah and need not arouse any difficulties in relation to faith and halakhah: 'Since from this work of mine neither impurity nor purity, neither prohibition nor permission emerge, my heart empowered me to put my mind to the task of writing this book.'[20]

This attempt to legitimize history by neutralizing it provided an opening for a study of the historical past *per se*, as an autonomous and secular sphere, as well as for critical research seeking historical truth independent of any religious or value-laden factors. Gans himself did not develop this idea beyond the sentence quoted above, but his words presage the change that occurred in attitudes towards the historical past. Gans found this view ready at hand in Azariah de' Rossi's *Me'or einayim* (1573). De' Rossi (*c*.1511–*c*.1578) made use of the neutralistic concept of history in order to apply critical methods to this secular sphere while avoiding any conflict with faith and halakhah. To underscore this approach, he went further and rejected the classical approaches that sought pragmatic benefit and exemplary models in history. De' Rossi even contested Livy's view that history can supply lessons from which a nation can learn what is best for it and its people. He believed this view was applicable only to the non-Jewish nations. The pragmatic and exemplary benefit, in de' Rossi's view, is not relevant to the Jewish

---

[19] Capsali, *Seder eliyahu zuta*, 10. In the 16th c. historical romances in Hebrew also began to appear. On 'popular' historical literature, see Bonfil, 'How Golden was the Age of Renaissance?' and n. 28 in the bibliography; Amadis de Gaula, *Alilot ha'abir amadish de ga'ulah*.

[20] Gans, *Tsemaḥ david*, introd. to pt. I, p. 7, and see the ruling of Moses Isserles in *Shulḥan arukh*, *Oraḥ ḥayim, Shabat*, 307: 16. See also Elbaum, *Openness and Insularity*, 257–60.

people since they possess the Torah, which includes all the models and guidance necessary for life. Post-biblical history, therefore, can add nothing in the way of experience or lessons for the Jews. This enables us to understand why the Sages showed so little interest in history and even erred in relation to various historical facts: 'For in all other things in which there is neither commandment nor transgression . . . if they are in keeping with the halakhah, that is all to the good, and if not, then fantasies will neither add nor detract.'[21]

De' Rossi's negation of any theological as well as practical legitimization for Jewish historical study was exceptional in his time, and was intended to justify his scholarly historical–philological study and his criticism of the Sages. At the same time the traditional concept persisted in the seventeenth and eighteenth centuries and was reinforced by the reprintings of sixteenth-century chronicles, including introductions by the authors in which they suggested a list of the 'benefits' of history.

Rabbi Jacob Emden (1697–1776) returned to the halakhic question and grappled with it on the eve of the Haskalah. In his youth Emden had shown an interest in learning the 'stories of their history'. In his halakhic responses he discusses in detail the prohibition of the *Shulḥan arukh* on the reading of history books on the Sabbath, and draws a distinction, as did Isserles, between books written in Hebrew, each of which must be examined on its own merits, and books in foreign languages. Reading the latter is a waste of time; at the very most, they may be scanned at random. In an additional distinction, Emden argues that 'there is no need at all to have any knowledge of [universal history], and it is forbidden to read about it on a regular basis', in contrast to Jewish history, parts of which were important and essential. Emden regarded the first parts of *Tsemaḥ david*, *Sefer yuḥasin*, and the Book of Josippon as sacred books and permitted them to be read even on the Sabbath, since 'they deal only with matters of Bible and Talmud' or with the miracles performed for the people of Israel. In his view, the 'foolish tales' (such as the legends about Alexander the Great) which he believed had been introduced into Josippon as a later addition should not be read on the Sabbath, and should not be read regularly even on weekdays. Emden forbade the reading of the sixth book of Josippon on the Sabbath; because it tells of the tribulations of the Jewish people and includes a description of the destruction of the Temple, he felt it ought to be reserved for reading during the three weeks of mourning over the destruction of the Temple, between 17 Tammuz and 9 Av. It was also forbidden to read Solomon Ibn Verga's *Shevet yehudah* on the Sabbath because of its sad stories, but Emden did recommend that it should be read on weekdays. He felt that the book had merits because it imparted a knowledge of the wonders worked by the Almighty for His people and provided arguments that could be

---

[21] De' Rossi, *Me'or einayim*, 263. On de' Rossi, see Bonfil, 'Some Reflections', 23–48; id., ed., *Writings of Azariah*, 62–77; Baron, *History and Jewish Historians*, 205–39, 'Azariah de Rossi's Historical Method'.

used in a religious dispute: 'every person is commanded to be familiar with this excellent book'. He had a much more qualified attitude towards *Seder hadorot dorot*; since a considerable portion of the book did not deal with Jewish history, it was of little benefit, and the same was true of the second parts of *Sefer yuhasin* and *Tsemah david*. Nonetheless, Emden did permit these books to be perused when the reader 'is travelling, is feeling too weak to study Torah, and when the teachers are on vacation', in order to acquire a certain familiarity with universal history, so that the Torah scholar could reply to his questioners without appearing to be ignorant and could also gain some understanding of the affairs of this world.[22]

Despite Emden's interest in history and his relatively liberal ruling, the legitimization he granted historical study can hardly be viewed as a significant departure from traditional views. Religious considerations remained the dominant criterion, the Jewish people was still the focus, and only on the periphery was it possible to use historical knowledge for pragmatic purposes, as did Gans, Amelander, and others who preceded Emden. In his book *Mitpahat sefarim* (1768) Emden went even further, and in the course of a polemic with Azariah de' Rossi, he rebuked him for occupying himself with tales of secular history: 'Heaven forbid, these are profanities and must not touch upon the holiness of heaven. They are as distant from us as earth is from the heavens . . . hence the Jew should remove himself far from the foolishness of the gentiles.'[23] History that could not be employed for religious-ethical purposes, which did not bear a significant religious message, did not reinforce the validity of tradition, or did not serve as a religious, value-laden example for emulation—in short, history that was not 'sacred history'—could scarcely be given any legitimization, and if so, only *ex post facto*.

THE 'JUDGEMENT OF REASON': LEGITIMIZATIONS FOR A NEW HISTORY

While traditional Jewish society continued to rely upon concepts of traditional history, which affirmed religious values and provided grounds for recognition of the uniqueness of the Jewish people, eighteenth-century Enlightenment thinkers and historians embarked on a struggle against 'Christian history' and proposed new legitimizations for the study and writing of history.[24] The French *philosophes* regarded the *Discourse on Universal History* (1681) by J. Bossuet, a clergyman and tutor to the dauphin, as the main target of their criticism. This was a popular and

---

[22] Emden, *Mor uketsiah*. On Emden's curiosity, see his autobiography, *Megilat sefer*, 126.

[23] Emden, *Mitpahat sefarim*, 33–4. Cf. Shohet, *Changing Eras*, 220–41.

[24] A vast literature exists on the historical and historiographical concepts of the European Enlightenment. Among others, see Arieli, 'The Modern Age and Secularization', 165–216; id., 'New Horizons', 145–68; Reill, *The German Enlightenment*; Cassirer, *The Philosophy of the Enlightenment*, 197–233; Bury, *The Idea of Progress*; Butterfield, *Man on his Past*; Gay, *The Enlightenment*; Iggers, *New Directions*; C. Becker, *The Heavenly City*.

well-known work in the eighteenth century, whose structure and content served as a typical model of the Augustinian interpretation of history.[25] Augustine's dualistic and dichotomous concept of history, which firmly separated the 'sacred history' of the 'City of God' from the 'secular history' of the 'temporal city', provided very scant justification for any history that did not relate the annals of the Church or contribute to man's knowledge of the Deity. While Bossuet adopted the Augustinian legitimization, he combined it with humanistic concepts that provided legitimization for exemplary and pragmatic history. His 'universal history' was intended to serve both as 'Catholic history' and as a history that dealt with the affairs of rulers: 'If they are in need of any experience in order to acquire the wisdom necessary for a good ruler, they can find no greater benefit to guide them than by adding the examples of past eras to the experience they have every day.'[26] Bossuet emphasized that this was merely a secondary benefit, and that the main benefit of history lay in plumbing the depths of the divine plan. In this way, history became an effective tool in the training of a Christian ruler, who should manage his kingdom with pragmatic wisdom but never forget his duty to submit to the will of God, the creator of kingdoms.

The revolution in the Enlightenment's historical thinking was expressed in a shift of the major emphasis from 'sacred history' to man and his works. For example, in Voltaire's view the main justification for historical study lay in the benefit to be gained from man's self-knowledge: 'It is not merely the life of Louis XIV that we propose to write; we have a wider aim in view. We shall endeavour to depict for posterity, not the actions of a single man, but the spirit of men in the most enlightened age the world has ever seen.'[27] This sentence, which opens Voltaire's book *The Age of Louis XIV*, aptly expresses the conceptual challenge that was flung at the historiography that preceded it. Voltaire and other European men of the Enlightenment proposed a new and alternative legitimization, without renouncing the basic classic assumption: history offers a pragmatic and exemplary benefit. The change, then, lay not in the fundamental concept of the benefit of studying history, but rather in the new contents and didactic aims for whose service history was being recruited. These were drawn from the world of thought and values of the Enlightenment, and were linked to social and ideological struggles aimed at shaping a new society and a new man, using historical examples alongside other methods.

Philosophers and writers of the Enlightenment employed history to construct a historical reckoning in which reason and morality were used as a yardstick for positive or negative judgements of the events, societies, religions, cultures, and values of the historical past. History was depicted as an unceasing battle waged by the elements of reason against the elements of anti-reason that threatened to de-

---

[25] Bossuet, *Discourse on Universal History*. On the Augustinian concept of history, see Markus, *Saeculum* and Löwith, *Meaning in History*.   [26] Bossuet, *Discourse on Universal History*, 3.
[27] Voltaire, *The Age of Louis XIV*, 1.

stroy them. 'The city of light' fought the 'city of darkness', and history provided numerous examples of this struggle. Negative historical examples were drummed into service to express reservations about and rejections of periods, figures, and events that represented superstition and ignorance, while positive examples encouraged identification with exemplary rational and ethical models.[28] Hence, the demand for change in the present underpinned the legitimization of the study of the past. History was like a mirror for humanity, reflecting its real image and enabling a new identity to take shape. The men of the Enlightenment found many positive models for emulation in classical Graeco-Roman history. On their way to the secular world, Gay asserts, the men of the Enlightenment set up 'road signs' made up of classical images, which directed and guided them towards a new world of values.[29]

In addition to its role in the formation of ideology, history was also endowed with philosophical legitimization. From John Locke and Henry Bolingbroke to Christian Wolff and Immanuel Kant, historical thinking was combined with philosophical thinking, and the view that experience, along with pure and abstract reason, was essential in order to acquire a coherent knowledge of truth and values gained wider currency. Human experience was divided into personal and historical experience, opening the way for the assumptions that the store of historical human experience provides examples that constitute experiential–factual raw material, and that rational judgement can extract ethical rules of behaviour from this store of experience. History thus became an empirical part of ethical philosophy, a source of authority for a knowledge of reality and for moral education.[30]

Naphtali Herz Wessely (1725–1804), a Hebrew poet and author regarded by the young maskilim as their spiritual mentor, was a contemporary of Moses Mendelssohn (1729–86) in Berlin. He was the first maskil to propose new possibilities of using historical knowledge for didactic purposes, breaking away from traditional legitimizations. In his *Divrei shalom ve'emet* (Words of Peace and Truth, 1782), the most important ideological work of the German maskilim, he tried to mobilize Jewish public opinion to support the reforms in the condition of the Jews proposed by the Austrian emperor Joseph II. In this work Wessely first outlined his ideal of the 'new Jew', to be moulded in modern educational settings. In this new programme of studies history ('a knowledge of the chronicles of the generations') was given a place alongside geography in 'human knowledge'.[31] Wessely cited a lack of interest in history as one of the negative aspects of Jewish society and a striking example of the 'dark realm of stupidity' in which it dwelt.

[28] C. Becker, *The Heavenly City*, 121–2; J. Rosenthal, 'Voltaire's Philosophy of History', 166–7.
[29] Gay, *The Enlightenment*, i. 31–8.
[30] Kant, *Critique of Pure Reason*, 670–2. See also Yovel, *Kant and the Philosophy of History*; Nadel, 'Philosophy of History', 292–315; C. Becker, *The Heavenly City*, 147; Gardiner (ed.), *Theories of History*, 35–49. On Herder and his historical thinking, see I. Berlin, *Vico and Herder*.
[31] Wessely, *Divrei shalom ve'emet*.

In assigning history a place in his new curriculum, Wessely clearly considered it an element in a far-reaching programme to heal Jewish society. As an additional means of persuading his readers of the vital importance of historical knowledge, he set out a list of arguments which, in his view, upheld the legitimization of history and proved its value. First, however, he repeated the sixteenth-century statements by Gans and de' Rossi and argued that 'these sciences have nothing to do with faith', that history and geography were neutral from the standpoint of religion, nor was there any halakhic prohibition against learning from history books written in German.[32]

The ideal of the new Jew, which Wessely thought should be nurtured by the new schools, was derived from the complex identity that the first maskilim wanted to adopt for themselves and impose upon the whole of Jewish society. This identity preserved religious Jewish culture and the shared national destiny, adding to it the identity of the Jew as a citizen of the state and as a member of human society with the capacity for rational thought.

Thus, in his list of the 'benefits of history', Wessely tried to link each feature of maskilic identity to a specific benefit offered by history, while his main interest lay in universal history rather than in Jewish history. To the Jew as a citizen, history was beneficial because it provided him with a store of knowledge that enabled him to converse in a cultured manner with members of non-Jewish society, and to transact his affairs as a ordinary citizen with prominent representatives of the state, its officials, and its ministers. It was the duty of parents to ensure that their children were well prepared for the new situation, expressions of which Wessely found in the policies of the enlightened absolutist regime, particularly after the publication of Joseph II's Edict of Tolerance. They must ensure that whenever they participated in a conversation about 'matters of war, or events that have occurred in the world in the past . . . they will not seem like "sleepers in the ranks of stupidity"'.[33] Historical knowledge would thus play a role in improving the image of the Jew among his neighbours.

To the Jew as a Torah scholar, history was beneficial in that it was an essential tool in understanding the narrative parts of the Bible and in acquiring a knowledge of the historical context of the time and place in which they occurred:

Hence for those who go to study in the *beit midrash* it is fitting that they should also learn the order of the generations and the events of the times, so they will know how things have come to be from the beginning, who occupied the states from the beginning, and how the kingdoms were established . . . for this knowledge will help them to understand the words of the Torah . . . and for anyone who is not familiar with the books of ancient history, these things seem to him as a dream without an interpretation and he will not be able to consider them carefully.[34]

On the surface, the objective—greater understanding of the Torah—did not deviate from tradition. However, the argument that the historical context of the

---

[32] Wessely, *Divrei shalom ve'emet*, ch. 1.   [33] Ibid., ch. 5.   [34] Ibid.

Bible should be taken into account was based on an important element in the historical revolution; namely, that a true understanding of facts and texts from the past could only be gained through study of their historical contexts.[35]

To the Jew as a human being, history contributed by helping him develop qualities of curiosity, criticism, and scepticism: 'And they will become accustomed to think of all matters with insight, and will not indulge in vain imaginings, nor will they believe old wives' tales or those who tell them strange and wondrous stories.'[36] Wessely employed history as a weapon in the struggle against irrational thought, superstition, and obscurantism, and as the foundation for nurturing independent thought.

To the Jew as a member of the Jewish people, history provided a rational explanation of the destiny and chosenness of the Jewish people. Universal history enabled the Jew to draw comparative conclusions, and anyone who studied the history of ancient peoples could see how they all deviated from *torat ha'adam* ('the law of man', signifying humanistic values), and hence did not endure, whereas Abraham was chosen by God because of his qualities and his dedication to *torat ha'adam*. By stressing that this criterion had influenced God's decision, Wessely shifted the centrality of the judgement, evaluation, and understanding of the acts of Providence from the theological plane of man's relations with the Almighty to the humanistic plane (*torat ha'adam*), thus secularizing it.

To the Jew as a maskil, history was beneficial because it provided illustrious examples that proved the importance of humanism, morality, and wisdom in personal and political success. Wessely revealed his didactic and moralistic aims, which were no longer dependent on religious values:

From [studying] history a man will become wise, by reading in it of the deeds of men of all nations who went before us, their leaders, thoughts, and counsel; and when he comes to understand the end of their affairs, he will see the effect of good counsel, and how through it entire kingdoms have succeeded, and have also raised up great men who became renowned; and on the other hand, he will see the effect of bad counsel, through which great kingdoms have declined and collapsed.[37]

This moralistic and intellectual mechanism of historical explanation was a major feature of the historical thought of the Enlightenment, and also reflects the way history functioned in moral education. Wessely, who laid the foundations of 'maskilic history', adopted a viewpoint from which the struggle between rationalism and prejudice, between virtue and 'evil counsel', was the main feature of human history.

The criticism levelled against *Divrei shalom ve'emet* by Rabbi David Tevele of Lissa (d. 1792), one of Wessely's many opponents, in a sermon he delivered on Shabbat Hagadol (the Sabbath before Passover) in 1782, shows that a new sense

---

[35] Funkenstein, 'Continuity and Renewal', 105–31.

[36] Wessely, *Divrei shalom ve'emet*, ch. 7.   [37] Ibid. and at the end of ch. 2.

of the past was indeed emerging. In his sermon David Tevele decisively rejected several of Wessely's arguments in favour of the study of history.[38] The rabbi presented two main objections: first, he complained bitterly about what he considered an attempt to turn the Torah into a collection of stories. Basing his argument on the Zohar, David Tevele asserted that the historical stories in the Torah were merely a mantle covering lofty and profound secrets and ideas, and that care must be taken to avoid turning them into 'history'. Certainly it was impossible to arrive at an understanding of the Torah by studying its historical context, since it was not in the least relevant to narratives so charged with meaning and sanctity. The Torah was not intended as a historical narrative, and those who chose to interpret it as history would reach neither understanding nor truth. David Tevele's second objection makes it clear that he astutely discerned Wessely's attempt to introduce maskilic values (the essential nature of *torat ha'adam*) in the example he had given, namely that the reason that Abraham was chosen by God would be obvious in light of the general historical context and a comparison of his way of life with that followed by other peoples.

David Tevele accused Wessely of a deed tantamount to desecration and an affront to the honour of the father of the nation: 'Our father Abraham, of blessed memory, was a unique man. So without reading of the abominations of the gentiles, would the righteousness of our father Abraham of blessed memory, the wondrousness of his piety, his asceticism, and his sanctity not be known?'[39] It would be unthinkable to portray the figure of Abraham as relative to his time and place, thus allowing for the possibility that had he lived in a generation strictly adhering to *torat ha'adam*, his unique qualities would have gone unnoticed. The conclusion of David Tevele's sermon is a thorough repudiation of Wessely's legitimizations for the study of history. In Tevele's view, universal history and historical thought were neither relevant nor legitimate, and might even constitute a threat and a danger to the 'sacred history' of the Jewish people.

Wessely did not fail to respond in kind. In his epistle *Reḥovot* (1785), published as the fourth part of *Divrei shalom ve'emet*, he replied to his opponents. In his response to David Tevele's arguments, Wessely seems to have retreated somewhat from what he had written three years earlier. Although he still maintained that history was essential ('Anyone wishing to be a good friend to his peers, to enjoy their company, and to have them enjoy his, must know a few things about the history of the world and the order of the generations'), he no longer felt that it was necessary to broaden one's study of history excessively, and thought a limited knowledge would suffice:

I am not saying that a man should spend his time reading books of history about each and every nation until he knows the annals of each, the wars and changes that took place in

---

[38] Louis Lewin, 'Aus dem jüdischen Kulturkampf', 182–94. See also Samet, 'Mendelssohn, Wessely, and the Rabbis of their Generation', 223–57; Eliav, *Jewish Education in Germany*, 39–51.
[39] *Jahrbuch der jüdisch-literarischen Gesellschaft*, 12 (1918), 193.

them, the names of their kings, their generals, and the like; for all this is good only for idlers, and bad for those concerned with the welfare of society, and even worse for serious students of the Torah, who would be wasting their time on matters of no significance.[40]

With these words, Wessely curtailed the legitimization of historical study to a certain extent, and apparently reverted to the position taken by Jacob Emden and his predecessors. In Wessely's opinion, the intensive study of history was completely legitimate for those wise men of the nations who 'specialized in history'. It was both fitting and desirable that they should devote time and energy to historical research, since they earned their livelihood by studying, investigating, and teaching, and also because the work of professional historians was vital for a state and its rulers. Jews, whose first obligation was the study of Torah, and who did not bear the responsibility of running a state, could rest content with 'abridged works'. Wessely therefore recommended that a Jew should acquire a certain familiarity with the 'substance of the major events that have occurred on the globe', rather than with the details. He ought to read traditional books that relate the history of the Jews; in universal history books, he 'should also read in brief' of 'what has happened to our people since the day the Second Temple was destroyed until the present', as well as the 'highlights' in the history of the various governments throughout the ages. What had originally been Wessely's main interest—the history of the nations—now became only secondary. The justification for this interest was hardly a real departure from the traditional one: a literal understanding of the Bible and the recognition that the prophets' predictions about the fate of the various nations had indeed been realized: 'Whosoever is wise, let him understand these things, for the ways of the Lord are right, His faith is perfect, and He rules the world with justice and equity.' In practice, in the curriculum of the new school that Wessely proposed, half an hour was allocated to the study of history each day—the same amount of time that was devoted to geography. There was no need to devote much more time to subjects which did not call for rigorous thought: 'For they are not like *hokhmot limudiyot vetiviyot* [logical and natural sciences] that call for much concentration and profound thought . . . but geography and history are very easy and are an amusement for young boys, both to look at the drawings of maps, and to hear news of past events.'[41]

Wessely rejected David Tevele's second objection in a restrained spirit, while attempting to represent his own view as one consistent with the words of the Zohar and David Tevele's interpretation of them. Wessely agreed that the Torah contained hints of secrets and esoteric knowledge, yet he insisted that the secret significance did not cancel the *peshat* (literal meaning) of the text, and asserted

---

[40] Wessely, *Divrei shalom ve'emet*, 4th letter, 51a–53a. Wessely's awareness that historiography was flourishing in Germany is also expressed in his article, 'Magid hadashot', 133.

[41] Wessely, *Divrei shalom ve'emet*, 53a.

that historical knowledge could be helpful in studying the Torah according to the *peshat*. Wessely came even closer to David Tevele's position in agreeing that the historical stories included in the Torah could not be compared to the secular stories found in the history books of other peoples. The Torah taught a moral lesson and the ways of the Almighty, a characteristic absent from other types of history. One can easily discern here the re-emergence of the traditional distinction made by Gans, Emden, and others between the history of Israel and that of other nations, a distinction between the sacred and the profane that ruled out almost any legitimization of secular history. Wessely continued to believe in the value and importance of history in the domain of worldly matters, in the reinforcement of faith, and in understanding the literal meaning of the Bible.[42]

While Wessely, a conservative in Haskalah circles, wavered between the two worlds, apologizing, hesitating, and retreating, his young friend Isaac Euchel (1756–1804) proposed a legitimization based on quintessentially Enlightenment concepts. Euchel, editor of *Hame'asef* and the moving spirit in organizing circles of maskilim in Germany, was a student of Kant's at Königsberg University, where he was exposed to Enlightenment views and concepts which he tried to transplant to the Haskalah.[43]

In an article entitled 'On the Benefits Provided by History', printed in *Hame'asef* in 1784, Euchel formulated the maskilic legitimization for historical study. This article can be regarded as the first modern theoretical Jewish work on 'history'.[44] The premiss for his thesis was a philosophical theory couched in the terms of medieval rational Jewish philosophy and Kantian concepts, and designed to expound the importance and benefits of history, its place in the sum total of human knowledge, and its goals in the Jewish context. Euchel asserted that both logic and the Torah called for rational inquiry in order to arrive at the real truth. This investigation employed 'the two fundamentals of human knowledge, which are intelligence and experience based on concreteness and accepted views'. Knowledge based only on a priori concepts was hard to acquire, whereas exclusive reliance on the senses was misleading and uncertain; hence a combination of the two was required, as well as evidence derived from experience. It was history that supplied the necessary experience in relation to chronologically distant facts, those things that were known through the tradition passed down from generation to generation, which existed thanks to the writers of history: 'And in order to know things distant in time, we avail ourselves of stories of past events, which constitute the history of everything done on earth, the deeds of each and

---

[42] Wessely, *Divrei shalom ve'emet*, 56; id., 'Magid hadashot', 130–3. On Wessely's standing in the circles of German maskilim, see Pelli, *The Age of Haskalah*, 113–30.

[43] Feiner, 'Isaac Euchel', 435–40.

[44] Euchel, 'Davar el hakore', 9–14, 25–30. Euchel identified himself as the writer of this article in his book *Toledot harav* (Vienna, 1814), 13. See also Hevrat Dorshei Leshon Ever, *Naḥal habesor*, 1783.

every nation, from the time of the Flood to this very day.' From this fundamental position, which made history an essential category of thought, Euchel derived four possibilities of extracting benefit from the study of the historical past. Two of these were in the domain of distinguishing truth from falsehood, and two in the domain of drawing a moral distinction between good and evil.

The first, *to'elet hakiri*, was philosophical use, consisting of the rational use of the store of facts gained from historical experience in order to test the truth of tradition. History was viewed as a yardstick by which to gauge Jewish tradition; by its light one could distinguish between truth and falsehood 'so that you may choose the one closest to your reason'. Euchel was aware of the radical consequences liable to result from this critical philosophical approach, so he added a qualification which appears at first glance to contradict his premiss, protecting Jewish tradition from almost any critical approach: 'Our inherited tradition is our faith. You must not deviate from it either to the right or to the left.' Rational inquiry, as practised by the medieval Jewish philosophers, was legitimate, but only in order to clarify one's thoughts and dispel any doubt, or in order to reply to an apostate who would not be content with answers based on faith but demanded empirical evidence. In this manner, Euchel pointed the blade of rational historical criticism towards the attackers of Jewish tradition (explicitly mentioning Voltaire), granting history legitimacy as a means of explaining and defending that tradition. However, the principle obviously remains valid, ready to hand for more radical uses.

The second possibility, *to'elet tori'i*, was literary benefit, similar in meaning to the benefit Wessely found in history: in a universal historical context it would lead to a more correct and profound understanding of the Scriptures and, according to Euchel, also of the Mishnah and Talmud. Perhaps in response to the words of David Tevele, Euchel reproached the rabbis, whom he described in harsh terms as 'perverting the right way', for their obstinacy, and in particular for their claim that they were able to distinguish between truth and falsehood without the aid of 'external' learning. In his view, it was impossible to achieve a correct understanding of Scripture if one ignored its historical and geographical contexts.

The third possibility, *to'elet medini*, was political benefit—of practical use in economic and social spheres. By studying history one could learn to distinguish between good and evil in business affairs; the merchant aspiring to gain maximum profit could base his actions on important information provided by historical experience 'and every astute man will have the knowledge to consider what is most profitable'. Moreover, historical knowledge was beneficial to the Jewish bourgeois merchant who 'arranges his actions in the correct order', in social meetings with Jews and non-Jews alike: he could make use of his knowledge 'to entertain his circle of friends with useful and pleasing stories'.

The fourth possibility, *to'elet musari*, was ethical in nature and was regarded by Euchel as the most significant benefit afforded by history. Man's purpose in life was to attain spiritual and practical perfection, and the most desirable way to this goal was to follow the golden mean between the extremes of good and evil. In order that man might be able to choose his way he had to be able to recognize good and evil qualities. Moral distinctions could not be made on the basis of the senses or the emotions; history could provide examples from the past which would serve as the basis for reasoned judgements: 'And seeing this in the light of reason, I will know how to judge whether this person's quality is natural or habituated, whether it depends on his temperament, or past history, or on the climate in which he was born. For this, we have need of reasoned judgement based on experience, which originates in history and geography.'[45]

Euchel did not cite the sources he used in formulating his theoretical essay, but it seems that the concepts and ideas it contains were taken from the words of his teacher Immanuel Kant. The definitions of history and geography, the benefit gained from their knowledge, and their place in the human epistemological system in the category of experience are included in Kant's series of lectures devoted to physical geography.[46] These lectures were only published after Kant's death; Euchel was apparently present when they were delivered during his student days at the university of Königsberg, and his article in *Hame'asef* was written under the influence of Kant's words. As is well known, Kant had a broad and profound philosophical concept of history, as Yirmiyahu Yovel demonstrates in his study, although only occasional echoes of this approach are discernible in Euchel's writings.[47] Several of the key texts on Kant's philosophy of history had not yet been published at the time; however, neither Euchel's Jewish audience nor his own intellectual level enabled him to formulate a more complete historical–philosophical theory. Euchel's assimilation of Kant's concepts and his transmission of some of them to a Hebrew-reading Jewish audience can be seen as an example of the attempt to popularize and adapt various historical concepts and to bring them down from an academic to a lower level—in this case to the level of the maskil.

Euchel was so convinced of the immense importance of history that he attempted to recruit Moses Mendelssohn to prove how essential it was for the Jewish intellectual to possess historical knowledge as an integral part of his spiritual repertoire. In his biography of Mendelssohn, written in 1787, Euchel included a remark which seems to contradict the evidence suggesting that Mendelssohn was indifferent to history. In his youth, Euchel states, Mendelssohn studied the 'chronicles of past ages': 'He was very well versed . . . in the knowledge of geography and history, and I have heard that in the days of his youth when he began to engage in wisdom, he also began to study history . . . and he knew all the principles of its tales by heart at the time.'[48]

---

[45] Euchel, 'Davar el hakore', 20–9, and cf. Nadel, 'Philosophy of History', 311–15. There is also a reference to this important article by Euchel in Yerushalmi, *Zakhor*, 83.

[46] Kant, 'Physische Geographie', 156–65.

[47] Kant, *On History*; Yovel, *Kant and the Philosophy of History*.   [48] Euchel, *Toledot harav*, 137

Euchel's tendentious claims apart, there is evidence in Mendelssohn's own writings of his broad knowledge of history, in particular of classical history, comparative historical comments, and historical schemas which he describes. These attest to his historical education, as well as to his acceptance of the historical concepts current among the maskilim. The scholarly view that stresses Mendelssohn's indifferent or derisive attitude towards history may thus need to be qualified. Although his philosophical approach certainly did not place any emphasis on a study of the historical past, it is difficult to accept at face value Mendelssohn's statement in a letter to Thomas Abbt that he found all branches of history boring.[49] Mendelssohn based his conclusions on traditional assumptions, such as the need to recognize the hand of Providence guiding history, and thus felt that the field of history had but scant relevance for the Jewish people. History as a 'civic science', as the 'chronicles of political regimes', was of no interest to the stateless person, unless it encompassed the 'annals of mankind', which included the Jew as well. In response to the German biblical critics, Mendelssohn asserted that the Jew was unable to relate to the Bible 'as to a book of history, to know events in ancient times, and to understand the ways of the Almighty and Supreme Providence in each and every generation'. This approach was relevant for the wise men of the nations; the Jew, however, would not seek to find pragmatic benefit or to satisfy his historical curiosity in the Bible, but rather would seek to study the commandments he was obliged to keep.[50] As a rule, Mendelssohn was sceptical about 'historical truths', which he regarded as a medium of knowledge inferior to 'eternal truths'. Although in his opinion the story of revelation from Abraham to the giving of the Torah on Mount Sinai was beyond question, in principle 'the authority of the narrator and his reliability are the only source of certainty in historical matters; without evidence we lack the ability to know any historical truth'.[51] In matters of faith, and for the purposes of understanding and observing Judaism, human history had no influence whatsoever, just as it was irrelevant to the individual's path to perfection, which was an ethical–biographical, intellectual, and ahistorical path. Mendelssohn rejected the maskilic–Christian schema of his friend, the philosopher and dramatist Gotthold Ephraim Lessing (1729–81), who placed Judaism at a lower stage of development than Christianity; he also asserted in his *Biur* (Commentary on the Torah) that historical time, both past and future, had no theological significance, since before God there is no past or future, but only present.[52]

[49] Mendelssohn's letter to Abbt, dated 16 Feb. 1765, *Gesammelte Schriften*, vol. xii/1, 75; Wiener, *Jüdische Religion*, 70–3; Berney, 'The Historical and Political Conceptions', 99–111, 248–70.

[50] Mendelssohn, 'Or lenetivah', *Gesammelte Schriften*, xiv. 243.

[51] Mendelssohn, *Jerusalem*, in *Gesammelte Schriften*, viii. 99–204, and in English translation: Mendelssohn, *Jerusalem and Other Jewish Writings*, 95.

[52] Thus, for example, in the commentary on the book of Exodus 3: 14. See Schweid, *Jewish Thought*, 140–3; Altmann, *Moses Mendelssohn*, 537–42; Liebeschütz, 'Mendelssohn und Lessing', 167–79.

Mendelssohn's stance did not amount to a return to the traditional position. He rejected Lessing's approach of the 'education of humankind', as well as that of biblical critics, and wanted to award pre-eminence to philosophy above all other disciplines. When he engaged in polemics with Voltaire and others who described biblical figures in pejorative terms, he did in fact maintain a historical view, opposing the ahistorical approach which failed to take into account the concepts of the ancient world.[53] Nor was Mendelssohn opposed to the use of history for 'popular' educational purposes: in his home in Berlin, in the 1780s, discussion centred on the question of what book would be most useful for the education and edification of the Jews of Poland. One of the maskilim participating in the discussion asserted that 'for this purpose nothing is more useful than a book of Jewish history, so that our people may learn from it the commencement of the laws of their religion and how they were later corrupted, the causes for the destruction of our state, and the persecutions and miseries that befell them due to their ignorance and opposition to every enlightened reform'. Those present proposed to Solomon Maimon (1753–1800) that he translate Basnage's book on the history of the Jews.[54] Mendelssohn saw a sample of the translation, and Maimon stated that it was a good piece of work 'even in the view of Herr Mendelssohn'; nevertheless, it is difficult to conclude from his account whether Mendelssohn was actually in favour of the didactic objective assigned to the history book by the maskilim.

Maimon, who rose from his post as a Lithuanian teacher to become a well-known German philosopher, was sceptical about the translation task offered him by the Berlin maskilim. He believed that history provided scant benefit and would not further Jewish education:

I myself am convinced that for the purpose of educating the Jewish people one ought not to begin with history nor with matters of natural religion and ethics, since these sciences can easily be understood by everyone, and hence are not capable of arousing a sentiment of respect for sciences in general in the hearts of the scholars among our people, who only respect those matters that require one to exert an intellectual effort. That is one reason, and the second is that these matters will surely come into conflict with their ancient religious laws and hence will not evoke a warm response. And furthermore, the truth of the matter is that the Jewish people has no true history, since this people has hardly ever had political relations with other civilized peoples.[55]

In light of the meagre intellectual challenge that history could offer to Torah scholars in Poland, the religious dilemmas likely to arise, and his own radical view denying post-state Jewish history any real sense of 'history', Maimon concluded that this field was left with only a small measure of legitimacy. Instead, he chose to translate, from Latin into Hebrew, a book on mathematics: an example of a neutral science that provided an intellectual challenge. Nonetheless, skimming

---

[53] Liebeschütz, 'Mendelssohn und Lessing', 169.
[54] Maimon, *Autobiography*, 134–5.   [55] Ibid. 135.

the pages of his memoirs back to an earlier period, one finds that history books were among the important milestones on his path to higher education. *Tsemah david*, Josippon, and a book describing the persecution of Jews in Spain (apparently *Shevet yehudah*), which he found in his father's library, served as his introduction to an alternative path to that of tradition. 'Let us compare, then,' Maimon wrote, 'the tedious subjects dealt with in the Talmud, such as whether an animal should be slaughtered at the neck or at the tail; or whether the High Priest puts on his shirt or his breeches first . . . with history, in which natural events are related in an instructive and agreeable manner.'[56] Even if the reference here is to traditional historical literature, Maimon evidently regarded it as a realistic, natural domain and an appealing and fascinating alternative to the Talmud, which he viewed as divorced from reality. This was his first step towards breaking free from the restrictions of traditional Jewish culture.

Although Mendelssohn and Maimon rejected the pragmatic–exemplary approach to history and thought it afforded little benefit to the Jews, either as Jews or as men and citizens, many maskilim carried on the approach suggested by Wessely and Euchel, which viewed history as a vital and extremely important field. The relatively unknown Joseph Baran, a young member of the Hevrat Shoharei Hatov Vehatushiyah who often contributed to *Hame'asef* until his untimely death in the 1780s, and Aaron Wolfsohn-Halle (1754–1835), a teacher in the new school in Breslau (where history was included in the curriculum), were among the maskilim who continued to repeat Wessely's claim: the decline of interest in history was a matter that needed to be addressed as part of the process of correcting the flaws of traditional Jewish society. Wolfsohn-Halle upheld Euchel's philosophical assertion of the importance of experience as a category of understanding and knowledge: 'Experience is the father of all crafts and most of the sciences. With its aid, man attains all the manifold treasures of wisdom and rises above all the creatures of the earth; in the absence of experience, man would be inferior to the dumb animals.' History, which provided part of human experience, served to guide man so that he had no need to rely on a heavenly, supernatural authority.[57] Using this concept of the pragmatic benefit of history, the lessons of history might be applied immediately in the life of the individual and the state. Joseph Baran published in *Hame'asef* excerpts of ancient world history, from which, in his view, clear-cut moral lessons could be extracted:

For this is the great benefit: to read in history, to inquire into and search for the thoughts of the gentiles and the nations, their concepts and their beliefs, and to weigh their innermost idea on the scales of justice, and to see what is good and what is not good, what is truth founded on reason, and what is falsehood and vanity; and thereafter to pave a pure and honest path to follow.[58]

[56] Ibid. 28–9.
[57] Wolfsohn-Halle, 'Sihah be'erets hahayim', in Y. Friedlander (ed.), *Studies in Hebrew Satire*, i. 182. [58] Baran, 'Divrei hayamim vehakorot leha'ir kartago', 346–8.

Here history also becomes a touchstone and an ethical guide. In ancient history the young maskil located islands of wisdom and reason and persons of high moral standing, and even succeeded in extracting from them mature and enlightened notions, such as reformed education and religious tolerance, evidence of which he found in ancient Greece and Carthage. The historical examples were proposed as being worthy of emulation, as well as the lessons from political history, whose vicissitudes arose from the tension between unrestrained passions and corrupt morals, on one hand, and virtues, on the other: 'When we see these, we shall know and understand that good lies only in following a straight path, and that true happiness comes only to the innocent and the righteous.'[59]

The maskilic legitimization of history, which turned *torat ha'adam* (in its broad sense as a store of knowledge, a mode of thought, and a system of humanistic ethics) into the organizing principle of history, was perceived as a threat to the values of traditional culture. This is demonstrated by the battle against the Haskalah waged by Rabbi Eleazar Fleckeles of Prague (1759–1826), the disciple and later the heir of Rabbi Yehezkel Landau (1713–93). In a sermon delivered in 1783, Fleckeles levelled a harsh attack against the role in education and lifestyle assigned by the maskilim to *torat ha'adam* and repeated his repudiation of any perusal of the 'books of the heathen', citing the traditional halakhic prohibition. In his sermon he repeatedly condemned history books (at least those written in a foreign tongue and dealing with world history), referring his listeners to the ruling in the *Shulḥan arukh* and the comment of Obadiah of Bertinoro, which, as I have already noted, drastically narrowed the legitimate scope of historical study. Fleckeles particularly despised the maskilic argument that these books contained ethical lessons: 'Heaven forfend, may the mouths be stopped of those who hold the opinion that much moral learning, fear of the Almighty, culture, and proper conduct can be learned from the books of the heretics.'[60] It seems that Fleckeles, like David Tevele before him, all too clearly discerned that the use the maskilim proposed to make of history had a secular significance. Jewish 'enlightened history', like the European version, increasingly regarded man as an autonomous creator of history, assigning him responsibility for his actions and seeking universal mechanisms to account for historical processes, and thus serving the new Jewish ideal which the maskilim wished to shape. The new justifications for curiosity about the past and for the study of history in schools as well as in general, were thus the first distinctive feature of 'maskilic history'. A comparison of these justifications with traditional apologetics for the writing and reading of history, on one hand, and the new roles played by history in the European Enlightenment, on the other, shows that from the 1780s onwards, the maskilim had begun to promote a new trend in the attitude towards history and historical thought. They cut themselves off from 'traditional history', juxtaposing it with the first modern alternative.

[59] Baran, 'Divrei hayamim lemamlakhot', 368–9.
[60] Fleckeles, *Olat tsibur*, i. 9. On Fleckeles, see J. Katz, *Out of the Ghetto*, 147–50.

RATIONALISTIC, REALISTIC, AND
MORALISTIC HISTORY

However, no maskilic historiography based on the new assumptions emerged, despite the new legitimization and the new roles assigned to history, and no Jewish historians focusing on the writing and study of history arose. This was in marked contrast to the eighteenth-century English and French philosophers and the enlightened historians in Germany, who created an extensive historiography, encompassing studies, monographs, and comprehensive works of universal history, giving expression to the new historical concepts. Unlike the men of the Wissenschaft des Judentums in the second and third decades of the nineteenth century, the circle of maskilim in Germany produced very little in the way of historical writing that deserved to be called historiography. 'Maskilic history' was expressed in the numerous references to the past, to be found throughout maskilic works, in both journalistic writing and belles-lettres; however, historical writing as such was relatively scarce. It included explanations of the importance of history, adaptations of biblical stories in textbooks for the new schools,[61] several translations of works dealing with ancient history, biographies of 'great men' who served as precedents for Jewish enlightenment, references to various episodes in Jewish history placed in the mouths of the heroes of maskilic satires, personal letters, formulations of historical schemas outside the framework of a distinctly historical work, and discussions of historical issues, such as those in *Hame'asef*.[62]

Nonetheless, even in the absence of a distinctive historiography, and without having produced even one true historian, 'maskilic history' expressed a sense and picture of the past which can be identified and linked to the maskilic world-view, and which exemplify their severance from traditional historical patterns of thought. In terms of their self-image, as well as in the goals they espoused, the maskilim viewed themselves as researchers applying rationalistic criteria in theory and in practice.[63] Although their research did not lead them to achievements approaching, for example, those of historians in the University of Göttingen school of the same period, their awareness of historical context, their sensitivity to anachronisms, their critical attitude towards historical sources, and in particular their endeavours to provide realistic historical explanations alongside the traditional theological explanations all moulded the Haskalah's rationalistic sense of the past.

The maskilim regarded the anachronistic approach as a logical flaw characteristic of traditional society, and it became the object of their scathing criticism.

---

[61] For example, 'Toledot avoteinu' [The History of our Fathers], in Wolfsohn-Halle, *Avtalyon*, 17–37.

[62] In addition to the articles mentioned in nn. 58 and 59, see Baran, 'Divrei hayamim la'i sitsiliyah', 199–221; id., 'Divrei hayamim lemalkhei ashur vemadai', 66–78, 101–24; id., 'Divrei hayamim le'artsot yavan', 232–6.   [63] Euchel, 'Davar el hakore', 9–14.

Saul Berlin (1740–94) illustrated this trend in his satire *Ketav yosher* (A Certificate of Integrity, 1794), written as a defence of Wessely's *Divrei shalom ve'emet*. In the following excerpt he mocks the unrestrained freedom he found in halakhic literature:

> By way of example, in the tale of Haman and Ahasuerus there are some allusions to a controversy regarding the methods of the great *posekim*, and they claimed that the opinion of Haman followed the method of the Rif [R. Isaac ben Ya'akov Alfasi, 1013–1103], while Ahasuerus followed the method of the Rambam [Maimonides, 1135–1204]. And at times Ahasuerus posed a difficult question formulated by the Maharsha [R. Samuel Eliezer Eidels, 1555–1631] and Haman replied with the explanation of Maharam Schiff [Meir ben Ya'akov Hakohen Schiff, 1605–41] . . . and it is no anomaly to say that Haman and Ahasuerus knew of the controversies of the *posekim* and the laws of the Talmud.[64]

In his play *Siḥah be'erets haḥayim* (A Conversation in the Land of the Living, 1794–7), Aaron Wolfsohn-Halle places in the mouth of a character who represents a traditional Polish rabbi an anachronistic explanation of the greatness of the Greek philosopher Socrates; in a scene set in the 'world of truth' (the afterlife) Socrates' importance becomes clear to all, to the rabbi's sorrow and surprise. The only explanation he can think of is that 'undoubtedly the soul of a righteous man, one of the Jews killed during the Chmielnicki pogrom, was reincarnated in this Greek'.[65] Wolfsohn-Halle comments: 'This man also believes in reincarnation, but in a new way: in his view the soul of a holy man living in the time of Bogdan Chmielnicki [17th cent.] could pass to Socrates; in other words a kind of backward reincarnation to Socrates, who lived about 2,000 years before Chmielnicki.'[66]

The maskilim could not abide such cavalier attitudes to history. They preached the need for chronological order in historical events and insisted that a familiarity with geography and world history was a prerequisite for an understanding of Jewish history. Mendelssohn's *Biur* on the Bible (a German translation with a new commentary) was composed with the participation of a group of maskilim, and followed a very moderate critical approach, although it did make use of earlier German research. As already noted, Mendelssohn stated that the Bible was not a book of history but a book of God's commandments.[67] In his Introduction to the Book of Ruth (1788), Wolfsohn-Halle wrote that in regard to the books of the Prophets and the Hagiographa, it was essential to investigate their authors and dates, as it was for any historical story.[68] Joel Brill (1762–1802), another prominent representative of the maskilim in Prussia during the 1780s and 1790s and the principal of a modern Jewish school in Breslau, wrote a broader and more comprehensive historical introduction to the book of Psalms (*Be'ur lesefer tehilim*, 1791).

---

[64] S. Berlin, *Ketav yosher*. The satire was written ten years before being published in 1794; see edition in Friedlander (ed.), *Studies in Hebrew Satire*, i. 102.

[65] Wolfsohn-Halle, 'Siḥah be'erets haḥayim', 162.   [66] Ibid. 188.

[67] Mendelssohn, 'Or lenetivah', in *Gesammelte Schriften*, xiv; cf. Sandler, *Mendelssohn's Edition*.

[68] Wolfsohn-Halle, *Mavo lebe'ur*.

Under the influence of German biblical scholars, he placed the book in its appropriate historical context, appended a historical–philological survey of the history
of song and music in the ancient world, and attempted to clarify the identity of
the author and the date of the book. He did not even hold back from stating that
the book of Psalms is a collection of different writings, and that King David was
not its sole author. He reached this conclusion on the basis of critical and philological criteria, such as an examination of the various poetic styles in the book,
for, after all, 'there can be no greater perversity than to insist that David knew
through his prescience the poetic style that would be employed by other poets to
be born a long time after his death'.[69]

The beginnings of a critical-contextual approach to texts and events from the
Jewish past appear mainly in the radical wing of the German maskilim. Wolfsohn-
Halle, for example, in a satire written in the 1790s, placed in Maimonides' mouth
harshly criticisms on kabbalah: Maimonides knows nothing about the existence
of the Zohar nor about kabbalists, and is convinced that Rabbi Shimon bar Yohai
would not have written anything so vacuous. The ideas of kabbalah stem, in his
view, 'from the obscure and incorrect concepts of that age'. In Wolfsohn-Halle's
writings one can also find some idea of the chronological and spatial relativity of
the halakhah, and again he bases this on Maimonides: the commandment of
sacrifices depended on historical circumstances 'and had it not been for that particular time and place, the commandment might not have been given at all'. Similar
arguments were very prevalent in the writings of David Friedländer (1750–1834),
and Euchel also believed that *minhagim* 'are not governed by the laws of God and
will alter with changes in place and time'.[70]

Wessely's less well-known article 'Magid hadashot' (The Teller of News,
1790) provides an interesting example of the treatment of historical sources.[71] In
this article Wessely published what he regarded as a startling historical discovery:
a Hebrew translation of a German copy of an abbreviated chronicle of the history
of Cochin Jewry that came into his hands from Göttingen through circuitous
routes, which he described. The translation was accompanied by footnotes and
annotations, in which chronological errors were pointed out and an essential historical background furnished, 'to edify the reader in understanding these matters
that we are copying for him'. Wessely was uncertain whether this was actually an
authentic chronicle, but asserted that painstaking examination had failed to disclose any weighty reasons to suggest that it was a fabrication: the historical context
was plausible and there was no motivation for forging such a document. Nevertheless, he was troubled by doubts; after all, Basnage had discovered that the existence
of Jews in Cochin had been known a century earlier and this raised the question

---

[69] Brill, *Be'ur lesefer tehilim*, introd., 29–30.

[70] Wolfsohn-Halle, 'Sihah be'erets hahayim', 160–7, 188; Friedländer, *Sendschreiben an seine
Hochwürden*; Euchel, 'Igerot meshulam', in Y. Friedlander (ed.), *Studies in Hebrew Satire*, i. 42.

[71] Wessely, 'Magid hadashot', 129–60, 257–76.

of why no direct contact had been established between them and the Jews of
Europe. Wessely wavered between a positive and negative attitude towards the
chronicle, hoping to find confirmation from a different source which would
prove the document's veracity. Did the Jews of Cochin really stem from the Ten
Lost Tribes, some of whom had reached Yemen after the Assyrian exile, had
been expelled from there, and had then arrived in India? Wessely was particularly
anxious to see the original book of chronicles preserved by the Jews of Cochin
with his own eyes. Despite his scepticism, he was so swept up by his enthusiasm
that he drew some far-reaching conclusions: he suggested that Hindu teachings
might have originated in Judaism, since 'in their faith they recognize the existence of the Almighty, and their priests are called Brahmin [a word allegedly
derived from the name of Abram] and by that name the ancient Jews called every
wise man of the gentiles when he abandoned his idols and called on the name of
the Almighty, and that is Brahmin or Abrahmin'. It was also possible, he added,
that the Chinese Confucius was none other than a Jewish sage from the Assyrian
exile.[72]

Christian and Jewish 'sacred history' could only be explained by reference to
the divine, and the arena of historical events was the exclusive stage of God.
Hence the historical explanations of 'traditional history' were mainly theological
and attempted to reveal the workings of the divine plan. These principles no
longer sufficed for the men of the European Enlightenment, and in the wake of
the humanistic historiography of the Renaissance and the seventeenth century
they searched for natural, realistic, secular, and rational historical explanations.[73]

In general, the maskilim did not deny divine intervention in history, but they
no longer regarded it as a full and sufficient historical explanation. Wessely, for
example, on one hand, upheld the traditional theological explanation and accepted
the existence of a divine plan: 'And from that time the Creator prepared heaven
and earth, in His supreme wisdom arranged the seasons of the earth, times for
good and times for evil, for He reads the generations in advance . . . and sets
kings on the throne to be the instrument of His faith, through them to work His
deeds and his laws'; however, on the other hand, it was man's moral actions that
determined the fate of kingdoms and, in his view, *torat ha'adam* was the basis for
their success.[74] The contradictions in Euchel's writings arise from the fact that he
no longer distinguished between theological explanation and natural and rational

[72] Wessely, 'Magid ḥadashot', 147, 153–6. On the question of the authenticity of the chronicle,
see Bar-Ilan, 'Books from Cochin', 74–100.
[73] Montesquieu, *Considerations on the Causes*, 24–5, 35–91, 97–9, 158, 169–70; Cassirer, *The Philosophy of the Enlightenment*, 209–16; Pocock, 'Gibbon's *Decline and Fall*', 287–303. On the historical
method of the historians in 18th-c. Germany, see the discussion in Reill, *The German Enlightenment*. On Kant's historical concept, Kant's essay, 'The Idea of a Universal History from a Cosmopolitan Point of View', 22–34; Thompson, *A History of Historical Writing*, ii. 117–19, 137.
[74] Wessely, *Divrei shalom ve'emet*, ch. 4 and end of ch. 2.

explanation. In his eyes, God was indeed the primal cause of every event, but His actions were carried out in a natural way. For Euchel, Mendelssohn himself provided an example of the ways in which natural providence operated:

And if you knew how to discern the connection between cause and effect in all the Almighty's deeds, and to find in this connection a sign and wonder greater and more marvellous than all the wonders that run counter to or lie outside nature, then you would also know that each and every day the Lord heaps upon us wondrous kindnesses without overturning the order of Creation . . .[75]

As for the explanation of Mendelssohn's appearance on the stage of history and his great success, Euchel, Mendelssohn's first Hebrew biographer, suggested that one ought to analyse the historical context that provided the fertile soil for his advent:

His parents' home, his place of birth, the period during which he grew up and was educated, his situation and that of the people in his life . . . the quality of his place of birth, whether sages and writers lived there, and [one should] inquire into the period of his education, whether that was a generation of knowledge or whether the Lord endowed him with sufficient spiritual gifts to feed his spirit.[76]

Although Euchel concluded that Mendelssohn attained his greatness despite the laws of history, the very fact that he was conscious of the importance of historical context is in keeping with the development of historical thought at this time. Euchel's maskil hero in his satire 'Igerot meshulam' placed even greater emphasis on secular factors at the expense of theological explanations. Perusing the history of Spanish Jewry Meshulam muses about the reasons for their expulsion from Spain: 'I knew that the Lord had smitten his people for having violated His commandments and for their unwillingness to follow His paths,' but this explanation does not satisfy him. He wants to inquire into the roots of evil, and finds an explanation similar to that proposed by Solomon Ibn Verga in his book *Shevet yehudah*, interpreting the expulsion as the result of the jealousy of the masses and the Jews' own provocative behaviour. Their ostentatious lifestyle aroused the fury of the masses, and the edict was not actually issued for religious reasons, since Christianity was opposed to forced conversion; he asserted that there were no logical considerations in support of the 'religious' theory:

It was neither religious zeal nor the love of their teachings that led the nations to do this to Israel, but rather envy of their grandeur and haughtiness. When the masses saw the men of Israel rising to heights, taking pride in their wealth and provoking them, succeeding greatly and amassing honour in the land, they [the Jews] became an impediment to them; so as a pretext they pointed the barbs of their evil intentions at their different religion, falsely accusing them until they were entirely banished from the land.[77]

---

[75] Euchel, *Toledot harav*, 15, 17.   [76] Ibid. 17–19.
[77] Euchel, 'Igerot meshulam', 49–50.

The blame is placed squarely on the Jews themselves. This was not a decree from heaven, and different and more restrained behaviour would have prevented the expulsion. Obviously this explanation, based on social, economic, and psychological causes, cannot be viewed in isolation from its maskilic context but must also be seen as an indirect criticism of the rich Jewish élite in Berlin, where Euchel lived. More radical maskilim turned these secular explanations of the fate of the Jewish people into a permanent motif. To Solomon Maimon, the ignorance of the Jews and their opposition to rational reforms explained the persecutions they suffered, and in David Friedländer's view, the Jews' hostility towards the Christians stemmed from their intolerance and their particularistic social insularity.[78]

As a matter of fact, Maimon no longer had any need of theological explanations. In sketching the historical context in which Maimonides had emerged in twelfth-century Spain, he described a figure who was a natural product of the place and the time—a product of flourishing Muslim Spain, in which the arts, the sciences, the wealth of the state, the education of its inhabitants, and the academies and renowned universities were thriving. The freedom enjoyed by the Jews, which enabled them to take an active part in the general prosperity and enlightenment, and the fine education that Maimonides received in Talmud, languages, and sciences constituted the circumstances that accounted for his exemplary qualities. In contrast, the opponents of science and philosophy gained the upper hand in France, where 'unparalleled political upheaval, ignorance, and vulgarity' prevailed.[79] Maimon employed similar criteria in explaining the rise of the hasidic movement in Poland. After examining its ideological and social foundations, he concluded that it was a movement that rose up against the Jewish aristocracy and aspired to dominate the Jewish people. Its leaders had a programme that was 'both moral and political', which succeeded thanks to a combination of social and psychological factors: the natural tendency towards idleness and a contemplative lifestyle, the burdensome yoke of the religious leaders, the penchant for fantasies and miracles, and the aridity of rabbinical study.[80]

THE MODERN PERIOD IN THE MASKILIC PICTURE OF THE PAST

A new sense of the past only develops when a significant change occurs in the way in which the present is viewed. Yehoshua Arieli's studies have shown how great an impact the terms 'modern era' and 'Middle Ages' made when they first appeared. They expressed the awareness of European intellectuals in the fifteenth and sixteenth centuries, and later in the seventeenth and eighteenth, of the onset of a new era, distinct from its predecessor. At this point European historiography also

---

[78] Maimon, *Autobiography*, 134–5; Friedländer, *Sendschreiben an seine Hochwürden*, 8.
[79] Maimon, *Lebensgeschichte*, ii. 1–14.   [80] Ibid. 81–93.

began to use the three-phase periodization (the ancient era, the Middle Ages, and the modern era). A great deal more than a historiographic system, it was tantamount to a rebellion against the Christian theological picture of the past. In Arieli's opinion, the introduction of the term 'modern era' provides 'important evidence of the self-awareness of the period' which coined it, implying a definite trend towards secularization.[81] From this standpoint, the self-awareness of the maskilim in Germany at the end of the eighteenth century was almost identical to that of the French *philosophes* and the German *Aufklärer*. They also shared in the belief, which soon became unquestioned Enlightenment dogma, that they were witnessing a highly significant historical shift in their own time. The new approach to the continuum of historical time, new images of periods, a new concept of the dynamic of time, and the formulation of new historical schemas all stemmed from the awareness of this shift. Even though there was no general agreement on whether the eighteenth century was an orderly, perfect, and enlightened century or simply one in the throes of a historical process that would lead to this happier condition, the men of the Enlightenment, Jews and non-Jews alike, shared the feeling that 'mankind [had] at last emerged, or [was] emerging, from the dark wilderness of the past into the bright, ordered world of the eighteenth century'.[82]

A similar historical approach can be found in Christian Wilhelm von Dohm's *Über die bürgerliche Verbesserung der Juden* (1781); in this instance it supported his demand for a changed attitude towards the Jews. This work was extremely influential in teaching historical concepts to the maskilim. It provided them with the grounds for distinguishing between the barbaric age that had passed and the new age, characterized by reason, justice, and merciful monarchs. It also lent support to the 'environmental theory', which claimed that historical circumstances were the sole cause of the economic, cultural, and spiritual decline of the Jews, and that a change in circumstances would make possible their reform and rehabilitation, allowing them to take their place as useful and moral citizens of the state.[83]

One can easily view the Enlightenment's images of the historical past as a projection onto the past of an enlightened vision of the future, which sometimes takes on the dimensions of a secular messianic vision. The social-ideological stance of the Aufklärer and their participation in a propaganda battle on which they pinned their hopes (but which also led to disillusionment), as well as their strivings for social and cultural change, were reflected in the historical systems they created. The mixed elements of optimism and pessimism, the antagonism between

---

[81] Arieli, 'The Modern Age and Secularization'; cf. also Hampson's view on the crucial importance of an awareness of historical reorientation, in *The Enlightenment*, 146–50. On the new periodization, see Nadel, 'Periodization', 581–4.

[82] C. Becker, *The Heavenly City*, 118. See also Montesquieu, *The Spirit of the Laws*, ii. 54–6.

[83] von Dohm, *Über die bürgerliche Verbesserung*; see also Liberles, 'Dohm's Treatise on the Jews', 29–42; Möller, 'Aufklärung, Judenemanzipation und Staat', 119–49.

reason and a misplaced faith in tradition, the abyss between their age and the medieval 'dark age', as well as the concept of progress, all served to bolster the Enlightenment belief that historical reorientation would be more than an intuition, and would be fulfilled in reality. Thus the new sense of the past that arose in the eighteenth century was directed towards the establishment of a new reality, and in this sense it served all branches of the European Enlightenment, including the Aufklärer in Germany, who were the chief source of influence on the maskilim there.

Wessely, in his *Divrei shalom ve'emet*, was the first writer to articulate a new evaluation of the present, together with a consciousness of modernity, a new attitude towards the past, the use of the maskilic picture of the future to measure the past, and a strong sense of a contemporary historical shift, which he welcomed, pointing to the possibilities it held for altering the destiny of the Jewish people. This work attempted to imbue Jewish society with a consciousness of change—a motif which accompanied the Haskalah from this point until the end of the nineteenth century, becoming dogma, the intellectual hallmark of the maskil, and a permanent feature of 'maskilic history'. The Creator 'in His supreme wisdom arranged the seasons of the earth, times for good and times for evil', and to the maskilim's joy they were privileged to live in an auspicious time, marked by the achievements of science—the invention of printing, the discovery of America, the invention of gunpowder and the telescope—achievements that in the view of the European Enlightenment also denoted the shift to the modern era. In the social–ethical sphere an opportunity presented itself 'to uproot hatred from the hearts of men, senseless hatred about a quarrel that is not their own, which originates in changes in faith and worship'. In his view, religious tolerance was the main and most revolutionary expression of the new era, and the people of Israel would be positively affected by the winds of change.

In the light of this assumption Wessely had already sketched out the general lines of the maskilic historical schema, based on the principle of rational thought: in ancient days, before the exile, the people of Israel had lived a perfect life based on *torat ha'adam*. The exile put an end to this period of glory, bringing a wave of pogroms, expulsions, and wandering, and in the medieval period the Jewish people declined, just as the European world declined, through long centuries of religious intolerance and the abandonment of rational thought. Only in recent years had 'merciful kings', enlightened absolutists, come to power, changing the face of history and presaging a new era for the Jewish people too—a restoration in the sense of reforming Jewish society, redressing the flaws that had marred it in the previous period, and restoring it to the right path of the wisdom of man: 'for what you are doing is but reviving the proper customs that were ours in ancient times, forgotten only because of the hostility of our persecutors'. For the last two centuries a new attitude of Jews had been emerging in Europe, now 'that the kings have joined together to remove the iron yoke from our necks'.

For their part, the Jews had only to respond by awakening from their slumbers. This new attitude first appeared in the Netherlands after her war with Spain, when she granted asylum to all religions and faiths in keeping with her adherence to the principle of religious tolerance. Following in the Netherlands' footsteps, England adopted a similar line, allowing Jews to settle there again in the seventeenth century. In the lands of the Holy Roman Empire it was the king of Prussia, Frederick II, who had reached the rational conclusion that 'it is fitting for a king to rule over free men and not over those enslaved to slaves'. Von Dohm's work, calling for tolerance towards the Jews, could only have been written under the rule of such a 'merciful king', guided by rational considerations. Wessely also discerned the first intimations of religious tolerance in the rule of the French king Louis XVI; even in the policies of Catherine the Great of Russia and the king of Poland he saw indications that the situation of the Jews would be improved. Head and shoulders above all these was the figure of Joseph II, Holy Roman Emperor from 1780 to 1790, 'who does much to further tolerance . . . and all of his royal decrees are replete with knowledge and love of mankind and charity'.[84]

Euchel made a key contribution to the maskilic picture of the past by singling out Moses Mendelssohn as the key figure of the new period in Jewish history. From then onwards Mendelssohn appeared in every maskilic periodization at the end of the 'dark' period and at the opening of the new era of light, reason, tolerance, and moral regeneration of Jewish society. Euchel's biography of Mendelssohn explains why the latter was regarded as representing the historical turning-point: Mendelssohn had 'restored [Judaism] to its pristine condition', reinstated study of the Torah to its rightful place, and urged the adoption of a pure Hebrew tongue, the study of foreign languages, and the love of sciences. It was Mendelssohn who had proved that 'There is still hope for the Jews, and they will no longer be put to shame by the gentiles saying: this is a heartless, good-for-nothing nation.' Mendelssohn's crowning achievements were in the sphere of improving and altering the Jewish image in the eyes of the surrounding culture; hence the encounter between Mendelssohn and Lessing became one of the major expressions of the historical shift. Mendelssohn's fame encouraged a tolerant attitude towards the Jews, culminating in the removal of several 'obstacles that were stumbling-blocks for the Jews in the early days, when every man was bowed under the wicked yoke of the priests who seek to do harm to this people . . .'. The Christian theological view had undergone a change along with the change in the image of the Jews, and all this was to a great extent due to Mendelssohn, who had so adeptly demonstrated in his own life that the Jew 'is not inferior to any other person in the teachings of man', and this without 'moving even one step away from the religion of his forefathers'.[85]

[84] Wessely, *Divrei shalom ve'emet*, chs. 3, 4, and 8; id., 'Magid hadashot', 133.
[85] Euchel, *Toledot harav* (Vienna, 1814), 27–8, 41, 136–7.

In the pages of *Hame'asef* the maskilim constantly reiterated these basic concepts of the maskilic picture of the past:

To our joy! For the hand and sword has been taken from the priests and the swindlers, and the king's sceptre shall govern with clemency . . . the man who believes in a good and loving God for humankind is our brother and friend . . . How goodly is our lot, for the era dominated by false prophets and priests who have corrupted religion for their own egoistic ends has been replaced by a happier time for all humanity—an era of religious tolerance.[86]

They extolled Europe, attributing to her an ideal image as a place in which brotherhood between men prevailed, power was in the hands of merciful kings, laws were tolerant, sciences and arts flourished, and citizens adhered to the Christian religion, the best of all religions (except, of course, the Jewish religion). In sharp contrast, Africa was peopled by 'very stupid men' and Asia by unlettered 'boors'.[87]

The news from France that reached the editorial offices of *Hame'asef* in 1789–90 further reinforced the new maskilic consciousness. 'Now when the sun of wisdom is shining over a people and a kingdom, their eyes will be opened to see justice and law and they will cast aside all vanity and frivolity.' For the maskilim, the French Revolution was an affirmation of their optimistic outlook and a new opportunity for the Jewish people: 'For now comes a time of hope that perhaps the days to come will be better for the Tribe of Israel than the days gone by.' The editors of *Hame'asef* welcomed the news from France and appealed to the Jews to respond to historical changes by acquiring knowledge and wisdom, which would prepare them everywhere in Europe to move from the status of foreigners shunned by society at large to the status of brethren, whose religion would no longer be a stumbling-block to those who wished to participate in the 'political well-being'.[88]

Moses Mendelssohn, depicted as the key figure at the opening of the new era in Jewish history, did not himself live to see the French Revolution, but it is doubtful whether he would have regarded it as a fundamental historical change. While he did not deny the existence of historical changes nor overlook the uniqueness of his period in contrast to both the recent and distant past, his interpretation of historical change was moderate and sceptical, even though he did use some of the accepted maskilic images and modernistic rhetoric. He viewed the classical past as an admirable epoch, the 'splendid morning' of philosophy, and the Middle Ages as a time of the decline of philosophy and the rule of dark minds, barbarism, superstition, and religious intolerance. 'Those cruel accusations [against the Jews], imprinted with the stamp of the times and of the monks' cells, the place where they were conceived', were in his view evidence of the medieval

---

[86] Baran, 'Divrei hayamim vehakorot leha'ir kartago', 344–8.

[87] Id., 'Divrei hayamim le'artsot yavan', 195–6; id., 'Divrei hayamim lemamlakhot', 369–85.

[88] Anon., 'Toledot hazeman', 365–7; *Hame'asef*, 4 (1788), 187–8. See also Michael, 'Triumph of the Ideas of "The Enlightenment"', 275–98; Feiner, 'Did the French Revolution Influence the Development of the "Berlin Enlightenment"?', 89–92.

barbarism inspired by Christianity.[89] In his age, Mendelssohn asserted, 'times [had] changed'. The revolutionary invention of printing and the emergence in the Netherlands of the idea of religious tolerance had paved the way to the eighteenth century. Mendelssohn thanked Heaven for having been privileged to see 'the auspicious hour, in which the full rights of humanity in their correct measure are taken to heart'.[90] He regarded Reimarus, Lessing, and von Dohm as the intellectuals and theoreticians who foreshadowed religious tolerance in Prussia, where he resided, and Frederick the Great as an enlightened ruler, open to the consideration and implementation of new ideas: 'I reside in a country in which one of the wisest sovereigns ever to rule over men has caused the arts and sciences to flower so abundantly and made the freedom of enlightened thought so attainable by the general public that their influence extends even to the lesser of the inhabitants of our lands.'[91] The favourable and rational atmosphere created by Frederick, as well as the decline of religious intolerance, enabled philosophers like Mendelssohn to sit in their studies writing their learned tracts, while observing this beneficial process with exhilaration.

However, Mendelssohn was also troubled by more than a few doubts: every period was characterized by the struggle of opposing forces, and in his view, it was by no means clear that the second half of the eighteenth century deserved to be described as a happy time. The invention of the printing press, for example, was indeed a revolutionary development, but this expression of modernism also had negative implications, first and foremost the declining value of the human aspect of man. Men no longer saw any need for close personal contact, in conversation, or for a first-hand knowledge of nature. The intellectual world had become a world of correspondence through lifeless letters. This was not the case in ancient times; 'maybe we cannot say they were better, but they certainly were different'. Man was more urgently in need of man then; life was fuller and more vibrant. Hence, material plenty might actually endanger the human spirit, even degenerating and debasing it. The triumph of religious tolerance was also not yet certain: 'Reason and the spirit of inquiry of our century have still not entirely eradicated the traces of the barbarism of history.' Superstition and anti-Jewish prejudice persisted in Christian consciousness, impeding the true integration of Jews into society at large. The status of Jews was still inferior, and here and there barbarism still burst forth into the modern world in the shape of blood libels and dreadful torture, religious intolerance, and the exercise of barbaric laws, as had occurred in the infamous case of the Frenchman Jean Calas, which had aroused enlightened public opinion in Europe in the 1760s. Mendelssohn suggested that it would be wiser to wait and see whether the improved conditions would really endure, and whether their potential would be realized and lead to a change in the situation of the Jews, since despite the processes of enlightenment and the trends

[89] Mendelssohn, *Gesammelte Schriften*, viii. 6–7 (Preface to 'Vorrede, Menassah Ben Israel Rettung der Juden').   [90] Ibid. 3–4, 6–8.   [91] Ibid. 3–4.

of toleration, 'even in our own times, which are better than those, enlightenment has by no means progressed yet to the point where those same crude accusations will no longer have any effect'.[92] True brotherhood among men had not yet been attained. Mendelssohn revealed a changing and ambivalent attitude towards Joseph II's Edict of Tolerance. Unlike Wessely, for instance, he was not particularly enthusiastic about it, and his attitude vacillated between hesitation, joy, and rejection. He concluded his introduction to Manasseh ben Israel's *Vindication of the Jews* on a hopeful note: 'The delusion that religion can only be maintained by iron force is gradually vanishing. Nations are now tolerating one another; they show a measure of kindness and forbearance towards you, an attitude which, with the help of Him who fashions the hearts of men, may ultimately grow into genuine brotherly love.'[93] However, in his letter to Naphtali Herz Homberg (1749–1841) in 1783, he revealed his suspicion of a Jesuit subterfuge, 'through which they encourage us, with ostensible friendship, to unite—while in truth what they desire is to entice us to convert'. If these temptations were heeded, Mendelssohn wrote, 'in fifty years' time everything [would] sink again into barbarism'.[94]

Mendelssohn's scepticism also led him into an argument about progress with his friend Lessing. Mendelssohn, in his *Jerusalem*, disagreed with the progressive synopsis of history that Lessing had outlined in *Die Erziehung des Menschengeschlechts*, and refused to accept it: 'I, for my part, cannot share the view of mankind's education into which my late friend Lessing was misled by who knows which scholar of history.'[95] In Mendelssohn's view, mankind stood at the same level in every historical period: 'in nearly every century mankind is simultaneously youthful, mature, and old, but in different places and regions of the world'. Each people had its own developmental pattern, and passed through life cycles that are independent of those of other peoples. Continuous progress towards perfection and happiness was possible only for the individual. Mendelssohn regarded the progressive schema as a historical–philosophical speculation with no basis in historical reality. For example, there was no need to assume that artistic and technological progress would be accompanied by moral progress. Historical reality revealed the intentions of Providence, and 'If you take mankind as a whole, you will not find that there is constant progress in its development that brings it ever nearer to perfection.' History was replete with advances and regressions. Each step forward was followed by a step backward, while here and there points of light flickered and then faded away: 'Individual men make progress, but mankind oscillates continually within fixed limits. Seen as a whole, however, mankind has clearly maintained virtually the same degree of morality through all fluctuations and periods—the same mixture of religion and irreligion, of virtue and vice, of happiness and misery.'[96]

[92] Mendelssohn, *Gesammelte Schriften*, viii. 3–10.

[93] Ibid. 23–5.

[94] Ibid. iii. 132–4; cf. J. Katz, 'To Whom was Mendelssohn Replying?', 127–38.

[95] Mendelssohn, *Gesammelte Schriften*, viii. 67.

[96] Ibid. 61–8.

Several basic assumptions in Mendelssohn's thought determined his relatively pessimistic concept of history. First, he rejected the view that Judaism was an anachronistic and inferior stage in religious development, in contrast to Christianity. He asserted that this was a reversal of reality—Christianity was a degenerate form of Judaism and a corruption of pure religion. He placed a greater stress on the individual's personal progress, regardless of his religious beliefs, and assigned less importance to the processes affecting larger groups, such as states, peoples, and humankind.[97] According to Mendelssohn's picture of the past, the Jewish people in its ancient time of glory possessed the potential of being 'a nation of priests'—'a nation which, through its constitution and institutions, through its laws and conduct, and throughout all changes of life and fortune, was to call wholesome and unadulterated ideas of God and His attributes continuously to the attention of the rest of mankind'.[98] Unfortunately, however, the process of deterioration had soon set in. The sin of the Golden Calf was its first manifestation, and the people's demand for a king in the time of Samuel was the second: 'Before long, this luminous cycle had also run its course. Matters were soon back or near the low point from which they had started, as the events of many past centuries have unhappily shown only too clearly.' It seemed that the period of glory had been no more than a meteor that glowed briefly and was extinguished: 'The Mosaic constitution did not persist long in its original purity.'[99] Mendelssohn ended *Jerusalem* with a mixture of hope and despair: 'At least prepare the way for your more fortunate descendants to [reach] that height of culture, that universal human tolerance for which reason is still sighing in vain.'[100]

Mendelssohn's cautious and pessimistic approach to historical time and to the eighteenth century did not ultimately become the dominant maskilic view.[101] Most of the maskilim in Germany shared the optimism and awareness of the shift represented by Wessely, Euchel, Baran, Wolfsohn-Halle and others. They felt it was incumbent upon them to persuade Jewish society to accept their stance and their concept of history. At the same time voices challenging the maskilic approach were heard. In the famous sermon delivered by Yehezkel Landau, the rabbi of Prague, immediately after the publication of Wessely's *Divrei shalom ve'emet*, he made favourable mention of the event that Wessely viewed as a historical shift—the publication of the Edict of Tolerance—and praised Joseph II as a merciful king for the Jews. However, Landau hastened to stress that one ought not to draw any conclusion—radical, practical, or theoretical—from this, since it did not constitute a substantive change in the basic situation of the Jewish people as exiles.[102]

---

[97] Altmann, *Moses Mendelssohn*, 539–42.   [98] Mendelssohn, *Gesammelte Schriften*, viii. 87–9.

[99] Ibid. 91, 103.   [100] Ibid. 110.

[101] Pelli, *Moses Mendelssohn*; Altmann, 'A New Evaluation', 47–58.

[102] Landau, *Derushei hazelah*, sermon 39, p. 53: 'We will feel no pride even though we have a merciful king who does much for our sake; nonetheless, as we are in a land that is not our own, it befits us to submit to the inhabitants of the country.' Substantive change can only take place in the era of redemption.

His disciple and heir Eleazar Fleckeles, mentioned above as taking a stand against the innovations of the maskilim, expanded on this theme in his sermons in the 1780s, denigrating the idea of progress: 'Oh, this evil generation, which views itself as wise, haughtily declares there is none wiser or more intelligent; nor has there ever been one like it, for in each and every generation wisdom multiplies and intelligence grows greater.' Fleckeles rebuked the maskilim for having developed a lofty image of their time, and also for believing that in this happy era there was hope for a change in the fate of the Jews:

In its own eyes, this generation is as pure as the heavens themselves; they are all wise, all clever, perfectly endowed with excellent virtues and good deeds, all well-versed in the administration of men's spiritual affairs, the administration of the home, the administration of the state, and in their misguided view, this time offers respite and salvation for the Jews, and the land will be filled with wisdom and knowledge of the natural sciences, mathematics, and philosophy.

Fleckeles wanted to prove that the doctrine of progress was basically flawed and that the true historical dynamic was its very opposite. The decline in life expectancy from the figures recorded in the book of Genesis, for example, was, in his view, evidence that the constant decline of generations was a divine law; hence those who believed in progress erred and would mislead others: 'Please, my brethren, lovers of truth, distance yourselves from these new inquiries; they are but vain acts of deception. How much more beautiful is the everyday talk of the ancients on sacred topics.'[103] Like his mentor Landau, Fleckeles was wary of a radical interpretation of the Austrian regime's attitude towards the Jews, which might undermine the foundations of Jewish tradition:

For here, in this generation in which the kings of the land and the nations have together nullified the previous sore tribulations . . . and have agreed that all nations should be equal, for their benefit, and will act together in love and affection, for although their religions differ, the people do not . . . and the Almighty will reward them; but much to our distress, because of this many are casting off the yoke of the Lord's words, saying that by royal authority they are permitted to eat animals which have not been ritually slaughtered, and the flesh of pigs, and they welcome the fact that the Almighty has kept us alive and sustained us and brought us to these days, in which every man can do as he sees fit, and weighty opinions are crushed.[104]

The merciful kings did not intend, he asserted, to destroy the distinctive traditions and faiths of each people; their sole aim was to introduce religious tolerance. If the outcome was to be the abandonment of all restraint, he would have preferred to return to the days of the old troubles, which were better than these. Despite the burden of the exile and the harsh enslavement of the monarchies, the Jewish people had not formerly estranged themselves from their God, while

---

[103] Fleckeles, *Olat tsibur*, 84.   [104] Ibid. 86*b*.

'now we sit calmly, for there is no trouble or outcry in our streets . . . and each and every year we hear of new violations of which our forefathers never dreamed.'[105]

The traditional stance, which refused to draw the necessary conclusions from the historical shift, was stridently denounced by the maskilim. Maskilic polemic against the traditional outlook is interwoven in Saul Berlin's witty satire *Ketav yosher*, written in 1784 with the aim of supporting Wessely against his opponents. To take matters to an absurd extreme, he places words of almost nostalgic yearning for the darkest periods in Jewish history in the mouth of the representative of traditional society:

For now all that remains to us is to distance ourselves far from them [the gentiles]. Nor shall we ever wish them anything good, and if thanks to their hatred of us the troubles that arise to spell our end should multiply, then that is all to the good, for in this way we shall gain an opportunity to sanctify the Holy Name before the very eyes of the gentiles. For from the day that the Temple was destroyed and the sacrifices were abolished, God, blessed be He, can have no greater satisfaction than to see us being killed and slaughtered like a sacrifice to consecrate His great Name, and our forefathers in former days rejoiced when the hatred of the nations became relentless . . . and may it come to pass that I, so poor and humble, will be found worthy to be killed or hung in sanctification of the Lord's Name. And it befits any man called a Jew to desire that the nations will despise us, so that we may attain the status of those righteous ones. And if, because of our numerous sins, the kings of the nations should abolish the decrees and the annihilations and killings, then we ought to think of this as a punishment and beg them to change their minds . . . how great a privilege was given to the dead of Betar [in the second-century Bar Kokhba revolt] . . . and the victims of Chmielnicki in [seventeenth-century] Poland were also so fortunate.[106]

Consciousness of the historical shift and the concept of the 'modern age' inevitably created a new picture of the past that broke the continuity of the exile and eased the historical tension between Jew and non-Jew. And yet traditional society was portrayed as determined to retain its picture of the past, 'for the bitter exile and the hatred of the nations burnish our sins and are better than all wisdom and science in glorifying and elevating the Almighty'.[107] Another traditional argument which Berlin attacked in *Ketav yosher* was self-disparagement in relation to the authority of the ancient Sages, and the belief that the generations that followed them had declined. The maskilim believed that these two views—failure to recognize the historical changes that had occurred and the inability to accept the notion of progress—stood in the way of any possibility of social reform. They thus attributed great importance to the new historical images that they presented as a way of changing the traditional world-view.

Aaron Wolfsohn-Halle's play *Siḥah be'erets haḥayim* can be seen as one of these attempts. In the land of souls a Polish rabbi representing traditional society debates with Maimonides, and is unwilling to accept the premiss that phenomena such as thunder and lightning are based on laws of nature. Referring to the Talmud,

---

[105] Ibid. 86*b*, 87*a*.   [106] S. Berlin, *Ketav yosher*, 95.   [107] Ibid. 95–6.

he claims these are supernatural phenomena: 'Shall I not rely on the words of our Sages? Shall I contradict the righteous ones who excel by far all the philosophers who have lived from the time of Adam until today?' To this argument he adds the traditional opinion: 'If the ancients are like humans, then we are like asses, for what are we when compared to them?'[108] Maimonides rejects the talmudic statement, claiming it was not accepted by the majority of the Sages but was merely a legend that was not binding, while Wolfsohn-Halle seizes the opportunity to make a long marginal comment attacking self-deprecation in relation to the ancients. Man was given an opportunity to acquire experience during his life-time, and this experience enabled him to advance with accelerating speed in the arts and sciences. Every generation benefited from the experience of its pre-decessors:

The relationship between the ages of humans is like the relationship between the genera-tions of mankind, the earlier and the later, between fathers and sons. The ancients were by no means capable of penetrating the secrets of nature as their descendants did, and of course, these were surpassed by the generations that came after them, for each generation acquires new experiences and extracts from them new inventions and discoveries.[109]

The saying in the Talmud which contradicts this view was in his eyes tantamount to a superstition which people were now casting off. It should not be interpreted as meaning that 'human intelligence is lessening with each generation', or that 'everything must remain as it was 1,500 years ago . . . for we with our ass-like intelligence dare not touch what those with human reason had determined'. Wolfsohn-Halle suggested a different, less restricting and inhibiting interpreta-tion of the problematic saying of the Sages: Rabbi Pinhas ben Meir, who made this statement, was comparing his own generation to that of the Sages of the mishnaic period merely from the standpoint of supernatural traits, and did not mean to say that men's intelligence was dwindling.[110] In his play Wolfsohn-Halle also introduced the enlightened historical synopsis, which from then on, by using von Dohm's environmental theory, became the most prevalent: the Jewish people was plunged into exile, marked by external pressure, hatred of religion, spiritual–religious deviation, and disillusionment with the 'learning of man', but now a more promising present had appeared, 'when the king and his ministers in our time have begun to lift the yoke from the shoulders of the Jews and to raise them from the ashes and instate them as men'.[111] In Wolfsohn-Halle's play these words are placed in the mouth of Moses Mendelssohn, as he explains to Maimonides what has happened to the Jewish people in recent gener-ations. Mendelssohn himself, with Maimonides' 'sanction', marks the historical turning-point. The first step in reforming Jewish society was taken by Maimon-ides in his time, and the second complementary step was taken by Mendelssohn.

[108] Wolfsohn-Halle, 'Siḥah be'erets haḥayim', 155–6.   [109] Ibid. 179–84 n. 14.
[110] Ibid. 184.   [111] Ibid. 173–4.

'For if indeed I first began to mark a path leading to our God,' says Wolfsohn-Halle's fictitious Maimonides, 'then you, thank the Lord, have cleared it, and have removed from it every obstacle that was hidden from my sight.'[112]

In the 1790s four maskilim—David Friedländer, Solomon Maimon, Lazarus Bendavid (1762–1832), and Shaul Ascher (1767–1822)—proposed historical outlines that were much more radical and philosophical in nature. Several factors were common to all four: they attempted to grapple philosophically with the key concepts raised by Mendelssohn in his *Jerusalem* (religious truths, the history of the Jewish religion, the validity of the halakhah); they used contemporary philosophical terminology in formulating their ideas; they were not afraid to draw the conclusion that faith and religious ritual must be reformed; and they wrote most of their theses in German, demonstrating their involvement in Christian social circles and their interest in addressing their writings to the non-Jewish reader in particular.[113] Their historical outlines had a philosophical cast and focused on the history of the Jewish religion. Their portrayal of the break in historical continuity and their sense of a historical shift were particularly perceptive, and their image of the future was accompanied by far-reaching conclusions regarding the radical reforms required of the Jewish people if they wanted to enter the world of European culture and gain civil rights.

In 1792 the young Shaul Ascher published *Leviathan*, which he dedicated to the king of Prussia, Frederick Wilhelm II, expressing his gratitude for 'the generous benefits awaiting my nation in the Prussian lands'. Ascher sketched a historical–philosophical synopsis in which he delineated several stages in the history of the Jewish religion:

1. The regulative stage, from the days of the Patriarchs until the Torah was given to the Jews, during which the substance of Judaism, its elements of faith, and the symbols of its observance were crystallized.

2. The constitutive stage, from the revelation at Mount Sinai, when the religion was turned into 'regulations' and it became necessary to act according to dictated norms, i.e. laws.

3. The stage of decline and defilement, beginning with the Second Temple period, when the substance, which had become institutionalized in the second stage, was forgotten. The laws became the major focus, the 'Pharisaic' trend intensified, and the spirit of factionalism corroded Judaism. This stage, in which Judaism became a 'constitution totally different from the original constitution', continued through the Middle Ages until the eighteenth century.

4. The future stage, in which an effort would be made to 'purify Judaism', and to 'abandon the old constitution', which Ascher regarded as 'the complete

[112] Ibid. 164.
[113] Meyer, *The Origins of the Modern Jew*, 57–84, 115–25; M. Graetz, 'The Formation of the New "Jewish Consciousness"', 219–37.

degeneration of our faith'; it would be replaced by a 'new constitution which will teach us the true nature of Judaism'.[114]

This provides yet another example of the historical dynamic characteristic of the Haskalah: an original golden age which gradually degenerated, the sense of a turning-point in the eighteenth century, and expectations of change—although in this case the scheme was applied to Judaism as a system of belief and halakhah, rather than to the historical destiny of the Jews.

A similar historical synopsis, positing deviation, degeneration, and decline in Judaism, is reflected in the periodization of the history of Jewish religion outlined by Solomon Maimon:

1. The period of natural religion, from the time of the Patriarchs to the giving of the Torah.

2. The period between the giving of the Torah and Rabbi Shimon Hatsadik (Simon the Just), the last of the men of the Great Assembly, during which the laws of the Torah were interpreted and new laws were added as required by contemporary circumstances.

3. The period of the Mishnah, during which the additional laws were committed to writing by Rabbi Judah Hanasi.

4. The period of the Talmud, during which the brief and succinct words of the Mishnah were interpreted.

5. The fifth period, which began with the completion of the Talmud and 'continues to this very day, and is destined to continue for ever . . . until the coming of the Messiah'. This period, as already noted, was marked by decline and degeneration and was characterized by a multiplicity of new laws and the adoption of alien customs, which, in Maimon's view, originated among other peoples.[115]

The basis of this periodization was the changes in halakhah, and, in Maimon's view, a dynamic characterized by degeneration from an age of reason: 'Thus the religion, which was originally a natural religion and in accord with reason, became unsightly.' The blame for this process, which was not inevitable, lay with the rabbis, who had perverted the pure religion, and Maimon looked forward to an age in which it would be possible 'to re-establish the harmony between religion and reason, which had been destroyed by prejudice'.[116]

In 1793 Lazarus Bendavid wrote in an extremely pessimistic tone that 'Since the destruction of the Temple in AD 70 Jewish history has sunk for over 1,700 years into an oppressive, impenetrable darkness.' David Friedländer's well-known anonymous letter to Teller in 1799, in which he suggested joining the Church on

---

[114] Ascher, *Leviathan, oder über Religion*, dedication to the king: bk. 2, ch. 5, bk. 3, ch. 5.
[115] Maimon, *Lebensgeschichte*, i. 245–8.   [116] Ibid. 244, 264.

the basis of common natural religion, is also replete with melancholy historical reflections. Friedländer regarded it as a historical certainty that 'Moses had already found among the fathers of his nation pure and pristine teachings, religious concepts free of any trace of heresy or idolatry', and that he had transmitted the idea of the pure divine essence and the undefiled concepts to the Israelites when they left Egypt. Moses was unable to remain content with an abstract, pure religion, however, and as a leader saw a need to educate the people through the rituals of the commandments. From that moment, when the constitution was formulated like a shell 'enveloping the great principles of the religion which are the content of the entire constitution', the primeval purity of the 'golden age' was marred, and with the destruction of the Jewish state and the exile of the Jews, decadence and decline began to set in. The first manifestation of this decline was the writing down of the Oral Torah: 'From the moment when the customs stopped having any real meaning or arousing any thought leading to moral or social activity, everything degenerated and turned into hypocrisy.' From this stage onwards the Jewish historical past was nothing but a succession of sad pictures: 'With grief and sorrow we now cast our glance down at the history of the Jews, who are no longer a nation nor recognized as such. Sharing their misery, we walk about among the ruins of their Temple and their state, which in the days of their flowering were so interwoven that they formed a single unit.' Loss of respect for reason and lofty truth and excessive attention to the 'shell'—the practical commandments, messianic faith in a miraculous redemption, religious concepts that became more and more mystical—all corrupted the minds and morals of the people. Friedländer's image of the condition of Judaism is akin to the image of the dark Middle Ages popular among Enlightenment historians, who viewed the period as a time when the Christian Church had sunk into a bleak state even worse than that of Judaism:

A vast darkness overpowered everything and man's reason was pinned under the yoke of superstition and fanaticism. One passes through many centuries devoid of any morals or virtues, when coarse manners and unrestrained passions were dominant and not a single bud of humaneness had shown itself as yet. True scholarship vanished, replaced by nit-picking scholasticism . . . all bearing the imprint of a distorted mind, of contorted common sense, awakening in us both pity and revulsion.[117]

However, the parallel between general history and Jewish history ended in the sixteenth century with the Reformation. European Christian history had succeeded in shaking off the gloom and climbing out of the depths of the dark period: 'After a long night, the daylight of reason shone forth slowly, but with an irrepressible intensity.' The new era was marked by reason, humaneness, and religious tolerance, and the Jews too desired to become a part of it and to end their own 'age of darkness'. History demonstrated mankind's steady march towards the develop-

[117] Friedländer, *Sendschreiben an seine Hochwürden*, 21–37; Bendavid, *Etwas zur Charackteristick der Juden*, 11.

ment of intellectual and moral forces, and these changes called for a response by the Jewish people. In Friedländer's vision, the Jews in the final analysis would merge 'in one way or another with the broad society of the state', as they freed themselves of their 'bonds' and introduced religious reforms. This picture of the future was much closer to the ideology of German Jewry's movement for religious reform in the nineteenth century and to the ideology of the emancipation than to that of the Haskalah of the eighteenth century.[118]

THE PANTHEON OF HISTORICAL HEROES

'It is well known that a legend evolving around a personality at any period of history and under all circumstances forms an integral part of that figure.' These words of the historian Ben-Zion Dinur, echoing the well-known distinction made by Ahad Ha'am between 'historical truth' and 'archaeological truth', are supported by the Haskalah's image of the past.[119] Most trends of 'maskilic history' were embodied primarily in individual historical figures, by means of their presentation in a pantheon of heroes or anti-heroes and by the manner in which they were actually used by the maskilim. These individual figures manifested the didactic, exemplary historical trend, serving a double function: through identification with them, the maskilim imitated these exemplary models that exhibited such maskilic values as virtuousness, rational thinking, dedication to the struggle for truth and justice, and participation in beneficial political and social action. In addition, the historical personality granted legitimacy to the methods and values of the maskilim themselves, frequently endowing them with authority; these values were projected retrospectively, recasting historical personalities, often anachronistically, into figures closely resembling the eighteenth-century maskilim. The free use made of historical figures, termed by Voltaire 'the tricks played with the dead', is a reflection of the historical attitude that considered it legitimate to evaluate the past, for better or for worse, in accordance with the maskilic standards of the day. A parallel naturally appears between historical outlines, images of the various eras, and the maskilic system of studying individual historical figures.

Since the inventory of Jewish biographies available to the eighteenth-century maskilim did not suit their inclinations, there was a need to build a new pantheon of heroes. The Middle Ages supplied legendary versions of biblical figures based on the midrashim of the Sages, Hellenistic–medieval legends, such as the wondrous figure of Alexander the Great described by Josippon, and hagiographic literature about the Jewish Sages. This heritage was passed on to seventeenth-century historical literature, with the addition of encomiums to more recent

---

[118] Friedländer, *Sendschreiben an seine Hochwürden*, 36–44; 64. See also Meyer, *The Origins of the Modern Jew*, ch. 3; Sorkin, 'The Impact of Emancipation on German Jewry', 177–98.

[119] Dinur, 'The Great Man and his Age', 9–10; Ahad Ha'am, 'Moses', 342–7; Rosman, 'The History of a Historical Source', 175–214.

tsadikim, such as the kabbalist Rabbi Isaac Luria Ashkenazi, known as Ha'ari (1534–72).[120] Through typological exegesis, historical figures frequently became symbols in the sense of the traditional saying 'the deeds of the ancestors are role models for their descendants', while kabbalistic symbolism focused on their metaphysical significance.[121] The traditional chronicles cite only the name, the period, and the major activities of the figures and do not normally provide detailed biographical descriptions. More extensive biographical outlines appear in Amelander's *She'erit Yisra'el*, which combines life histories of several rabbis and *geonim* with those of 'great people who held positions of importance in the courts of great kings and ministers'. Amelander devoted an entire chapter to the biographies of the medieval sages, including wondrous tales attesting to their greatness in Torah scholarship. Heilprin, the author of *Seder hadorot*, on the other hand, was primarily interested in the question of the spiritual origins of the historical figures appearing in his book and wished to discover the identities of their various reincarnations. Bar Kochba, for example, who considered himself the messiah, was 'a reincarnation of Ganon who delivered tens of thousands [from Egypt] before their time'.[122] In this manner, historical figures were endowed with significance through mythologization and symbolic linkage to an essentially theological system.

The maskilim endowed historical personalities with new significance and exploited them for new purposes, even though the traditional, didactic system encouraging individuals to learn from exemplary heroes persisted, as it did in the European Enlightenment. The tradition of literary encomiums also persisted in maskilic biographies, although now it was the maskilic attributes of the hero that were lauded, attesting to the substantially secular nature of the praise. Euchel, for instance, considered the field of history that recounted 'the story of one person from among all the people (biography)' to be the most effective type of historical account in educational terms. Indeed, the first historical writings to appear in *Hame'asef* were in the section entitled 'The Lives of Great Jews', which described only those historical figures who met the following four criteria: they had to be great in Torah, great in wisdom, wealthy men who had used their riches for the benefit of all the Jewish people, and politically active in ruling circles in order to promote Jewish interests.[123]

A central position in the pantheon of heroes of the Haskalah was allocated to Maimonides, who more than any other figure exemplified the breakthrough into the world of external culture. The maskilim believed that his wisdom and expertise in the Torah anticipated the maskilic ideal, and they discerned innovative

---

[120] Halevi, *The Historical–Biographical Tale*; Dan, *The Hebrew Story*; id., 'The Beginnings of Hebrew Hagiographic Literature', 82–100.

[121] Funkenstein, 'Nachmanides' Typological Reading of History'.

[122] The quotation is from Heilprin, *Seder hadorot*, 160. See also Amelander, *She'erit yisra'el*, 113–23, 144–6, 181–8.   [123] Hevrat Dorshei Leshon Ever, *Nahal habesor*, 2–3.

perspectives in his writings. Maimonides was portrayed in a historical biography, 'Toledot rabeinu mosheh ben maimon', published in *Hame'asef* in 1786. It was written by Shimon Baraz, a young maskil from Königsberg and a member of Hevrat Dorshei Leshon Ever in that city, as an exemplary biography projecting maskilic values for the eighteenth century.[124] Maimonides' approach to traditional learning was described as a critical one, and his *Mishneh torah* was seen as 'opening a new path to Torah study'. His commentary on the Mishnah in Arabic had made it possible to learn it not merely by rote, but with understanding. His codification system was lauded for its distinctly rational approach—its methodicalness, order, and improved organization. While Maimonides' purpose had been religious, to purify faith and religion, to study Torah, and to instil its love in the people, he had also wished to spread *torat ha'adam*, decorum, and lofty moral standards that would improve Jewish behaviour and be esteemed by all. As an educator, Maimonides had been aware of the failings of his contemporaries—a blind generation that had strayed from wisdom—and had acted out of a sense of responsibility and leadership 'to reform and improve those who walk in darkness'.

Although Maimonides was granted a place within the maskilic pantheon, his fate was seen as resembling that of Socrates and others who, in their time, constituted islands of rationality, forced to struggle against the leagues of the 'benighted': 'Men, clever and wise in their eyes, who in their power and pride ruled the foolish masses, who accepted their words unquestioningly . . .'. These represented those who objected to enlightenment in all eras, who were unable to understand the maskil, especially rulers who were leading the masses away from the true path. The dispute surrounding the philosophical writings of Maimonides, led by the sages of Montpellier, was described by Shimon Baraz as a war between the children of light and the children of darkness. He himself was certain who had been right and sharply condemned those who held false and foolish opinions.[125]

This theme, which emphasized the struggle against Maimonides, was important to Solomon Maimon too. According to him, Maimonides and his writings were the impetus for the spiritual shift that ultimately led him to the world of the Haskalah and helped him to move from a melancholy and visionary frame of mind to one of rationalism: 'My admiration for this illustrious teacher was great; I considered him the ideal of human perfection and his teachings to be spoken in the voice of divine truth.'[126] This was the reason he adopted the name Maimon for himself when he shrugged off his identity as a Lithuanian *talmid ḥakham* and *melamed* in favour of that of a modern German philosopher. He regarded the dispute surrounding the writings of Maimonides as characterizing two schools of thought, each of which sprang from different political and cultural soil—Spain

---

[124] Baraz, 'Toledot rabenu moshe ben maimon', 19–27, 35–47. Cf. Lehmann, 'Maimonides, Mendelssohn and the Measfim', 87–108.   [125] Baraz, 'Toledot rabenu moshe ben maimon', 39–43.

[126] Maimon, *Autobiography*, 260–1. Cf. Lahover, *Between Old and New*, 97–107, 'Maimonides and the Hebrew Enlightenment in its Beginning'.

and France, leading to a conflict between 'orthodox theologians' and 'an enlightened theologian'. The analogical leap from this thirteenth-century episode to the
world of the eighteenth century was easily made, as was the parallel of the contrast
of the enlightened Spanish, who developed in an enlightened country (Germany)
and the ignorant French, who developed in an ignorant country (Poland)—as
Maimon described his native land. This is a perfect example of the maskilic use
of the historical past, through which Maimonides appears as a maskil in a supra-
historical conflict with the prejudices of Jewish society, his objective being 'to
re-establish the harmony between religion and rationality'.[127]

Another major element of the historical image of Maimonides emphasized by
the maskilim was his contact with the non-Jewish world and its culture. They
praised Maimonides for having written several of his works in Arabic and used
this fact as justification for writing philosophical treatises in the vernacular of the
countries in which they lived. They were impressed by his close relations with
the Egyptian sultan and credited him with universalist views. The great esteem
in which the philosophical writings of Maimonides were held by non-Jewish sages,
who even translated them into their own languages, was a source of pride to
them. The maskilim considered Maimonides an example for all generations in
terms of the maskilic values he expressed, as well as in the perfection of his character and his moral dimensions. They enumerated his virtues: he aspired to
truth and justice and was repelled by evil; he was humble and diligent; he was
involved in society; he fled from radical extremes to central, moderate positions.
He was a figure of such perfection that 'He resembles the heavenly bodies whose
like will not reappear in the skies for hundreds of years.' Just as Maimonides
served as a source of inspiration to Mendelssohn and Maimon, others were encouraged to imitate this ideal figure: 'Those who follow in his path and love
truth and peace and desire the good of man, Jew and gentile alike, shall be the
glory of all peoples.'[128]

In the literary corpus of the Haskalah, the figure of Maimonides was exploited
in Wolfsohn-Halle's play 'Siḥah be'erets haḥayim' in the dispute between a traditional rabbi on one side and Maimonides and Mendelssohn, constituting a united
front holding similar positions, on the other. The debate revolved around several
basic questions preoccupying the world of the Haskalah of the 1780s and 1790s,
with Maimonides functioning as the authority and legitimizing source, confirm-
ing the authenticity of maskilic values and explaining their consonance with the
genuine Judaism he represents. Through the figure of Maimonides, Wolfsohn-
Halle lambasts the traditional values represented by the rabbi, thus further bolstering Mendelssohn's historical image. Maimonides is portrayed as an enraged maskil

---

[127] Maimon, *Lebensgeschichte*, ii. 1–10. See also Werses, 'The Expulsion from Spain', 48–81;
Schorsch, 'The Myth of Sephardic Supremacy', 47–66; Funkenstein, *Perceptions of Jewish History*,
234–47.
[128] Wessely, *Divrei shalom ve'emet*, ch. 7; Baraz, 'Toledot rabenu moshe ben maimon', 47.

whose rejection of the rabbi borders on loathing. He rebukes him and the members of his generation severely: 'I have known the men of your land. I knew they were untrustworthy sons and their deeds and laws were disordered.' Maimonides groans with sorrow upon hearing the accepted religious values of traditional society, thus granting approval to the maskilic view that the traditional Judaism of the period was a perversion of the original form of the religion. He disputes the criticism voiced against Mendelssohn's *Biur*, legitimizes the translation of the Torah into a foreign language, and gives support to Wessely's *Divrei shalom ve'emet*, besides backing one of the most mordant statements in the work ('A *talmid ḥakham* with no mind of his own is no better than a carcass'), and rejecting the alleged antiquity of the Zohar, branding kabbalistic ideas as false. By sanctioning criticism of the Sages and objecting to self-abnegation in relation to the authority of the ancients, Maimonides represents the rational approach in which recognition of God is based first and foremost on intellectual speculation and observation of His deeds. Maimonides is placed in opposition to the traditional world of values, along with Socrates and Plato, the Greek sages who had also been granted a place in heaven by the maskilim, and Mendelssohn, who had only recently ascended skywards. A new typological image evolves in this work: Moses ben Maimon and Moses Mendelssohn almost blend into a single figure in terms of the maskilic messages they project. They are 'slotted in' to the maskilic historical synopsis at the turning-point of Jewish history, riding on the wave of reformation and the restoration of light to the Jewish people: Moses the legislator gave the Torah in its pure form, Maimonides began to see 'the path of light', and Mendelssohn, drawing on the teachings of Maimonides, continues to 'clear the path'. The author thus creates the desired literary propagandist effect: the Haskalah appears as a continuation of original Judaism, even gaining God's seal of approval, while traditional society is delegitimized. The mythical Maimonides, in his historical, maskilic guise, is almost entirely alien to the world of the traditional rabbi, who is profoundly shocked and appalled by his views. Indeed, in Wolfsohn-Halle's work Maimonides seems to have become a card-carrying member of the group of eighteenth-century German maskilim.[129]

It was the radical maskil David Friedländer who voiced certain reservations regarding this much-admired figure. He demanded that a distinction be made between the Maimonides of *Moreh nevukhim* (Guide of the Perplexed), who was worthy of admiration, and the Maimonides of the *Mishneh torah* (Code of Jewish Law), whom he considered a negative symbol of intolerance and rigid halakhic formalism. However, this view did not go beyond the contents of a private letter, which was not published until many years later.[130]

'Toledot harav don yitsḥak abrabanel' (1784), the first biography to appear in the 'Lives of Great Jews' section of *Hame'asef*, was devoted to the life of Rabbi

---

[129] Wolfsohn-Halle, 'Siḥah be'erets haḥayim', 136, 151–5, 160–4, 173–4; cf. Werses, 'Echoes of Lucian's Satire', 84–119.   [130] D. Friedländer, 'Brief zu Meir Igger'.

Isaac Abrabanel (1437–1508); the author's name does not appear, but it conformed almost exactly to the four criteria for great historical figures determined by Euchel. In his maskilic incarnation Abrabanel was considered a hero on the basis of the events of his life, and almost no attention was paid to his writings or theoretical views. The maskilim stressed his image as a harmonious combination of greatness in Torah scholarship, piety, financial wealth wisely used, expertise in foreign tongues, and wisdom in external matters. Once again the maskilic biographer focused on the close contact Abrabanel maintained with the Christian world—his connections, the respect he was shown, and the high positions he held in the ruling courts of Portugal, Spain, and Italy. He exploited these contacts for the benefit of all Jews, to whose aid he came in times of distress, as he did during the expulsion from Spain. As was fitting for a personage of his great reputation, extending beyond the Jewish world, Abrabanel's death was mourned not only by the people of Israel, but also by all the sages of Venice. The historical figure of Abrabanel is captured in these words:

Rabbi Yitshak Abrabanel was an honest, God-fearing man all the days of his life, a pleasant companion who desired the good of his people. And although all his writings demonstrate his objection to the beliefs of the Christians and his efforts to overthrow the strongholds of their religion, he nevertheless loved all Christian people who were honest in their hearts and he enjoyed their company, and wished them well, and this is the way of a truly wise man who should be revered and followed by all who those who love mankind and seek wisdom.[131]

As the paradigm of a 'truly wise man', Abrabanel the humanist, man of society, and possessor of exalted attributes knew how to maintain the balance between the rejection of Christianity as a theology and the ability to establish social relationships with Christians on a humanistic basis, thus embodying the maskilic demand for a more appropriate attitude towards the surrounding Christian society.

Apart from Abrabanel, other figures from the Sephardi Diaspora were greatly admired, including Azariah de' Rossi, Moses Raphael D'Aguilar (d. 1679), and Joseph Delmedigo of Candia (1591–1655). David Mendes of Amsterdam contributed most of the biographies of Sephardi Jews and the great men of Amsterdam published in *Hame'asef*, through the good offices of Wessely; in 1778 he added an account of Isaac Orobio de Castro (1620–87), an exemplary figure who combined the personae of a learned doctor, a philosopher, and a God-fearing Jew respected by non-Jewish sages and their kings.[132] Manasseh ben Israel (1604–57) was one of Moses Mendelssohn's historical heroes, primarily by virtue of his apologia for the Jewish people. According to Mendelssohn he possessed three laudable qualities: 'He was an eminent Torah scholar and learned in other

[131] Anon., 'Toledot harav don yitshak abrabanel', 38–42, 57–61. The quotation is from p. 61. Cf. Lehmann, 'Maimondes, Mendelssohn and the Measfim', 103–8.

[132] Mendes, 'Toledot hehakham moshe rafa'el daguilar', 16–17, 26–7; id., 'Toledot harav yosef', 124–7; id., 'Toledot hehakham hamefo'ar', 219–23. Cf. Barzilay, 'The Italian and the Berlin Haskalah', 17–54.

sciences, and he laboured assiduously for the welfare of his brothers.' In the wake of the publication of Dohm's *Über die bürgerliche Verbesserung der Juden* and the ensuing discussion of the 'Jewish question' in Germany, Mendelssohn chose to write an introduction to a German translation of Manasseh ben Israel's *Vindication of the Jews* in 1782, as an apologia for Jews and Judaism and a rebuttal of the Christian prejudices that had not yet died out.[133] The seventeenth-century heretics from Amsterdam Uriel da Costa (1585–1640) and Baruch Spinoza (1632–77) did not hold particularly pre-eminent positions in the maskilic pantheon of individual historical figures. Neither of them had his biography written in the eighteenth century, though we shall see below that they were recruited in the struggles for religious freedom and freedom of conscience in a later era. Nevertheless, the maskilim alluded, directly or indirectly, to their belief that Spinoza's excommunication was groundless, asserting that he apparently 'did not intend to deny the existence of the Creator'.[134]

Contemporary heroes of the Haskalah to a great extent paralleled those chosen by the European Enlightenment. Solomon Maimon, for example, adopted the philosophical 'line of descent' accepted since the *Encylopédie*, the major work of the French Enlightenment, published from 1751 onwards. In *Mafte'ah korot hafilosofiyah* (The Key to the History of Philosophy), which preceded his *Givat hamoreh* (The Hill of the Guide; his exegesis of the first part of Maimonides' *Moreh nevukhim*, published in Berlin in 1791), the Jewish reader could become acquainted with the essence of Copernicus's innovations and the theories of Galileo and Kepler, which complemented the Copernican theory. Following them were Francis Bacon, who 'decided to construct his theories on strong foundations taken from observation and experience', Descartes, Newton, and Leibniz, 'who made greater strides than all who came before him, particularly in the wisdom of philosophy'.[135] The more popular eighteenth-century heroes, images that bore the message of the future, were those who symbolized the historical shift for the maskilim. Placed at the point where European humanism, enlightened government, and the modern maskilic idea intersected were Lessing and von Dohm, such 'angels of mercy' as Joseph II, Frederick II, and Catherine the Great, and, of course, the supreme hero of the Haskalah, Moses Mendelssohn. These figures gradually became part of the basic repertoire of maskilic consciousness. They were seen as helping to direct history towards the common goal of universal tolerance based on humanistic morality and rationality. This new tolerance

[133] Mendelssohn, 'Vorrede, Menasseh Ben Israel Rettung der Juden', in *Gesammelte Schriften*, viii. 1–25.

[134] Euchel, *Toledot harav*, 113–14. Euchel also writes about Spinoza, 'The philosopher Baruch de Spinoza, one of the Jews of the Sephardi community who was born in Amsterdam in the year 1632; the men of his generation injured him, slandering him and saying he had denied the existence of God.' See also Maimon, *Givat hamoreh*, 161; cf. Lahover, *Between Old and New*, 109–22, 'Spinoza in the Hebrew Enlightenment Literature'; Dorman, *The Spinoza Dispute*.

[135] Maimon, *Givat hamoreh*, 11–16.

was manifested in the changing relations between Jews and the surrounding society.

Among the maskilic 'angels of mercy', Joseph II had already been given prominence by Wessely in his *Divrei shalom ve'emet*. Because of his Edict of Tolerance, which demonstrated the monarch's humanistic and rational approach, Wessely placed him at the gateway of the new historical era, in the hope that he would become an example 'to all the angels of the earth in spreading peace through the world'.[136] Joseph II was not an exceptional figure: Frederick II of Prussia, Louis XVI of France, Stanislaw Poniatowski, king of Poland, and Catherine the Great of Russia were also held up as examples of enlightened rulers. These European 'angels of mercy' exemplified the maskilic belief that the ideals of love of mankind and universal tolerance had crossed the line from concept and aspiration to realization. The maskilim used this belief in their internal campaign, calling for greater allegiance to be shown by Jews to their native lands. The ideological foundation that served as a platform for the Jewish policy adopted by enlightened rulers was attributed by the maskilim almost exclusively to the figure of the German writer and philosopher Gotthold Ephraim Lessing. The maskilic image of Lessing was composed of two complementary elements: he was the first sage to 'write favourably of the Jews' and, in his *Nathan der Weise*, he proclaimed the principle of religious tolerance, that all men are men before they are members of any particular religion. However, Lessing was granted his dominant historical position not on the basis of his ideological teachings, but rather because of his encounter with Mendelssohn, his Jewish friend. Their friendship was considered a welcome and exhilarating relationship that symbolized the victory of maskilic principles and the certainty that the barriers separating the Jewish people from the rest of society would be removed: 'Take pleasure in the peaceful relationship between your camps and in the love and brotherhood between these two wise men . . . The greatest sage of Israel and the greatest sage of the nations are seated together.'[137] In Wolfsohn-Halle's fictional paradise in 'Siḥah be'erets haḥayim', for example, Mendelssohn is about to be reunited with Lessing, after both have been granted a divine reward, together with Socrates and Plato: 'For you too, dear brother, will I find there,' cries Mendelssohn. 'You, Lessing, whose soul is bound to mine! I shall find you, embrace you, and never leave you!'[138]

In this respect, the figure of Lessing was less important in and of itself than as an essential element in the historical image of Mendelssohn. In Euchel's view, his biography of Mendelssohn, which may have been the major influence in moulding the image of Mendelssohn that was admired for generations, was a 'holy work'. Euchel was aware of his mission: to create a figure destined to serve as

---

[136] Wesseley, *Divrei shalom ve'emet*, ch. 3. On Joseph II's greatly admired image, see also Herz Homberg's letter quoted in *Hame'asef*, 4 (1788), 329; B. Jeiteles, *Ma'arakhei lev*; anon., 'Ḥadashot hazeman', *Hame'asef*, 6 (1790), 188.   [137] Euchel, *Toledot harav*, 27–8.

[138] Wolfsohn-Halle, 'Siḥah be'erets haḥayim', 163; cf. Shoham, *Nathan der Weise*, 13–91.

the maskilic 'pillar of fire'. Euchel's Mendelssohn was 'the master teacher, the analytic sage, the divine Rabbenu Moshe ben Menahem', a Jew depicted as having a weak physique and unprepossessing looks: 'He was not comely, but nevertheless all took pleasure in seeing him because his countenance was illuminated by his wisdom.' His physical weakness only accentuated the greatness of his spirit, and his spiritual and moral strength surmounted physical obstacles. As an eminent sage and educator, he served as a living example to his students: 'Since each and every step he took expressed his morality and ethos, he sowed enough truth to take root in a wise heart and succeed in bearing fruit.' As befitted a representative of the best of the bourgeois ethos and the German *Bildung* ideal, he was modest and polite, satisfied with little, never raised his voice, never became angry, and was never greedy. Mendelssohn was involved in society and divided his time wisely between work and reflection. All of his actions were circumspect and balanced, manifesting the decency and honour typical of a person of perfect character and exalted attributes. The story of his life, its sharp contrasts, and the tortuous path he travelled to become the 'first among his people and the only one of his generation to be recognized and glorified', demonstrated that the hand of Providence was at work here 'and [that] it was the desire of God to exalt his name in the land'. Thus, in the cause of Providence, Mendelssohn opened a new era in the history of the Jewish people 'because God commanded His people to release their wisdom that had been imprisoned by the fetters of sloth'. Mendelssohn is depicted as the student of rabbis, a *tsadik* and a consummate teacher himself, who, though all his actions were performed in the name of God, nevertheless represented the ideal synthesis of loyalty to Judaism and involvement in general culture and society. The admiration of non-Jews for the maskilic Jew reached its peak with Mendelssohn's death. All of Berlin held its breath upon hearing the terrible news, and all the sages of the time mourned him deeply. Jews and non-Jews alike attended his funeral, and the king's poet eulogized him. Mendelssohn, who brought about the positive turning-point in the history of the Jewish people, left behind a binding legacy. We rejoice, cried Euchel, 'that we were privileged to stand before him and hear him utter his teachings, we rejoice that God gave us eyes to see and a mind to understand his pure words that give life to those who live by them'. The maskilim were committed to passing on his image and his teachings to future generations and to teaching them to follow in his path and live by his principles. This exemplary figure did not belong to his generation alone, but should also serve as a source of inspiration and authority for all generations.[139]

Other maskilim also penned tributes to Mendelssohn, using literary means to enhance his commanding image. Many titles and epithets were affixed to Mendelssohn's name: his first name, Moses, was supposed to confirm the parallel to the

---

[139] Euchel, *Toledot harav*, 17–24, 41, 45, 122–7, 133–6.

prophet Moses and to Moses Maimonides, and the use of the acronyms Rambeman (R. Moshe ben Menaḥen) and Ramad (R. Moshe Dessau) placed him in the same league with the Rambam (Maimonides) and the Rema (R. Moses Isserles, the great Polish halakhist). His resemblance to Moses and Socrates (he was called 'the German Socrates') elevated his reputation, and the application of Alexander Pope's well-known words, originally describing Newton—'Nature and Nature's laws lay hid in night | God said, *Let Moses* [Newton] *be!* and all was Light'—to Mendelssohn endowed him with a central position in history as the saviour who brought light to the dark night in which the people of Israel were immersed. This glorification of Mendelssohn, which had already begun during his lifetime, intensified after his death. In Wolfsohn-Halle's 'Siḥah be'erets haḥayim' the desire to exalt Mendelssohn's name reached its zenith: Mendelssohn is depicted as winning the support not only of Maimonides but of the archangel Michael, who tells him of the dispute among the heavenly saints concerning which of them would have the privilege of welcoming Mendelssohn and ushering him into the celestial entourage. King Solomon, a spokesman for wisdom, claims the right on the basis of the fact that Mendelssohn was the author of works of wisdom. King Solomon's father, King David, author of the Psalms, declares: 'I will go out and receive this man of God who gives pleasure with songs and whose language is melodious' (an allusion to Mendelssohn's translation of the book of Psalms), and Moses claims the right, saying, 'For this is Moses, my chosen one; I yearn for him, for he placed his teachings before the people of Israel like a precious ornament. I shall go forth and guide him to the holy abode'—implying that the teachings of Mendelssohn are in fact the pure Torah of Moses. If this were not enough, the argument reaches new heights at its conclusion, this time with direct intervention of God, saying, 'To my son! My precious son Moses, who expunged the thoughts of the evildoers of the land who did not comprehend the deeds of the Almighty and whose machinations contained nothing of God. For this he will be rewarded. His righteousness goes before him, and he will be gathered into the bosom of God.'[140]

The biographical image of Mendelssohn, which was more detailed than those of other figures, also summed them all up. It included all the basic principles that the maskilim, particularly the moderates among them, wished to present as the maskilic ideal, an example to be emulated. Other historical images, such as those of Maimonides and Abrabanel, developed from that of Mendelssohn, and the figures of Lessing and Socrates contributed in turn to the Mendelssohnian image. Socrates, for example, was merged with Mendelssohn to create 'the Jewish Socrates'. This mutual influence of maskilic historical figures was based more on the maskilic vision of the future than on their picture of the real past, a fact

[140] *Hame'asef*, 3 (1786), 161. See also Pelli, 'The Image of Moses Mendelssohn', 269–82; Wolfsohn-Halle, 'Siḥah be'erets haḥayim', 163–76. On the image of Moses as a maskilic figure, see Wessely, *Shirei tiferet*, i. 28–9, 32–7, 41–2, ii. 7.

particularly apparent when various historical cycles are 'compressed' in Wolfsohn-Halle's 'world of souls'. Here historical time loses its dynamism and a literary encounter—anachronistic in historical terms, but comprehensible in light of the maskilic world-view—takes place between Socrates, Plato, Lessing, Maimonides, and Mendelssohn. In these encounters the maskilim receive the appreciation that eluded them on earth; in the 'world of souls' the bearers of light, spread throughout history, are singled out, and contacts between Jews and sages of all the nations are extolled, all for the purpose of adding further emphasis to the maskilic demands for ideological and social changes in the future.

THE DISSEMINATION OF MASKILIC HISTORY IN THE EARLY NINETEENTH CENTURY

'Maskilic history', developing in the circle of German maskilim during the last two decades of the eighteenth century, thus broke with 'traditional Jewish history'. Historical speculation was not only intended to reveal the deeds of divine Providence, and the theological messages of history were pushed aside in favour of a secular historical past in which human, rational and moral activity was dominant. Just as the European Enlightenment had constructed a new picture of the past and proposed a kind of 'philosophical history', the Haskalah, functioning within the framework of its critical goals and demands for a reformed society, also created a new image of the past that presented a clear alternative to the traditional version. The new legitimization of historical study, the new division of history into periods, the belief in the historical turning-point and the shaping of 'a modern age', stemming from awareness of modernity, together with progressive programmes and realistic explanations, all characterized maskilic awareness of the past and made it possible to identify 'maskilic history' as a specific historical phenomenon and an element of the consciousness of those Jewish intellectual circles that made pragmatic and didactic use of history. 'Maskilic history' presented exemplary types, elevated historical heroes, and proposed moral explanations of events, all aimed at realizing the maskilic aspiration of creating a new, ideal Jew who would also be a universal man and a citizen of his country.

The early maskilim did not create a new historiography as did their non-Jewish counterparts; this had to wait for the 1820s and the foundations laid by the new generation of German Jewry—the members of the Verein für Kultur und Wissenschaft des Judentums (The Society for the Culture and Science of Judaism)—and Marcus Jost's comprehensive and well-written work *Geschichte der Israeliten* (History of the Jews), which appeared from 1820 onwards. In my view, this was not a case of two stages, with one serving as the basis for the other, although several historical concepts of the Haskalah did filter down into the society, including the critical, rationalistic approach, belief in the 'modern age', and the Mendelssohn legend. However, with the exception of a few isolated links with the radical branch of the Berlin maskilim, 'maskilic history' had almost no impact on the formation of the society, whose spokesmen even came out openly against it and the maskilim of the previous generation.[141]

Thanks to the rapid acculturation of German Jewry in the nineteenth century, there was almost no need to popularize or translate portions of universal history from German into Hebrew, for example, or even to adduce any special legitimizations to prove that a knowledge of history was essential. When the generation of self-taught maskilim, who still had one foot in the traditional *beit hamidrash*, was replaced by an intellectual élite of modern university graduates, little room remained for 'low', unprofessional 'maskilic history' in Hebrew. Thus modern Jewish awareness of the past developed on two fronts. The later of the two was that of the Wissenschaft des Judentums, which flourished in Germany among the generation born in the 1790s and during the struggle for emancipation; and it focused on defending Judaism from external criticism, as well as searching for a theoretical legitimization of Jewish existence in the modern state. On this front, awareness of the past was characterized by scientific research, an idealistic philosophy of the Jewish religion, and historians with systematic, formal academic training. Mature Jewish historiography and the historiography employed by advocates of religious reform, or in the formulation of a new Jewish identity, flourished in the nineteenth century.[142]

The second front was that of 'maskilic history', which developed in German maskilic circles at the end of the eighteenth century during the struggle for internal reforms in Jewish society and the break with traditional habits and thought. The maskilim sought legitimization for their approach and their image of the future, but their relative remoteness from historical research institutions apparently limited their ability to create a genuine historiography. Points of contact between the two fronts and the manner in which the Wissenschaft des Judentums was integrated into the eastern European Haskalah during the nineteenth century will be among the subjects discussed in the following chapters.

The optimism and enthusiasm of Isaac Euchel, who was the first to organize a group of German maskilim and formulated a plan for the establishment of a supra-community organization of maskilim, gave way to a sense of disappointment and pessimism during the last decade of the eighteenth century. In post-Mendelssohnian Berlin processes were taking place that must have disappointed the maskilim, who believed in the internal reform of Jewish society, the cultivation of Hebrew literature, and the moderate maskilic path. The loosening of their ties to wealthy men, the increase of deistic views, and the non-intellectual modernization processes taking place outside the sphere of the Haskalah, such as

---

[141] Schorsch, 'Breakthrough into the Past', 3–28.
[142] Michael, 'The Renewal of Interest'; id., *I. M. Jost*; Meyer, 'Abraham Geiger's Historical Judaism', 112–21; Myers, *Re-Inventing the Jewish Past*.

social integration and behavioural acculturation, turned the maskilim into a marginal group lacking a social base.[143]

However, 'maskilic history' did not disappear, even after the fading of the Haskalah in Germany, but continued to serve the maskilim throughout the nineteenth century, even when the Jewish historiography of the Wissenschaft des Judentums was flourishing in central and western Europe. 'Maskilic history' was the heritage of every maskil who considered himself an heir of the 'Berlin legacy', and formed a central element of his intellectual baggage as a tool for elucidating his world-view and an expression of his self-awareness as a maskil. We can already see examples of this during the first two decades of the nineteenth century, even before the appearance of the Wissenschaft des Judentums, in the Austrian offshoots of the Haskalah, in Galicia and Russia, and even in the short-lived attempt to revive the Haskalah in Germany through the Hevrat Ohavei Leshon Ever (Society of Lovers of the Hebrew Tongue). Despite the uniqueness of each of these offshoots, and the products of local historical circumstances that shaped the image of the maskilim in each particular place, their shared characteristics reflect the common source that inspired and nurtured them.

Shalom Hacohen (1771–1845), the maskil who was the editor of *Hame'asef* during its second reincarnation from 1808 to 1811, continued to write 'maskilic history' in his translations of episodes from ancient history, 'Divrei hayamim lebavel' (The History of Babylonia, 1810), and in poetry containing biblical and historical motifs. His essay on the expulsion of the Jews from Spain, the first of its kind in Hebrew, was based primarily on several chapters of J. S. Semler's book, which was itself a translation into German of an English book on world history. As will be seen, during the 1830s Hacohen tried to compete with Jost's historiographic enterprise, in the meantime continuing maskilic trends both in his search for rational explanations for the expulsion and in his periodization of the history of Hebrew poetry, which was influenced by Herder and the British Lowth.[144] The crisis of the German Haskalah was manifested in this periodization, just as it was in the version created by Judah Leib Ben-Ze'ev (1764–1811), one of the 'refugees' of the Berlin Haskalah who settled in Vienna, in his history of the Hebrew language. Both versions identify a turning-point in the history of the modern age, dividing it into two periods: the first witnessed the heyday of the Haskalah, which symbolized the flourishing of literature, poetry, and the Hebrew language; while the second saw the Haskalah's decline. 'Great was the hope reflected by that generation,' wrote Ben-Ze'ev, 'but who could believe that

---

[143] Feiner, 'Isaac Euchel', 456–69.

[144] S. Hacohen, 'Divrei hayamim', 23–30, 35–9; id., 'Gerush hayehudim', 20–48, 72–80; the source for Hacohen's article was Semler, *Übersetzung der Allgemeine Welthistoire*, 487–96. S. Hacohen, *Mata'ei kedem*, 3–9; see also ibid. 4–5, 20–1, 33, 'Hatsalat avraham be'ur kasdim'. Cf. T. Cohen, *From Dream to Reality*.

that spectacle, like the sight of a flash of lightning, would glitter momentarily and then disappear?'[145]

Ben-Ze'ev's introductions to *Hokhmat yehoshua ben sirah* (The Wisdom of Joshua ben Sira, 1798) and *Megilat yehudit* (The Scroll of Judith, 1799) and his adaptation of Eichhorn's study *Mavo el mikra'ei kodesh* (Introduction to the Holy Scriptures, 1810) already displayed the characteristics of critical historical research. Ben-Ze'ev's writings bore out Wessely's claim that the study of the Bible required historical knowledge, and he even reiterated this claim in almost the same words: 'If you are an understanding reader . . . [you must] know the situation, the time, the issue, and the author you are dealing with. And particularly in texts containing stories and events of our nation which are dependent upon time and place; all the more so when these events are related to matters of other nations.'[146] In his survey of the history of the Hebrew language, Ben-Ze'ev explained the changes it underwent on the basis of its general historical context, 'because language undergoes the same periodical vicissitudes as its speakers'; he also pointed out the vital interaction between the legal and political status and educational level of the Jews on one hand, and the flourishing and decline of Hebrew on the other.[147] Ben-Ze'ev continued the trend of adapting the history of the Jewish people for new textbooks to be used in schools, including a short paraphrase of the ancient history of the Jewish people in *Mesilat halimud* (The Path of Learning, 1802). The better-known *Sefer toledot yisra'el* (History of Israel, 1796), written by the Bohemian teacher Peter Beer (1758–1838), was a maskilic adaptation of the biblical story, which became very popular and was reprinted in the nineteenth century.[148]

Although the Prague maskilim continued to cultivate Hebrew literature, they also wrote in German. A long article discussing the Haskalah which appeared in the short-lived journal they published, *Jüdisch-Deutsche Monatsschrift* (1802), contained a section that summarized the benefits of studying the historical past. The anonymous author underscored the importance of historical study, which provided a plethora of exemplary types, a picture of the past characterized by the conflict between reason and its absence and between exalted qualities and a degenerate moral sense, and also espoused a belief in progress—all characteristic features of 'maskilic history'.[149] Interest in history grew in this circle of maskilim, among

[145] Ben Ze'ev, *Otsar hashorashim*, i, introd. from 1807; cf. the more optimistic schema in his book *Yesodei hadat*, introd.

[146] Ben Ze'ev, *Mavo el mikra'ei kodesh*, general introd.; see also id. (ed.), *Hokhmat yehoshua ben sirah*; id., *Megilat yehudit*.

[147] Ben Ze'ev, *Otsar hashorashim*. Note that Ben Ze'ev's periodization is not congruent with that of the Enlightenment. In his case, 'the dark centuries' are rather the 16th–18th cc. (up to Mendelssohn), while the 7th–16th cc. are regarded favourably as a time 'notable for the knowledge of language'.

[148] Ben Ze'ev, *Mesilat halimud*; P. Beer, *Sefer toledot yisra'el*.

[149] *Jüdisch-Deutsche Monatsschrift*, 152–7. See also Toury, *Die jüdische Presse*, 1–6; Kestenberg-Gladstein, 'A Voice from the Prague Enlightenment', 295–304.

whose leaders were Meir Fischer (d. 1858) and Solomon Loewisohn (1789–1821), who contributed several of their historical writings to the Jewish German-language journal *Sulamith*.[150] The articles by Fischer and Loewisohn contained passages on both general and Jewish history, including Roman history, a history of the Jews of North Africa, and biographies of Uriel da Costa, Isaac Orobio de Castro, and the grammarian Elijah Levita (1468/9–1549), though these last were sketches rather than fully developed articles. Loewisohn even outlined a synopsis encompassing the history of the Jewish people from the time of Hadrian. Loewisohn's periodization was characeterized by consciousness of the historical shift that had occurred in the eighteenth century, whose pivotal figures were Joseph II and Moses Mendelssohn. While the gloom of the Middle Ages had lifted in Europe, the Jews remained immersed in darkness, although Loewisohn was convinced that 'the memory of the thousands of years of shame that had passed' was about to be obliterated from the earth; the lectures he published in 1820 on the modern history of the Jews were written in a similar spirit.[151] Loewisohn demonstrated his abilities as a research scholar in his geographical-historical lexicon of the Land of Israel in biblical times *Meḥkarei erets* (A Biblical Geography, 1819), in which he attempted to identify biblical sites through philological examination, based on a large number of sources.[152] The historical writings of the Prague maskilim were also of a more scientific nature, as manifested in the incorporation of chronological tables, the large number of footnotes, and the bibliographical lists. For example, a bibliography containing twenty-two items in French, Latin, and German was appended to Meir Fischer's short monograph *Toledot yeshurun taḥat memshelet mahadi ve'imam aderis* (Jewish History under the Rule of the Mahdi and Imam Aderis, 1817). Fischer's access to the Prague library apparently allowed him to reach a relatively large selection of sources and studies, including up-to-date research from the end of the eighteenth century and the beginning of the nineteenth.[153]

However, despite his ability to carry out research, which far surpassed that of the German maskilim of the previous century, his historical works were written from a definitely maskilic point of view. Fischer called upon the reader to judge historical events and personages and learn the lessons they teach because, in his view, historical example is preferable to any other sort of moral preaching as a didactic method. 'The chronicles of the world and its history', wrote Fischer, 'will instruct us in the thoughts and deeds of the upright and virtuous and

[150] Michael, 'The Contribution of *Sulamith*', 86–113; id., 'Solomon Lewinsohn', 147–62; id., *Jewish Historiography*, 121–59.

[151] Loewisohn, *Vorlesungen*, 5–6, 9–13; see also Michael, 'The Contribution of *Sulamith*', 107–13. A Hebrew translation of Loewisohn's *Vorlesungen* appears as 'Shiurim bahistoriyah haḥadashah shel hayehudim', in Loewisohn, *Mivḥar ketavav*, 23–55, and the introd. by R. Michael, 7–38.

[152] Loewisohn, *Meḥkarei erets*.

[153] Fischer, *Toledot yeshurun*, 9–15. See also id., *Historische Taschenbuch*; id., *Korot shenot kedem*.

apprise us of the machinations and libels of deceivers and wrongdoers.'[154] Having lived through the Napoleonic era, Fischer claimed that leaders have a major impact on historical events. He assembled a gallery of corrupt and evil rulers (including Caligula, Nero, and Demetrius) who had led their kingdoms to ruin, as well as a contrasting pantheon of moral leaders (the most prominent being Joseph II, once again) who had guided their countries to prosperity. In Fischer's view, a similar dynamic could be traced in the history of the Jewish people, and he therefore blamed its leaders for the destruction of the Jewish state at the end of the Second Temple period.[155] Thanks to Fischer's moderateness and his efforts to avoid attacking traditional attitudes, Fleckeles, who by then was head of the rabbinical court in Prague, sanctioned his historical work *Korot shenot kedem* (Ancient History) in 1811. Fleckeles stated that he found nothing at all in this book, which dealt with Roman history, 'that contradicted, heaven forbid, God's Torah and its commentators', and he even ruled that the book could be read on the Sabbath as entertainment.[156]

'Man's senses are stimulated before his intellect,' explained Solomon Loewisohn in *Melitsat yeshurun* (The Poesy of Jeshurun, 1816), claiming that, in addition to teaching rational lessons, stories of the past could stir the soul, arousing in it a sense of loftiness and awe, 'because the great gap of time that separates us from them will exalt them in our imaginations'.[157] Influenced by the 'school of the sublime' and the spirit of Herder, Loewisohn hoped that history would provide not only the educational benefit of a historical world brought close enough to be an almost active presence, but also the aesthetic values inherent in observing it from a distance. The emotional dimension was projected onto the Jewish national sense as well, infusing Jewish history with a sense of pride and arousing a feeling of love for the Jewish people. Meir Fischer considered Loewisohn's historical writings as a new page in Jewish historiography, which had been so long in decline, and the fulfilment of the natural desire of every nation to document its history.[158] Issachar Baer Schlesinger (1773–1836) of Kolin, Bohemia, author of the historical poem *Haḥashmona'im* (The Hasmoneans, 1817), went even further by using his poetry in the struggle against assimilation. Schlesinger chose a historical subject hitherto undeveloped by the maskilim in order to create a group of Jewish heroes, a source of Jewish pride with whom Jews could identify. His aim was to re-create the tales of their heroism in a way that would bring tears to the eyes of 'men with feeling souls'. Aware of the importance of historical context, Schlesinger was careful to keep his verses faithful to historical truth, and his poems included scholarly

---

[154] Fischer, *Historische Taschenbuch*, 67; id., *Toledot yeshurun*, vol. i.; id., *Korot shenot kedem*, 9–15.

[155] Fischer, *Toledot yeshurun*, 17–18, 27, 62–5.

[156] Fleckeles's approbation at the beginning of Fischer's book *Korot shenot kedem*, 5. On the close relationship between the rabbi and Fischer, see Michael, 'The Contribution of *Sulamith*', 98.

[157] Loewisohn, *Melitsat yeshurun*, 28–9. See also T. Cohen, *Solomon Loewisohn's* Melitsat Yeshurun.   [158] Fischer, *Historische Taschenbuch*, 5–10; Kievael, 'Caution's Progress', 77–105.

marginal notes elucidating historical issues; he clarified dates, identified geographical sites, criticized the account of Josephus, expressed surprise at anachronisms
found in Mendelssohn's work, and questioned the identity of 'Mattathias, son of
Jochanan the high priest'. Schlesinger challenged the maskilim's veneration of
classical heroes, replacing them with the Jewish heroes of the Hasmonean revolt:
'Epaminondas was highly successful in saving his country from the Lacedaemon-
ians, Leonidas died a despotic hero with the 300 Spartans . . . but the Maccabee
surpassed the Athenian in glory.' Schlesinger also rejected Socrates as a historical hero and attempted to prove that those who believed him to be a monotheist
had erred. Socrates' last request before his death—to sacrifice a rooster to the god
of medicine—proved he should not be viewed more favourably than any of the
fools and dreamers of the ancient world.[159]

   Prominent in the Hungarian branch of the Haskalah at the beginning of the
nineteenth century was the attempt of Rabbi Moses Kunitz of Buda (1774–1837)
to sketch maskilic biographies of sages from the mishnaic period. Almost no Jewish
figures from the time of the Sages had previously been included in the pantheon
of maskilic heroes. Kunitz, like Schlesinger, believed that their inclusion would
counterbalance the pantheon of classical philosophers. In contrast to Schlesinger,
Kunitz did not attack the image of Socrates as a maskil who had sacrificed his life
for the truth, but claimed that 'the lives of the talmudic Sages and their history'
had been neglected, even though they too provided exemplary images of wise
and righteous men who suffered martyrdom for the sake of the truth.[160] In *Beit
rabi* (The Rabbi's House), which he wrote at the end of the eighteenth century
and published in Vienna in 1805, the figure of Rabbi Judah Hanasi appears in a
play and a biography. Kunitz intended this to be 'the first notebook' in a series of
biographies. However, except for *Ben yoḥai* (Vienna, 1817), written in defence of
the Zohar rather than as a biography of Rabbi Shimon bar Yohai, the enterprise
was abandoned. Kunitz's biography of Judah Hanasi was based exclusively on
Jewish sources, and was the result of his great admiration of this exemplary
figure of Jewish history. In *Beit rabi* Judah Hanasi was transformed into an
exemplar of the moderate maskil: great in wisdom and knowledge of the Torah,
blessed with moral qualities and genteel manners, and, as one of his students
describes him, 'a learned doctor'. Kunitz's Judah Hanasi demands reform in
Jewish education, preaches productivity, and urges the poor to engage in agricul-
tural work. Expert in Hebrew, he also advocates the study of pure languages
—Hebrew, Greek, or Latin—but not impure ones such as Aramaic: 'Study the
Torah of God, acquire a pure understanding of the languages of your lands, each
land its own language.' Judah Hanasi's relationship with the Roman emperor
Antoninus played a major role in his life, and Kunitz emphasized that the

---

[159] Schlesinger, *Haḥashmona'im*, introd. 3–4, 24*b*, 54, 75.
[160] Kunitz, *Beit rabi*, introd., 6–9. On Kunitz, see Fahn, *Selected Essays*, 70–99. On the Haskalah
in Hungary, see Silber, 'The Historical Experience of German Jewry', 107–57.

spiritual enrichment characterizing this relationship was mutual. Judah Hanasi even promises the emperor that all monotheists will be granted life in the world to come. When rumours of the emperor's death reach him, the rabbi expresses his hope of meeting his beloved friend in the afterlife. The non-Jewish world's appreciation for the work of Judah Hanasi is also emphasized, just as the encounter between Mendelssohn and Lessing was underscored in maskilic history. In Kunitz's view, the encounter between the Jewish sage and the Roman emperor served as an impetus for change in the attitude of non-Jews towards the Jews, legitimizing it and proving its feasibility.[161]

Maskilic history was also adopted in the Russian Jewish context in Shklov and later in St Petersburg during the early years of the nineteenth century. It appears that Judah Leib Nevakhovich (1776–1831), who wrote under the patronage of the wealthy government merchants Abraham Peretz and Nathan Nata Notkin, identified with the maskilic picture of the past in its entirety. In his apologia *Kol shavat bat yehudah* (The Daughter of Judah Cries Out), written in Russian and then translated into Hebrew (1804), Nevakhovich included a 'short history of the Russian people' in an attempt to persuade the Jewish reader to believe in the historical shift taking place in Europe in general and in Russia in particular.[162] In this work, too, history is placed within a moralistic system as an element of divine law and, in a direct continuation of Wessely's thought, Nevakhovich declares that 'only a nation which lives by *torat ha'adam* shall not stumble, and influence shall pass from those who betray *torat ha'adam* and stray from the straight path'. Nevakhovich was the first writer to apply the maskilic picture of the past, evaluation of the present, and vision of the future to the Russian empire. The German Haskalah provided him with the concept of the polarization between the dark ages, characterized by religious fanaticism and the corrupt rule of the clergy,[163] and the modern age, with its slogans of universal peace, tolerance, justice, and law. In the eighteenth century, Nevakhovich points out, the maskilim became guides for enlightened rulers: 'And in the previous generation, from 1700 to 1800, wisdom made greater strides in Europe, and this was an age of knowledge unparalleled in any nation from the first day of man's presence on earth.' Just as the darkness of medieval times determined the bitter destiny of the Jewish people, so the new epoch heralded a gradual change for the better, towards greater rights and freedom. Several countries had already 'liberated [the Jews] and given them a place in their land'.

---

[161] Kunitz, *Beit rabi*, 7–10, 19, 32–3, 43, 48, 59, 66–7, 75. Mendelssohn's picture hung on the wall of Kunitz's room, alongside those of Wessely and Baruch Jeiteles: Fahn, *Selected Essays*, 97–8.

[162] On Nevakhovich, see Mahler, *History of the Jewish People*, iv. 57–63. On the maskilim in Shklov, see Fishman, *Russia's First Modern Jews*.

[163] 'All those who read the chronicles of history will be horrified by the many calamities caused by these perversities, and give up counting the number of slain men, women, and children who were felled by the sword in that chaos' (Nevakhovich, *Kol shavat bat yehudah*, 3–7).

Nevakhovich depicts the history of Russia according to a similar formula of emergence from ignorance and darkness into light. The Russian people had long been immersed in darkness until the rise of enlightened emperors: Peter the Great, 'who called wisdom his sister', and Catherine, 'who continued to increase wisdom in her land and taught men to love one another and extirpate the religious hatred in their hearts'. Catherine also 'called for us to be liberated as other peoples were' when she granted permission for the Jews living in the annexed Polish regions 'to sit in judgement and judge our brethren by the laws of the land'. While the 'disease of ignorance' afflicting the hearts of the masses had not yet been cured and the 'worthless attitudes' of antisemitism had not disappeared, Nevakhovich was optimistic about the continuation of the historical process, and he praised Russia for the rapid pace of change:

It appears that the Russian people are behaving with the wisdom and decorum of the giants who preceded them, and nowhere in history can we read of a people who, before less than a century had passed, began to imbibe from the well of wisdom and increase their knowledge like the Russians of today. They will soon be like the Germans or the French, who have followed in the path of wisdom for several centuries.[164]

Russia, late in climbing on the bandwagon of the Enlightenment and slow to match the strides being taken in Europe, was still lagging behind Germany and France. However, in Nevakhovich's view, she was ahead of other countries in all matters concerning religious tolerance. In an apologia directed to the Russian people, he outlined the bitter fate of the Jews, replete with persecution and victimization, and attempted to impress upon them the maskilic recognition of the need for religious tolerance (quoted by him in the words of Lessing's hero Nathan the Wise). Nevakhovich praised the policies of Tsar Alexander I and claimed, rather oddly, that enlightened absolutism was better for the Jews than free, republican governments. He called for the Jews 'to throw off the dust of our forefathers who, in the early generations, destroyed you with the sword of ignorance and made you the target of their arrows. Awaken and see that these are not those days of yore'—a summons that anticipated by a generation the maskilic programme formulated in Russia in the 1820s.[165]

While Nevakhovich's historical outline drew its principal elements from that created by the moderate maskilim in Germany, it appears that the version incorporated by the doctor Jacob Elijah Frank into his memorandum of 1800 to the Russian senator Gabriel Derzhavin (which ultimately provided the foundations for Alexander I's 1804 edict) was based more on the radical historical blueprint of David Friedländer and Solomon Maimon. Frank focused on the destiny of the Jewish religion and proposed an additional version of the break between a pure, distant Jewish past, when belief in God was honest and moral obligations undefiled, and the recent past and the present, in which pure religion had been

[164] Nevakhovich, *Kol shavat bat yehudah*, 3–7, 10–11, 29.   [165] Ibid. 22–8, 34–6.

falsified and its concepts distorted by the rabbis through their 'talmudism' and mystification. The rabbis, portrayed as 'benighted' medieval priests, were presiding over a meaningless cult and had deluded the people, leading them blindfold into espousing foolish beliefs, thereby creating a barrier between Jews and other peoples. On the face of it, the negative attitude of the Christians could even be justified as an act of defence against the Jewish hatred of Christians. The time had come, Frank claimed, to arouse the Jews from their deep religious sleep and to enact reforms that would restore their ancient purity of belief. Mendelssohn's work had proved that it was possible to achieve the moral renaissance of the Jewish people—a mission the Russian government had to take upon itself, and which would be carried out, in Frank's view, on the basis of the recommendations of Mendelssohn's Jewish followers in Russia, including himself.[166]

These isolated examples of the offshoots of the Berlin Haskalah in Vienna, Prague, Buda, and Shklov at the beginning of the nineteenth century indicate that these thinkers were beginning to internalize the maskilic picture of the past first formulated by the German maskilim during the 1780s. The role of the maskilim in each of these places as lobbyists for change and interpreters of the present led them to adopt 'maskilic history', which served to support, justify, and legitimize them. Several of them who were teachers and writers were inspired to try their hand at various types of historical writing, which no longer bore any resemblance to accepted 'traditional history'.

In Berlin itself there was hardly any need for Hebrew adaptations or translations of episodes in universal history; anyone dissatisfied with works written in the style of *She'erit yisra'el* could turn to a German history book. In eastern Europe, however, the maskilim found a wider audience among scholars and the middle class, and their writings in the 'lower', more popular style of 'maskilic history' may have been the only books that could open a window onto the unknown historical world for readers with little education.

History was included in the curricula of the modern Jewish schools in Germany, beginning with the first schools established at the end of the eighteenth century. In this sense, Wessely's plan was indeed implemented. In effect, history was divided into two separate subjects: world history, which was studied with the aid of German textbooks, almost always in a single lesson that included geography as well, and biblical history (*biblische Geschichte*), taught with the aid of several books, written especially for this purpose, that abridged and adapted the Bible (with the addition of later chapters of ancient history) into historical stories and pedagogical texts. Most of these books, dozens of which were written in the nineteenth century, appeared in Germany; some of them were written in German transliterated into Hebrew characters. Only a few, such as *Toledot ha'avot* (The History of our Forefathers, 1820), by the teacher Joelson of Frankfurt-am-Main,

---

[166] Frank, 'Tazkir'. See also Ettinger, 'Principles and Trends', 20–34, esp. p. 31; id., 'The 1804 Regulation', 87–110.

or *Nahar me'eden* (River from Eden, 1837), by David Zamosc of Breslau (1789–1864), were published in Hebrew.[167]

In the following chapters I shall trace the development of the maskilic awareness of the past and the ways in which history was used in those centres of the maskilic movement in eastern Europe whose members saw themselves as the nineteenth-century followers and perpetuators of the Berlin Haskalah.

[167] Eliav, *Jewish Education in Germany*, s.v. 'Biblical history'. On the teaching of history in Breslau, see Reicheneu, 'Hadashot hazeman', *Hame'asef*, 7/1 (1794), 74. See also the list of textbooks on 'biblical history' from the 19th c. in Strassburger, *Geschichte*, 282–4.

TWO

The Manipulation of History in Nineteenth-Century Galicia

THE GALICIAN MASKILIM

IN the mid-1810s, a circle of maskilim gradually formed in eastern Galicia that included Jewish intellectuals and writers, most of them young men in their twenties or thirties, born after the Austrian empire had annexed Galicia from Poland in 1772. This group of maskilim, most of whom lived in the three large communities of Brody, Lvov, and Tarnopol, introduced the Haskalah movement to eastern Europe. Although there were individual maskilim before this period, no cohesive maskilic movement with literary forums and clearly formulated world-views was yet in evidence. The Galician Haskalah may be viewed as one segment of a Haskalah network that encompassed the maskilim of the entire Austrian empire. The reformist policy of the enlightened absolutist regime in the time of Joseph II, Herz Homberg's tireless activity to establish new Jewish schools, and the support of the maskilim by wealthy Jews in Vienna and Prague were salient features of the historical background to the growth of the Haskalah in Austria at the end of the eighteenth century and its spread to provincial cities in Bohemia, Moravia, and Hungary.[1]

In their development and activity the Galician maskilim were closely allied to the Austrian Haskalah. Anton Schmidt's printing-house, for example, was an important focal point uniting the Haskalah movement throughout the entire empire, and it published a great many works by Galician maskilim. Samson Bloch Halevi (1784–1845), one of the leading figures of the Galician circle of maskilim, worked there for a short time as a proof-reader.[2] The 'Vienna press' was regarded as a maskilic institution and symbol by both the maskilim themselves and their hasidic

---

[1] On the Haskalah movement in Austria–Galicia, see Kestenberg-Gladstein, *Neure Geschichte der Juden*; Mahler, *Hasidism and the Jewish Enlightenment*; id., *History of the Jewish People*, vi. 86–175; Gelber, *The Jews of Brody*, 173–219; id., 'The Haskalah Movement', 215–23; id., 'The Jews of Tarnopol', 46–95; Silber, 'The Historical Experience of German Jewry'; Bartal, 'The Heavenly City', 33–42; Zinberg, *A History of Jewish Literature*, vi. 25–100; Etkes (ed.), *Religion and Life*, 25–88.

[2] Bloch, *Shevilei olam*, vol. i, letter to Nahman Krochmal; J. Klausner, *History of Modern Hebrew Literature*, ii. 350–68.

opponents, as is evident from the satires written by Joseph Perl (1773–1839) and Isaac Baer Levinsohn (1788–1860).[3] During their travels to other lands to sell subscriptions to their books, the maskilim enjoyed the support of the communities of Bohemia, Moravia, and Hungary.[4] Some maskilim studied at universities in Vienna and Prague. Isaac Erter (1791–1851) studied medicine in Budapest, and Hayim Ginzburg, the son of Dov Ginzburg, one of the founders of the Haskalah in Brody, studied art at a Viennese academy.[5] Solomon Judah Leib Rapoport (1790–1867) maintained contacts with maskilim in Moravia; for example, he gave much encouragement to Joseph Flesch (1781–1841) for his research and his translations of Philo's writings.[6] Rapoport moved from Galicia to Prague in 1840 to serve as a rabbi there, and Meir Letteris (1800?–71) moved to Vienna, where he engaged in extensive literary activity.[7] Judah Leib Pastor and Samson Bloch were among those addressing queries to the maskilic rabbi Moses Kunitz of Hungary, while Wolf Meir (b. 1778) and Judah Loeb Jeiteles (1773–1838), from Prague, provided approbations for *Kinat ha'emet* (The Zeal for Truth, 1828) by Judah Leib Mieses (1798–1831).[8] From 1820 to 1831 the maskilim of Austria had at their disposal an all-Austrian literary forum, an annual entitled *Bikurei ha'itim* (First Fruits of the Times), founded at the initiative of Shalom Hacohen, who came to Austria from the declining centres of Haskalah in Germany.[9] Many Galician maskilim—Rapoport, Erter, Mieses, Jacob Samuel Bick (1772–1831), Abraham Goldberg (1790–1850), Mordechai (Marcus) Strelisker (1806–75), Abraham Notkis (d. 1862), and others—sent their writings to the editors in Vienna; works by some sixty authors, including poems, biblical commentary, translations, and historical essays, were published there during the twelve years of the annual's existence. The editors, who changed frequently, also reflected the exclusively Austrian scope of *Bikurei ha'itim*: Shalom Hacohen was replaced in 1823 by Moses Landau, a school supervisor from Prague (1778–1852); he was succeeded by Solomon Pergamenter, Issachar Baer Schlesinger of Kolin, Isaac Samuel Reggio (Yashar; 1784–1855) of northern Italy, and Judah Loeb Jeiteles of Prague. The editors had very modest goals, which did not include the genuine cultural struggles that might have been expected of men who thought of themselves as the heirs and followers of the German *Hame'asef*. '*Bikurei ha'itim*', the annual's title-page proclaimed, 'contains some delightful pieces on science and practical matters, intended for parents who wish to give a gift to their well-

---

[3] I. B. Levinsohn, 'Emek refa'im', 136; id., 'Divrei tsadikim', 147–8.

[4] See the list of subscribers in Bloch, *Shevilei olam*, vol. ii.

[5] Letteris, 'Toledot hameḥaber', p. xv.   [6] Flesch, *Ḥayei moshe*.

[7] On Rapoport, see J. Klausner, *History of Modern Hebrew Literature*, ii. 215–66; Barzilay, *Shlomo Yehuda Rapoport*. On Letteris, see J. Klausner, *History of Modern Hebrew Literature*, ii. 369–400.

[8] Kunitz, *Sefer hamatsref*, i. 200, ii. 131–8, 194, 580. The approbations were published by Mieses separately: *Bikurei ha'itim*, 11 (1830), 126–31.

[9] Kestenberg-Gladstein, *Neuere Geschichte der Juden*, 289–92; Gilboa, *Hebrew Periodicals*, 61–6; J. Klausner, *History of Modern Hebrew Literature*, ii. 30–7.

behaved children, so they may hear wisdom and learn some lessons'.[10] It was a forum for teachers and educators with a didactic aim, which addressed itself to *gebildete Hausväter und Hausmütter* (educated fathers and mothers) and to bourgeois Jewish families, and also encouraged students aged 15–17 to send in their early attempts at writing.[11] The writers' main efforts were directed towards shaping Jewish youth in keeping with a maskilic ethos, moderate and bourgeois in nature. A strong emphasis was placed on family life, 'the success of the home', and restraining the passions. One of the periodical's writers addressed its readers with the words: 'Happy is the man who follows the precepts of his forefathers, seeks goodness and truth, and follows righteous paths.' 'A hard-working man, who eats in moderation, and keeps a tight rein on his passions' was the maskilic moral ideal promulgated by the Austrian teachers.[12]

Only about a quarter of those participating in *Bikurei ha'itim* were maskilim from Galicia, but their contribution reflected the unique nature of the Galician Haskalah. A comparison of Erter's 'Moznei mishkal' (Scales, 1822) and Rapoport's review of Perl's *Megaleh temirin* (The Revealer of Secrets, 1819)—two works by Galicians in this Austrian forum—with the material routinely printed in the annual shows that the Galicia maskilim were imbued with a different spirit from that of their colleagues in the rest of the Austrian empire.[13] The special circumstances surrounding the maskilim's activity in Galicia, in the midst of a traditional Jewish society that was hostile to them, and in particular the dominant presence of the hasidic movement, did not allow them to develop a lukewarm, neutral, and individualistic Haskalah, like that in those regions of the empire where the hasidim posed no threat. For the Galician maskilim, creative writing in Hebrew was not only an aim in itself; it also served as a vehicle for a social and cultural struggle and as a propaganda tool. This difference also underlay the short-lived attempt of the Galician maskilim to establish a literary forum of their own, which would be better suited to their objectives than *Bikurei ha'itim*. At the age of 23 Meir Letteris founded a maskilic journal entitled *Hatsefirah* (The Dawn), but he only succeeded in publishing one issue, in 1824. In contrast to *Bikurei ha'itim*, *Hatsefirah* had an aggressive editorial policy and addressed a different readership—not the 'educated Jew', but the young, upright reader not attracted by the 'inanities' of the hasidim, nor afraid of the 'perverse' elements attempting to frighten him. It was the aim of *Hatsefirah* to bring young maskilim out of their isolation and to bolster their confidence: 'Now the maskilim will no longer conceal their search for knowledge, for now they are imbued with the right spirit.'[14] Letteris regarded *Hatsefirah*

[10] *Bikurei ha'itim*, 1 (1820).

[11] Among these were, for example, Robel from Austerlitz, aged 17, Hayim Guenzburg, aged 16, and Aharon Yosef of Trieste, aged 15, who studied with Samuel David Luzzatto in Padua.

[12] Rapoport, 'Hatslahat habayit', 110–13; B. Shenfeld, 'Ha'adam', 83–7; Siedefeld, 'Hashivui', 82–4.

[13] Erter, 'Moznei mishkal', 166–9; Rapoport, Review of Perl's *Megaleh temirin*.

[14] Letteris, 'Davar el hakore', introd.

as the heir to *Hame'asef*, though he asked contributors not to send the journal only literary material or translations and commentaries. He thought it more important to print 'articles opposed to and challenging the corrupt customs that have sprung up in our midst'.[15] *Hatsefirah* was printed in Zolkiew and all who contributed to it, except for Shalom Hacohen, were maskilim from Galicia. A list of the journal's agents in various cities also reveals a segment of the Haskalah movement that differs from that catered for by *Bikurei ha'itim*: the cities of Bohemia and Moravia do not appear on the list, which actually sketches a map of the branches of the Haskalah in Galicia, in Brody, Zolkiew, Tarnopol, and Jaroslaw. There were also agents in Vienna (Hayim Ginzburg from Brody) and in Odessa (Leibush Landau from Brody), and in Berdichev, Uman, and Kremenets in Russia. Despite the political boundary, there were close ties between the maskilim of Galicia and those of Russia, who jointly created a Haskalah network in eastern Europe. After the demise of *Hatsefirah*, the maskilim of Galicia had to wait for nearly a decade for their own literary forum, which was founded at the end of 1833 and called *Kerem ḥemed* (Delightful Vineyard). However, this journal, founded by the young Samuel Leib Goldenberg (1807–46), gradually lost its Galician character and became a general forum for the Wissenschaft des Judentums until, in the mid-1840s, another attempt was made, this time with a journal called *Yerushalayim* (Jerusalem).[16] In 1843 discussions were held between maskilim in Galicia (Isaac Erter), and in Russia (Isaac Baer Levinsohn), regarding the publication of a joint maskilic periodical, but the idea never came to fruition.[17]

The militant nature of the Galician Haskalah was determined by the very process of enlightenment. In personal testimonies and biographies the experience of becoming enlightened is described as a revelation and conversion that occurred at a young age and engendered great excitement in the heart of the maskil. In addition, there was the heady sense of belonging to an intellectual élite trying, against enormous odds, to combat a hostile and obscurantist majority. Erter, for example, was 'converted' to the Haskalah under the influence of Joseph Tarler, who had apparently studied at a European university before coming to the small town where Erter was living; he was the first to 'give him life, the life of the spirit and deep thought, and to set his soul free to guide him in the paths of reason'.[18] Bloch became a maskil at the age of 18, when he moved from his native Kulikow to Zolkiew, where he met Nahman Krochmal (Renak; 1785–1840). Bloch describes his conversion as a dramatic turnabout from folly to wisdom: 'Like one of the lambs in the flock of my people, in my inadequacy I was an empty-headed youth, devoid of any morals and lacking any insight . . . my mind was empty of any wisdom and resourcefulness . . . it was immersed in the depths of stupidity . . .

---

[15] Letteris, 'Davar el hakore', introd.

[16] On *Hatsefirah*, *Kerem ḥemed*, and *Yerushalayim*, see Gilboa, *Hebrew Periodicals*, 66–8, 70–3, 84–5.

[17] Weinryb, 'On the Biography of R. Isaac Baer Levinsohn', 201–5; B. Nathanson, *Sefer hazikhronot*, 70–1.   [18] Letteris, 'Toledot hameḥaber', 9–10.

until I found you, so beautiful in nature!'[19] Krochmal, who was the same age as Bloch, was delighted to find a partner in enlightenment, and the two went for long walks in the mountains, their hearts fired with their longing to spread the Haskalah far and wide: 'We imagined ourselves purifying our hearts, cleansing our minds, and then turning darkness into light and the shadow of death into coherence, for we would be the bearers of the torches of justice and a reason in the land of darkness, a candle illuminating the way for the people walking in darkness and a light on their path.'[20]

Gradually meeting-places were set up, channels of communication were established, and a world of shared experiences was created; all these gave the circles of maskilim in Galicia a sense of social cohesion and fostered their collective consciousness of being a unique group within the larger Jewish society. Individual maskilim enjoyed the social support of 'a fraternity of comrades who serve wisdom and are fired by the flame of their zeal', as had been the case in the 1780s among the maskilim of Prussia. The homes of several prominent maskilim and of patrons of the Haskalah served as gathering-places for young maskilim, and sometimes resembled the 'courts' of the hasidic rabbis to which disciples came for spiritual sustenance. One such home, for example, was that of Dov Baer Ginzburg, the secretary of the Jewish community in Brody. Among his guests during the 1820s were Mendel Levin (1749–1826), Krochmal, Rapoport, Bick, and Levinsohn. In the Brody home of the Trachtenberg brothers, rich merchants who were also the patrons of Erter and Letteris, 'all the maskilim and those seeking wisdom always gathered'.[21] The homes of Mieses and Rapoport in Lvov, and particularly those of Perl in Tarnopol and Krochmal in Zolkiew, were a lodestone for many maskilim. The need for closer contacts and meeting-places increased when it became clear how militant and hostile was the attitude of the hasidim and mitnagedim towards the maskilim. The ban of excommunication issued in 1816 by Rabbi Jacob Orenstein in Lvov against a group of maskilim there, on the charge that they had been corrupting the youth with their propaganda advocating the study of secular 'wisdoms' and languages, became a pivotal experience in the evolution of the Galician Haskalah movement. It was described again and again, and the maskilim's triumph over the humiliated rabbi, who was forced to withdraw his ban publicly, nurtured their hope that this example would typify cultural and social progress everywhere until they achieved a complete victory.[22] Attempts to thwart the maskilim's efforts to establish schools in Tarnopol and Brody, the charge of heresy against Krochmal arising from his contacts with Karaites,[23] and other similar incidents increasingly hardened the boundaries between the circles of maskilim and their opponents.

[19] Bloch, *Shevilei olam*, vol. i, a letter to Nahman Krochmal. [20] Ibid.
[21] Gelber, *The Jews of Brody*, 175, 179; B. Nathanson, *Sefer hazikhronot*, 8–9.
[22] Letteris, 'Toledot hamehaber', 10; Gelber, 'The Haskalah Movement', 217–19.
[23] N. Krochmal, letter to Ze'ev Shiff (July 1816), in id., *Collected Writings*, 413–16.

A number of young maskilim, including Bloch and Letteris, became 'enlightened' as a result of their semi-clandestine contacts with Krochmal.[24] Young
students of the Talmud secretly sneaked into his home to learn, receive encouragement, and engage in intellectual conversation with him, often on walks in the
open fields outside the town.[25] The maskilim also pinned their hopes on Krochmal, in the expectation that he would guide, organize, and unite all the maskilim
throughout Galicia, an expectation which was never fulfilled.[26] Instead of giving
rise to an orderly organization, Krochmal's home continued to serve as a magnet,
attracting many young maskilim. According to one account:

> several times a year, on a clear day, under the pure heavens, groups of young people would
> go on foot from Lvov to Zolkiew to the home of Rabbi Krochmal, of blessed memory, and
> at eventide they came back with happy hearts, having taken farewell of him, to the homes
> of the scholars mentioned [Rapoport and Benjamin Tsevi Notkis], for one spirit, the spirit
> of wisdom and insight, the spirit of knowledge and enlightenment, and the aim of seeking
> truth revived and united all hearts![27]

In addition to the private meeting-places at the 'courts' of maskilim or in the
homes of wealthy supporters of the Haskalah, two maskilic schools, founded in
Tarnopol (1813) and Brody (1818), were also influential centres for maskilim.
These schools afforded an opportunity to educate the young generation according
to a maskilic curriculum. They offered foreign languages, such as German,
French, and Italian; general education, including geography and history; Jewish
studies, and, in Brody, bookkeeping and banking for the children of merchants.
They also provided teaching jobs for maskilim.[28]

Mention has already been made of the maskilic journals *Hatsefirah* and *Kerem
ḥemed* as attempts to create forums for literary and journalistic writing. *Kerem
ḥemed*, for example, edited by Samuel Goldenberg, turned his native Tarnopol
into a centre of maskilic literary activity, and opened channels for communication
and avid discussion among maskilim. However, the most important element in the
development of the Galician Haskalah into a cohesive movement was the exten-

---

[24] Letteris described the meetings as a formative experience: 'From time to time some sanctimonious men would come forth to tattle to my father about me, disparaging me for following in
Krochmal's path, but I did not desist, and would secretly go to his home for the joy of sharing some
words of wisdom with him'; *Toledot avi*. See also Letteris, *Zikaron basefer*, 35.

[25] David Lachsher, for example, a young talmudic scholar, studied Maimonides' *Moreh nevukhim*
with him. See *Otsar hasifrut*, iii. 7.

[26] Rapoport's article appears in id., 'Al mot harav heḥakham . . . hafilosof rabi naḥman krokhmal',
Kerem ḥemed, 6 (1841), 46–8; editor's introd. to N. Krochmal, *Collected Writings*, 65–87.

[27] Triebesch, *Korot ha'itim* (Lemberg, 1851) (unpaginated). When Krochmal's daughter was
married, the entire group of maskilim travelled to the wedding (Bick's letter to Bloch (1821), in
Letteris, *Mikhtavei ivrit*, 178).

[28] On the schools, see Gelber, 'The Jews of Tarnopol', and Berish Goldberg, *Sefer ohel yosef*.
Erter, for example, was a teacher in the school in Brody until 1825. On Gottlober's visit to Perl's
school in Tarnopol, see Gottlober, *Zikhronot umasaot*, i. 222–8.

sive network of personal correspondence between its members. Anyone perusing the correspondence between maskilim can only conclude that nearly all of them wrote to each other. By means of these letters, the social relationships of this maskilic 'republic' were formed, young people seeking their way were given guidance, information about the publication of new books was disseminated, manuscripts were transmitted, views were exchanged, and reactions to various publications were expressed. Some of these letters were actually written as articles for publication, and some were even of a distinctly scholarly character. Meir Letteris, recognizing the importance of the maskilim's correspondence, saw to it that a number of collections of letters were published,[29] and his initiative helped to preserve the legacy of the Haskalah, as did his biographies of maskilim.

I was despised by my Jewish brethren! For thus is every seeker of reason persecuted mercilessly by the fanatics of that wretched bird [hasidism] which has spread its wings over our land, spanning the length and breadth of Galicia . . . And the sanctimonious purifiers would block out the rays of the sun of wisdom, they rebel against its light. They strive to hold it back with bolted doors, and with their folly they cover the face of the earth. And thus I and my friends have become the most hated of all. They quarrelled with us over our demands to know something of the teachings of reason . . . however I maintained my position; I fear neither them nor their masses.[30]

These words, referring to the 1830s and 1840s, from a letter by Zelig Mondschein of Bolechow (1812–72), faithfully reflect the 'maskilic predicament' in Galicia and the maskilim's self-image as a small, isolated circle of persecuted seekers of truth. On one hand, they were competing for the minds of Jewish youth, as they endeavoured to expand their circles, and on the other, they were engaged in an unrelenting struggle against the hasidim, whom they regarded as the most abhorrent socio-cultural element in Jewish society.

Young people were the target population of the Haskalah propagandists: both yeshivah students, whom they felt it was imperative to educate in the sciences and to teach the needs of the time in a new historical era, and sons of the wealthy merchants, students, or doctors, who spent much of their time among non-Jews and were liable to abandon their Jewish identity totally. Rapoport's letters reveal his sensitivity towards young people who were uncertain about the path they should choose. In 1815, in his long letter 'Ner mitsvah' (Lamp of the Commandment), he attempted to dissuade a young talmudic scholar (perhaps Mordecai, Rabbi Orenstein's son) from turning to hasidism. In other letters, some answering questions and requests for advice addressed to him, he sent detailed lists of programmes of study to young maskilim:[31] 'I knew it was no easy matter to enter the hall of wisdom in

[29] Examples of these collections include Letteris, *Mikhtavei ivrit*; id., *Sefer mikhtavei benei kedem*; id., *Mikhtavim*; Bloch, *Shevilei olam*, vol. iii (appendix); Harkavy and Halberstam, *Zikaron larishonim*, vol. i; Rapoport, *Igerot shir*.

[30] Mondschein, *Imrei yosher*, 17–41. On Mondschein, see Hendel, 'Maskilim and Haskalah', 35–40.

[31] Rapoport, 'Ner mitsvah'; Holish, 'Letter to Rapoport', 133–8; Rapoport, 'Mikhtav 23', *Kerem ḥemed*, 1 (1833), 83–7.

this land of darkness,' Rapoport wrote to a 'dear friend' in distress, 'I know the tribulations you will encounter, I have myself experienced them.'[32] Rapoport also admitted that on more than one occasion the maskilim were bitterly disappointed and frustrated when promising young men, usually serious students who had already begun to absorb the values of the Haskalah, became hasidim.[33] Joseph Perl regarded the young as his only hope of seeing the fulfilment of the maskilic vision of the future: 'You are delightful young men who have not borne the burden of worrying about earning a livelihood . . . and whose minds have not been corrupted by the malice and wickedness that are destroying our people.' Drawing an analogy from the Second Temple period, he expected that these young men would save their people just as had the young Hasmoneans then.[34]

Hasidism was an obsession among the Galician maskilim, and they would resort to almost any means to block the expansion of the 'sect', which before their very eyes was sweeping up the Jewish masses, even spreading to the central urban communities.[35] Hasidism aroused an outburst of hostile emotions among the maskilim, and the struggle against it was portrayed as a war of light against darkness, on which the future of the entire Jewish people depended. Perl's memoranda to the Austrian authorities, his proposals for legislative and police measures, and his anti-hasidic satires are but an acute expression of the dominance of the 'hasidic problem' in the minds of Galician maskilim in the nineteenth century.[36] Hasidism was depicted as a huge, menacing movement whose tsadikim and emissaries were running a massive campaign of persuasion to win over young people and whose success would ruin any chances of Jews integrating into the state, human society, and European culture. The hasidim figured prominently in maskilic correspondence. The maskilim gathered information about them, reported various events related to them, and gloated over any setbacks they suffered. Not only did they accuse hasidim of religious fanaticism, disloyalty to the regime, opposition to modernism, and the promotion of superstition (*Schwärmerei*), but they also denounced them as sexual perverts, adulterers, and even as capable of committing murder.[37] Particularly rancorous feelings were directed towards the 'scoundrel and sinner from Zhidachov', the hasidic *tsadik* Rabbi Tsevi Hirsch Eichenstein (1785–1831), to whom the maskilim imputed control of more than 100,000 hasidim.[38]

[32] Rapoport, 'El re'a yakar', 75–7.

[33] Ibid.; id., 'Mikhtav', *Bikurei ha'itim*, 7 (1827), 23–4; Krochmal's letter to a young maskil, in id., *Collected Writings*, 416–18; Bloch, 'Mikhtav leyehudah vorman', 81–5.

[34] Perl, 'Katit lamaor', 38–9.

[35] Mahler, *Hasidism and the Jewish Enlightenment*; Werses, 'Hasidism and Haskalah Literature', 379–91.

[36] Mahler, *Hasidism and the Jewish Enlightenment*; Perl, *Über das Wesen der Sekte Chassidim*, 1–49; Shmeruk, 'Authentic and Imaginative Elements', 92–9; Werses, *Story and Source*, 3–45, 'The Satirical Methods of Joseph Perl'.

[37] S. Katz, 'Letters of Maskilim', 266–76; Rapoport, 'Mikhtav lebik' (1830), 486.

[38] Bick makes this assessment in his letter to Rapoport in 1828 ('Mikhtav leshir', 29). On Galician hasidism, see Mahler, *Hasidism and the Jewish Enlightenment*; Werses, 'An Unknown Satirical Work', 224.

These features of the social history of the Galician Haskalah, in particular from 1815 to 1840, left their mark on the way the maskilim manipulated history. During this period in Galicia even those maskilim who professed to be serious historians engaged in critical research, like the historians of the Wissenschaft des Judentums in Germany, deliberately and consciously employed history to prove the truth of maskilic ideology. The maskilim's precarious situation, so fraught with ferment and tension, induced them to search for their distinctive identity in the past and to use historical examples to denounce their opponents. However, before examining their attempt to incorporate the conflict between the Haskalah and hasidism into a broad picture of the past, and discussing the special dialogue that developed between the maskilim and the Wissenschaft des Judentums, I will first present the thread of continuity in the Galician maskilim's sense of the past, which was a continuation of 'maskilic history'.

THE UNFOLDING OF MASKILIC HISTORY

The conscious, declared intention of the Austrian maskilim in general and of the maskilim of Galicia in particular of carrying on the German Haskalah was manifested in their attitude towards 'history' as a field of knowledge, literature study, and instruction that fulfilled eminently didactic functions. In the late eighteenth century 'history' still required legitimization, which it received in independent articles and introductions to historical writings. The maskilim's link to 'Berlin' literary formats, their desire to pick up where the Berlin Haskalah had left off, their need to persuade a traditional society that it was essential to forge a path to European culture and create a new ideal Jew, as well their internalization of the popular German historiography of the day, all combined to influence the way in which the maskilic consciousness of the past was shaped.

Euchel's 1784 article 'Davar el hakore', containing the first attempt to formulate the didactic objectives of 'maskilic history', which he called 'the judgement of the mind built upon experience', was reprinted verbatim in 1820 in *Bikurei ha'itim* and once again served as a basis for the interpretation of universal and Jewish history in a characteristically rational and moral light.[39] Seven years later Reggio even recapitulated Wessely's view of history, almost half a century after its original exposition in *Divrei shalom ve'emet*.[40] History continued to function as a guide for Jewish society: 'By means of this observation, we shall be shown the path we must take after comparing era to era and man to man and class to class.'[41] The historical analogies made a contribution to the national moral inventory

---

[39] Euchel, 'Davar el hakore', *Bikurei ha'itim*, 1 (1820), 69–73, 80–4; Letteris (ed.), *Hame'asef lashanah harishonah*.   [40] Reggio, *Hatorah vehafilosofiyah*, 64.

[41] Bick, 'El maskilei benei ami!', 71–2. On Bick, see Werses, 'Between Two Worlds', 27–76; id. (ed.), *Trends and Forms*, 110–59.

demanded by the maskilim, particularly since they clarified the correlation between the outward status of the Jews and their cultural and scholarly accomplishments. The maskilim believed that all civilized peoples who had begun to
emerge from 'the darkness of folly into the light of science' did so by studying
their past: 'For the benefits of this inquiry will be strongly entwined with the
success of our people and will awaken the minds of its sages to consider: What
were we? How did we rise from the depths of our situation in ancient times to
that in which we find ourselves today? And how can we further advance ourselves?'[42] Universal history was seen as a pragmatic, moral compass providing an
answer to the question 'Did the people act wisely and innocently, thus rising to the
heights, or did they act foolishly and immorally, thus descending to the depths?'[43]
The maskilim believed in the ultimate victory of 'virtue' and advised young Jews
to discover the 'great people' of the past and emulate their behaviour.[44]

A short article written by Mordecai Strelisker, a young maskil from Brody and
a friend of Krochmal's, contains a concise, four-point summary of the maskilic
perception of history and its functions during this period: the commemoration of
great people and their deeds; the positive or negative moral evaluation of historical heroes ('including tyrannical rulers who, while still alive, were feared and
flattered at the gates, and who will be judged truly and honestly after their deaths
by the history books according to their deeds; for these books favour no one and
take no bribes, and are honest judges of the kind we know not here in our land');
ethical education according to positive models; the discarding of negative images;
and the recognition that progress is not inevitable: 'These will instruct men in a
pleasant way to recognize and know that violence, folly, sin, disobedience, and
deceit will for centuries repeatedly prevent men from rising to rationality and
soaring to the heights of skill and science that would enable them to achieve perfection.'[45]

These four goals of history presented by Strelisker accurately reflect the continuity in the historical perception of the maskilim, and are in keeping with the
view of the eighteenth-century maskilim. However, against the backdrop of the
new historiographic trends in nineteenth-century Europe and the efforts of historians and philosophers to break away from the pragmatic, didactic, rationalistic, and moralistic history of the Enlightenment and to write scientific, objective
history instead, the maskilic approach to history appears rather anachronistic. Did
the nineteenth-century maskilim continue to adhere to obsolete concepts? The
question has a twofold answer. First, a description of the 'maskilic situation' in
Galicia during the first half of the nineteenth century reveals that the historical

---

[42] Reggio, 'Shenei hakhamim gedolim bilti mefursamim', 12 n. Cf. Mieses, 'Al devar sibat he'ader',
54–69.   [43] B. Shenfeld, 'Mikhtav mito'elet', 71. Cf. S. Hacohen, *Kore hadorot*, introd.
[44] Shenfeld, 'Mikhtav mito'elet', 70–2; Reggio, 'El hahokerim', 39–52; Flesch, *Reshimat anshei
mofet*; Rapoport, introd. to 'Toledot rabeinu natan', 3–6.
[45] Strelisker, 'Al devar hato'elet', 142–6.

function of the maskilim, as a minority aspiring to influence and shape society according to maskilic values, resembled the role of the eighteenth-century maskilim of Berlin and Königsberg in the previous generation. It is thus no wonder that the mode of thinking, the concepts, and even the purposes for which they mobilized the historic past were similar. However, in addition to this resemblance, the maskilim also had access to historical works that were not entirely divorced from the historical literature of the nineteenth century. They possessed volumes of the most popular 'universal history' in all of Europe at the time—the secondary, popular German historiography written by second- and third-rate historians whose names, for the most part, became marginal in the history of European historiography.

Written in 1830, Strelisker's article was not original, but rather summarized the introduction to a book written by a very popular historian, Karl Heinrich Pölitz (1772–1838), whose writings were extensively used by other east European maskilim, some of whom even tried to translate and adapt them.[46] Pölitz, a professor of history and statistics at the University of Leipzig, was a prolific historian, who wrote some 150 works intended for all educated readers, not only academics. His four-volume *Die Weltgeschichte für gebildete Leser und Studierende* appeared in 1804, and by the 1830s it had been reprinted six times and 12,000 copies had been distributed.[47] He himself admitted that this was not an original historical work based on primary sources but an adaptation, based on the newest and most outstanding studies of German historiography from the end of the eighteenth century onwards. In his historical perceptions, Pölitz remained largely an eighteenth-century man, a fact that made it easier for the maskilim to digest his writings and pass them on to the Jewish reader. In Pölitz's view, history reflected the great achievements of mankind, which alternately progressed and regressed. The desire for liberty was the predominant value of history, and historical events passed before the eyes of the historian like a dramatic, impressive parade. He observed, described, and also judged them according to rational and moral criteria. Pölitz adopted the common dichotomy between eras of light and darkness, with political and civil liberty contrasted to suppression and superstition, as well as the didactic approach and the exaltation of heroes. His liberal, humanistic, and universal views were combined with something of the nineteenth-century spirit, particularly the Protestant–nationalistic approach that placed Germany at the centre of universal history. However, the maskilim chose those views that best suited their purpose, selecting eighteenth-century approaches and ignoring the rest with relative ease. Strelisker recommended history, particularly exemplary biographies, as an enormously beneficial and educational field for young Jews, not only using the historical past to direct them towards the Haskalah but also providing his readers with a popular, contemporary historical approach, which he borrowed from one of the many volumes of secondary German historiography.

[46] Pölitz, *Die Weltgeschichte*.   [47] *Allgemeine Deutsche Biographie*, xxvi. 389–92.

Maskilic historical writing drew first and foremost upon maskilic ideology and its goals. However, as Hebrew writers, the maskilim also satisfied the ever-increasing curiosity of early nineteenth-century Jews about world history and geography, which was intensified by the political upheavals of the Napoleonic era. Two prominent Galician maskilim, Rapoport and Perl, began their literary careers with this type of history: in 1814 Rapoport published a short piece on Napoleon intended for 'all men whose hearts were touched by the new and marvellous events of our times'.[48] Perl's *Luaḥ halev* (Calendar of the Heart), appended to the calendars he published, recorded historical events. This *kronik*, as it was called, combined episodes from 'traditional Jewish history' (the history of the Patriarchs, the building and destruction of the Temples, the expulsion of the Jews from England and Spain) and incidents from universal history. It was intended to disseminate historical knowledge, praise inventions and discoveries that attested to human achievements, and preach patriotism (in Perl's case, in Galicia in 1816, Russian patriotism): 1,386 years since the building of the city of Kiev; 1,192 since the beginning of belief in Muhammad; 669 since the building of the city of Moscow; 474 since the discovery of gunpowder; 376 since the discovery of printing; sixty-four years since Franklin discovered how buildings could be saved from lightning—these are just a few of the events included in Perl's *kronik*.[49]

Mendel Levin's adaptation of the wondrous travels of the educator, philanthropist, and prolific writer from Dessau Joachim Heinrich Campe (*Merkwürdige Reisebeschreibungen 1781–1785*) was another addition to this genre of dramatic historical stories. In 1818 Levin's book appeared in Zolkiew under its Hebrew title, *Masaot hayam* (Sea Journeys), and it was reprinted several times during the nineteenth century. It included adventure stories: 'the events and hardships that befell [a captain] of the land of the Netherlands on the northern sea of ice in the year 1696' and a journey on the 'southern sea of ice' in 1786.[50] Stories of the exploits of great explorers in unknown continents and of their adventures and encounters with natives, particularly the experiences of Columbus, attracted great interest. Indeed, there were several nineteenth-century versions of the story of the discovery of America, most of them based on Campe's *Entdeckung von Amerika*, written between 1780 and 1782.[51] In the maskilim's view, the discovery of America was one of the symbols of the modern age, an example of man's

---

[48] Rapoport, *Tekhunat ha'ir paris*.

[49] Perl, *Luaḥ lishenat 1816*. On Perl's calendars, see Mahler, *Hasidism and the Jewish Enlightenment*, 149–68.

[50] Mendel Levin, *Masaot hayam*. See also Ofek, *Hebrew Children's Literature*, 92–3; Z. Shavit, 'Literary Interference', 41–61.

[51] Ofek, *Hebrew Children's Literature*, 79–87. The first translations–adaptations were M. Mendelson (Hamburg), *Metsiat ha'arets*; Horowitz, *Tsofnat pa'ane'aḥ*; Guenzburg, *Gelot ha'arets haḥadashah*. See also Zinberg, *A History of Jewish Literature*, v. 278–80, vi. 227–9; Feingold, 'Haskalah Literature', 91–104.

tremendous ability and an event that opened a new historical era, as described in all the books on 'universal history' that they used. Furthermore, it provided readers with an exotic and fascinating story about an unknown culture and heroic deeds, as indicated in the title of a book by Abraham Menahem Mendel Mohr (1815–68): *Columbus: The Story of the Discovery of the Land of America some Four Hundred Years Ago*. In his Hebrew translation (apparently based on other Hebrew adaptations) Mohr attempted to stir the hearts of his readers with biblical language, transforming a historical event into a historical adventure story:

It was midnight, and Columbus stood in the bows of the boat and saw in the distance what appeared to be a gleam of light and the flame of a candle, and he called to one of the queen's slaves who was with him, and they looked upon the wondrous sight in the distance. And as they stood and looked, the shouts of the sailors on board the *Pinta* sailing before them could be heard: Land! Land! And all the people rejoiced and fell upon their knees to give thanks to God and bowed down at the feet of Columbus, begging him to forgive their crimes that had angered him on their voyage.[52]

Mohr, a prominent Galician maskil, was an expert in the genre of historical stories and geographical descriptions intended for a relatively large cross-section of readers, not necessarily maskilim, and his writings were widely distributed from the 1840s to the 1860s. He was preceded, however, by Samson Bloch in the 1820s and 1830s. The sections devoted to the countries of Asia and Africa of Bloch's *Shevilei olam* (Ways of the World), which combined geography and history, were published between 1822 and 1827. The book was an anthology of existing German geographic literature and brief historical surveys of each country. Bloch had taken upon himself an ambitious, encyclopaedic task: to provide the Hebrew reader with a comprehensive description of the 'characteristics of all the nations of the world—their boundaries, climates, and peoples, their rivers and seas, the religious beliefs of their inhabitants, the customs of their governments, their wisdom and knowledge, their language and deeds'. The work was never completed, although the book was a success and had a sizeable number of readers, as shown by the list of subscribers and the approbations. Bloch fulfilled 'the desire of many of the educated among our people who long to learn about the lands in which our forefathers lived and the sites of our Temple, and about the rest of the countries known through Holy Scripture and the writings of the Sages'.[53]

The maskilim translated and adapted those sections of popular, secondary German historiography dealing with ancient times, continuing the work of their German predecessors that had begun in the journal *Hame'asef*. Baruch Schenfeld (1787–1852) translated several lexicographic passages for *Bikurei ha'itim*, including the history of the Phoenicians, the history of ancient commerce, mummification in ancient Egypt, and a piece on 'the development of authority' from the tribal, patriarchal family to the appearance of 'national leaders'.[54] Although the maskilim

---

[52] Mohr, *Kolombus*, 3*b*.   [53] Letter from Bloch to Krochmal in Bloch, *Shevilei olam*, vol. i, introd.
[54] Shenfeld, 'Orḥot kedem', 60–70; Shenfeld, 'Hithavut haserarah', 158–67.

considered the acquisition of a store of knowledge of the past to be an important goal *per se*, they did not miss any opportunity to exploit that knowledge to prove the correctness of their ideas. Perl's survey of the progress of human civilization from the farming and building stage to the higher level of refined culture, science, philosophy, and art concludes with a typically maskilic remark urging the Jews 'to become wise and educated, to cast off the shameful opinions of others, and not to appear foolish in conversations with other peoples in public'.[55] Perl added a short translation of Jost's book on the history of the Khazar kingdom to his anti-hasidic *Bohen tsadik*, exploiting it to prove the feasibility of true religious tolerance, which, in his opinion, had been achieved in that kingdom in the past.[56]

Apart from these and numerous other historical sketches, only a single attempt to write a comprehensive book on Jewish history was made within the sphere of the Austrian Haskalah during this period: the first part of Shalom Hacohen's *Kore hadorot*, published in 1838. Hacohen's objective, as he himself put it, was to provide the Hebrew reader, maskilic and traditional alike, with a succinct, factual account that would answer the needs of those who found it difficult, for example, to read Jost's book in German: 'And I said I would write a book in clear, easy Hebrew chronicling the entire history of the Jews from the reign of the first king of the house of the Hasmoneans and until the present day.'[57] The book is primarily an adaptation of secondary sources, based almost entirely on Jost's *Geschichte der Israeliten*, as will be discussed later, and contains many maskilic messages. Though *Kore hadorot* was written from a maskilic historical perspective, the author considered his work to be a revival of Jewish historiography in Hebrew in the tradition of the Bible, *Sefer yuhasin*, *Tsemah david*, and *Seder hadorot*. The emphasis he placed on the Sanhedrin's mastery of external wisdom, his belief in the historical turning-point of the modern age, exemplified by religious tolerance, his criticism of the negative customs (such as early marriage) of contemporary east European Jews, and his idealization of Jews engaged in working the land furnish a few examples of his maskilic approach. The first part of his book, chronicling events up to the destruction of the Second Temple, was published with rabbinic approbations and had a respectable advance list of subscribers, in which Russian, Galician, and German Jewish communities were represented. The introductory letter by Rapoport, who was then rabbi of Tarnopol, praised the initiative of this historiographic project and wished Hacohen a long life 'in order to see, in his lifetime, the remaining parts of this book published to enlighten the Jewish people'.[58]

[55] Perl, 'Rashei hahokhmot', *Luah lishnat 1816*, 2–5. Perl was probably influenced by Murhard, 'Früheste Geschichte', 152–70.

[56] Perl, *Bohen tsadik*, 89–91. Cf. Jost, *Geschichte der Israeliten*, vi. 111–20, 365.

[57] S. Hacohen, *Kore hadorot*, introd.

[58] Rapoport, letter prefacing S. Hacohen, *Kore hadorot* (unpaginated). Among the rabbis who gave their approbation to the book were R. Solomon Zalman of Tiktin, R. Dov Barish Meizlisch of Krakow, and R. Tsevi Hirsch Chajes of Zolkiew. R. Michal Kristianpoller of Brody was among the subscribers.

His wish, however did not come true. Although the three-part work was apparently completed, the book remained in its manuscript form and its fate is unknown to this day, apart from two separately published chapters, from the second part, which covered Jewish history from the destruction of the Temple to the Crusades, and from the third part, which described the period from the Crusades to the nineteenth century.[59]

Little changed in the maskilic pantheon of heroes. Biography continued to play a central role in the maskilic picture of the past, providing exemplary and didactic models. In the first half of the nineteenth century even leading European historians such as the British Thomas Carlyle still paid considerable attention to historical heroes. However, more complex theories of the philosophy of history were already portraying such heroes as less autonomous and free in their actions on the stage of history. Hegel's hero, for example, is unaware of the fact that he is being manipulated for higher purposes by the cunning of reason and is acting as an 'agent' of 'the spirit'. The French philosopher Auguste Comte linked heroes to collective processes and historical laws.[60] In any case, secondary historiography, such as that of Pölitz, maintained the centrality of the hero, crediting him with the ability and power to effect change and to act with complete autonomy and freedom of choice. Great individuals were regarded as the dynamic element that brought about change, while the masses were merely dragged along behind them.

Pölitz's pantheon included Zarathustra, Moses, Alexander, Julius Caesar, Muhammad, Charlemagne, John Huss, Columbus, and Luther—figures belonging, in his opinion, to the cultural heritage of all humankind. The maskilim chose only a few figures from this pantheon, however. Classical figures embodying wisdom and morality, such as Socrates, Pythagoras, Alexander, and Diogenes, continued to appear in maskilic historical literature,[61] but the spotlight shone mainly on heroes of the modern age, principally Columbus and Napoleon. These two heroes were exploited to demonstrate man's ability to forge new paths through the power of reason, while also pointing out the limitations of human ability and the inevitable failure of excessively ambitious men like Napoleon.[62]

The pantheon of Jewish heroes was much broader and more varied. Shalom

---

[59] Ch. 3 of vol. xvi (of pt. III) appeared in *Bikurei ha'itim haḥadashim* (Vienna, 1845), 25–6. It deals with the history of European Jewry in the 18th c. and is parallel to pt. VIII of Jost's *Geschichte der Israeliten*. The introduction and chs. 1–7 of vol. vii of pt. II appeared in J. Mezah (ed.), *Gan peraḥim*, 19–37. Mezah's note (ibid. 19) indicates that the MS of pt. II at least was sold by Hacohen in Warsaw to R. Isaac Ze'ev Cohen, who gave it to his brother R. Moses Cohen, who in turn gave it to the library of a synagogue in Warsaw. See also P. Lahover, *Researches and Experiments*, 207. It is important to note that Hacohen's book was the first and only work in Hebrew that covered the entire history of the Jewish people until the publication of Ze'ev Jawitz's books at the end of the 19th c.

[60] Hegel, *The Philosophy of History*, 29–32; Löwith, *Meaning in History*, 52–9, 67–90; Carlyle, *On Heroes*.   [61] J. Jeiteles, 'Siḥot ḥakhmei amim', 147–8.

[62] Mohr, *Kolombus*; id., *Dagul merevavah*; id., *Ḥut hameshulash*. For a completely different position, cf. Schlesinger, 'Pitagoras', 84–101. Letteris took the same position in his 1840 poem on Napoleon on the island of St Helena: 'Masa i hasela', *Bikurei ha'itim haḥadashim*, 19.

Hacohen promoted figures from the Hellenistic and medieval periods, particularly Josephus, Philo, and Abrabanel. In his view, Josephus was the most important; Hacohen called him 'our Jew', whose achievements as a historian were universally acknowledged. The example of Abrabanel bore the message that Jews could draw closer to non-Jewish society without relinquishing their Judaism. In a historical comparison that presented a model of Jewish leadership and also demonstrated a certain cyclical approach to Jewish history, Hacohen drew a parallel between Jeremiah, Josephus, and Abrabanel: 'They were great *tsadikim*, sages and writers, as was Abrabanel. Abrabanel too was close to the royal court and beloved among the nations. They experienced poverty and exile, Jeremiah after the destruction of the First Temple, Josephus after the destruction of the Second Temple, and Abrabanel during the bitter expulsion from Spain.'[63]

The maskilim used medieval figures in their polemics against those who opposed any contact whatsoever with secular studies and foreign languages. A constant feature in many ideological articles and even in personal letters was the list of examples 'proving' that the Haskalah was not engaged in any activity that had not been undertaken in the past, and moreover, by personages held in the highest esteem. For example, Rapoport responded to a young man seeking his advice about a career with a long list of Jewish sages and doctors from the past, in an attempt to substantiate his claim that the study of medicine was not forbidden.[64]

Bloch, Mieses, Bick, Perl, Rapoport, and others provided lists of medieval figures which generally included Sa'adiah Gaon (882–942), Sherira Gaon (906–1006), Samuel Hanagid (993–1055/6; 'the *talmid ḥakham* among the great learned men and an expert in Arabic literature, which gave him the strength to stand in the hall of the king'), Judah Halevi (before 1075–1141), Abraham Ibn Ezra (1089–1164), David Kimhi (1160?–1233?), Rabbenu Bahya Ibn Pakuda (eleventh century), Joseph Albo (fifteenth century), Obadiah Sforno (c.1470–c.1550), and above all, Maimonides (1135–1204): 'Whosoever shall read his history will tire of his efforts to find another person on all the earth who can compare to him.'[65] In addition, Rapoport dealt with the history of the *geonim* and the figures of Eleazar Kallir, Rabbenu Hananel ben Hushiel (d. 1035/6), and Rabbenu Nissim (c.990–1062), chronicling the lives of great men who had contributed to 'proving the truth of the lessons of the Talmud and books of wisdom', in the sense that they represented the ideal blending of Torah and general culture.[66]

The lists of great men usually concluded with key figures of the eighteenth-

[63] S. Hacohen, 'Toledot heḥakham'.

[64] Rapoport, 'Mikhtav lem. a.', 8–24. The letter dates from 1822.

[65] Rapoport, 'Bikoret', 175–6; Bick, 'El maskilei benei ami!', 77; Mieses, 'Al devar sibat he'ader', 63; Bloch, *Teshuat yisra'el*, introd.; Spitz, 'Toledot rabi avraham', 49–55.

[66] Rapoport, 'Toledot rabenu natan', introd. Rapoport also provided a brief list of Jewish women who had acted courageously when the Jewish people faced great affliction; these included Esther, Bathsheba, the prophetess Huldah, Queen Helena, and Esterka, the legendary mistress of Casimir the Great, king of Poland, in 'Mikhtav lem. a.'

century Haskalah and even those of the nineteenth century who were still alive and active. The first was Moses Hayim Luzzatto (Ramhal, 1707–46), who was admired as a maskilic poet, though the maskilim attempted to downplay his devotion to kabbalah as unsuited to Haskalah ideals.[67] Overshadowing them all was the figure of Moses Mendelssohn, whose image had already been shaped in the eighteenth century. The centenary of Mendelssohn's birth occurred in 1829, providing a perfect opportunity for several maskilim to re-emphasize the historical importance of this hero of the modern age. Reggio, the editor of *Bikurei ha'itim*, announced the anniversary in a grandiloquent introduction to the ninth issue:

The year 5589 brings us to the hundredth year since the birth of the great eagle, may his memory be blessed, and it is a sacred year, a festive year for all those who espouse our cause, a holiday year for those who yearn for the good of our people; you who are eminent for your wisdom, the first fruit of your thoughts in this year will be an offering of thanks in honour of our Master, the light of Israel.[68]

To these words he added a paean of praise, describing Mendelssohn as the figure who had inaugurated an era of light after one of darkness, brought the Jewish people from folly to wisdom, fostered the Hebrew language, fought talmudic casuistry, and acted as the messenger of Providence.[69] Another laudatory poem, written by a young student of Samuel David Luzzatto's, underscored Mendelssohn's universal contribution: 'Prince of all those who love wisdom, from the day of your birth all peoples saw in you a shining light, a fountain of wisdom that cast off the night.'[70] The Mendelssohnian cult reached its zenith in the centenary sermon written by Judah Jeiteles of Prague, which described Mendelssohn in messianic terms. Jeiteles suggested that Mendelssohn's birthday should be turned into a day of worship and thanksgiving for all generations, a day on which the Jewish people would give thanks to God for giving them a 'redeemer' in the person of Mendelssohn:

For this day a child was born unto us to increase wisdom among the people of Yeshurun, and who would become the father of all the children of Jacob, the prince of peace . . . this is the day God brought light unto us and cast off darkness . . . to open blind eyes that had strayed from the true path and were lost in the land for many years, and the gate of wisdom was closed before them . . . this is the day we had hoped for, when the shackles of our imprisonment were removed, the hope of Israel in its time of tribulation.[71]

The use of messianic concepts, taken in part from the prophecies of Isaiah, strengthened Mendelssohn's mythological image and assigned religious meaning to the shift that had taken place. In his second concrete proposal Jeiteles called for the erection of stone monuments in all Jewish schools. The monuments would

---

[67] Bick, 'El maskilei benei ami!', 77; Almanzi, 'Toledot r. moshe hayim luzato', 53–4; Letteris, *Migdal oz*, introd.

[68] Reggio, 'Introduction', *Bikurei ha'itim*, 9 (1828), 3.   [69] Ibid. 4.

[70] Avshalom, 'El tiferet yisra'el', 97.   [71] J. Jeiteles, 'Reshit bikurim', 23–6.

be engraved with the dates of Mendelssohn's birth and death and the well-known verse (originally describing Newton) 'Nature and Nature's laws lay hid in night; God said, Let Moses be! And all was light.' This would help to transmit Mendelssohn's legacy to future generations and to incorporate it in the historical memory of the Jews as a model to be admired and emulated:[72]

And the time will come when your children ask, what is the meaning of this stone? And you will say that this stone commemorates a man who opened our eyes, Moses ben Menahem, to whom God gave the ability to teach Torah, and if he had not been here to open the path of learning before you . . . you would have remained in darkness and ignorance like the generations before you, and the light of wisdom would not have shone upon you . . . he is the man who gave us a place among other nations and was our voice and intercessor, casting off the libels fabricated against us . . . and that is why we have erected this monument, to perpetuate his memory for all the generations to come.

A kind of summary of all the lists of historic heroes can be found in *Reshimat anshei mofet* (List of Exemplary Men), an extraordinary lexicon published by Joseph Flesch in Prague in 1838.[73]

Flesch states in his introduction that he was influenced by Pölitz in everything related to the didactic function of 'exemplary men', and, in his view, all the figures in his lexicon expressed the ideal of 'the maskilic talmudic scholar'. The twenty-six pages of the lexicon list, in alphabetical order, the names of some 500 individuals, from the time of the destruction of the Second Temple to the 1830s: *tana'im*, commentators, poets, *geonim*, philosophers, and German and Austrian maskilim. The lexicon's innovation, beyond the fact that it contained the entire pantheon, was the legitimization it granted to contemporary maskilim by including them with famous and admired figures of Jewish history. It placed rabbis, kabbalah scholars, and maskilim in the same category, with almost no distinction between them. The Vilna Gaon (1720–97), Euchel, Ephraim Luzzatto (1729–92), David Friedländer, Mendelssohn, Spinoza, Perl, Moses Hayim Luzzatto, Maimonides, Shimon bar Yohai, Isaac Luria, Rapoport, and Levin rub shoulders in Flesch's lexicon. Viewed in this way, the Austrian–Galician maskilim appeared as the legitimate heirs of an ancient historical tradition.

In general terms, the picture of the past imagined by the maskilim was shaped by their perspective of the historical turning-point in the modern age—a shift whose crucial importance to maskilic consciousness has already been discussed. The following comment, made by Bick in 1823, is a typical expression of this view of the past:

When God took pity and cast off the obstinacy of the people of Europe and pierced the clouds of folly, the lights of wisdom began to break through in Germany, France, Spain,

---

[72] Jeiteles, 'Reshit bikurim', 25. Jeiteles also printed a letter from the talmudist and kabbalist R. Jonathan Eybeschuetz (c.1690–1764) to Mendelssohn to demonstrate the high regard in which Mendelssohn was held by rabbis; *Kerem ḥemed*, 3 (1838), 225.   [73] Flesch, *Reshimat anshei mofet*.

and the other countries, and when their people rose to higher levels of education and became worthy of the name 'civilized', then the enlightened ones joined the wise men of all nations and they nourished one other in science and reason and all the works of art for the benefit of human society . . . and so too did the Jewish people grow and progress. For it is the nature of wisdom to benefit all the people of the earth. Religious hatred ceased, replaced by the love of mankind, and all the nations began to look favourably upon the people of Israel, who are also men.[74]

The maskilic picture of the past, in contrast to that of the present, emphasized the dark hues of that gloomy time which was marked by persecution of the Jews in the name of 'religious revenge', turning them into the victims of endless libels, oppressive edicts, and expulsions. Von Dohm's theory explained the horrors of the past by placing them within the general context of the nations of Europe, which were then 'very foolish and ignorant'. This explanation also served as a justification of Jewish separatism, Jewish cultural decline, and Jewish involvement in unproductive activity.[75] Since Jewish history was conditioned by 'external' developments, a link was also created between Jewish history and universal history. During their period of exile 'the Jews absorbed many ideas from other peoples', a phenomenon that could be judged as negative, since it led to the infiltration of foreign views into Judaism, or as positive, since it proved Jewish open-mindedness. From its inception Judaism was universal, advocating 'the love of mankind'. Examples of this, such as the alliances formed with other nations in ancient times (David and the kings of Tyre and Hamath, the Hasmoneans and the Romans), constituted evidence of an anti-separatist trend.[76] Even on a local level there was interaction between Jews and their immediate surroundings, as, for example, among the Jews of Poland: as long as Poland was a 'discriminatory country' that placed little value on culture and education and had a undeveloped economy, the Jews were able to maintain their Torah culture; however, when the country was partitioned and imbued with a Western spirit, not only did the situation of the Jews begin to change in the direction of enlightenment and economic productivity, but Poland's status as a centre for Torah study was diminished. Bloch's words, for example, imply that Jewish society was shaped almost entirely by environmental conditions: 'We are people of little means, caught between the wealthy and the indigent of all the nations among which we have been dispersed . . . we are like putty in their hands and they easily leave their mark upon us, with their morals, their customs, and their deeds.'[77]

However, the maskilim were far from obscuring the historical uniqueness of the Jews. The miracle of Jewish survival throughout history was the cornerstone of the maskilic picture of the past and a constant source of wonder and pride.

[74] Bick, 'El maskilei benei ami!'
[75] See Perl, *Bohen tsadik*, 108–9; Mieses, 'Al devar sibat he'ader', 54–7; Bick, 'El maskilei benei ami!', 71–3; Reggio, 'Shenei ḥakhamim gedolim', 12–14.
[76] B. Shenfeld, 'Ma'amar hahanhagah', 34–44.
[77] Bloch, letter to Rapoport (1828), in *Shevilei olam*, vol. i.

Do you know, brothers, [cried Rapoport] that the existence of our chosen people for several thousand years has been a source of wonderment among all the peoples on the face of the earth, for they saw that all the ancient nations which, in their time, ruled the populated countries of the world—Assyria, Babylonia, Persia, Media, Greece, and Rome—and which were feared by all, passed from the world as if they had never been [?][78]

In the maskilic view, the Jewish people were wise enough to maintain the proper balance between absorbing external influences and preserving their own uniqueness, between drawing upon the culture and wisdom of other nations and 'dwelling alone'. Krochmal, who believed that Jewish history had run a unique course, made a particular effort to prove this uniqueness: while all other nations underwent a single biological life cycle, ending in their decay, the course of Jewish history had been multicyclical and, in effect, eternal. The Jewish nation had always had the ability to regenerate itself, since it was nourished by its 'general spiritual' strength. According to Krochmal's *Moreh nevukhei hazeman*, and in the opinion of other maskilim as well, the explanation for the historical uniqueness of the Jewish people was ultimately a matter of divine choice, divine mercy, and the divine mission 'to teach humankind the great and absolute belief in the Torah'.[79] Krochmal, like his fellow maskilim, saw the course of Jewish history as a complex path along which the Jewish people confronted external influences, absorbing some and defending themselves against others. He considered Jewish uniqueness to be merely the consolidation of the truths of all those cultures with which the Jewish people had come into contact throughout its history.

This historical uniqueness thus presented no obstacle to changes and improvements in Jewish society and culture, nor to the integration of the Jews as citizens of the state. Time and time again the maskilim attempted to prove that Jews had always been patriotic subjects and that the yearning for Zion could go hand in hand with life as full citizens, based on the universal recognition of Jews as human beings:

The Jewish people have always been solitary and strange among the gentiles. We ask only a small thing from you. Do not increase your oppression for our people. See us as human beings like all others, begotten by men and women, as you are. Test us, give us a chance, compare us to yourselves, and see us as people like all others, aspiring to be free. Though we yearn to return to Zion, we also desire the good of the country. We poor prisoners of privation pray for peace in your country.[80]

This combination of Jewish uniqueness, national patriotism, and humanistic universalism as characteristic of the Jewish past and present underpinned the maskilic demand and expectation that the situation of the Jews in the state would be improved. However, this was only one front on which the struggle was pursued: the Galician maskilim focused the bulk of their efforts on the home front

---

[78] Rapoport, 'She'erit yehudah', 173.   [79] N. Krochmal, *Moreh nevukhei hazeman*, 35–40.
[80] Rapoport, 'She'erit yehudah', 244–5.

in their confrontation with hasidism, and the picture of the past they created was used primarily in the service of this conflict.

A NATURAL HISTORY OF HASIDISM

There were some similarities between the maskilim and the mitnagedim in their attitude towards hasidism. In this respect, the maskilim followed the same lines as the polemical writings of the mitnagedim at the end of the eighteenth century. This is not surprising: the mitnagedim in Lithuania and the maskilim in Galicia shared a common aim—to prove that the hasidism of Israel ben Eliezer, the Ba'al Shem Tov (c.1700–60), was devoid of any legitimacy.[81] However, from this point onwards the two movements went their separate ways. The mitnagedim argued that hasidism was a heresy, contradicting true Judaism, marring religious aesthetics, and deviating from the mainstream. In their polemical writings they made scant use of historical arguments. They did so for three purposes: to demonstrate the difference between the authentic hasidim of early times and the modern hasidic movement that purported to be their successor; to portray the Ba'al Shem Tov as being 'no scholar' and hence possessing no legitimacy as a religious leader, especially since he was poor and could lay no claim to an illustrious lineage; and to assign hasidism to the category of dangerous phenomena that occasionally erupted among the Jews: 'the wicked among God's people', who included the Sadducees, the Christians, the Shabbateans, and the Frankists.[82] The maskilim adopted some of the arguments put forward by the mitnagedim, but they were not satisfied with polemical writings. The mitnagedim, according to Mieses, 'were opposed to this sect entirely on the basis of the fact that their leaders' customs and views . . . were contrary to the words of the Sages'.[83] The maskilim's major line of attack was to challenge the legitimacy of hasidism by comparing it to their own system of values and by making a rational enquiry into its roots, history, doctrine, and modes of operation. The maskilim's historical study of the hasidic movement was designed to compare it to other historical phenomena and to portray it as a deviation from the stream of pure Judaism. Their aim was not to defend the 'old', as the mitnagedim wished to do, but to fight against those endangering the 'new', or to uphold what the maskilim regarded as the 'authentic' old.

The sources employed by the Galician maskilim fighting against hasidism in the first three decades of the nineteenth century were works written at the end of the previous century. The most influential of these writers were Solomon Maimon, Mendel Levin, and the *magid* from Lithuania, Israel Loebel. Maimon's fascinating autobiography was one of the basic texts of the east European maskilim, and his

---

[81] Perl, *Über das Wesen der Sekte Chasidim*.
[82] Wilensky, *Hasidim and Mitnagedim*, ii. 268, 292, and 198–200, 235–6, 301.
[83] Mieses, *Kinat ha'emet*, 98–9.

lucid description and analysis of the early hasidic movement were an invaluable source of information. Maimon was one of the first to apply the tools of rational thought to hasidism, and his writings also influenced the maskilic image of the hasidic *tsadikim*, explaining their success by their cynical exploitation of the naïvety of the Jewish masses in Poland.[84]

Israel Loebel, whose anti-hasidic crusade received additional impetus when his brother became a hasid, added information about the origins of hasidism and its founder. In a German text apparently written in Lvov and addressed to the Galician authorities during his travels there in 1797–9, this departure from the arguments of the mitnagedim is already very apparent: it portrays hasidism as an anti-humanistic movement, separating itself from the state and non-Jewish society and arousing the hatred of non-Jews. To the emerging image of the Ba'al Shem Tov Loebel added more negative aspects, claiming he was hungry for power, but that his lack of talmudic and general knowledge made it impossible for him to attain a position of influence and power. Instead he chose a different way, becoming a 'master of spirits'. Following the eighteenth-century rationalist model, the Ba'al Shem Tov was depicted as deceitful and hypocritical priest, attracting the masses through his machinations:

In order to achieve his aim of acquiring disciples, he painted his face with the tint of sanctity and appeared in the guise of a devout person. This mantle of holiness in which he wrapped himself; the strong tendency of men towards the esoteric (which cannot be learned in the customary way, but seduces the ignorant and the naïve); all these and more brought Rabbi Israel Ba'al-Shem, in a short time, that is, less than ten years, more than 10,000 devotees.[85]

In the anti-hasidic memorandum that Mendel Levin sent to the Polish Sejm in 1791 hasidism was portrayed as the malodorous fruit of the kabbalistic branch of Judaism. In his historical explanation of how the movement came into being, Levin traced two parallel lines of development of the Jewish religion. One was the canonical, legitimate line extending from the Torah of Moses to the Talmud, Maimonides, and in the eighteenth century to Mendelssohn; the second was the popular line of mystical concepts that reached its peak in the Zohar. This 'deviant' line, in his view, had a strong impact on the ignorant lower classes, and hence was taken up by Polish Jewry, especially in Ukraine, as a continuation of the earlier deviant mystical movements of Shabbetai Tsevi (1626–76) and Jacob Frank (1726–91).[86] Levin's historical outline became the keystone of the maskilic sense of the past in eastern Europe and the basis for viewing Jewish history as a

---

[84] Maimon, *Autobiography*, 81–93.

[85] Loebel's pamphlet in Wilensky's Hebrew translation; Wilensky, *Hasidim and Mitnagedim*, ii. 326–38. See also Michael, 'R. Israel Loebel's German Booklet', 315–23.

[86] In Levin's memorandum to the Polish Sejm in 1791 (Mahler, *History of the Jewish People*, vi. 266–8), and in his introd. to Maimonides' *Moreh nevukhim*: M. Levin, *Alon moreh*. See also Werses, 'On the Track of the Lost Book', 379–97; Levine, 'Menahem Mendel Lefin: A Case Study', 179–97; Gelber, 'Mendel Lefin of Satanow's Proposals', 275–305; Sinkoff, 'Tradition and Transition'.

dualistic past evolving along two tracks, one enlightened and the other its opposite, seen in terms of light and darkness, or of rationalism and superstition. Viewed from this perspective, the contrast between Haskalah and hasidism was merely a continuation of these opposed historical tracks. This historical approach also enabled Levin and other maskilim to prepare a programme to combat hasidism. As soon as it was clear that these were not two legitimate streams but rather a legitimate one and a deviant one, any means could be used to wipe out the deviant path.

Levin's and Loebel's works, mitnagedic polemical articles, Maimon's autobiography, and hasidic writings were all to be found in the Tarnopol library of Joseph Perl, the most prominent opponent of hasidism at the time. Perl, who waged his battle mainly against the current manifestations of hasidism in Galicia, had relatively less need of historical precedents, but he did base several of his anti-hasidic arguments on a broad historical background, as well on a typology of the development of religions.

Perl proposed a three-stage model of the development of every religion: the formation of the religion in the society's age of innocence was inevitably followed by its corruption by false religious zealots, who introduced mystical notions, thus causing it to degenerate and decline. This era also witnessed the excommunications and persecutions of all those who did not accept the religion in its new form. Only when the situation improved could the third era begin, when leaders would arise to purge the religion of its flaws and dispel the 'mystic darkness'. Did the Mosaic religion also go through a similar history? Its first era ended with the Jewish people's military and political defeat at the hands of the Romans, and the second began with the compilation of the Oral Torah in the Mishnah and the Talmud. In the Talmud there were already myths, superstitions, and tall tales, intermixed with serious studies, but it did not yet contain a foundation for the teachings of hasidism. The third stage, when the first attempts were made to purify the Talmud and to extract from it the important things appropriate for the 'spirit of the time', began with the early days of Islam, a relatively tranquil time for the Jews, during which they lived in safety and developed science and philosophy. Among the sages noted by Perl as having been active in this era were the lineages of the rabbis who did not engage in factionalism; Maimonides and Joseph Caro (1488–1575), author of the *Shulḥan arukh*. All the rabbis who followed them merely interpreted the rulings they had laid down, in order to make them conform to the spirit of the time and the situation of the Jews in each period. Perl also harshly criticized the Orthodox rabbis for lacking enlightenment, in particular for their ignorance of languages and the humanities, but he praised them in comparison to the hasidim since they were free of any superstition, at least in his opinion.[87] Against this background, the hasidic deviation was all the more

---

[87] Perl, *Über das Wesen der Sekte der Chassidim*, 63–8. See also A. Rubinstein's introd. to this edn. (p. 32), which notes that Perl ignored the kabbalistic stream. Nonetheless, in this work Perl did devote an appendix to the kabbalah (pp. 159–62).

conspicuous, for the Jewish religion was passing through its three stages of development and was apparently capable of proceeding into the future, in keeping with the spirit of the time and the status of the Jews, like any other religion. Hasidism had no rightful place in this theory of the development of religion. Moreover, it was opposed to the purification of religion, which ought to characterize the third stage, in which the Jews now found themselves.

By stressing the Ba'al Shem Tov's lack of any known lineage or family connections, Perl was able to delegitimize hasidism further. No one knew the founder's life history or parents' origin for certain, nor could anyone ignore the fact that he was an ignorant boor.[88] Perl regarded the Ba'al Shem Tov as a simple miracle-worker and sketched an image of him based on the book *Shivhei habesht* (Praises of the Besht (Ba'al Shem Tov)). Although he denied that the book was reliable, Perl used it to denigrate the Ba'al Shem Tov's image. He commented, for example, in *Megaleh temirin*: 'It is no wonder that he was regarded . . . as merely a simple miracle-worker, for anyone perusing the sacred book *Shivhei habesht* will see that at that time no one held him in esteem, and several God-fearing and upright persons even jeered at him.'[89] In a more extensive critical historical note Perl argued that the hasidim had constructed a mythical image of the Ba'al Shem Tov, but were unable to support it with evidence that would stand the test of criticism. In his view, their aim in trying to clothe the Ba'al Shem Tov in scholarly garb was to prove to the mitnagedim that he was in no way inferior to them. However, in fact this was a distorted image; the Ba'al Shem Tov had made no pretence of being anything other than a healer and magician.[90]

It is quite clear that Perl was addressing his anti-hasidic writings to the mitnagedim. He was drawn, through a kind of romantic nostalgia, to the Torah-suffused past of Polish Jewry, regarding it as an ideal past that had ended:

If in bygone days, great men of Ashkenaz and Italy in Poland addressed their complaints to the rabbis and heads of yeshivot, that is because at that time there were really God-fearing men of valour, aristocrats famed for their morality and knowledge of the Torah in the land of Poland, but this is no longer the case, and now we do not have the rabbis and teachers needed for our communities in Poland.[91]

Like the mitnagedim in the early eighteenth century, Perl pointed an accusing finger at the hasidim, whom he blamed for having weakened the centres of Torah study in Poland. For example, he deplored the fact that in hasidic-'occupied' Ukraine there was not a single rabbi issuing rulings, so that halakhic questions

---

[88] Ibid. 70–5. On the question of the Ba'al Shem Tov's lineage, see Rosman, 'The History of a Historical Source', 201–2.   [89] Perl, *Megaleh temirin*, letter 57 (p. 22*b*).

[90] Perl, 'Katit lamaor', 27–8. This work, which had already been written in 1821, was only published in 1836. See Rubinstein, 'The Booklet *Katit Lamaor*', 140–57. Perl repeats this claim in *Bohen tsadik* and produces a historical document to prove that the Ba'al Shem Tov was a witch doctor and a simple peasant (p. 20).   [91] Perl, *Bohen tsadik*, 88.

about what was forbidden and what was permitted were addressed to the *tsadik*, who gave mystical replies which were not based on accepted rabbinical thinking. It is thus no wonder that the Vilna Gaon and his disciples became ideal figures in Perl's mind, or that his maskilic view of the future envisioned mitnagedim accepting maskilic values, as in the ideally depicted farming communities of mitnagedim–maskilim in southern Russia in his *Bohen tsadik* (The Test of the Righteous, 1838).[92]

If it were at all possible to find historical precedents for the hasidic sect, Perl believed they should be sought among 'people who had lost their way in the faith and learned false studies and new paths of worshipping the Almighty'. The perceptive Jewish community leaders had exposed these holders of 'distorted views' immediately, revealing their sins before they could endanger the pure faith. These religious deviants had never been atheists, but had rather claimed to possess their own religious truth. Perl counted among them the worshippers of the golden calf in the Sinai desert, as well as the Shabbateans and the Frankists. Hasidism was a similar phenomenon. Perl even suggested that it was swept along on the wave of Frankism, and could not be defeated even by all-out war. Frankism was credited with considerable influence on hasidism: 'the pestilence of leprosy began to spread from these distorted views in recent times . . . these injurious views that consume our pure and sacred faith have remained to this very day'.[93]

In the 1820s Perl's extensive knowledge of the hasidic movement, as well as his attitude towards it, found its way into the books of two historians with whom he had corresponded: Peter Beer and Marcus Jost.[94] Beer, from the radical wing of the Austrian Haskalah, regarded hasidism as one more religious sect among the others whose history was described in his book *Geschichte, Lehren und Meinungen aller Bestandenen und noch bestehenden religiösen Sekten der Juden* (1822–3).[95] He did not attempt to hide his negative attitude to hasidism. He viewed it as a sect with roots in kabbalah, whose adherents practised acts of piety and asceticism (as he had learned from Maimon), which had added one innovation: the introduction of a miracle-working *tsadik* seeking influence over the masses. The circle of naïve seekers after God was joined by charlatans pursuing prestige and wealth, who succeeded in misleading the ignorant. It was clear to Beer, as it had been to Perl, that hasidism had managed to establish a foothold only in those backward regions where the Haskalah had not yet penetrated, and thus it spread in Poland, Wallachia, and Moldavia, but not in Germany, France, or Italy. The information Beer included in his book served as the basis for the entry 'Chassidäer' that he

[92] Ibid. 107, 113.

[93] Perl, 'Katit lamaor', 34–5; id., *Bohen tsadik*, 113. See also Werses, *Haskalah and Shabbateanism*, 106–8.

[94] On Perl's relations with Jost and Beer, see A. Rubinstein's introd. to Perl, *Über das Wesen der Sekte der Chassidim*, 1–2.

[95] P. Beer, *Geschichte, Lehren und Meinungen*, 96 ff. See also Werses, *Haskalah and Shabbateanism*, 146–8; Michael, 'Peter Beer', 1–8.

wrote for the encyclopaedia published by J. S. Ersch and J. G. Gruber.[96] This entry, in volume xvi, which appeared in 1827, was the first encyclopaedic entry about hasidism. At the time this encyclopaedia was one of the major sources of general knowledge for the Galician maskilim. In this circuitous manner, they were able to find the essence of the maskilic view of hasidism, as well as several of Perl's ideas, in a German encyclopaedia published in Leipzig.

In 1828 hasidism was included in an account of modern Jewish history for the first time, in the last volume of Jost's *Geschichte der Israeliten*.[97] Since Jost had connections with the virulently anti-hasidic Galician maskilim Mieses and Perl, and did not rely on hasidic writings but made use of Beer's book and his radical views of the rabbinic world, it would not have been surprising if he had adopted a negative attitude to hasidism. However, in this instance Jost was careful not to draw conclusions based on the material placed on his desk. He dissociated himself from Beer's subjective and derisive judgement as well as from the anti-hasidic article Perl had sent him.[98] Since Jost was far removed from the centres of the maskilic–hasidic controversy and was doing his best to place hasidism in its historical context, he distinguished between the information he had received and the maskilic tendentiousness prevalent in eastern Europe. The impression he gained from the sources was one of a successful movement sweeping up the masses, and hence he chose to place it among the modern changes affecting the Jews from 1740 to 1815. In the chapter on the history of Polish Jews in this period Jost sketched a historical process that began with the rabbis' efforts to preserve traditional values, especially Torah learning, and ended with the Emden–Eybeschuetz controversy in the 1750s and opposition to hasidism. He believed that the new era must lead to the decline of 'rabbinism' and the victory of science and emancipation, and that hasidism had actually contributed to this trend. On this point Jost completely abandoned the Galician maskilim's approach to hasidism, with his suggestion that it ought to be regarded as an anti-rabbinic movement and a phenomenon that was advancing modern Jewish history rather than retarding it. At the very hour when the fountainhead of rabbinical Jewry in Poland was drying up, kabbalah offered an alternative path of development, which was adopted by the hasidim.[99]

Of all the Galician maskilim Judah Leib Mieses, author of the anti-hasidic book *Kinat ha'emet*, published in Vienna in 1828, became the most outspoken opponent of hasidism. One of the prominent members of the circle of Galician maskilim in the 1820s, he lived in Lvov, but apparently frequently visited the other centres of Haskalah in Galicia and elsewhere. Perl was a close friend, Erter was his pupil, and he seems to have served as a patron of young maskilim who desired to pursue higher studies. Mieses maintained close contact with scholars

[96] P. Beer, 'Chassidäer', 192–6.   [97] Jost, *Geschichte der Israeliten*, ix. 40–57.
[98] Ibid. 45 n. 2; 46 n. 1. See also Michael, *I. M. Jost*, 54.
[99] Jost, *Geschichte der Israeliten*, ix. 43; Michael, *I. M. Jost*, 66–8.

in Germany (including Friedländer and Jost), Vienna (Homberg), and Prague (Jeiteles, Meyer Wolf, Peter Beer) and obtained approbations from them for his book.[100] The source material used in his book is most impressive: from the Jewish philosophy of the Middle Ages and the Renaissance to the literature of the European Enlightenment and the historical and philosophical literature of the eighteenth and nineteenth centuries—Maimonides, Sforno, de' Rossi, Emden, Spinoza, Bayle, Locke, Kant, Michaelis, Mendelssohn, Maimon, Friedländer, Fichte, Eichhorn, Schiller, Neander, de Wette, and Pölitz are but a few of those whose works Mieses consulted in writing *Kinat ha'emet*. Mieses was probably the first east European maskil, perhaps even the first Jewish historian in the nineteenth century, to base a discussion of hasidism on such a varied range of thought and scholarship.

Taking the hasidic movement as his focus, Mieses composed a 200-page work, an intellectual attempt to examine hasidism with the tools and concepts drawn from his sources and to anchor it in a historical context, both in the history of religions and in the history of the Jewish people and its religion. He chose to examine hasidism through an investigation that would expose its historical roots and reveal to all its negative and deviant nature. In hasidism he found a consummately Jewish test case, to which he could apply the eighteenth-century maskilic model of a struggle of reason against folly and superstition, which he could exploit to direct 'Jewish youths' to the path of reason: 'so their hearts will no longer be seduced to believe in the fools and cheats of the generation who, according to the mob's belief, have the power to move spirits and devils as they wish and to work endless miracles'.[101] To Mieses, hasidism was the embodiment of rampant superstition, and like Perl and others, he regarded the hasidim as the main obstacle in the way of improving the political, moral, and cultural situation of the Jews. The fight against hasidism and its roots thus became the foremost objective for every maskil: 'And it is impossible to annihilate any evil without finding the cause that engendered it; hence it is fitting and proper, even a duty for every maskil . . . to write against the belief in demons . . . and to prove with evidence the error of those believing in these follies.'[102]

In *Kinat ha'emet* Mieses followed the maskilic literary model of conversations in heaven, the 'world of truth', conducted between characters from the past who are invested with authority. In the land of souls true opinions are not concealed and 'it is here that every maskil will reveal the truth from the depths of his heart and will speak . . . without . . . placing any restraint on his tongue'.[103] In his book Mieses arranged a meeting between Maimonides and Rabbi Solomon Chelm

---

[100] The life of Mieses, who died of the plague at an early age, has, in great part, remained obscure. See J. Klausner, *History of Modern Hebrew Literature*, ii. 267–82. Bick alludes to Mieses' contacts with German scholars in a letter written in 1829 (*Otsar hasifrut*, iii. 27). An annotated edition of two parts of *Kinat ha'emet*, which includes a discussion of Mieses' satirical work, has recently been published by Y. Friedlander, *Hebrew Satire in Europe*, iii. 17–144.

[101] Mieses, *Kinat ha'emet*, 4–5.   [102] Ibid. 8.   [103] Ibid. 21.

(1717–81), author of *Mirkevet hamishneh* (a commentary on Maimonides' *Mishneh torah*, 1751), for a tranquil dialogue. The appearance of Maimonides is not surprising. Mieses depicted him in line with the historical image shaped by the German Haskalah during the 1780s, and used him as a maskilic ideal and exemplary figure. He projected the plight of the persecuted Galician maskil onto Maimonides, as a figure fighting for the truth, taking no notice of his adversaries and the reactions of the foolish mob. Mieses' version of Maimonides makes a statement about the goal of 'the maskilim in the world, all of whose labours . . . [are intended] only to dispel the cloud of stupidity by the spirit of their understanding'.[104] Why was Solomon Chelm chosen as Maimonides' interlocutor? First of all, the author of *Mirkevet hamishneh*, who was president of the *beit din* in Chelm and from 1771 onwards rabbi of Lvov, revealed an affinity for Maimonides' *Mishneh torah* in his writings, and could consequently be portrayed as Maimonides' disciple in the world of souls despite the period of time that separated the two. The rabbi from Chelm had also won a reputation as one of the sternest opponents of hasidism as early as the lifetime of the Ba'al Shem Tov. This fact, based on the description of the hasidim in the introduction to *Mirkevet hamishneh*, had already been noted by Loebel and Perl, and Mieses had probably learned it from them.[105] The words that Mieses placed in Solomon Chelm's mouth suggest that he regarded him as some sort of early maskil, opposing hasidism because of its enthusiasm and deviation from reason.[106] Perhaps it is also significant that he served as rabbi in Lvov, the city where Mieses lived. He was assigned another important role in Mieses' book, preventing the introduction of an anachronism. Obviously Maimonides could not have known anything about the later hasidism, so it is Solomon Chelm who provides him with information about the movement, as well as about the Zohar and kabbalah in general. In the literary situation that Mieses constructed, Solomon Chelm represents the later generations and asks penetrating questions about them, and Maimonides analyses the situation and replies at length.

For Mieses, historical thought was the impetus for correcting erroneous concepts about the faith and a weapon in the struggle against leaders who, in his view, had remained frozen in a particular stage of history, achieving authority by dint of historical tradition. What was the great importance of history in Mieses' view? It was not merely another science in which Jews ought to become well versed, nor was it only a storehouse of models for emulation; rather it was a mode of thought for the purpose of 'examining faith and customs to see how they had progressed and changed'.[107] History was the greatest teacher since it revealed

---

[104] *Kinat ha'emet*, 14, 21. Mieses also defended Maimonides in 1827 against Bick's attack on him: 'Mikhtavim', *Bikurei ha'itim*, 11 (1830), 131–42.

[105] Perl, *Megaleh temirin*, letter 109 (pp. 41*a*, 41*b*).

[106] Mieses, *Kinat ha'emet*, 108–9. Cf. Mahler, *History of the Jewish People*, iv. 25–6; Scholem, 'The First Two Testimonies', 228–40.   [107] Mieses, *Kinat ha'emet*, 108–9.

dynamics, variation, and constant changes, and hence played an important role in shattering sacrosanct concepts:

It is well known that it is only this knowledge that will teach man to know the condition and customs of each and every nation, and to see how most of them have advanced, for petty reasons, and were born from a corrupt source. And it will show how to find the causes that made the people of one nation leave the way they inherited from their fore-fathers and to follow in the ways of another nation with which they dwelled in one society, and to understand why some peoples have not altered most of their old ways and habits that they inherited from their forefathers from then until today . . . if they lack the know-ledge of these things, men cannot know the origins from which their ways, deeds, and moral state sprang, and will think that the customs they have followed to this day are the very ones followed by their ancient forefathers and which, from the earliest generations until the present, have changed not one whit, and that they all originated from the Torah, and hence are sacred in their eyes and they will cling to them strongly.[108]

Mieses believed in historical progress and objected to the nostalgic yearning for a 'golden age' and the tendency to view the ancients as superior to men of the present. His thinking about hasidism and its place in history was informed by his awareness of historical change, recognition of the interactions between the Jews and other peoples, denial that the past possessed any authority, and championing of the idea of progress. In *Kinat ha'emet* Solomon Chelm tells Maimonides that since his death 'the pure faith has been dwindling away, wisdom is absent from the children of Israel, and each and every day superstition and foolish thoughts multiply among them'. The principal culprit responsible for this regression in recent generations 'was a certain man, lacking in knowledge, whose name is Israel ben Eliezer, called by the masses the Ba'al Shem Tov'.[109] In relating how hasidism came into being and in describing its founder, Mieses followed in Perl's footsteps, but added a great deal more detail. He too portrayed the Ba'al Shem Tov as an anti-hero from the standpoint of the Jewish Enlightenment: he came from Poland, 'a place of darkness and folly', his education was meagre, and even in religious studies he was 'bereft of any knowledge of the Torah and understood nothing of any saying in the Talmud and all the more so in the Bible'. From the peasants among whom he lived the Ba'al Shem Tov learned folk medicine, based, Mieses emphasizes, not on the intelligence of these peasants but on their practical experience. This skill helped him to gain control over the masses.[110] Several rabbis erred in relation to the Ba'al Shem Tov, and this bolstered his authority in the eyes of simple folk and enabled him to succeed in the gross deception he devised. With amulets, witchcraft, magic, and kabbalistic practices the Ba'al Shem Tov and his successors, the *tsadikim*, managed to win the hearts of the people. At the

[108] Ibid. 109. This also opened the way to historical relativism, which served as a justification for religious reform.

[109] Ibid. 22.   [110] Ibid. 22–6.

same time they fought against study of the sciences—a clever tactic, designed to ward off potential opponents.[111]

The success of hasidism, over which the Galician maskilim in their frustration never stopped agonizing, was interpreted by Mieses in the context of the natural history of religion as the cynical manipulation of deceitful priests pursuing wealth, prestige, and power over the common people by exploiting their weakness and ignorance. It was not the first time in Jewish history that this had happened; this phenomenon had historical precedents and was a manifestation (as Levin also claimed) of the historical struggle between pure rational religion, generally the province of the élites, and popular, mystical religion. Mieses employed several of the concepts and outlines of the eighteenth-century European Enlightenment, such as those proposed by David Hume in *The Natural History of Religion* (1757).[112] Hume depicted religion in terms of secular and natural processes, rather than in terms of divine revelation or philosophical truths, and based his argument on anthropological evidence in order to explain why polytheism preceded monotheism. In his view, psychological traits such as fear, hope, and imagination underlay religion. Polytheism was appropriate to the pre-rational stage of primitive man, who feared supernatural forces and hoped to divert them for his own benefit. Under the entry 'religion' in Voltaire's *Philosophical Dictionary* (1764) a mirror image of this sequence appeared. According to this, monotheism came first as the natural form of religion, but in this version, too, the history of religion was a natural history, the result of human vicissitudes, the manipulations of priests, and the weakness of the masses.[113]

Even before Mieses wrote *Kinat ha'emet*, his writing had already moved in the direction of a natural and secular history of religion very similar to Hume's. In primitive society, he wrote, men lived like wild animals (like Hobbes's 'state of nature'), without any social frameworks, science, or vocation, because in the warm climate of Asia, where they lived, they did not suffer any physical deprivation which would have motivated them to learn and to change their lives. In this historical stage humans were savage and ignorant, and felt no need for religious faith. Impelled by their animal instinct of fear, they gathered into small groups, from which larger kingdoms eventually grew. At this stage polytheistic idolatry also developed: man's inability to explain natural phenomena led him to attribute each phenomenon to a particular god. As the challenges facing humankind increased, man's intelligence was sharpened, particularly in view of the need to

[111] Mieses, *Kinat ha'emet*, 27: 'The words of these deceivers and fools were received by nearly all Jews [in Poland] with complete faith; they believed in their nonsense and followed in their evil ways. Thus, the people of Israel have lost their pure devoutness . . . have forsaken their study of the wisdom of Judaism . . . and every man who knows how to read a book will tirelessly seek after knowledge of the kabbalah; and nearly all of the people are fascinated by tales of demons and the lives of the deceivers and fools and their power over the spirits.'

[112] See also Cassirer, *The Philosophy of the Enlightenment*, 160–96.

[113] Voltaire, *Philosophical Dictionary*, 350–4.

overcome his enemies and to search for sources of sustenance. During this historical stage beliefs in evil and benevolent divinities emerged, and priests added the details of rituals. Political needs and the formation of empires contributed to a new phase in the history of religions, bringing about an alliance between the priesthood and royalty and agreement on a unified religion for the empire.[114] Needless to say, in this natural history Providence or divine revelation played no part. In *Kinat ha'emet* Mieses further refined this developmental synopsis, and moderated it by including divine revelation.[115] According to Mieses' natural history, the five stages in the gradual development of religion were:

1. Idolatry: belief in many idols in a primitive society, born of ignorance, fear, and awe in the face of natural phenomena.

2. Ditheism: The dualistic belief in a wrathful god and a merciful god and the development of religious ritual, expressed in the offering of sacrifices in order to appease the gods.

3. The formation of a religious priesthood: 'In the course of time, men arose who set themselves apart (either out of innocence and foolishness and a passionate desire to draw near to their gods, or out of great fear of them) and withdrew from all the matters of this world and its affairs, devoting their souls and all they had to the gods.' These men took upon themselves the function of prayer and worshipping the gods and urged others to engage in this as well. To the masses they appeared to be holy men, possessed of a divine spirit, pious and pure. In a marginal note Mieses asked the reader to conjure up an association with the figure of the hasidic *tsadik*, who also seemed to be a wondrous being to the common people.[116]

4. The penetration of deceitful priests into the religious establishment and the corruption of that establishment: the hypocritical priests acted like 'the foolish clerics, and in order to mislead the people they behaved as their fellows did . . . but this was only for outward show in order to deceive the masses, to acquire a reputation and accumulate vast riches'. They employed natural means to manufacture false miracles; enacted laws and commandments, claiming they had received this doctrine in a revelation; ordered the construction of temples and churches; and established complicated rites. In this stage, religion degenerated seriously: the idols were no longer conceived as a symbol of spiritual forces but were worshipped as gods. In another marginal note Mieses again drew the reader's attention to hasidism and drew an analogy: this type of deceitful priest was the model according to which 'most of the great Beshtians and the *tsadikim* of our time' behaved.[117]

---

[114] Comment by Mieses on David Caro's *Sefer tekhunat harabanim*, 7–9.

[115] Mieses, *Kinat ha'emet*, 29–38. The synopsis was also influenced by S. Muller's work *Ḥeshek shelomoh*.   [116] Mieses, *Kinat ha'emet*, 34.   [117] Ibid.

5. The inception of monotheistic religion with the appearance of Abraham, who was 'the first to prove with his reason and intelligence the existence of one Creator of the entire universe', without any divine revelation. The Israelites bore the message of the true faith, and idolatry began to dwindle. In order for monotheism to become the province not only of the sages, but of the common people too, there was need of a revelation, and herein lay the importance of the revelation on Mount Sinai.

How was it, Mieses asked, that even after the revelation, idolatry, superstition, and the entire imaginary world of spirits and magic was not uprooted from people's hearts—not even from those of the Jews, the bearers of monotheism? Here Mieses incorporated popular religion into his outline of the history of religion. Alongside the rational religion, polytheistic and anti-rational beliefs persevered among the masses, in the manner of 'the common folk who do not possess a clear and correct knowledge that verifies the existence of the Almighty', and who found it difficult to conceive of an abstract idea, preferring some tangible illustration.[118] The absorption of false beliefs and alien religious concepts that infiltrated into Judaism from outside, particularly from Persia and Greece, and the encouragement of popular beliefs by the deceitful priests also played a role in nurturing the 'mass religion'.

It would also seem that Maimonides himself had deviated from pure monotheism; in his writings he spoke about spheres and separate intelligences, and hence could not serve as the spokesman of pure reason. As a solution to this problem, a completely anachronistic speech appears in Mieses' book, which shows the lengths to which the Galician maskil went in trying to cleanse his maskilic ideal of any impurities. The 'Maimonides' of 1828 apparently tries to atone for having believed in such nonsense and for having failed to cut himself off from the ideological and social climate of his own time:

I am not ashamed to confess that I erred in many things, for I adhered more than was fitting to the philosophy of the wise man, Aristotle, without deviating from it either to the right or to the left. I thought then (for I read many of his books and was constantly in the company of sages who accepted the views and methods of his philosophy as truth, and I did not scrutinize his views well in my own mind) that all his words and statements were true and that his opinion was perfection itself. And that led him to accept the faulty notion that there are in the world celestial spheres and separate intelligences, a belief which undoubtedly came from the Chaldaeans [astrologers] and the people of Persia. How I wonder now at myself for having been capable of believing them in such foolishness![119]

---

[118] 'And although they believed in one God, they did not entirely give up their belief in spiritual beings. This belief remained in the hearts of the masses with some slight changes. Instead of holding to the beliefs they had before the knowledge of one God was revealed to them, that these spirits are truly free gods who do as they wish and do not submit to a higher unity . . . they later thought that they submit to the authority of a single king . . . and even later, when they grew more intelligent, they called them good and evil spirits or demons' (Mieses, *Kinat ha'emet*, 37).

[119] Ibid. 61–7. See also Mieses' letter to Bick, in Letteris, *Mikhtavim*, 53–9; Mieses, 'Mikhtavim',

Mieses' broad and detailed historical survey of all stages of kabbalah revealed its roots and devoted much space to proving that it was alien to Judaism and a vestige of idolatrous beliefs. According to Mieses, from Maimonides' death to the nineteenth century kabbalah grew stronger and attracted many supporters, marking the constant deterioration of the Jewish religion. The Zohar was a work by 'one of the charlatans who wrote books of folly and vain ideas, either to gain fame among the Jews or to amass great wealth', and was but the product of a wild imagination, unrestrained by reason. One source of major idolatrous influences on kabbalah was Alexandria of the Second Temple period. When the Jews were dispersed in the period of exile, they came into cultural contact with pagan religions, and hence kabbalah was one of the deleterious effects of the exile. Mieses drew on a great deal of information about pagan religions, and using a detailed comparison of concepts and ideas from Gnosticism, Zoroastrianism, and Alexandrian philosophy, tried to prove that some of their concepts had passed into kabbalah.[120] He also included a long list from the words of the Sages, from Sa'adiah Gaon to the seventeenth century, denouncing these beliefs. In any event, in the course of time the true source of kabbalistic ideas had been forgotten, and the Jews imagined that kabbalah was a tradition of their forefathers handed down to them at Mount Sinai. This error led many sages to find allusions to these secrets in the Pentateuch and the Prophets. The flow of kabbalistic creation did not cease and there was no rational restraint to curtail its innovations and variegations. Hasidic teachings were a further stage in the kabbalistic sequence, from *Sefer yetsirah* (Book of Creation), through the Zohar, the works of Moses Cordovero (1522–70) and Isaac Luria, the Ari (Lion), to the 'great ones of the sect of the Beshtians [hasidim]'. In Mieses' picture of the past, dominated by an unceasing confrontation between folly and reason, between ignorant, reactionary masses and an enlightened, progressive élite—a confrontation that had exposed the Jewish religion to deviant, alien influences—hasidism was placed in the most negative category. It was the very embodiment of foolishness, a religion of the masses, a deviant religious trend, idolatrous mysticism foreign to Judaism, and a product of the machinations of cunning religious leaders, hungry for power over the masses.

This view of the past is a cogent expression of the hostility of maskilic ideology to hasidism, but it also reflects the frustration of the Galician maskilim, who, faced with the success of hasidism, could only take refuge in history, consoling themselves with the fact that every enlightened élite has always suffered the same fate. 'There were then,' Mieses wrote in 1824, in an article later included in *Kinat ha'emet*, 'as there are now and have been in each and every generation, many fools and deceivers, scoundrels, men of low families, wise in their own eyes, pretending

---

Bikurei ha'itim, 11 (1830), 131–42. Cf. T. M. Rabinowitz, 'The Attitude of the Kabbalah', 279–87; Scholem, 'From Philosopher to Kabbalist', 90–8.

[120] Mieses, 'Igeret 2', *Kinat ha'emet*, 138–51. See also id., 'Mikhtav 2', 129–34. In this article, printed after his death, Mieses again discussed the history of the kabbalah.

to be pious, whom the credulous masses indiscriminately regarded as the great men and sages of the land.'[121] Even the golden age of Jewry in Spain was not free of such phenomena, and only a minority engaged in intellectual activity, which had but a faint resonance among the masses. Identifying with the persecuted maskilim, Mieses continued:

These deceivers and fools in their wrath devised false accusations against the authors of books who, zealous in their passion for truth, wished to wage a war of reason and to write against foolishness and deception; [the hasidim] have tried to discredit the sages and have libelled them and illicitly opened their mouths wide against them, saying that they have deviated from the path of the Jewish religion and have transgressed the commandments of the Almighty.

Mieses found only one ray of light in the modern age, springing from the historical shift that had occurred in Europe, in particular the appearance of the 'merciful kings', who were 'adopting the paths of reason and struggling to expel the darkness of stupidity'. In his opinion, the key achievement of the period was the annulment of the religious leadership's privilege of excommunication, which allowed everyone 'to walk in the paths of wisdom and justice' without any fear.[122]

Mieses died in the 1831 cholera epidemic, leaving behind a faithful devotee, Isaac Erter, to carry on his cause, transplanting several of Mieses' basic ideas from the field of historical research to that of biting social satire. In his satires hasidism and wisdom are portrayed as two opposite poles, or as two forces competing for the minds and souls of young Jews in Galicia.[123] Erter's satires employed literary devices to make the choice easier: to prove the superiority of wisdom beyond any doubt the typological character of the Ba'al Shem Tov, as portrayed by Mieses in *Kinat ha'emet*, became the figure of the 'woman of hasidism', a false prophet pursuing wealth and misleading the masses. The figure of 'Wisdom, daughter of God' invites a young man, hesitating in front of different paths through life, on a journey through history, culminating in the victory of the Haskalah.[124] Erter presented a dramatic story, rapid and dynamic, replete with changes, surprises, fear, and joy, and moving in a progressive direction. Following in Mieses' footsteps, and using the literary device of a nocturnal journey, he dramatized the formation of human society 'as men grouping together after emerging from caves in rocks and cliffs and the depths of the forest, in which they wandered about without any society like the wolves of Arabia'; this was followed by the formation of the state, necessitated by the dangers of physical existence, then by the formulation of laws, and the development of pagan religions. When the journey reached the Middle Ages, Erter described the hegemony of the Church as a grim, dismal scene, for which the Pope bore the principal responsibility:

[121] Mieses, *Kinat ha'emet*, 165–6. These words had already been printed verbatim in *Hatsefirah* in 1823, in Mieses 'Al devar sibat he'ader', 54–63.   [122] *Kinat ha'emet*, 165–6 and 197–8.
[123] Letteris, 'Toledot hameḥaber'; J. Klausner, *History of Modern Hebrew Literature*, ii. 321–4.
[124] Erter, 'Ḥasidut veḥokhmah', 99–100; id., 'Gilgul hanefesh', 40–1.

Your soul will be afflicted by anxieties, when a wicked fool puts on the garb of holiness (like the one now standing before you) and sits on a throne above the kings, a sword of vengeance in his right hand in place of a sceptre, and in his left, a key to the gate of heaven. He has brought down nobles and has led tens of thousands to slaughter, in his arrogant desire to dominate all corners of the globe; he will crush into dust all the corpses of the earth, and on its pyre will place all men of intellect.[125]

Erter explicitly singled out the hasidic *tsadik*, 'an evil fool in holy garb', as a figure similar in nature to the Pope, and pinned his hopes on the continuation of the historical analogy in modern times as well. The liberation of monarchs from the yoke of the Church, the rise of the human spirit, and the victory of reason over folly were the signs of the modern age. The maskil was also engaged in a struggle to guide the Jews to this positive historical track, and the defeat of hasidism was one of the prerequisites for success.

The historical synopses of Perl, Mieses, and Erter may seem over-simplistic, both in their presentation of the hasidism–Haskalah dichotomy and in the sole solution they proposed, which they viewed as the express objective of the course of history: the total disappearance of hasidism. In contrast, Rapoport, a more moderate and central figure in the Galician group of *maskilim*, revealed other shades of opinion and new considerations. Sensitive to the complex implications of the acculturation and modernization of European Jewry, and aware of the contemporaneous social and cultural crisis, Rapoport was more concerned with the historical fate of the Jewish people than with the militant struggle against the hasidim.

Rapoport's anti-hasidic arguments, which first appeared in his pamphlet 'Ner mitsvah', were still focused mainly on his concern about adverse effects on talmudic learning. He was then a typical east European Torah scholar, 25 years old, still supported by his parents and his father-in-law and engrossed in Torah study, although he had already imbibed some 'external literature' and values of the Haskalah. Hasidism was a glaring folly, Rapoport claimed in his attempt to dissuade a young scholar from joining the movement, and it was also a digression from the legitimate path of Jewish scholarship. Like Jost after him, in 'Ner mitsvah' Rapoport explained the success of hasidism against the backdrop of the crisis in talmudic learning and as a reaction to it, although he viewed its appearance as a deepening of the crisis, not as the beginning of a change. Moreover, in his view, hasidism was a movement of the ignorant masses, seduced by deceiving *tsadikim*. Rapoport regarded the lower stratum of society, which he despised and feared throughout his life, as 'an ugly beast with many mouths and no eyes'.[126] The escape route he offered the would-be hasid was through Maimonides, 'who leads the one who has lost his way', and whose rationalistic teachings, profound knowledge of the Torah, and élitism would perhaps return the perplexed young man to the path blazed by the Vilna Gaon and his disciples.[127]

[125] Erter, 'Hasidut veḥokhmah', 105.   [126] Rapoport, 'Ner mitsvah', 19, and also 2, 10–11.
[127] Ibid. 24–5.

Rapoport's 1815 pamphlet seems to have marked a turning-point in his life. Coming on top of the incident of the Lvov excommunication, which took place about the same time, it clearly showed that Rapoport's place in Jewish society was among the Galician maskilim. Even as a maskil, however, Rapoport attempted to examine the problems of his time from a broad historical perspective, revealing his concern about the signs of division and discord within the Jewish people in the past as well as in the present. He addressed his first article on Jewish history, published in 1823 in *Bikurei ha'itim*, to 'all those who have not cast off the bonds of love, have not undone the ties of the covenant that bind the entire Jewish people, each man to his brother; [and to those] who even in the Diaspora have been pained by all that has happened to their fellow Jews in distant lands and in various nations, in whose sorrow they have felt despondent and in whose joy they have found comfort'.[128] In his opinion, the 'diminished love of one's nation', which he regarded as one of the negative products of the modern age, endangered the very existence of the Jewish people. The historical survival of the Jews was ensured not only by Divine Providence, which preserved the eternal quality of the nation, but also by shared ideas and the ties of brotherhood.[129]

Until the modern age a common mode of thought and frame of mind had prevailed among Jews, bridging the geographical distances between the dispersed communities and uniting the Jews in every land. In the eighteenth century, however, this uniformity had been shattered. Rapoport did not inherit the optimistic faith of the German maskilim in the previous century, fired with enthusiasm by the historical shift taking place before their very eyes. He tended more towards the pessimism of the moderate German maskilim of the late 1790s. In his view, the roots of the crisis lay in hasidism and the Haskalah, and the basic experience of Jewish existence in the 1820s and 1830s was one of divisiveness, controversy, and social discord. The divisive elements far outnumbered the unifying elements, resulting in a sense that the common denominator, which until then had been the cohesive factor, was vanishing.

Rapoport viewed the rift between the hasidim and the maskilim as the first crucial split in Jewish history, and as a maskil who believed in the centrality of prominent personalities in history, he portrayed it as a conflict between two figures, Mendelssohn and the Ba'al Shem Tov:

These two famous men, one radiating light and the other wrapped in darkness shot through by lightning, stirred the hearts of the [Jewish] people in the generation before us, just as the wind stirs reeds in the water. Their rays reached every Jewish soul throughout our lands, and naught was hidden from them. In indirect ways, these rays came to them, and as they were transformed, so were the views and thoughts of those who followed one or other of these two men.[130]

Despite his negative opinion of hasidism, Rapoport did not suggest a one-sided solution to resolve the schism. Instead, he hoped that once the impaired

[128] Rapoport, 'Al devar yehudim ḥofshi'im', 51.   [129] Rapoport, 'She'erit yehudah', 173–4.
[130] Ibid. 174.

common denominator was restored, on the basis of 'love of the nation', it would
be able to surmount the ideological differences:

But this I ask of you, be of one heart in your love together with the children of your
mother, Zion, who is now so abandoned and unwanted; then there is hope that you will
soon unite in so far as other matters are concerned too. The love of the nation is the
cornerstone of its existence and greatness. It is the main prop and stay for a strong foundation for the Jewish religion, so that it may never falter . . . fan the sparks of love of faith
and nation among your brethren.[131]

His conclusion that the bond to the Jewish people was no longer self-evident,
and hence had to be specially nurtured and turned into a conscious link through
literary and propaganda means, is one of the early harbingers of the modern
nationalist idea. Rapoport's blend of anti-hasidic, maskilic rationalism and romantic
concern for the nation's unity was put to a severe test in 1826, compelling him to
sharpen his ideas and to formulate a new historical outline to justify his absolute
repudiation of hasidism. In that year Jacob Samuel Bick, a member of the Galician
group of maskilim, left the Haskalah movement and began to exhibit pro-hasidic
sympathies.[132] The Galician maskilim found it very difficult to swallow this act
of 'conversion' in what they regarded as the wrong direction, from the maskilic
camp of 'enlightenment' to the hasidic camp of 'obscurantism'. They hoped Bick
would recant, 'for since the dawn of the earth, no reasonable man has honestly
deviated from the path of wisdom; and if such a thing did happen, he returned to
it before many years passed'.[133] However, Bick's 'deviation', which seemed to
contradict the laws governing the progress of history and to place weapons in the
hands of those opposing enlightenment, was not temporary. The maskilim—first
and foremost Rapoport—were forced to cope with Bick's criticism of the
Haskalah and championing of hasidism.

   Bick the maskil had already expressed thoughts that were later characteristic
of Bick the hasid, and these may also have led him to take this step. The most
prominent of these ideas was his sympathy for the common people. Unlike
Rapoport, who had scoffed at the masses and expressed his contempt for them in
his 1815 pamphlet, in the same year Bick wrote about the popular historical forces
that create culture, about the language of the Jewish rank and file, and about the
close relations that should exist between intellectuals and the common people.[134]
When Bick underwent his 'conversion', his picture of the past also changed, as is
obvious from the following example: in 1824 he had portrayed the three to four
centuries before Luzzatto and Mendelssohn as an era of darkness, during which
the sciences had been neglected and emphasis had been placed on intensive
Torah study; but after he had reached his anti-maskilic conclusion that 'study of
the Torah and observance of the commandments' were the 'soul of the nation' and

---

[131] Ibid. 175.   [132] On Bick's polemic, see Werses, 'Between Two Worlds'.
[133] Mieses, 'Mikhtavim', *Bikurei ha'itim*, 11 (1830), 132–3.
[134] Bick's letter to Tobias Feder (1815), in Werses, 'The Unknown Original Version', 181.

ought not to be spurned in favour of the 'free sciences', he regarded the same period as the era of innocence. Only the cosmopolitan maskil would regard this period as dark; the observant Jew took a different view:

Of this also I have no doubt, that we are obliged to increase our study of the Torah and observance of the commandments . . . that is what our forefathers did in the years of innocence (termed the years of darkness by the cosmopolitan Ben-Ze'ev) until the generation of the revered Rabbi Moses Hayim Luzzatto, of blessed memory.[135]

These words constitute Bick's attempt to refute one of the best-known maskilic historical outlines, formulated by Judah Leib Ben-Ze'ev early in the century.

Bick's maskilic views were greatly influenced by French literature, and in his polemical letters from 1826 onwards he made many hostile references to the French Revolution, using it as a basis for his criticism of the supposed tolerance, rationalism, and élitism of the French Enlightenment and the Haskalah. The revolution was denounced by the maskilim in Galicia; they regarded it as an arbitrary act by an illegitimate group which had abused the legitimate absolutist monarchy. This view can be understood in light of several factors: the maskilim's support of enlightened absolutism in Austria, on which they had pinned their hopes for the reform of Jewish society, the post-Napoleonic reaction of the time, and the relative moderation of the maskilim on political issues and their opposition to political radicalism. Bick accused the maskilim of waving the flags of 'tolerance' and 'cosmopolitan love', while stirring up strife and agitation within Jewish society, 'boiling their brethren's blood, raising the people's temper to fever pitch', and castigating the hasidim.[136] Radical maskilic criticism, Bick warned the maskilim, was liable to upset the internal balance of Jewish society and to lead to bloodshed as had happened during the French Revolution, whose initiators and advocates had also been philosophers. Now, Bick believed, the French regretted the awful events of the revolution:

The French curse the memory of the philosophers Voltaire and Rousseau for their habit (due to their desire to gain fame and admiration) of crying out in despair over those vilifying them (who existed not only in their imagination); for the members of their generation became fastidious about the slightest flaw, and grew accustomed to clamouring, and because of them the people of France raged in a passion, like a man endangered by fever, and a revolution arose in their land, and in Europe many thousands were killed, and the blood of children, young men, and the old flowed like water.[137]

The results of the revolution, which was motivated by a critical ideology and demands for radical reform, were diametrically opposed to its original slogans. Bick stressed the revolutionary dynamic that turned the revolutionaries into men

---

[135] Compare Bick's letter to Rapoport (1827) in Kupfer, 'Jacob Samuel Bick', 546, to Bick's article of 1823 'El maskilei benei ami!', 71–7. Ben Ze'ev discussed this in the periodization of the Hebrew language that he suggested in the introduction to *Otsar hashorashim* (unpaginated).

[136] Bick's letter to Bloch (Sept. 1827), in Letteris, *Mikhtavei ivrit*, 173–6.   [137] Ibid. 173–4.

who were anti-humanist, intolerant, and immoral, battling ruthlessly against any deviation: 'Woe to the land that loses its finest sons, in which a man voicing an opinion that totally disagrees with another's will be judged as if he had sorely affronted him.'[138] He called on the maskilim to put the principle of tolerance into practice, and to apply it to the hasidim as well, and of course to 'deviant maskilim' like himself. With regard to Rapoport, his opponent, he argued that his unfair criticism of hasidism and his readiness to judge it without truly examining it closely resembled 'the trials in the lethal courts of Marat and Robespierre in the revolution of France'.[139] This led him to conclude that the 'quality of tolerance praised in the books of the new writers' had remained a theory which had not been put into practice.[140]

Bick invoked the French Revolution not only to prove the Haskalah's lack of tolerance but also to justify his idea that the common people were preferable to the élite, feeling superior to reason, and love of one's nation better than cosmopolitanism. Hasidism, he claimed, represented positive values since it was a movement of the masses with an emphasis on the soul and was a particularistic Jewish movement, while the Haskalah was élitist, remote from the common people, and rationalist and universalist. For Bick, the revolution provided incontestable proof that rationalist philosophy could lead to bloodshed and hence ought to be opposed: 'It is quite clear', he wrote to Rapoport at the end of 1829, 'that you adhere to the view that philosophy . . . has never shed blood; but the revolution in France in 1789 did indeed arise from philosophers!'[141]

For this reason, Bick severely attacked maskilic élitism, demanded that the maskilim show sensitivity towards the common people, called for tolerance towards hasidism, and placed love of the Jewish people at the top of his scale of values. It was unthinkable to hate 200,000 hasidism, our brethren, part of the Jewish people, Bick argued. Nor could hasidism be compared to Shabbateanism, which the Jewish people had cast out of its midst. The fact that the whole Shabbetai Tsevi affair had petered out in three years, while hasidism had been in existence for over eighty years, proved that the latter was a legitimate popular movement, and that the people, with their healthy instincts, had not identified it as an alien element, as the maskilim had claimed.[142]

Rapoport completely rejected Bick's anti-maskilic claims and the picture of the past he presented. In his view, there was no truth to Bick's argument that the maskilim did not love the Jewish people; rather, Rapoport believed that such particularistic love should not completely supplant the love of universal mankind, as it had in Bick's case, since 'for him [Bick], good, genuine love means the hatred of other nations'. Rapoport believed that the continued absorption of the best of universal culture would improve Jewish life:

---

[138] Ibid. 173.   [139] Bick, 'Mikhtav leshir', 25–6.   [140] Letteris, *Mikhtavei ivrit*, 175–6.
[141] Bick, 'Mikhtav leshir', 267. See also Werses, 'Between Two Worlds', 67–9.
[142] Bick, 'Mikhtav leshir', 264, 267. Cf. Werses, *Haskalah and Shabbateanism*, 116–18.

Many enquiries into Jewish history have demonstrated for me that the separation of the Jews from other peoples, from their wisdom, their teachings, and their principal writings, did not elevate them to the heights they were meant to attain. Only if they learn the good from all lands and peoples and surpass all others in the foundations of their pure and genuine faith—only then will they become a wise people, as promised in the Scriptures.[143]

According to Rapoport, it was also untrue to say that the maskilim hated all the hasidim for it was well known that, in their naïvety, the masses were drawn to those who presumed to lead them. The maskilim were enemies not of the common people, Rapoport stressed, but of their leaders: 'Our souls are pained to see many of our people erring, but we would not say they were evil because of it, God forbid. And this is my expression of true tolerance.'[144] The *tsadik*'s incitement of the common people, which occasionally led to bloodshed, seemed to Rapoport to be similar to the Pope's call for the Crusades that brought about the pogroms of 1096. The unrestrained masses, inflamed by the *tsadikim*, were likely to engage in murderous acts.

Rapoport claimed that the increasing numbers of hasidim and the continued existence of their movement for several decades did not constitute proof of their legitimacy; 'a heretical cult' is one which sooner or later disappears. In analysing Jewish history, importance should be attributed to the quality of a phenomenon and not to its ability to survive. Though Shabbetai Tsevi had disappeared relatively quickly, other deviant cults, such as the Sadducees and the Samaritans, had endured:

It is not as you think, that it is the length of time that a cult endures that has importance, such as the cult of Shabbetai Tsevi, may his name be cursed. The years of its existence should not even be mentioned as evidence, nor should one speak of the growing number of members of any heretical cult, for truly, if such a cult should exist among the Jewish people for only two weeks, that is sufficient in the eyes of the One who chose us from among all other peoples to bring much evil upon us, God forbid . . . and even the three years of Shabbetai Tsevi were enough to lead to disaster . . . however, whether the number of years is small or great, even if such a cult endures more than 1,800 years, we pray to God that the time will come when He shall wipe them from the face of the earth.[145]

Rapoport's maskilic apologia, expressed in his disputation with Bick as an attempt to detract from the importance of the masses, is yet another illustration of the situation of the Galician maskilim as a minority fighting against the ascendant hasidic movement. Seen from this perspective, all history was a battlefield in the conflict between mass movements and minorities made up of sages and maskilim, who were usually powerless to halt the masses. Rapoport believed that the common people possessed a latent potential for destruction and violence, acting with no rational judgement whatsoever, easily incited, driven by the power of imagination, and governed by potent emotions and urges. It was the dominance

[143] Rapoport, 'Mikhtav 23', *Kerem ḥemed*, 1 (1833), 83–4.
[144] Rapoport, 'Mikhtav lebik'.   [145] Ibid. 487–8.

of the common people that had brought about such historical disasters as the Islamic conquests and the Crusades, and, in Jewish history, had led to the destruction of the First and Second Temples: 'and how many people were killed and how much blood was spilled on the numerous occasions when the masses were carried away and their imaginations took control and their hearts raged, and they rose as a sea and destroyed cities and countries and killed their inhabitants, something science and even sophistry had never done'.[146]

As Rapoport interpreted it, the French Revolution had also been a catastrophic event characterized by an unrestrained outburst of the common people. In his opinion, the revolution was not the product of masikilic ideology at all, which therefore could not be held responsible for its degeneration into terror and bloodshed. The causes of the revolution derived from the socio-economic tensions in France that had led to the uprising of the masses, who were merely trying to satisfy their material needs:

The basic cause of the French Revolution of 1789, known to all those who enquire into that period, is that the majority of the people lived in poverty while the wealthy allowed themselves every indulgence and satisfied every desire, and that is what brought the tribulations upon them. The rebels did not shout that they were hungry for science, but only for bread.[147]

Like many previous revolutions, the French Revolution was a rebellion of slaves against their masters, like the sixteenth-century Peasants' Rebellion. In other words, such revolutions had taken place in periods pre-dating the Enlightenment, 'when the sun of wisdom had not yet begun to shine in those countries'. The Reformationists had described the Peasants' Rebellion as a religious war, although religious ideology was essentially secondary and served only to add fuel, in the form of religious fanaticism, to the frenzy of the masses. In such historical situations, Rapoport replied to Bick's claims, the enlightened élite, guided by their reason, must take on the important role of restraining the common people, disseminating enlightenment, and waging a life-and-death battle against religious fanaticism. Bick had therefore erred in his understanding of the concept of tolerance; it did not signify the capacity to ignore or be indifferent to foolish beliefs or the deplorable behaviour of the masses. Enlightenment and rationality did not lead to appalling behaviour and bloodshed; irrationality, superstition, enthusiasm, and the slavish obedience of the common people to their leaders, which characterized the hasidic movement, did. They were the true danger. History had proved that the élite was right and the masses were usually wrong. The concept 'tolerance' was interpreted by Rapoport to mean maskilic responsibility for the fate of the misguided masses: 'For the Almighty enlightened our minds only so that we could

[146] Ibid. 488.
[147] Ibid. These words are also quoted by Rapoport in a polemic with Samuel David Luzzatto in 1831; see also Harkavy and Halberstam, *Zikaron larishonim*, vol. ii, pt. 1, pp. 47–8; Werses, 'The French Revolution'.

give light to the masses who are in darkness, and we should not go mad and caper wildly just because all around us men have taken leave of their senses; and this is not opposed to tolerance.'[148] In this way, Rapoport broke the causal link between revolution and the Haskalah, making instead a critical connection between religious fanaticism and the common people, a connection that led to rebellion, destruction, and murder: 'Indeed, hypocritical religion and faith will always be used as a weapon and as an instrument of war.'[149] It was not the ideas of the Haskalah that led to political and social radicalism, but rather the enemies of Haskalah that did so—the masses and their fanatical leaders, historically manifested in Jewish society by the hasidim. Hasidism was not merely an expression of authentic popular power, as Bick believed, but a violent, fanatical, introverted, and destructive mass movement.

Rapoport's *Toledot* (Biographies) established his reputation, which endured for generations. This was a series of biographies that began to be published in 1829 in *Bikurei ha'itim* and guaranteed him a place in the annals of the Wissenschaft des Judentums and in the regard of Jewish historians in Germany as well. One innovation of *Toledot* was his inclusion of medieval biographies. He may have done this under the influence of romanticism or Zunz's biography of Rashi, or as a result of his own conservativeness, which led him to choose a period that allowed him to use critical tools with impunity.[150] However, it appears that Rapoport did not choose any particular period at all, but rather chose particular people who typified exemplary maskilim. Rabbenu Nathan ben Jehiel (1035–c.1110), Sa'adiah Gaon, Hai Gaon (939–1038), Rabbenu Hananel ben Hushiel, Rabbenu Nissim, and Eleazar Kallir were recruited by Rapoport, using a significantly higher level of critical research than in earlier maskilic biographies, in order to legitimize his ideal image of the wise rabbi, learned in languages and averse to kabbalah. A unique feature of the period he chose was the multitude of examples he could muster to serve his purpose: 'However, not many eras can equal that one, from the time of the *geonim* until the time of Rabbenu Nathan, in the truth of their commentaries on the Talmud and other books of wisdom, and also in the dissemination of those commentaries from country to country and from nation to nation.'[151] Sa'adiah Gaon was lauded as 'a man of great wisdom, famous for his talmudic and scientific studies', who prevailed over those who opposed science and philosophy. Rabbenu Nathan, who compiled an Aramaic lexicon, was knowledgeable in foreign languages: 'there is some reason to believe that he loved science and also read books of medical wisdom in Arabic'. Though Hai Gaon may have studied kabbalah, he tried to dissociate himself from its foolish beliefs, even though in his time 'there was not yet mixed in it much dross and additions from the secrets of the East and Spain'. With regard to Eleazar Kallir, Rapoport

[148] Rapoport, 'Mikhtav lebik', 29–30.   [149] Ibid.
[150] See Barzilay, *Shlomo Yehuda Rapoport*, 48–53.
[151] Rapoport, 'El hakore', introd. to 'Toledot rabenu natan', 3.

was able to announce that his writings contained not even the slightest hint that he had any knowledge of the kabbalistic mysteries.[152]

It is easy to discern in *Toledot* yet another attempt to transmit the anti-hasidic message that Bick refused to accept: leaders and sages must prove their greatness through intellectual creativity, and their ability to attract the common people is insufficient:

Most of our brothers in some countries will rightly want to call men great and wise luminaries only because they behave unusually . . . and the masses will not notice if they have any wisdom or are superior to others and what qualities make them worthy of repute. I hope the examples that I have presented here of the histories of several wise and excellent men will demonstrate the true qualities and virtues that earned them the homage of their people for all generations.[153]

Rapoport also perceived the great struggle between hasidism and Haskalah in terms of the doctrine of the soul, as a struggle between intellect and passion. Though both existed within a man's soul, the soul could attain wholeness only through a harmonious balance of power between them. His comment that emphasis on passion alone, or total dependence on the intellect, led to a lack of wholeness indicates that Bick's criticism had penetrated the maskilic consciousness:

The intellect sheds light upon the night of confusion and it is the guide for achieving knowledge in all sciences. However, it is not sufficient to lead men to the designated goal without the power of passion that stirs and awakens them to all studies and deeds. . . . As it is with a man, so it is with many nations in different periods, according to changes in place and time.[154]

Making use of geographic–climatic theories of history, Rapoport classified the various nations according to their character traits, which he saw as determined by their natural environment. Inhabitants of eastern and southern nations lived in a hot climate, which intensified their passions and weakened their intellect. Therefore, their emotions were easily stirred, the masses went to war, and religious fanaticism dominated. The Muslim conquests were an example of 'the time when the Arabs were incited to madness, sweeping across countries and claiming endless numbers of victims'.[155] The opposite was true for the people of western and northern countries: the climate was cold or temperate, passions were relatively weak, and the power of the intellect prevailed. This explained the flowering of Graeco-Roman culture, art, literature, and classical poetry. However, granting absolute superiority to the intellect was also destructive, and this was what had led to the political instability of Greece and Rome, and, ultimately, to their downfall.

---

[152] Rapoport, 'Toledot rabenu se'adyah'; id., 'Toledot rabenu natan', 70–2; Rapoport, 'Toledot rabenu hai gaon', 80, 89–90, nn. 15, 17; Rapoport, 'Zeman umekom', 98. On Rapoport's attitude to kabbalah, see Lahover, 'Visible and Hidden', 298–9.

[153] Rapoport, 'Toledot rabenu natan', 5.

[154] Rapoport, 'El hakore'—introd. to 'Toledot rabenu hananel', 6.   [155] Ibid. 6–8.

In the Middle Ages the power of the intellect, as well as that of the passions, was weakened, which caused almost complete deadlock: 'that enormous period of time they called the Middle Ages that divided ancient times from modern times, when men crawled and crept on the earth with no memory and no interest in anything, neither things of passion nor things of the intellect.'[156]

In contrast to Eastern and Western nations, the Jewish nation had developed in an ideal natural environment, and its eventual perfection was predetermined. The location of the Land of Israel between Asia and Europe, and the eastern and north-western climatic influences upon it made possible a balance between the powers of passion and intellect: 'And thus the temperament of the people of Israel was a mixture of passion and intellect and reached the desired goal in the proper time . . . for signs of the power of the intellect were very visible in them, as is well known.'[157] Exile, the political pressures exerted by the Romans, and religious disputes during the time of the Second Temple (a natural historical phenomenon occurring during 'the immature years of every nation, before their wisdom has developed') prevented the potential inherent in the natural circumstances of the Jewish people from being realized. However, the attributes of a people did not disappear, even when it was cut off from its land, and therefore the internal struggle between the forces persisted:

In the country in which I live and in neighbouring countries to the east, I saw the disgrace of my people. As is well known, my people have been divided into two parts for more than sixty years and a discerning eye will see that division concerning the matters we have discussed. Half of my people will listen only to the voice of the hero who arouses them to action . . . and it is the power of the passions that always motivate the soul to rise up over worldly matters and to continue to exalted heights . . . and the other half will heed only the power of the mind.[158]

Here the hasidim were presented as lacking moral judgement and the maskilim were shown to have lost their creativity because they had deviated from the harmony that characterized the Jewish people. Hence, not only the love of one's people and the fear that they would become divided, but also the nature of their authentic national and spiritual character, demanded a renewed balance of powers.

Rapoport presented this historical, psychological, and climatic theory in the early 1830s. At the end of this decade he endured the most difficult experience of his life—a short, unsuccessful term as the rabbi of Tarnopol, which he left because he was unable to withstand the wave of hostility and vilification directed towards him.[159] In the wake of this experience Rapoport left Galicia to become rabbi of Prague. In Tarnopol he summed up the problem of hasidism in Galicia,

---

[156] Rapoport, 'El hakore'—introd. to 'Toledot rabenu ḥananel', 8. Only the Crusades lit a spark that aroused passions, but that soon died down too.

[157] Ibid. 9.   [158] Ibid. 10–11.

[159] On the difficult situation in Tarnopol, see Rapoport, 'Mikhtav 3', *Kerem ḥemed*, 3 (1838), 38–53; S. Hacohen, 'Ḥeshek shelomoh', 253–6.

sounding much more pessimistic, for he was once again unable to bridge the yawning gap in any way. In 1839 he revealed that all hope was gone: 'Although we had hoped the numbers of the hasidim would grow smaller until they disappeared, they have greatly increased in number, and like the frogs of Egypt, they have infested every house and every bedroom.'[160] In the battle between Haskalah and hasidism the latter was the overwhelming victor and, in his frustration, Rapoport could only revile the hasidim from a distance as 'a disgrace to humanity'.

Krochmal's death in 1840, shortly after the death of Perl, seemed to Rapoport to mark the end of an era in Galicia. The domination of hasidism, the egotism of the wealthy élite, the imperviousness of the scholars, and the disintegration of a binding sense of brotherhood all symbolized for Rapoport a profound conflict, for which he blamed primarily the hasidim, 'the oppressors of the people'. Rapoport, who felt he had been exiled from his homeland, which had been conquered by 'the foul and the despicable [hasidim]', sent his brothers in Galicia what sounded like a final, pessimistic message: 'My brother, fellow countrymen, and sons of my native city! Behold, the time has come for you to remove this heavy burden from your shoulders, to destroy the sorcerers and soothsayers. Be no longer seduced in your foolishness and wander no more along their paths, for they have already felled many casualties and have 'killed' a vast number.'[161]

NAHMAN KROCHMAL
THE MIDDLE-OF-THE-ROAD MASKIL

Nahman Krochmal (1749–1840) was the unacknowledged leader of the Galician maskilim, even if only a few principles of his major ideological doctrines were known to them during his lifetime. From the moment his book *Moreh nevukhei hazeman* (The Guide of the Perplexed of the Time) was printed in Lvov in 1851, it was recognized as an exemplary work of Jewish historical thought. Several central themes emerging from research on Krochmal lend credence to the claim that he occupied a unique historical position in his generation: as a philosopher opening a new era in Jewish thought, drawing on the idealistic philosophy of his time that was influenced by Hegel, Kant, Fichte, and Schelling; as a scholar in the field of Jewish studies, poised on the threshold of the new critical approach to the historical study of Judaism and making a pivotal contribution to the development of modern historical consciousness; as a man of modern Hebrew literature during its transitional period between rationalism and romanticism; and also as the harbinger of modern Jewish nationalism.[162]

---

[160] [Rapoport], *Kerem ḥemed*, 4 (1839), 46. This was in an anonymous review, written by Rapoport, on Perl's *Boḥen tsadik*.

[161] Rapoport's eulogy on Krochmal's death, 'Al mot harav heḥakham', *Kerem ḥemed*, 6 (1841), 41–9.

[162] Rotenstreich, *Jewish Philosophy in the Modern Era*, 52–70; Schweid, *Jewish Thought*, 177–211; Gutmann, 'Foundations', 259–86; Buber, 'A People and its God', 287–95; Taubes, 'Nachman Kroch-

Studies of Krochmal have limited discussion of him to theoretical, philosophical, and literary issues such as: Was he a Hegelian? Who influenced his cyclical conception of history? Was he a nationalist and a romantic? Did he aspire to write a new *Guide of the Perplexed*? What were the limits he set for his criticism? However, it appears that one essential aspect has been neglected: namely, the social circle within which Krochmal functioned as one of the moderate maskilim of Galicia during the first third of the nineteenth century. When his life is discussed, however, it is presented almost completely separately from his book, thus confining him to the history of Jewish thought and ignoring his involvement in the Haskalah. Krochmal's intellectual history is one of interaction between his maskilic experiences, the heritage of the Haskalah, and his worldview and maskilic values, on one hand, and the new ideas and philosophical systems of thought he employed in his book, on the other. The mould into which Krochmal poured his maskilic views was new and unprecedented. However, his awareness of the past, despite its innovations, still bore the stamp of the Haskalah. The attempt to portray Krochmal as a representative of a circle of scholars in Jewish studies, living on some kind of desert island of academic study and writing outside the particular context of his time and place, obscures his uniqueness. Unlike central and west European scholars of Jewish history (Wissenschaft des Judentums), who considered the improvement of Jewish life to be directly linked to legal emancipation and social integration, the Galician maskilim were not seriously troubled by the 'Jewish question'. Krochmal's concern was not comparable to that of Leopold Zunz (1794–1886), for example, who lamented the delay of emancipation. The problems of Zunz and the Western Jewish sages were essentially post-maskilic, and they confronted them within the ideological framework of the emancipation. Krochmal and the Galician maskilim, on the other hand, grappled with internal Jewish problems and strove to forge a path for the maskilic intellectual in an increasingly diversified reality.

Of all the western European maskilim, it was Zunz (who published Krochmal's *Moreh nevukhei hazeman* in 1851, after the author's death) who directed the reader to the especially problematic nature of Krochmal, a scholar who addressed internal Jewish problems at a time when the light was already shining on the German Jews, 'but the darkness in the Polish valley had deepened'.[163]

In Zunz's opinion, Krochmal was motivated to write his book by the difficulties facing a divided, crisis-ridden Jewish society 'so that they will attain absolute truth and do good because they are aware that the image of God in man is his spirituality, and pure wisdom and clear knowledge are the spiritual wings that raise us above the evil extremes'.[164] Zunz believed that Krochmal's aims were didactic and that he sought an antidote to hasidism, heresy, and assimilation. This belief,

mal and Modern Historicism', 150–64; Bat-Yehudah, 'R. Nachman Krochmal', 419–30; Harris, *Nachman Krochmal*.

[163] Zunz, publisher's introd., in N. Krochmal, *Collected Writings*.   [164] Ibid.

however, indicates that Zunz was unable to free himself from the philosophical concepts of Wissenschaft des Judentums. In fact, Krochmal was not satisfied with the study of pure faith alone, but strove to enable the men of his generation to understand the crisis of their time against the backdrop of the Jewish and universal historical past. At this point we must address ourselves to Krochmal himself, his view of the 'perplexities of his time', and the link between them and his scholarship and outlook.

The available letters reveal that Krochmal was no less obsessed by hasidic fanaticism than were Perl, Mieses, Erter, and Rapoport, and that his responses to it were strong and emotional. In 1816 the hasidim of Lvov accused him of heresy, citing as evidence his links with Karaites. Krochmal was deeply offended by the accusation, and defended himself against 'the hot fire of foolish fanaticism with which [he] had been attacked by some hypocrites in the community of Lvov'.[165] Krochmal's characterization of the hasidim as zealots and drunken fanatics preaching folk religion to the ignorant masses of eastern Europe was similar to that of other Galician maskilim. When he became aware of the distress of a young maskil (apparently Abraham Goldberg) who had fallen victim to hasidic intrigues, Krochmal was enraged. He called the hasidic *tsadik* 'one of those stubborn and mutinous fleas' and wrote to the youth, 'I was angered and dismayed to learn that you have fallen prey to their intimidation and that they have weakened your heart.' Krochmal was even willing to accept the assistance of Austrian officials in the struggle against hasidism. He despised the hasidim and suggested to his colleagues that they adopt the methods of Maimonides, who knew how to stand up to the ignorant masses.[166]

Hasidism aroused in Krochmal the sense of an imminent crisis, which also greatly influenced his historical outlook. If the maskilic picture of the past, originating in the 1780s, was underpinned by an optimistic sense of the present and the perception of a positive historical turning-point, then Krochmal's picture of the past took shape against the backdrop of a profound internal crisis in Jewish society. In his opinion, 'the corruption of principles and morals', the defilement of 'the essence of the Torah', and the undermining of pure faith, on one hand, and a counter-reaction that took the form of tendencies towards heresy, on the other, were all manifestations of the decline of Jewish history.[167] We have already seen a similar sense of crisis in Rapoport, stemming from the moderate maskil's fear of a divided society and the loss of an ideological–religious consensus. This also occupied Krochmal's mind as he began to write *Moreh nevukhei hazeman*. He discussed his hesitations about writing a book dealing with history and faith that would be acceptable to the various factions—'and who knows how to

---

[165] Krochmal, letter to Ze'ev Shiff (1816), in id., *Collected Writings*, 413–16.

[166] Letter from Krochmal, ibid. 416–18. On this episode, see also *Memorial Book of Mosty-Wielkie*, i. 21, 88.

[167] Letter from Krochmal to Rapoport (1838), in id., *Collected Writings*, 430–1.

contend with a world so full of different sects?'—with Samuel David Luzzatto (1800–65) of Padua, who he thought shared his moderate maskilic position.[168] The correspondence between the two holds the key to an understanding of the social and ideological context of Krochmal's book.

Krochmal observed that the dynamics of the present were more difficult to grasp than those of other periods. Changes had occurred throughout the course of Jewish history. However, if it were possible to chart these changes on a diachronic time axis, with each period and its changes shown in relation to its predecessors, then today we would have to add those changes that are occurring synchronically in other places. 'All is whirled away by the spirit of the time, in different directions', wrote Krochmal to Luzzatto.[169] How could one write simultaneously for 'the Italian Jew and the oriental Jew, for the wise men of Germany and the hasidim of the northern kingdom', Krochmal asked Luzzatto, coming to the conclusion that only the moderate, 'middle-of-the-road' maskil was capable of doing so.[170] Luzzatto demanded that Krochmal take an unequivocally critical position and avoid compromise. Krochmal heeded his exhortation and in *Moreh nevukhei hazeman* he uncompromisingly took 'the extremes' to task and attempted to persuade his readers of the correctness of the path of the 'true believer', as opposed to those of the hasid and the scholar, of the young Jews who had strayed from their people, and of the merchants who scorned Jewish tradition and those who perpetuated it.[171] The opening of *Moreh nevukhei hazeman* charts a labyrinth of paths before which a nineteenth-century Jewish youth stands bewildered. The middle-of-the-road maskil not only tries to guide the youth along the right path of the moderate Haskalah, the path of a wise and God-fearing maskil, but also attempts to explain the meaning of the labyrinth itself. This was one of Krochmal's innovations: he found that historical–philosophical thinking could satisfactorily address the problems of those who were perplexed by their time.

In the section 'Sha'ar hasamim' (Gate of Remedies) of *Moreh nevukhei hazeman* Krochmal presented his readers with the negative extremes through six types of believer and non-believer. The first are the two types whose religious behaviour seemed to him to be particularly abhorrent: the hasidic *tsadik* and his devoted disciple. The former was characterized by his hallucinatory tendencies (*Schwärmerei*), a rationalistic concept that eighteenth-century maskilim had already employed in their attacks on religion and the religious establishment. A believer who displayed this attribute

would remove his thoughts from worldly occupations and delights and be repulsed by all things governed by the senses; then the achievements of the intellect will become diminished in his eyes. He will spend his days concerned only with the state of his inflamed soul

---

[168] Krochmal's letter to Luzzatto (Sept. 1835), in id., *Collected Writings*, 424–6.   [169] Ibid. 425.

[170] Ibid. 'It is up to us, who sit in the middle and see what is being done and said to the right and to the left, to say: it is time for the Lord to act, for thy law has been broken on every side.'

[171] Luzzatto's letter to Krochmal (1837), in Letteris, *Sefer mikhtavei benei kedem*, 65–9.

. . . he will think he sees with his inner eye angels of heaven and transparent or invisible objects . . . he will go mad thinking he is a partner of the Creator.[172]

In Krochmal's view, this type of Jewish believer was the main cause of the weakening of pure faith during his time. The other five types of believer and nonbeliever were mainly defined on the basis of their response, whether adoring or hostile, to the *tsadik*. The second type was represented by the hasid, whose religious belief was defined as superstition (*Aberglauben*). While the *tsadik* was a member of the élite developing within the circle of scholars and pious Jews, the hasid came from 'the masses who were weak in religion and strong in imagination . . . just as a hallucinating man seeks the company of spiritual men for a less lofty purpose, for his pleasure and to be rescued from evil'.[173] His religious world was populated by *tsadikim*, demons, sorcery, spirits, and angels, and while such a world might be suitable for the common people, who were driven by emotion and imagination, it struck a serious blow to pure faith, 'darkening the glory of religion and making men resemble monkeys'.[174] The third type of believer—perhaps the best of the three, although he too had many failings—was the talmudic scholar, the *talmid ḥakham*, who aspired to nothing more than a life defined by meticulous observance of the *mitsvot*, which would eventually lead him into developing negative tendencies: 'The multiplicity of deeds loses direction,' wrote Krochmal, 'or it leads to sanctification of action and denigration of thought.'[175]

In contrast to these three types of believer there were three opposing types who were, in Krochmal's opinion, 'obliterators of moral reality, whose overemphasis of a single quality leads to the development of a diametrically opposed quality'. Reaction to the hallucinating *tsadik* led to the emergence of those who denied the existence of God, materialists who degrade the image of man and 'ascribed the nature of a man's soul to his bodily fluids and temperature'; in reaction to the hasid arose the sceptics who no longer believed in common sense, inner feelings, and tradition, including critics of the Bible who doubted 'the reality of the faithful shepherd, our master Moses, and his handing down of the Torah . . . [and say that] perhaps a deceitful rabbi wrote it'; and as a reaction to the scholar, there emerged those who abandoned all observance of the *mitsvot*. Krochmal summed up the problem of his time: 'Both extremes lack proper faith in our generation. They all consider true belief to be what they were taught in their youth.'[176]

The 'middle-of-the-road' maskil was situated between the extremes and proposed that those who were 'perplexed' should take the same middle position.[177]

[172] N. Krochmal, *Moreh nevukhei hazeman*, 7.   [173] Ibid. 7–8.
[174] Ibid.   [175] Ibid. 8.   [176] Ibid. 6, 8–9.
[177] Krochmal constructed his concept of the middle path on the basis of a statement in the Jerusalem Talmud (*Ḥagigah* 2: 1): 'This Torah resembles two paths, one of fire, the other of snow; he who inclines towards the first dies in the fire, he who inclines towards the other dies in the snow. What ought he to do? Walk in the middle.'

However, Krochmal's perception of the 'middle' differed from Maimonides' well-known view of the golden mean. Krochmal sought the middle road in the spheres of science and the arts, based on intellectual effort, but not in moral and spiritual matters, for this could only be attained through self-education, virtue, and morality. In fact, Krochmal expressly opposed Maimonides' 'golden mean', claiming that, in the latter's time, the geometric mid-point between the extremes was simply an unacceptable compromise that combined the objectionable principles of both poles. Krochmal strove for the 'essence', a synthetic point reached through philosophical and historical study. Such study attempted to get at the root of ideological schisms, to discover the historical source of undesirable divergence, to explain differing opinions by understanding how they had formed, and to show that conflicting positions were the outcome of later developments. Krochmal's 'middle' thus meant an understanding of present phenomena based on historical thought:

And this was the profound and true meaning of the suggestion that we choose an exalted path in our enquiries, rising along it until we reach the primary source and the beginning of things, so that our questions are clarified and the contradictions deriving from them fade away—and we shall reach knowledge with no hallucinations and no denial of spirituality, and no conflict of this kind . . . for the scholars, the intellectuals, and those who seek truth with all their hearts, there can be no counsel or stratagem except for profound study of the source and the origin of the matters in question and of the method in which all contradiction will be obliterated. Thus will their souls and minds be put at rest, and this exalted way will unite the two extremes. We shall metaphorically call this path the middle road.[178]

Krochmal sought to make the concept of historical time a basic yardstick for thought. Like other maskilim, he cautioned against anachronism: 'Nothing causes greater harm than intermingling times and deeds in such a way that there remains no difference between them.'[179] Young people of that period had already mastered popular history books, primarily those 'abridged history books that they usually had in their possession', and so they scorned any approach that ignored history. Critical, scientific research into tradition, by which Krochmal meant traditional texts, would arrange the various strata according to periods and would present each stratum as a product of its time, so that 'the private opinions' of 'a particular time' would not be regarded as eternal truths. This was the method Krochmal applied in his study of the aggadah, the Oral Torah, philosophy, and kabbalah in the final chapters of his book. Historiographically, he attempted to present Jewish history against its universal backdrop as a monumental vision of changes occurring in time. Krochmal also emphasized the stages of its development and demonstrated the historical implementation of 'the general spirit of the nation'.

---

[178] N. Krochmal, *Moreh nevukhei hazeman*, 16–17.   [179] Ibid. 211.

In contrast to standard maskilic history, Krochmal rarely used didactic examples, nor did he discuss biographies of great people or create a periodization
that was characterized by sharp reversals from period to period. He preferred to
enquire into historiographic perceptions, sought to understand the larger processes involved in the development of the Jews and other peoples, and conceived
an organic biological rhythm of life cycles according to which history proceeded.

However, Krochmal's maskilic approach is unmistakable, even when he formulated his writings in terms of new historical concepts. Especially characteristic is his practical use of history as a storehouse of lessons to be learned. Thus,
for example, Krochmal claimed that historical study of the interaction between
the Jews and other nations was 'compulsory for all men of wisdom and great men
who wish to understand their essence and their source'. Those who studied this
interaction would 'arrive at a clear impression and ultimately an awareness of our
essence, the soul of the Jewish people, how we appear to the world through our
history and our writings, throughout the vicissitudes of time to this very day,
and from this we shall infer what is to come'.[180] Historical study was a guide for
the future, and Krochmal used the great cyclical pattern of history to reassure
the perplexed of his time, who were experiencing a crisis in the present. His
emphasis on the Jewish people's ability to be reborn and to set out on a new historical path at each new renaissance (in contrast to other peoples, who only had a
single life cycle) was meant to inspire hope; for then, as in the past, a new, in-
vigorating life cycle awaited, and with it, new germination and growth. While
Krochmal's pragmatic tendencies led him to draw historical analogies that would
provide the Jews of his day with a compass, he did so with great caution, so as
not to obscure the uniqueness of historical phenomena.

Krochmal's basic model of the historical life cycle postulated that the germination and growth stages of every nation (and of all humankind) resulted from
developing the potential inherent in the 'spirit of a nation'. Every cycle began
with intensive activity in the realm of material needs and moved towards ever-
increasing humanism, science, religion, and spirituality. The dynamics of degeneration and destruction were inevitable, for the seeds of calamity and decay had
already been planted during the nation's formation. Moral, psychological, social,
political, and religious flaws brought about the destruction of all peoples: the
growing numbers of property owners led to greed, moral corruption, the disrup-
tion of judicial and governing procedures, and struggles for control. Schisms
among people and conflicts between ideas were accelerated by the infiltration of
foreign customs and concepts; excessively comfortable and pampered lives soft-
ened the heart and weakened a nation's fortitude and power of endurance. It was
always during such periods of crisis that false mystical religious beliefs flourished. These afflictions struck a blow so fatal to the 'spirit of the nation' that it
totally disintegrated: 'The truth is that the strength of a nation does not lie in the

[180] Ibid. 167.

fact that it is a nation, but in the spiritual strength it possesses,'[181] and no social group could exist after the spiritual ties that bound it had crumbled.

An examination of Jewish history through the prism of this model revealed that it, too, was subject to the same historical principles which, according to Krochmal, derived from Divine Providence. Despite the complexity of Krochmal's historical outline, two fundamental, interrelated, and relatively simple maskilic principles are perceptible in it: a historical picture replete with contrasts that are classified as good or bad, positive or negative; and an assumption that there is an ideal, exemplary model of the Jew and a proper path to be followed, deviations from which are to be condemned. Like his maskilic colleagues, Krochmal was not satisfied with merely describing 'what really happened', but also revealed his excitement or sorrow about what was taking place.

On the basis of the first two cycles of Jewish history that Krochmal described in his book, a series of tensions extending throughout history can be distinguished:

1. The principal process is the tension between trends of social–national consolidation and those of division and disintegration. The cyclical fluctuations move from consolidation during the period of growth to disintegration during the period of decline and destruction. In Krochmal's view, these contradictory trends were the heartbeat of Jewish history. Various political and religious tactics might be employed to preserve consolidation. During the growth period of the first cycle, for example, the revelation at Mount Sinai strengthened 'national bonds'; and during this cycle's period of 'power and achievement' Solomon halted the separatist tendencies of the tribes to hold 'private beliefs' by establishing the Temple and centralizing of the kingdom around a single religion and a single government.

2. This first major process was also linked to the dynamics of the Jewish people's relationships to other nations, and occasionally events in this area had a decisive impact on the disintegration process. Like other moderate maskilim, Krochmal attempted to determine how much fruitful influence could be absorbed before absorption became emulation or assimilation. He found several examples in Jewish history that could serve as lessons for later generations. During the growth period of the first cycle and the florescence of the second the absorption of foreign influences was fruitful and beneficial: during the Egyptian exile the Jewish people acquired the best of a material and scientific civilization, while their strength, the tradition of the Patriarchs, and the memory of their homeland guaranteed their continued national separateness. The encounter with Greek civilization turned the Hellenistic period into a golden age, for it brought about material and spiritual perfection. In contrast, during the period of decline contact with foreign cultures led to self-abnegation. Such was the case during the period of decline of the first cycle, when 'Such evil kings as Ahaz, Manasseh, and Jehoiakim sought to better their situation

---

[181] N. Krochmal, *Moreh nevukhei hazeman*, 40.

by emulating the idolatory of the gentiles.' Krochmal stressed that this was an instructive example for posterity: emulation of the gentiles was 'the evil that always grows so wildly and uncontrollably among the people'.[182] On the other hand, Krochmal the maskil condemned the response of the Sages, who, at the end of the Second Temple era, issued prohibitions aimed at halting assimilation and preventing contact with the Romans. In his view, their lack of open-mindedness led to the Romans' negative image of Jews, as well as to Jewish religious fanaticism.

3. A key problem in cultural interaction was the potential damage to pure faith, and the tension between the preservation of pure Jewish monotheism and the infiltration of idolatry and superstition had always existed in Jewish history. When faith was preserved during periods of florescence and power, the result was cultural and political success (for example, during the times of Solomon and the Return to Zion), while the corruption of faith led to political instability, moral deterioration, and cultural decline.

These principles re-emphasized the moderate, middle-of-the-road maskil's awareness of the past as he came to grips with internal division, absorption of external culture, deviation from pure faith, superstition, and the unruly masses. These were issues of Krochmal's time that had existed in the past too. Krochmal attacked fools, evil rulers, and religious fanatics in Jewish history. Thus, for example, when he described the zealots of the Second Temple era, Krochmal undoubtedly had in mind the hasidim he hated so bitterly:

From among the sages themselves arose multitudes of sects of falsely pious, sanctimonious pupils. They became cruel murderers, calling themselves zealots and servants of the one and only God. They called the leaders of the sages and the priests and all good and peaceful men by the name of flatterers and servants of idol worshippers. They manipulated the ignorant masses, doing whatever they wished with them.[183]

If, in this example, the negative model of the *tsadik* and the hasidim was projected onto the past, it was because Krochmal also saw the positive model of the maskil in the past. His description of the second cycle, which began with the flowering of the Babylonian exile, contains maskilic images of the transition from darkness to light and from foolishness to wisdom. It was a period in which Jews proficient in philosophy and science were recognized for their achievements by rulers of nations:

Even during the time of the Temple and the days of Josiah and later, God succeeded, through his prophets, in gradually dispelling more clouds of the folly of idolatry and the false faith related to it; and a spark of reason was ignited among all the people until later, at the beginning of exile, their unique aspect, free of any hint of idolatry, was fixed in their hearts. And still, most of the people of this exile were noble and virtuous, men of knowledge and industry . . . and among them were also men educated in all the wisdom of philosophy and science.[184]

[182] Ibid. 49.   [183] Ibid. 93.   [184] Ibid. 52.

In Krochmal's view, therefore, the beginning of the growth cycle of the Jews was linked to the appearance of enlightened men who spread light, reason, and science, and fought against folly. He offered a similar explanation for the role of the Judaeo-Hellenistic centre in Alexandria, which he considered the symbol of an unparalleled exemplary period (the stage of 'power and achievement' of the second cycle).[185] In contrast, according to Krochmal's interpretation, the seeds of the destruction that occurred in the third stage of the entire cycle had already been planted during the cycle's growth stage. During the First Temple era this process began in the time of the Judges and Samuel, and was expressed in the isolationist tendencies of the tribes. In the Second Temple era the process began during the final days of Johanan Hyrcanus, with the revival of the Pharisee, Sadducee, and Essene sects. Krochmal also applied the word 'sect' to the hasidim of his time, which explains his pessimistic historical view of the development of sects. He saw historical regularity in the dynamics of religious sectarianism: it began in a pure, ideological dispute over matters of religion and faith (which was positive in itself), spread to the area of politics as opposing forces competed for power and governmental authority, and ended in fanaticism and mutual hatred. Citing an example from the Pharisees and the Sadducees, Krochmal claimed that they were 'sects that had different ideas . . . only in matters of religion and faith, and they both sought to acquire governmental power and authority over the public, and intervened in the leadership of the state and its councils. And their enmity and fanaticism were a constant source of ceaseless evildoing at the end of this period and at the beginning of the decline that followed it.'[186]

The undesirable and inevitable consequences of the sects that had sprung up among the Jewish people led Krochmal to the conclusion that they were invalid in principle. They did no harm as long as they remained within the province of ideological argument. However, the history of sects demonstrated that the masses were always mobilized for the struggle, which ultimately led to the perversion or neglect of ideology.

The deterioration and the 'vast night of darkness' of the third historical cycle of Jewish history, described very briefly in *Moreh nevukhei hazeman*, continued from the thirteenth century, the time of Nachmanides, until at least the middle of the seventeenth century. Did Krochmal regard the 1830s as the beginning of the fourth cycle? His book does not discuss the eighteenth century, leaving the issue open to speculation. It seems that the maskilic situation in which Krochmal lived did not allow him to define his time as one of revitalization. The conflict with the 'hasidic sect', his perception of internal divisions, deviation from pure faith, and cases of heresy and assimilation among the Jews of his time combined to give him a sense of crisis, and he seems to have regarded his own time as a continuation of the period of decline of the third cycle. As in previous eras, only the maskilim, whom Krochmal called 'the few flashes of light', might make possible

---

[185] N. Krochmal, *Moreh nevukhei hazeman*, 61–2.   [186] Ibid. 72.

the future development of a new cycle in which unity, pure faith, and reason would be restored to the Jewish people.

WISSENSCHAFT DES JUDENTUMS IN GALICIA

In 1849 Tsevi Hirsch Chajes (1805–55), the enlightened rabbi of Zolkiew, summed up the impressive achievements of the Jewish scholars who had 'studied the events of world history' in the preceding thirty years. Chajes, who considered himself a member of this circle of scholars, did not conceal his excitement at and admiration of this new phenomenon: 'And during our own time, Jewish scholars from the lands of Italy, Galicia, and Germany have refined all aspects of the science of criticism, in all its roots and widespread branches, leaving not a single item, be it small or large, without subjecting it to their meticulous scrutiny, and reaching a conclusion about everything hitherto obscure.'[187]

He attempted to review the results of the research conducted by all the scholars of his time, while suppressing the personal bitterness he felt as a result of the friction between him and several of them. Among others, Chajes listed Moses Kunitz, Rapoport, Zunz, the Italian scholars Luzzatto, Reggio, and Jost, who 'uncovers in the proper order unknown facts about the condition of the Jewish people wherever they have settled', as well as Julius Fuerst of Leipzig (1805–73), Solomon Lewisohn, Samson Bloch, Zacharias Frankel (1801–75), Yehoseph Schwarz (1804–65), and Krochmal, who had already shown Chajes two chapters of *Moreh nevukhei hazeman*.

And they grow ever more numerous [Chajes added] in the lands of Italy, Germany, Galicia, Lithuania, and the Netherlands, great scholars and enlightened men, well versed in the sciences, attempting to clarify every unknown aspect of Jewish history . . . by using everything found in the chronicles of the nations and their leaders in former times; [and they] also make an effort to publish books by Jewish sages from earlier generations, which are stored in the royal treasuries.[188]

Chajes' descriptions reflect a dynamic period of research and study, marked by growing intensity, as the realm of Wissenschaft des Judentums extended throughout the European Jewish world, from the Netherlands to Lithuania. In Chajes' view, this development was evidence of a great change, in contrast to the maskilim of the previous generation: anyone comparing the achievements of *Hame'asfim* or *Sulamith* with those of contemporary scholars 'will realize that while the [earlier scholars] excel in their knowledge of the sacred tongue and in rhetoric and poetry, in so far as the knowledge of the history of the nation and the science of religion are concerned, they are but dwarfs when compared to us'.[189] Chajes was a master of traditional learning, as well as possessing historical knowledge and an education in philosophy, acquired at the university in Lvov, and

---

[187] Chajes, 'Imrei binah', 871.   [188] Ibid. 874.   [189] Ibid.

was a member of the circle of maskilim established in Zolkiew under Krochmal's leadership, to which he had belonged since his appointment as the community rabbi in 1829. He regarded the Wissenschaft des Judentums not only as a successful republic of scholars spreading throughout the Jewish world, but also as a cohesive society. Although the network of reciprocal relations, the correspondence, and the joint publications of these groups support this assumption, the maskilim of Galicia followed their own unique path in regard to Jewish studies in the nineteenth century, and in this sense Chajes himself belonged more to the Galician maskilim than to the circle of Jewish scholars in Germany. Indeed, his survey of the achievements of Wissenschaft des Judentums was intended to endow scientific research on Jewish subjects with legitimacy in the eyes of the traditional rabbinical world and the moderate maskilim, stressing the tradition of unbroken continuity:

And I have also attempted to summarize here the essence of the art of criticism and its history among our people, for it is not a new method of our time, as some rabbis would claim, but one employed by the authors of the Mishnah and the Talmud and by rabbis from then on, to investigate every obscure matter in one place and to cast light upon it from another.[190]

Based on this point of view, the history of Wissenschaft des Judentums did not begin with Zunz nor with the establishment of the Verein für Kultur und Wissenschaft des Judentums in Berlin in the 1810s, but rather with the *tana'im*, who were pioneers in developing an original Jewish method of study. In Chajes' view, this approach also solved the problem of dealing with biblical criticism, since if the 'scholars' among the *tana'im* and the *amora'im* had already engaged in biblical research, contemporary scholars were no longer called upon to do so. Although non-Jewish scholars had devoted much attention to the Bible, among the Jews 'the tradition is unreservedly accepted and one must not deviate from it, neither to the right nor to the left'. Chajes also added a survey of the succession of 'scholars' who arose after the Sages, including Sherira Gaon, Maimonides, Abraham Zacuto (1452–*c*.1515), Azariah de' Rossi, Moses Isserles, David Gans, Hayim Joseph David Azulai (1724–1806), and Jehiel Heilprin (1660–1746). This nineteenth-century harmonistic approach to Jewish history, implying continuity and uniformity in space and in time, enabled the enlightened rabbi from Galicia to offer an extremely moderate interpretation of the Wissenschaft des Judentums and to gloss over the substantive difference between the study of Judaism in his own time and the interpretation of the Scriptures and the halakhah that preceded it.

However, while traditional research (*ḥakirah*) was essentially a form of scholarship subject to an authority external to the sources and lacking any conceptions of historical thought, in the nineteenth century the term 'research' had an entirely different meaning and content. Nor did Chajes use the term 'research' in the

---

[190] Chajes, 'Imrei binah', 872.

maskilic sense, as a form of critical-rationalistic philosophical study aiming at objective knowledge of the truth and of virtue, an approach that made every maskil a 'researcher' (*ḥoker*). Chajes substituted the term 'research' for 'science' (Heb.: *mada*; German: *Wissenschaft*), a term based on the aspiration to gain an objective, unbiased knowledge of the historical truth and implying a critical approach employing historiographical methods developed in late eighteenth-century Germany.

Immanuel Wolf was one of the founders of the Verein für Kultur und Wissenschaft der Juden which first coined the term Wissenschaft des Judentums, later translated into Hebrew as *ḥokhmat yisra'el* (the wisdom of Judaism); he defined this science in words far removed from the concepts and ideas embodied in Chajes' writings, assuming that any object could become the subject of a special science:

And the essence of this special science will then be to describe that object in its entire scope and all the phases of its systematic formation *per se*, and for this sake alone, not for any other purpose. If we apply this rule to the sciences of Judaism, we shall find that the following are the principles underlying its essence: A. The science of Judaism investigates the entire scope of Judaism; B. It develops Judaism according to its own terms and describes it methodically . . . C. It deals with the subject *per se* and for its own sake, not for any special interest or for a particular purpose. There is no prejudice in its inception nor any bias in regard to the results at its conclusion. Its aim is not to show the topic of its study in either a positive or a negative light from the standpoint of prevailing views, but rather simply to describe it as it really is. Science is an end in itself and in itself constitutes a vital need of the human spirit, and hence it does not make use of any benefit whatsoever that is external to it.[191]

This conception of the science of Judaism was not adopted by the circles of Galician maskilim; those engaged in historical research there also imposed certain rigid limits on their research and criticism, as we shall see, remaining within the bounds of didactic 'maskilic history'. We must now examine how the science of Judaism, mainly the product of German Jewish scholars, was absorbed by the maskilim of eastern Europe.

The gap in formal education between the historians in Germany, who were trained to engage in scientific study in universities and modern educational institutions, and the maskilim, most of whom were self-educated and had never studied outside traditional schools, sometimes made the latter feel inferior. Rapoport, for example, expressed dissatisfaction with the results of his research and hoped that Western scholars would be more successful in shedding light on certain matters still veiled in obscurity: 'and one should indeed expect this of the renowned maskilim, the new colleagues from Berlin who now publish a journal to spread knowledge among the Jewish people, for they apparently possess a great desire

---

[191] Wolf, 'Über den Begriff'.

and the intellectual capability to single out significant places and times relating to the history of our people'.[192] A letter by Krochmal contains a similar expression of self-abnegation and the feeling that the German scholars surpassed the maskilim in Jewish studies. He revealed that his greatest dream was to teach in Berlin, the city of wisdom: 'My dearest wish is to seize any opportunity to obtain an appointment, even one that is not permanent, to teach some portions of Jewish science.' Like Rapoport, Krochmal relied on the German scholars to resolve complex research issues: 'How fortunate that our colleagues the Jewish scholars in Germany have taken an interest in this matter, for we lack the necessary means to do so.'[193]

Other than the disparity in formal education, there would seem to have been no reason for the maskilim to feel inferior to their German colleagues. An examination of the literature they read shows that the maskilim in no sense lagged behind Western intellectuals and were quite well informed about all the works published in Germany during the first half of the nineteenth century. Rapoport, for example, received nearly every newly published book from his friend, a professor of history at Lvov University; Krochmal subscribed to the 1832 edition of Hegel's works and read the best of the German philosophers, including Kant, Herder, Schelling, and Fichte; and in *Kinat ha'emet* Mieses referred to a long and very impressive list of books on philosophy, studies in biblical criticism (De Wette, Eichhorn), books on the history of religion (Neander, Spitteler), encyclopaedias, and history books.[194] In nearly every historical study they wrote, the Galician maskilim used the works of Basnage, Pölitz, Heern, and the well-known popularizer Johannes von Müller.[195] But even though the shelves in both East and West contained the very same books, there was a difference in the way they were used. While the Jewish scholars in Germany absorbed the new research methods that had originated in German academies, the Galician maskilim regarded the historical literature in their possession as a store of historical knowledge rather than as a source of method, historical thinking, or a specific outline of history. Secondary popular historiography was more to their liking, and the style of von Müller, who wrote an enlightened didactic history, was eminently suited to the Haskalah.[196] Given this attitude, they would surely have rejected the criticism levelled by Hegel, who regarded von Müller as a negative example of a historian pursuing moral and political aims. Hegel asserted that the events of the past ought not to be con-

[192] Rapoport, 'Al devar yehudim ḥofshi'im', 77.

[193] Letteris, 'Toledot r. naḥman', 109; N. Krochmal, *Moreh nevukhei hazeman*, 456.

[194] On Rapoport, see M. N., 'Letoledot harav hagaon', *Hayahadut*, 1 (1885), 47; on Krochmal, see J. Klausner, *History of Modern Hebrew Literature*, ii. 207; Mieses, *Kinat ha'emet*, bibliography.

[195] Bick, 'Mikhtav 22', 79. Rapoport referred to Heern, *Handbuch der Geschichte*. On Heern, see Thompson, *A History of Historical Writing*, ii. 127–30.

[196] See, for example, a quotation from von Müller's universal history in Luzzatto's letter to Rapoport (21 May 1841), in Luzzatto, *Igerot shadal*, v. 738–9. On von Müller's book, *Vierundzwanzig Bücher allgemeiner Geschichten*, published from 1811 onwards, see Thompson, *A History of Historical Writing*, ii. 140–83; *Allgemeine Deutsche Biographie*, xxvi. 587–610.

sidered in the light of current events; nor should one try to derive moral lessons from them. In his view, didactic history was an inferior and anachronistic form of historical writing.[197] The maskilim, on the other hand, like the broad public of readers of German in Europe, continued to read von Müller, Pölitz, and their ilk omnivorously, combing history for examples and lessons.

Unlike their colleagues in Germany, the maskilim were selective in their exploration of German historical literature. Several factors dictated the special nature of the east European version of the Wissenschaft des Judentums: the maskilic writers of history had no professional academic training, remained within the bounds of maskilic history, wrote in Hebrew mainly for a scholarly Jewish public, and adopted a relatively moderate attitude towards the Jewish religion.

In practice, much of the Galician maskilim's writing was historical criticism, and they frequently made declarations affirming the right to engage in objective investigation for the purpose of attaining the truth. However, with the exception of Mieses, who argued for absolute freedom of enquiry, they were very sensitive to the permissible bounds of research.[198] Krochmal was particularly cautious and hesitant:

My heart trembles within me when I propose such new premisses, so totally opposed to all that prevails today among the people and the élite, and since there are now fewer true God-fearing men, there are a growing number of fanatics waiting in ambush along the road to see if any should utter a word that is the reverse of that to which they have been accustomed, or should reject their poor store of knowledge, and they will declare war on him.[199]

The maskilim in Galicia did not conceal their fear that they were liable to encounter the outright hostility of the Orthodox if they were to draw all the conclusions implicit in their research. Consequently, they were forced to resort to apologetics: to argue that hokhmat yisra'el sought not to challenge the tradition, but rather to enrich it and establish it more firmly. Krochmal exercised even greater caution, stating that the conclusions of his research were merely hypotheses: 'And I do not insist that all of my words, claims, and conclusions are clearly and irrefutably true.'[200]

Of all the Jewish intellectuals in Germany, the Galicians had the highest regard for the historian Marcus (Mordecai) Jost (1790–1860), and his book Geschichte der Israeliten, first published in 1820, was read widely in Galicia. The maskilim's attitude towards Jost can thus be examined in detail as a test case for the selective way in which they accepted the work of Wissenschaft des Judentums. On one hand, Jost enjoyed vast popularity, but on the other, his picture of the past and his positions on various issues were not consistent with the maskilic sense of the past. In Jost's books the maskilim found a source of reliable historical information;

[197] Cf. Hegel, The Philosophy of History, 1–6.
[199] N. Krochmal, Moreh nevukhei hazeman, 157.
[198] Mieses, 'Mikhtav 2', 129.
[200] Ibid. 149, 158.

they admired him as the greatest Jewish historian, corresponded with him, and measured their own achievements against his research studies.[201] An anecdote about Chajes told by Jacob Bodek reflects how studiously Jost's books were read in Galicia:

Once when I travelled with him to Brody, and we came at night to an inn in the city of Zloczow, I rested upon my bed, reading the eighth volume of a book on the chronicles of the Jews by the great and wise rabbi Mordecai Jost, which I had with me on my journey so that I might read it when the travellers stopped to feed the horses or for an overnight stay. And when Rabbi Chajes saw that book in my hand, he asked me about various interesting matters written about in this book and what I thought of them, and if I did not recall them at that moment, he said to me: But they are written for you in that book, in such and such a volume, on such and such a page, or in such and such a footnote, and he spoke to me of all the first seven volumes which I had read as if they lay open before him, just as the pages of the Babylonian and Jerusalem Talmud and the books of the *geonim* and the ancients were open before him.[202]

However, the maskilim did not always agree with Jost's historical judgement, criticizing him and proposing other modes of understanding. It was Luzzatto who levelled the severest criticism at Jost, even stooping to *ad hominem* arguments and totally repudiating his method of research.[203] Although Luzzatto, who taught in the rabbinic seminary in Padua, did not actually belong to the circle of Galician maskilim or take an active part in the maskilic struggle, his extensive correspondence with key figures of the Galician Haskalah earned him a special status as a fellow proponent of a moderate version of enlightenment.[204] For his part, Luzzatto tried to organize the Galician maskilim into a cohesive front to counter what he regarded as the objectionable tendencies of Wissenschaft des Judentums, as expressed in Jost's books, and was glad to find allies and colleagues in the study of Jewish history among them. The strongest tie was formed between Luzzatto and Rapoport; in his first letter Luzzatto praised Rapoport, 'for you have followed the path of critical investigation . . . you have approached it with integrity, your scrutiny of it is lucid, your enquiry into it is extremely profound, and the efforts you invest in it are blessed by the Almighty'.[205] In fact Luzzatto was attempting to create an alternative to the Wissenschaft des Judentums established by Jost and his fellows in the West, and he believed that Rapoport

[201] Rapoport, 'Al devar yehudim ḥofshi'im'; Flesch, *Ḥayei moshe*, introd.; Chajes, 'Imrei binah', 874; Perl, *Boḥen tsadik*, 89–91, trans. from Jost, *Geschichte der Israeliten*, vi. 111–20, 365.

[202] From the biography of Tsevi Hirsch Chajes in the unpaginated supplement added by J. Bodek to Triebesch, *Korot ha'itim* (Lemberg, 1851).

[203] On Luzzatto, see J. Klausner, *History of Modern Hebrew Literature*, ii. 47–127; Horwitz, 'Rationalistic and Anti-Rationalistic Motifs', 287–310; Margolies, *Samuel David Luzzatto*; Myers, *Re-Inventing the Jewish Past*, 26–8, 93–4.

[204] Krochmal's letter to Luzzatto, in Krochmal, *Collected Writings*, 425–6; and Luzzatto's letter to Rapoport (12 Oct. 1831), in id., *Igerot shadal*, i. 222.

[205] Luzzatto's letter to Rapoport (27 Aug. 1829), in id., *Igerot shadal*, i. 165–6.

would be prepared to join him in renouncing Jost, and in his lonely stand as an opponent of the Jewish scholars in Germany—a hope which did not bear fruit at first.

Despite his numerous contacts with contemporaneous maskilim, which earned him a key position in Haskalah circles and in Jewish intellectual life in Europe from the 1820s to the 1860s, Luzzatto was an exceptional figure. The title of 'scholar' or 'researcher' (ḥoker) suited him better than that of 'maskil', for, as he himself stated, his investigations were more in the nature of research for its own sake, devoid of both the didactic maskilic orientation and the ideological character of Wissenschaft des Judentums. 'My heart has told me', Luzzatto wrote, 'that there is but one truth, and it alone is worthy of our service, it alone deserves to be fought for, and it alone merits casting aside the joys of the world . . . and this inner call . . . is the life of my spirit and the breath of my soul.'[206] As part of his self-imposed asceticism, zeal for the truth, and avid and prolific research in linguistics, philology, and literature, Luzzatto conducted an intensive search for ancient books and manuscripts and made an important contribution to the Wissenschaft des Judentums. 'If Satan were to come to me', Luzzatto wrote to Zunz, 'and say "Give me a manuscript and I will print it on the printing press of Hell," I would kiss his hands and give him whatever he asked for.'[207] His ideological point of departure set clear boundaries defining the uniqueness and superiority of Judaism. For this purpose he drew a series of essential distinctions between Jewish culture ('Judaismus') and European culture ('Atticismus'), placing the two in absolute opposition—an approach which was a salient departure from the Haskalah. His historical and cultural distinctions were accompanied by a value system that distinguished between the good and the beautiful, between emotion and intellect, and between the authentically Jewish and the alien which deserved to be rejected, as well as a list of arguments against attitudes such as faith in moral progress, an idealistic view of the present, admiration of European culture, and denial of the authority of the ancients. 'The voice of Judaismus is opposed to the intellect', and '"Kultur" does not necessarily contribute to ethics and justice' are examples of Luzzatto's anti-rationalistic dicta.[208] In his view, a distinction had to be made between negative historical research with a 'Greek' orientation, of the sort taking shape among German Jews, and positive historical research which had a 'Jewish' orientation. In a letter to Rapoport, Luzzatto enunciated this view:

The Jewish wisdom in which some scholars of Germany of this generation are engaging will not last, since they themselves do not regard it as precious in itself, for in their eyes Goethe and Schiller are greater and more worthy of respect than all the prophets, tana'im, and amora'im; they also study the ancient past of Israel as others study the ancient past of

---

[206] Luzzatto, Ketavim, i. 16 (introd.).

[207] Luzzatto's letter to Zunz (15 Mar. 1852), in id., Igerot shadal, viii. 1130. See also Werses, 'Samuel David Luzzatto', 703–15.

[208] Luzzatto, 'Derekh erets o atikismus', 43, 69. See also Y. Shavit, Athens in Jerusalem, esp. ch. 6.

Egypt, Assyria, Babylon, and Persia: namely, for the love of science or the love of honour. They also have another aim in mind: to obtain favour and respect for Israel in the eyes of the gentiles . . . to hasten the coming of what they regard as the first redemption—the emancipation . . . however, the Jewish wisdom that will endure for eternity is that which is based on the faith, which enquires in order to understand the Torah and the Prophets as the words of the Almighty, and to understand the history of this unique nation, which consists of special events, and to understand throughout all ages the war of the divine spirit, which is [this people's] inheritance, against the spirit that enters into it from without, and how in each and every generation the divine side has overpowered the human.[209]

As part of his struggle against 'Atticism', Luzzatto attempted to tarnish the venerated images of Maimonides and Ibn Ezra, who, in his view, exemplified the pernicious penetration of alien elements into Judaism. He wished to supplant them with alternative ideal models, first and foremost Rashi and Judah Halevi, men who embodied authentic Jewish qualities, had enhanced Judaism, and were eminently worthy of admiration. Judah Halevi was Luzzatto's historical hero, whom he described as 'the delight of my soul, the friend of my heart . . . my being is bound up with his'.[210] To the Galician maskilim, any attacks on Maimonides' image were unacceptable, and when these first appeared in Kerem hemed, including the severe judgement 'Maimonides with all his philosophizing has caused us grievous troubles', they responded by attempting to contradict Luzzatto, who 'was assailing the great men of past generations with the sword', expressing perplexity regarding his motives. As far as they were concerned, Maimonides was still a maskilic hero, whose work had paved the way for young men joining the ranks of the maskilim and served as a propaganda and polemical weapon against opponents of the Haskalah.[211]

Luzzatto's criticism of Jost was part and parcel of his overall attitude towards Wissenschaft des Judentums. Luzzatto ordered a copy of Jost's Geschichte der Israeliten from Germany, planning to use it in the history classes he taught at Padua, but as soon as he began turning its pages, he realized that the book contained views he could not accept. He was shocked by the insult to the honour of great Jews, and by the adoption of the conclusions of De Wette and other biblical critics that the Bible was composed of various fragments rather than being the product of divine revelation. He warned against the dangers inherent in such a critical and destructive Jewish historiography, particularly in light of the fact

---

[209] Luzzatto's letter to Rapoport (5 June 1860), in id., Igerot shadal, ix. 1367; Luzzatto's letter to Steinschneider (1847), in id., Igerot shadal, viii. 1087.

[210] The quotation is from Luzzatto's letter to Gedaliah Brachar (1839), in id., Igerot shadal, iv. 593. See also Luzzatto, Mehkarei hayahadut, i. 159–90, 193–7; ii. 243; Luzzatto's letter to Rapoport (1833), in id., Igerot shadal, ii. 245–7; Luzzatto's letter to Rapoport (1848), id., Igerot shadal, vi. 760–1. On Luzzatto's criticism of Maimonides, see J. Klausner, A History of Modern Hebrew Literature, ii. 108–9; Rostovsky-Halpern, History of Hebrew Literature.

[211] N. Krochmal, 'Mikhtav lishemuel goldenberg', Kerem hemed, 4 (1839), 260–74; id., Kerem hemed, 5 (1841), 92–4; Chajes, 'Tiferet lemoshe', 432.

that Jost's books were gaining in popularity and circulating among 'cultured Jews' and young people.[212] Luzzatto did not spare Jost, 'the heretic scholar', harsh words of abuse: 'I hated and despised Jost, and as long as I live and I still have a pure heart within me, I shall go on hating him.'[213] Luzzatto classified his friends according to their attitude towards Jost, and did his utmost to convince others to share in his strong feelings, albeit without much success.[214] However, from 1839 onwards Luzzatto became more moderate, and at Jost's initiative, the two men began corresponding with one another.[215] Luzzatto overcame his personal hatred and even gained some respect for Jost, but continued to stress the disparity between his views and Jost's. His critical tone began to sound more pacific, with a touch of reconciliation and regret, although his criticism was still pungent:

And when, my dear scholars of Germany, will the Almighty open your eyes? And how long will you fail to see that in following the mob and allowing national pride to be extinguished, and the tongue of our forefathers to be forgotten by our offspring, and Atticism to gain in strength daily in our midst, and in permitting your brethren to entertain the false notion that perfection is nothing other than becoming like their neighbours and being important in their eyes, your hearts will not be uplifted with zeal for God, zeal for the truth and zeal for brotherly love, to teach them that the good is not visible but is what is felt in the chambers of the heart, and that the success of our nation does not depend on emancipation, but rather on the love of each man for his brother, and that we are bound by the ties of brotherhood like the members of one family. And herein lies our success.[216]

Of course Rapoport, like Luzzatto, was also far from accepting a vision of the future that predicted assimilation, the dissolution of national cohesion, and the abandonment of the Hebrew language. However, his attitude towards Jost was at first quite moderate. Rapoport greatly admired Jost because he respected him as a historian, and felt that he himself was mediocre in comparison; he was also pleased by the praise Jost accorded him. This caused Luzzatto grave disappointment, and Rapoport had to explain that he really did not concur with Jost's views on all matters, but still did not consider Luzzatto's harsh attack on him to be justified.[217] In his defence of Jost, he enlisted arguments in support of tolerance and the 'love of Israel'. He remonstrated with Luzzatto, asserting that in his rash and hot-tempered attitude towards Jost he was displaying intolerant arrogance, on one hand, and, on the other, was ignoring Jost's love of the Jewish people. The

[212] Luzzatto's letters to Rapoport 1830–1, in id., *Igerot shadal*, ii. 170–1, 176–7, 178–80, 187–8. See also Michael, *I. M. Jost*, 79–81; Barzilay, *Shlomo Yehuda Rapoport*, 106–15; Mahler, 'Tolerance and Freedom', 85–94.

[213] Luzzatto's letter to Rapoport (22 Oct. 1830), in id., *Igerot shadal*, ii. 176; Luzzatto's letter to Rapoport, ibid. 178.

[214] Luzzatto's letter to S. Goldenberg (28 June 1831), ibid. 190–1; Luzzatto's letter to Rapoport (11 Mar. 1831), ibid. 187–8: 'If he is your friend, I cannot possibly be your friend.'

[215] Luzzatto's letter to Jost (26 Mar. 1839), in id., *Igerot shadal*, iv. 600.

[216] Luzzatto's letter to Jost (24 Jan. 1840), in id., *Igerot shadal*, v. 660.

[217] Rapoport's letter to Luzzatto (1830), in Rapoport, *Igerot shir*, 13–15.

real enemy, he reminded Luzzatto, was the camp hostile to the Haskalah; that was where the battle should take place, not within the maskilic camp. The criticism levelled at Jost was likely to rebound like a boomerang, causing injury to the maskilim: 'Someone else, from one of these two extremes, the hasid at one end and Jost at the other, may say that he alone has tested everything and knows how to judge, and the former will call you by the very name you have called the latter'.[218]

Rapoport also saw far less danger in Jost's writings, since he knew there were relatively few men in Galicia capable of reading and understanding his books. His views, Rapoport believed, would not leave an imprint on the religious consciousness of the common people or of the scholars. If any danger did exist, it lay in the ideological fanaticism that could lead to a split within the nation, and Luzzatto's polemics would have the effect of inflaming these deplorable tendencies. As a matter of fact, Rapoport took exception to Luzzatto's views about the opposition between 'Atticism' and Judaism, and he continued to adhere to an optimistic maskilic approach, advocating openness to the best of European culture, in response to the Zeitgeist.[219]

Although Rapoport took Jost's side during the 1830s, he, like Krochmal, Luzzatto, and Chajes, had a very different conception of Jewish history from that of Jost and the other representatives of Wissenschaft des Judentums in Germany. Although Rapoport stated that whenever he approached the task of 'inquiring into such matters', he freed his mind of 'all prejudice and all anger that arise from religious zeal';[220] in fact he placed certain restrictions on himself, and as we have seen, also consciously exploited his research for maskilic purposes. He aspired to enhance the status of the Torah, to preserve the honour accorded the Jewish people by non-Jewish intellectuals, and to propose exemplary figures as models for emulation. This led him, like Luzzatto, to formulate an alternative concept of the Wissenschaft des Judentums.[221] In his letters to Zunz he emphasized the effectiveness of historical research in illuminating the thought and consciousness of the Jewish reader, but added the caveat that historical criticism must be constructive, not destructive; the scholar must take care to avoid undermining religion and causing a radical revolution with his sharp tools of criticism, and in particular he must avoid applying the critical method to the Bible.[222]

Rapoport warned that the scholar must accept the authority of the halakhah as

---

[218] Rapoport's letter to Luzzatto (1833), in Rapoport, *Igerot shir*, 14.

[219] Rapoport's letter to Luzzatto (1831), in Harkavy and Halberstam, *Zikaron larishonim*, vol. ii, pt. 1, 43–54.

[220] Rapoport's letter to Luzzatto, in Rapoport, *Igerot shir*, 53–8; Pitlik, 'S. L. Rapoport's Historical Method', 123–39.

[221] Rapoport's letter to Luzzatto, in Rapoport, *Igerot shir*, 234–6; Rapoport, 'El hakore', introd. to 'Toledot rabenu natan', 4. Cf. Schorsch, 'The Emergence of Historical Consciousness', 423–4.

[222] Rapoport's letter to Zunz (1833), *Allgemeine Zeitung des Judentums*, 236. See also Rapoport, *Erekh milin*, introd. 4.

well as that of the rabbis of his time and restrain his drive for enquiry, 'for if an intellectual angel should ever think of rising up into the heavens and flying in the face of riders in the chariot of the Mishnah and the Talmud, I would clip his wings and send him downward'.[223] But it was not only his inner faith that guided Rapoport in his research; the social situation also inhibited his inclination towards free enquiry. In a letter from Tarnopol written in 1838, he revealed his inner uncertainties and his fear that others would believe that his historical work followed the same lines as Jost's. A scholar, Rapoport felt, had to know which boundaries he must never cross, and he certainly ought not to publicize radical conclusions, for fear of hostile Orthodox reactions:

As you well know, all of my enquiries into the ancient past of Israel have only been made in order to know when and where events occurred, but not to know their causes. I shall speak of the history of the babe, from youth to old age, but not about his qualities before his birth. These, thank God, exist in profusion in the Bible, intelligently expounded upon, but they remain a secret with me, sealed among my treasures. And great is the distance from my heart to my tongue, from my tongue to my pen, and also from my poor pen to the printing press, 'because I stood in great fear of the multitude, and the contempt of families terrified me, so that I kept silent'.[224]

These words were written during a painful period for Rapoport when many in Tarnopol opposed his appointment as the district rabbi, and he obviously feared that the publication of his research on the biblical period would only add fuel to the flames. However, beyond his personal considerations, Rapoport sought to shape historical research along moderate lines. He strenuously attacked 'those who speak out with arrogance, whose number is growing from day to day, all of whose wisdom can be summed up as mockery of the true scholars'.[225] The degree of objectivity advocated by Western scholars—in Rapoport's view, out of a sense of inferiority in relation to the non-Jews—was leading them to disparage the great men of Jewry for no purpose. In their zeal for objectivity, they tended towards a degree of subjectivity, which had the opposite effect, so that by 'making so great an effort to appear disinterested, they end up by taking an interest [in the matter]'.[226] Although Rapoport mentioned no names at the time, years later he admitted he had been referring to Jost. In the early 1840s Rapoport lost his relative equanimity after Jost said some highly critical things about him in the course of a scholarly dispute between the two, about the period of Judah Hanasi's life and the identity of the Roman emperor Antoninus referred to in the Talmud. From then on the tables were turned: Luzzatto was reconciled with Jost, and Rapoport, no longer an admirer of the German model, became one of his harshest critics. Jost cast doubt on Rapoport's ability and reliability as a historian, claim-

---

[223] Rapoport's letter to Luzzatto (1830), in Rapoport, *Igerot shir*, 13–15.
[224] [Rapoport], 'Mikhtav 3', *Kerem ḥemed*, 3 (1838), 38–53.
[225] Rapoport, 'El hakore', introd. to 'Toledot rabenu natan', 4.
[226] Ibid. 5. Cf. 'Mikhtav 5', 150.

ing that, unlike modern historians, he did not know how to make proper use of non-Jewish sources but was confined within the bounds of the talmudic text like a traditional Torah scholar.[227] These claims, as well as the denigration of Rapoport as a 'Pole' who had insinuated himself into the territory of the scholars, where he did not belong, were also made by other scholars, even after he had left Galicia to take up his position as rabbi of Prague.[228]

Rapoport used these attacks on him to emphasize the boundaries between the German Wissenschaft des Judentums, represented by Jost, and his own preferred approach. Jost's greatest shortcoming, in his view, lay in the very flaw he had attributed to Rapoport—the fact that he had cut himself off from the Jewish sources:

If, as he would have it, I have not followed the paths of foreign fields in my studies, I have not been so harmed by that as I would have been had I wandered aimlessly in the paths of the Hebrew fields. And, just as I do, he knows that enquiry into the times and lives of the wise men of Jeshurun has emerged from the wellspring of Judah, and that is where it belongs.[229]

Not only did this approach of drawing exclusively upon foreign sources fail to promote historiography, it actually caused it to regress. Rapoport believed that Jost's sycophantic behaviour towards non-Jews and his attempts to appear disinterested were leading him to adopt a distinctly anti-Jewish viewpoint. He thus personified the great danger of historical criticism, whose barbs seriously injured the image of the Jewish people in the eyes of others.[230]

With Rapoport's blessing and encouragement, the elderly Shalom Hacohen made an attempt to translate the alternative science of Judaism into a language of historical writing that would compete with Jost's. The pioneering nature of his book *Kore hadorot*, the first history book written in Hebrew in modern times, has already been noted. Although it was closely modelled on Jost's work, it opposed Jost's ideas and is a good example of the selective absorption of Wissenschaft des Judentums by the maskilim. The book is really an adaptation, abridgement, and translation of Jost's work. Its structure is similar to that of Jost's *Geschichte der Israeliten*, and Hacohen admitted that he had 'followed a book of Jewish history written by a scholar, a member of our religion, in the German language, in nine volumes'.[231] However, in regard to historical judgement as opposed to facts, their ways parted and the maskil was unable to accept what he regarded as Jost's extremist positions:

In so far as his judgements in praising or disparaging the actions of this generation, or in seeking the causes of events and the like are concerned, his thoughts are not mine, nor are

[227] Jost, 'Megilat mordekhai', 10–14, 27–32, 41–6; Barzilay, *Shlomo Yehuda Rapoport*, 106–15.
[228] Jost had the support of M. M. Mohr, who was in favour of radical biblical criticism. See also anon., 'A Letter from a Polish Sage on the Critique', *Zion*, 1 (1841), 188–92.
[229] Rapoport, *Kerem ḥemed*, 7 (1843), 144–5 (editor's introd. of 1842).
[230] Ibid. 150–1.   [231] S. Hacohen, *Kore hadorot*, 4.

his views mine; for although we cannot accuse him of failing to show partiality for illustrious men, in this he greatly exaggerated, and ventured to speak out against the tradition of our Sages, who did not say the same. Hence, although I did copy from his writings, I made many changes in them as I saw fit, and added to them statements from the Talmud which do not contradict the statements of other writers of history.[232]

Hacohen adopted the bounds set by Rapoport, and painted a different picture of the past from that in Jost's book. For example, both men began their histories with the time of the Hasmonean Hyrcanus, but while Jost regarded the preceding period as an insignificant era of childhood, Hacohen perceived it as a time of 'sacred history' recorded in the Holy Scriptures, which relate absolute truth. Hacohen believed there was no room for Jost's brand of biblical criticism, nor could he accept the evidence of Josephus Flavius in his *Jewish Antiquities* unless it accorded with the words of the Bible. Jost's picture of the past continued the ideas of the radical Haskalah that had emerged in Germany in the 1790s: during the period of exile the Jews were a religious community which endured because of the pressures exerted by the surrounding societies; the history of the Jews merely recounted the fate of separate Jewish groupings; the halakhah served as a bulwark for the religion, but its development and ramification marked the negative course of the rabbinic stream, which placed restrictions on thought and enquiry; in the modern era the anti-rabbinic forces had embarked on a struggle, and in the end they would prevail and purify Judaism.[233] Hacohen, in contrast, preserving older maskilic concepts, foresaw a brighter Jewish future, marked by unity, national solidarity, relief from the burden of exile, and consensus among the factions about the true nature of the faith, in the spirit of the Torah. In his image of the past, he attempted to uncover signs that might point to that future, stressing the unity and continuity of history and extolling the awareness of collective uniqueness.[234] It is no wonder, then, that the first part of *Kore hadorot* was so well received by rabbis and maskilim, particularly in eastern Europe, where the book was printed.

The historical circumstances and the different views and aims of the Galician maskilim led to their development of a distinctive approach to the Jewish historical research taking shape in Germany. In the 1820s and 1830s they even began to develop an alternative science of Judaism, whose studies, written in Hebrew, were used for internal didactic purposes and remained faithful to the traditional sources. Conscious of the difference between the two divergent paths taken by the science of Judaism, the Galician maskilim even claimed a position of precedence

---

[232] Ibid. 6.

[233] Michael, *I. M. Jost*, 41–2, 69–76, 102; Dinur, *Historical Writings*, iv. 105–8, 'Israel in the Diaspora'.

[234] S. Hacohen, *Kore hadorot*, 6; introd. to vol ii. 19–20; vol. vii, ch. 2, p. 23. See the criticism (probably by Joshua Heschel Schorr), published as an anonymous letter from Galicia in *Israelitische Annalen*, 2 (1840), 240–1, 250.

for themselves. Their version of the development of scientific research into Judaism began with Rapoport and then moved to Germany, not the other way round, as had actually happened. As they would have it, 'Thanks to him, many scholars of Germany have again begun to peruse the books of the Talmud and the writings of the ancients, which they had previously abandoned.'[235] This debate about precedence, rooted in the ideological tension between the Jews of eastern and western Europe, continued into the latter half of the nineteenth century and the beginning of the twentieth.[236]

THE STRUGGLE FOR FREEDOM OF THOUGHT

In the shift that occurred in the 1830s and 1840s there was a palpable sense of pessimism among the Galician maskilim, who felt that an era had come to an end. The deaths of Perl and Krochmal, Rapoport's defeat in Tarnopol and his move to Prague, the dominance of the hasidim, the continuing internal rift, and the acculturation that they perceived as a 'pseudo-Haskalah' all fuelled their feeling that failure was destroying their circle.[237] This, however, was not a reflection of the decline of the Galician Haskalah but rather the result of two different processes: the replacement of one generation of maskilim by the next and the acceleration of modernization. Joshua Heschel Schorr (1818–95), a member of the new generation of maskilim, portrayed the socio-cultural map of Galician Jewry in 1838, describing the established camps of Orthodoxy, divided into Torah scholars and hasidim, and the *Aufklärer*, or 'enlightened'. In his view, only a tiny minority of the second group was actually worthy of the title; the rest were merely 'ultra-liberals' who denied tradition out of hand, or 'pseudo-maskilim', whose enlightenment was expressed solely in their behaviour and lifestyle. Schorr used marital patterns to illustrate the social dividing lines, since each group preferred to marry among its own: marriages between the families of hasidim and yeshiva students were rare; marriages between families of maskilim and talmudic scholars were unusual; and maskilic and hasidic families never intermarried.[238] Other descriptions of Galician society, such as those of Solomon Rubin (1823–1910), another maskil of the new generation, placed particular emphasis on the growth of the religiously indifferent merchant class, which included intemperate and unethical opportunists who nevertheless sought recognition and respect from the rabbis.[239]

---

[235] Supplements added by J. Bodek to Triebesch, *Korot ha'itim* (Lemberg, 1851).

[236] On this dispute, see Bernfeld, 'Dorshei reshumot', 203–4 n.

[237] For contemporary reactions, see Rapoport, 'Mikhtav 3', *Kerem ḥemed*, 3 (1838), 38–9; Rapoport, 'Mikhtav', *Kerem ḥemed*, 4 (1839), 46, 241–59; S. Hacohen, 'Ḥeshek shelomoh', 253–9; Rapoport, 'Mikhtav 3', *Kerem ḥemed*, 6 (1841), 41–9; Bloch, letter to the editors of *Yerushalayim*, 12; Bloch's letter to Bodek, 1841, in Bloch, *Shevilei olam*, vol. iii, appendices.

[238] Schorr's anonymous article 'Carakteristik', 283–4; his authorship was traced by E. Spicehandler, 'J. H. Schorr', 199–200.   [239] Rubin, *Uriel Acosta*, 3–6.

The Jewish population in Galicia increased from 250,000 in 1830 to 449,000 in 1875. In the large cities, such as Brody, Lvov, and Tarnopol, the growing class of merchants, clerks, and other professionals supported the Haskalah. An increasing number of Jews attended secondary school and university, more maskilic schools were established, and leadership was gradually transferred to men of the more modern classes, and even to modern rabbis. In 1840 it was decided to establish a synagogue in Lvov for the 'enlightened', modelled on those in Vienna and Prague. Abraham Cohen (1807–48) was invited to Lvov from Bohemia to serve as preacher, teacher of religion, and principal of a modern school, which he did until he was poisoned by his opponents, dying in 1848. The maskilim failed in their attempt to train a young rabbi, Dr Jacob Goldenthal, who was sent to Germany to be educated in order to return to the Brody rabbinate in full compliance with the law requiring that a rabbi have a general formal education.[240] In Tarnopol, Solomon Goldenberg (1807–46) investigated the possibility that Dr Hyman Jolowitch, who tended towards reform, might come from Germany to serve as a teacher of religion.[241] In any case, by 1851 the maskilim were pleased with the rabbis of the communities, taking pride in the fact that many of them were 'children of the spirit of the time that had begun to prevail in the land'.[242]

There was a discernible tendency among the young generation of maskilim, which included the children of Perl, Rapoport, and Krochmal, to migrate from Galicia to Vienna, Rome, Berlin, and Odessa. Many members of this generation had already received an academic education and did not have many employment opportunities. Like some merchants, several of them moved to cities outside Galicia, or remained in the places where they had studied. For example, when Goldenberg's son reached the age of 14, he consulted Zunz about his future. The boy had completed secondary school in Tarnopol, but Goldenberg was not satisfied with the calibre of the institution and even feared the influence of the Christians who taught there. His greatest fear, however, was that his son might ultimately follow in the wake of other young men of the new intelligentsia:

The fate of Jewish students in this land will be that a vast number will become doctors or will study the laws of the land and become advocates, and they will be pressured by the enemies of our nation without giving them the benefit of a fair trial. For then they will abandon their people and religion and will adhere to the God of the gentiles.[243]

---

[240] Gelber, 'The Haskalah Movement', 226–64, on Lvov; id., *The Jews of Brody*, 258–96; id., 'The Jews of Tarnopol', 95–103; Friedmann, *Die galizischen Juden*. See also Zinberg, *A History of Jewish Literature*, vi. 73–7, 347; Bader, *Medinah vehakhameiha*, 116.

[241] Goldenberg's letter to Zunz (1844), in Schorsch, 'The Production of a Classic', 203. In 1845 M. Steinschneider was put forward as a candidate for the rabbinate of the Tarnopol community: Gelber, 'The Jews of Tarnopol', 98.

[242] Supplement added by Bodek to Triebesch, *Korot ha'itim* (unpaginated). On Krochmal's family, see Rawidowicz, introd. to N. Krochmal, *Collected Writings*, 59–67.

[243] Goldenberg's letter to Zunz (1844), in Schorsch, 'The Production of a Classic'.

Ultimately Goldenberg decided to send his son to Berlin and place him under Zunz's supervision so that he would remain part of Jewish society and be instructed by teachers who walked 'the straight path'.

During this period, however, the maskilim continued their activities as Hebrew writers seeking to perpetuate maskilic ideology and principles, rejecting hasidism, which continued to grow stronger, as well as 'pseudo-maskilim'. After *Kerem hemed* was closed down, attempts were made to create a new forum for the Haskalah. In 1840 Schorr, Erter, and Luzzatto planned an alternative journal, which, however, never materialized. In 1845, after discussions between several young maskilim, including Letteris, Mohr, and Schorr, the journal *Yerushalayim* (Jerusalem) was published, though only for three months.[244] It was intended as a continuation of *Hatsefirah* and *Bikurei ha'itim*, and most of those involved in it came from the ranks of the Galician maskilim: Jacob Bodek (1819–55). Mohr, Bloch, Nahman Fishman (1809–78), Moses Blumenfeld, Schorr, and Abraham Goldberg. After *Yerushalayim* was closed down, the maskilim made use of the platform provided by the Austrian journal *Kokhavei yitshak* (Stars of Isaac), edited by Mendel Stern (1811–73), and also contributed to the Jewish journals published by Jost and Philippson in Germany.[245] A Galician journal was established once again during the 1850s: this was *Meged yerahim* (Blessing of the Months), edited by Joseph Cohen Tsedek (1827–1903), with contributions from young Galician maskilim, although it was only published between 1855 and 1857.[246]

Schorr was the most prominent of the Galician maskilim. He was a radical maskil and owned his own personal, almost exclusive forum, *Hehaluts* (The Pioneer), founded in 1852. Born in 1818 into the wealthy and well-connected upper class of Jewish society in Brody, he established many contacts with maskilim, most notably with Luzzatto. However, he burned all his bridges, levelling his iconoclastic tendencies on the moderate maskilim. In *Hehaluts* he lashed out at Orthodoxy, publicized the Wissenschaft des Judentums, engaged in polemics with maskilic opponents, and championed religious reform—attitudes that only a few contemporary Galicians were prepared to share.[247]

The maskilim viewed the events of 1848 as a turning-point that aroused expectations of full emancipation, even after it became clear that there was still a long road ahead:

And if the children of Israel in Galicia attain only a small part of this heritage of liberty, for the sunlight of liberty has not shone upon them as it has upon their brothers in the lands

[244] Luzzatto, *Igerot shadal*, v. 675; Letteris, *Mikhtavei ivrit*, 192; Gilboa, *Hebrew Periodicals*, 84–5.
[245] On *Kokhavei yitshak*, see J. Klausner, *History of Modern Hebrew Literature*, ii. 40; Gilboa, *Hebrew Periodicals*, 89–91.
[246] On *Meged yerahim*, see Gilboa, *Hebrew Periodicals*, 110–11. In the mid-1860s, with the growing political tension in Galician Jewry, a more stable periodical was founded by Baruch Werber, called *Ivri anokhi*.
[247] On Schorr and *Hehaluts*, see J. Klausner, *History of Modern Hebrew Literature*, iv. 58–77; Spicehandler, 'J. H. Schorr', 181–422.

of Austria, our hope is strong that the emperor will soon bestow his mercy upon the Jews of Galicia . . . and that the light of emancipation will shine upon all the children of Israel, wherever they may dwell.[248]

From 1848 onwards the maskilim strengthened their foothold in community institutions and Jews became increasingly aware of the need to adopt modern patterns of political activity. During the 1860s this activity became party-oriented in all respects, which further aggravated the polarization between Orthodoxy and modern elements such as merchants, professionals, and maskilim.[249]

While many changes were taking place in urban centres in the 1840s and 1850s, the maskilim still had to contend with the typical maskilic situation in the small rural communities of Galicia. They had to grapple with a hostile society (hasidic, for the most part) and maintain belief in their ability to attract young people to their ranks. From the point of view of the maskilim in the outlying areas, Galicia was still a cultural desert in the 1850s, and the prospects for the spread of the Haskalah were dim. Solomon Rubin, a native of Dolina who was excommunicated by the hasidim of the Zurawno community, expressed this in dire terms: 'Our land, Galicia, is still appalling and horrible, battered and held captive in the stinking sewers, in the darkest depths of the world. The mighty men of valour mourn, walking tortuous paths covered with thorns and barbs.'[250]

Rubin's early experiences influenced his development as a maskil. He saw his mission as a struggle against superstition, hasidism—the source of all sin—hypocritical rabbis, and those who would deny freedom of thought. Two other maskilim had similar experiences: Zelig Mondschein of Bolechow, who was elected a community official and attempted to reform the community's organization from a position of strength within the establishment, and Jehiel Meler (1822–93) of Stanislawow, where the 'leprosy of hasidism' still flourished, who, as a maskil, felt unbearably isolated.[251] Only during the shift of the 1850s and 1860s did the maskilim admit that signs of positive change were visible in the outlying areas. Schorr thought that in the small towns too the authority of the rabbi had declined: 'His voice is barely heard, his power is weakened and depleted.'[252] However, the maskilim continued to see themselves as martyrs, destined to travel an

---

[248] References to the 1848 pogroms appear in Morpurgo, 'Korot hazeman', 35; Jacob Topover of Brody, 'Kol haderor', 64–7; Goldshtof, *Korot ha'olam*, ii. 150–2; Chajes, 'Minḥat kana'ut', 975–6. Cf. Gelber, *The Jews of Brody*, 390; Baron, 'Samuel David Luzzatto', 40–63.

[249] See Gelber, *The Jews of Brody*, 173–219; id., 'The Haskalah Movement', 215–23; id., 'The Jews of Tarnopol', 46–95; Friedmann, *Die galizischen Juden*, 52–68.

[250] Rubin, *Uriel Acosta*, 9. See also Rubin, 'Mikhtav mishelomoh rubin', 103–307; Schorr, 'Odot maskilim', 67–8.

[251] Mondschein, letter to Letteris (1850s), *Imrei yosher*, 17–41; id., 'Mishpat emet', 27–36; Maller, 'El ir moladeti', 34–7; anon., Toledot heḥakham shimon blokh', *Kokhavei yitshak*, 7 (1846), 40–5. See also Hendel, 'Maskilim and Haskalah', 435; Gelber, 'The Jews in Stanislav', 27–37. Several anti-hasidic satires appeared in *Kokhavei yitshak* in the 1840s and 1850s. Abraham Goldberg also belonged to this group; Teleks, 'Abraham Goldberg', 43–4; Zohar, *Olelot mibatsir*, 113–45.

[252] Schorr, 'Odot maskilim', 68.

arduous road, to act courageously, and to confront their enemies with unwavering faith in their world-view.[253]

During the 1840s and 1850s the maskilic awareness of the past also reflected these trends of continuity and change. The historical past continued to play an educational role as a reservoir of vital knowledge and exemplary models. Historical research developed on an even higher plane, since several of the maskilim had acquired a university education. Studies by Rubin, who received a doctorate from the University of Göttingen, and by the self-educated Schorr, who investigated Babylonian and Persian influences on Judaism, illustrate this trend. Working within a social context still fraught with the hasidic 'menace', the maskilim continued to view history as the arena of conflict between reason and folly, mining it for analogies of the struggle for liberty, tolerance, and freedom of thought against conservative forces and religious fanatics of all kinds.[254] Having interpreted the events of 1848 as a historical turning-point, maskilim such as Erter and Schorr concluded that the bulk of their efforts from that point onwards should be focused on the struggle against rabbis and on demands for leniency and religious reform. It was this historical perspective that induced Galicians to join the central European stream that called for religious reform, in opposition to moderate maskilim, such as Rapoport and Chajes, who sought to create a picture of the past that would justify their objections to religious reform.

Hebrew readers became more familiar with universal history during this period, as books translated and adapted from secondary German historiography were added to their bookshelves. In Lvov, Jacob Bodek reissued Abraham Triebesch's chronicle *Korot ha'itim* with an update of recent history: the Napoleonic Wars, the history of the Habsburg empire during the first half of the nineteenth century, and the revolutions of 1848.[255] His brother-in-law Abraham Mohr of Lvov was a prominent popularizer of historical and geographical works intended for readers who, though unable to read foreign literature, were nonetheless very interested in reading detailed accounts of historical heroes and their dramatic exploits. In 1855 Mohr published *Dagul merevavah* (One in a Thousand), the most detailed account up to that time of the history of Napoleon, written in praise of him, with the traditional reader in mind: 'He is the lofty, exalted man that God appointed to fill the universe with the glory of his heroism and to alter the picture of Europe.'[256] In addition, Mohr published a history of Napoleon III (*Hut hameshulash* (A Triple Thread), 1853), the history of Field Marshal Radetsky (*Gibor milḥamah* (A War Hero), 1856), and a new edition of Bloch's *Shevilei olam*, which

---

[253] Nahman Fishmann's letter to Feivel Goldshtof in Goldshtof, *Korot ha'olam*, vol. ii: 'It is not only your fate, my dear friend! For it is the lot of every maskil, of every seeker of wisdom who follows the path of reason to pluck in the Garden of Eden some of the fruits of knowledge.' This was written following the burning of Goldshtof's books by hasidim.

[254] A. Goldberg, *Masa tsafon*, 13–14, 15–16, 27–30; Mondschein, 'Gemar ḥasid', in id., *Imrei yosher*, 48–9; Maller, 'Yedid hanetraliyut', 58–74.   [255] Bodek, suppl. to Triebesch, *Korot ha'itim*.

[256] Mohr, *Kolombus*; id., *Dagul merevavah* (quotation from the introd., 'Magid mibereishit').

contained an updated section and copious geographical and historical information about the world. It also included a summary of the history of the Jews in different lands.[257]

In 1858 and 1860 Feivel Goldshtof of Krakow published the first two parts of his work *Korot ha'olam* (History of the World) in Vienna and Lvov. This was a lucid and detailed universal history running 'from the earliest days of the world up to the present'.[258] *Korot ha'olam* was a translation and adaptation of one of the most widely distributed books of this type of popular universal history in the nineteenth century, written by Gottfried Gabriel Bredow of Halle University. First published in 1803, Bredow's book was reprinted dozens of times in various translations and revisions, and was also used as a textbook.[259] Another book that was of great assistance to Goldshtof was *Allgemeine Weltgeschichte für alle Stände*, by Carl von Rotteck, a statesman and historian from Freiburg; the work appeared in 1812–27 and was later reissued thirteen times.[260] Bredow and von Rotteck were affiliated with the same historiographic stream, whose members included Pölitz and von Müller. These writers, whose books were addressed to the enlightened reader, continued to record didactic history that endorsed liberal and patriotic values. Von Rotteck, for example, was one of the prophets of a liberal Europe in the post-Napoleonic era, and, since he was a 'son of the Enlightenment', the maskilim felt justified in transmitting his message to the Hebrew reader.[261]

Goldshtof's translation deviated very little from the original source, adopting Bredow's periodization and identifying with the attitude that history was 'human experience' which served as a never-ending source of 'knowledge and common sense' in matters where reason alone was insufficient. He even went so far as to provide an extensive account of the Reformation, which, in German Protestant historiography, was the cornerstone of the transition to the modern age. Goldshtof's universal history, following the example of his sources, consisted of three major elements: the actions of 'many renowned people'; 'momentous events connected with the rise and fall of powerful kingdoms'; and the development of human civilization through the taming of the wilderness, technological inventions, and the settlement of towns and cities. The picture of the past depicted in his book was almost identical to that of the eighteenth century: a breathtaking narrative at the heart of which is man, who develops his abilities, attains momentous achievements, and moves ever forwards. The Middle Ages was a time of darkness and ignorance, while the fifteenth and sixteenth centuries represented the shift to the modern age, a new dawn. This shift was symbolized by 'two visions',

[257] Mohr, *Ḥut hameshulash*; id., *Gibor milḥamah*; id., in Bloch, *Shevilei olam*, vol. iii.
[258] Goldshtof, *Korot ha'olam*. On Goldshtof, see Busak, 'Jews of Krakow', 101–2; Bader, *Medinah vehakhameiha*, 61.
[259] Bredow, *Umständlichere Erzählung*; on Bredow, see *Allgemeine Deutsche Biographie*, iii. 282–3.
[260] On Rotteck and his book *Allgemeine Weltgeschichte für alle Stände* (1812), see *Allgemeine Deutsche Biographie*, xxix. 385–9.   [261] Gooch, *History and Historians*, 98–102.

'the discovery of America, and the termination of papist rule brought about by the Reformation', and by the two people responsible for them, Columbus and Luther. 'Who would have believed that a man of the people could cast off the Pope's influence in so many countries? But such was he! Read the history, such was he! . . . Luther, who, with only his staff and mantle, left the monastery and found the courage to smash the sceptre of the ruling priests.'[262]

It would seem, however, that Goldshtof was rash in presenting Luther to the Jewish reader as an admirable historical figure. The facts that many Jews from Galicia subscribed to the first part and that it also received approbations from the rabbis of Krakow did not prevent attacks on the author and his book. He was only able to finish writing it in Lvov, with the encouragement of the maskilim there. It apparently fell into the hands of some hasidim, who complained, 'Behold, this Jew has brought us a book in which he also speaks of matters relating to a faith which is not ours.' In one *kloyz* (house of study) his book was burned because of the passages dealing with the history of Christianity, and Goldshtof himself told of Jews cursing him as he walked through the streets. Once again the maskil was compelled to resort to apologetics to in order to justify the fact that he was writing history, to anchor this writing in legitimate traditional sources, and to defend the importance of a knowledge of general history. In Goldshtof's view the schism in Christianity, for example, could teach readers about the danger of an ideological rift, in the light of the religious fanaticism that arose with the Reformation, the Thirty Years War, and the massacre of St Bartholomew's Day. Nor was the historian entitled to disregard those chapters of history that did not accord with his views or those of his readers, but he must give a faithful and unbiased depiction of all events.[263] The case of *Korot ha'olam* shows that, in the 1850s and 1860s in Galicia, history had not lost its militant function as one of the tools for disseminating the Haskalah and its values.

Through universal history and its heroes the maskilim promulgated the modern ethos, centring on man as creator of progress, despite all the obstacles placed in his way by reactionary forces. An example of how the modern ethos was used in the struggle for freedom of thought and opinion can be found in the work of two maskilim, Solomon Rubin and Meir Letteris. These two introduced two heroes who had previously played only minor roles on the stage of maskilic history: Uriel da Costa and Baruch Spinoza. Within a short time these two figures became an integral part of the useful past for those maskilim who completely identified with their historical fate. Solomon Rubin translated Karl Gutzkow's play *Uriel da Costa* in 1854, while he was in Galatz in Romania, where he had fled from

---

[262] Goldshtof, *Korot ha'olam*, ii. 10. On the hero, see ibid. 9. Goldshtof also published a poem about Napoleon in exile: 'Napoleon al i hasela', 55–7.

[263] On Goldshtof's opponents and his attempts at apologetics, see Goldshtof, *Korot ha'olam*, ii, introd.; id., 'Hatelunot al sifri *korot ha'olam*', 31–2; id., *Leket ma'amarim*, 13 ff. See also Sobel, *Sefer dorot olamim*, introd.

Galicia after being excommunicated by the hasidim.[264] Gutzkow was the quintessential representative of the Young Germany movement, which advocated personal freedom, preference for the present, anti-idealism, and anticlericalism, and in his play Rubin found a literary and intellectual response to his situation as a persecuted, enlightened Jew. In line with the methods of 'maskilic history', Rubin chronologically transposed da Costa from seventeenth-century Amsterdam to both ahistorical time, making his hero a universal example of 'the war between blind faith and pure ideas', and to the mid-nineteenth century in Galicia. Rubin transformed da Costa into a radical, sceptical, anticlericalist maskil fighting to defend his views:

> Uriel: the standard-bearer of the young, enlightened heroes among our people, searching into the certainties of faith, adapting and assembling the thoughts of the sages of other nations to gain a greater understanding of the Torah and the Talmud; finding it hard to believe and easy to doubt, he will enquire into and evaluate each and every tradition down to its very foundation. He is a painful thorn in the side of the rabbis, who are angered for fear of losing their position and their power, for only in darkness and in the ignorance of the people can they grow stronger, standing like the cedars of Lebanon among the common forests of the masses . . . any man who holds freedom of thought dear to his heart will take umbrage at the blindness with which they have struck the masses.[265]

Rubin expected that da Costa's life story would be read in the light of current events, revealing the true face of contemporary society to the Hebrew reader. Rubin built a model like those of Mieses or Rapoport, who had constructed a Jewish picture of the past that expressed the struggle between the deviant stream (hasidism) and the legitimate stream, and had recruited examples from other periods to this struggle. However, Rubin's model contained a series of analogous conflicts between a religious establishment and an enlightened individual seeking freedom of thought: the prophet Isaiah fell victim to King Manasseh; Jeremiah to the priest Pashhur; Maimonides was attacked and banned by 'obscurantist' rabbis; the medieval philosopher Jedidiah ben Abraham Bedersi (c.1270–1340) was attacked by opponents of philosophy; and Moses Mendelssohn was the target of a barrage of hatred, curses, and bans from the 'hypocritical rabbis'. Thus, the history of the Jewish people provided a long list of 'martyrs' on the altar of enlightenment, who fell into the hands of the 'obscurantists'. Uriel da Costa became just one more link in this chain.

   In Rubin's opinion, the rabbis' misuse of excommunication led to internal wars in Jewish society and contributed to an unusual martyrology. The annals of many other nations were replete with victims of war, who fell at the hands of leaders such as the Roman emperors, Muhammad, and the popes. In Jewish history, however, there were many 'victims of the spirit', who had fallen under the ban of

---

[264] Rubin, *Uriel Acosta*, introd. in German; see also D. Kaufmann, 'Hebrew and Yiddish Drama', 60–1; J. Klausner, *History of Modern Hebrew Literature*, vi. 305–8.

[265] Rubin, *Uriel Acosta*, i, 4–5.

excommunication: 'Your executioner is not a mighty soldier clad in armour and helmet or an archer in the vanguard', Rubin wrote, 'but rather a stupid and ignorant old judge, blowing a crooked *shofar*, in the temple of God, in the synagogue.'[266]

Other Galician maskilim joined Rubin and accepted the analogy he drew between da Costa and the Galician maskil.[267] Schorr, for example, used this new image in describing the victory of the maskilim who succeeded in overcoming Rabbi Orenstein's ban in Lvov in 1816. Schorr stressed, 'They no longer turned their backs to the assailants and their cheeks to the attackers, as in the days of Uriel da Costa.' This time it was not a maskil who recanted and regretted his action, but the rabbi, which in Schorr's view presaged a reversal of the relative strengths of the two camps in the nineteenth century, in comparison to the seventeenth.[268]

'The History of the Wise Scholar Baruch Spinoza, may his Memory be Blessed', by Letteris, published in *Bikurei ha'itim haḥadashim* in 1845, completely exonerated the excommunicated philosopher and identified him as a 'maskil', thus opening a polemic that continued for nearly twenty years. The maskilim were already familiar with Spinoza and his philosophy.[269] To mark the bicentenary of his birth, a biographical sketch by Ludwig Philippson (1811–89) had appeared in *Sulamith* in 1832. In 1837 Berthold Auerbach wrote a play about Spinoza and translated his writings into German, and Isadore Kampf translated his *Tractatus Theologico-Politicus* for *Literaturblatt des Orients*.[270] Just as the maskilim had used Uriel da Costa, identifying him with the figure of the persecuted maskil, they employed Spinoza for the same purpose, displaying more interest in his biography than in his philosophy. Letteris added Spinoza to the pantheon of the Haskalah, thus clearing him of the charge of heresy. His Spinoza was an illustrious scholar among the sages of Israel, who diligently fostered the spirit of enquiry, attained great achievements despite all who conspired against him, and through his own efforts aspired to free himself of the oppressive community education and institutions. There was nothing heretical in his views, nor was there a total breach with the words of the sages. As a 'maskil', Spinoza had encouraged the trend of productiveness ('he learned the art of grinding and polishing lenses . . . that he might earn his livelihood by working at this trade without compromising his principles') and he suffered the same fate as other enlightened men throughout the generations: 'for this is the case with human beings throughout history, that all who hate wisdom and abandon its pleasing paths, and choose to walk in dark-

[266] Rubin, *Uriel Acosta*, 7–12.

[267] For another image of da Costa, see Bodek, 'Toledot uriel da kosta', 26–9.

[268] Schorr, 'Masa rabanim', 56.

[269] Letteris, 'Toledot heḥakham haḥoker barukh di spinoza', 27–33. On the polemic, see Lahover, *Between Old and New*, 109–22; Sokolow, *Baruch Spinoza*, 86–99; J. Klausner, *History of Modern Hebrew Literature*, ii. 104–7; Schweid, *Jewish Thought*, 349–55; Dorman, *The Spinoza Dispute*, 96–152. A favourable attitude towards Spinoza appears as early as 1828, in Mieses, *Kinat ha'emet*, 20.

[270] Philippson, 'Baruch Spinosa', 336–7; Kampf, 'Spinosas *Theologisch-Politischer Tractat*', 524–31.

ness, with great animosity cruelly persecute every enlightened man who seeks out God with broad-mindedness and reason.'[271] Spinoza confronted all these fanatics and sanctimonious men and demanded the right to 'be free of his oppressors so he might seek wisdom and knowledge in peace'.[272]

Senior Sachs (1815–92), whose life and education combined east European Haskalah and German Jewish scholarship, joined the pro-Spinozists, but placed greater emphasis on Spinoza's philosophy. He asserted that the philosopher's pantheism incorporated an authentically Jewish philosophical vein.[273] Abraham Krochmal, Nahman Krochmal's son, was also attracted by Spinoza's philosophy. He regarded himself as a 'disciple of Rabbi Immanuel Kant and Rabbi Baruch de Spinoza', and also tried his hand at an apologetic approach to Spinoza's method.[274] In 1857 Solomon Rubin published his *Moreh nevukhim hehadash* (New Guide of the Perplexed), which included Hebrew translations of some of Spinoza's writings and an additional biography.[275] The book's title indicates that, in Rubin's opinion, Spinoza deserved to be thought of as the modern Maimonides. Like Krochmal, Rubin aligned himself with the camp of 'lovers of Spinoza' and was pleased by the positive reversal in the attitude towards him that had emerged in recent years. To his mind, Spinoza's biography was one more example, nearly identical to that of da Costa, of a great personality victimized by religious fanatics. Rubin found analogies for Spinoza in Seneca, Herodotus, Cicero, Dante, Colombus, Gutenberg, Copernicus, and Galileo, and he denounced the 'fire of religion', that bloodthirsty monster 'that imbibes the blood of men and eats away their flesh, burning with the flame of the Holy Divinity like shining amber'.[276] In his opinion, religious fanaticism had never been absent from Jewish history, and if reward and punishment existed in history, then the Jews had been punished for their deeds, according to the dictum 'an eye for an eye':

The children of Abraham exiled the children of Ishmael, and they will avenge themselves on them at the end of days. The children of Israel slew the idolatrous Canaanites with the sword of religion, and the latter also returned and killed the offspring of Israel; they are the Christians in the kingdoms of Rome; and the Christians thereafter persecuted their Jewish brethren, while they were being ruthlessly persecuted by the Ishmaelite.[277]

Unlike Letteris's Spinoza, Rubin's was not a legitimate bearer of Jewish tradition but a religious revolutionary relying solely on his intelligence. Spinoza was

---

[271] Letteris, 'Toledot hehakham hahoker barukh di spinoza', 27–9. [272] Ibid. 31.

[273] Sachs, 'Kol kore', 213–20; Lahover, *Between Old and New*, 119–21, 'Spinoza in Haskalah Literature'; J. Klausner, *History of Modern Hebrew Literature*, ii. 143–7; Dorman, *The Spinoza Dispute*, 146–52.

[274] A. Krochmal, *Iyun tefilah*, 70, 164. See also J. Klausner, *History of Modern Hebrew Literature*, iv. 93. Krochmal's dialogue 'Even haroshah' is an interpretative apologia on pantheistic philosophy. Smolenskin published this article in *Hashahar*, 2 (1871), special suppl.

[275] Rubin, *Moreh nevukhim hehadash*. [276] Ibid. 1–10. [277] Ibid. 26–7.

an example of Kantian man, proclaiming his own full freedom and autonomy. In the light of Spinoza's teachings, Rubin suggested to the 'young maskilim of our people' that they introduce revolutionary changes in the ideological foundation of their education. Hitherto they had studied the 'scholarly books of the sages of Spain and the Arab lands, whose brows were wrinkled with age; the pages of these books on natural sciences and astronomy are as reliable as a broken reed in the hands of a shaky old man'. In his view, students ought to forsake Maimonides and obsolete medieval philosophy. The alternative 'guide of the perplexed' must be Spinoza: 'Young Jewish men who have only now left the house of talmudic studies, their hearts still yearning for wisdom, their minds thirsting to imbibe the truths of philosophy . . . should from the outset place their trust in this new guide . . . and thus he will lead them to the gates of the shrine of the new philosophy.'[278] Rubin's comparison of Spinoza and Maimonides revealed several similarities between the two: they were both philosophers sent by the Almighty to illuminate the minds of the men of their generation, they were nonconformist, wrote in foreign languages, were persecuted and banned, and both were towering figures in history: 'The Torah of Moses [Maimonides] was a curtain dividing a thousand years of darkness before him from a thousand years of light after him; but the lamp of Spinoza sent forth rays of brightness that separate two thousand years before him and many generations after him.'[279] However, the differences between them were more numerous and tilted the scale in favour of Spinoza: his philosophy was independent and original, while that of Maimonides was based on Muslim and Spanish wisdom. Spinoza was a totally rationalistic philosopher, while Maimonides incorporated some non-rationalistic elements in his philosophy. Above all, Spinoza was an unmitigated maskil, who disdained the opinions of the masses and fought uncompromisingly for the sake of truth, while Maimonides hesitated, vacillated, and attempted to placate the rabbinical establishment. Rubin called for an innovative, radical, and unaccommodating Haskalah, so for him Spinoza was the ideal model, rather than a 'moderate maskil', like Maimonides: 'let us believe in the Almighty and Barukh His servant, rather than in Aristotle and in Moses [Maimonides] his disciple'.[280]

However, the moderate maskilim could not bear the idea of Spinoza as a major historical hero. Reggio had already noted on the margins of Letteris's article that it was impossible to conceal the fact of Spinoza's heresy. He consequently warned the reader against words that would 'destroy the foundations of his faith and darken the light of religion'. In the mid-1840s Luzzatto turned his struggle against Spinozist trends into a war in defence of the values he cherished, which now seemed to him to be seriously threatened.[281] The excommunicated philosopher's advocacy of rationalism and pure intellectualism and his denial of God's

---

[278] Rubin, *Moreh nevukhim hehadash*, 13.   [279] Ibid. 14.   [280] Ibid. 15–17.

[281] Reggio, 'Haḥoker barukh di spinoza', 31 n. Luzzatto's main arguments against Spinoza are summed up in his book *Meḥkarei hayahadut*, i. 198–222.

existence meant that he had negated the basic principles of Jewish faith as Luz-zatto understood them. Luzzatto was opposed to any attempts to depict Spinoza as a faithful Jew who had distanced himself from religious ritual only because of the pressures brought to bear by his persecutors. He emphasized that 'this philosopher, who was of the seed of Israel, estranged himself from his people, and did not live with them or die among them'.[282] The translation of Spinoza's writ-ings into Hebrew, undertaken by Rubin, angered Luzzatto even more and led him to emphasize the disparities between Spinoza's teachings and Judaism. Luzzatto once again drew a dichotomy between 'Judaismus' and 'Atticismus', presenting Spinoza as the consummate representative of the latter, who had abandoned the straight path of Judaism. Luzzatto defined the supporters of Spinoza, Rubin first and foremost among them, as 'pseudo-maskilim' who belonged to the radical Voltairean rationalistic branch of the Enlightenment.[283] The issue of Spinoza became the criterion by which he classified other maskilim as either colleagues or adversaries. Luzzatto did not view his struggle as a mere intellectual exercise, but revealed a profound emotional involvement: 'This man is despicable in my eyes', he wrote, and the fact that Rapoport, for example, did not take up arms against Letteris, the author of Spinoza's biography, or break off relations with him, infuriated him: 'If a man like you does not rise up against such an abomina-tion, and if a man who dearly loves you praises and lauds Spinoza, while you stand by silently, can there be any hope for Israel?'[284] 'As long as I have a heart in my breast, I shall persist in my controversy with the lovers of Spinoza', Luzzatto declared in 1862, and he behaved like a witch-hunter, suspecting that every maskil with whom he spoke had somehow been contaminated by Spinozan heresy.[285] Things went so far that Luzzatto even suspected there might be a conspiracy, based in Bolechow, where Rubin resided, plotting some sort of Spinozan revolu-tion:

I am not unaware of a conspiracy of evil men attempting to spread the views of Spinoza throughout Jewry. The spider sits in Bolechow spinning its webs and expanding its fortress in order to ensnare souls, and it sends its tracts to the sages of this generation, inciting them to join it, to pierce the eyes of fools, and to aggrandize the man of Amsterdam in their opinions.[286]

---

[282] Luzzatto, Meḥkarei hayahudut, i. 200.

[283] Ibid. 204–7, 212–17. Rubin replied to Luzzatto in his Teshuvah nitsaḥat.

[284] Luzzatto's letter to Sachs (22 Apr. 1853), in id., Igerot shadal, viii. 1197; Luzzatto's letter to Rapoport (22 July 1845), ibid., vi. 953. See also praises in Luzzatto's letter (23 June 1854), ibid., viii. 1241. For the threat by M. Stern, S. Sachs, and N. Keller that they would not take any part in Kokhvei yitshak if any words praising Spinoza were printed in it, see Luzzatto, Igerot shadal, ix. 1359–60, 1409.

[285] Luzzatto's letter to Werber, in id., Igerot shadal. ix. 1399; Luzzatto's letter to Tsevi Hirsch Bodek (1863), ibid. 1408.   [286] Luzzatto's letter to Mordecai Dushak (1863), ibid. 1406.

ICONOCLASM:
ATTITUDES TO RELIGIOUS REFORM

The religious reform movement, perhaps more than any other ideological stream in nineteenth-century Jewry, was attended by a strong historical awareness, especially in its use of history to justify its view of religion as open to change in response to contemporary conditions, which underpinned its ideological justification.[287] As is well known, this religious trend became a major factor in central and western European Judaism during the 1840s. In eastern Europe, however, it hardly gained a foothold, appearing only in a moderate form, manifested in the establishment of reformed synagogues based on the Viennese model. The aesthetic changes made in the synagogues of Tarnopol, Krakow, and Lvov were not at all anti-halakhic, and were perceived both as a response to the needs and tastes of the Jewish élite, and as yet another step in maskilic reform.[288] In 1841 Rapoport, the moderate maskil, unhesitatingly added his voice to those calling for the establishment of a 'temple' in Lvov, and encouraged the initiators of this project to throw off their fear of the hasidim: although the latter prayed like wild men and believed that worship was possible only through 'madness and confusion', squalor and contamination, the maskilim would prove that cleanliness and aesthetics were vital to pure-hearted prayer.[289] However, from the moment the Council of Reformed Rabbis met in Germany in 1844–6 Rapoport, by then rabbi of Prague, concentrated all his energy and maskilic values in a struggle against the nascent Reform movement. For him, as for Jacob Bodek and for Chajes, reforms were being introduced in a different country, and it was thus not yet clear what implications they would have for Galician Jewry. Nonetheless, these men felt they ought to begin preparing to grapple with the dangers they posed. In 1845 Jacob Bodek wrote a letter to his brother-in-law Abraham Mendel Mohr, which was published the same year in *Yerushalayim*. In it he reported the latest news he had learned on his visit to Vienna and Prague, which had the Jewish world in an uproar. In reaction to the first Conference of Reformed Rabbis, held at Braunschweig in 1844, and in anticipation of the second, Bodek sought to inform the Galician maskilim and rabbis of the fateful events:

The time has come to act! Who knows what the reformers in Frankfurt am Main will decree? Geiger has promised to act in this gathering to cancel *halitsah* . . . the Torah and religion are being ground into the dust . . . like an epidemic carried by the wind, it will kill all those in its path, moving freely from city to city and from state to state . . . and soon it

---

[287] Rotenstreich, *Jewish Philosophy*, 90; Meyer, 'Abraham Geiger's Historical Judaism', 112–21; Meyer, *Response to Modernity*.

[288] Meyer, *Response to Modernity*, 196–200; Silber, 'The Historical Experience of German Jewry', 50–69; Meyer, 'The German Model', 67–91. On new synagogues in Galicia, see Gelber, 'The Jews in the Krakowian Republic', 81–2; id., 'The Haskalah Movement', 230–7; id., 'The Jews of Tarnopol', 49–50.   [289] Rapoport, 'Al mot harav hehakham', *Kerem hemed*, 6 (1841), 43–4.

will come here as if on the wings of an eagle, to the homes and chambers of our rabbis, and there will be no escape![290]

Although the Galician maskilim themselves were in the vanguard of a historical trend that demanded change and modernization, they perceived German religious reform as destructive and totally unjustified. During the 1840s and 1850s Rapoport's war against reform in general, and against Abraham Geiger (1810–74) in particular—a war that left the impression among his opponents that he had defected to Orthodoxy—was merely the result of his moderate maskilic position. In Rapoport's view, reform constituted an existential danger to the Jewish people, just as hasidism threatened it from the opposite extreme. This emerges clearly from his paper *Tokheḥah megulah* (An Open Reproach), sent in 1845 to participants in the second Conference of Reformed Rabbis, held at Frankfurt.[291] Rapoport did not address the issues that concerned the reformers—the development of the Jewish religion, the concept of Judaism, the relativism of the commandments—but rather elaborated on the historical significance of reform, as he had previously done with regard to hasidism. He warned against the danger of sectarianism and national division, expressed his fear of the historization of Judaism, which would impair its historical continuity and unity, and, as a maskil, cautioned that Orthodox reaction would put an end to even the moderate Haskalah: 'For we shall move backwards along the path of world history. This terrible dispute will cause us great harm . . . and the masses of our people, who are honest and faithful, will be thrown ten degrees backwards, and, in later generations, rather than rising, they will fall, heaven forbid.'[292]

Just as Rapoport believed that hasidism would ultimately disappear, so he believed that the Jewish people would overcome the obstacle of reform. However, historical analogies, such as the disputes during the Hellenistic period and the sectarian controversies that preceded the destruction of the Second Temple, indicated that reform would worsen the situation of the Jewish people among other nations.[293] In any case, it seemed clear to him that the reformers were striving for assimilation, and that, at the most, only a few would remain to form a cult of 'dissidents' similar to those in England and France.[294] As far as actual religious reforms were concerned, Rapoport categorically denied the authority of the reformers to effect changes, stressing that the survival of the Jewish religion despite 2,000 years of persecution was undeniable proof of its strength and stability. The Jewish religion had proved itself and had helped preserve Jewish existence;

[290] Bodek, 'Mikhtav le'avraham mendel mor', 14–15.

[291] Bernfeld, *Toledot shir*, 108 (who asserts that Rapoport changed his mind when he came to Prague); J. Klausner, *History of Modern Hebrew Literature*, ii. 249–50; Rapoport, *Tokheḥah megulah*, also cited in Horwitz, *Zacharias Frankel*, 202–42. Cf. Meyer (ed.), *The German Rabbinical Conferences*, 7–13, introd.; Barzilay, *Shlomo Yehuda Rapoport*, 150–1.

[292] Rapoport, *Tokheḥah megulah*, 202–4.

[293] Rapoport's letter (undated), in Letteris, *Mikhtavei ivrit*, 160–2.

[294] Rapoport, *Tokheḥah megulah*, 206.

any deviation from it might damage the eternal life of the nation. In keeping with his maskilic picture of the past, Rapoport also disagreed with the image of the past implied by a speaker at the Braunschweig Conference, who depicted the history of the Jewish people up to the modern age as one of decline and stagnation. Rapoport re-emphasized the continuity of illustrious Jews, who had never been lacking, not even during the Middle Ages: 'Not one generation has passed from that time until the present in which the light of many exalted and enlightened Jews did not shine.'[295]

Chajes' reaction was very similar to Rapoport's, except that he was more intent on preparing a well-reasoned halakhic argument against the suggested reforms. He put forward hardly any maskilic arguments; his defence of religion as an ahistorical system and his aggressive attitude towards Geiger and Samuel Holdheim (1806–60), two of the main Reform leaders, were largely Orthodox in nature. In addition to the claim that the reforms were destructive and threatened to sever a 3,000-year-long adherence to one Torah, Chajes accused the reformers of clashing with the spirit of the time. Pointing to the revolutions and European nationalist ferment of the 1840s, Chajes asserted that at the very time when other nations were nurturing and preserving their national past and trying to uncover their historical roots, the Jewish reformers were promoting an opposite trend: dissolving national unity and impairing the historical heritage, by which he meant the commandments. Chajes also believed, in light of the 1848 revolutions, that religion in Europe was regaining respect and appreciation; while the French Revolution had lashed out against religion and the religious establishment, the 1848 revolutions were not accompanied by anti-religious sentiments. The reformers, he asserted, were adopting an anachronistic approach: 'Today faith and religion are seen as the cornerstone of society everywhere in the world; only the Jewish reformers stand alone in their actions and efforts to tear down the ancient edifice.'[296]

As mentioned before, the Reform movement struck hardly any roots in Galicia, and even moderate attempts to change customs in the 1840s were met with a militant Orthodox reaction.[297] However, in addition to the moderate maskilim, there were others who accepted the reformist approach, a tendency expressed in the pages of *Hehaluts*. As far back as the 1820s Mieses in his *Kinat ha'emet* had advocated religious reforms in Galicia, but only with the appearance of Schorr's *Hehaluts* in 1852 did a small group of maskilim coalesce that was radical in its attitude to religion and fought for reform. However, these men were unsuccessful in exerting any real social and cultural influence.

The first article in the first volume of *Hehaluts* was a didactic one, written by Isaac Erter and completed by Schorr after Erter's death.[298] There was a difference

---

[295] Rapoport, *Tokhehah megulah*, 216–23.   [296] Chajes, 'Minhat kana'ut', 973–1031.
[297] Kluger, *Toledot shelomoh*, 87–95.
[298] 'Toledot Hehaluts', and in Letteris's edition (Erter, *Hatsofeh leveit yisra'el* (Vienna, 1864), 6–14), which includes a full and far more radical version.

of twenty-four years in their ages, but nonetheless Erter, a Galician maskil of the 'old generation', agreed at Schorr's urging to collaborate with him on the new periodical. The events of 1848 and his personal meeting with German Jews at the Carlsbad spa had led Erter to conclude that the Haskalah must bring pressure to bear on the Galician rabbis to convince them that 'now is the time to ease restrictions and to rescind antiquated regulations, replacing them with new ones', on the assumption that emancipation was near at hand.[299] In his opinion, the notion of historical progress justified the denial of the authority of the ancients, who had lived in the childhood of the human species, and the transference of this authority to religious reformers and to recent, more mature sages. Talmudic and rabbinic literature was destined to lose its mandatory social status and to become the province of scholars in the science of Judaism, who were interested in the historical and cultural heritage of the Jewish people. The religious pluralism that would prevail after the reform of Judaism seemed to him both desirable and consistent with earlier periods of history, such as the Second Temple period. The changes in religion would not endanger national unity, as the moderate maskilim and the Orthodox feared, for that unity was firmly based on two other foundations—monotheism and universal ethics, which the Jews had transmitted to all humanity throughout history.

After Erter's death Schorr worked in nearly total intellectual isolation, lashing out at the rabbinic and hasidic leadership of Galicia and demanding religious reform as a vital need of the time, while basing his arguments on critical historical research. Schorr's financial independence, the fact that he had his own forum, *Hehaluts*, and his audacity enabled him to express his radical views openly, even without support from the circle of maskilim in Brody or elsewhere, as well as to criticize other maskilim for their excessive moderation. Geiger and Zunz, the Reform movement, and Jewish studies in Germany were an inspiration, a model, and a source of envy for Schorr, but he did not think of himself as part of the German movement for religious reform and was even critical of it.[300] In the maskilic situation prevailing in Galicia, the path Schorr chose to follow was that of a radical maskil. But although he waged a lone campaign for reform in Galicia, Schorr indirectly ushered in changes in the attitudes of the Orthodox and of moderate maskilim, as well as new options of reformist thinking in eastern Europe.

The idealistic term Zeitgeist ('spirit of the time'), interpreted both as the concrete historical circumstances of a specific period and as an autonomous suprapersonal force that drives history, was a keystone of Schorr's historical awareness. While earlier maskilim had been greatly influenced by the events of the eighteenth century, which they perceived as a historical transition, Schorr, adopting the progressive maskilic picture of the past, located the turning-point in the nine-

---

[299] Erter, 'Toledot *Hehaluts*', 6–11. The quotation comes from Erter, 'Mikhtav lesaks', 157–8.

[300] Erter, 'Toledot *Hehaluts*' (Letteris's edn.), 10–14. This excerpt does not appear in *Hehaluts* at all. Geiger, 'Eleh shivrei luhot munahin ba'aron', 50–2.

teenth century, pinpointing it to 1848. In that year, the Zeitgeist brought not only scientific achievement and moral advancement but also the emancipation of the Jews. According to Schorr, this process was one of the laws of history, for the spirit of the time affected universal history and Jewish history equally. It was impossible to stand against the Zeitgeist and to try to stem its tide. When it was marked by oppression, religious fanaticism, and clericalism, then Jewish life would also witness a rise in oppression, and not only from without external forces; the rabbis would also dare to 'tyrannize their people ruthlessly, with excommunication, bans, and ostracism'. Now, however, when liberalism was growing in Europe, the rabbis' authority was reduced and new opportunities were presenting themselves to Jewish society.[301] The problem, however, was that the Jewish leadership was not marching to the tune of the Zeitgeist; this was the important function of 'writers', who must act as a 'whip', remonstrating and warning against any attempt to oppose the spirit of the time.[302] In Schorr's view, there could be no doubt that, ultimately, Orthodoxy would also give in to the compelling force of 'time', for nothing maintained its absolute validity beyond its allotted time, not even the halakhah.[303]

The past with which Schorr dealt in his studies of the Bible and rabbinic literature, as well as in his biographies of medieval sages, was a 'functional past' *par excellence*. Jewish sources, particularly the Talmud, were considered in relation to their time and place of origin; examples from the past that legitimized religious reform were harnessed to this objective in Schorr's studies, as they were in those of his colleague at *Heḥaluts* Abraham Krochmal (d. 1888). Schorr defined the divergence between rabbinic thinking, which extolled the past, and modern historical thinking as the polarization between authority and criticism (*Streit zwischen Autorität und Kritik*), and urged 'Ignite the fire of criticism in the field of Jewish heritage to devour the briars and thorns.'[304] In his writings he strove first and foremost to prove that the Talmud was written by men and should be understood in the context of the time in which it was composed—the period following the destruction of the Second Temple—and in the light of the failure of the revolutions of the second century CE. The talmudic Sages were not larger-than-life super-humans projecting their authority onto later generations; they were 'people like us, and their words are not the words of a living God'.[305] The ascetics of that period had constituted the cultural, enlightened element of the people, and they had acted according to the spirit of that time. Although their enterprise had served an important function during that period, this historical work should be

---

[301] Schorr, 'Masa rabanim', 37–8.

[302] Erter, 'Toledot *Heḥaluts*, 17–18 (Schorr's supplement to Erter's article).

[303] Schorr, 'Davar be'ito', 43, 56; id., 'Masa rabanim', 48.

[304] Schorr, 'Streit zwischen Autorität', 169–72; Erter, 'Toledot *Heḥaluts*', 17 (Schorr's supplement).

[305] Schorr, 'Davar be'ito', 49; id., 'Simat ayin al hamishnah vehagemara', 50–65; id., 'Shenat taryag', 1–12.

taken only as an example for the sages of the current generation as they introduced new reforms in keeping with present conditions.[306]

Schorr and Abraham Krochmal made a special effort to destroy the image of Judah Hanasi, who was seen as a great obstacle on the path to religious reform, due to his claim that one court cannot overrule another. In the second volume of *Heḥaluts* Krochmal published 'The Biography of Rabbi Judah Hanasi', whose aim was to 'judge all his deeds . . . and examine whether his disciples and his disciples' disciples were righteous and blameless in their adoration and glorification of him'.[307] The Judah Hanasi of Krochmal's biography is an anti-hero: he lived during a relatively comfortable period in which external pressures were weakened, peace had been restored, and the sages had begun to re-establish their power. From the maskilic point of view, he possessed many positive attributes: he had an excellent élitist education; he was educated in Torah studies and in languages; he loved Hebrew; and he could hold his own 'in the halls of the kings'. However, he was sullied by his quest for power and the opportunistic considerations that underlay his desire to 'be loved and trusted by his people'. His rabbinic authority did not stem from his intellectual greatness, but rather was acquired by terrifying his students and silencing all criticism; and he used his right to confer ordination as a rod to suppress all opposition. Thus it came to pass that 'what was unworthy of becoming a law for the generations . . . was nonetheless accepted as an eternal law, because Rabbi Judah was the greatest of the age, and governed with almost as much power as a king, and all the men of wisdom bowed to his will and could not summon the strength to oppose him'.[308] Schorr employed familiar maskilic literary methods to strengthen these damning claims: he resurrected the third-century *amora* Rabbi Shimlai, who was depicted as becoming 'convinced' that the criticism of Rabbi Judah was justified, adding his 'endorsement' of the facts: 'Indeed, Beit Hanasi boasted of surpassing the Jewish people, terrorizing the sages of his generation.'[309]

Counterpoised against this negative image of Rabbi Judah was the positive figure of Samuel Yarhina'ah, a member of the first generation of Babylonian *amora'im*, sketched in a biography by Abraham Krochmal.[310] Samuel was born at the end of the second century CE into a world that provided security, stability, and opportunities for spiritual renewal. However, then too, most of the sages were not in step with the spirit of the time: they remained immersed in the study of Torah 'and placed no importance on the welfare and success of the Jewish people as a whole'. At that unpropitious time Samuel was an exception, taking upon himself the role of a maskil: to break through the darkness and bear the torch of light and science. Samuel was 'a spiritual man, sent by God to the people

[306] Schorr, 'Davar be'ito', 37–40; id., 'Shivrei luhot', 60; id., 'Peshatei dikara', 95–7.

[307] A. Krochmal, 'Toledot rabi yehudah', 63–93. Cf. Schorr, 'Davar be'ito', 49–50.

[308] A. Krochmal, 'Toledot rabi yehudah', 83. Krochmal added a continuation to this article entitled 'Bi nesiah', 118–40. [309] Schorr, 'Shenat taryag', 1–2.

[310] A. Krochmal, 'Toledot shmuel yarhinai', 66–89.

of the Babylonian exile to preserve life', a maskil who aspired to a thorough knowledge of Torah and Jewish wisdom, dared disseminate new ideas among the people, studied foreign languages, enquired into science, tried his hand at writing poetry, and established good relationships with Persian rulers and sages. He was both lenient in his halakhic decisions and a halakhic reformer, and his struggle for the acceptance of a permanent calculation of the calendar, which he reached through scientific computation, was perceived as the struggle for a young rebel against Judah Hanasi and the rabbinic establishment.

The fact that *Heḥaluts* dared to criticize the great figures of the Mishnah and the talmudic Sages, as well as the extremes to which Schorr took his historical biblical criticism,[311] presented a challenge to both Orthodoxy and the moderate Haskalah. A remarkable Orthodox response appeared in the form of an alternative to *Heḥaluts*, which also emulated Schorr's style. Rabbi Solomon Kluger (1775–1869) of Brody supported this book, *Haḥolets* (The Deliverer), written by Moses Harmelin, which, among other things, attempted to correct the picture of the past portrayed in *Heḥaluts*: Samuel Yarhina'ah, for example, returns to being 'truly righteous and blameless', an exemplary figure for the Orthodox, who, through the evil of the maskilim, had been unjustly recruited to their cause.[312] Rapoport's response reflected the stance of the moderate maskilim, re-establishing the boundaries Schorr had overstepped. In particular, Rapoport came to the defence of Judah Hanasi in order to strengthen the authority of the Talmud and halt the trend towards halakhic reform, yet another step in the battle he had been waging since the 1840s. Rapoport saw Schorr and his associates as 'evil animals and predators', characterized by destructive tendencies and fatal methods of research that 'did not spare the honour of the ancients of thousands of years ago, fathers of the Torah, and described the father of the Mishnah, who is considered sacred by all Jews, as lacking any virtue, morals, or knowledge, and vilified him'.[313] As described above, Rapoport and other maskilim constructed a picture of the past that was populated by exemplary maskilic figures, and assisted the maskilim in their struggle within a Jewish society that was indifferent or hostile to them. However, the iconoclastic tendencies of Schorr and *Heḥaluts*, which served religious radicalism, seemed to go too far and threatened not only traditional values, but also the values of the moderate Haskalah. The radical picture of the past, which isolated the 'deviants' and destroyed the traditional pantheon, was not consonant with the moderate maskil's picture of the past, which was intended to present the traditional pantheon in a new maskilic light rather than to shatter it completely.

[311] Schorr, 'Mikhtav leḥaver', 97–116. Cf. Shelly, *The Study of the Bible*, 93–102.

[312] *Inter alia*, Schorr, 'Shenat taryad', 17–18; A. Krochmal, 'Toledot shmuel yarḥinai', 84; Reggio, 'Al teudat zera', 51–4.

[313] Rapoport, 'Mikhtav larabanim', 40–6; Schorr, 'Shivrei luḥot' (a harsh criticism of Rapoport, portrayed as a hypocritical turncoat maskil who deserted the Haskalah and went over to the Orthodox camp).

THREE

Optimism under Oppression:
Maskilic History in Russia,
1825–1855

THE IDEA YEARNING TO BE REALIZED

THE historical context in which the Russian Haskalah was established and developed was marked by a constant struggle with political issues raised by the Russian rulers' policy towards the Jews. In the early 1820s Isaac Baer Levinsohn called for changes in the nature and values of Jewish society, particularly in relation to Jewish occupations and education. He based his demands on what he considered to be the far-reaching promises of Tsar Alexander I's 1804 edict.[1] The close involvement in Jewish affairs of Nicholas I (1825–55) and the members of his government, as well as their attempts to redefine the status of the Jews with regard to military service, autonomy, economics, and education, considerably strengthened the link between government policy and maskilic activity.[2] The maskilim's desire for progress and their hope that what they saw as a 'maskilic–governmental alliance' would be strengthened are strikingly apparent in their propaganda, programmes, poetry, literature, and correspondence. In the maskilic consciousness and in the repertoire of images and common expressions used by the maskilim the term 'benevolent emperor' was not merely an expression of loyalty, obedience, and flattery but also the cornerstone of their ideology. They truly believed that the 'benevolent emperor' would 'heal the wounds and end the tribulations of the Jewish people and the injuries which had crushed them for thousands of years and were as yet unhealed'.[3] Although the facts indicate that the 'maskilic–governmental alliance' was more of a one-sided, optimistic image than a reality,

[1] Levinsohn, *Teudah beyisra'el*, 182–4 (written in 1823).

[2] Mordechai Levin, *Social and Economic Values*; Etkes, 'Compulsory Enlightenment', 264–313; Zinberg, *A History of Jewish Literature*, vols. vi–vii; Stanislawski, *Tsar Nicholas I and the Jews*.

[3] Fuenn, 'Mikhtav lebetsalel stern' (1840), 150–1. The letter is also included in Fuenn, *From Militant to Conservative Maskil*, 173–8. See also Mordechai Levin, *Social and Economic Values*, 110–13; Etkes, 'Between Change and Tradition', 4–5; Lederhendler, *The Road to Modern Jewish Politics*.

the very existence of the image was important as a source of confidence and hope for the maskilim, and it left its mark on their consciousness of the past.

Russian maskilim of the 1820s and later, including Isaac Baer Levinsohn, Samuel Joseph Fuenn (1818–90), Abraham Baer Gottlober (1811–99), and Benjamin Mandelstamm (1805–86), based their ideology on the perception that the difficult situation of the Jews—their inferior position in the country as well as the quality of their education and characteristics—was the product of political, economic, and religious circumstances, and, in particular, the result of the oppression and intolerance of the pre-modern rulers. Better treatment, religious tolerance, and an acceptance of the precepts of the Haskalah would deliver the Jews from their troubles and the abnormal circumstances of their lives. Although 'the Jewish people in this time and in this country are still on the lowest rung of the ladder of national and moral enlightenment, on a level with the other non-Christians in Christian countries and the rest of our brethren in other countries',[4] the maskilim felt that government initiatives, which were destined to change the climate and redress the external conditions responsible for the relative retardation of the Russian Jews, would allow their innate potential for renewal to be realized. As government intervention increased, reaching a peak in the 1840s in government-sponsored education (the establishment of modern government schools for Jews), the maskilim could proclaim, enthusiastically and in vivid rhetoric, that their expectations were indeed already being realized: 'Now our master, the emperor, has taken upon himself to be the tiller of our soil, to uproot from it all rank and bitter weeds, to cleanse the hearts of the Jewish people of all evil schemes, and to sprinkle blessed dew upon the thirsting, yearning soil.'[5]

As enthusiastic supporters of the government's plans and propagandists seeking to accelerate the reform of Jewish society, the maskilim lashed out against those who did not respond positively to the new trends of the 'modern age'. There should be no obstructions to the path of the ship being steered 'towards the good port' the government aspired to reach, and the Jews should prepare by cleansing themselves of 'the defiling scum' before they crossed over from 'darkness' to 'great light'.[6]

The Russian Haskalah acquired its critical attitude towards Jewish society from the earlier German centres of Haskalah as well as from Galicia. The Russian maskilim saw themselves, as did their Galician counterparts, as part of a continuous movement, stressing that they were the third stage in the history of the Haskalah, a movement founded in Berlin and carried on by maskilim in Austria and by the 'Berliners' of Volhynia and Lithuania. The poet Adam Hacohen (Abraham Dov Lebensohn, 1798–1878) expressed this maskilic sense of uninterrupted continuity in his response to the establishment of the short-lived Hebrew

[4] Koifmann, 'Mikhtav al devar hahinukh', 55–6.
[5] Fuenn, 'Mikhtav lebetsalel stern', 152; Koifmann, 'Mikhtav al devar hahinukh', 55–6.
[6] Fuenn, 'Mikhtav lebetsalel stern'; Mandelstamm, Ḥazon lamo'ed, ii. 7.

journal *Pirhei tsafon* (Northern Flowers) in 1841: 'From the gatherers (*Me'asefim*) of many seeds to the planters of a beautiful vineyard (*Kerem hemed*), from the first fruits of Yemen (*Bikurei ha'itim*) to the flowers of the north (*Pirhei tsafon*)'.[7]

When in 1828 Levinsohn published his book *Teudah beyisra'el* (A Testimony in Israel), a work that became the springboard for the formation of the Haskalah movement in Russia, he was already addressing a public that included many who had already 'converted' to the Haskalah ideology.[8] *Teudah beyisra'el* was a source of great encouragement to the young maskilim, particularly the learned élite and those gifted in Torah study who became involved in the Haskalah, influenced by the literature of the Berlin Haskalah and by medieval and Renaissance Jewish rationalist philosophy, or, more directly, influenced by individuals who had already been exposed to the German Haskalah. Levinsohn 'proved' to them that by doing so they were not absorbing an external, foreign culture, and showed them that a 'Russian Mendelssohn' could arise, speaking in a language familiar to the scholars of eastern Europe.

However, among the growing Jewish population within the Pale of Settlement (2,350,000 in 1850) the maskilim were, at first, a relatively marginal minority—small circles of writers and intellectuals who earned their livelihood from writing and publishing, usually in dire economic straits and in need of wealthy patrons. According to one estimate, in the 1840s the maskilim in Lithuania alone numbered 200 men, but this would appear to be a highly exaggerated assessment. An examination of the records listing the names of those who subscribed to maskilic books might in fact yield this number, and perhaps even a larger figure, but such subscribers were not necessarily maskilim themselves. Moreover, the fact that wealthy merchant families were involved in 'maskilic politics' and supported the maskilim does not justify considering them members of maskilic groups themselves, even though there are some indications that these families were becoming acculturated.[9] A more precise indication is provided by the number of writers who were actually writing and active in maskilic literary public affairs, participating in the correspondence between maskilim, and, from the 1840s onwards, teaching in modern Jewish schools. Investigation of those individuals reveals that there were several groups of maskilim, scattered primarily among the communities of Vilna, Berdichev, Mohilev, Kishinev, Dubno, Uman, Kremenets, Odessa, and other towns, and that their numbers varied from a few individuals to several dozen in each place. Levinsohn's home in Kremenets was a important meeting-place

[7] Adam Hacohen, 'Shirei sefat kodesh', in *Kol shirei adam*, i. 243–5. See also *Pirhei tsafon*, i. 92–5; Gottlober, *Zikhronot umasaot*, i. 75–82; Mordechai Levin, *Social and Economic Values*, 74–7; Mahler, *History of the Jewish People*, vol. i, pt. iv, pp. 9–13.

[8] This is obvious from the approbations of the book and the list of subscribers attached to it. On Levinsohn, see J. Klausner, *History of Modern Hebrew Literature*, ii. 33–115, and Etkes, 'Between Change and Tradition'.

[9] Shatzky, *Kultur geshikhte*, 87; Zalkin, 'The Vilna Haskalah'.

for the maskilim. It was the address for neophyte maskilim finding their way, for writers of literary works seeking first opinions, and for advice regarding governmental plans. It also served as a 'court' for visiting maskilim, like Mendelssohn's home in Berlin and Krochmal's in Zolkiew. Almost every prominent maskil of the time seems to have corresponded with Levinsohn. In many ways, this correspondence not only created strong personal contacts between Russian and Galician maskilim, but also established a maskilic republic of letters.[10]

The Russian maskil, like his Galician counterpart, was not only affiliated with a minority in Jewish society but was also usually regarded as a heretic by the traditionalist. Until the 1840s and even later autobiographical evidence and letters portray the maskilim as socially isolated, persecuted (particularly in small communities), hesitant to identify themselves openly with the Haskalah, and in search of maskilic society or the patronage of a wealthy man.[11] 'How sweet are the moments we are together, each providing strength and courage to his fellow, to turn away from darkness and seek the light of science'—thus Gottlober recorded memories of his world at the time of his visit in 1833 to a group of maskilim in Dubno.[12] Benjamin Mandelstamm breathed a sigh of relief when, to his surprise, he discovered a few isolated maskilim in Berdichev—a city 'built in a disordered fashion on a dunghill':

You will surely understand from this, my brother, the joy in my heart when I found in this city . . . these virtuous few of good thoughts and common sense, and became their companion during my stay there; yes, in their eyes, I too was like a gift of God to whom they could pour out the troubles of their heart. They could not speak thus to the barbarians who inhabit the city, and so they rejoiced in my coming as if I were a fresh spring of water in this parched land, come to quench the thirst of their souls with the news and prospects before us regarding schools and the working of the land.[13]

These means of communication—the exchange of letters, meetings and visits, 'pilgrimages' to Levinsohn—did not satisfy the social needs of the maskilim, and from the 1820s onwards attempts were made to organize them into local groups and into a wider movement. In a number of communities groups of maskilim organized 'reading societies', and groups associated with new schools were formed in Vilna, Odessa, and Kishinev. Although there were occasional proposals, some made with the participation of Galician maskilim, to establish a nationwide organization, nothing came of them.

---

[10] These preliminary conclusions are based primarily on collections of letters by maskilim, including B. Nathanson (ed.), *Be'er yitshak* and id. (ed.), *Sefer hazikhronot*, and letters in the Ginzberg Collection. On the Vilna circle of maskilim, see I. Klausner, *Vilna: 'Jerusalem of Lithuania'*; B. Nathanson, *Sefer hazikhronot*, 49–57.

[11] On the maskilic autobiography, see Werses, 'Autobiography in the Haskalah', 175–83; Mintz, 'Guenzburg, Lilienblum and the Shape of Haskalah Autobiography', 71–110; Gottlober, *Hanitsanim*, 7–8.   [12] Gottlober, *Hanitsanim*, 185.

[13] Mandelstamm, *Hazon lamo'ed*, ii. 72. The description relates to the early 1840s.

A major change, which to some extent strengthened the position of the maskilim in Russia, began in the early 1840s, with the government's new plans for sweeping reforms in Jewish society. The decree calling for local committees to convene to discuss the problems of the Jewish population, Max Lilienthal's (1815–82) mission to persuade the Jews to accept the government's educational programme, the plans for government-sponsored education, and the opening of rabbinical schools in Vilna and Zhitomir all stirred Jewish public opinion and led to increased activity among the maskilim.[14] In 1840 the maskilim in Dubno wrote a letter asking Levinsohn to assume leadership of the maskilic movement and to serve as its spokesman at the opportune moment provided by Nicholas I; they likened the situation in Russia to the situation in central Europe in 1782, when Joseph II's Edict of Tolerance was issued.[15] However, Levinsohn declined their request to play the role of Naphtali Herz Wessely, preferring to leave the field open to others. The dispute that erupted over the government's plan to establish a new Jewish educational system strengthened maskilic identity and reinforced the negative image of the maskilim in the eyes of traditional society. The new schools that were ultimately established also provided teaching jobs for maskilim and a forum for disseminating the Haskalah. The first Russian maskilic journal *Pirḥei tsafon* was published during this period and, although it did not last very long, its very appearance indicates that some of the earlier obstacles had been removed. Nicholas I's policy confirmed the maskilim's predictions regarding the tendencies of the enlightened absolutist government. Encomiums of Nicholas and Uvarov, the minister of education, were written in the most enthusiastic language.[16] The Vilna of the 1840s appeared entirely different to Mandelstamm, who returned there after several years of absence: 'The dark cloud that then hovered over the Jewish people is gone, the light has begun to shine through the layers of folly, and the dawn has burst upon them!' The synagogue of the maskilim of Vilna, Taharat Kodesh, which opened in 1846, was also a source of self-confidence and unity for the maskilim, serving as proof that, backed by government fiat, they could free themselves of the fear that had hitherto been inspired by 'the prodigious numbers of people who abhor science'.[17]

However, in the 1840s and 1850s, too, the maskilim were not accepted by the traditional élite, who could not countenance the daring and innovativeness of people 'who did not study the Torah and upon whom the light of the Talmud had not shone'.[18] Nor was there a radical change in the status of the maskilim on the social level, and they continued to be persecuted in small communities. In the Russian Haskalah, as in that of Galicia, hasidism was identified as the main obstacle

[14] In addition to Etkes and Stanislawski, see Shohet, *The Crown Rabbinate*.

[15] L. Glazberg's letter to Levinsohn (1840), in B. Nathanson, *Be'er yitsḥak*, 60–1.

[16] Among others, in the poem by Gottlober, *Hanitsanim*, 2–6.

[17] Mandelstamm, *Ḥazon lamo'ed*, ii. 4, 77–89; Gottlober, 'Kirot libi homeh', 215–16.

[18] Lilienthal, Letter to his father (1842). Cf. Lipschitz, *Zikhron ya'akov*, i. 74–84.

to the reform and healing of Jewish society, and the anti-hasidic literature of the Russian maskilim carried on the Galician tradition.

It is nonetheless important to point out that the maskilim were aware of the complex reality of Jewish life in Russia and did not ignore its less ideal aspects. They did not restrict their pens and their talent to internal Jewish propaganda, but also used them to produce an apologia for Jews and Judaism addressed to the non-Jewish world. Levinsohn, for example, wrote against the blood libel and the attacks of converts and missionaries like Alexander McCaul on the Talmud.[19]

The poetry written by Adam Hacohen and his son Mikhal (Micha Joseph Lebensohn; 1828–52) did not express the optimism of the maskilim, but portrayed the present as a time in which cruelty had not yet passed from the world and played a central role in human history. Wars, slavery, and conquest also characterized the present, and the fate of the Jews was not as bright as the maskilic vision would suggest.[20] Adam Hacohen's 'Kol na'akat bat-yehudah' (The Daughter of Judah Cries Out, 1842) is a poem of remonstrance against God for the fate of Jews in the present, and only in the second edition of *Shirei sefat kodesh* (Poems of the Holy Tongue, 1861) were footnotes added, indicating that the poet was referring to the Middle Ages and not to the present era of benevolent kings; the footnotes were apparently added under the influence of Alexander II's accession to the throne in 1855.[21] An additional example of this sober, realistic view can be drawn from the visit made by Moses Montefiore (1784–1885) to Russia in 1846. Publicly the government as well as the maskilim painted a picture for the visitor that was far rosier than the reality. Privately, however, after Montefiore's departure the maskilim made sure that the real truth was passed on to him. 'We wiped away the tears on the faces of the orphans and widows, who wept bitterly, for they wanted bread and there was none,' Benjamin Mandelstamm wrote to Montefiore, 'and we also alleviated the suffering of many of the impoverished. We did all of this without stirring your heart and without grieving your gentle soul.'[22] After Montefiore had gone, the dreams and hopes the Jews had pinned on his visit faded, and they returned to stark reality: severe poverty, limited means of livelihood, governmental edicts, and hostile officials, who in the maskilim's opinion were turning the tsar against the Jews and preventing him from learning the truth about their situation.

The maskilim were more realistic than they seemed; they knew only too well that they were living the frustration and tension of the conflict between their ideal image of the present and the bleak reality of Nicholas's reign. However, the

[19] Levinsohn, *Ahiyah hashiloni*; id., *Yemin tsidki*; id., *Efes damim*.

[20] Adam Hakohen, 'Hahemlah', 165–200.

[21] Adam Hakohen, 'Kol na'akat bat-yehudah', 152. Cf. Vilna 1861 edn., as in id., *Shirei sefat kodesh: Mivhar*, 101–3. Alongside this poem are others singing the praises of the rulers of Russia; id., *Shirei sefat kodesh* (1842), 69–78.

[22] Mandelstamm, *Hazon lamo'ed*, ii. 55. On Montefiore's visit, see Dick, *Ha'ore'ah*; Etkes, 'Compulsory Enlightenment', 301–4.

Haskalah could not have existed without an optimistic picture of the future, without the awareness of a historical shift, or without the maskilim's conviction that they could change the face of things, for the major part of their effort was directed internally: to guide ambivalent young people, to introduce reformed curricula to students who sought enlightenment, and to acquire positions of influence and leadership. The maskilim lived the present very intensely, were highly sensitive to the events of their time, and felt committed to a struggle to help their people. In the 1840s Mordecai Aaron Guenzburg (1795–1846), a well-known Russian maskil, called for a militant Haskalah that would focus primarily on the problems of the present and would not shrink from 'confronting the enemy at the gate'. The maskil could neither remain passive nor hide and the Haskalah could not remain a theoretical system of ideas and principles. In Guenzburg's view, the Haskalah was the fuel that would fire irresistible activism, and he described this in picturesque terms:

The ideas we conceive in the depths of our heart are the bare souls that will haunt us and force us to provide them with bodies, to give them a form of expression so they may be felt by the senses of man, for when the idea yearns to be realized, when the thought longs to be put into practice, woe to the man who conceals his feelings within himself, for they will be like a boiling cauldron inside him, they will bubble like water on the flame, until they burst forth.[23]

The historical context of Nicholas's reign, the social status of the maskilim, their self-awareness, and their vision determined the maskilic situation in Russia. It was this situation which largely dictated the direction of maskilim's interest in history and the nature of the picture of the past that they created. From the maskilic point of view, the past had two aspects: the political past, which was essentially universal and dominated by the transition to the 'modern age'; and the maskilic Jewish past, which they used to persuade their audience that the need for internal change and reform was of vital importance. Knowledge of universal history, the identification of the place of the Jews within it, and the creation of 'roots' for the maskil, in order to counter his image as someone who wished to uproot traditional values and supplant them with new ones, were among the aims of maskilic study of the past in Russia up to the mid-1850s.

A UNIVERSAL HISTORY FOR A MODERN ERA

In 1833 Mordecai Aaron Guenzburg completed the translation and adaptation of two short historical works, 'Toledot napoleon bonaparte' (The Life of Napoleon Bonaparte) and an introduction to Karl Heinrich Pölitz's *Weltgeschichte*, to which he gave the Hebrew title *Toledot benei ha'adam* (History of Mankind), and submitted them for approval to Wolf Tugendhold (1796–1864), the Jewish censor appointed by the Russian administration in Vilna. The Vilna censor was very

---

[23] Guenzburg, *Devir*, ii. 11–25.

familiar with the subject matter; he had attended Breslau University, where he had studied history under Ludwig Wachler, and had later taught Jewish history at the rabbinical seminary in Vilna.[24] But Guenzburg was terribly disappointed by Tugendhold's decision: 'Toledot napoleon bonaparte' was totally rejected for publication, and the author was required to introduce many changes and to delete entire sections from his introduction to *Toledot benei ha'adam*. 'To tell you the truth, the harsh criticism of our honourable friend the rabbi and censor', Guenzberg wrote to a friend, 'has greatly discouraged me in so far as this pamphlet is concerned, as well as the book of general history which I intended to write, because if I am forced to refrain from mentioning any matter relating to politics, I shall never be able to achieve any success.'[25] The censor apparently chose to exercise great caution and to water down any political discussion that could be interpreted as having topical implications. The cowardice and 'faint-heartedness' that Guenzburg imputed to the censor were commonplace during Nicholas I's rigid rule, and Tugendhold naturally baulked at approving any work dealing with the French Revolution and Napoleon so soon after the 1831 Polish revolt against Russian rule.

Guenzburg was anxious to acquaint the Jewish reader in Russia with the entire sweep of universal history, 'including the chronicles and events in the life of each and every nation'. In his eyes, the political arena was the focus of all historical events.[26] He nearly despaired because of the obstacles placed in his way by censorship, but nevertheless carried on translating and adapting historical works. Guenzburg was the author of most of the fifteen works of universal history written between the 1820s and the early 1850s by maskilim in Russia. He translated Campe's *Die Entdeckung von Amerika* (The Discovery of America) (1780–2), and published it in 1823 under the title *Gelot ha'arets hahadashah* (Discovery of the New Land). From the subtitle we learn that the description of the dramatic exploits of Columbus, Cortés, and Pizarro in the fifteenth and sixteenth centuries were 'for the benefit of Jewish children so they may learn to speak eloquently at an early age'. But Guenzburg regarded it as more than a textbook. In his view it was the first example of a universal history; if *Gelot ha'arets hahadashah* was warmly received by Hebrew readers in Russia, particularly among those 'with an understanding of science', then he would undertake to translate a complete book of universal history.[27] 'Toledot napoleon bonaparte' and the introduction to *Toledot benei ha'adam* were merely samples of his ambitious translation project.

Guenzburg chose to translate one of the most popular books of universal history written in Germany at the time: Pölitz's *Die Weltgeschichte* (World History), the first edition of which had appeared in 1805. I have already dealt with the nature

---

[24] Fuenn, *Safah lane'emanim*, 665.   [25] Guenzburg's letter (May 1833), in id., *Devir*, ii. 82–3.

[26] Guenzburg, *Gelot ha'arets hahadashah*, introd.

[27] Ibid. On Guenzburg and his essays, see J. Klausner, *History of Modern Hebrew Literature*, ii. 120–70; Bartal, 'Mordecai Aaron Guenzburg', 126–47.

of the book and its author in my discussion of the maskilim of Austria–Galicia. In 1830 an abridged translation of Pölitz's introduction prepared by M. Strelisker was printed in *Bikurei ha'itim*,[28] and in 1833, after inserting the required corrections, Guenzburg published his translation of the entire introduction as a preliminary prospectus. In 1835 the first part was published in Vilna, covering universal history from the creation of the world until the fall of the Roman empire to the barbarians at the end of the fifth century.[29] By 1842 Guenzburg had completed three more parts, covering the Middle Ages and the modern era until after the Napoleonic Wars. This was the first Hebrew book since Abraham Triebesch's *Korot ha'itim* that presented a consecutive universal history. Only the first part of Guenzburg's book was published in its entirety, and a few of the chapters describing the time of Muhammad and the origins of Islam, the reign of Charlemagne, the Crusades, and other periods were printed posthumously, over forty years after his death. Guenzburg himself also published a few chapters about the modern era under various titles, without any mention of the fact that they were excerpts from his translation of Pölitz. During the reign of Nicholas I the only historical works considered suitable for publication were those dealing with relatively neutral periods of history which had little relevance to the present, such as ancient times and the age of discoveries, or chapters about modern history that glorified the Russian state and its rulers.[30]

One of the aims underlying the Russian government's offer of new educational frameworks to the Jews was to nurture Russian history. Universal history was introduced into the curriculum in the new Jewish schools in Russia. At the school in Odessa, for example, the first principal, Ephraim Zietenfeld, taught universal history to the third-year students in 1826, and Bezalel Stern (1798–1853), a maskil who had come there from Galicia, taught this subject in 1834.[31] In Riga the students' achievements in history were examined in 1840, and in a memorandum sent to the governors in the Pale of Settlement the importance of teaching Russian history and history was emphasized as the most effective way to unite non-Russians and minorities with the ruling nation.[32] Guenzburg's book *Itotei rusiyah* (The Chronicles of Russia), published in Vilna in 1839, fitted in well with this aim, and was intended for use as a textbook for the new school in Vilna where Guenzburg later served as a teacher. In 1842 Guenzburg carefully selected the historical period most flattering to Russia from part IV of *Toledot benei ha'adam*: 'Hatsarfatim berusiyah: divrei yemei 1812–1813' (The French in Russia 1812–

[28] *Bikurei ha'itim*, 11 (1830), 142–6.
[29] Guenzburg, *Toledot benei ha'adam*. For the praise heaped upon it by Lilienthal, see Philipson, *Max Lilienthal*, 289–90.
[30] A few chapters from vols. ii and iii were printed in the collection Zederbaum, *Leket ma'amarim*, 53–81. During his lifetime, Guenzburg published sections of pt. 4 of Pölitz's translation; see Guenzburg, *Hatsarfatim berusiyah*, and id., *Pi haherut. Sefer yemei hador* was published after his death, as was 'Toledot napoleon bonaparte'.
[31] Gottlober, *Zikhronot umasaot*, ii. 87, 94.   [32] Slutsky, *The Haskalah Movement*, 39, 71.

1813), and published it as a separate book. Encouraged by the praise lavished on him by the minister of education, Uvarov, who was inordinately pleased by this attempt to teach the Hebrew reader about the defeat suffered by Napoleon at the hands of Alexander I, Guenzburg decided to publish the continuation, describing Napoleon's last years: 'Pi haḥerut: milḥemet ha'ashkenazim veharusim betsarfat 1813–1815 ad galut kaisar napoleon me'al admato' (The Advent of Freedom: The War by Germany and Russia against France 1813–15 up to the Exile of Napoleon).[33] It was only after Guenzburg's death, during the rule of Alexander II at the end of the 1850s, that the censor approved the publication of the chapters on the history of the French Revolution (*Sefer yemei hador*, 1860) and the biography of Napoleon before his great battle with Russia (*Toledot napoleon bonaparte*, 1878). Guenzburg's desperate attempts to publish *Toledot benei ha'adam* in its entirety outside Russia, with financial support from Moses Montefiore, also failed, and except for the chapters mentioned above which were published as separate books, none have survived.[34]

Guenzburg was not the first to translate Russian history into Hebrew. A less well-known Vilna maskil, the teacher Judah Leib Germaisa, preceded him by a few years. In 1836 Germaisa published his *Toledot rusiyah* (History of Russia). Its forty pages summarized the major points of Russia's political history from the early Middle Ages to the reign of Nicholas I. The central figures in the book were the rulers of Russia and their exploits: 'The chronicles of the rulers who governed this land in the past from the time the Russian people became a nation, and the circumstances and wars in this land from then until the rule of our lord, the merciful emperor Nicholas Pavlovich, his exalted excellency'.[35] Germaisa dwelt on Peter the Great's contribution to Russian history and particularly emphasized Russia's victory over Napoleonic France; of the book's forty pages, ten are devoted to a description of Alexander I's triumph. This historical event also formed the centrepiece of the two works published by the teacher Feivel Schiffer of Warsaw in the 1840s. In the first Schiffer wrote a paean to the ruler of Poland for his heroism, 'The chronicles of our lord Paskievitch, the grand duke and hero, president of Warsaw', and in the second he wrote the life of Napoleon from a pro-Russian point of view.[36] The detailed biography, which ran to over 250 pages, included expansive descriptions of 'the war in the land of Russia' and praised the courage of 'Russia's heroes'—a slant that probably made it easy for the censor Tugendhold to approve the book for publication. The last Hebrew historical work written in this period, relating episodes of universal history and entitled *Nidḥei yisra'el* (The Outcasts of Israel), was written by Samuel Joseph Fuenn. It was actually written as a book of Jewish history, but the author's historical approach

---

[33] See Adam Hakohen, *Kinat soferim*, 44.

[34] Guenzburg's letter to Montefiore (Jan. 1847), in Guenzburg, *Devir*, ii. 28–9; apparently id., 'Melekh asur berahatim' also formed part of the book.

[35] Germaisa, *Toledot rusiyah*.   [36] Schiffer, *Devar gevurot*; id., *Toledot napoleon*.

led him, as will be discussed later, to include the history of Europe and the Orient from the fifth to the thirteenth centuries. All in all, the universal history of the Middle Ages, partly based on the German historian Friedrich Christoph Schlosser's *Weltgeschichte für das deutsche Volk*, took up almost a quarter of Fuenn's work.[37]

The historical literature that introduced universal history to the circles of maskilim in Russia, who in turn made it available to the Hebrew-reading public and students, was the same as that which the maskilim of Austria–Galicia had read in the first half of the nineteenth century. Despite the cries of distress uttered by maskilim like Levinsohn, bemoaning the lack of books and the difficulties of obtaining them, contemporaneous popular German historiography was readily available, as in Galicia. In those years, when European historiography was pursuing new paths and moving towards academic institutionalization, the study of documents, and the development of romantic and nationalistic concepts, the maskilim were relying exclusively on secondary historiography, which was still following eighteenth-century trends. This is clear from a detailed examination of the books to which Levinsohn referred in his writings in the 1820s and 1840s. Nearly all the historical works were in German. As sources of ancient history, Levinsohn used German translations of Eusebius, Herodotus, Pliny, Origen, Aristotle, and others, as well as textbooks on Greek and Roman history and lexicons published in Vienna, Halle, and Leipzig. The most important seventeenth- and eighteenth-century authors he read were Bossuet, Bayle, Herder, Michaelis, Rousseau, Voltaire, Dohm, Kant, and Semler. The books on universal history most often referred to by Levinsohn were those by A. L. Schlözer, the historian from Göttingen; Johannes von Müller, the great popularizer of history; Pölitz, of Leipzig University; L. Wachler; and Schlosser, the Heidelberg historian.[38] Not one of these history books adhered to a purely scientific–objective approach. Schlözer, for example, pursued a pragmatic and didactic historical method. The same was true of von Müller, who, as already noted, was soundly rebuked by Hegel as a result.[39] Schlözer was, to a great extent, Pölitz's heir, and he openly opposed the 'Ranke school'. Like Pölitz, Schlözer adopted a liberal, moralistic, and cosmopolitan conception of history, and the principles of 1789 guided him in his historical writing.[40] The Russian historian in this group was Nikolai Karmezin, whose book *The History of the Russian State* (1818–26) was read by the maskilim either in the original or in German translation. His book inspired Russian pride and patriotism in the years after the Napoleonic Wars, and his conception corres-

---

[37] Fuenn, *Nidḥei yisra'el*. On Schlosser's books and historiographic approach, see Gölter, 'Die Geschichtsauffassung'; Iggers, *The German Conception of History*, 29–43; Thompson, *History of Historical Writing*, ii. 142–3; Gooch, *History and Historians*, 99–102.

[38] The list is based on Levinsohn's bibliographical references in his various books, in particular in *Teudah beyisra'el* (1828), *Efes damim* (1837), and *Beit yehudah* (1839).

[39] See Hegel, *The Philosophy of History*, 5–7.

[40] Iggers, *The German Conception of History*, 96–8.

ponded to the trends of the Haskalah: on one hand, he continued the tradition established by Schlözer, von Müller, and Pölitz, characterized by the use of examples from didactic purposes; on the other, he stressed Russia's status as a major force in universal history.[41]

The maskilim of Russia turned to the past in search of a store of didactic examples and precedents. Although their motive in doing so was not merely to escape the present, nonetheless their historical conception was not entirely free of a sense of nostalgia for the past and the lure of antiquity—the hallmark of the Romantic stream in Europe.[42] Guenzburg, for example, wished to accord due honour to the 'aura of venerability' that surrounded the 'ancients', 'for it is in the nature of the beautiful soul to be aroused to honour, modesty, and all virtue, when it sets its eyes upon something of antiquity that has existed on the earth for thousands of years'.[43] In Napoleon's battle in Egypt he found an example that proved 'how powerful is the effect of an ancient thing upon the soul':

We heard about one of the military leaders of our time, whose enemies surrounded him and waged a mighty battle against him at the feet of the ancient pyramids in Egypt, and when he saw his soldiers, fearful and failing in battle, he called unto them: 'Soldiers, from the summit of these pyramids forty centuries look down upon you!' No sooner had he spoken than his hard-pressed warriors took courage in their zeal to prove their heroism before the eyes of those venerable witnesses, as they struck back at their enemies.[44]

The maskilim held archaeology in high esteem, and reported to Hebrew readers on the finds made in the East during Napoleon's campaign; first and foremost was the decipherment of Egyptian hieroglyphics with the help of the Rosetta Stone. They also informed their readers about the discovery of the city of Pompeii in 1748, and about the excavations conducted there early in the nineteenth century. With great excitement, Gottlober related that 'in these very days buildings have been found under the earth, in which many books and various implements have been preserved, and the people in them have turned to stone'.[45] Nostalgia for more recent events can be found in the travel tales of Benjamin Mandelstamm, who in the 1830s toured several of the 1812 battle sties. At Borodino Mandelstamm, alighting from his carriage, conjured up a picture of the bitter battle waged on that field, which was now covered in flowers. The discrepancy between the past and the present inspired him to offer a moralistic explanation denouncing Napoleon and the French:

For they imagined they could destroy this plot, and now the marrow of their bones waters its clods of earth, and the sight is a cause of joy to their enemies. And the flowers and

[41] Thompson, *History of Historical Writing*, ii. 625–6; Raeff, *Russian Intellectual History*, 117–24; Walicki, *A History of Russian Thought*, 53.

[42] See Schenk, *The Mind of the European Romantics*, 30–45.

[43] Guenzburg, 'Mikhtav' (Vilna, 1837), 20.   [44] Ibid. 21.

[45] Gottlober, *Pirhei ha'aviv*, 26; Guenzburg, *Toledot benei ha'adam*, 251–2; id., 'Mikhtav', 22; id., 'Melekh asur berahatim', 62–5.

plants, now blooming before my eyes on the mountain and on the plain, are but the tufts of hair upon the heads of the young men of France who, stabbed by our soldiers, bled upon the field.

In Smolensk Mandelstamm saw, in a dreadful dream, the death of Napoleon's soldiers who fell in the Russian winter: 'Camp after camp of naked, barefoot soldiers . . . corpses like statues of wood and stone, their eyelids open wide, and bitter tears, like clods of frost and ice, in them . . . and one man took the roasted flesh of another and ate it to assuage his pangs of hunger.'[46]

However, in the 1840s, with the growing agitation over the issue of the 'government-sponsored Haskalah', it was Mandelstamm who warned the maskilim to stop descending into the nether world to exhume 'ancient, time-worn ideas . . . dead bones that have already turned into dust'. He encouraged them instead to grapple with contemporary challenges. The present was the only significant time for the Haskalah, for only in the present could one show initiative, engage in activism, and engender change: 'Man may dislodge the generation of the past and transfer the mountain of the future together, but you—the present—exist and endure for ever . . . only you are the regent of man's changes of fortune . . . only in you reside both his happiness and his success.' In Mandelstamm's imagery the present was the 'lifeline' and the past was 'the thread that is interwoven in it'; the maskil lived with a constant awareness of a present in which events occurred quickly, one after the other.[47] For example, in Levinsohn's eyes, the fifty years between Mendelssohn and his own *Beit yehudah* seemed a briefer age than all the periods that preceded it, and yet the period was 'packed with innumerable changes that affected the Jews living in Europe'.[48]

History was the arena where man could act autonomously and exercise freedom; unlike nature, which was subject to natural laws, human rational and moral processes operated in history. This was also the main claim made by Guenzburg in the introduction to his *Toledot benei ha'adam*.[49] Although the article was largely a literal translation of the introduction to Pölitz's book, Guenzburg made several additions, altering it to make it reflect the maskilic concept of history. To the maskil, history provided insights into the nature of man, his reason, spirit, and morality. Consequently, historical research was of supreme importance: 'It is extremely valuable to study the words of mankind, dispersed in all corners of the globe, the reach of man's intelligence, and the flight of his spirit to rise higher and higher like a child of God, and the copiousness of his quandaries that cast him lower and lower, until he descends to the level of a beast in the valley.'[50] There were two ways of acquiring knowledge of man's nature: philosophy showed 'how much man may attain with his monumental spirit' and history showed

---

[46] Mandelstamm, *Ḥazon lamo'ed*, i. 23–4, 28–9.   [47] Ibid., ii. 5–9.

[48] Levinsohn, *Beit yehudah*, ii. 161.

[49] Guenzburg, *Toledot benei ha'adam*, 1–24 (preface). Cf. the introd. in the original: Pölitz, *Die Weltgeschichte*, vol. i (written in 1823).   [50] Guenzburg, *Toledot benei ha'adam*, 1.

'how much man has really achieved'. By combining these two modes of knowledge, the historian could judge to what extent man had realized his innate potential. History was made up of a series of great events which utterly changed the face
of the world—such as the migration of peoples, the Crusades, inventions, and
discoveries—and of the great figures of the past, whose moral integrity, patriotic
deeds, universal contribution, and struggle for justice had earned them an eternal
place in the temple of history. The ideal historian was still the judge who applied
rational and moral yardsticks to determine who was worthy of praise and who
merited denunciation, but he also needed to possess a large measure of objectivity
and professionalism.[51] Man stood at the centre of history and was 'the great purpose upon which history rests'. The greatness of man did indeed attest to the
greatness of his Creator, but God appeared in history more as the primeval creator
than as the moving force behind events. This realm seemed to be left to the spirit
of man who, through his own faculties, was 'king and ruler over this land and his
desires are forever paramount'.

Guenzberg tried to tone down the historical role that Pölitz had attributed to
the German people in his book, and those parts of Pölitz's introduction which
emphasized the decisive part played by the Germans in history were omitted in
Guenzburg's Hebrew introduction. The maskil was interested in advancing the
idea of a single universal history, with common traits that enabled all human
beings, including the Jews, to identify with it and to develop a sense of belonging. At the very most, he was prepared to underscore the importance of Russia,
out of a sense of political loyalty or as a sop to the censor's demands. Another
change that Guenzburg made was to 'Judaize' Pölitz's introduction by deleting
every mention of the historical role of Protestantism, to which Pölitz had imputed
a revolutionary role at the dawn of the modern era, and which he viewed as a
modernizing, liberal, liberating, and enlightening element. Guenzburg also made
some significant changes in the list of great men cited by Pölitz, choosing to delete Charlemagne, John Huss, and Martin Luther from the list, which included
'universal' figures such as Zoroaster, Confucius, Alexander the Great, Julius
Caesar, Muhammad, and Columbus. Luther was removed from another list and
replaced by Copernicus and Galileo. Guenzburg found men of science, who had
made a universal contribution, more worthy of mention than the controversial
founder of a religious stream that had caused a schism. However, at the same
time Guenzburg stressed his view that great men actually exist outside their time
and their national affiliation, as a great human asset: 'They will not be regarded
as members of their nation or of their generation, for they are the property of the
entire human species.'[52]

The maskilic concept of history continued to be pragmatic in both senses of
the word: first, events were interconnected and explained on the basis of their

[51] Guenzburg, *Toledot benei ha'adam*, 1–3.
[52] Compare Guenzburg's preface, ibid. 9, 14, to Pölitz's, *Die Weltgeschichte*, i. 12.

context and the other of their occurrence, and secondly, lessons were extracted from the examples provided by the past. Fuenn, for example, combined these two aspects in elucidating the benefit to be gained by studying universal history in the introduction to his book *Shenot dor vador* (History of the Generations, 1844): 'May all the history books of all mankind be open before us, that we may learn from them the course of events and the various interrelated causes, the successes, and the hardships that follow one upon the heels of the other in consequence of the just and evil deeds that men perpetrate.'[53]

Since the maskilim were particularly intrigued by the changing aspects of history—the crises, transitions, and shifts—their historical writing took the form of a very dramatic narrative. For example, the 'explorers of history' were particularly interested in the changes and events that had occurred in the ancient world between the time of Alexander the Great and the reign of Augustus.[54] The recent Napoleonic Wars also stirred the feelings of the maskilim, who described them at length and in great detail. But beyond relating narrative history, the translators and adapters of universal history, in particular Guenzburg and Fuenn, tried to depict historical processes in broad strokes and to present the reader with a complete account of the course of universal history.

Following Pölitz, Guenzburg divided history into four periods: the ancient era and the Middle Ages were followed by a 'modern age' and a 'newest age' (*die neueste Zeit*). The course of universal history began on the Asian continent in 'the days of darkness and doubt'. Cyrus, king of Persia, caused the first shift, but because of his ignorance in 'matters of statesmanship' his kingdom crumbled. Alexander the Great, Aristotle's pupil, was more adept than Cyrus in the art of establishing an empire, but his also fell into disarray. The following period belonged to the emperors of Rome, until they fell prey to the Germanic tribes. The fall of Rome was given the standard eighteenth-century moralistic explanation, along with a certain nationalistic German element, which Guenzburg did not omit: when 'the spirit of Rome was vitiated by their corrupt morals and their feeble rulers, the pageant of peoples burst forth like a strong current of water sent by the era to infuse new blood into the veins of the weakened sons of the West and to create a race of healthy, solid folk'. During the period of mass migrations civilization declined and only gradually, as the bourgeois class grew stronger and trade developed, did events take a turn for the better. The spread of science, scientific inventions, and the discovery of America were some of the signs of the 'spirit awakening from its slumber', which brought in its wake the Reformation, absolutist rulers, and colonialism. All this had taken place in the 'modern age', while the French Revolution had opened yet another era—the 'newest age'.[55]

[53] Fuenn, *Shenot dor vador*, preface.
[54] Guenzburg, *Toledot benei ha'adam*, 226. As a child Guenzburg was fascinated by history, especially descriptions of war, which he found in the Book of Josipon or in *Shevet yehudah* (Guenzburg, *Avi'ezer*, 36–7, 41). [55] Guenzburg, *Toledot benei ha'adam*, 16–22.

Since Fuenn never completed his *Nidhei yisra'el*, we have only a partial picture of the way he depicted the course of universal history. In any event, even his relatively brief work shows that his approach was far more complex than Guenzburg's. The nation was the basic active element in history, in Fuenn's view, and the role of history was to record the 'events in the life of the entire people from its inception, the changes it underwent from the day it began to walk in the paths of time, moving towards its desired destination—its independence'. Starting from the familiar assumption that the individual biography is analogous to the history of a people ('as is the case with each and every man, so is the case with each and every people'), Fuenn arrived at the principle of dualism, according to which every people had a political history and a spiritual history which interact. Historiography should describe each history separately as the fruit of a distinct 'spirit', but the ideal was to arrive at an overall picture. Fuenn wrote his book before the publication of Krochmal's *Moreh nevukhei hazeman*, but even though he was not directly influenced by it, he had apparently absorbed the idealistic historical terminology, and perhaps also a touch of Hegelian terminology:

As history goes forth to search for all events in a people's past . . . it will divide in two the spirit that sustains the people: the spirit of the deeds of the people in its land and in the life of its state, the actions of its rulers and leaders, and these will be called the political spirit; and the spirit of the people's doings in its part of the divine realm, the life of its faith and enlightenment, the doings of its teachers and sages, the story of its teaching and wisdom, and this part will be called the moral spirit. However, while these are the two parts of the people's spirit, we must know that they are parts of one unity, two branches spreading from one trunk, nourishing one another and influencing each other. The political spirit will act upon the moral spirit, and the latter will also reach out to act upon the former. And if history should separate the two, it will not divide them completely; it will step back only in order to draw closer, and when it chooses to observe the course of each aspect separately and simultaneously, it will do so only in order to reunite the separate views into one overall, distilled, and purified view, for comprehensive, overall knowledge is grounded in individual pieces of knowledge.[56]

As far as the maskil was concerned, the 'political spirit', and the 'moral spirit' were not historically equal, nor did they have the same value. He preferred to deal mainly with the history of the spirit, the culture, and the universal religions rather than with political history. The priority assigned to moral history was also helpful to the maskil in discussing Jewish history in the Diaspora, where the Jewish people had hardly any political history, in Fuenn's view. Although one ought not to belittle 'political history', the 'aspects of moral history are far loftier, for they reveal to us the splendour of God, the doctrine of the spirit that emanates from the heavens . . . the destiny of man as a child of the Almighty and the glory of the kingdom of heaven'.[57]

Metaphors from the world of biology, such as those adopted by Krochmal,

[56] Fuenn, *Nidhei yisra'el*, 1–2, preface.   [57] Ibid. 3–4.

were yet another expression of the analogy between the history of the individual and that of nations. They provided a historical explanation for the flowering and decline of nations: 'Each and every nation passes through the various ages of life: it flowers in boyhood, grows in youth, wilts in its dotage.'[58] This explanation was useful to Fuenn in grappling with a question which he felt had weighty implications for Jewish history: how to understand the divergent historical course taken in the Middle Ages by the Christian peoples, on one hand, and the Muslim peoples, on the other. Fuenn's simplistic description of this disparity was that 'history of the Europeans is marked by the tendency to cast out members of other religions, to dim the light of wisdom and science. The history of the Orientals is marked by the tendency to draw members of other religions closer, to kindle the life of wisdom and enlightenment.' And he asked, 'Along what path did the spirit pass in order to overturn their foundations, making Christianity, based on love and compassion, into a religion so far from righteous, and Muhammedanism, founded on the sword and warfare, into a religion full of blessings and all that is good?' Fuenn's basic assumption was that the flaw did not lie in the essence of the Christian religion, but rather in the historical circumstances and in the particular state of the 'spirit of the people' that had accepted the principles of Christianity.

Another of Fuenn's assumptions was based on the idea that the Europeans were superior to the peoples of Asia and Africa: the ability of Europeans to develop, to advance, and to make use of reason far exceeded that of the 'sons of Asia and Africa', who by their nature were indolent and culturally backward. The analogy between the ages of 'individual man' and the 'history of mankind' was the key that helped Fuenn understand the historical disparity between Christians and Muslims. In each biological-historical phase, the people also took on the characteristics of each particular age: in the age of childhood, 'natural desire' predominated, free of any social or rational restraints; in the age of boyhood there were violent fluctuations, characterized by instability, contradiction, and extreme emotions; and in the age of maturity man's intelligence finally gained the upper hand and 'with the force of his reason and understanding', he became capable of suppressing his anger and emotions and placing them in the 'refining and purifying crucible'. The Christian peoples had appeared on the 'stage of history' just when the Roman empire was ageing, degenerating, and dying, 'like new sons of the land of Europe, coming to inherit the legacy of the dead'. The Germanic peoples were then in a state of boyhood, filled with youthful vigour, and when they reached the phase of their early manhood, they engaged in conquest and the establishment of empires. Throughout the Middle Ages, the Christian peoples had remained in the phase of historical youth; hence they were incapable of properly interpreting Christianity and even distorted it, descending into religious fanaticism. To a certain extent, Fuenn's historical explanation absolved the Christians of any moral responsibility and revealed an understanding of their behaviour as

[58] Ibid. 7.

the inevitable outcome of historical circumstances: 'Since it was not through rebelliousness and treachery that they committed evil acts . . . We will cast our eyes not upon their sins but will be mindful of their youthfulness, for they moved in the path marked out for them by their Creator.'[59]

Unlike the Christian peoples, who embraced their new religion in their youth, the Muslim peoples embraced theirs at the end of their historical boyhood, when 'their emotions had already been somewhat illuminated by the beam of the enlightenment'. That is why they had a more positive attitude towards other religions and cultures than the Christians, although even in that era they were still benighted, and it was their ignorance that led them to spread their religion through the power of the sword. In the late Middle Ages new peoples, with a childlike mentality—the Ottomans and the Seljuks—had gained control over Islam, and this had led to the decline of the nations of the East.[60]

Fuenn's sole reason for describing the historical, biological, and deterministic outlines in *Nidḥei yisra'el* was to provide a natural explanation for the historical transition taking place in Europe in the modern era. In his view, this was the period in which the Christian people had attained maturity, something they could not have done without first going through the earlier stages. The modern era, as an age of reason, was inevitable; this was the message the Russian maskilim reiterated to their target audience. In Fuenn's words:

Suddenly the skies of Europe were lit up and the entire land illuminated because of the Christian peoples; wisdom and enlightenment meet, justice and peace converge . . . Now the people of Europe have attained adult intelligence, having passed through the boyhood stage, after the turmoil of their youth has been subdued, after their lusts have been melted in the crucible of experience. Their tempered desires have become a sovereign's sceptre borne by monumental reason.[61]

Fuenn's *Nidḥei yisra'el* did not survey the modern age; Guenzburg, on the other hand, not only translated sections from Pölitz's work that discussed the modern era, but in the published parts of his translation dealt mainly with the 'most modern era', focusing on the French Revolution and the Napoleonic era. How were these historical phenomena portrayed and assessed by Guenzburg and other Russian maskilim, whose hands were tied by stringent censorship and whose books had to be written from a pro-Russian perspective? During the first half of the nineteenth century, when the maskilim in Russia were working on Hebrew translations and adaptations of these episodes of the recent past, the French Revolution and Napoleon were also the subject of intensive discussion in European literature and historiography. The controversy over 'the legend of Napoleon' and the merits of the revolution raged among liberals, conservatives, romantics, and nationalists, and its echoes reached the maskilim as well.[62] Their major source

---

[59] Fuenn, *Nidḥei yisra'el*, 111–15.   [60] Ibid. 61–3, 115–16.   [61] Ibid. 115.
[62] Ben-Israel, *English Historians*, chs. 7–8; Geyl, *Napoleon: For and Against*.

of information was, of course, the German literature on the subject, which they translated; Guenzburg's source was Pölitz's book. His universal history was completed before hostile relations between Germany and France had intensified. However, in later, updated editions Pölitz, like Rotteck and Schlosser, continued to view the revolution as an auspicious event, to support the political liberty and liberalism it had brought in its wake, and to view Napoleon as a historical hero, 'the giant of the newest age' (*der Riese der neuesten Zeit*).[63]

Politically, the Russian maskilim (like their Galician counterparts) supported the absolutist regime, on which they pinned all their hopes and expectations for both internal and external reform of Jewish life in Russia, and this prevented them from embracing political radicalism and republican government.[64] In his adaptation of Pölitz, therefore, Guenzburg was forced to temper as much as possible the praise Pölitz had lavished on the French Revolution. In his introduction to *Toledot benei ha'adam* Guenzburg makes only a casual reference to 'the time of the French conspiracy' as the beginning of the eighth period of universal history, moving directly on to a discussion of the wars that followed in its wake and a description of the deeds of the 'spirit of might' (in effect, a metaphor for Napoleon), which threatened all of France's neighbours until it was destroyed by Russia. What emerges is a distorted picture of the revolution, in which the victory of Alexander I (who was not mentioned at all in Pölitz's work) appears to be the culmination of the process that began with France's weakness during the reign of Louis XV. On the other hand, Guenzburg emphasized his sympathy with the absolutist regime. Describing ancient governments, he concluded that the ideal form, preferable to aristocracy, democracy, or republicanism, was 'the ancient, chosen regime desired by good people of all generations, a powerful monarchy controlled by just laws'.[65]

In *Sefer yemei hador*, written during the 1830s but only published in 1860, Guenzburg translated those chapters of Pölitz's book dealing with the French Revolution and 'the history of the new era, from the beginning of the changes in France in 1770 and up to the journey of Napoleon to the land of Russia in 1812'. Although the translation is essentially accurate, albeit abridged, Guenzburg's maskilic adaptation is unmistakable. The Russian reader of Hebrew could find in the book not only a description of the course of events but also an analysis of the causes of the revolution: the economic crisis, the extravagances of the monarchs, the privileges of the nobility, and the impact of the American Revolution.[66] Nevertheless, Guenzburg, who supported the legitimacy of the monarchist regime, did not identify with the revolution. While the causes of the revolution were understandable, a stronger ruler than Louis XV would have been able to find a solution

---

[63] Pölitz, *Die Weltgeschichte*, i. 4, 25, 32.

[64] Mahler, 'Sociological and Political Roots', 61–77.

[65] Cf. Guenzburg, *Toledot benei ha'adam*, p. xxii, and Pölitz, *Die Weltgeschichte*, i. 3–4.

[66] Guenzburg, *Sefer yemei hador*, 3–4. Cf. parallel chapters in Pölitz, *Die Weltgeschichte*, iv. 33 ff.

to France's problems and prevent revolution. The king did not use his power to nip revolutionary activity in the bud at the convocation of the Estates-General, and 'owing to the meagreness of his power, he was unable to find the strength in his soul to bring the rebels and insurgents to justice'. The revolutionaries, therefore, were depicted as criminal rebels, a gang of 'shameless' traitors. He could more easily and more accurately translate the passages in which Pölitz himself denounced the fanatics, particularly in his description of the radical stages of the revolution, the Terror, and the execution of the king.[67]

Napoleon rose from the darkness and chaos of the revolution, and Guenzburg portrays him against his tarnished backdrop as a commendable figure and historical hero. Napoleon's biography was translated and adapted into Hebrew several times in eastern Europe during the nineteenth century, and in every version one senses the same vacillation between admiration for a self-made hero who achieved greatness, on one hand, and condemnation of his inordinate ambition to control and dominate Europe, on the other.[68] Although Guenzburg's Napoleon was 'an exemplary man' of 'monumental spirit', he was also an opportunist who abused the ideology of the revolution: 'Liberty and equality were the magic words on French lips, catchphrases to sway the heart of the masses to desire [French rule].' Napoleon was a product of the revolution. The fact that he was transformed into an emperor was explained by the maskilim as a voluntary act of subjugation by a people whose soul had revolted against 'the yoke of the conspirators who continuously arose to destroy the land'.[69] Since the concepts underpinning the revolution had never been internalized, it was easy for a despot to take control of the masses. The maskilim lost whatever sympathy they had previously felt for Napoleon the moment he embarked upon his wars. It was clear to them that his every action was immoral and illogical, bringing him closer to his collision with Alexander I. The hero, carried away by his quest for power and homage, must ultimately be judged before the tribunal of history.

From the moment Napoleonic and Russian history crossed paths, the maskilim explained history from the Russian perspective. The writings of Germaisa and Guenzburg, as well as the observations of Fuenn, Levinsohn, and others, are filled with praise for the course of Russian history and the enterprises of the Romanov rulers.[70] Even such an aggressive step as the partition of Poland was portrayed as one of Catherine the Great's achievements and a punishment for the Poles, and was described quite matter-of-factly: 'And in 1779[!] eastern Poland was united with the land of Russia and an additional 1,600 square Persian miles were annexed

---

[67] Cf. Guenzburg, *Sefer yemei hador*, 6–8, 11, 20 and Pölitz, *Die Weltgeschichte*, iv. paras. 615–30; cf. Guenzburg, ibid. 20, and Pölitz, ibid. 65; Guenzburg, ibid. 5, and Pölitz, ibid. 35.

[68] Schiffer, *Toledot napoleon*, 4; Mohr, *Dagul merevavah*.

[69] Guenzburg, *Sefer yemei hador*, 130; id., 'Toledot napoleon', 12–13, 16, 25, 27–8.

[70] See Guenzburg, *Itotei rusiyah*, 16, 25–7; Germaisa, *Toledot rusiyah*; Fuenn, *Nidhei yisra'el*, 124; Levinsohn, *Efes damim*, 20–1.

to Russia.'[71] The failure of Napoleon's invasion of Russia was predictable because of Russia's power and because it contradicted the laws of history:

Those who study history have proven, by speaking the truth, that from the day nature began to lead man throughout the world, his path was marked before him from north to south . . . Napoleon, in his desire to overturn this system, strove to change the laws of nature, and this brought him to judgement and punishment, just as nature punished powerful sovereigns who preceded him, monarchs who rebelled and did deeds that were contrary to natural laws.[72]

Feivel Schiffer, for example, described Napoleon's defeat in 1812 as a battle filled with heroic deeds:

And twelve years [into the century] was the year of the great war . . . and the spirit of war touched the four corners of the universe, and a murdering star arose, and there sprang up a wrathful tribe that overran the boundaries of kingdoms and destroyed all the people of Europe. Roaring like a young lion, Napoleon, leader of a great army, went to war . . . Napoleon declared that one king alone would arise in the land, and there would be a single ruler over all the people. All the inhabitants of the coast obeyed him, fearing the great havoc that would be wrought by the sweeping, all-consuming, burnished sword in the hands of the slaughterer, who gathered up in his fist all the countries of Europe and who longed to subjugate to his will the hero of the north . . . Bonaparte said, Come, let us do battle! Napoleon raved and ranted with fury, and a fearful storm raged.[73]

The maskilim's anti-Polish attitude was yet another manifestation of their monarchist stance, their loyalty to Russia, and their admiration for its rulers. The Polish Revolt of 1831 was compared to the French Revolution of 1789, and the insurgents were depicted as lawbreakers influenced by French ideas, who had learned nothing from the 1793 'school of blood'. The Polish rebels demonstrated a lack of political intelligence—for there was no chance that the small Polish Republic could exist, surrounded as it was by three enormous kingdoms—as well as ingratitude towards the Russian government for its just policies towards the Poles.[74] Just as Schiffer, the maskil from Warsaw, admonished the Poles for not acknowledging Russia's benevolence towards them, the maskilim reprimanded Jewish society for failing to recognize the presence of 'the modern era' in the Russia of Nicholas I's reign.

In the maskilic view of the past, universal history was perceived as surging powerfully and irrevocably towards the maturity, enlightenment, and wisdom of the modern era. This movement appeared to be taking place throughout Europe, including both Russia and the Jews living there. In the 1840s Guenzburg wrote a strongly worded warning, based on his interpretation of history, to the rabbinic leadership: 'Your eyes have dimmed from seeing what these times have taken

[71] Germaisa, *Toledot rusiyah*, 11.   [72] Guenzburg, *Pi haherut*, 1, preface.
[73] Schiffer, *Toledot napoleon*, 195; id., *Devar gevurot*, 16–17.
[74] Schiffer, *Devar gevurot*, 72–86.

from you; that is why you love darkness and fear the light.'[75] Historical dynamics would not cease, and if the maskilic leadership did not mobilize to divert the new streams to more promising directions, the modern era would be attended by terrible destruction. Guenzburg couched his prophetic caveat in military terminology, taken from the history of the wars he so frequently translated:

Behold, you stand at the threshold of the modern age, and we, the writers, walk about to herald its coming and command you to provide it with a resting-place and prepare for it whatever it lacks; for its way is the way of soldiers who come to the city, and the quartermaster evacuates houses for their encampment and provides as much food as their heart desires. If the people of the city hearken and prepare what the army desires, it will arrive in an orderly fashion and take what has been made ready for it. It will not despoil, nor will it destroy. However, if the people do not believe in the quartermaster, as you do not believe in us, and prepare nothing, the new era will come like bold soldiers entering a city which has not made preparations for their coming. The army will do whatever it wishes and will evacuate houses for its encampment and take whatever crosses its path, and it will destroy and plunder a thousand times more than it needs, and will fill the land with death and chaos; heed my warning![76]

The maskilim's perception of their role as pioneers of the modern era thus derived from their interpretation of history. They saw themselves as the front-line reconnaissance team, whose social and cultural role as writers was to prepare society for its approaching rendezvous with the changes of the modern era, to ease this epic encounter, and to hasten its arrival.

THE MASKILIC CHAIN OF TRADITION

Levinsohn, the dominant figure in shaping the maskilic world-view in Russia from the 1820s onwards, was instrumental in imbuing the maskilic consciousness with faith in the modern era. 'The first days are already behind us', he wrote in *Teudah beyisra'el*, and, employing contrasting metaphors of night and day, darkness and light—a leitmotif of the Haskalah from its beginnings, he proclaimed the historical transition in Europe:

After an overcast, sombre night the dark clouds of ignorance that had hitherto hovered over the inhabitants of Europe were dispelled, and from the East, the sun of wisdom and the Enlightenment peeped forth, left the canopy that had covered it at eventide, and established its palace in the kingdom of Europe. Then the masses who had walked in darkness also saw a bright light, were purified in the crucible of the Enlightenment, and filled their hearts with wisdom. Ethics, knowledge, and the sciences found an abode among them, and the kings and princes who arose to rule them were merciful monarchs and wise men, in no way like the earlier kings in whose lands we lived, in Spain, France, Portugal, and elsewhere. And now all the peoples have cast out their stone hearts and capricious nature. The religious fanaticism and intolerance that once ruled their hearts have been extirpated too,

[75] Guenzburg, 'Kikayon deyonah', 38–48.   [76] Ibid. 47–8.

and all the nations of Europe, large and small, are endeavouring to reform their ways and are seeking the love of all men, irrespective of nationality and religion.[77]

How would the Jews become active participants in the new age? What significance did it have for them? And was an internal revolution called for in Jewish life? Levinsohn, who wholeheartedly believed in the dawning of a new era in the Europe and Russia of his time, invested enormous effort in explaining to Jewish society, and in particular to the learned élite, how the Jews could gain entry into the 'new era'. While he had depicted the course of universal history as one marked by drastic, revolutionary, and unprecedented change, in relation to the history of the Jewish people he proposed a restorative historical course, stressing continuity and succession. In Levinsohn's view, the upheavals in European history had provided the Jews with the essential conditions, not for launching an internal revolution, but for returning to the original, authentic path of their history, from which they had strayed at a certain stage. According to this view, all the distortions in the economic structure, education, and ethics of the Jews were products of historical circumstances, and not inherent in the character of the Jewish people or the course of Jewish history. Levinsohn greatly expanded this idea; he did not hesitate to point to the shortcomings of the Jews themselves, who shared responsibility for the deviations (for example, the spread of Lurianic kabbalah, the rise of the hasidic movement, and the predominance of the *pilpul* method of Torah study). He also supplied his readers with a great deal of evidence to prove that 'the deeds of your forefathers are eternally successful and are a goodly and just heritage'.[78]

He thus concluded that justification for the maskilic creed lay in Jewish history and that it was the maskil's duty to try to reconstruct an accurate picture of the past. The maskil constructed his picture of the future and his plans for social reform as he looked back into the Jewish past. He did not think of himself as a revolutionary rebelling against history, but as a man carrying on Jewish tradition and drawing upon the roots of Jewish history throughout the ages. To prove that this was truly the case, Levinsohn had to formulate a new structure of Jewish history, and to present what amounted to an alternative Jewish history. His purpose was twofold: to provide legitimacy for the path taken by the Haskalah and to refute the anti-maskilic arguments that depicted the maskil as a modern and alien phenomenon. The aim of this alternative history was to give credence to the idea that Jewish history had always been consonant with the ways of the

---

[77] Levinsohn, *Teudah beyisra'el*, 182. *Teudah beyisra'el* made a considerable impact on maskilim as well as on the young men who aspired to join their ranks. In the 1830s, for example, it was studied as a textbook in the new school in Odessa, with Zalman Dins as the teacher (see Werbel's letter to Gottlober, in Gottlober, *Zikhronot umasaot*, ii. 93–4). On the formative influence of this book on Fuenn, see his autobiography, 'Dor vedorshav', 264. For more on Levinsohn and his book, see Etkes, 'Between Change and Tradition'; Stanislawski, *Tsar Nicholas I and the Jews*, 52–5.

[78] Levinsohn, *Teudah beyisra'el*, 182.

Haskalah, and to invent a tradition with which the advocates of the Haskalah could identify and also claim to be following.

In *Teudah beyisra'el* Levinsohn included a vast inventory of examples presented as historical precedents, in accordance with the fundamental concept of maskilic history. A comparison of these precedents with the present situation would instantly reveal the great discrepancy between the ideal past and the present, and would convince his readers that 'we have rebelled against the Almighty, and walked an unpaved path'.[79] The method of historical precedent that underpins *Teudah beyisra'el* actually predetermined what was worthy of emphasis and which precedents could be recruited for the maskil's purposes.

Time was seemingly condensed in this history, which took an overview of different periods without distinguishing between them and subjected them to a single criterion derived from nineteenth-century maskilic values. The existence of a 'chain of Haskalah' was assumed, as an alternative to the accepted 'chain of tradition', and Levinsohn and the other Russian maskilim were seen as constituting the last links in this chain. They had inherited the 'torch of enlightenment' from their predecessors and were charged with passing it on. The basic issues that the 'chain of Haskalah' had to resolve were taken from the maskilic platform formulated by Levinsohn and other maskilim. These related to six topics on the maskilic agenda: education, language, *ḥokhmot* (i.e. secular, scientific fields of enquiry), occupation, attitude towards the state, and Jewish leadership.[80]

Education

The 'chain of Haskalah' showed that as far back as the Second Temple period there were Bible schools in every city, where children studied the books of the Bible in their order without skipping any parts, including the Prophets and the Hagiographa. Following a graded method, appropriate to the age of each pupil, the teachers also taught Hebrew, literal interpretation of the Bible (*peshat*), grammar, and cantillation.[81]

Language

Levinsohn regarded Hebrew as the cornerstone of Jewish identity, both as a language of communication for all Jews that preserved the 'religious link and the nation's existence', and as an ancient 'national' tongue, 'the mother of all Eastern languages', a knowledge of which would help to nurture Jewish self-respect. In *Teudah beyisra'el* the 'chain of Haskalah' bore witness to the fact that from the time of the Sages, through the *geonim*, the sages and kabbalists of the Middle Ages, and up to the Vilna Gaon, the great men of Israel had taken a favourable view of the study of the Hebrew language and Hebrew grammar—a point of con-

---

[79] Ibid. 152. Levinsohn, who wrote his book a short time after returning from Galicia, believed like other Galician maskilim that hasidism bore the major blame for the crisis besetting east European Jewry.

[80] See Levinsohn, *Beit yehudah*, ii. 148–54.   [81] Levinsohn, *Teudah beyisra'el*, 4–10.

tention in the confrontation between the maskilim and the representatives of the east European non-maskilic society, particularly the hasidim.[82] In addition, the 'chain of Haskalah' claimed that the sages of Israel had never disapproved of the study of the language of the surrounding society, 'and without a doubt, all the sages who knew the languages of the gentiles, like the Sanhedrin and the *tana'im* and their ilk . . . learned these from books and from schoolteachers'.[83] In the Second Temple period, for example, Jews in Palestine had employed a trilingual system: Hebrew, Greek as the language of the state, and Aramaic as the vernacular. Rabbi Yossi's objection in the Talmud to the use of Aramaic was exploited by Levinsohn to draw an analogy in support of the maskilim's demand that Yiddish be abandoned as the spoken language: 'In this land, why use the Yiddish language? Either the pure German tongue or the Russian language, for that is the language of the state.'[84]

Secular Studies

On the study of *hokhmot*, referring mainly to the natural sciences, Levinsohn claimed that the great men of the Jewish nation not only were actively engaged in this domain, but were also scientific pioneers. Moses, for example, was the 'father of the natural *hokhmot* and an important inventor, and David and Solomon delved into the wonders of nature'.[85] However, Levinsohn's efforts to prove the legitimacy of the sciences by way of historical precedent led him into a contradiction. On one hand, he rebuked traditional society for its anachronistic approach, but on the other, he himself was guilty of an exaggerated use of anachronisms. A good example is his discussion of astronomy. Levinsohn was prepared to assign a place in his gallery of the savants of astronomy to Noah as well as to Abraham, who was, according to the Sages, 'a great astrologer'; according to the sixteenth-century *Sefer yuhasin* (Book of Genealogy), he 'taught astrology in Egypt'; and according to Abrabanel, he 'was very well versed in the lore of the zodiac'. Abraham's image as a maskil was further reinforced, in Levinsohn's view, by other 'evidence' attesting to the fact that Abraham was also the author of books of philosophy and the inventor of writing. Nonetheless, owing to the loss of the ancient Jewish books of wisdom and the advance and accumulation of knowledge, the Jews now had no choice but to turn to non-Jewish wisdom literature, which in many cases was just a revised version of original Jewish wisdom; hence those Jews who engaged in it were not venturing into a sphere alien to Judaism, but rather were returning to a forgotten source.[86] To substantiate the Jewish past, Levinsohn appended a lexicon of almost 160 historical figures, which took up forty pages (about a fifth of the entire book). According to Levinsohn, these

---

[82] Ibid. 21–8, esp. 22 n. 2.   [83] Ibid. 42.   [84] Ibid. 37–9.   [85] Ibid. 69–73.
[86] Ibid. 13 (n.), 79–88, 109–12. Levinsohn's anachronism has already been noted by Etkes, 'Between Change and Tradition', 14.

men passed on the 'Haskalah', in the sense of fostering the *ḥokhmot* (sciences), from one to another in an unbroken historical sequence. This, then, amounted to a 'chain of Haskalah' arranged in chronological order, like the classic Jewish 'chain of tradition', and even incorporating some of the men that appeared in the latter. The 'chain of Haskalah' began with David, Achitophel, Solomon, and the Prophets, and ended with Mendelssohn, the Vilna Gaon, and Rabbi Baruch Schick of Shklov (1744–1804). A brief item was devoted to each figure, relating his achievement to science or languages, or Levinsohn's attitude towards him. The scholarship and piety of these figures was incontestable, and was familiar from traditional historical literature. The most exemplary trait of the 160 men in the lexicon, defining them as historical heroes, was their adherence to ideal mas-kilic values. The construction of a pantheon of maskilic heroes was, as seen earlier, a hallmark of 'maskilic history'. Levinsohn, however, went much further than his predecessors. Instead of 'screening' the various figures and choosing the maskilim among them, he took nearly all the well-known men in Jewish history and attested to their maskilic traits. A young scholar reading *Teudah beyisra'el* might have been surprised to learn that anyone adopting the path of the Haskalah was not rebelling against tradition but was actually faithfully continu-ing it, following a well-paved path walked by most of the great men of the nation in the past.

Occupation

Levinsohn employed a similar tactic in his attempt to prove that if the Jews were to turn to new, productive types of occupation, particularly agriculture, as recom-mended in Alexander I's 1804 edict, this would not amount to a revolution in the pattern of Jewish life but would rather correct an anomaly and bring about a return to the ways of their forefathers. In this domain, too, Levinsohn proposed a 'chain of Haskalah', which, in his words, demonstrated that 'all the holy and great men of the generation did their utmost to eschew the charity and gifts of the people, and earned their livelihood from their craftsmanship or their wisdom'. Until the end of the Second Temple period, agriculture had been the dominant Jewish occupation, and it was only due to the political crisis of the time that Jews gradually became craftsmen. The excessive and unnatural concentration of Jews in branches of commerce was an outcome of their exile, their insecurity, and their impermanence—the result of the decrees forbidding them to work in agri-culture or the crafts, and of the need to be mobile. While the Jews had engaged in the sciences throughout their history, they had not worked in agriculture in all periods but only during an ideal era in the distant past. In the nineteenth century, however, circumstances were favourable, making it possible for the Jews to re-turn to a life of agriculture after a long break. In *Teudah beyisra'el* agriculture was depicted as an occupation that would guarantee the success of a nation and even improve its morals; in Jewry's golden age:

our nation was at the height of its success as long as most of its people worked the land, with each man dwelling safely under his vine and under his fig tree, knowing no fear. They were accustomed to a life of hard labour, and grew so mighty they angered the nations of the world . . . their hearts were perfectly attuned with God and men, none among them cheated their brethren nor knew any prevarication . . . false oaths were also alien to them.[87]

This period lasted from the time of the Jews' exodus from Egypt until Solomon's reign. From that time onwards they strayed, digressing into trade, and agriculture was no longer their dominant occupation. In the eyes of Levinsohn and other maskilim, only large-scale commerce seemed a vital and fitting occupation in which one could adhere to moral precepts; they believed that petty trade led to lawbreaking and corruption. Why, then, Levinsohn wondered, 'should we not follow in the footsteps of our ancient forebears and work the land as they did?'[88]

Attitude towards the State

Levinsohn felt that in light of historical precedents, the maskilim were justified in demanding loyalty and obedience to the Russian government. By taking this stance, the Jews would once again be continuing the tradition of their fore-fathers, following in the footsteps of the ancients. Even more: while in the past the Jews had prayed for the welfare of an idolatrous monarchy, the benevolent kings of the present were monotheistic and pursued justice and tolerance. In regard to the internal Jewish debate on service in Nicholas I's army, Levinsohn provided evidence from the past attesting that Jews in various periods (such as Samuel Hanagid, who had served as a general in eleventh-century Granada) had not abstained from military service, but had even been ready to lay down their lives for the sake of their rulers.[89]

Leadership

In all generations almost up to the present Levinsohn claimed, 'no man could ever have attained a high position as one of the heads of the community if he had not possessed these qualifications [a knowledge of science and languages], in addition to excelling in the Torah'. Hence the requirement laid down in the 1804 edict, which made knowledge of the state language a prerequisite for the appoint-ment of rabbis and heads of the congregation, was not a harsh decree, for it was consonant with Jewish tradition. Even Moses was a 'great statesman', well versed in languages and science, as were other ideal figures such as Mordecai, Philo, Manasseh ben Israel, and Mendelssohn.[90]

How did the opponents of the Haskalah react to the maskilim's attempt to take over the Jewish past and present it as a maskilic past? Non-maskilic society in

---

[87] Levinsohn, *Teudah beyisra'el*, 161–8, 173–4. On the maskilim's views of the economic occupa-tions of Jews, see Mordechai Levin, *Social and Economic Values*.

[88] Levinsohn, *Teudah beyisra'el*, 173, 184–5.

[89] Ibid. 130–1, 186.   [90] Ibid. 105–7, 157 (n.).

eastern Europe did not leave a wide range of sources reflecting its attitudes towards the Haskalah during this period, but there are two examples that relate directly to *Teudah beyisra'el* and to Levinsohn's mode of argumentation.

The first source is a virulent anti-maskilic pamphlet entitled *Sefer makhnia zedim* (Subduing the Evildoers) written by Rabbi Nathan Sternharz of Nemirov (1780–1845), one of the principal disciples of Rabbi Nahman of Bratslav.[91] The pamphlet was apparently written in the late 1820s or 1830s. 'And now just recently we have heard', Sternharz wrote, 'that they have printed some defiled book and called it T.B. [*Teudah beyisra'el*] to show that several great scholars and *tana'im* knew their sciences'. Sternharz referred to this claim with derision and tried to disprove Levinsohn's 'chain of Haskalah' by demonstrating that the real situation was just the opposite: the trends espoused by the Haskalah had always been rejected. In his eyes, Levinsohn's approach was absurd; 'and I do not know why they do not produce evidence showing that all the great men, the *tsadikim* and the *tana'im*, never shaved their beards, and that not a single one of them studied their science and their languages'.[92]

It was true, Sternharz admitted, that there were some sages who made use of secular sciences to serve them in their study of the Torah, 'for certainly in the external *hokhmot* there are also several words of truth and several things which the great can use'. This, however, clearly referred to *hokhmot* that were subservient to the principal Jewish activity—the study of the Torah—and to sciences that had not been learned in 'their evil churches'. In his view, there were no grounds for introducing changes in the traditional Jewish educational system, and certainly one could find no legitimacy for this in tradition and history. 'Greek wisdom', which was forbidden by the Sages, was interpreted by Sternharz in its broadest sense to encompass all of 'their evil *hokhmot*'. He also found an alternative historical precedent with which to goad Levinsohn:

Then, too, in ancient times, everyone who followed their evil ways would cast off all restraint and abandon prayer entirely, and hence all men whose hearts were truly filled with the fear of God would rebuke them. And Rabbi Shlomo ben Aderet, may his memory be blessed, excommunicated them . . . yet in each and every generation there were a few men who were so overpowered by evil that they did not hearken to the voice of the truly learned men, the holy ones, and they behaved licentiously, and some in ancient times even converted to another religion by learning their alien sciences.[93]

With these words, which echoed Rabbi Nahman's hostile attitude towards non-Jewish studies, Sternharz attempted to 'restore' the Jewish past to those whom he regarded as its legitimate owners—the opponents of the Haskalah—and to employ it as an anti-maskilic weapon. He summed up his criticism of *Teudah beyisra'el* by commenting that it was preposterous for the maskilim presumptu-

[91] Sternharz, *Sefer makhnia zedim*, 5–6; see Feiner, 'Sola Fide!', 65–88.
[92] Sternharz, *Sefer makhnia zedim*, 2   [93] Ibid. 21–2.

ously to 'state their opinions based on the ways of the Holy Torah', when they are the very ones who had deviated from it, whereas 'we are following in the ways of our sacred forefathers'.[94]

Another anti-maskilic reaction may be found in *Adat ya'akov* (The Community of Jacob) by Rabbi Jacob Eichhorn of Krakow, written in 1844 and printed with the approbation of the town rabbi.[95] While the immediate impetus for writing the book was the tension between the traditional leadership and society and modern groups in Krakow, Eichhorn directly referred to *Teudah beyisra'el* in the course of his attack on the writings of the maskilim. He described it as a book by 'one of the residents of Kremenets in the Ukraine', written with the sole purpose of undermining the study of Torah from within and distorting the image of the Jews in the eyes of their non-Jewish neighbours—namely, as an unprecedented act of calumny. Like Sternharz, Eichhorn was enraged by Levinsohn's historical claims: 'He cites evidence from the ancient luminaries, who lived 800 years ago, like Rabbi Sa'adiah Gaon and his fellows, who knew many languages and much science, and usurps a share in the ancient chronicles to vindicate his way, the way of sinners and fools who cast off piety.'[96]

Eichhorn was convinced that the Haskalah would lead Jews to abandon the ways of the Torah, and that the reality of Jewish life offered no hope for true social and economic integration into the society at large. He did not believe that the study of languages and science would help in this regard, and as for engaging in agriculture, the Jewish religion almost completely prevented that at the time. If indeed there were in the past exceptional men who studied external *hokhmot*, that had no bearing on this generation. The great achievements in Torah study of those few sages who would have regarded the sciences as subordinate to their scholarly activity could not be compared to those of later generations.[97]

Criticism of the 'historical precedent' method, used by Levinsohn in his maskilic propaganda, also came from within the maskilic camp. Although Guenzburg did not make specific mention of Levinsohn in his criticism, he did refer to all those maskilim who tended to 'impute to the writings of the ancient sages recent philosophical thoughts and theories, the meaning of which was not known to the ancients'.[98] With these words, Guenzburg not only enunciated a concept of history that eschewed anachronisms, but also revealed an approach that was much more radical than Levinsohn's. Anyone seeking the truth, in his view, should not adopt a strategy of deception and disguise that made the ancients into representatives of the maskilim:

I would have had no trouble taking a simple figure of speech from one of the legends and dressing it in the foreign garb devised by the philosophers, and beautifying it with lovely words so that it would find favour with all who see it . . . but I am a lover of truth and I will

---

[94] Ibid. 23. [95] See also Gelber, 'The Jews in the Krakowian Republic', 80–1.
[96] *Sefer adat ya'akov*, 3b, 4a. [97] Ibid. 4a. [98] Guenzburg, *Kiryat sefer*, 115–16.

not resort to any falsehoods in order to confer the honour of the later sages upon the ancients, who never laboured to achieve it.[99]

To counter Levinsohn's restorative historical concept of Jewish history, Guenzburg proposed a radical concept of the modern era that applied the principle of the 'new age' in universal history to Jewish history as well. Not only did he aver that the device of the 'historical precedent' was not underpinned by historical truth, but he also believed that it ran counter to the maskilim's aim of persuading Jewish society that the new was of value in its own right, in the achievement of progress, and in the need to make a break with the past:

And instead of endeavouring to plant intelligence in the hearts of our people so that they will understand that wisdom [science] is of great value even if there is no allusion to it in the aggadah or the midrash, they are being led by vain efforts to despise any wisdom or knowledge that the ancients did not possess, as if wisdom had time limits set upon it, and was told: Until this time, and no later, shall you make yourself known to men.[100]

These differences of opinion about the tactics the maskilim ought to adopt in their propaganda efforts deepened in the 1860s and 1870s and became one of the criteria differentiating the moderate and the radical streams of the Haskalah. In this debate Levinsohn represented the historical consciousness typical of the moderate Haskalah, that looked back to the Jewish past and reshaped it along maskilic lines. Guenzburg, on the other hand, represented a maskilic orientation that turned to the 'modern era', a period that was not necessarily the authentic heir of the Jewish past but was capable of surpassing it. However, both streams shared a belief in the turning-point that had occurred in universal history. As a writer of philological and historical works, Levinsohn belonged to the circle of the east European Wissenschaft des Judentums. In the middle of the century he wrote to Fuenn that 'my research into Jewish antiquity has always been my pleasure and my sole preoccupation', and his keen interest in the past is clearly reflected in the scores of historical issues he discussed in his works and the lengthy notes he attached to them.[101] Major issues he tackled included the history of Hebrew grammar from the time of the *geonim* onwards, the early history of Polish–Russian Jewry, the history of European languages and writing, the life of Josephus, Jews in remote lands (the Khazars, the Ethiopian Jews, and the Jews of India), and many geographical–historical topics and bibliographical questions (the date and author of the book of Ben Sira, the Zohar, etc.). After Levinsohn became famous as a 'researcher of antiquity', he received many requests from maskilim asking him to provide them with information about Jewish history. Traditional Jews also turned to him in the hope of benefiting from his copious knowledge of history, as well as from what they regarded as his connections with the authorities. These requests were the impetus for Levinsohn's apologetic books *Efes damim* (No

[99] Guenzburg, *Kiryat sefer*, 115–16.   [100] Ibid. 115.

[101] Levinsohn's letter to Fuenn (1851), in B. Nathanson, *Sefer hazikhronot*, 92–4.

Blood, 1837), written in reaction to blood libels, *Yemin tsidki* (In Support of my Justification, 1837), and *Ahiyah hashiloni* (Ahijah the Shilonite, 1863), condemning missionaries and anti-Jewish converts.[102] Here too, he made use of historical proof and precedent to counter Christian claims against the Jews.

Levinsohn's optimistic view of the modern era compelled him to find some excuse for the appearance of the blood libel in Russia, so that his overall schema of universal history, and in particular his faith in the historical turning-point, would not be impaired. His historicization of the blood libel, by separating it from early Christianity, on one hand, and delegitimizing it in the modern era, on the other, played the central role in the argument of *Efes damim*. From the formal standpoint, in choosing the formula of a literary confrontation between a Jew and a Christian, Levinsohn was ostensibly continuing the tradition of the Jewish–Christian disputation. However, in this dialogue the two disputants are on the same side of the controversy. Instead of portraying a conflict, Levinsohn described an encounter, in keeping with the maskilic conception, shaped along the lines of the Mendelssohn–Lessing encounter: an interdenominational meeting on the basis of religious tolerance and agreement about the values of the European Enlightenment. The heroes of *Efes damim*—Maimon, the chief rabbi of Jerusalem, and Simias, the Greek Orthodox patriarch of that city—share a common goal: to free themselves from 'the Kingdom of evil, which is cruel religious hatred'. During their meeting, which is characterized by mutual respect, they kiss, drink coffee, and smoke together.

The question debated by Maimon and Simias was: has the blood libel existed since antiquity and is it one of the foundations of Christianity? The roots of the blood libel, in Levinsohn's view, lay in medieval mentality, with its religious fanaticism and superstition, but were certainly not ancient: 'I am surprised to hear you, a wise man,' Maimon argued, 'so well-versed in all branches of history, and in particular the history of the Christian church, say that this has existed from the foundation of the Christian religion. Heaven forbid! There is not the slightest hint of this accusation against the Jews in any of the ancient chronicles.'[103] There is a sort of role reversal in the blood libel: the Christians, who had been persecuted by the pagans, became persecutors in their turn when Christianity became the dominant religion, and the blood libel against the Jews was a variant of an accusation that had been levelled against the Christians in the distant past.[104] Its beginnings lay, in Levinsohn's opinion, in the reign of Alfonso X, king of Castile in the mid-thirteenth century, and in the future the blood libel would gradually disappear as enlightenment grew stronger. The historical mechanism seemed to be quite simple: the better the attitude towards the Jews, the

---

[102] Levinsohn, *Efes damim*; id., *Yemin tsidki*; id., *Ahiyah hashiloni*. See also J. Klausner, *History of Modern Hebrew Literature*, iii. 52–3; Lederhendler, *The Road to Modern Jewish Politics*, 100–10.

[103] Levinsohm, *Efes damim*, 13, 43–5.

[104] Ibid. 16–18. Cf. a similar conception in Guenzburg, *Ḥamat damesek*, 2–3.

more progress would be made towards a future of world peace between Jews and their neighbours: 'For since the time that the blood libel has become a thing of the past, some fifty or sixty years now, the Jews have drawn closer to the Christians, living with them in amity, and the degree to which the Enlightenment has taken root among the Jews is beyond measure.'[105] Levinsohn hoped that the fictional encounter between Maimon and Simias would serve as an ideal model for an enlightened European Judaeo-Christian world.

Levinsohn believed history attested that the Jews were superior to their non-Jewish neighbours, in their achievements as well as their moral standards. He depicted a Jewish history that could successfully compete with any other, maintaining that biblical historiography was true, objective, and more exact than any other historiography, that Jewish historical consciousness was more profound than that of any other nation, and that the Jewish people itself was one of the most ancient on the globe. He claimed that one of the most important qualities of an 'honourable and happy nation' was its antiquity and 'its definite knowledge of its ancient lineage, going back to the very quarry from which it was hewn'.[106] In his quarrel with Voltaire's anti-Jewish views, Levinsohn overturned the deist claim about the cruelty of the Jews as depicted in the Bible:

The reader of the history books of the Greeks and Romans and of the other ancient peoples will see the magnitude of the cruelty the nations inflicted upon one another, in particular through religious hatred; and even close to our own time, we have heard and learned what was perpetrated on a single night in Paris [the St Bartholomew's Day massacre], not to mention the brutal Inquisition in Spain.[107]

As examples of the Christians' abject level of morality, Levinsohn cited the St Bartholomew's Day massacre, the Crusades, and Luther's words about burning the Jews. Earlier periods of history were characterized by the ignorance of the non-Jews, whereas the Jews, the only monotheists, were the 'enlightened' of the ancient world. At the very hour when the various nations were 'still lying dreamlike . . . in the slumber of ignorance, like the insects of the forests, seeking prey like the evening wolves, and like cattle eating the plants of the land, barefoot and naked without shame, and resembling beasts as they walked', there was only one nation working towards the enlightened age: 'Only the family of Jacob walked alone in the path of the more advanced nations then, but it was far loftier than they were in its pure faith, so free of all defilement and superstition.'[108]

Levinsohn's version of Jewish history, accompanied by examples cited for polemic and apologetic purposes, was thus the history of an 'honourable and happy nation', in which one could take pride. Its antiquity, historical awareness, endurance, spiritual achievements, and high moral standards rendered the 'Israel-

---

[105] Levinsohn, *Efes damim*, 47–8.   [106] Levinsohn, *Beit yehudah*, i. 1–3, 44–5.
[107] Ibid., ii. 34–5; id., *Aḥiyah hashiloni*, 107–8.
[108] Levinsohn, *Beit yehudah*, i. 36–7; id., *Teudah beyisra'el*, 110; id., *Efes damim*, 65–6.

ite nation' superior to all the Christian nations, both in the past and in the present. Levinsohn asked all the attackers and persecutors of Jewry to take a second look at Jewish history, in the belief that it would convince them to adopt a more favourable attitude towards the Jews and to abandon their prejudice against them.

In *Beit yehudah* (The House of Judah), written in 1827–8 but only published ten years later, Levinsohn reconstructed the history of the 'Israelite nation'. He also grappled with one of the fundamental elements of modern Jewish historical awareness: the distinction between religious and political elements in Judaism and Jewish history. In the final analysis, Levinsohn chose to write what he called 'the annals of the Jewish religion from its inception to the present day', but he expanded the concept of 'religion' to embrace not only 'divine religion', which dealt with beliefs and commandments, but also 'civic religion', which encompassed everything the maskilim defined as *derekh erets* (literally 'way of the world', signifying courtesy, cleanliness, respect for parents, proper decorum, etc.) or the 'teachings of man': languages, crafts, literature, science, and economic affairs. 'Religion', in Levinsohn's interpretation, encompassed all those spheres which the maskilim had urged the traditional society to accept as legitimate alongside the more narrowly defined religious tradition. In his historical survey of the 'annals of the Jewish religion', Levinsohn also proposed an alternative history that legitimized the Haskalah. In his own words, 'The Israelite nation has always differed from other nations, for in its case the Torah-oriented religion, political affairs, all the fields of study and sciences, and all modes of behaviour and manners are intertwined, interconnected, and joined together, so that there is no difference between them and they all fall within the scope of religion.'[109]

However, one must avoid misinterpreting Levinsohn's concepts. His inclusion of the 'political' sphere in 'religion' does not mean that he viewed Jewish history as political history, but rather that he drew a distinction between the internal political content of the nation's history, i.e. culture, economy, and the like, and its political status. For Levinsohn, Jewish history was first and foremost the history of the Sages, Jewish literature, and ideological streams, whereas a separate 'political history' would only include the external framework which determined the 'political status' of the Jewish people in all periods and places.

The structure of *Beit yehudah* reflects this approach. To his 'annals of religion' Levinsohn added a brief preface entitled 'The Vestibule of the House: The History of Jewry from the Standpoint of its Political Status'. This described the political regime of the Jewish people when it resided in its own land, and its status in Christian Europe and in the modern era. The reader must pass through the 'outer vestibule', as Levinsohn put it, before entering the 'house' itself. In principle, he believed there was a connection between the political and the external, on one hand, and the religious and the internal, on the other: 'A reader of

[109] Levinsohn, *Beit yehudah*, i. 5.

this book will, from time to time, need to have some knowledge of the political standing of the Jews in the past, apart from the issue of their religious standing',[110] but in fact there is scarcely one example of such a connection in the book (except, of course, in the modern era).

In fact, his periodization of the 'external history' also differed from that of the 'history of the religion'. The political form of government was Levinsohn's criterion for dividing 'external history' into seven periods: the patriarchal period, from the time of the Patriarchs to Moses, during which the Jews were nomads; the democratic period, during which God was the sovereign and Moses and the elders served as a senate or parliament, managing the life of the people according to the Mosaic law; the period of the Judges, who were analogous to the Roman emperors; the government of the kings, until the destruction of the First Temple; the period of sharp fluctuations between slavery and freedom during the Second Temple period; 1,700 years of exile; and the seventh era, beginning at the end of the eighteenth century, which had produced signs of change leading to the granting of freedom and civil rights to the Jews.[111] The 'internal history', in contrast, was divided into 'ten epochs', based on the criterion of 'the great changes that took place in religion, the Torah, and wisdom'. It began with natural religion or philosophy during the period from Adam to Abraham, and continued with revealed religion, prophecy, the Oral Torah, the *geonim*, kabbalah, and philosophy, ending with the Vilna Gaon, Mendelssohn, and the changes that had taken place in the early nineteenth century.[112] Levinsohn acknowledged the interdependence of the 'history of religion' and the history of 'political status', but he did not succeed in integrating the two in his book.

Just as he constructed a 'chain of Haskalah' in *Teudah beyisra'el* and the concept of the superiority of Jewish history in *Efes damim*, Levinsohn employed his 'history of religion' in *Beit yehudah* for the purpose of apologetics directed at non-Jewish society and for internal propaganda. Again and again he returned to the anachronistic images of renowned Jewish figures: Abraham was portrayed as the great teacher of the human race, particularly for having made the transition from 'natural religion' to 'revealed religion'. Moses made his contribution to universal civilization as an enlightened man of science, and the prophet Samuel established a 'general school' and societies of prophets which were actually 'societies of writers or scholars'.[113] A typical example of Levinsohn's manipulation of history to support the maskilic platform is his interpretation of the emergence of sects during the Second Temple period. He asserted that the fundamental difference between the Pharisees, the Sadducees, and the Essenes was in their attitude towards the introduction of alien culture into Judaism. While the Sadducees regarded the study of external *ḥokhmot* as a sin, and hence totally prohibited it,

---

[110] Levinsohn, *Beit yehudah*, i. 5.
[111] Ibid. 5–17. Cf. B. Shenfeld, 'Ma'amar hahanhagah', 34–41.
[112] Levinsohn, *Beit yehudah*, i. 19–22.   [113] Ibid. 29–30, 30–3, 38–40, 146–65.

concentrating solely on Torah learning, the Pharisees and Essenes were closer to the maskilic ideal. The Pharisees 'delved deeply into the wisdom of the Torah', and never shrank from using secular studies for this purpose, even accepting ancient philosophy as a framework for understanding the Torah and as a desirable sphere of wisdom in its own right. According to Levinsohn, the Pharisees assumed that philosophy was a system of rational and conceptual methods originating in divine intelligence, and that although these were not handed down at Sinai, they were planted in the hearts of men by God—a notion close to Mendelssohn's well-known distinction, in *Jerusalem* (1783), between rational truths and revealed truths. In Levinsohn's view, the Essenes were moderate maskilim who tried to bridge the gap between the other two positions and believed that the fundamental elements of secular studies were alluded to in the revealed Torah. 'In each and every generation', Levinsohn asserted, 'these three positions hold sway over the Jewish people.'[114] The distinctions he drew between Sadducees, Pharisees, and Essenes were, of course, no more than an anachronistic model for the divisions that Levinsohn saw in his own time. The distinction he drew between the 'Pharisee maskil' and the 'Essene maskil' was in fact one between the ideal Mendelssohnian maskil, who argued that European culture, science, and philosophy embodied rational truths worthy of legitimization on their own merits, and the moderate maskil, like Levinsohn himself, whose thinking was constantly coloured by the claim that enlightenment also existed immanently in the Torah and in Jewish history.

It is these digressions on topical issues, of which there are quite a few in *Beit yehudah*, that give Levinsohn's 'history of religion' its polemical nature. After praising the talmudic period as one in which the Jews were anxious to acquire knowledge and wisdom, Levinsohn commented that in the present era such enthusiasm was considered shameful: 'As a matter of fact, they regard the absence of such knowledge as great wisdom, devoutness and sanctity.'[115] Levinsohn also used Maimonides as an exemplary model of a maskil who succeeded in creating the perfect synthesis between intelligence and religion, science and Torah, and he regarded the banning of Maimonides' philosophy in the thirteenth and fourteenth centuries as an outrage. Levinsohn blamed a group of 'uncultured' youth for the ban imposed by Rabbi Solomon ben Aderet (1235–1310) on the study of philosophy, stating that their extreme behaviour, superficial education, and deviation from the middle road ('so patently obvious in our times in this country') had aroused an emphatic counter-reaction on the part of the rabbis.[116] Levinsohn classified the art of magic as a 'natural wisdom', like the 'magnetism' and 'mesmerism' of his own time, and asserted that while kabbalah may have begun as a true theory, it was distorted by frivolous men who 'delude the masses'.[117]

Levinsohn's interpretation of Jewish history was thus a recasting of the past in the mould of the 'moderate Haskalah'. The purpose of his 'history' was to persuade, to remonstrate, to testify, and to justify to Jewish society—particularly its

[114] Ibid. ii. 27–9.   [115] Ibid. 59–60.   [116] Ibid. 124–5 (n.).   [117] Ibid. 126–33.

intellectual élite—the maskilic platform, together with all its proposed reforms in the spheres of organization, education, occupation, language, and even modes of thinking. Levinsohn was so carried away by his propagandist aims that, despite his broad knowledge of historical literature, he was only capable of delving into the past with the aid of his maskilic criteria. Consequently, in the final analysis, although he was sharply critical of the traditional use of anachronisms, he created his own 'maskilic anachronism'. Nonetheless, the maskilic awareness of the historical transition taking place in the political and universal 'external history' of Europe linked the 'modern era' with the 'internal history' of the Jewish people and called for a restoration, or regeneration, of Jewish society. This restoration, however, was of course selective. It was based on the values and aims of the maskilim, and hence did not include, for example, any ideas about rehabilitating and reconstructing Jewish political frameworks.

THE USE OF HISTORY IN MASKILIC PROPAGANDA

Levinsohn's keen interest in Jewish history was not unique among Russian maskilim during Nicholas I's reign. There were numerous publications dealing with the Jewish past, and several instances illustrating the practical use of examples from the past can be cited.

In 1828 Bezalel Stern arrived from Tarnopol to take up his position as principal of the maskilic school in Odessa. In the speech he gave in German before Russian representatives of the government, teachers, and students on the day he took office, he preached loyalty to the government and to the ideal of 'educated Jews'. He apparently found justification for this ideal in Levinsohn's *Teudah beyisra'el*, and his argument again revolved around the maskilic awareness of the historical transition:

Then he recalled the early days of the world, the Middle Ages, the time of darkness that passed without bringing any good to the Jewish people, whose lives were wretched for they were relentlessly persecuted by the gentiles of Europe. And wherever the people of Israel settled, they were isolated and separated from other peoples and they lived in fear. In the depths of the darkness which engulfed them, they saw nothing of what was happening in the land. Then God removed the mask of darkness that covered the people, and the dawn of wisdom rose, and light illuminated the eyes of the nations and their rulers. Blessed be God, who changed the times and replaced the darkness with light; blessed be He who swayed the hearts of the kings and rulers to better the lives of our people and to bless us with the salvation and justice of their great benevolence in the present day. How fortunate we are to live under the rule of our lord, his exalted majesty, the emperor, who is a wise, God-fearing ruler. And, like him, his truth-loving servants do all in their power to raise us from the dust that overspread us in the time of darkness and death.[118]

The government's campaign from 1840 onwards to organize a system of reformed schools confirmed the maskilim's recognition of the historical turning-

[118] Gottlober, *Zikhronot umasaot*, ii. 90.

point. They urged the Jews to accept this new initiative, calling upon them to compare the dark past with the light of the present: 'My people! Open your eyes,' Gottlober exhorted, 'and see your happiness in these times as compared to ancient times, and take cognizance of how God has blessed you.'[119] In a letter to Lilienthal written in 1843 Gottlober sketched his plan for writing a book about 'the history of the wise men' who had lived in Poland during earlier generations. The book was intended for students, and using Levinsohn's method, he intended to claim and prove that there were maskilim among Polish Jewry too, and that their presence in Russia was not a revolutionary innovation.[120] With the approach of the convocation of the Rabbinical Committee at St Petersburg in 1843, which was charged with promoting government-sponsored education, maskilic optimism increased even further, and maskilic propaganda depicted Nicholas I not only as a benevolent king belonging to the 'modern era' but also as an unprecedentedly liberal ruler, even in comparison to such ideal models as Frederick the Great and Joseph II, and certainly in comparison to Napoleon: 'For which of them cast a benevolent eye upon the children of Israel, to rule them compassionately before they were cleansed of their defiling scum? Before they returned from darkness to blazing light?'[121] As far as Russia was concerned, Nicholas's policy was described as benevolent and lenient, because it was not made conditional upon internal change among the Jews:

And did Frederick the Great take the time to show this people the path they must take before Moses Mendelssohn risked his life to lead them and remove the obstacle? And Napoleon I, who gave all peoples equality under his rule, did not find it in his heart to give them civil justice until he found them worthy and ready for this . . . and King Joseph did not, of his own volition, establish schools in his kingdom for our youth until the great people of our nation pleaded for his compassion.[122]

Another example of maskilic propaganda supported by historical arguments was the 'clothing edict' affair. In the early 1840s taxes were levied on Jewish dress, and in 1845 Minister Kisilev announced that, starting in 1850, traditional Jewish dress would be absolutely forbidden. The maskilim, who supported government policy and urged the Jews to abandon traditional dress, which was the most conspicuous barrier between Jews and their neighbours, stressed in their propaganda that this was not a halakhic matter but a historical one. Traditional dress was a product of the Middle Ages and had come about because of Christian hatred: 'The source of the hatred of the Jewish people harboured by all the nations in the Middle Ages, who did not want the Jews to clothe themselves in the same garb as they, was their desire to place a mark on the forehead of the Jews as a sign of their religion.'[123] The improvement in the Christian attitude towards the

[119] Gottlober, *Hanitsanim*, 88–90; id., 'Mashal shelosh hatabaot', 33–65.

[120] Gottlober, *Zikhronot umasaot*, ii. 141–4.   [121] Mandelstamm, *Ḥazon lamo'ed*, ii. 7.

[122] Ibid.

[123] Fuenn, 'Mikhtav lebetsalel stern', 152–3. See I. Klausner, 'The Decree on Jewish Dress', 11–26; Mahler, *History of the Jewish People*, vi. 107–9.

Jews eliminated the historical basis for traditional dress, and there was no longer anything to prevent a positive response to the demands of the Russian government and the intentions of the tsar to turn the Jews into 'people fit for the society of men'.[124]

The venerated image of Mendelssohn and the pioneering status assigned to the 'Berlin Haskalah' continued to function as cornerstones of the maskilic picture of the past in Russia too. Adam Hacohen, for example, in his poem 'El bozei hahokhmah' (Those who Scorn Wisdom), took pride in being called a 'Berliner', as the maskilim were dubbed by their adversaries, and envisaged a historical continuum from 'the learned Moses', who championed *hokhmah*, to the Russian maskilim.[125] In 1845 Joseph Hertzberg of Mohilev published his Hebrew translation of Mendelssohn's *Morgenstunden* (*Mo'adei shahar*), which included an introduction lauding 'the Jewish Socrates'. He dedicated his book to Moses Montefiore in honour of his successful intervention in the 1840 Damascus blood libel, comparing him to the biblical Moses, who had saved his people from their suffering in Egypt.[126] During Montefiore's visit to Russia in 1846 his name was once again linked to that of Mendelssohn. Adam Hacohen's poem 'Shemesh, yare'ah vekokhavim' (Sun, Moon, and Stars), mentioned three luminaries—the biblical Moses, Maimonides, and Mendelssohn—as the three historical heroes of the Jewish people, and added an additional one: Moses Montefiore. 'For there, along with ben Menahem, ben Maimon, and the redeemer, ben Amram, shall your name be the fourth, Sir Moses Montefiore.'[127] Although this fourth hero was of a new class, being a political rather than a spiritual saviour, in the simplistic maskilic typography Montefiore possessed the 'Mendelssohnian' capacity to save the Jews from their era of decline, delivering them from their afflictions.[128]

POLITICAL HISTORY AND MORAL HISTORY

Samuel Fuenn's historical work *Nidhei yisra'el* is a striking contrast to the relatively simplistic attempts in Russia to employ history and its enlightened figures in maskilic propaganda. Fuenn, a teacher in the rabbinic seminary of Vilna, was a central figure in the maskilic circle there. In his book, published in Vilna in 1850, shortly before the publication of Krochmal's philosophical study of Jewish history, Fuenn set himself a far-reaching and hitherto unattained objective: to encompass 'all the history of the children of Israel and the wisdom of its sages, from the time of their exile from their land until the present generation, in all the

---

[124] Guenzburg, 'Al devar habegadim', 90–1.

[125] Adam Hakohen, 'El bozei hahokhmah', 154–60.

[126] Herzberg, *Mo'adei shahar*, 5–7, 12–13.

[127] Adam Hakohen, *Shirei sefat kodesh*, ii. 133–5.

[128] Cf. historical analogies in Guenzburg's poem in honour of Montefiore, quoted by Dick, *Haore'ah*, 51–5.

nations of their wandering'.[129] This was, in effect, the first attempt after Shalom Hacohen's endeavour to produce a Hebrew overview of Jewish history. Fuenn took the bulk of his historical material from secondary sources and, like Hacohen before him, based his work primarily on Jost's books. He studied the works of central European scholars of Wissenschaft des Judentums, and was especially influenced by the young Graetz's article 'The Structure of Jewish History', which had appeared just a few years earlier. Fuenn, like Rapoport, disagreed with Jost's views and attempted to pave the way towards an east European maskilic alternative to Wissenschaft des Judentums.[130]

Fuenn's theoretical introduction to *Nidhei yisra'el* indicates that, in his opinion, the same historical forces governed both universal and Jewish history. I have already noted that he perceived universal history as the didactic history of all peoples, moving along the time axis 'towards the goal of independence', and ultimately submitting to the biological fate of all men: decline and death. With regard to Jewish history, Fuenn asked several basic questions: what is the relationship between the political sphere and spiritual–ethical foundations? How continuous and uniform was Jewish history during exile? What was the connection between Jewish and universal history? He also considered a fundamental historiographic question: what was the most appropriate way to write Jewish history?

In Fuenn's idealistic philosophy of history, the active force in history, guided and controlled in principle by Divine Providence, was 'the spirit of the people', which consisted of two parts, political spirit and moral spirit, unified by their constant interaction.[131] Historiography, therefore, had to describe both 'political history' and 'moral history', and must ultimately provide a synthesis of the two. However, the 'political spirit' had ceased to exist in Jewish history from the moment the Jews were exiled from their land. In Fuenn's words, 'It ceased living the life of an independent state, and no longer had anything whatsoever to do with political history.' The political history of an exiled people naturally blended with the history of the countries in which it settled, and only occasionally 'a few things concerning it are mentioned in the written history of those who ruled it'. Even then, however, its history was a passive, non-autonomous one: 'it is only active in the sense of being influenced by the actions of others, and does not itself initiate actions'.[132] It was Fuenn's intention, however, to prove that in the post-political era of the Jewish people the second, 'moral' element of history had succeeded in preserving the Jews as an active, autonomous body. Exile did not radically interrupt historical continuity, in his opinion, and as long as a people were able to nurture the 'moral spirit', their history deserved to be inscribed on the pages of universal history.

[129] Fuenn, *Nidhei yisra'el*, vol. i, pt. 1.
[130] For example, Fuenn took sides with Rapoport in the controversy with Jost about the chronology of the Second Temple period; ibid. 16–17; cf. more examples on pp. 22, 24.
[131] Ibid. 1–2.   [132] Ibid. 2.

'During seventeen centuries of dispersion, Judaism took shape in the intellectual realm', Graetz asserted, and Fuenn unquestioningly adopted this view. The historical life of the Jewish people did not end, for, unlike ancient peoples who lost not only their 'political spirit' but their 'moral spirit' as well, the Jews lost only the former: 'Although the power of its government and political spirit were gone for 2,000 years . . . nevertheless, its moral spirit . . . [and] the fire of its religion and faith remained a part of it.' It must nevertheless be noted that, while Graetz stressed intellectual and philosophical speculation as the substance of spiritual history, Fuenn emphasized the 'spirit of faith and religion'. Like Graetz, however, he used the concept 'moral history' not only to prove the historical continuity of the Jewish people through time but also to affirm its unity in space: religious and spiritual creation also bound the Jews together during times of geographical dispersion.

Although Fuenn came nowhere near depicting the absolute uniqueness or isolation of Jewish history, he does seem to have been one of the first Russian maskilim to adopt the idea of 'mission' formulated by Jewish intellectuals in central and western Europe. In Fuenn's view, the purpose of writing 'the history of the people of Jacob' during the period of exile was to prove 'the sanctity of pure religion, [and] its authority and power'. From the dawn of history, the Jewish people had been chosen to 'bear the standard of pure faith, faith in the single God . . . to spread the blazing light of wisdom and science over all the darkness of the land'.[133] This was a 'holy mission' that could be accomplished without physical or political power, since it required only spiritual might. The fact that Christianity and Islam had grown out of Judaism was proof that its universal mission had succeeded. However, although the 'mission' and monotheism of the new religions ostensibly required them to honour and respect the Jews, the historical reality was quite different. Fuenn believed that he had discovered the reason for this, as well as the central driving force of the Jewish people in exile.[134]

Loss of autonomy had led the Jews to become dependent upon 'the spirit of faith' of the peoples in their host countries. Once again, there was no political bond of the sort that had existed in the pre-exilic period between the Jews and their neighbours, and so 'political history' had a relatively tenuous effect on the Jewish people. Fuenn also believed that he had found the law governing the history of the Jewish people during its exile—the correlation between 'spirit of the faith of non-Jews' and 'the moral history' of the Jews. Such a correlation was not, of course, a new idea in the maskilic picture of the past, and it served to distinguish between modern era, characterized by its rationalism and tolerance, and the previous era. Fuenn, however, introduced these common maskilic perceptions into a more conceptual mould and placed greater emphasis on the link between Jewish history and the dynamics of universal history:

---

[133] Fuenn, *Nidḥei yisra'el*, i. 4.   [134] Ibid. 5.

Jewish moral history must also pay heed to the standing of the spirit of faith among the various peoples in whose midst they dwell, to observe the path it has taken to reach its destination, whether it has walked a straight path or a crooked one. Jewish moral history must consider all the various periods of their innocence and purity, the time of their confusion and deviation, and the return to their pristine state. All these have influenced, for good or for ill, the spirit of the faith of the Jewish people; and the rise and decline of the faith of the ruling people, in all aspects of truth and reason, has determined the success or failure of its subjects. Thus, its rights and laws have changed and the strength of its dominant spirit has grown or declined. And only when the deeds of the political spirit are intertwined with the moral spirit in every ruling people, and they govern according to reason, can moral history influence their political standing and take its proper place, whence it will observe all of the causes, and will know and explore the source of all the deeds of the Jewish people.[135]

These basic theoretical assumptions led Fuenn to an impasse regarding the most critical historiographical issue: how could a historian write a comprehensive history of the Jewish people? How could one adhere to the rules of historiography, which required a full and unified description that combined details into one cohesive pattern and did not skip from time to time or place to place? The nature of Jewish history, Fuenn emphatically asserted, does not allow this. When he began to divide Jewish history into periods, it became clear to him that this was not merely a case of geographical dispersion, but also involved historical processes taking place at different times. He therefore reached the conclusion that normal chronological periodization could not be applied to a history that had developed at different rates:

When we attempt to divide this vast period of time into different sections, we see once again that one general division is not possible, and that one cannot assign a single rhythm and set of borders to the history of the people of Jacob in all the countries in which they settled, for they did not reach these lands at the same time, nor were all peoples noted in the history books of the land, nor did they all rule from that time until the present day.[136]

On the other hand, Fuenn's belief that the 'moral history' of the Jewish people was contingent upon 'the spirit of the faith of non-Jews' led him to conclude that the criterion for periodization must be taken from outside rather than from within the course of Jewish development: 'It is worth while learning from the spirit of faith the character of the various periods and the main changes in religions, in order to use them as the criterion for dividing this large period of time from the destruction of the Temple until the present into various eras, distinguished from each other by their nature and spirit.[137]

The different dynamics of Jewish and non-Jewish history further exacerbated the problem of periodization. As mentioned earlier, Fuenn believed in a cyclical, biological-historical schema similar to Krochmal's. He too distinguished between biological stages that progressed according to age and ended in death for all

---

[135] Ibid. 6.   [136] Ibid. 6–7, 9.   [137] Ibid. 6.

peoples, on one hand, and in the unique historical development of the Jewish people, which he regarded as eternal and multicyclical, on the other:

The Jewish people that, as an eternally powerful, living spirit, takes on and discards the outward forms of the changes in nations and periods of life, is different at the beginning from the way it is at the end, revolving like the revolutions of a wheel. And just as each time the land renews its youth when new peoples come to live in it, so the epochs of its history will again be renewed.[138]

This unusual historical situation made it difficult to organize the history of the Jewish people into clearly defined periods, for the cycle of Jewish historical life did not move synchronically with that of non-Jews.

To make the situation even more complex, the dynamics of Jewish history were not only cyclical, but also linear: 'It is not possible to straighten its curves; it proceeds as crookedly as a dance before two armies, so it is not possible to devise a straight and true way of dividing it into sections of a whole.'[139] In the modern era, when different Jewish communities were at completely different stages of growth, and general 'external' history and Jewish 'moral history' were not moving at the same pace, it was particularly evident that historical developments were not all occurring according to the same rhythm. He described this metaphorically:

Here time will harvest the blessing of its sheaves, and there it will continue to bear its seeds; here blossoms and flowers will lift their heads from the soil towards the rays of the spring sun, and there gusts of stormy winds will smash the splendour and glory of the vintage and terrible ice will cover the riot of colours, the hope of so many days. And how can we choose a single measure of time and a single rhythm for all the events and situations of all the Jews in every country?[140]

Fuenn's struggle with this historiographic question stemmed in great part from his reservations about Jost's *Geschichte der Israeliten*, which served as his primary source for data on medieval Jewish history. Jost, however, did not propose a clear periodization, choosing instead to write a history remarkable for its fragmentary nature and lack of unity.[141] Fuenn, too, ultimately adopted the division between Jewish communities in Christian countries and those in Islamic countries, although he had first attempted to put forward his own historiographic method, which seemed to him to be the lesser of two evils. He suggested that Jewish historians should organize their material in two general sections: the first section should trace historical development along a chronological axis 'from the day the thread of the story began until the time of the generation preceding ours', and the second should describe history on a geographical basis, 'according

---

[138] Fuenn, *Nidḥei yisra'el*, i. 7. Cf. H. Graetz's conception, which represented the Jewish people as a passive observer of the rise and decline of nations in history, in *The Structure of Jewish History*, 96–7.
[139] Fuenn, *Nidḥei yisra'el*, i. 7.   [140] Ibid. 8.   [141] Michael, *I. M. Jost*, 39–40.

to the places the children of Jacob could be found'. The construction of an appropriate chronological framework could be based on two criteria: 'major events' that influenced the majority of Jews, and 'episodes of the moral spirit', in both its active and passive forms and under the influence of the 'spirit of the faith of non-Jews'. With regard to the geographical aspect, the historian should isolate each country and describe all facets of the Jews living in it: their external situation, their lifestyle, and their spiritual attainments, linking this to the impact of the lands in which they lived and the influence of 'the general spirit reigning then in all their places of habitation'. Fuenn admitted that his proposal was not a perfect solution, one of its disadvantages being the possibility that the same events might be described in both sections, although the continuity and unity would be preserved: 'At the very least, we shall find a full picture of the episodes of the moral spirit over the course of time, and an unbroken knowledge of their history and standing in each and every land.' The incisive reader would perhaps himself synthesize the two aspects and solve 'the conundrum of the movement of time around one of these axes according to the information provided by the other'.[142]

Fuenn drew up a comprehensive plan for *Nidhei yisra'el*, which was to be comprised of two parts. He wrote two pamphlets from the first part, only one of which was published. It described Jewish history moving along a chronological continuum, but only from the destruction of the Second Temple until 1210. The second pamphlet was supposed to complete the chronological survey up to the nineteenth century, and the second part of the book was to have included monographs on Jewish communities in various countries.

In the chronological section that was published, Jewish history was divided into three periods. The first, from the destruction of the Second Temple until the completion of the Talmud (in Fuenn, AD 68–500), was characterized as 'the destruction of the political government'. Fuenn believed that this process had begun even before the destruction of the Temple, with the dispersion of the Jews. The Hellenistic and Roman occupations of the Land of Israel and the constraints of trade relations created a universal culture into which Jews too were integrated. The break between the 'political' and the 'religious', according to Fuenn's analysis, had already begun at this stage: 'The ties binding political and religious matters into a single entity were broken; religion and political leadership separated from each other. Each one chose the path along which it desired to travel.'[143] This split was also stressed by Graetz, who noted the power play in Jewish history between the religious and the national elements. In Fuenn's view, this was evidence of the intervention of Divine Providence: during the stage of

---

[142] Fuenn, *Nidhei yisra'el*, i. 8–9. Fuenn's reply to Levinsohn's criticism of the book (B. Nathanson, *Sefer hazikhronot*, 94) shows that, in his view, the main importance of *Nidhei yisra'el* lay in the original structure he proposed for Jewish history—'I conceived and gave birth to the programme and the wise men will judge it'—and less in the precise presentation of historical facts.

[143] Fuenn, *Nidhei yisra'el*, i. 10–12.

political decline, it was necessary to save at least the 'spirit of faith', 'so that the
political spirit, as it fell, would not pull the religious spirit down with it'.[144] He
considered the wars leading to the destruction of the Temple to be wars of faith
that were not fought for political control. In this respect, he explained, the defeat
was military, not spiritual. The spirit survived, and was embodied in the centre
for Torah study in Yavneh, led by Rabbi Yohanan ben Zakai. Fuenn did not disdain military valour, and he even called Bar Kokhba 'the prodigious hero'. However, it was obvious to him that the revolt was merely the final flicker of the
'flame of the political spirit'. From this period onwards, although the Jews were
erased from 'the book of political history', the door was opened to their spiritual
renewal. 'The spirit of the time' spurred the Sages to write the Mishnah and the
Talmud, and led to the strengthening of yeshivot. The Talmud was not only 'a
memorial to ancient times worthy of respect', but also became a refuge for 'the
religious spirit'.[145]

Fuenn designated the second period, from AD 500 to 1037, as the time of 'the
general dispersion', marking the beginning of the history of Jewish exile and all
its attendant historiographic problems: 'None of the periods of the chronological
cycle had any distinguishing features.'[146] This period began when the wellspring
of 'the intellectual spirit' dried up and the danger of annihilation threatened the
dispersed Jews. However, it was also during this period that a positive historical
mechanism began operating: the Jews' openness to their surroundings and ability to draw upon alien culture while still maintaining their Jewish uniqueness,
which kept them from passing into oblivion. This idea, which characterized the
approach of the moderate maskilim, was formulated by Fuenn in his history of
the Middle Ages: 'We have already learned from the history of the moral spirit
that all destruction and internal upheaval bring about a new strength and endeavour', a situation similar to what Fuenn expected would occur in Russia as a
result of the war waged by the maskilim to establish a new educational system.[147]
According to this principle, the Jews' confrontation with 'the traits of the non-
Jewish spirit' strengthened their own spirit even further, purified their faith, and
prevented them from stagnating. The constant struggle ensured that 'the spirit
of the time' would arouse the Jews 'to know the deficiencies of this era, to understand what they faced, and to recognize and use their own potential'.[148] It was
this openness that, at the end of the period in Muslim Spain, brought about the
awakening of interest in *ḥokhmot* and science, and spurred Jewish sages on to
study all areas of *ḥokhmot*—the perfect expression of the maskilic ideal.

In Fuenn's opinion, during the eighth and ninth centuries of the geonic period
Jewish creativity flourished thanks to the efforts of the caliphs of the Abbasid
dynasty to promote culture, education, and even religious tolerance. He considered the Karaites to be quasi-maskilim, lovers of *peshat* (literal interpretation),

[144] Fuenn, *Niḏḥei yisra'el*, i. 12.   [145] Ibid. 16–18, 24–5, 36.   [146] Ibid. 37.
[147] Ibid. 47.   [148] Ibid. 38–9.

who tended towards innovation and possessed 'simple intelligence'. Although they had left the ranks of the Jewish people, they nevertheless contributed dialectically to its history. The confrontation with the Karaites awakened several sages to a new mode of thinking 'in which love of the new took root in their hearts'. It also led to the development of rationalistic philosophy to counterbalance Karaism. Influenced by Hegelian concepts, Fuenn explained that historical phenomena ceased to exist because they had completed their historical function. Thus, for example, the period of the Sanhedrin came to an end in the Land of Israel after having completed its function of glorifying the Oral Torah, and the geonic period in Babylonia ended after it had achieved its goal. The end of a historical phenomenon, however, does not wipe all trace of it from the historical record, since it has a cumulative effect on later phases. The explanation did not satisfy Fuenn, and he added more realistic ones to account for the decline of the Babylonian academies in the period of the *geonim*, such as loss of income, conflicts, and the inferior quality of the *geonim*, for the effect of 'political reasons and external matters' should not be ignored.[149]

The third period (1037–1210) did not differ greatly from its predecessors, for then, too, Jewish history was in a state of 'total dispersion in all countries'. Fuenn nonetheless saw signs of stability in these two centuries, following the great fluctuations in both 'universal' and Jewish history in the preceding centuries. He called this period 'the time of gathering the fruits of the dispersion': after the 'general dispersion' the Jews began the slow process of striking roots in the lands in which they were living, adapting to their surroundings, and reconciling themselves to their situation. Although 'the darkness of night' ruled them from without, this was a period of incandescence for the internal life of the Jewish people. 'Political history holds no interest whatsoever for the historian writing about this period in Jewish history, for it was merely a repetition of what had already happened in preceding eras.' On the other hand, 'moral history . . . is very important and valuable to us: for in this sphere great heights of achievement had been reached in all categories of scientific study'.[150] In the spiritual creativity of Spanish Jewry, there had been an encounter between 'the light of intellect' and 'the light of faith', marked by confrontation, receptiveness, conflict, and productivity. At the end of this period the Jewish 'moral spirit' came close to reaching its peak in the Hegelian sense of self-consciousness—the ultimate goal of history, according to Hegel.

Despite Fuenn's intensive involvement with medieval Jewish history and his relatively complex explanations of the fate of the Jews, his maskilic vision was not altered. He too perceived the Middle Ages as a harsh, dark era, the tempestuous boyhood of the Christian peoples—a stage that was already behind the Jews, replaced, to their great joy, by 'the modern era'. Indeed, Fuenn's historical

[149] Ibid. 85.   [150] Ibid. 126.

view was intrinsically maskilic. His awareness of the transition that had begun in the modern era, his faith in the power of reason, his belief that the maskilic ideal had existed in the past, and the fact that he linked the normal development of the Jewish people to the positive behaviour of the surrounding society all place *Nidḥei yisra'el* in the tradition of maskilic historical writing. However, in Fuenn's work, as in Krochmal's *Moreh nevukhei hazeman*, maskilic history was underpinned by profound and innovative historical thinking. Both Krochmal and Fuenn employed idealistic historiographic concepts and dialectical explanations, traced the long-term course of history, and attempted to place Jewish history within a comprehensive historical structure. Fuenn also proposed a kind of work-plan for the Jewish historian who encountered difficulties, despite his intentions, in applying this perception of the unity and continuity of the Jewish people to the period of exile.

Fuenn's *Nidḥei yisra'el* provides a consummate example of the east European maskil, in thrall to various concepts and perceptions of idealistic historiography and historical thinking, who attempted to reshape what he had drawn from the German Wissenschaft des Judentums into a maskilic literary format. Like Graetz and Krochmal, Fuenn stressed the power of the continuity of Jewish existence in history, as opposed to the Christian and Hegelian historical concepts, but this historical approach was not merely defensive in character. For example, while Graetz wrote his programmatic article in 1846 as a polemic against the attempt 'to erase Judaism from the book of life', and against 'the new tendencies growing among our own people to see Judaism as an abstraction . . . to move it from the vitality of action to the vagueness of the emotional religiosity' of those who supported internal religious reform,[151] Fuenn was more concerned with the need to change the face and stance of traditional Jewish society in Russia. In the 1840s Fuenn was involved in efforts to persuade Russian Jewry of the necessity to respond positively to the reforms initiated by Nicholas I's government, particularly in education, and he believed that the reign of this 'benevolent ruler' expressed the progress and growth of 'the spirit of faith' of the people among whom the Jews of Russia lived. In *Nidḥei yisra'el* Fuenn linked the Jewish 'moral spirit' to the 'spirit of faith' of the ruling people, thereby creating the ideological basis and legitimization for the Vilna maskilim's belief in the necessity for spiritual–cultural changes and the rehabilitation of the Jewish 'moral spirit'. From the 1860s onwards, the theoretical and abstract historical concepts of *Nidḥei yisra'el* were translated into the language of maskilic journalism and ideology in Fuenn's editorials on contemporary Russian problems, published in his Hebrew journal *Hakarmel*. In these editorials he urged the Jews to find the proper balance between preserving 'the special essence' of the Jewish people and 'joining with all the peoples of the land . . . neither to be distant from each other, nor to inter-

[151] H. Graetz, *The Structure of Jewish History*, 123. See also Schorsch, 'Ideology and History', 1–62.

mingle excessively'. Fuenn asserted that the course of Jewish history up to that point had proved that the mission of the Jewish people lay solely in the preservation of 'the bond of faith', and that 'the other desires of an enlightened man and those of a citizen of the land are the same everywhere in the universe; not to be isolated in the conduct of his life nor to be separated from his neighbours, the people in whose shadow he finds refuge'.[152]

[152] Fuenn, 'Yisra'el ba'amim', 41–2, 49–50.

FOUR

Reaching the Masses:
The Dissemination of Maskilic History

THE CHANNELS OF DISTRIBUTION

'A NEW LIFE', wrote Shalom Abramowitz, better known by his pen-name Mendele Mokher Seforim (1835–1917), as he looked back nostalgically at the past, 'was in store for the Jews, beginning with the sixties of this century, a life marked by an uplifted, light-hearted spirit, full of hopes for the future.'[1] Although the hopes that the maskilim pinned on the reign of the Russian tsar Alexander II (1855–81) were not always realized, and while maskilic faith in Russia's 'benevolent government' gradually crumbled from 1870s onwards, changes did actually take place. The Jewish population increased (from 2,350,000 in 1850 to 3,980,000 in 1880); gradually, on a selective basis, more Jews were allowed to reside outside the Jewish Pale of Settlement; some of Nicholas I's edicts were abolished, chief among them the cruel conscription of Jewish boys and young men to the army; economic patterns fluctuated, with poverty and distress increasing, on one hand, and a small class of wealthy entrepreneurs developing, on the other; and processes of acculturation were intensified, particularly in the large cities that were the destinations of internal immigration.[2]

Changes also took place within maskilic circles. Young maskilim were exposed to Russian culture, a new generation of maskilim was affected by the prevailing spirit of modernity, and secondary streams were formed in the Haskalah movement. The numbers of maskilim grew, there was a substantial increase in works of Hebrew literature, the Jewish press offered vastly greater opportunities for publication and communication between maskilim, and the Society for the Promotion of Enlightenment among the Jews of Russia, founded in 1863, provided financial support for initiatives to bring the Jews closer to Russian culture.[3]

[1] Abramowitz, *Sefer hakabtsanim*, 197.

[2] Dubnow, *History of the Jews in Russia and Poland*, ii. 154–242; Slutsky, 'The Emergence', 212–37; Tcherikower, *Jews in Time of Revolution*, 127–200; Dinur, *Historical Writings*, iv. 202–28; Zipperstein, *The Jews of Odessa*; Greenberg, *The Jews in Russia*, i. 73–186; Nardi, 'Transformations in the Enlightenment Movement', 300–27.

[3] Zinberg, *A History of Jewish Literature*, vii. 91–126; Bartal, 'Radical Enlightenment', 13–20; Feiner, 'Jewish Society, Literature, and Haskalah', 283–316; I. Kovner, *Sefer hamatsref*; Lilienblum, *Letters*, 133.

While my reconstruction of the maskilic sense of the past in the first half of the nineteenth century was based on a handful of prominent writings, some of which were never completed, in the second half of the century the maskilim produced a large number of historical works of different types. In this chapter I will attempt to find some order in these writings, and to classify them according to their aims and the particular audiences to which they were addressed. The expansion and diversification of the Jewish reading public enabled maskilic writers to impart the major messages of 'maskilic history' to various types of readers at different levels of popularization.

This chapter focuses on the channels through which maskilic history was disseminated in Russia, particularly in the 1860s and 1870s. Most of the maskilim who were active in furthering this aim had been influenced by the changes taking place in the reign of Alexander II, and regarded themselves and were regarded by their younger, more radical colleagues as belonging to the moderate stream of the Haskalah. In the 1840s they had advocated a militant Haskalah and inveighed against traditional ways, but now they favoured a conservative Haskalah that eschewed radicalism.[4] This chapter then is devoted to the moderate maskilim, while the radical trends that subverted the original principles of the Haskalah are the subject of the next.

The historical literature written by the maskilim during the reign of Alexander II was part of a growing Jewish book market with an expanding readership. In 1859, for example, the Romm Press in Vilna planned to print 3,000 copies of each of Guenzburg's books *Sefer yemei hador* and *Kiryat sefer*; 2,000 copies of the fourth part of the translation by Kalman Schulman (1819–99) of the French writer Eugène Sue's adventure novel *Mystères de Paris*; and 3,000 copies of Schulman's *Shulamit*.[5] *Ahavat tsiyon* (The Love of Zion), by Abraham Mapu (1808–67), came out in five Hebrew editions, although its author could hardly conceal his envy at the more dazzling success enjoyed by *Mystères de Paris*. The most successful author of all was Isaac Meir Dick (1814–93), whose Yiddish stories sold in their thousands. The Hebrew periodicals, published from 1856 onwards, had close to 4,000 subscribers and a even larger readership, since every copy was read by several people.[6]

This expansion of the reading public does not necessarily imply that the situation had changed drastically and that the numbers of maskilim in Russia had increased dramatically. The maskilic circle itself, which included the 'creators', activists, and writers of the Haskalah, remained relatively small and continued to

[4] In order to emphasize their link to the 18th-c. German Haskalah, the moderates called themselves 'the 1783 maskilim'. Eliezer Zweifel applied this term to Idel Sharshavsky; see Paperna, *Collected Writings*, 277.   [5] Kohn, 'Romm's Printing House', 109–14.

[6] Miron, *From Romance to the Novel*, 231–8; Werses, *Yiddish Translations of 'Ahavat Tsiyon'*, 15–48; Dick, 'Mikhtav leḥ. y. gurland', 408. The figures are based on Sokolow's estimation; id., 'David Frishmann', 281–3. For the expanded Hebrew readership, see Miron, *When Loners Come Together*, 56–85. Additional statistical data on the circulation of Hebrew books in Russia in the 19th c. can be found in Dinur, *Historical Writings*, iv. 217–20.

represent only an élite group of intellectuals, although it was joined by a new generation. A large proportion of the new readers were neither maskilim nor supporters of the Haskalah but came from traditional society, which also witnessed change during the reign of Alexander II. One innovation was the appearance of what Dan Miron, the scholar of Hebrew literature, later called a 'normal Hebrew-reading public'. It was composed of individuals who had acquired their education in the traditional houses of study (*batei midrash*) but were induced by their bourgeois lifestyle to expand their horizons. There were no intellectuals or ideologues like the maskilim among these readers, who were content to read the latest news and pleasant tales. Judah Leib Kantor (1849–1915) defined the readership of a Hebrew periodical at the close of the 1870s as:

Men who are no longer afraid to read 'external' books and are unable to read foreign languages—mostly people who will pay in full for the pleasure they gain from reading Hebrew periodicals when they are resting and relaxing. These people want news, pleasing stories, views about Jewish life, and the biographies of famous men, but not scholarly enquiry into history.[7]

Hence a maskilic writer desirous of attracting these readers could not limit his writing to historical studies, which would only appeal to the small readership of maskilim. Indeed, the most successful historical literature had a purely popular orientation: stirring historical tales, translated and adapted from German, and historical novels and stories in Yiddish that appealed to an even lower socio-cultural level of readership that included boys and women. Some of the maskilim were contemptuous of this low type of literature and found it hard to reconcile themselves to its dissemination. Mapu, Schulman, Dick, and others, however, understood that these popular works not only helped them earn their livelihood by writing but also enabled them to expand the target audience for maskilic propaganda.[8]

In quantitative terms, historical literature was very well represented in the Jewish book market in Russia at the time. The lists and catalogues of Jewish booksellers are an invaluable source of knowledge about the share of the market commanded by the various types of historical literature. A very large selection was offered to the reading public by the bookseller Aaron Faust of Krakow. His catalogue (1876–7) contained close to 1,700 books, most of them in Hebrew and some in Yiddish and German.[9] There were scores of booklets of Yiddish tales, not included in the catalogue, that could be ordered by mail like all the other books. Most of the books on the list were works of traditional religious literature:

[7] Kantor, 'Mikhtav el ha'ozer beharedaktsien', 68–9.

[8] Miron, *When Loners Come Together*, 62–4.

[9] *Hamagid*, 20 (1876), 397–8, 407, 433–4; *Hamagid*, 21 (1877), 39–40, 59–60, 69–70, 79, 89–90, 99–100, 109–10, 155–6, 173–4, 201, 211, 230. Additional publishers' and booksellers' booklists appeared in *Hamagid*, 15 (1871), suppl. to no. 6; 18 (1874), no. 9; 18 (1874), 97, 125, 152, 162, 187, 235; 19 (1875), 179–80; 22 (1878), 289.

Ḥumash (the Pentateuch), Mishnah, Talmud, Midrash, *musar* (ethical teachings), and kabbalah. Only a quarter of the books (over 400) could be defined as modern literature, produced by maskilim in Russia and Galicia or by Jewish intellectuals from Germany. About 120 books (close to 7 per cent of all the available books) were history books or historical tales, though this group also included new editions of traditional historical literature or traditional biographies of great Torah scholars. In the final analysis, close to 100 works can be defined as new historical literature.[10]

The lists of historical literature available to the Jewish reading public in Russia in the 1870s reveal an accumulation of works from various periods and a great diversity in the types of works. Stacked together on the shelf of available history books were several levels of historical literature. It seems that the chronicles and chains of tradition written during the Middle Ages and the Renaissance continued to serve as a source of historical knowledge and a basis for the traditional picture of the past at the close of the nineteenth century. The fact that these traditional history books were constantly reprinted attests to their relevance for the reading public. Gedaliah ben Joseph Ibn Yahya's *Shalshelet hakabalah* (Chain of Tradition, 1587), for example, went through eight editions in eastern Europe during the nineteenth century, five of them between 1862 and 1890; David Gans's *Tsemaḥ david* (Offspring of David, 1592) came out in ten editions (eight in Lvov and Warsaw between 1847 and 1878); and *Shevet yehudah* (Rod/Tribe of Judah, 1554) by Rabbi Solomon Ibn Verga appeared in no fewer then fifteen editions. In Lvov, for example, it was reprinted every three to five years from 1846 to 1874. Jehiel Heilprin's chronicle *Seder hadorot* (The Order of the Generations), which first appeared in 1769, went through ten more editions. Unquestionably the most popular 'bestseller' was the book of Josippon; it was printed twenty-five times by various printing-houses in eastern Europe throughout the nineteenth century, seventeen of them in the second half of the century. In the 1870s, for example, Josippon was printed six times in Warsaw—every year or two! Amelander's *She'erit yisra'el* (Remnant of Israel, 1743), regarded as a sequel to Josippon, appeared in sixteen editions.[11]

The publishers did not delete the introductions from any of the later editions of these books, so that the traditional view of the past, formulated several centuries earlier, continued to make its presence felt and to exert its influence in the nineteenth century. At the very most, a few attempts were made to update these works. For example, the story of the Damascus blood libel of 1840 was added to *She'erit yisra'el*, and 'Additions to the Sixth Millennium', which preserved the style of traditional chronography, were added to the later editions of *Tsemaḥ david*.[12] The traditional approach underlying this historical literature is clearly apparent

[10] This calculation includes the list of the bookseller Abraham Zuckerman of Warsaw which appeared in *Hashaḥar*, 8 (1877), suppl. to no. 5.

[11] The data on the editions comes from H. D. Friedberg, *Bibliography: Catalogue*.

[12] Gans, *Tsemaḥ david*.

when compared, for example, with Meir Wiener's edition of *Shevet yehudah*, published in Hanover in 1855. Here the editor made an effort to produce an annotated academic edition, using first editions to correct errors that had found their way into the later Warsaw and Lvov editions, and adding references, indexes, and names of people and cities.[13] Against this backdrop, the role of this traditional historical literature in eastern Europe becomes increasingly clear. It served as popular history, on one hand, and as sacred, canonical, and legitimate history, on the other. But popular history was transmitted not only in books but also in oral stories, as Perez Smolenskin demonstrated: 'terrifying stories' from the distant and more recent past were the topic of lively conversation in the *beit midrash*, telling of

the war of Alexander the Great, who subdued the entire world under his feet until he came to the Garden of Eden and read, written clearly upon the gate, 'Ye shall come here but no further' . . . they sat together and conversed about Alexander and Rothschild, about the greatness of Moses Montefiore or the wars of Napoleon, they spoke of the heroic deeds of the Ten Tribes and the children of Moses, who resembled the sons of giants in their height and the sons of the gods in their righteousness.[14]

Similar comments about the stories current among the idle young men sitting around the stove at the house of study are expressed by Abramowitz's heroes in his *Ha'avot vehabanim* (Fathers and Sons, 1868). They mock the superstitions and the folk tales about 'the red-headed Jews, the mountain of darkness and the Sambatyon river, about the deeds of Alexander the Great, the tree he spoke with, and the formidable eagle he rode upon . . . about Sammael and his wife and the chronicles of Gog and Magog'.[15] The maskilim condemned the popular, folkloric approach to the past, and their historical writings were intended to provide reliable and rational historical information in order to combat the traditional, popular view and to offer an alternative to it.

Among the books listed by the booksellers Faust of Krakow and Zuckerman of Warsaw were such eighteenth- and nineteenth-century works as Euchel's biography of Mendelssohn, *Toledot yeshurun* by Meir Fischer of Prague, *Toledot napoleon* by Feivel Schiffer of Warsaw, Krochmal's *Moreh nevukhei hazeman*, and Feivel Goldshtof's *Korot ha'olam*. Close to forty books were penned by Russian maskilim, and readers could choose books of universal history translated by Kalman Schulman, scientific historical studies such as *Likutei kadmoniyot* (Compilations of Antiquities) on the Karaites by Simhah Pinsker (1801–64), original historical novels such as Mapu's *Ahavat tsiyon* and *Ashmat shomron* (The Guilt of Samaria), and Hebrew translations of historical stories, such as Samuel Fuenn's *Ya'akov*

---

[13] Ibn Verga, *Shevet yehudah*.

[14] Smolenskin, *Kevurat ḥamor*, 43–4; it first appeared in *Hashaḥar*, 4, (1873).

[15] Abramowitz, *Collected Writings*, 28. On the diffusion of 'history' from the level of the historian to the general public, see Stanford, *The Nature of Historical Knowledge*, 146–72.

tirado (Jacob Tirado), and those written in Yiddish by Dick. Booksellers also sold Graetz's series *Geschichte der Juden* in the original German immediately upon publication of each volume, as well as German books by Levi Herzfeld, Ludwig Philippson, Meyer Lehmann, Abraham Geiger, and others. The lists also included several history textbooks in Russian.[16]

Historical studies written by Russian maskilim in the nineteenth century reached only a very limited circle of maskilim. An example is Fuenn's *Divrei hayamim livenei yisra'el* (The History of the Children of Israel), which was intended to be a scholarly Hebrew version of the history of the Jews from the time of the Second Temple onwards.[17] In 1871 Fuenn wrote to Judah Leib Gordon (1830–92) in frustration: 'I have invested so much labour in it, and for whom have I laboured and toiled? Believe me that I have not yet sold even thirty copies, and who knows if I shall succeed in selling enough to recoup the 250 roubles I spent on printing it?' Fuenn was wealthy enough to sustain the loss, and the limited number of buyers did not prevent him from continuing his project. 'As long as the breadth of life is within me,' he wrote, 'I shall not cease from my labours for the enlightenment of our people and the expansion of the boundaries of Jewish wisdom, which I shall carry on to the best of my ability, for it seems to me that I was created for this purpose.'[18] The circle of maskilim thus remained relatively small; in his efforts to reach a wider audience Fuenn also translated several historical books which had more dramatic and appealing plots.

The Society for the Promotion of Enlightenment among the Jews made special efforts to disseminate maskilic historical literature. Established in St Petersburg, in 1863, the society became an focal point for the initiation of various maskilic projects, as well as the address to which maskilim could turn for advice or financial assistance.[19] Mapu, for example, proudly bore the title 'worker and writer' awarded him by the society; Eliezer Tsevi Hakohen Zweifel (1815–88), a former teacher at the rabbinic seminary of Zhitomir, persuaded Abraham Harkavy (1835–1919), an eminent member of the society, to lobby for an annual stipend that would support him in his old age; and Gottlober, with the assistance of his student Hayim Jonah Gurland (1841–90), requested funds from the society to publish his writings. Gottlober was deeply hurt by the fact that the society had not included him among their numbers, thus denying him his due as a member of the maskilic movement: 'It grieves me that they did not call upon me to join them, thus dishonouring me. Why, I was a member of the movement before that group was formed; for thirty years I have sown its seeds in tears. How could I have been forgotten by the members

[16] See booklists in nn. 9 and 10 above.

[17] Fuenn, *Divrei hayamim livenei yisra'el*; letter to Gordon, in Fuenn, *From Militant to Conservative Maskil*, 197–8.

[18] Feigensohn, 'The History of the Romm Printing House', 278.

[19] L. Rosenthal, *Toledot ḥevrat marbei haskalah*, introd. to vol. i; Greenberg, *The Jews in Russia*, 109–10; Zipperstein, 'Transforming the Heder', 87–109.

of this new society, as the dead are erased from the heart?' He was quick to forgive this affront to his honour, however, and shortly afterwards he asked the society to arrange a teaching post for him at the rabbinic seminary in Zhitomir.[20]

The statutes of the society stated that it planned to publish or assist in publishing 'beneficial books . . . both in Russian and Hebrew, whose purpose is to disseminate enlightenment among the Jews'.[21] Strengthening Russian patriotism was the first priority of the society's directors, and to achieve this goal they attached great importance to promoting an awareness of both universal and Russian history. As early as 1864 the society decided 'to endeavour to print a book of Jewish history written in Russian', since the contents of such a volume 'affect every Jew, and will stir in many the desire to read it'.[22] Fuenn sent the society a letter in which he proposed publishing such a book in Hebrew as well, to be disseminated in two versions, one to students and a more popular version to the masses.[23] In the same year Schulman also wrote to the society requesting financial support for the publication of his translations of Josephus's writings, and stressing the universal importance of these books.[24] Although the society's committee did allocate 100 roubles to Schulman, it expressed greater interest in a project the society itself had initiated: two Hebrew translations, one of universal history and the other of Russian history. It put the project up for tender, as it were, asking several maskilim to take on the assignment. Eventually Schulman was chosen by the orientalist and Christian convert Professor Daniel Chwolson (1819–1911) and Dr Malis to carry out the first part of the project, and Abramowitz was chosen to execute the second part. Concurrently, the society entered into negotiations with Jewish printers to publish a large number of copies at a low price.[25] Abramowitz's work was halted almost at its inception; nor did any other books of Russian history meet the society's expectations. In 1868, therefore, Solomon Mandelkern (1846–1902), still a student in St Petersburg, was given the task of writing a comprehensive book of Russian history, under the close supervision of Professor Chwolson.[26] Another member of the society proposed that the Russian translation of Peter Beer's *Sefer toledot yisra'el* (Book of Jewish History) be used as a textbook.[27] The society's priorities become clear when the different amounts of financial support given to various maskilim are compared. Books written solely at the initiative of the writers, with no involvement on the part of the society, and books written in Yiddish did not receive a great deal of backing. Samuel Resser (d. 1880), for example, received 25 roubles for his Yiddish translation of *Sefer toledot yisra'el*, and Mikhel Gordon (1823–90), who sent his Yiddish history of Russia to the society, received merely

[20] Mapu, *Mikhtavei avraham mapu*, 229; Zweifel, 'Mikhtavo leharkavi', 512–13; Gottlober, letter to Gurland (1871), in id., '13 mikhtavim me'et gotlober', 414–15, 423–42. See also Lilienblum's criticism of the society in his letter to Gordon in 1872, Lilienblum, *Letters*, 132.

[21] L. Rosenthal, *Toledot ḥevrat marbei haskalah*, i. 204.   [22] Ibid. 3.

[23] Ibid. ii. 33.   [24] Ibid. 31.

[25] Ibid. i. 4, 7, 12–13, 17, 36; ii. 36.   [26] Ibid. i. 54, 59.   [27] Ibid. 71.

a promise that they would buy 30 roubles' worth of books from him. Mandelkern, on the other hand, who was being cultivated by the society, was granted a monthly allowance of 15 roubles for as long as it took him to complete his *Sefer divrei yemei rusiyah* (Book of Russian History).[28]

OPTIMISTIC AND PATRIOTIC HISTORY

During the reign of Alexander II most maskilim became more intensely aware of the positive historical turning-point.[29] The belief that 'the time of evil for the people of Israel has passed, the time when only disgrace, shame and scorn were their fate among other nations'[30] became widespread, allowing the Russian maskilim to hold fast to the picture of the past that had been shaped in the 1820s, and to pass it on to the second half of the nineteenth century. The relative relaxation of governmental pressure on the Jews and the liberal image of the tsar enabled the maskilim to pursue their campaign for the adoption of this picture of the past, by pointing out the clearly visible changes taking place in the present, harbingers of a better future.

The concepts of Zeitgeist ('the spirit of the time') and the 'hand of time' were expounded by the maskilim at every opportunity in order to explain historical changes and persuade their readers of their inevitability. 'The hand of time' was responsible for progress: it ensured Jewish rights in Europe, abolished superstition, and toppled the barrier that had separated Jews from other peoples for so many years. It was futile to oppose the spirit of the time, and the maskilim compared those attempting to turn back the clock to 'the dead opposing the living'.[31] Like Guenzburg in the 1840s, the maskilim continued to warn Jewish leaders against attempts to halt the Haskalah or the maskilim. Joshua Steinberg (1825–1908), the son-in-law of Adam Hacohen (Abraham Dov Lebensohn) and a graduate of the rabbinic seminary in Vilna, published *Or layesharim* (A Light to the Righteous), a didactic maskilic book of ethics in which he exhorted his readers to study science, to be faithful to the homeland, and to cultivate other maskilic values. He pictured the Haskalah being carried along a 'river of the Zeitgeist' and asserted that efforts to fight against it were futile or would have radical and destructive results. Steinberg, who was then serving as the government-appointed rabbi in Vilna, admonished the traditional leadership: 'Have you not yet learned that endeavouring to halt the Haskalah at this time is like trying to dam the monumental waters of the river by throwing stones into it?'[32]

[28] Ibid. 43, 64, 59.   [29] Gottlober, 'Semel hakinah', 496–507.

[30] *Hamagid*, 7 (1863), 1–2; *Hamagid*, 9 (1867), 354 (editorials).

[31] Tarnopol, 'Hashpa'at hamamlakhot', 87–8, 96, 103–4, 107–8, 110–11, 115–16. See also Plungian, *Sefer ben-porat*, 56.

[32] J. Steinberg, *Or layesharim*, 1–6. Cf. Plungian, *Sefer ben-porat*, 59–62; editorial, 'Hegyonei hamagid', *Hamagid*, 6 (1862), 145–6, 153–4, 160–1, 169–70; and Gordon's famous poem 'Hakitsah ami', 17.

On the other hand, maskilic optimism, based on an awareness of historical transition and on the concept of the spirit of the time, was rejected by spokesmen for Orthodox Judaism, a trend that had been developing in Russia as a reactionary force trying to influence public opinion, particularly after the dispute on religious reform at the end of the 1860s. In the 1870s Jacob Lipschitz (1838–1921), an Orthodox journalist and historian from Kovno, had already introduced an anti-maskilic picture of the past. He saw a terrible, cruel fanaticism at work in both universal and Jewish history, being used as a weapon to victimize the weak and undermine 'the tree of life' built on religious faith and wisdom. The noxious element could take on a number of forms, depending on the spirit of the time: in the Middle Ages the sword of religious fanaticism dominated, while 'in this generation . . . the clouds of folly have cleared like drifting smoke, and almost no memory of the disgrace and ignominy of religious fanaticism has remained. The sun of civilization has rays long enough to illuminate the land and its inhabitants.'[33] Is this yet another expression of maskilic consciousness? It would appear that even if the concepts were the same, Lipschitz forced them into an Orthodox mould, attempting to reverse roles: he claimed that the Haskalah was merely a new disguise for religious fanaticism. He believed that the radical articles in Hebrew journals directed against the rabbinical establishment and the tendency towards religious reform demonstrated that the Haskalah was destructive in nature and formed part of the same malevolent historical force. Lipschitz argued with the maskilim about the true substance of the spirit of the time, claiming that they had fabricated a spirit antithetical to religion. He did not seem to reject an awareness of the historical turning-point, although by asserting that the success of the Haskalah was totally incompatible with the contemporary spirit of the time, he ascribed a counter-modernist meaning to the concepts 'Haskalah', 'spirit of the time', and 'a wise and intelligent generation':

Are these the fruits of the Haskalah!? Has such a thing ever been heard of, that in the wise and enlightened nineteenth century, which champions knowledge and tolerance, those who presume to represent these values wreak vengeance through coercion and force, persecution, and defamation, to extirpate and desecrate the laws of the Talmud and the *Shulḥan arukh* . . . clever barbs . . . [borne] on the wings of the new literature in the Zeitgeist they themselves have invented saying this is the true spirit of the times. It is as if nature has altered its dominion, and the new time is so lacking power and potency that it cannot bear the burden of religion.[34]

The maskilim, for their part, continued to present maskilic history that they believed justified their stance. Dialectic thinking encouraged those who used it and offered consolation: the maskilim's struggle against opposing forces was merely a necessary stage in the historical process that would end in victory for the Haskalah. Levinsohn's method of historical precedent was also applied in the

---

[33] Lipschitz, 'Lahat haḥerev', 265–75. On Lipschitz as the creator of Orthodox historiography, see Bartal, 'Zikhron ya'akov', 409–14.   [34] Lipschitz, 'Lahat haḥerev', 266.

1860s and 1870s for similar purposes of persuasion and legitimization, and history continued to act as a critically important guide to the present. The eternal life promised to the Jewish people and its historical uniqueness as embodied in its ability to pass through several life cycles were fundamental maskilic concepts.

'Integration without self-abnegation' was the moderate Fuenn's slogan during the reign of Alexander II. In thus simplifying the desired goal, Fuenn was claiming that two forces are at play in the soul of every people: the urge to preserve their unique identity and the desire to unite with all other peoples. Throughout the course of history, the Jews too had manœuvred successfully between their distinctive nature and openness to their surroundings. 'Coming closer to enlightened peoples' did not harm 'the spirit of the nation' but strengthened it: 'When the Jewish people settled among wise and enlightened nations, they rose above them in scientific and civil education, and scientific education breathed its spirit also upon religious and moral education, and purified and refined the articles of faith and the concepts of religion, thus adding to it strength and power.'[35] Fuenn returned from his musings on history to the Russia of 1868, admonishing the Jews 'to draw closer to other peoples . . . to be the active, vital limbs of the gentile body we have joined, and together to do good and beneficial work for its success, honour, and glory'.[36] This was similar to Gordon's entreaty to the Jews in his poem 'Hakitsah ami' (Awake, My People!), that had appeared two years earlier in Fuenn's journal *Hakarmel*: 'Be . . . a brother to your countrymen and a servant to your king.'[37]

Almost every year at Hanukah the maskilim felt the need to justify the Jewish military and political rebellion against Hellenistic rule in the second century BC. Since the maskilim perceived Jewish existence as spiritual, based on 'the union of faith', and considered 'the spirit of the nation' was incompatible with the art of government or war, they endeavoured to prove that the festival of Hanukah was not simply a national holiday. More than we recall the physical valour of the Maccabees, wrote *Hamagid* in 1857, we understand the war as a struggle for spiritual deliverance from Greek culture.[38] Apart from this and similar political–military events that had taken place when the Jews were living in their homeland, Jewish heroism had been entirely spiritual in nature during the period of exile: 'Spirit, not force, ensured the safety of the children of Jacob; its sword was a page, its strong bow was a tablet. Its valour has never been forgotten.'[39]

The journals *Hamagid*, *Hakarmel*, *Hamelits*, and *Hashahar*, published during the reign of Alexander II, were manifestations of an expanding maskilic circle of both writers and readers, and a forum for scores of articles dealing with history.[40] In most cases these were neither scholarly articles nor original ones, but rather

[35] Fuenn, 'Yisra'el ba'amim', 41–2, 49–50.   [36] Ibid. 50.
[37] J. L. Gordon, 'Hakitsah ami' first appeared in *Hakarmel* (1866), issue 1, p. 1.
[38] 'Mai ḥanukah?', *Hamagid*, 1 (1857), 205 (editorial).   [39] Berman, 'Mipi olalim', 13–16.
[40] On the Hebrew periodicals, see J. Klausner, *Hitory of Modern Hebrew Literature*, iv. 111–25; Elkoshi, 'The Hebrew Press in Vilna', 59–97, 105–52; Gilboa, *Hebrew Periodicals*.

translations and adaptations of secondary or tertiary sources: popular German historiography, Russian literature, and German Jewish journals. This was informative history intended to enrich knowledge and disseminate it to a relatively large audience of readers of the Hebrew press. This informative universal Jewish and Russian history constituted one channel through which maskilic writings were popularized. They were directed at traditionally educated, well-to-do men and educated young students of rabbinic seminaries, who had not yet gained direct access to European literature.

Until the appearance of Kalman Schulman's book, Feivel Goldshtof's *Korot haolam* (History of the World) was almost the only Hebrew volume of universal history on the shelves. In 1861 *Hamagid* recommended to its readers that they purchase the book, because up to that point, 'no other person had had the courage to put into a book the entire history of the world'. In the 1850s and 1860s *Hamagid* itself published several articles on the archaeological discoveries that had been made in the East. Two of their regular contributors provided readers with accounts of the ancient Egyptian, Babylonian, and Assyrian excavations. Both wrote with satisfaction that none of the findings contradicted the contents of the Holy Scriptures. On the contrary, 'Stones from ancient times corroborate the fact that the words of our Scriptures are right and true.'[41] The reports on archaeology aroused widespread interest in ancient history, and the articles published on these subjects in Hebrew journals described ancient Egypt, the Hyksos kings, and 'the ancient land of Babylonia and its sages'.[42]

In the field of natural history the maskilim sought to demonstrate the enormous progress of science, and a Jewish student from Kovno who was studying at the vocational school in Potsdam submitted a short biography of Copernicus to *Hamagid*.[43] For background on the stormy political events in Italy, which was fighting for its independence, the reader could scan a condensed history of contemporary Italy. Joseph Epstein (1821–85), a schoolteacher in Shavli, published a biography of Garibaldi, 'the father of all the events currently taking place in Italy'. During the political and military conflicts in the Balkans in the 1870s readers were provided with historical information that shed light on 'the history of the Slavic people residing in the Balkan peninsula and fighting against the Turks'.[44]

As mentioned, the Society for the Promotion of Enlightenment, which had initi-

---

[41] Advertisement, *Hamagid*, 5 (1861), 8; Widover, 'Mifalot hakhmei dorenu', 69, 73–4; Brook, 'Ginzei nistarot', 169–70, 175; Rubin, 'Avnei miluim', 49–55. See also Y. Shavit, 'Truth Shall Spring out of the Earth', 27–54.

[42] Orenstein, 'Toledot goyei yemei kedem'; Rubin, 'Ma'aseh bereishit'; id., 'Menahem habavli'; Minor, 'Toledot yemei kedem', 118–20; N. Halevi, 'Malkhei haro'im hiksas'; J. L. Gordon, 'Erets bavel ha'atikah', 241–60.

[43] Zalkind, 'Korot yediat toledot hateva', 106–7, 230–1, 237–8; Y. Levinsohn, 'Korot hokhmat hatekhunah', 336 ff.; *Hakarmel*, 5 (1865), 6–8, 15–16; Granowitz, 'Toledot kopernikus', 100.

[44] *Hakarmel*, 1 (1860), 7–8, 15–16; 91–2, 99–100; *Hakarmel hahodshi*, 3 (1876), 478–83. On accounts of contemporary events in the Hebrew press, see Y. Shavit, 'Window on the World', 3–10.

ated the project of translating a book of Russian history into Hebrew, considered
a knowledge of Russian history a necessary step towards the integration of the
Jews into Russian society. In May 1864 the society decided to translate some
single-volume works of Russian history; books written by S. Solovyev (1820–79)
and D. Ilovaiskii (1832–90) were selected as possible candidates.[45] Ilovaiskii was
the more conservative of the two, and his books portrayed autocratic Russia by
glorifying the Romanov dynasty. Apart from a six-volume history of Russia, he
wrote several textbooks and popular history books, one of which he submitted to
the committee of the society.[46]

As noted above, in November 1864 the society proposed to the young
Abramowitz that he translate Ilovaiskii's book into Hebrew, and four years later
his *Divrei hayamim levenei harusim* (History of the Russian People) was published
in Odessa. His translation was intended to provide the Jews with clear and basic
information about 'the history of the people in whose land they lived'.[47]

For reasons that are not clear, however, Abramowitz translated only a small
portion (covering the ninth to the seventeenth centuries) of the book, and he did
not receive the society's backing upon its publication.[48] In 1866 the society was
already looking for a different translator, and published a tender for the composi-
tion of a work to be titled *Toledot erets rusiyah* (History of the Land of Russia),
which would incorporate the history of the Jews of Russia and would be based on
the new edition of Ilovaiskii's work. Joseph Epstein was finally chosen as the
translator, and he sent his manuscript to the committee in St Petersburg in 1868.
The book was reviewed by the committee and found to merit a 50 rouble prize.
After the manuscript had been sent to the writer for revisions, the committee withdrew its offer for some reason, deciding not to publish the book under its aegis,
just as it had in Abramowitz case.[49] Epstein's book was not published until five
years later,[50] and in the meantime a new contract was signed, this time between
the society and the 22-year-old Solomon Mandelkern, then a university student
in St Petersburg. This time the translator was not required to follow Ilovaiskii's
book, though once again the proposed history of Russia had to include the history
of the Russian Jews. The writing, which was to have taken a year, extended far
beyond the deadline. It was not until 1872 that a contract for printing the volume
was signed with a printing-house in Warsaw, and the book was held up by the
censors for another two years. When Moses Montefiore visited St Petersburg in
the summer of 1872, Mandelkern was photographed holding several pages of the

[45] L. Rosenthal, *Toledot hevrat marbei haskalah*, i. 7; ii. 36.

[46] Gooch, *History and Historians*, 414–15; Thompson, *A History of Historical Writing*, ii. 626–7; *Great
Soviet Encyclopedia*, x. 146.

[47] Abramowitz, *Divrei hayamim*; L. Rosenthal, *Toledot hevrat marbei haskalah*, i. 12–13; ii. 42.

[48] Abramowitz, *Collected Writings*, 6.

[49] Announcement, *Hakarmel*, 5 (1866), 312; L. Rosenthal, *Toledot hevrat marbei haskalah*, i. 54, 59.

[50] Epstein, *Divrei hayamim lemalkhei rusiyah*. The author was a teacher in a government school in
the Vilna district. The 200-page book also discusses Russian Jewry.

book which, at that time, was being proof-read. In an act of self-aggrandizement he presented Montefiore with the photograph, winning the Englishman's praise. It was only after the intervention of Gordon, the society's secretary, that the book was finally published in 1875, more than ten years after the society had first proposed a Hebrew translation of Russian history.[51]

Mandelkern's book comprised more than 800 pages in three parts. This was one of the first works to be written by this scholar, who eventually completed his doctoral studies at the University of Jena in Germany and wrote a monumental biblical concordance. His *Sefer divrei yemei rusiyah* (Book of Russian History) is packed with details, names, events, dates, and geographical locations and, in this respect, he achieved his goal: to provide extensive and detailed information about the history of Russia and its Jews. The book, however, contains no evidence of a profound historical conception, and was written, in accordance with the requirements of those who initiated and funded it, as the story of Russia, 'the benevolent kingdom'. The Jews identified with this Russia and were proud of its achievements. The maskilic tendency towards patriotism is apparent in the designations Mandelkern gave to the various periods: 'After Ancient Times', 'The First Rulers of the Rurik Dynasty', 'The Mongolian Yoke', 'The Muscovite Rulers', 'The Time of Anger and the Time of Perplexity', 'A New and Glorious Era Begins with the Romanov Dynasty'. The chapter titles proclaim gradual but constant improvement towards the climax, which was reached in the present: 'Days of the Kingdom's Renewed Strength', 'Days of the Reform and Renewal of Russia' (the period of Peter the Great), 'The Days of Valour and Glory' (Catherine the Great and Paul I), and 'The Days of Eternity and Grandeur', the period of Alexander I, at the heart of which was the defeat of Napoleon.[52]

'Informative history' about the Jewish past appeared during the reign of Alexander II in the form of scores of articles in the Hebrew press. The maskilic authors, most of whom were teachers in government schools and rabbinic seminaries, generally adapted historical literature from secondary sources: Jewish magazines published in Germany, or the writings of Marcus Jost, Leopold Zunz, Heinrich Graetz, Meyer Kayserling, and others. The history of the expulsion of the Jews from Spain, the monarchy and the rabbinic establishment in Portugal, Spain during the Inquisition, the history of the Jews of Sicily, France, Morocco, South America, and the Ottoman empire are examples of the subject matter of these articles.[53]

---

[51] L. Rosenthal, *Toledot ḥevrat marbei haskalah*, i. 59, 94, 116. See also J. L. Gordon, 'Pirkei zikhronot', 311. Gordon was opposed to Mandelkern's publicity campaign for his book and expressed some doubt about the author's integrity and ties to Judaism.

[52] Mandelkern, *Sefer divrei yemei rusiyah*. See also Y. Levinsohn, *Erets rusiyah*; Schulman, *Kiryat melekh rav*; Deinard, *Sefer masa kerim*.

[53] Kanel, 'Lekorot gerush hayehudim', 419–21; anon., 'Hamelukhah veharabanut beportugal', 138–40; Y. Levinsohn, 'Shenot ra'inu ra'ah', 118–19, 134–6; anon., 'Hayehudim besefarad', *Hamagid*, 5 (1867), 3–4.

Not only was the Jewish history reflected in these articles entirely informative in nature, with almost no effort made to analyse, draw conclusions, or incorporate it into a wider schema, but the rhetoric employed lacked the dramatic quality that usually characterized maskilic history, with the exception of some scattered proclamations of joy at the improved lot of the Jewish people, or some emphasis placed on the 'maskilic character' of the medieval sages. It would thus appear that these historical articles served as chapters of a textbook on Jewish history intended to enrich the historical education of readers of Hebrew journals. They were intended, as mentioned, particularly for those who were still unable to read books by Jost and Graetz in the original German.[54]

SCIENTIFIC KNOWLEDGE OF THE PAST

The picture that has emerged up to this point might lead one to conclude that the Russian maskilim left historical research to the 'wise men of the West', and were content to copy or adapt already existing material in order to recast it into literary forms requiring relatively less intellectual effort. This, however, was not the case. The popularization of universal historical Russian Jewish knowledge through textbooks and journalistic channels existed side by side with maskilic efforts to develop scholarly history, making an original contribution to the nineteenth-century Wissenschaft des Judentums.

It was once again Samuel Fuenn, undeterred by the failure of his *Nidḥei yisra'el* in the 1850s, who began a new, comprehensive book of Jewish history. In 1870 Fuenn informed the readers of *Hakarmel* that he was about to print the first part of a planned series called *Divrei hayamim livenei yisra'el* (History of the Children of Israel) that would survey Jewish history from the Babylonian exile to contemporary times. 'This book of ours', Fuenn prefaced his work, 'is not copied from the books written by contemporary historians, but it is based upon their words and on the results of many investigations and researches that we have conducted at length in this field, by studying the *midrashim*, the *agadot* and the books of the earlier and the later sages of Israel and of the nations.'[55] Fuenn planned that this series of books would comprise seven or eight parts and considered it an important enterprise that would fill the void in Hebrew literature. Why did Fuenn begin a new book rather than completing his *Nidḥei yisra'el*? His abandonment of the earlier book once again reveals the frustration of east European maskilim attempting to write Jewish history, with their eyes turned constantly in the direction of Western scholars—a phenomenon already observed among the Galician maskilim. The publication of a great number of studies in the 1850s and 1860s,

[54] A popular textbook was written by the Odessa maskil Isaac Warshavsky, *Sefer toledot yisra'el*. Warshavsky was a Hebrew teacher in Odessa, and in his book for young people he adapted the biblical story from the Creation to the construction of the Second Temple. Nine editions had been printed by 1910.   [55] Fuenn, 'Kol kore', 209.

particularly in Germany, led Fuenn to conclude that *Nidḥei yisra'el* did not meet the scientific criteria of modern historical research. Dissatisfaction with the quality of his book caused him to decide to begin the new series, *Divrei hayamim livenei yisra'el*, twenty years after the publication of the first part of *Nidḥei yisra'el*:

> We became aware that, in that book, we did not live up to our obligation to the science of history, and therefore, we should not live up to our obligation if we completed it in the same manner we began it. And with God's help and with renewed strength, we have undertaken to labour faithfully in the field of the science of Judaism.[56]

The criticism levelled at *Nidḥei yisra'el* by Levinsohn, the figure Fuenn most admired, may also have weakened his desire to continue the project. This time Fuenn decided to base his work on that of the best scholars, including Rapoport, Krochmal, Zunz, Jost, Geiger, Herzfeld, Graetz, and Kayserling. In addition, he would study and enquire into 'the primary sourcebooks of that wisdom'.[57] The influence of Krochmal's *Moreh nevukhei hazeman* is obvious. Fuenn sketched the broad outlines of the unique course of Jewish history: the antiquity of the Jewish people ('a people that has always been, a people much older than all other peoples of the world'), the marvellous and diverse forms its history took ('its ages have been miraculous throughout all its existence'), God's revelation to the Jewish people at Sinai, and the Jews' survival despite the loss of their political life. This was a chronological history, 'a great and monumental chain of momentous actions, commencing in the past, moving and spreading until it encompasses all times and places'.[58] The Jewish people's singular ability enabled it to be reborn and to return to the cycle of historical life, even after its decline.

Acquisition of a 'scientific knowledge' of the past naturally entailed a much greater effort than that required for writing 'informative history' or the historical tales discussed below. Fuenn took upon himself the tasks of a scientific historian as he understood them from the works of Wissenschaft des Judentums, setting a hitoriographic challenge for himself:

> to present a complete whole, not one composed of various materials that are independent of each other, but one in which the organs are interdependent, act and are acted upon, influence and are influenced by one another . . . to paint the spectacle of history as a great chain made up of many, many interconnected links . . . joined by cause and effect.[59]

However, a careful reading of the book reveals Fuenn's almost total dependence on previous studies and, except for the polemical comments and assessments that he appended to the views and conclusions of those studies, this work is simply yet another Hebrew adaptation of the Western Wissenschaft des Judentums. Fuenn's contribution lies in his annotated criticism and comments rather than in any original

---

[56] Fuenn, *Divrei hayamim livenei yisra'el*, 6. In 1860 Fuenn was still planning to continue *Nidḥei yisra'el*; see Fuenn, *Kiryah ne'emanah*, 18.

[57] Fuenn, *Kiryah ne'emanah*, 5–6; I. B. Levinsohn, *Pituḥei ḥotam*, 18–20.

[58] Fuenn, *Kiryah ne'emanah*, 3–6.   [59] Ibid. 4–5.

and independent study of primary sources. Particularly striking is Fuenn's affinity for the work *Geschichte des Volkes Israel*, by Levi Herzfeld (1810–74), whose three volumes on the Second Temple era were published in Germany between 1847 and 1857.[60] Herzfeld was a perfect example of Wissenschaft des Judentums in Germany in the mid-nineteenth century; trained as a historian at the University of Berlin and serving as a Reform rabbi in Braunschweig, he had also participated in the conferences of Reform rabbis in the 1840s and worked alongside Ludwig Philippson in the Israelitische Literaturgesellschaft. The first part of Fuenn's book coincides with the structure of the first part of Herzfeld's work: both open with the destruction of the First Temple and end with Alexander the Great. The body of Fuenn's text follows Herzfeld's step by step, and only occasionally does he allow himself a comment that runs counter to the latter's conclusions. As a typical representative of the east European version of the Wissenschaft des Judentums aspect of the Haskalah, Fuenn refrained from criticizing the traditional sources too sharply. Thus, for example, he rejected Herzfeld's claim that Nehemiah was an envious man who banished Ezra because he wanted no interference in his affairs. Heaven forbid, Fuenn argued with Herzfeld, that we should denigrate Nehemiah, a great benefactor of the Jewish people, who risked his life for the nation and acted in the name of God.[61]

This is only one of many examples. Fuenn rejected criticism that cast doubt upon the sources, people, and events. He wrote favourably, defensively, and admiringly of the Jewish past, and identified with it.[62] In his view, for example, the Hasmoneans were defeated because they had abandoned the guiding principle of the revolt; the moment they lost sight of the fact that their forefathers had given their lives for 'the revival of the faith' and chose to pin their hopes on the political regime, the revolt was doomed to fail. Fuenn's description of the revolt is based on those of Herzfeld, Graetz, the books of the Maccabees, and Josephus. His discussion of the figure of Judah, however, is an almost literal translation from Graetz, reiterating his portrait of Judah as 'an enlightened and prodigious hero' in both his faith and his valour.[63]

The discrepancy between Fuenn's claim to be writing an original, scientific history and his dependence on the studies of Jewish historians from Germany points up the dilemma of the Russian maskil. Fuenn knew that if he wanted to write as a historian, he had to conform to the scholarly and scientific works of Jewish history. However, he did not succeed in achieving anything beyond translations and adaptations, annotated with his own comments. His independently acquired,

---

[60] On Herzfeld and his book, see Baron, *History and Jewish Historians*, 322–43.

[61] Fuenn, *Divrei hayamim livenei yisra'el*, i. 41, n.   [62] Ibid. 93–4.

[63] Ibid., vol. iii, ch. 5, pub. separately in *He'asif*, 5 (1889), 180–204; id., *Divrei hayamim livenei yisra'el*, ii. 66–8, 98. Cf. H. Graetz, *Geschichte der Juden*, ii. 296–300. In contrast, on other issues Fuenn tended to accept Herzfeld's opinion and to reject that of Graetz. See Fuenn, *Divrei hayamim livenei yisra'el*, ii. 3–4 (nn.), 162–7.

informal education and his distance from the centres of Jewish historical research made it difficult for him to grapple successfully with the enormous task he had set for himself. This enterprise of Fuenn's was yet another failure, and only two parts of the seven or eight he had planned were published: the first appeared in 1871 and the second in 1877. He stopped writing after he had reached the end of the Hasmonean era. Apparently, his attempt (discussed below) to translate Graetz's book into Hebrew in the 1870s discouraged him from continuing to write a book whose chances of competing successfully against that of Graetz were very slim indeed.

In 1860 he had undertaken a less ambitious task, and his book *Kiryah ne'emanah* (Faithful City) was published ten years before *Divrei hayamim livenei yisra'el*. It was intended to present the history of the Jewish community of Vilna as part of 'the general history compiled from the details'. Noah Magid Steinschneider (1829–1903) was his research assistant; he spent a year copying inscriptions from ancient gravestones and passages from the community registers for Fuenn, and both of them collected oral testimony from the community elders.[64] Their joint research resulted in a short chronological survey of the community's history and a history of the sages of Vilna, organized chronologically, in the form of a biographical lexicon.

Fuenn's *Kiryah ne'emanah* also manifested the maskilim's growing interest in the roots of east European Judaism and in their identity as east Europeans. The maskilim saw themselves as breaking new ground in this area of historical research, since they were dealing with subjects that had not received their rightful due from Western Jewish scholars. An outstanding example of this trend was the great amount of attention given to the history of the Karaites and the Khazars— historical topics which were also linked to the question of the origins of east European Jewry and its relations with the Karaites in Russia. The learned Crimean Karaite Abraham Firkovich (1786–1874) undoubtedly provided the main impetus for a historical discussion of the Karaites. It eventually became clear that the Karaite books, journals, documents, and inscriptions published by Firkovich were 'adjusted' or forged to support the claim that the Russian Karaites were descendants of the Ten Tribes of Israel, had no connections to rabbinic Judaism, and thus were not responsible for its transgressions.[65]

Firkovich had a loyal friend in Simhah Pinsker, the Jewish maskil from Odessa, who incorporated dozens of manuscripts he received from Firkovich in his book *Likutei kadmoniyot* (Compilations of Antiquities), published in 1860. Pinsker's book, which was primarily an annotated edition of manuscripts from Firkovich's

[64] Fuenn, *Kiryah ne'emanah*, 5–8 ('El hakore'). See also Beilinson, *Alei hadas*, 26. Cf. works that may have served as exemplars for Fuenn, such as Luzzatto, *Avnei zikaron*; Lieben, *Sefer galed*.

[65] As far back as 1851 Levinsohn had asserted that Firkovich's version of Karaite history did not pass the test of historical scholarship: I. B. Levinsohn, 'Ta'ar hasofer', 176–94. On the Karaites in Lithuania, see Bartal, 'The East European Haskalah and the Karaites', 15–22.

collection, did not methodically explicate Karaite history. The book was written within the 'literary republic' of the Wissenschaft des Judentums in the nineteenth century: Pinsker was in contact with Graetz and even sent him sections of his book in manuscript before it was sent to be printed in Vienna, where Pinsker was assisted by A. Jellinek. Regarding the key issue of the origins of Karaism, Pinsker admitted that it could not be considered a movement until the time of Anan in the eighth century; however, in his opinion, Anan had not created Karaism *ex nihilo* and Karaite views were already being circulated among individuals at a much earlier period. As far as an assessment of the significance of the Karaites in Jewish history was concerned, Pinsker claimed that Karaism served as an 'opposing power' necessitated by 'the course of history', whose function was to awaken the Jewish religion from its torpor. As had happened during the Second Temple era, religion had become so degenerate that sects had emerged to 'introduce new ideas which, unlike religion, impugned tradition, availing themselves of Hellenistic wisdom to destroy its foundations'. This had compelled the Pharisees to gather strength and join forces. In the same way, the Karaites had become the second opposing force to emerge, after the completion of the Talmud. In terms of a 'historical equation', therefore, the Karaites were a positive force, because they forced the rabbis into new patterns of thought. In an annotation that he did not develop further, Pinsker also alluded to the interdependence of such 'opposing forces' and to various stages in universal religious history: the sects of the Second Temple era appeared during the birth of Christianity; the Karaites were linked to the emergence of Islam; and the hasidim, whom Pinsker considered yet another opposing force, appeared in reaction to the development of Protestantism.[66]

Gottlober's *Bikoret letoledot hakara'im* (A Critique of the History of the Karaites) appeared four years after Pinsker's *Likutei kadmoniyot*. While writing this book, Gottlober had kept not only a copy of Pinsker's book on his desk but also the fifth part of Graetz's *Geschichte der Juden*, Jost's book, and *Geschichte des Karaerthums* ('History of the Karaites'), written by Julius Fuerst, a Jewish linguist, bibliographer, and historian from Leipzig. In fact, a substantial part of Gottlober's book is taken up by a Hebrew translation of sections of these three works, with the addition of critical and polemical annotations—a literary form quite similar to that of Fuenn's *Divrei hayamim livenei yisra'el*. Gottlober described the aims of his polemics:

I did not wish to write a history of the Karaites according to Graetz and Jost, such as Fuerst did, for when laid in the scales, their words (or at least some of them) are together lighter than breath; and they seem to be history because of the beauty and arrangement of their language, that is to say, their external attributes do not attest to the value of their contents.[67]

He accused Fuerst of basing his book entirely on Graetz and Jost, and believed that the latter two were in debt to Pinsker, from whom they drew inspiration.

[66] Pinsker, *Likutei kadmoniyot*, 2–13.
[67] Gottlober, letter to Gurland (May 1865), in id., '13 mikhtavim me'et gotlober', 417.

Gottlober therefore defended the representative of Russian Wissenschaft, and at least with regard to this particular historical issue, demanded recognition for the Russian maskilim's superiority over the Jewish historians in Germany. His critical discussion was intended first and foremost to prove that Jost, Graetz, and Fuerst had erred and to support Pinsker. Gottlober continued with a challenge to the German Wissenschaft des Judentums, and with self-confidence containing more than a scintilla of arrogance, says of himself:

I translated Graetz's words from his book, and so I am not responsible for them; and in several places I commented on them justly and disproved his words, as I also did with Fuerst, who hastily based his work on those who preceded him and did nothing but re-arrange their writings; and for the most part, whatever he did change is not true, as I have clearly demonstrated. Finally, it seems to me that the work of these wise men was done neither by day nor by night, nor at the Sabbath twilight, for they wrote nothing whole and proper. If God grants me life, I shall show them how a history should be written, and the truth shall guide me like a pillar of fire to illuminate this dark night before me.[68]

Gottlober eventually produced a complex, intricately structured scholarly work based on a short study he had submitted to Levinsohn in the 1850s. Studies of the 1860s, however, forced him to provide a detailed discussion, expanding the original work.[69] Gottlober tried to pave an independent path, not only in his criticism of Jost, Graetz, and Fuerst but also in his reservations about several of Pinsker's hypotheses and conclusions. For example, he raised a well-founded fear that Firkovich had distorted the words of ancient sources and even falsified parts of them. He did, however, welcome Firkovich's involvement in the intellectual world of the Russian maskilim and believed that it was worth while to 'mediate peace between the two sects, at least by drawing the people, if not the religions, closer'.[70] In an era of growing religious tolerance, he believed the Jews and the Karaites should move closer together. He did not conceal his sympathy for 'the new sect' and even found similarities between it and the Haskalah. His assessment of the beneficial historical role played by the Karaites went far beyond Pinsker's, and he claimed that 'The way of every new sect . . . is to acquire wisdom and under-standing, and not to follow all old things blindly. Indeed, in our time, the enlight-ened—that is to say, the people for whom intelligence is their guiding principle, lighting their path—have been called the *Aufklärer*.'[71]

Firkovich's forgeries were unmasked in the mid-1870s, and the maskilim's

[68] Gottlober, letter to Gurland (May 1865), in id., '13 mikhtavim me'et gotlober', 417.

[69] Gottlober, *Bikoret letoledot hakaraim*, 6 n. With great caution, Gottlober accused Levinsohn of having copied from his research in writing his 'Ta'ar hasofer'.

[70] Gottlober, *Bikoret letoledot hakaraim*, 3–6.

[71] Ibid. 22, 126 n. See also his letter to Gurland, in Gottlober, '13 mikhtavim me'et gotlober', 419. In 1830 Gottlober met Karaites in Odessa, who even tried to persuade him to join their community (Gottlober, 'Zikhronot miyemei ne'urai', in id., *Zikhronot umasaot*, i. 261–8). His poem dedicated to a Karaite sage in Odessa (1839) also demonstrates his favourable attitude towards the Karaites (Gott-lober, *Kol shirei mahalalel*, 28).

image of the Karaites was tarnished. The Karaites were favoured over the Jews when they were granted civil rights in 1863, damaging the relationship between the two groups. The young maskil Ephraim Deinard (1846–1930) returned from his journey to the Crimean peninsula having met Firkovich, convinced that his version was at odds with 'stories of the history of the world and the judgement of common sense'. 'I thought', Deinard wrote, 'that the time has come for our people to unmask this man, who shocked the whole world with his amazing findings.'[72] In his *Sefer masa kerim* (Travels in the Crimea) he claimed that Pinsker, Chwolson, and even the Russian government had fallen into Firkovich's trap. All the sources used by the Karaites to prove their antiquity were invalid, and he believed that an examination of their race would reveal that the Russian Karaites were of Mongolian or Turkish origin. They were nothing at all like the maskilic image they projected, and were possessed of extremely unpleasant traits; they were a greedy, obsequious people who practised strange customs.[73]

Not all the maskilim were convinced of the truth of Deinard's harsh claims. At least one outstanding representative of the moderate maskilim in Russia, Eliezer Zweifel (1815–88), found it difficult to swallow Deinard's acrimonious approach and categorical conclusions. Zweifel continued to advocate a closer relationship between the maskilim and the Karaites, and *Sefer masa kerim* came as a blow to him. He felt that Deinard 'had had the effrontery to destroy all that is sacred and true, and demolish all peace and brotherhood, and dispel all hope that we might gradually unite with these brothers of ours who are so far off'.[74] Zweifel accused Deinard of being a provocateur and a government informant, and of burning the bridges between Jews and Karaites. For him, the Jewish origins of the Karaites were indisputable, and he had no doubt whatsoever that the Karaites were 'sons of our people'. Zweifel even tormented himself for being among those who had provided an approbation for Deinard's book before he had even read it.[75]

Although Deinard planned to continue *Sefer masa kerim* to include accounts of the Khazars and the Jewish inhabitants of Crimea, these sections were never published. The history of the Khazars, on the other hand, was the subject of the first book written by Joseph Judah Lerner (1847–1907), a young maskil from Odessa. He discovered that there was no Hebrew version of the history of the Khazars, and sought to make his contribution to the subject of their origins as part of his study of the roots of Jewish settlement in Russia. In Lerner's version the Khazars, also possessed of maskilic traits (reason and morality), had deliberately converted to Judaism. In the eleventh century, however, increased Russian pressure had led the Khazars in the Crimea to adopt the Karaite religion. Lerner's sources were Graetz, Chwolson, and Rapoport, and he called for scholars, especially Abraham Harkavy, to continue their more detailed studies to shed light on the matter.[76]

[72] Deinard, *Sefer masa kerim*, 1.   [73] Ibid. 2, 54, 58–9.   [74] Zweifel, *Sanegor*, 39.
[75] Ibid. 17, 40–1.
[76] Lerner, *Hakuzarim*, 5–6, 21. On Lerner, see Malachi, 'Joseph Judah Lerner'. See also Werses, *Haskalah and Shabbateanism*, 181–2.

In contrast to Fuenn, Gottlober, and Lerner, Harkavy was a historian who, although nurtured by the Haskalah, received academic training at the universities of St Petersburg, Berlin, and Paris, which put him on a different level in terms of historical research.[77] Though Harkavy's treatment of the history of Russian Jewry continued to demonstrate the maskilic trend observed in Fuenn and Gottlober, his approach was philological. His expertise in languages and his reliance on primary sources made him a historian in the full sense of the word. Together with Ilya Orshanski (1846–75) and others, Harkavy was already part of a post-maskilic phenomenon: the beginnings of Russian Jewish historiography, written primarily in Russian and based on professional, scientific research.[78]

THE AUTOBIOGRAPHY OF THE HASKALAH MOVEMENT

The Russian maskilim opened a new avenue, in addition to their writing of scholarly history, with the aim of documenting and preserving the heritage of the Haskalah. This trend, which began with Euchel's biography of Mendelssohn in 1788, continued with Letteris's writings in Galicia and Levinsohn's 'chain of the Haskalah'. The biographies of German maskilim—Wessely, Solomon Maimon, and the physician and philosopher Marcus Herz (1747–1803)—were printed in instalments in the Hebrew press.[79] The first volume of *Hame'asef* was available in Letteris's edition, published in 1862, and Fuenn occasionally printed various letters from the Haskalah period in Germany in *Hakarmel*. Later maskilim were also the subjects of biographies: in 1863 Gottlober decided to write Levinsohn's life story along the lines of Euchel's biography of Mendelssohn, but before he could carry out his plan an anonymous maskil anticipated him and published his version in *Hamagid* in serial form.[80] Abraham Kaplan (1839–97) of Riga dedicated a book to Mapu's life a short time after the author's death, in the belief that his biography was the story of one of the nation's great heroes.[81]

In addition to the preservation of the Haskalah heritage in order to bolster the self-confidence of the maskilim and unite them around their common origins, an attempt was made in the 1850s to deepen the roots of the Haskalah in Russia by promoting and enhancing the image of the maskilic hero Rabbi Manasseh ben

[77] T. Harkavy, 'Abraham Harkavy', 116–36.

[78] Magid, 'List of Articles and Books by Abraham Harkavy', 14–15, 18. Among his first works on the Jews of Russia are 'Derishot vehakirot' and 'Rusiyah besifrut hayehudim'. On the beginnings of Russian Jewish historiography, see Maor, 'Historians of Russian Jewry'; Slutsky, *The Russian Jewish Press*.

[79] Joseph Kera, 'Toledot rabi naftali', 101–202; N. K., 'Devarim ahadim mitoledot shelomoh maimon'; Langbank, 'Toledot rabi mordekhai ben rabi herts', 37–9.

[80] Y. Sh. P. A., 'Yitshak ba'er levinson mikremnits', 357, 373, 381, 389, 397–8. See also Zinberg, *A History of Jewish Literature*, vi. 328.

[81] A. Kaplan, *Hayei mapu*. Luzzatto's autobiography was published in *Hamagid* during 1858–60: id., 'Toledot shadal', 66–7, and then in instalments until *Hamagid*, 4 (1860), 174–5.

Joseph of Ilya (1767–1831). Manasseh was scarcely known to the maskilim and was not included in their pantheon until the publication in Vilna in 1858 of *Sefer ben-porat*, by Mordecai Plungian (1814–83), in which he presented, for the first time, Manasseh's biography and views. Plungian, who belonged to the group of Vilna maskilim, was a brilliant Torah scholar who was attracted by secular studies and absorbed the values of the Haskalah. For a while he worked as a Talmud teacher at the rabbinic seminary in Vilna, and he later became well known as a proof-reader at the Romm Press.[82] He found it easy to identify with Manasseh of Ilya, another Lithuanian talmudist who had absorbed outside influences, and had dared to express original ideas that were unacceptable to the traditional élite and consequently aroused its antagonism.

The author of *Sefer ben-porat* was aware that he was creating a new maskilic hero, or at least redeeming a forgotten one.[83] According to his view of history, the fate of peoples and nations was the outcome of a lengthy process, replete with struggles against adversaries and enemies. Only after periods of oppression and humiliation could the end of the long road to success be attained. In Plungian's view, this was a divine form of education, teaching men to struggle and to achieve success through arduous efforts. He believed that this dynamic was given a consummate expression in Manasseh's life. He had lived during a historical stage in which the struggle had not borne fruit; nevertheless, it was an essential stage since it paved the way for the mid-nineteenth-century Haskalah. Plungian wanted to revive this forgotten figure, whose ideas had fallen on deaf ears during his lifetime, since he believed that people were now ready to heed Manasseh's message and that the modern generation would enthusiastically embrace it.

Another reason for creating this new hero was the need to venerate the memory of great Jews in Russia. All nations, including the Jews in other countries, Plungian asserted, commemorated their wise men, but the Russian Jews had neglected theirs. To correct this oversight, he suggested that the Haskalah had begun in eastern Europe. His *Sefer ben-porat* was an early and deliberate attempt to establish the legitimacy of the Haskalah via the biography of an early maskilic hero.[84]

Plungian's biography of Manasseh displayed all the usual maskilic hallmarks: a brilliant Torah scholar from Lithuania, whose tendencies to broaden his horizons were blocked from an early age; a youthful marriage that ended in divorce; religious scholarship that rejected *pilpul* and adopted a critical approach. Manasseh's rationalistic critique of the religious sources made him a target of persecution. He had many enemies, but many pupils too. Manasseh was aware of the decay of Jewish society and foresaw that wisdom would triumph, and that in the end the changes brought by time could not be halted. However, he was ahead of his time; his generation was not yet prepared to absorb innovations, and he had to carry out

---

[82] N. Nathanson, *Sefat emet*; Mapu, 'Mikhtavim le'avraham kaplan', 573; Werses, 'Mordechai Plungian'.   [83] On Manasseh of Ilya, see Barzilay, *Menashe of Ilya*.

[84] Plungian, *Sefer ben-porat*, pp. iii–iv, 4.

the mission of the maskil, courageously advocating change and new ideas in a hostile environment. He fearlessly urged Jewish youth to cleave to the Torah as well as to wisdom and science—the essence of the modern maskilic ideal—and laboured to save the 'glory of our people which is being trampled under the feet of the boors among them'.[85]

However, Plungian's *Sefer ben-porat* did more than just construct an east European maskilic hero; it also served as a moderate maskilic alternative to a Haskalah with roots in the Vilna Gaon's house of study, advocated by Joshua Heschel Levin (1818–83). In this sense, *Sefer ben-porat* was a counter-history, written in direct response to Levin's *Aliyot eliyahu* (a biography of Elijah ben Solomon, the Vilna Gaon). Published in Vilna in 1856, Levin's book lavishly praised the Vilna Gaon, holding him up as a model for emulation and instructing the young generation to shun evil ways and follow in the path of *tsadikim* and sages. In *Aliyot eliyahu*, he was depicted as a hero of giant proportions, and much more than a brilliant Torah scholar; he was the true maskil, who combined Torah and wisdom, was well versed in all the sciences, but eschewed the pitfalls of philosophy. Levin, himself a member of the mitnagedic Lithuanian élite, tried, on one hand, to endow the Gaon with the qualities of a maskil in order to advance his claim that the mitnagedic stream was consonant with the Haskalah; on the other hand, however, he criticized the maskilim, urging them to return to the path of the Vilna Gaon.[86]

Plungian, who objected to the maskilic image that Levin attempted to foist on the Vilna Gaon, chose Manasseh of Ilya as a counterweight, arguing that he embodied the quintessential maskil. In *Sefer ben-porat* Plungian did not conceal the fact that Manasseh was an intimate of the Gaon, and to a certain extent depicted him as his disciple, but he stressed that Manasseh preferred the path of the hasidim to that of the mitnagedim: 'he said there is hope for a man who thoughtfully considers his ways, tortuous and devious as they may be, for he will prepare his steps in the future to walk upright, but there is no hope for a man who shuts his eyes and sees not where his ways lead him'.[87]

Plungian was more open in levelling harsher, albeit indirect, criticism at the Vilna Gaon in other parts of his book. The Gaon not only refused to see the changes taking place in his time, and consequently did not merit the title of 'maskil', but, in Plungian's view, he erred in not taking responsibility for the Jewish community. The Gaon engaged in scholarly pursuits for his own sake, but hardly accepted any pupils: 'He kept his thoughts and his path concealed in his heart and did not reveal them to any man, and hence his wisdom died with him.'[88] Manasseh, on the other hand, fought all his life for the sake of maskilic ideals and laboured to impart them to his pupils. Plungian sharpened the boundaries between maskilim

---

[85] Plungian, *Sefer ben-porat*, 6–7, 43–6, 59–67, 73–4, 127–8.

[86] On Joshua Heshel Levin, see Zitron, 'The Dynastic Struggle'; Etkes, 'The Vilna Gaon and the Haskalah', 195–6. Cf. Mapu's criticism of Levin: Mapu, *Mikhtavei avraham mapu*, 21; I. Kovner, *Sefer hamatsref*.   [87] Plungian, *Sefer ben-porat*, 14; see also 13, 33.   [88] Ibid. 90–1.

and non-maskilim and denigrated the maskilic image of the Gaon. He did not believe that the roots of the Russian Haskalah were embodied in the Gaon, but rather in Manasseh of Ilya, the prototype of the true maskil.

Many in the Vilna community took exception to this maskilic image of Manasseh. A short time after the appearance of *Sefer ben-porat* complaints were heard that Plungian had in fact falsified the true image of a peerless talmudist by ascribing a series of maskilic traits to him. An anonymous writer in *Hamagid* reported that some of the community's rabbis and leaders were up in arms, and critics were asking how Plungian had dared to turn Manasseh into a maskil and a philosopher as if he were a Spinoza or a Solomon Maimon.[89] The maskilic camp was quick to react to these protests, arguing that the maskilic image was justified.[90] In spite of the controversy, from the publication of *Sefer ben-porat* onwards the new maskilic hero took his place in the consciousness of Russian maskilim, both those who sanctioned the maskilic image of the Vilna Gaon, like Fuenn, who regarded Manasseh as the Gaon's loyal disciple, and the followers of Plungian, like Reuben Asher Braudes (1851–1902).[91] Braudes regarded Manasseh as one of the two potential reformers of Judaism in eighteenth-century Poland: Manasseh, along with the Ba'al Shem Tov, recognized the need for change among the rabbis and wished to see the halakhah and the way of life made more lenient. Both men wanted to kindle a sense of vitality in the people's hearts and to introduce direct study based on literal interpretation and logic. The Ba'al Shem Tov's aim was to expel despair and to ease the severe strictures imposed by the rabbis. The good intentions of these two reformers were maliciously defeated by the Vilna Gaon. Braudes believed that had it not been for the Gaon's intervention, Manasseh's maskilic pupils and the Bal'al Shem Tov's hasidic disciples would, in the final analysis, have joined forces: 'for then they would surely have joined together, would have shared common views and methods, and all the children of Israel would have had vitality and light in their religion'.[92]

In the 1870s two more works were written on the history of the Haskalah. In 1878–9 *Haboker or* printed, in instalments, Gottlober's 'Hagizrah vehabeniyah' (History of the Development of the Haskalah in Russia and Poland),[93] and in *Hakarmel* Fuenn published his book *Safah lane'emanim* (Language for the Faithful), also in instalments (1879–80). Gottlober and Fuenn, two of the oldest and most venerable of Russian maskilim, were both sworn advocates of the moderate Haskalah, but each employed a different historical schema to depict the history of the Haskalah in general and of the Russian Haskalah in particular.

According to Gottlober's narrative, the Haskalah in Russia was not a native product of east European Jewry. Instead, it came there from Germany, via Galicia, on its way to revolutionize Jewish society. Gottlober distinguished seven periods

[89] Anon., 'Hatsofeh', 34–5.   [90] Ibid. 50–1.
[91] On the maskilic image of the Vilna Gaon, see Etkes, 'The Vilna Gaon and the Haskalah'.
[92] Braudes, *Hadat vehahayim*, 25–43.   [93] Gottlober, 'Hagizrah vehabeniyah' 25–149.

in the history of the Haskalah movement. To designate the first, the period of pre-Enlightenment ignorance, he used the kabbalistic term *tohu shekodem hatikun*, 'the chaos preceding the restoration'. This period was characterized by the static and uniform life of the Jewish communities, who adhered faithfully to the religious faith and its discipline, either willingly or out of fear of their leaders. In Gottlober's view, this was an illusory peace: 'that calm was like the peace of a field of graves, devoid of any life or joy, feeling or movement . . . reason had concealed its face under the cloak of faith, knowledge had shyly withdrawn'. The next three periods were marked by grave crises in the history of Polish Jewry: the Chmielnicki massacres of Jews in 1648–9 and the catastrophic Shabbatean movement and its religious radicalism, followed by Jacob Frank and his sect, who were 'a catastrophe compounded'. Hasidism was depicted as the successor of Shabbateanism, but also as rebelling against it. The mitnagedic trend led by the Vilna Gaon did not, in Gottlober's view, hold out a promise of any change or reform whatsoever. Only the last three periods in his synopsis were pervaded by light and brightness, and they originated in the Haskalah of Berlin and the work of Moses Mendelssohn. Levinsohn was the first to absorb the message coming from the West, and the Russian government, for its part, galvanized the Haskalah.[94]

A sharp contrast is presented by the book by Fuenn, who at the time was compelled to defend the basic values of the moderate Haskalah, which were no longer self-evident, particularly the observance of the commandments and the promotion of the Hebrew language. He chose to represent the Russian Haskalah as emanating from an authentic unbroken tradition, deeply rooted in Jewish history and the history of Russian Jewry. In *Safah lane'emanim* Fuenn did not attempt to uncover the historical circumstances that gave rise to the Haskalah; following Levinsohn's method, he merely presented a chronological list of Hebrew writers and books, which for him served as examples of the continuity of Hebrew literary works. In Fuenn's mind, the history of the Hebrew language and literature corresponded with the history of the Haskalah; thus his book opened with the Bible and worked its way through time until, in the last chapter, it reached the Haskalah in Germany and Russia. Fuenn also supported the maskilic image of the Vilna Gaon, and consequently placed him alongside Mendelssohn as one of the fathers of the Haskalah in Russia. By characterizing the Haskalah as a religious enlightenment that embraced all things—Torah, commandments, ethics, and secular sciences—Fuenn was able to argue that the Haskalah had begun even before the Vilna Gaon, that the course of its development was free of any friction or upheavals, and that it had originated in the early days of the nation. The dissemination of religious enlightenment had thus always been the mission of the Jewish people.[95] Hence, in Fuenn's view, the history of the Haskalah was not a particular section of Jewish history but rather the one and only spiritual history of the Jewish people throughout all epochs.

[94] Gottlober, 'Hagizrah vehabeniyah', 25–6, 30, 34–5, 69–149.
[95] Fuenn, *Safah lane'emanim*, 573–88, 591–8, 657–77.

ABRAHAM MAPU AND THE POPULARIZATION OF
MASKILIC HISTORY

The literary works of Abraham Mapu, the Lithuanian maskil from Kovno, and in particular his historical novels *Ahavat tsiyon* and *Ashmat shomron*, which placed him at the very centre of the stage of Hebrew literature in Russia in the 1850s and 1860s, could perhaps be regarded as marking a significant shift in the maskilic sense of the past. His choice of Palestine during the period of the monarchy as the setting for the plots of his enormously popular novels and his idyllic depictions of ancient pastoral life might have led one to conclude that Mapu, yearning for the distant past, had written a national historical epic, departing significantly from the traditional goal of the maskilim to transform society.[96] The truth is, however, that Mapu remained within the boundaries of the maskilic consciousness, both from the standpoint of the picture of the past implicit in his work and as regards the topical functions of the past in his work. Mapu saw himself as a 'visionary author', a writer constructing fictional plots to capture the reader's imagination and enthral him with the adventures of his heroes. Mapu felt that by adopting the new literary genre of the romantic novel he would acquire an extremely influential propaganda tool and reach a much broader readership:

For the fable possesses great power, and drama strongly affects the masses of the people and will attract their hearts to wisdom . . . a multitude will heed the visionaries, but not many will find wisdom, and only a few among the people will ascend the mountain of wisdom; but the people will not live according to their ways and they will not light the way for the multitude . . . for as a remedy is for the flesh, so is this a remedy for the soul, and those struck by fancy will be healed by fancy, and those wounded by a false vision will be cured by a true vision.[97]

Mapu's novels were philosophical books, whose fanciful plots were underpinned by maskilic logic.[98] In *Ahavat tsiyon* and *Ashmat shomron* the ancient past in the Land of Israel served as a backdrop for social and cultural models that were typical of nineteenth-century Jewish society, and very far removed indeed from the seventh and eighth centuries BC, in the days of King Ahab and King Hezekiah. Mapu did not even try to conceal his objectives: of *Ashmat shomron*, for example, he wrote that this was a work that would 'express ancient riddles about Judah and Israel, the brothers separating into two inimical kingdoms . . . these plots are also relevant for us at this time and they call aloud to us: how good and pleasing it is for brethren to dwell together'.[99] For decades, lessons learned from

[96] Klausner, *Creators and Builders*, 182; Cohen, *From Dream to Reality*, 93–153; Kleinman, *Figures and Ages*, 55–6.
[97] Mapu's letter to the heads of the Society for the Promotion of Enlightenment (1864); Mapu, *Mikhtavei abraham mapu*, 230–1. Cf. Miron, *From Romance to the Novel*, 59–62. See too Mapu's letter to A. Beilinson (1860); Mapu, *Mikhtavei avraham mapu*, 180.
[98] Miron, *From Romance to the Novel*, 146. See also Patterson, *Abraham Mapu*.
[99] Mapu's letter to the heads of the Society for the Promotion of Enlightenment (1864); Mapu, *Mikhtavei abraham mapu*, 237. The same words were printed in the preface of his *Ashmat shomron*, 79.

precedents in the past had been one of the hallmarks of the maskilic sense of the past. Mapu's novels set in the biblical period, as well as the story 'Ḥozei ḥezyonot' (The Visionaries), set in the time of Shabbetai Tsevi, provided a new and attractive literary wrapping for familiar maskilic contents. In this sense, Mapu was one of the chief popularizers of the maskilic sense of the past.

Mapu chose to set his historical novels in periods of crisis. Unlike other maskilim, his optimism was qualified and he offered it as an ideal solution in his novels, more as a hope than as a realistic ending. He belonged to the older generation of moderate and self-taught Russian maskilim and did not gain fame as an author until he was in his fifties. Even after his books began to sell well to readers of Hebrew literature, his correspondence reveals him as a morose, bitter man, living a solitary, modest, and rather drab life.[100] During the reign of Alexander II Mapu was one of the first maskilim to reject the simplistic, dualistic maskilic view of contemporary Jewish society as one divided between the opponents of Haskalah and its supporters. The problem of the 'new generation' was a prevalent motif in his writing, expressing the moderate maskil's frustration at the emergence of a generation most of whose members had adopted a modern lifestyle but did not adopt the ideas of the Haskalah or belong to its circles. These were the 'pseudo-maskilim', the sons of the wealthy, educated in the new schools, and young women who learned Russian and French. Their behaviour demonstrated their rejection of tradition and their acculturation into the surrounding society; nor were they intellectuals following the maskilic example of fostering Hebrew literature and language.[101]

Like Krochmal in Galicia in the 1830s, Mapu viewed the sharp polarization in Jewish society as a threat to its very existence, and gave this growing sense of danger expression in his literary work. He feared that the members of this new generation were likely 'to flee from the burning house', because they 'love life and luxury, and speak slander by saying: billows of smoke will rise up from the chimneys of the old house; ah! Fire is secretly consuming it, let us escape with our lives.'[102] Mapu's three historical novels are set in times of historical crisis—an hour of 'fusion and annihilation' in Krochmal's terminology, which had a strong influence on Mapu. The plots of *Ahavat tisyon* and *Ashmat shomron* unfold at the close of the eighth and the beginning of the ninth centuries BC, during the reigns of Ahab and Hezekiah, kings of Judah; the central events are Sennacherib's siege of Jerusalem after Samaria had fallen to the Assyrians (in *Ahavat tsiyon*) and the death throes of the kingdom of Israel and its conflict with the kingdom of Judah (in *Ashmat shomron*). *Ḥozei ḥezyonot* tells of the state of crisis provoked by Shabbateanism in the

[100] B.-Z. Dinur's introd. to Mapu, *Mikhtavei abraham mapu*; J. Klausner, *History of Modern Hebrew Literature*, iii. 269–360; cf. Bartal, 'Gentiles and Gentile Society', 47–52.

[101] On the distinction between 'enlightenment', 'assimilation', and 'acculturation' in Russia, see Zipperstein, 'Haskalah, Cultural Change', and Feiner, 'The Modern Jewish Woman'.

[102] Mapu, *Ḥozei ḥezyonot*, 455.

seventeenth century, in 'a generation great in deeds . . . a sacred generation led astray by vain hopes and enticements whose foundation lies in the mountains of darkness, in the delusions of Shabbetai Tsevi . . . truth is stumbling through the streets, and falsehood has taken up a high place on the mountains of Israel'.[103]

How did Mapu characterize hours of crisis in the distant past as well as in the present? This is clear from the foreword to his *Hozei hezyonot*, which appeared almost verbatim at the beginning of the first part of *Ashmat shomron*:

In the days of Ahaz, king of Judah, Pekah, son of Remaliah, and Hoshea, son of Elah, kings of Israel, the voices of the prophets grew hoarse from calling upon the defiant sons; and they grew weary of pleading with a rebellious nation that erred in its heart. At that evil time Ephraim rebelled, Judah betrayed . . . Torah vanished from Zion, and truth and honesty fled from the gates of Samaria . . . righteousness dwelt in the forest, and faith found refuge in the caves.[104]

Crisis was explained by Mapu according to the antithetical model of maskilic historical thinking: right and wrong, light and darkness constantly contest with one another in a struggle that ends with the victory of the good and the upright. Even in a generation of evil and sin there were islands of justice and reason, and these were embodied by the maskilim in every generation, who provided a source of hope for future redemption. Apparently, as far as Mapu was concerned, the moderate maskilim in Russia the 1850s and 1860s filled the role that had been taken by their predecessors the prophets in the eighth century BC and the first maskilim in the eighteenth century. The figure of the ideal maskil was projected back into the distant past and onto his fictional heroes. In *Ahavat tsiyon*, for example, there were the figures of Yoram, 'chief of a thousand', and the generous Yedidiah: 'Yoram and Yedidiah burned brightly like jewels in the crown of the generation of perversity, the generation of Ahaz, for their spirit was loyal to God and to His holy ones, and they were among the disciples of the Lord; the testimony of the prophet, son of Amoz, was bound up with them and the teaching of God was inscribed in them.'[105] These literary heroes were also compelled to grapple with the opponents of the Haskalah, the hypocrites and impostors, and the other social forces that were so repugnant to the maskilim.

Political strife, differing religious beliefs, and personal quarrels were the hallmarks of the 'generation of perversity' during the period of the monarchy and the generation of Ahaz, just as they were in Mapu's novel *Ayit tsavua* (Hypocrisy), set in nineteenth-century Russia. In it Nehemiah, the maskil of the 'old generation', decries the divisiveness in his generation and longs for a leadership that will heal the rifts and unite the people. Similarly, in *Hozei hezyonot* the angel Michael

---

[103] Ibid. 457–8. See also Werses' discussion of the background and content of *Hozei hezyonot*, Werses, *Haskalah and Shabbateanism*, 228–35.

[104] Mapu, *Ashmat shomron*, 73; id., *Hozei hezyonot*, 458.   [105] Mapu, *Ahavat tsiyon*, 3.

blames Satan for having imposed the same state of divisiveness in Jewish history in general, and during the time of Shabbetai Tsevi in particular.[106]

Mapu divided the battlefield on which the maskilim were struggling into two fronts: one facing inwards, confronting the hasidim and the 'pseudo-maskilim', and the other facing outwards against the external enemies of the Jews. Scattered throughout all Mapu's stories are the negative characters of the 'old generation', who are hostile to the Haskalah, with emphasis on the figure of the hasid. In the period of the monarchy this character was represented by the priests of Ba'al— vain and reckless villains, plotting evil and holding to superstitions. In *Ashmat shomron* the priests of Beit El are denounced as responsible for the many sins of the kingdom of Israel and the widening internal rift that led to its demise. They are accused of deviating from the Jewish religion and imitating alien faiths, and are denounced for their greed and low morals: 'There is no truth, no mercy, no knowledge of God in the land, for all they desire is to fill their bellies, to wax fat on the choicest part of every offering of the people of Israel.' In this way, they were turned into the 'hasidim' of the eighth century BC; the same is true of the descriptions of the debauchery and drunkenness of these priests.[107] By depicting them as wisdom-hating men who entice the masses with vain delusions, Mapu turned his novel into a virulent piece of anti-hasidic propaganda. He was even more open in confronting hasidism in his *Hozei hezyonot*, and in a letter in 1858 he revealed his tactic: 'This lofty vision strikes at the hasidim purporting to do great and marvellous things . . . I didn't touch the hasidim themselves, but only Shabbetai Tsevi and his generation: "strike a scorner and the simple will beware".'[108]

Mapu also concurred with Levinsohn's view about the duty of maskilic writers to contend with anti-Jewish trends, and was probably also influenced by Levinsohn's apologetic writings. Michael, one of the protagonists in *Ayit tsavua*, leaves a sum of money in his will to finance writers who 'beat their pens into spears to fight Voltaire and Eisenmenger, our enemies, who have invented things that are not true about the people of Israel to blacken their name among their neighbours'.[109] In the third part of *Ayit tsavua* Mapu introduced a discussion that takes place in the salon of the pro-Jewish gentile nobility, where Jews are also welcome —a situation that expresses a maskilic picture of the future. Loira, the daughter of the Count, has been given one of Voltaire's books by one of the ministers, a jurist by profession, and she condemns his disparaging words about the Jews:

---

[106] Mapu, *Ayit tsavua*, 282; id., *Hozei hezyonot*, 469.

[107] Mapu, *Ahavat tsiyon*, 7, 41–2; id., *Ashmat shomron*, 98, 125, 166.

[108] Mapu's letter to his brother (Jan. 1858), in id., *Mikhtavei abraham mapu*, 26. Cf. Werses, *Haskalah and Shabbateanism*, 228–35; see also Mapu, 'Igeret le'ahiv'.

[109] Mapu, *Ayit tsavua*, pt. 5, p. 426. Voltaire's attacks on the Old Testament and its Jewish followers provided ammunition for later antisemitic campaigns; Johann Andreas Eisenmenger (1654–1704) wrote a book which had a formative influence on antisemitic polemics.

If the honourable advocate will listen, I would like to tell you what I think about Voltaire's book, which you have lent me and have highly praised. And I do not know as yet: why is he deserving of fame? For he is Voltaire, capable of abusing any who offend him. Is he the first to curse the Jews and to see in them only trouble? Our people is not like this today, nor are the Jews like this in this era, for they have chosen wisdom and all good ways.[110]

The minister who represents the Jew-haters enters into a debate with Loira about her enlightened and tolerant views. He counters her arguments by stressing the Jews' arrogance and their lack of productivity. Loira rebukes him, reminding him that the situation in Russia in the 1860s actually shows that the Jews are introducing reforms. Their economic role in trade contributes to the state, and their decision to take the path of wisdom obliges the surrounding society to change its attitude towards them. Did not Spain decline following her expulsion of the Jews? Elisheva, Loira's enlightened Jewish friend, has also read Voltaire's book, and has left her opinion of it in Hebrew among its pages. Mapu places three apologetic points in the mouth of his heroine to counter Voltaire's views: first, historians will find that every nation makes its own unique contribution to history—the Sidonians as merchants, the Babylonians as astronomers, the Greeks as philosophers, the Romans as jurists, and the Jews as the bearers of monotheism. Secondly, the Jews in ancient times far surpassed all other nations in their religion and ritual: 'Voltaire forgot all the deceits of the ancient peoples. Why did he not remember the Jew who afflicted his soul . . . why did Voltaire also forget the peoples who worshipped the forests and sanctified dross . . . and consulted the oracles and the dead and feared witches and wizards?' Lastly, the long and unbroken history of the Jews is worthy of the respect of the sages of all nations, and their antiquity attests to the Almighty's desire that they should endure.[111]

It has already been noted that Mapu's maskilic historical schema was based to some degree on Krochmal's *Moreh nevukhei hazeman*, particularly in relation to the Jewish people's capacity for renewal after a period of crisis and decline. His adoption of Krochmal's ideas was not merely a literary and intellectual choice but reflected the similar maskilic situation in which the two lived, one in Galicia in the 1830s and the other in Lithuania in the 1850s and 1860s. The anxiety that gripped moderate maskilim drove both of them to emphasize trends of divisiveness and disintegration and ideological controversies. They also expressed their anticipation of historical renewal, an attitude in keeping with their maskilic picture of the future.

Nonetheless, the very existence of the Haskalah movement encouraged Mapu in his belief that the direction of the future was already evident, even in the midst of the crisis. He felt that cultural renewal was imminent since the distant past provided proof that Jewish renewal was possible. The biblical period of the monarchy not only served as a basis for Mapu's consciousness of crisis but also presented a

[110] Ibid., pt. 3, p. 373. See the discussion of this meeting in Bartal, 'Gentiles and Gentile Society', 50–1.   [111] Mapu, *Ayit tsavua*, pt. 3, pp. 374–5.

utopia projected into the past, the idyllic picture of a society in which the wealthy supported the maskilim and Jews lived in peaceful villages, working the land.[112] Mapu's recommendation, in both *Ahavat tsiyon* and *Ashmat shomron*, was to remove the causes of divisiveness and to build a united leadership as the only solution that would ensure a harmonious future for the people:

A day unto the Lord that will surely come, a day of light for the children of Israel; and on that day He shall be the faith of their times, a store of salvation, wisdom, and knowledge; the fear of the Lord is their treasure. The old generation shall not do evil unto the new, and the new generation shall not mock the old, for the two will abide in peace together. A shepherd will lead them faithfully, by the springs of wisdom shall he guide them, and they will quench their thirst, drinking the pure waters of the source of Israel.[113]

This maskilic picture of the future, in keeping with the outlook of the moderate maskilim, was not reserved solely for the future. Mapu also believed that the reign of Alexander II in Russia provided ever greater assurance that the necessary conditions for internal renewal would be established. Tsar Alexander was, in his view, spreading serenity and tranquillity throughout the land and acting as 'moon and sun' to the entire generation. 'In the light of his countenance', Mapu ardently hoped, 'the worm Jacob, crawling from the top of ancient mountains, passing through many generations, will recover its strength, see the light, and make the crooked straight.'[114]

HEROICS AND SACRED MEMORIES IN POPULAR HISTORICAL FICTION

Although Mapu's romantic novels did not become as popular among the masses as he had anticipated, they did reach a relatively wide readership of both sexes (in Hebrew and in Yiddish translation) that extended beyond the circle of readers of scholarly Haskalah literature. The success of *Ahavat tsiyon* brought in its wake a wave of historical stories, most of them Hebrew translations from German, which now served as a new avenue for the dissemination of maskilic history in Russia.[115] The first to begin writing belletristic, popular historical literature was Kalman Schulman, who translated and adapted *Harisot beitar* (The Ruins of Betar, about Bar Kokhba) written by Rabbi Dr Samuel Meyer of Hanover. Schulman did not continue writing books of this genre, moving on to other areas, as will be discussed below. However, within a short time of the publication of *Harisot beitar* in 1858 more than thirty books, anthologies of stories, and individual short stories of

---

[112] Mapu, *Ahavat tsiyon*, 3; id., *Ayit tsavua*, pt. 3, pp. 253, 440–1.

[113] Mapu, *Hozei ḥezyonot*, 455; *Ashmat shomron*, 194; *Ahavat tsiyon*, 82.

[114] Mapu, *Hozei ḥezyonot*, 456.

[115] Halkin, *Modern Hebrew Literature*, 233–9; Ofek, *Hebrew Children's Literature*, 149–72; Werses, *Haskalah and Shabbateanism*, 145–91; Miron, *When Loners Come Together*, 56–85.

this type appeared. They were intended to provide the Hebrew reader with entertaining stories from the past that would 'educate and benefit young people'.[116]

Hardly any of these historical stories were the original creations of Russian maskilim, to whom they were readily available among the historical stories published in Germany in Jewish books and periodicals throughout the nineteenth century. Ludwig Philippson (1811–89), Marcus Lehmann (1831–90), Samuel Meyer, Hermann Reckendorf (1825–75), and Shalom Hacohen were among the authors whose stories were made accessible to the Jewish reader in Russia in Hebrew translation. In 1875 an attempt was made to encourage belletristic historical literature: the maskilic author and publisher Eliezer Isaac Shapira (1835–1915) established the series 'Beit ha'otsar' and commissioned translations of historical stories about the Jewish past from several maskilim.[117]

The historical stories were not all set in one particular period, but their plots were generally dramatic and grim, recounting the bitter fate of Jews in the premodern era or episodes of Jewish heroism in desperate situations. In *Harisot beitar* the reader followed 'the marvellous tale of Bar Kokhba's heroism and the destruction of Betar'. It was a tragic story about a doomed rebellion in the course of which supreme heroism was displayed and at the end of which rivers of blood were spilled, a tempest of emotion was unleashed, and Jews fell victim to horrendous tortures. The terrible fate of Rabbi Akiva, graphically described, vividly illustrates the florid language of these historical stories:

> Then Rabbi Akiva, horrified, said: Now I choose death so that my eyes will no longer look upon such a dreadful traitor and murderer . . . and the killers approached him and removed his clothes, leaving him naked. Then they shackled him to an iron pole, and with sharp-toothed combs of iron they tore his flesh slowly, slowly, so as to prolong his horrible suffering . . . but the holy Rabbi Akiva did not cry out, but only lifted his eyes heavenwards . . . until his pure and holy soul left the prison of his torn body, so sorely wounded and bloodied.[118]

Kidush hashem—sanctification of the Divine Name, even at the cost of one's life—was a common motif in the plots of these historical tales. There was also a marked tendency to deal with the great crises in Jewish history. Influenced by Mapu, Abraham Shalom Friedberg (1838–1902) began to write an original historical book entitled *Aharit yerushalayim* (The Last Days of Jerusalem), set at the time of the destruction of the Temple.[119] Other stories written in this vein included Marcus Lehmann's 'Bustenai' (1897), translated into Hebrew from German by Fuenn, set during the time of the *geonim* in Babylonia; *Hayehudim be'angliyah* (The Jews in England, 1869), translated by Miriam Markal-Mosesohn of Kovno

---

[116] From the title-page of Shapira, *Sipurim*.

[117] Ofek, *Hebrew Children's Literature*, 156–62; Ben-Ari, *Romance with the Past*.

[118] Schulman, *Harisot beitar*, 126–7.

[119] Friedberg's letter to Mapu, in A. S. Friedberg, *Sefer zikhronot*, 113. Friedberg wrote eight chapters of the story but never completed it.

(1837–1920), from I. A. Francolm, *Die Kreuzfahrer und die Juden unter Richard Löwenhert* (1842), which was set in the time of the Crusades; and a long list of others that related dramatic episodes from the lives of the *conversos* in Spain and Portugal.[120] Samuel Fuenn, who, in addition to writing scholarly historical works, believed in the importance of popular belletristic history, contributed several translations of stories of this type. In *Ya'akov tirado* (Jacob Tirado, 1872) he translated a story by Ludwig Philippson about the early settlement of Jews in the Netherlands.[121] The story recorded the exploits of the sixteenth-century hero, who manages to escape from the Inquisition, returns to Judaism, and after many adventures and adversities acquires the right for Jews to settle in a country that practices religious tolerance. This happens after the hero has proven his heroism and his value to the country by providing military assistance to the British navy and to the Dutch. Raphael Del Monte of Hamburg is the hero of *Hahiluf* (The Exchange, 1873), translated by Fuenn from a story by Lehmann. Raphael discovers he is a Jew, goes through a severe crisis, and is on the verge of committing suicide, but he slowly reconciles himself to his fate, and accepts his Jewish identity. Another short story, *Hakadish lifnei kol nidrei* (Kaddish before Kol Nidrei, 1876), which Fuenn chose from among Solomon Cohen's stories, recounts the fascinating tale of a military commander, a forcibly converted Jew, who wishes to regain his Jewishness. The reader is once again introduced to the horrible events of the Inquisition, but is also deeply moved by the fragile threads that still connect the forced converts to their Jewish origins.[122]

A young maskil from Polotsk, Abraham Rakowski (1854–1921), inaugurated Shapira's 'Beit ha'otsar' series with another of Philippson's stories, whose plot was designed to recall 'sorrowful memories from the days of darkness of the Inquisition that bathed our forefathers in blood'. In the story *Nidhei yisra'el* (The Exiled of Israel, 1875), the stages leading up to the expulsion of Spanish Jews are described, and the author stressed that 'the entire spectacle is based on the evidence of history' and was not a literary fiction.[123] The story *Emek ha'arazim* (Vale of Cedars, 1875–6), adapted and translated by Friedberg from *Vale of Cedars* by the English author Grace Aguilar (1816–47) as the second volume in the 'Beit ha'otsar' series, is set in Spain during the period of the expulsion. A romantic love affair between a Spanish nobleman and a Jewish woman reaches its tragic climax when the couple's attempt to flee is thwarted and their death draws near. At this point the young woman proclaims her Jewish identity with pride, revealing her

[120] Markal-Mosesohn, *Hayehudim be'angliyah*; see also the very favourable review of the book in *Hakarmel*, 7 (1869), 238.

[121] The quotations here are from the Vilna, 1881 edition. Philippson's story first appeared in 1855 and is included in the collection Philippson, *Gesammelte Schriften*, vol. i.

[122] On Solomon Cohen and his historical stories, see Kressel's introduction to Solomon Cohen, *Podeh umatsil*.

[123] Another story from the lives of the *conversos* was written by Philippson and translated into Hebrew; see Beilinson, *Galut sefarad*.

heroic readiness to die in sanctification of the Divine Name: 'I am a Hebrew! Your religion is not mine, your people are not my people, and your God is not my God.'[124] Another tragic human predicament is the topic of 'Haovdim vehanidaḥim' (The Lost and the Exiled) by Tuviah Pesah Shapira (1845–1924), in which a close friendship develops between a Jewish boy, the survivor of a massacre of a family of *conversos* in Portugal, and a Christian, who is trying to atone for his responsibility for this massacre.[125] In another story by Shapira, 'Hamistater o diego de agulars' (The Hidden One; or, Diego de Agulars, 1876), the surprising twist in the plot is that the head of the Inquisition in Madrid is of Jewish origin. He discovers this a short time after he himself has sentenced his sister to be burned at the stake. Just before she dies, she cries out, 'Don't harm me! I am a Jew! I was born a Jew and I will die a Jew in the name of the God of Israel! I will die but I will not convert; do with me what your cruel hearts wish, but I will not forsake my religion!' The Inquisitor flees from these 'immolators of humans', settles in the community of Spanish Jews in Vienna, and then moves to Amsterdam.[126]

Shapira's story 'Haperud' (The Separation) describes the conflict between Rabbi Saul Levi Morteira of Amsterdam and his pupil Baruch. Only at the end of the story, when the reader has already completely identified with the protagonist's human suffering, does it transpire that he is really Baruch Spinoza. Spinoza's excommunication is not presented in the story as the outcome of an ideological and religious dispute; the emphasis is rather on the personal and tragic aspects. The fundamental problem in this fictional story is not the charge of heresy or ideological deviation, but the dissolution of the bonds of love between Spinoza and the rabbi's daughter. Hence, all the reader's attention is directed to the young woman as she listens to the ban of excommunication being read out: 'In the women's gallery sat a beautiful damsel; down her rosy cheeks tears flowed like a powerful waterfall, and the pallor of death covered her face . . . In such dreadful circumstances did Baruch Spinoza, the sage and inventor of a new philosophical method, leave the city of his birth in 1660.'[127] This is a perfect example of the popular function of belletristic literature. By lowering the level of the Spinoza affair from the theological, philosophical realm to that of a romantic love story, and by presenting the excommunication as the personal tragedy of a young enlightened man, the author hoped to awaken feelings of sympathy for the hero in the reader's heart, as well as repugnance for the harsh rigidity of the leaders of the Amsterdam community. This made it possible to grant legitimacy to the excommunicated philosopher without going into the intellectual background of the affair. The sentimental and emotional aspect seemed to be stronger than any logical argument, certainly when it was presented to a readership who, for the most part, lacked any other source of information about the Spinoza affair.

Belletristic history, originally written in central Europe, in Magdeburg,

[124] A. S. Friedberg, *Emek ha'arazim*, 215.   [125] Shapira, *Sipurim*, 11–28.
[126] Ibid. 34.   [127] Ibid. 50–61 (quotation: 60–1).

Hanover, Heidelberg, Leipzig, and Prague by German Jewish authors, some of whom were modern rabbis and community leaders, had a clear purpose: to help preserve Judaism. Philippson, for example, realized in the mid-nineteenth century that, apart from attempting to introduce religious reforms, there was also a need to counter assimilation and to strengthen the Jewish identity of the general public. In 1855 Philippson's proposal for the establishment of a Jewish literary society (Israelitische Literaturgesellschaft) was printed in the *Allgemeine Zeitung des Judentums*. The purpose of the society was to publish Jewish literature of various levels, from classical Jewish literature and modern 'Jewish wisdom' (such as Graetz's and Geiger's books) to Philippson's own historical stories. The society issued some eighty publications between 1856 and 1874, with the declared aim of strengthening Judaism. Popular belletristic literature was intended to serve as an antidote to religious indifference and the harmful influences of secular life. In an era of materialism and spiritual limbo, Philippson wrote, the synagogue and the school no longer sufficed as centres to fortify Jewish identity, and literature should also be exploited for this purpose.[128]

To counter the criticism that these historical narratives were ruining the good taste of the masses and degrading scholarship, Philippson described his concept of this genre and its aims. He believed that, despite the disparity between the historian and the novelist, it was possible to combine the 'genius of poesy and the genius of history' in the historical novel. Both writers aspired to revive the historical truth accurately and to describe internal developments, but the novelist had more freedom to concentrate on the psychological motives of the historical characters. In the meeting between the historian and the novelist both had to make compromises and concessions. The novel took its external circumstances (time, place, events, names, and persons) from history, thus limiting its freedom of action; but having paid his debt to history, the author was entitled to delve into the inner lives of his characters. Philippson cautioned authors about the danger of slipping into fantasy. Particularly since the historical narrative was so widely distributed to such a large readership, the author had to be careful to avoid disseminating a false historical picture. And what was it that made the historical story popular? Readers loved the story because it opened up a palpable flesh-and-blood historical world. The narrative plunged them into a realm of emotions and thoughts that history could only sketch in broad, general lines. From the ideological standpoint, Philippson wanted to harness the historical narrative to current issues. In his view, the writer of historical novels was obliged to present the great historical riddle of Jewish survival and the existence of the Jewish people despite all their adversities. He had to write about the period of exile after the Jews had lost their spiritual and political centre, and focus on the struggles, hardships, and persecutions. It was these difficult times in Jewish history that could provide the key to the

---

[128] Philippson, 'Aufforderung an alle deutsch-lesenden Israeliten', 87–9; Kressel, 'A Chapter in Jewish Culture', 25–34; Toury, *Between Revolution, Reaction and Emancipation*, 100–1.

secret of Jewish survival and teach readers about the power of the human spirit, the virtues, the love, and the commitment to Jewish identity that typified the Jews. In this way, the historical narratives would become what Philippson called a *Volksbuch* ('book of the people'), that enabled the present to be reflected through the prism of the past, and provided encouragement and consolation for its readers.[129]

The maskilim in Russia who adapted German Jewish historical fiction and translated it into Hebrew not only found a collection of stories that could be transmitted with relative ease to Hebrew readers; they also found history that suited their own purposes. Letters, introductions to books, and readers' reactions all show that the maskilim were well aware of how appropriate this literature was to their efforts at popularization, and they used it to preserve the continuity of Jewish life (as had the original authors in Germany). The apprehension felt by the moderate maskilim in Russia for the new generation emerging during Alexander II's reign has already been discussed; they believed these stories would work against negative trends, such as the growing neglect of the Hebrew language, the abandonment of the halakhic framework of Jewish life, and the decline of the 'national spirit'. The identification with Jewish history, which had apparently been so self-evident in the previous generation, now seemed in need of reaffirmation and reinforcement. However, the aim of preserving the Jewish heritage, which was well served by belletristic history, did not blur the reformist aims that this history promoted in its maskilic Hebrew adaptation.

In 1875 Friedberg wrote from Grodno to the publisher Shapira to inform him that he had begun translating Grace Aguilar's book. It was a 'charming and enticing' book, he wrote, and its power lay in its ability to stir the reader's emotions.[130] In a letter to Perez Smolenskin, Friedberg related his impressions from his first emotional reading of the book: 'I was stirred by this wonderful story, which warmed my heart and aroused all my senses.' He hoped that his translation would affect readers similarly.[131] Friedberg realized that he was writing romantic literature that appealed to the emotions, and he did not hide his intention to pluck at the reader's heartstrings until tears flowed from his eyes. However, this romantic aim was coupled with the moderate Haskalah's ideological orientation towards national romanticism. In his *Emek ha'arazim* Friedberg also wished to arouse feelings of nostalgia by reviving the 'sacred memories' of the nation from the time of the expulsion from Spain, 'a period that has been dear to us since then, a time that saw the troubles of our forefathers in Spain'.[132] Friedberg summed up the aims he had in mind when translating *Emek ha'arazim* and explained the benefit to be derived from this story, particularly in a generation marked by the disintegration of Jewish identity:

This entire story is written in a national spirit mingled with sentimental feeling, fitting for the taste of our readers, who are just becoming acquainted with romantic literature, and

---

[129] Philippson, *Gesammelte Schriften*, ii. 7–13. [130] A. S. Friedberg, *Sefer hazikhronot*, 125–6.
[131] Ibid. 127. [132] Ibid.

for this period, to fasten the bonds of a strong faith to our hearts as in the distant past. Even the most cold-hearted reader will not be able to refrain from weeping; his tears will fall like pouring rain to soften his heart and awaken in him love and great affection for his people and his homeland, that national love which is growing weaker in our midst in this generation, affected by the wind of cosmopolitanism that has gathered all of us under its wings.[133]

Friedberg knew full well that these words would please Smolenskin, who was one of the outstanding exponents of early nationalism in the 1870s, as will be discussed in the next chapter.

Several responses by readers suggest that Friedberg did indeed achieve his aims. Mordecai Plungian wrote to him that reading *Emek ha'arazim* had been a very moving experience for him: 'I am hastening to tell you about the impression left on my heart and my emotions when I read your book. It filled me with both pleasure and sadness.'[134] In his journal *Hamagid* David Gordon (1831–86) praised the publisher for having chosen to provide the reader with 'sacred visions' instead of 'profane stories and sensual novels, for which there is no longer any demand since young people have begun to understand the languages of the gentiles'.[135] Gordon was among those who were very concerned about the 'Jewish national spirit which, Heaven forbid, must not get lost among the host of new winds now blowing in the Jewish camp', and he thought that historical novels were the best means of 'arousing young people's emotions, inducing them to love their faith, which has been our bulwark throughout all the generations, and to revive us, living as we do in the midst of many nations today'.[136] Gordon also commended Friedberg for the change he had made in his Hebrew translation of the book, by turning the Christian protagonist in the original into a forcibly converted Jew, which Gordon believed would remove any taint from the love affair between him and the Jewish girl.[137]

In addition to evoking national nostalgia, romantic excitement, and sacred memories, the historical stories were also used to sharpen the distinction between the past and the present and to nurture an optimistic approach to positive modern trends. In the publisher's foreword to Philippson and Rakowski's *Nidhei yisra'el* Shapira found it essential to emphasize that the memories of the dreadful past were of a historical period that had ended long ago. The Inquisition, which had steeped Europe in the blood of our forefathers, he argued, belonged to the days of darkness, and the reader was asked to dip into the stories of the Jewish past as if into a nightmare, and then to awaken and find with joy that it was only a dream.[138]

[133] Friedberg, *Sefer hazikhronot*, 127.

[134] Plungian's letter in A. S. Friedberg, *Sefer hazikhronot*, 129–30.

[135] D. Gordon, 'Besorat sefarim', 87. Cf. Miron, *From Romance to the Novel*, 232–9.

[136] D. Gordon, 'Besorat sefarim', 87.

[137] Ibid.; A. S. Friedberg, *Sefer hazikhronot*, 127.

[138] Publisher's note to Rakowski, *Nidhei yisra'el*. Cf. Shapira's introduction to A. S. Friedberg, *Emek ha'arazim*, and Gordon's letter to Miriam Markal-Mosesohn, in Markal Mosesohn, *Hayehudim be'angliyah*.

IMPROVEMENT OF THE MASSES:
HISTORY IN YIDDISH

In order to expand the target audience for maskilic propaganda, it was vital to create literature in the Yiddish vernacular. Thus, despite all ideological inhibitions, attempts were made in the 1860s and 1870s to make maskilic history accessible to wider sections of Jewish society in Russia by writing belletristic and informative history in Yiddish. The maskilim used this avenue of popularization to appeal to those Jews, particularly young girls and women, who found it difficult to read books like Mapu's historical novels in Hebrew, or the stories translated by Shapira, Schulman, and Fuenn.[139] They had to penetrate a market that for many years had been dominated by Yiddish translations of traditional history, in particular Josippon, *She'erit yisra'el*, and Nathan Neta Hannover's *Yeven metsulah* (Miry Pit, 1653).[140] Their writings had to compete with marvellous and miraculous tales about Alexander the Great and the exploits of the Ten Lost Tribes, and to bring the general public up to date about the 'modern age', which had hardly been mentioned in traditional literature.

This sphere of popularization will be illustrated here by the works of three maskilim: Isaac Meir Dick, who wrote a great number of widely circulated historical stories in Yiddish, Samuel Resser, and Mikhel Gordon (1823–90). The latter two were less well-known maskilim who tried their hand at writing comprehensive works on Jewish history, world history, and Russian history. The literary historian David Roskies has asserted that the popular literature written by Dick in Yiddish could be categorized as a genre that lay between 'subversive' maskilic writing and traditional folk tales, so that it was also tolerated by non-maskilim. Dick took advantage of this fact in order to put across maskilic messages in the guise of piety. To his male and female readers, he offered wondrous and frightening tales from the past, such as *Der vunderlekhe geshikhte fun der ershter hatoke vos unzere toyre hakdoyshe iz netak gevorn* (The Wondrous Tale of the First Translation of our Sacred Torah) or *Di shreklekhe geshikhte fun shabse tsvi* (The Dreadful Story of Shabbetai Tsevi, 1864).[141] Dick based his writings on a variety of historical material, which he found in the traditional chronicles as well as in German Jewish literature translated by maskilim into Hebrew. He introduced fascinating adventures and tales of love into his stories, as well as some ideas characteristic of the maskilic sense of the past.[142]

---

[139] On Mapu's translation into Yiddish, see Werses, *Yiddish Translations of 'Ahavat tsiyon'*.

[140] Erik, *The History of Yiddish Literature*, 373–91. *Yeven metsulah* described the massacres of 1648–9, carried out by the Ukrainian Cossacks under Bogdan Chmielnicki.

[141] Dick, *Hadrat zekenim*.

[142] Roskies, 'Isaac Meyer Dik', 7–47, 145–6, 157–61. Cf. Miron, *The Traveler Disguised*, 252–3; Sadan, introd. to I. M. Dick, *R. Shemayah*, 7–15; Werses, *Haskalah and Shabbateanism*, 143–5.

Dick adapted a historical chapter entitled *Der aroysgetribener un bald tsurik-gerufener yoysef* (Joseph—Expelled and Immediately Called to Return, 1877). The story tells of the Jews in England during the Crusades and the dreadful fate of the Jews of York in 1190. According to the story, when Richard the Lionheart was absent from England, the Crusaders were able to attack the Jews with impunity, since it was the monarchy that protected the Jews and the mob could only molest them when the king was absent. These and other events were portrayed as belonging to a past with no parallels in the modern world. Most of his story on the St Bartholomew's Day massacre of 1572 (*Di blut hokhtsayt fun pariz*, 1870) is devoted to detailed historical information: Dick explained the significance of the Reformation and the course of events from the time of Luther, through the Calvinists, the Huguenots in France, and the St Bartholomew's Day massacre, ending with the Thirty Years War. Dick thought this an especially important story, of great benefit to the Jewish reader. The story of Luther could demonstrate the great potential inherent in a poor young boy who had the power to challenge enormous forces such as the Pope and the Catholic Church. The significance of the Reformation for the Jews lay in the fact that it had weakened the Church and thus lessened the pressure on them. In his view, the Reformation had diminished religious fanaticism and contributed to an expansion of trade, science, and wisdom in Europe. Dick also employed the story of the Reformation to explain the phenomenon of religious sects in Christianity and in Judaism, during the Second Temple period as well as in the present.[143] In this way, he not only tried to spread historical knowledge but also attempted to encourage elementary historical thinking. He helped his readers to understand the socio-cultural reality of their time in general abstract terms as a historical phenomenon, with analogies in both the Jewish and the non-Jewish past.

In his popular works Dick waged a maskilic struggle against superstition, the fear of ghosts and devils, and the mystical conception of reality. In *Di shreklekhe geshikhte fun shabse tsvi* he continued the maskilic strategy of denouncing false messiahs and their followers and emphasized that Shabbetai Tsevi had misled the masses just as all charlatans manipulate the ignorant.[144] Dick's maskilic reformist aims and his attempt to shape a popular maskilic consciousness were even more pointedly expressed in his rhyming introduction to the collection of stories *Alte idishe sagen* (Old Jewish Sayings, 1876). Ostensibly longing nostalgically for the past, Dick characterized the pre-modern era as one of miracles and wonders, and as a world of magic, miracle-workers, and belief in wonder-working *tsadikim*. Unfortunately, Dick mockingly observed, this age of devils and spirits, reincarnation, and supernatural miracles was one that belonged exclusively to the past, to the 'old world'. In the new era, the age of Enlightenment, people were subject to the laws of nature and had their feet firmly planted on the ground.[145]

[143] Dick, *Di blut hokhtsayt fun pariz*.   [144] Werses, *Haskalah and Shabbateanism*, 143–5.
[145] Dick, *Alte yidishen sagen*, 4.

Awareness of recent historical change, the presence of a 'modern era', the identification of the present with the Enlightenment and rational maskilic values, realism
and negation of the imagination and the supernatural world were all new concepts
which Dick tried to adapt from the intellectual sphere of the maskil in order to
make them comprehensible and acceptable to the world of the Jewish woman and
the community at large. The historical story in Yiddish was one of the literary
means of disseminating the maskilic sense of the past on the lowest level to the
broadest stratum of the Jewish population in the Russia of Alexander II.

*

In 1864 Samuel Resser, who was born in Vilna and lived in southern Russia, where
he taught in a government school, wrote to the Society for the Promotion of
Enlightenment among the Jews asking for financial support to translate history
books into Yiddish.[146] Resser was already able to show the society his first book: a
translation from Russian into German, in Hebrew characters, of a book of universal history, which he called *Eine kurze allgemeine Weltgeschichte* (A Short General
History of the World, 1863).[147] He wrote his history books for a specific audience
of uneducated Jews and young people who knew no foreign languages, for whom
history had hitherto been a neglected and unknown field.

The book had more than 230 pages and in an informative, rather tedious exposition surveyed the history of the world from the Creation and the beginnings
of civilization until 1821. Chapter titles appeared in Russian too, and various concepts and names in the body of the text were translated into Russian or Hebrew.
Resser appended a 'Calendar of Olden Times', organized according to the well-
known four-part periodization: *die alte Geschichte* (Ancient History) up to the fall
of the western Roman empire; *die mittelere Geschichte* (History of the Middle Ages)
up to the discovery of America; *die neue Geschichte* (New History) up to the French
Revolution; and *die neuerer Geschichte* (Modern History) up to the Greek War of
Independence of 1821 (apparently the final year covered in the Russian book
which he used for his translation). Although it contains almost no interpretative
comments or historical explanations the book is clearly maskilic in character. It
ends with a chapter that could stand alone, a survey of the progress of enlightenment in the modern era.[148] The emphasis in this chapter is on literary works, the
development of science, changes in industry, and various inventions as the pre-
eminent and beneficial aspects of the period.

The Jews were not integrated into Resser's universal history; Jewish history

[146] L. Rosenthal, *Toledot ḥevrat marbei haskalah*, ii. 42. On Resser, see *Leksikon fun der nayer
yidisher literatur*, viii. 515–16.

[147] It received a favourable and encouraging review by Gottlober, 'Et lata'at', *Hamelits*, 5 (1865),
no. 12. On the discussion among the maskilim concerning the relative merits of Yiddish and German,
see Shmeruk, *Yiddish Literature*, 261–93. On the Resser, see Shatzky, *Kultur geshikhte*, 195–6.

[148] Resser, *Kurtze allgemeine Weltgeschichte*, 219–21.

occupied a separate place in his plans, and he produced another book, *Koroys yisra'el: di alte geshikhte funem folk yisroel* (Jewish History). The manuscript of the first part of this book—written this time, he said, in *prost yidish* (the Yiddish of the masses), and not in German transliterated into Hebrew, in order to expand its circle of readers—was sent in 1867 to the Society for the Promotion of Culture among the Jews, which decided to give Resser the minuscule sum of 25 roubles to help cover printing costs. The money, however, was insufficient, and the book, completed in 1866, was not published until 1869, in Vilna.[149] The approbations of the book reflected the maskilim's uneasy feelings about a book written in Yiddish. However, everyone, including the author, agreed that 'the language of the inarticulate' had to be used if the maskilim wanted to reach the masses. Abraham Margaliot wrote to Resser: 'I was very happy to see that you succeeded in improving the masses in their mother tongue . . . the Ashkenazi Jewish language, and you did not fall short of the target.' Why was a knowledge of Jewish history considered important for the ordinary Jew? Margaliot's reasons were similar in spirit to those used to justify historical stories: tales of antiquity would 'stir sacred feelings and love for their homeland' in the hearts of the Jews, arousing nostalgia for ancient times. Stories about the period of exile would intensify the Jews' memory of suffering and persecution and further sharpen their awareness of the great contrast between the past and the present. Readers would be convinced that Jewish life in Russia was preferable, and would understand 'that such is not the case in our land, the land of imperial Russia, in which the Jew can own property . . . and our great government does not strictly enforce the laws against us as do governments of other countries'.[150] In his introduction Resser specifically stated that he was impelled to write *Koroys yisroel* in Yiddish by a desire to disseminate knowledge of the past and, in particular, to cultivate an awareness of the spirit of the time among uneducated Jews, 'so that the simple folk who understand neither Hebrew nor other languages will know something about history'.[151]

*

Resser also planned to publish a Yiddish translation of Russian history, but another maskil anticipated him. In 1869 Mikhel Gordon's Yiddish book *Die geshikhte fun rusland* (The History of Russia) was published in Zhitomir. Gordon, the brother of Rabbi Israel Gordon of Vilna, belonged to the circle of moderate maskilim in that city and earned his livelihood as a private tutor. His numerous articles were published in Hebrew and Yiddish journals, and he also wrote textbooks, poetry, and translations.[152] *Di geshikhte fun rusland* was another book

---

[149] See L. Rosenthal, *Toledot hevrat marbei haskalah*, ii. 43.
[150] Approbations by Gottlober and Margaliot in Resser, *Koroys yisroel*.   [151] Ibid., introd.
[152] M. Gordon, *Di geshikhte fun rusland*. On M. Gordon, see L. Rosenthal, *Toledot hevrat marbei haskalah*, i. 64; *Leksikon fun der nayer yidisher literatur*, iii–iv. 129–34; M. Pines, *Histoire de la littérature*, 74; Reisen, *Lexicon*, 510–18.

intended to inform readers about the history of the homeland, although Gordon attempted to recount it in the form of tales that would appeal to the simple folk. Gordon's aim was to cover Russian history from its beginnings to his own time, an aim that was only partly achieved. The book began with the Slavic tribes and myths about the founding of Slavic countries and the beginnings of 'true history' in the ninth century AD, and continued up to the era of Tsar Michael Romanov in the seventeenth century.

Perhaps Mikhel Gordon was more aware than any other maskil who wrote popular history of the role played by the translator into popular Yiddish. His book had two introductions, one in Hebrew for the circle of maskilim to which he belonged, and the other for readers of Yiddish. In the first introduction he apologized to the maskilim who might wish to ridicule him for choosing to write in Yiddish and attempted to explain his maskilic attitudes. 'Historical tales', in his view, allowed for a great deal of manipulation, since the writer could do what he wished with them; in his hands, they were 'like a rubber cord that can contract to hold the tales of a whole year on one sheet of paper, or can expand, stretching one story over a hundred sheets of paper'.[153] Even before putting pen to paper, the writer of history selected his ideological goals and his target audience, and constructed his book accordingly. That was why, he explained, history books differed from one another, even though the events of the past could not be altered. Gordon was thus making the rather modern assumption that a historical tale changes in accordance with the writer's inclinations and his intended audience. He introduced his book as a new and original work because it was written 'according to the level of the readers for whom I laboured', and because of the maskilic messages it contained. The book's readers would be poor people who had no general education or knowledge of foreign languages, and were completely unfamiliar with universal history and biography. This reading public had difficulty exerting its mental powers, seeking only to derive pleasure from its reading. The writer who was aware of this had to reach out to the developed imagination and strong emotions of his readers, not to their dormant intellect. Gordon writes,

I caught the reader's heart by collecting pleasant and diverting stories that would please and amuse him, and I sometimes lengthened a pleasant story and shortened an uninteresting one . . . even though the second was important and the first irrelevant. I skipped over and omitted many names and events that were not pleasing and were not relevant, for I did not want the reader to tire of them, and to dislike the story and the book, and put it down.[154]

As a writer of popular history, Gordon was thus willing to sacrifice much of 'history' in order to appeal to the readers of his book, and he scrupulously defined his task:

[153] M. Gordon, *Di geshikhte fun rusland*, 1.   [154] Ibid. 2.

I have done this work for the simple folk, and therefore I was careful to make their labour simple. I called it 'simple' because the French call this labour *populaire*, since the simple folk are called the 'populace' and many of the wise men of other nations write books to teach wisdom and science to the 'populace', and they are called popular books. These wise men knew how to be very careful to speak to the people in their own tongue and in their own way, and their work was popular, that is to say, all the simple people could understand it.[155]

Gordon criticized Hebrew historical novels and romances, which were also intended for the masses, claiming that the writers of such history had erred and failed, because they 'did not observe the laws of popular writing'. Such history books could be read only by maskilim and remained unfathomable to the masses. 'For whom, therefore, did these wise men of our people labour and toil', he asked, 'and who in the world was made better by their labours?'[156]

Why did he choose to write history, of all things? In this, Gordon was an exponent of the maskilic view that historical knowledge had the power 'to enlighten man and improve his mind much more than any of the other *hokhmot* or sciences'.[157] However, he cited another reason related to his target audience: the poor were still at the pre-modern stage of development, their minds bound by 'Asiatic stupidity'. History would serve as a means of education that would persuade them to break away from the Asiatic mentality and draw closer to the European world of the modern era, as had the Russian and the European poor.[158]

In his Yiddish introduction, however, Gordon naturally did not reveal his maskilic guidelines. Instead, he attempted to cajole the reader into recognizing the importance of historical knowledge and to guide him towards reaching the right conclusions from the book. Familiarity with the course of universal and Jewish history, in his opinion, should arouse in his readers a sense of gratitude for their present situation. Gordon described Jewish history in the old pre-partition Poland–Lithuania as a series of decrees against Jews and deprivation of their rights, a time when they were forced into non-productive professions and given an inferior level of education and culture. He did not blame the Polish and Lithuanian peoples for this, but rather the religious fanaticism of the Church and the Jesuits. The Russian occupation of Poland (1772–95) totally altered Jewish destiny. Religious tolerance and the desire to turn the Jews into productive inhabitants of the country were the guiding principles of the Russian government's policy. A comparison of the Jewish past with its present under Russian control was therefore the main maskilic message of Gordon's history book, and its major objective was to weaken the Jews' fear and loathing of Russia's Jewish policy: 'First of all, you must thank the Creator for redemption and salvation, and then you must thank and bless the good Russian government and the Russian people for the perfect peace you enjoy in this country'.[159]

---

[155] M. Gordon, *Di geshikhte fun rusland*, 2.   [156] Ibid. 2–3.   [157] Ibid., p. iii.
[158] Ibid. 3.   [159] Ibid. 8–9.

The religious concepts Gordon used also suited his target population and gave his arguments religious legitimization. The entire course of history was ascribed to the Almighty. The sufferings of the past were described as punishment for the transgressions of the Jews, and the Christians did not bear sole responsibility for them. In general, it was advisable to forget the harsh past in order not to violate the biblical commandment 'You shall not avenge nor bear any grudge'. Accounts of the era of persecution, Gordon emphasized, were not meant to inspire hatred, but were to be used as the criterion for appraising the present situation and to draw closer in friendship to Russia and its people.[160]

We cannot know the impact the book had on the masses of the Jewish people Gordon was addressing. Perhaps the fact that the book was not highly publicized and was only printed once speaks for itself. Gordon did not complete his plans, although, like Dick and Resser, he provides an example of the maskilim's deliberate attempts to disseminate maskilic concepts of the past among the common people.

KALMAN SCHULMAN: THE FIRST PROFESSIONAL POPULARIZER

The most prolific popularizer of universal and Jewish history during the reign of Alexander II was undoubtedly Kalman Schulman, a moderate maskil from Vilna. In his modest apartment on Little Stephan Lane, in Vilna, Schulman wrote, adapted, and translated almost thirty books and many more articles, at his own initiative as well as under the aegis of the Society for the Promotion of Enlightenment among the Jews. These were all written in Hebrew, which Schulman believed ought to be diligently preserved and fostered. The Romm Press in Vilna printed most of his works, which sold well and came out in a number of editions. Schulman, who until the 1860s had earned his living by teaching Hebrew in the secondary school attached to the rabbinic seminary, was able to devote all his time to his literary pursuits and to earn his livelihood as a professional author thanks to his contacts with the Society for the Promotion of Enlightenment among the Jews. Schulman belonged to the Vilna circle of moderate maskilim, and his age, religious education at the Volozhin yeshiva, cultural baggage, traditional dress, religious lifestyle, and maskilic outlook made him a typical member of this circle, which included Samuel Fuenn and Mordecai Plungian. Schulman attended services at the maskilic synagogue, 'Taharat Kodesh', and corresponded with many maskilim throughout Russia.[161]

Thousands of copies of Schulman's books were sold. The secret of his success was unquestionably the fact that he did not address his books to the relatively limited circle of maskilim but managed to appeal to a wide readership. Thanks to his strongly religious approach, which was not merely a device to win the reader's

---

[160] Ibid. 10.

[161] Posner, 'Rabbi Kalman Schulman'; Zitron, *The Makers*, i. 143–66; Friedman, *Sefer hazikhronot*, 181–5; J. Klausner, *History of Modern Hebrew Literature*, iii. 361–88.

heart but a basic element of his maskilic outlook, expressed in all his writings, his books also found their way on to the bookshelves of non-maskilic homes. The prominent Jewish thinker Ahad Ha'am (1856–1927), for example, wrote in his memoirs that only Kalman Schulman's books had succeeded in getting past the stringent censorship imposed by his hasidic father on the books his son was permitted to read.[162] Schulman, it seems, stretched his Haskalah to its religious extreme, but still remained a maskil. He found his ideal in Naphtali Herz Wessely and identified with his moderate approach: 'The light of Torah, enlightenment, and pure devotion to the Lord all merged in his soul . . . like all true lovers of the faith of Israel, he knew that the Torah and wisdom are sisters and their Father is one and the same.'[163]

Like other popularizers, Schulman also regarded history as an excellent medium for educating the Jews.[164] His main aim was to fill the great void in Hebrew literature, which in his opinion lacked 'two areas of knowledge that are of the greatest importance to all wisdom and science, namely a knowledge of world history and geography'.[165] As will be seen, Schulman did succeed in fulfilling this task, particularly in his comprehensive nine-volume work *Divrei yemei olam* (World History), which opened a window on the vista of history for many Hebrew readers. The young Joseph Klausner (1874–1958), who later became the national historian of the Second Temple period and an expert on modern Hebrew literature, read Schulman's translation of Josephus' *Wars of the Jews* when he was about 12. According to his own testimony, it gave him 'the first impulse to a love of and addiction to the Second Temple period'.[166] The historian Simon Dubnow (1860–1941) recalled that Schulman's *Shulamit*, a book about travels in Palestine, was one of the first secular books he read, at the age of 10 while still a pupil at *ḥeder*. 'With delight I read and reread the lyrical descriptions, written in the flowery language of the Holy Scriptures', Dubnow recalled nostalgically. On one hand, he was interested in reading the historical stories and geographical descriptions of places familiar to him from the Bible, and on the other, he indirectly learned about later historical events. 'I was especially fascinated', Dubnow wrote, 'by the historical descriptions of the East after the period at which [Josephus] Flavius' book ends. I learned about the Crusades, Arab and Turkish rule . . .'. In retrospect, as a mature and professional historian, Dubnow did criticize Schulman's romantic approach, but he did not deny that in his youth that same 'naïve book . . . about the past glory that turned into a wilderness . . . captivated my tender heart!'[167]

---

[162] Ahad Ha'am, *Pirkei zikhronot*, 45.   [163] Schulman, 'Toledot harav naftali herts veseli', 1.

[164] Schulman, Letter to Gurland, in Schulman, 'Mikhtavim', 411.   [165] Ibid. 412.

[166] J. Klausner, *History of Modern Hebrew Literature*, ii. 384; Zitron, *The Makers*, 159; Nisanboim, *In my Lifetime*, 20.

[167] Dubnow, *Sefer haḥayim*, 46–7. More reactions to Schulman appear in J. Klausner, *History of Modern Hebrew Literature*, iii. 379–80. See also testimony by Werses: 'Even in my grandfather's home, in which there was a mixture typical of the moderate Vilna mode of enlightenment—Torah, Haskalah, and devoutness—I found in his bookcase the autobiography *Avi'ezer* and *Divrei yemei olam*'; Werses, 'Highways and Byways', 8.

Shulamit and Schulman's other books on Palestine were written for young readers, in particular pupils in *ḥeder* and yeshiva, to acquaint them with events that had taken place in the Holy Land.[168] The five books on Palestine that he published between 1854 and 1870 included extensive historical and geographical information, as well as a survey of conditions there in the mid-nineteenth century.[169] Schulman collected the material from travel and research books, in many cases also expanding its scope to include the general history of the East (Egypt, Assyria, and Babylonia). He contributed to the rediscovery of Palestine in the nineteenth century by imparting some of this information to Hebrew readers in eastern Europe. In doing so, Schulman laid the foundation for the study of Palestine and its historical past, which later served as an important element in the consciousness and ideology of the nationalist Zionist movement. However, despite later attempts to draw him into the modern Jewish nationalist movement, he illuminated the past of the Holy Land in a different spirit and with different objectives in mind.

What were the aims underlying Schulman's books on Palestine and what did he hope to instil in the young reader in Russia by providing him with a knowledge of its past? His treatment of Palestine linked it to three focal points: scientific archaeological research, the sanctity of the land, and its antiquity, which evoked romantic emotions. The first aspect perceived the past of the Holy Land and the past of the ancient East in general, which in the nineteenth century were being uncovered by archaeological excavations, as one more example of the importance of historical knowledge. This knowledge expanded the boundaries of human wisdom and also contained 'profound moral lessons and sage counsel'.[170] 'In such a wise generation', Schulman asserted, true to the maskilic tradition that lauded the accumulation of knowledge, 'all those uncovering the ancient past have added wisdom and knowledge to all that existed before them'. The archaeologists were carrying the 'torches of the light of research', 'digging under the soil of ruined lands, in felled forests, between the crumbling walls of abandoned palaces, and in the dark rooms of decaying temples and wrecked castles . . . they have removed from the very depths of the underworld their dearest friend: wisdom'; it was scientific reason that enabled men to use these findings in order to reconstruct a more complete historical picture.[171]

For the Jews, the past of the Holy Land which was being uncovered carried a special meaning. Schulman believed that Jews were obliged not only to appreciate the achievement of scientific progress but also to recall the religious significance of Palestine. On one hand, the historical and geographical past of the country could help clarify the language and content of the Bible, and on the other, Jews should cherish the memory of the land and learn about the ideal Jewish past. 'Oh, who is the man whose heart has been touched by the love of God, and the love of His

---

[168] Schulman, *Halikhot kedem*, 3.
[169] Schulman, *Harel*; *Shulamit*; *Sefer ariel*; *Shevilei erets hakedoshah*. See also T. Cohen, *From Dream to Reality*, 230–55.   [170] Schulman, *Sefer ariel*, 1.   [171] Ibid. 8–9, 113–25.

Torah and His people?', Schulman asked, in the spirit of the moderate Haskalah, 'and
does not long to know of the events of those happy days? [And of] the history of the
people of the God of Abraham in those sacred times?. . . how I would love to walk
in those places where God was revealed to your prophets and your visionaries!'[172]

For Schulman, beyond the findings of scientific research and its religious implications, Palestine was the stage for a romantic historical spectacle that deeply affected
the mind and emotions of the Jew. Here the scholarly, rationalistic, and moralistic
significance of history was relegated to the sidelines, supplanted by the moving experience of the Jew observing the past with a sense of the glory of the ancient world.
This was not an intellectual observation of the kind to be found even in Mapu's historical novels; it was clearly a romantic view that elevated the spirit of the beholder,
and not necessarily a source of philosophy or moral lessons. It was the antiquity of
the biblical past that was the source of its influence. In Schulman's view, a traveller
in the ancient world of Palestine could experience a spiritual uplifting that actually
transcended physicality: 'Whose heart will not be overflowing with thousands of
lofty ideas when he conjures in his mind's eye life in his precious land . . . exalted
majesty enfolds it all day long . . . awe-inspiring grandeur of antiquity envelops it for
eternity.'[173] Archaeologists, too, in Schulman's view, were motivated by this fierce
passion to uncover the roots of the ancient past. Antiquity had a stirring effect on the
mind: 'For something which is very ancient will engage our thoughts with the memory of its splendour and will excite our minds with the power of its grandeur.'[174]

In this way, Palestine blended modern scientific research, religious sanctity,
and antiquity in its past. One could look back with nostalgia at the antiquity of
Palestine, and the study of its history uplifted the spirit of the Jews, stirred their
emotions, and strengthened their identification with their ancient past.

Schulman was the first to undertake the task of translating Josephus' writings
into Hebrew, and in his eyes this endeavour also formed part of the redemption of
the age-old remains of the past of the Holy Land. When in 1864 he applied to the
Society for the Promotion of Enlightenment among the Jews for financial support
for this project, Schulman stressed the importance of Josephus' books, as 'vestiges
of sacred stones which in days gone by shone on the holy ground, and lit the way
for all the sages of the globe throughout the generations, and in their light will
walk all those delving into the ancient history of our people'.[175]

In 1854, in his *Halikhot kedem* (Ancient Customs), Schulman wrote about the
Second Temple period and what he regarded as the major historical dilemma of
that period: how to judge the Zealots who had rebelled against the Roman empire.
'Who can we blame for the destruction of the Temple', Schulman asked, 'the
Romans or the vile rebels?'[176] We ought not to forget, he reminded his readers,
that the Romans in the first century BC were different from the peoples living in

---

[172] Schulman, *Halikhot kedem*, 11.   [173] Ibid. 3–4.   [174] Schulman, *Sefer ariel*, 1–2.
[175] L. Rosenthal, *Toledot ḥevrat marbei haskalah*, ii. 31.
[176] Schulman, 'Divrei yemei yerushalayim', in id., *Halikhot kedem*, 61 n.

the nineteenth century, since they had no knowledge of monotheistic faith nor of the Enlightenment and humanism. Their ruthless behaviour was understandable against this historical background, but what was less understandable was the emergence of cruel fanatics and murderers from the midst of the Jewish people. Schulman had no compunction about blaming the Zealots for the destruction of the Temple and harshly rebuked them for not heeding the sages. In particular, Schulman denied the legitimacy of any revolt against the ruling authority: 'Anyone rebelling against his king is also rebelling against God who has enthroned him . . . kingship of the land is likened to the kingship of heaven, and he who lifts a hand against the throne of the king shall be reckoned as one who attacks the throne of the Lord.'[177]

When Schulman next addressed his fundamental dilemma, it was in his adaptation of *Harisot beitar* as a historical tale; as already mentioned, it dealt with the second-century Bar Kokhba revolt. This time he depicted the historical events in a more balanced manner, including arguments both for and against rebellion, and emphasizing the heroism of the Jewish rebels and their leader. Nonetheless, there was no change in Schulman's maskilic message; he believed these tragedies of the first centuries AD and thereafter actually attested to the Jews' duty to remain loyal to the government under all circumstances. In conversation with a friend, Schulman insisted that it was not censorship considerations that led him to express a negative attitude towards rebellion but rather his inner conviction.[178] His firm belief in loyalty to the ruling government and in its legitimacy, a belief supported by the moderate Haskalah, inspired him with an affinity for the character and fate of Josephus. This is why, in translating his writings, Schulman introduced an apologetic strain, with the aim of clearing the name of this Jewish historian and justifying him to all those who had labelled him a traitor to his people.

The first book of Josephus which Schulman translated (from a German translation) was *Toledot yosef* (The Life of Josephus), which came out in Vilna in 1859.[179] In a letter to J. L. Gordon, Schulman wrote that he had composed an introduction in which he vindicated Josephus, countering the unfavourable portrait sketched by other historians, such as Jost and Graetz. This introduction, however, was so long and costly to print that it was ultimately omitted from the book.[180] In its stead Schulman appended historical and geographical notes to the translation, giving the book the appearance of a scholarly study, and included a short introduction explaining the importance of Josephus' writings. Schulman believed that Josephus had possessed ideal attributes that justified his promotion to the status of a Jewish hero in the historical pantheon. He compared him to the prophet

---

[177] Ibid. 39.   [178] Ben-Ami, 'Kalman Schulman', 123.

[179] In Jan. 1859 Gordon told Schulman that Ze'ev Kaplan had also begun to translate this work. Schulman, who did not want to compete with him, was alarmed, but was prepared to accept the fact that there would be two translations. In the end only Schulman's was published; Schulman, 'Tseror igerot', 539.   [180] Ibid. 541.

Jeremiah, who had warned of present and future evil, and enumerated his virtues: he was beloved by his people, concerned about their fate, and acted for their benefit; he was an excellent writer and historian; he had been acquainted with contemporary sages and he was possessed of a valiant spirit, which he demonstrated in the Galilean War. In addition, Josephus' books had already been translated into many languages, and it was inconceivable that such an important historical source should remain inaccessible to the Hebrew reader.[181]

Immediately after the publication of this book, *Hakarmel* published a biography of Josephus written by Schulman, apparently taken from the unprinted introduction. In the biography Schulman underscored the superiority of the position Josephus had taken on the revolt against Rome and condemned the behaviour of the fanatic 'Jewish élite'. Nonetheless, Schulman lauded the battles in which Josephus fought in the Galilee. In his view, the Jotapata War was even more exalted than the Trojan War portrayed in Homer's epic, and merited inscription in the pages of universal history. It was only hostility towards the Jews that had caused this heroic conflict to be relegated to the sidelines of history.[182]

In 1861 Schulman published a manifesto in which he declared that he had undertaken to translate all of Josephus' writings into Hebrew. He intended to publish them in serial form, producing four pamphlets a year, and was looking for agents to enlist subscribers in advance in order to finance the enterprise.[183] In 1862 the first part of his translation of *Milḥamot hayehudim* (The Jewish Wars) appeared, and in 1863 the second and final sections were published. For the first time the Hebrew reader could read the principal historical source on the revolt against Rome, as if it were a fascinating historical novel. The approbation of Rabbi Abraham Simha of Mastislav also sanctioned the book for Lithuanian scholars. He linked his approbation to the Vilna Gaon's recommendation, reported by Barukh of Shklov, that the wisdom literature necessary for an understanding of the Scriptures should be translated into Hebrew, as well as to the specific request of Rabbi Hayim, the founder and head of the Volozhin yeshiva, who, according to Rabbi Simha, wished to see 'Josippon of the Romans' translated 'to enable us to understand the intentions of our great rabbis of blessed memory in the Talmud and the Midrashim'.[184]

In his introduction to the book Schulman described Josephus as a hero who could have prevented the destruction: 'If the Jews had heeded his words, Titus would not have crushed the Jewish people and made its garden a desolate waste.' He justified Josephus' actions at Jotapata, contending that it was not cowardice that kept him from committing suicide as the other surviving soldiers did, but rather, 'it was because of the sacred hope that it would enable him to be a mighty sanctuary for the remnants of the Jewish people against the enemy'.[185]

---

[181] Schulman, *Toledot yosef*, 3–5.   [182] Schulman, 'Toledot yosef ben matitiyah', 79–80, 95–6.
[183] Schulman, 'Kol kore', *Hakarmel*, 1 (1861), 252 (announcement).
[184] Schulman, *Milḥamot hayehudim*, ii. 4–6.   [185] Ibid. i. 3–4.

Schulman's abridged translation of *Kadmoniyot hayehudim* (Jewish Antiquities) appeared in 1864. He did not deem it necessary to translate the sections that covered the periods included in the Bible, so the book opens with the reign of Cyrus and ends with Herod. In the same year Schulman's translation project encountered financial difficulties; as noted above, he turned to the Society for the Promotion of Enlightenment among the Jews in St Petersburg, and with its aid *Kadmoniyot hayehudim* was printed.[186] The following year, when he considered his enterprise completed, Schulman proposed to the society that they issue all his books and translations dealing with the history of the Land of Israel, his translations of Josephus, and *Harisot beitar* as one comprehensive volume 'that would encompass the history of the ancient world'. This plan, however, was never carried out, and Schulman addressed himself to a new project initiated by the heads of the society: a translation of universal history into Hebrew.

Divrei yemei olam, which eventually consisted of nine volumes containing more than 2,000 pages of world history from antiquity up to the assassination attempt on Tsar Alexander II in 1881, was Schulman's greatest, most influential, and most widely distributed work.[187] It began with the society's decision in May 1864 to translate a two-volume Hebrew version of *Allgemeine Weltgeschichte* by Georg Weber (1808–88).[188] The heads of the committee offered the assignment to four maskilim, among them Schulman and Abraham Kaplan of Riga. The candidates were asked to send a number of translated pages to St Petersburg as a sample. Schulman and Kaplan responded positively to the proposal. Kaplan promised to finish the entire translation within a year if the society selected him, and Schulman replied that he did not possess a copy of the book, and therefore could not submit a sample translation. On the other hand, he promised that if he were chosen, 'the honourable members could rest assured that the translation would not fall short of the original in eloquence and grace of utterance and in all the virtues of language'.[189] In October 1864 Professor Chwolson decided to assign the task to Schulman, apparently because he had already proved his ability in his translations of Josephus, although Chwolson may also have been influenced by the fact that they knew each other from the time they had studied with Rabbi Israel Ginsburg in Vilna in the 1840s.[190]

Schulman happily accepted the assignment; once again, he did not have to depend on subscribers enlisted in advance, and he could finance his book in accordance with his agreement with the society. He even enthusiastically suggested that the project be expanded to include Jewish history. It was clear that Schulman was not independent; the Society for the Promotion of Enlightenment among the Jews not only financed the translation and its printing, but it also directed Schulman's

[186] L. Rosenthal, *Toledot ḥevrat marbei haskalah*, i. 4; ii. 31, 113.

[187] Additional editions were published for nearly half a century, until the eve of the First World War.   [188] L. Rosenthal, *Toledot ḥevrat marbei haskalah*, i. 7.

[189] Ibid., i. 7–8; ii. 36–9, 42.   [190] Ibid., ii. 37, 42. See also Friedman, *Sefer hazikhronot*.

writing through Chwolson, who was appointed as the head of the project. In November 1864 Weber's books were sent to Schulman in Vilna, along with Chwolson's comments and a list of topics he was to translate. Schulman was obliged to send every chapter to St Petersburg immediately upon its completion.[191] He reported to St Petersburg that he would begin work immediately: 'I have freed myself from all other work, and all day and night I write and translate only Weber's *Allgemeine Weltgeschichte*.'[192] In accordance with his agreement with the society, Schulman consulted Chwolson throughout his work. For example, he sought his permission to omit Weber's introduction because of the linguistic difficulties it posed, and he asked to expand Weber's abridged discussion of ancient Palestine. When Schulman began to translate the section on the Middle Ages, he even asked Chwolson what exactly he was permitted to write about Jewish history. Would the society's directors agree, Schulman enquired, to descriptions of antisemitism and detailed accounts of the edicts issued against the Jews? Schulman ultimately committed himself to presenting those 'days of darkness' from two well-known maskilic vantage-points that would tone down the harsh impression: on one hand, he stressed the contrast between that era of fanaticism and barbarity and the modern era, in which the sun of wisdom and religious tolerance shone over Europe, and, on the other hand, he 'proved to those who scorn science that in ancient times the rabbinic leaders and the scholarly *geonim* were not only sages but also skilled philosophers and writers, prodigious interpreters and poets'.[193]

In 1866 Schulman was nearing the end of his translation, and the committee began to consider its printing. Chwolson proposed that it be initially published in serial form as a special supplement to *Hakarmel*, and that after it was completed, 2,000 copies would be printed at the society's expense from the same print blocks. This proposal was apparently rejected, and the committee asked several printers for bids. The heads of the society's committee wanted the book to be distributed at a price that would not put off potential buyers. They therefore stipulated that the price of printing the book be low—no more than 2 kopecks per galley.[194] In January 1867 Schulman submitted the final chapters of his translation, which had taken more than two years to complete. He was invited to travel to St Petersburg so that agreement could be reached on the terms of printing.[195] For Schulman, the visit to the capital city was an exciting experience that heightened his sense of 'awe at the majesty' of the government, and stirred him to write about Russian history, culminating in a book he wrote in Hebrew on the city of St Petersburg and its history.[196] With regard to *Divrei yemei olam*, the committee decided to go over the translation, make revisions if necessary, and have it printed in three

[191] L. Rosenthal, *Toledot ḥevrat marbei haskalah*, ii. 47–9, 53.   [192] Ibid. ii. 57.

[193] Ibid. 53, 59–60, 120, 123.

[194] 'Report of the Society for the Promotion of Enlightenment among Jews for 1865', 49; L. Rosenthal, *Toledot ḥevrat marbei haskalah*, i. 12, 36.   [195] L. Rosenthal, *Toledot ḥevrat marbei haskalah*, i. 43.

[196] Schulman, 'Hamasa le'ir peterburg', 273–4. The reference is to Schulman's book *Kiryat melekh rav*.

volumes as soon as possible, at Schulman's expense. The society stipulated that high-quality paper and print be used, and gave instructions to print a minimum of 1,000 copies. Profits from the sale of the book would be Schulman's, but he had to promise that it would be sold at a low price. The society lent Schulman 300 roubles, paid directly to Romm Printers in Vilna, to cover printing costs, which he had to repay in three payments upon the publication of each of the three volumes.[197]

When the first part of *Divrei yemei olam*, from the creation of the world to the destruction of Carthage, was published at the end of 1867, it was already clear that at least four volumes, not the three originally planned, would be necessary to print the entire manuscript. Schulman asked his young friend Jonah Gurland, a student in St Petersburg, to write a favourable review for the Hebrew journals in order to promote sales of the book, and he also lobbied to have it accepted as a school textbook.[198] Schulman asked the society to try and obtain a specific order from the Russian minister of education requiring schools to purchase the book. The Alliance Israélite Universelle, for example, sent Schulman a congratulatory letter signed by Adolph Cremieux, and ordered thirty-two copies for its schools in Asia and Africa.[199]

The remaining parts of the book, covering the Middle Ages and the modern era up to 1852, continued to come out serially, one each year from 1868 to 1870, and sold quite well. 'The masses of our people rushed to get copies of this book,' Schulman boasted, 'as if . . . they were grapes in the desert and streams in the wilderness. A reliable indication of this is the fact that in but a few days all the copies were sold.'[200] Indeed, in 1872 a second edition of the first two parts was published, and in 1874–5 the second edition of the next two parts came out. By October 1872, according to Schulman, the entire first edition had been sold.

Encouraged by this success, Schulman asked the society whether he could translate works on geography and Russian history. He also planned to publish a book surveying the history of the Haskalah, based on material that, owing to its wide scope, had not been included in the fourth part of *Divrei yemei olam*. At the same time, Schulman asked the society's permission to add new sections to *Divrei yemei olam* that would update recent history, from 1852, the last year covered by

---

[197] L. Rosenthal, *Toledot ḥevrat marbei haskalah*, i. 44. Schulman haggled with the heads of the society, asking for 4 kopecks per folio sheet instead of the 2 kopecks the society offered. The society's board partly acceded to his demand, setting the price at 3 kopecks (ibid. 49). In the end Schulman did not repay the loan, and managed to convince the board that thirty sheets more than had been planned had been printed and that the sum of the loan was payment for these (ibid. 94).

[198] Schulman, letter to Gurland, 'Mikhtavim', 410–11.

[199] L. Rosenthal, *Toledot ḥevrat marbei haskalah*, ii. 196 (Apr. 1868).

[200] Schulman, letter to Gurland, 'Mikhtavim', 411. The publication and success of the book had an unfortunate effect on another Hebrew writer, Eliezer Rashkov, who had also written a universal history book. Rashkov apparently lost hope that his own book would be published, and it remained in manuscript form (Manuscript Dept., National and University Library, Jerusalem, 30828). On Rashkov, see Fuenn, *Keneset yisra'el*, 141–2.

the fourth part, up to the 1870s. The society rejected his proposal and his efforts
to influence J. L. Gordon, the society's secretary, were of no avail. He did not
give up, however, and in 1875, without the society's official consent, he prepared
the fifth part for publication. This section gave an account of contemporary
European political and military history of the 1850s and 1860s.[201] The book itself
was not printed until a year later, in June 1876, after a long delay at the censors.[202]
Other parts, covering all contemporary history up to 1881, were printed in a similar fashion: Schulman prepared the books at his own initiative and each time
received 100 roubles to help offset printing costs. Owing to both financial problems and censorship delays, this process was a great deal slower than at the first
stage, when the initial four volumes were printed, and the sixth to ninth volumes
came out in 1879, 1880, 1882, and 1884.[203] Although the final five parts of *Divrei
yemei olam* thus encompassed a brief period, 1852–81, these books enabled Jewish
readers to grasp the intricacies of the international relationships of their time.
The readers of Schulman's books learned, among other things, about the American Civil War, the unification of Germany, the Polish Revolt, the Crimean War,
and the rise of Louis Napoleon to power in France. In the sixth part Schulman
again moved to Asia, describing European colonialism as a beneficial policy
intended to save the East and deliver it from its ignorance, and the seventh part was
devoted to a detailed description of the war between Russia and Turkey.[204]

Weber's universal history book *Lehrbuch der Weltgeschichte*, selected by the
Society for the Promotion of Enlightenment among the Jews to be translated into
Hebrew, was one of the most popular works of its kind in Germany and throughout Europe during the second half of the nineteenth century, just as Pölitz's books
had been in the first half. Weber, who had received doctorates in philosophy and
theology from the University of Heidelberg and was a student and admirer of
Schlosser, wrote history for three readerships: scholars, school pupils, and the
general public. His great project *Allgemeine Weltgeschichte*, which comprised fifteen
volumes, was published between 1857 and 1881 and was supplemented by another
four volumes of updated information. Before embarking on this comprehensive
enterprise, Weber published two shorter, very popular books: *Lehrbuch der Weltgeschichte*, a textbook in two volumes, twenty editions of which were published
from 1846 until Weber's death; and an abridged, single-volume universal history,
which was also widely distributed, and passed through a similar number of edi-

[201] L. Rosenthal, *Toledot ḥevrat marbei haskalah*, i. 91, 123; Schulman, *Mosdei erets*, i. 3–4; Schulman,
Divrei yemei olam, iv. 22–4; Schulman, 'Tseror igerot' (Sept. 1872), 542–3.

[202] Schulman, 'Tseror igerot' (Jan. 1876), 545; (June 1876), 546. The sensitive nature of the political history covered in this part apparently lay behind the long delay at the censor's.

[203] L. Rosenthal, *Toledot ḥevrat marbei haskalah*, i. 141, 155, 184; Schulman, 'Tseror igerot', 550–1.

[204] Additional edns. of *Divrei yemei olam*: vol. i (1880, 1912); vol. ii (1974, 1884, 1886, 1911); vol. iii
(1911, 1914); vol. iv (1875, 1912); vol. v (1879, 1887, 1912); vol. vi (1912); vol. vii (1911, 1914); vol.
viii (1912); vol. ix (1914).

tions between 1851 and 1889. Schulman possessed all the volumes of Weber's large, comprehensive history that had been published up to 1864, as well as the two volumes of the *Lehrbuch der Weltgeschichte*. He translated the *Lehrbuch* into Hebrew, with the assistance of the larger work and other books, particularly the final volumes of the *Allgemeine Weltgeschichte*.[205]

Weber perceived universal history as a mirror that reflected all historical knowledge that existed at the time of its writing, and he therefore undertook to include in his book everything that had been uncovered by the new scientific research flourishing in Germany's universities.[206] On the other hand, he was careful to make a distinction between his scholarly, professional, and popular works, in contrast to Leopold Ranke, for example, whose studies were published in Germany at the same time. Weber stressed that he did not consider Ranke a rival, for each had different goals. While Ranke wrote for the professional historian, Weber endeavoured to make his books as popular as possible, and render them accessible to the educated classes—objectives similar to those that Pölitz had set himself at the beginning of the century. Weber attempted to cover all periods and the achievements, events, religious beliefs, ideas, cultures, and political and economic developments of all nations. In the manner of every nineteenth-century liberal and idealist, he regarded history as the stage for the struggle of the spiritual to dominate the material, and the story of the victory of liberty and equality in society—ideals which the maskilim found very easy to accept and identify with. In addition to writing history, Weber was active in the field of education and had clearly didactic aims. Carrying on Enlightenment concepts from the eighteenth century, he believed that history would supply examples of virtuousness and help teach young people to be moral and to shun evil and corruption. Like Pölitz, Weber combined liberalism and cosmopolitanism with German nationalism, and he added devotion to the Fatherland to the fundamental values of humanism and liberty. In his opinion, Germany deserved a central place in universal history because it had exerted great influence on other peoples in many periods. Germany's centrality in Europe, the Germans' aspiration to universal education, and their cosmopolitanism, Weber wrote in 1864, rendered the German historian particularly well qualified to write universal history. In Schulman's translation and adaptation, however, all allusions to Weber's Germanocentricity were expunged.[207]

Schulman did not translate Weber's introduction, in which the German historian elucidated his historical approach and outlined the structure of universal history, for, as noted above, he found it difficult to translate the terminology into Hebrew.

---

[205] L. Rosenthal, *Toledot ḥevrat marbei haskalah*, ii. 53. Another work he used was Karl Becker's popular textbook *Weltgeschichte für Kinder und Kinderlehrer*. The two parts of Weber's textbook are nearly the same size (about 2,300 pages) as Schulman's book (2,150 pages).

[206] Weber, introd., *Allgemeine Weltgeschichte*, 7; Weber, introd., *Lehrbuch der Weltgeschichte*, 30.

[207] Weber, *Allgemeine Weltgeschichte*, 8–10, 11–14.

The introductions to the various volumes were therefore all written by Schulman himself, and expressed his own views of history.

According to its subtitle, 'The History of Man and the Events that have Occurred in all the Nations of the World throughout all Time, the History of Wisdom, Sciences, and Industry', *Divrei yemei olam* was intended to encompass universal political, economic, and cultural history; in addition, it would contain 'the history of the Jewish people from the time of the Hasmoneans up to the present, the history of the great men of Israel, renowned figures of all the generations, and the history of the Haskalah in Israel from the time of Rabbi Moses ben Menahem Mendelssohn, of blessed memory, up to the present'. However, these last two subjects were not actually included in *Divrei yemei olam*. No history of the Haskalah was written, and the history of the great men of Israel was the subject of another book. Only parts of Jewish history were covered and the more ancient periods in particular were left out altogether.[208] Most of the book, therefore, remained in the realm of universal history, where the Hebrew reader encountered the culture and rulers of classical Greece, learned about the development of religions, the greatness of the Roman empire, feudalism and the Crusades, the Renaissance, the Reformation, and many other episodes. Schulman's dramatic and colourful style transformed historical events into stories brimming with adventures, wars, revolts, slaughter, acts of cruelty, and struggles for justice and liberty. The plethora of exclamation marks in the book made for lively reading and, as Schulman had intended, it aroused his readers' awe and excitement.

In the book's general introduction Schulman recapitulated the Haskalah's familiar justification for the study of history and the importance of historical knowledge: 'True history teaches and instructs us how to improve our ways so we may walk the right path of life'; 'This knowledge is the source of life for the spirit of man'; the Torah itself commanded us to remember historical events; and history reflected the hand of Providence that directed the world.[209] History stimulated the spirit and engendered the fear of God, and taught about the momentous transition that had occurred in the modern era. Weber himself did not deny that Providence was a dominant factor in history, but stressed that the historian was not qualified to study the ways of God. He saw history as an arena of action open to man's free will. In Schulman's introduction Providence played a much more central role in history, although he changed nothing in the general section entitled 'The Theory of History', translated from Weber, which claimed, as did the original, that the destiny of nations and people was determined by moral behaviour, patriotism, and other human factors. This section also asserted that the function of the historian was to study, criticize, and create a total picture of the history of man, with the assistance of geography and chronology.[210]

---

[208] Schulman, *Divrei yemei olam*, i. 228–47 (the Hasmonean revolt), ii. 40–84 (the Bar Kokhba revolt). Weber devoted only two pages to the topic: *Lehrbuch der Weltgeschichte*, i. 438–9.

[209] Schulman, *Divrei yemei olam*, i. 3–9.   [210] Ibid. 16–19.

Weber's periodization of universal history divided it into the four periods characteristic of earlier writings: the ancient world, marked by despotism, republics, and paganism; the Middle Ages, in which 'a cloud of death lay upon the countries of Europe', the aristocracy oppressed the lower classes, and the Pope subjugated them all; 'the modern era', which began with the Reformation and the discovery of America, 'when the sun of wisdom broke through and dispersed the darkness of folly from Europe'; and finally, 'the newest age', depicted as the ideal realization of Enlightenment ideas, 'when every desire and every aspiration is to deliver the same just laws to members of the various faiths, to mete out eternal justice under all the heavens'.[211] However, a more precise comparison between the structure of Weber's book and Schulman's adaptation of it reveals that the two do not completely correspond, and that Schulman did not fully implement the periodization that he himself had set out in the book's introduction. Schulman's expansion of his translation beyond the two sections planned at the project's inception also caused a break in the structure.

Schulman attempted to avoid Weber's term 'the revolutionary era' in referring to the period that encompassed the American Revolution, the French Revolution, and the Napoleonic era. This was a problematic and radical term in tsarist Russia, as it was for the moderate maskilim, for whom loyalty to the government was unequivocal. Moreover, it appears that since Schulman viewed universal history from a Jewish perspective, he was unable to include the fifteenth to eighteenth centuries in the modern era, as had Weber. In accordance with the maskilic awareness of the past, which Schulman faithfully preserved, the historical turning-point of the new era was much more closely linked to the end of the eighteenth century, with the rise of enlightened absolutism and the Enlightenment, than with the Reformation and the Renaissance. Hence he preferred to designate the period by a name he found ready-made in Weber; the 'harbinger of the modern era', although Weber himself used the concept solely to designate a relatively short period of history that included the era of geographical discoveries and the Renaissance.[212]

In his introduction to the Middle Ages Schulman showed complete independence from Weber. In his opinion, the entire period was a combination of 'marvellous and terrible times, the likes of which had never been before and would never come again'. The bright points of the Middle Ages were the elimination of idolatry, the establishment of universities, and towards the end, the invention of printing and the discovery of America. However, 'the papacy and fanaticism ruled over the gentiles, plunging Europe into a long period of darkness'.[213] Apart from these general comments, Schulman examined the Middle Ages from the vantage-point of Jewish history.

As noted above, Schulman consulted with Chwolson before writing the section

---

[211] Ibid. 19.   [212] Weber, *Lehrbuch der Weltgeschichte*, vol. ii, pt. 3, para. 1.
[213] Schulman, *Divrei yemei olam*, ii. 1.

on the Middle Ages, and in the introduction he reiterated his question: was there
any point in minutely describing the persecution of the Jews and the edicts issued
against them during this period? In his opinion, there were two key justifications
for an affirmative reply. First, an examination of this bleak time in light of the
modern era proved again and again the superiority of the present. Secondly, there
was a danger that any history omitting this chapter would cause it to be completely forgotten. Schulman feared that in the ideal future, the era in which all
men would be possessed of moral virtues and live within the framework of a perfect society, it would be impossible to imagine that the Jews could have endured
such grim and cruel hardships. No one would believe that a people showing such
exemplary loyalty to the kings, a people that had never been involved in political
revolutions, could have been discriminated against and harshly repressed. In his
view, therefore, there was a danger that the suffering of the Jews in the Middle
Ages would be denied, and that readers in the future might doubt the credibility
of the stories:

And thus he will deny the history of mankind in general, and of the Jews in particular, and
he will decide that all things written in the book about the Jews and their dreadful hardships in the Middle Ages never truly existed, and are simply the invention of great poets
with bold imaginations who have presented them as an example for the sake of capturing
the hearts of the readers, just as all dramatists do in their tragedies.[214]

Schulman's maskilic consciousness and profound conviction that the pre-modern
era was a closed chapter in history and could not be repeated led him to believe
that the memory of past episodes of Jewish suffering should be preserved so that
they would not be obliterated from memory in the future. His belief in the modern era was boundless, and his assessment of the Middle Ages was a blend of
elegy, romanticism, and nostalgia, on one hand, and maskilic optimism regarding
the present and the future, on the other:

With a soul bursting with sorrow and eyes exhausted with tears, I recall those days of
darkness and the terror of death, and with a joyous soul and eyes filled with light and happiness, we shall look upon these happy days in which all of us in this generation live . . . Ah,
who would have thought that the Jewish people who had been sacrificed by Europe, placed
upon the altar above the fire and the wood to be completely annihilated, who would have
thought then that a time would come when it would be liberated, the altar would be
destroyed, and the fire would be doused . . . and that it would have a glorious place in the
temple of liberty like all the nations of the earth, and that the kings and lords of the land
would walk before it bearing the torch of Enlightenment . . . Ah, now we can say to the
Jewish people that the day will come in which all the visions and prophecies uttered by its
prophets will come true. And the earth will be full of the knowledge of the Lord's glory as
the waters fill the sea.[215]

---

[214] Schulman, *Divrei yemei olam*, ii. 3–5.   [215] Ibid. 5–6.

Divrei yemei olam thus met the requirements of those who commissioned it and conveyed the spirit of its author's maskilic awareness of the past. It was a most optimistic book, written with an admiring eye towards the benevolent tsar Alexander II. Thus, for example, the monarch is mentioned in the chapter describing the massacre of the Jews by the Crusaders in 1096, to make readers aware of the enormous gap between the fanatic mentality of the Church in the Middle Ages and the tolerant rulers of the modern era.[216]

Schulman places 'two terrible spectacles' at the opening of the modern era (which, as mentioned, paralleled Weber's 'Revolutionary Era'): 'the French insurrection' and the 'exploits of Napoleon Bonaparte'.[217] Schulman regarded these as unprecedented and crucial events that had destroyed the existing order, undermined all conventions, and led to bloodshed and political and religious radicalism. As a moderate maskil, his world-view and belief in the legitimacy of the absolutist, monarchical government left him no choice but to condemn both the revolution and Napoleon, as its direct offspring, almost without reservation.

Weber, who was Schulman's principal though not sole source for the description of the revolution, also had reservations about it. In his opinion, the English deist and French Voltairean versions of the Enlightenment were decisive causes of the revolution, and his view of it was ambivalent. On one hand, eighteenth-century literature contributed to the promotion of liberty, the sovereignty of the people, equality, humanism, and religious tolerance; it succeeded in restraining the Catholic Church and striking a blow against the Jesuits. However, on the other hand, it swept away values essential to social stability. As a moderate liberal and a German Protestant, Weber looked askance at the revolution's total subversion of religion and its challenge to the state and its laws. It was impossible, Weber asserted, to act on the basis of reason alone, without ascribing importance to the past and to historical development.[218] It was on these points in particular that Schulman chose to moderate Weber's criticism of the Enlightenment. He apparently did not wish to attack an ideology that he himself was preaching. Schulman's tactic was, on one hand, to underscore the achievements of the European Enlightenment, particularly its war against ignorance, superstition, and fanaticism and its mitigating influence on the monarchs, while, on the other hand, he made a distinction between the moderate Enlightenment and its radical representatives. Schulman admitted— this time, in an exact translation of Weber—that the enlightened men of France subverted the foundation of social existence, did not exhibit sufficient sensitivity to the legitimate boundaries of criticism, and brought about religious and political anarchy.

The revolution itself was described in *Divrei yemei olam* as an illegitimate act, carried out by the masses of the French people, who were possessed by 'an evil

216 Ibid. 206
217 Ibid. iv. 3–4 (introd.).
218 Weber, *Lehrbuch der Weltgeschichte*, ii. 343, 351–2.

and destructive spirit and the driving force to open the way to lawlessness'.[219] It
was the inflamed masses who stormed the Bastille in July 1789, and members of
the indigent class who forced the king to leave Versailles for Paris in October
1789, greatly dishonouring him.[220] Louis XVI was portrayed as a pathetic king,
beloved by his people but possessed of a weak character, and an ineffectual ruler.
Schulman wrote an emotional condemnation of his execution by the 'accursed
insurrectionists'. This was, in his view, the great crime of the revolution and
a rebellious continuation of the cycle of bloodshed that characterized it. His
description of the 1793 execution was one of the most dramatic in his book, and
attempted to convey to the Hebrew reader the oppressive atmosphere pervading
Paris on the day of that 'terrible murder', the king's bravery, and his bitter end:

The silence of death prevailed over all the streets, and the city of Paris, usually so gay and
filled with the noise of the multitudes, became a desolate wasteland. That terrible silence
and the cloud that hung over that day were as harbingers of the disaster and dreadful evil
that would come to that city of blood at the time of the fearful murder. At the tenth hour,
the king's coach arrived at the place Louis XV, and there the executioner awaited him, and
the instrument of death known as the guillotine . . . The door to the coach in which the
king sat opened, and he stepped out and ascended to the platform of the slaughtering-
place with a tranquil heart and a spirit befitting an innocent, righteous man, who knew
that he was blameless and his hands clean. At that moment the executioners seized the
king and led him to the slaughter, and the priest knelt at the feet of the king and cried:
'Rise, son of the holy Louis: rise to the heavens!' Then the blade of the instrument of
death fell upon the neck of the king and severed his head from his body, and the head, covered in blood, rolled on the platform of the slaughterhouse . . . and the fierce tyrants
danced and leapt and capered on the platform of the slaughterhouse, cavorting like
drunken men, with happiness and merriment . . . But the French people whose hearts
were touched by the fear of God privately mourned for the blood of the righteous and just
king, which had been spilled by the wickedness of the despotic murderers of the land, and
secretly, in the innermost chambers of their homes, they spoke a bitter eulogy for their
beloved and exalted king.[221]

Through his descriptions of the French Revolution and the Napoleonic era,
Schulman defended two fundamental values that, in his view, ensured social order
and human existence: the sanctity of the monarchy and the sanctity of faith. He
believed that anything harmful to the monarchy inevitably harmed religion, as it
had in France. 'The French insurrection', which destroyed these two fundamental
values, was therefore an appalling historical event, and the struggle for liberty was
swallowed up by the unjustified radicalism. It was not surprising, therefore, that
Napoleon, a prodigious historical hero whose actions were destructive, was an

---

[219] Schulman, *Divrei yemei olam*, iv. 3.
[220] Ibid. 61–7. Schulman's complete description does not appear in Weber's book. Evidently he
relied upon a different source here.   [221] Schulman, *Divrei yemei olam*, iv. 81.

inevitable product of the revolution, and that his ambition, which lacked moral bounds, brought about his downfall as well as that of the revolution.

These two historical phenomena, 'the French insurrection' and Napoleon, could serve, according to maskilic perceptions, as negative examples from which lessons could be learned: one must remain faithful to the king and to God, out of obedience, discipline, and an awareness of the price of pride and defiance of the rulers of the country and the Kingdom of Heaven. Schulman, however, saw that the major significance of the revolution for the Jews lay in its implications for the course of Jewish history. While 'the French insurrection' should be condemned, it was nonetheless ultimately responsible for bringing about 'Jewish liberty'. The historical paradox of the modern era, in Schulman's view, was that this particular revolutionary era had decidedly helped to improve the status of the Jews in the country, even though periods of unrest had always previously augured badly for the Jews. From the outset it was to be expected that the French Jews would be harmed by the revolution, and that the Catholic clergy would exploit the opportunity to incite the inflamed masses against them. Circumstances did not seem to bode well for the Jews: the monarch and the nobility had lost all their power, and the Jews, unable to find protection, had become vulnerable to attack by the masses and the Church. However, this particular cloud had a silver lining. Influenced by the radical Enlightenment, an anticlerical and intensely anti-Catholic trend developed in revolutionary France and the Church suffered some harsh blows. These revolutionary developments, which the maskilim shunned in principle but welcomed in retrospect, toppled the iron wall that had separated Jews and Christians. The French people realized 'that they had hated them with a vicious hatred, and for no good reason had they laid a trap for them, for no good reason had they persecuted them with fire and swords, to spill their blood'.[222]

This profound change in attitude towards the Jews and the pressure applied by the National Assembly to grant them political rights culminated in the Emancipation Act of 1791. While the Napoleonic era brought with it some regression and the clergy regained some of its former power, Schulman's Napoleon nonetheless made an effort to maintain Jewish equality. Schulman even found a positive aspect to the 'infamous edict' of 1808, claiming that its purpose was to placate the anti-Jewish stream in France, and that Napoleon knew quite well that the edict would cause no serious harm, 'since most Frenchmen had already made great progress in enlightenment, and would close their ears to this cruel law in those days of light'.[223] Schulman was reluctant to spoil the pretty picture he had sketched, and, with his great optimism, was unwilling to imagine a severe reaction to 'Jewish liberty'. He believed that the revolution, an unjustified event in itself, had created an irreversible situation that promised a new era for the Jews. From that point onwards European Jewry made great strides forward, and during the nineteenth century 'would . . . rise to the heights in almost every area of science and know-

<hr>

[222] Ibid. 5–6.   [223] Ibid. 7–9.

ledge . . . and all of this in a very short time, while other peoples did not succeed in rising thus for many hundreds of years'.[224]

What should have been the attitude of Jews living in the Russia of Alexander II to the French Revolution? First, like all his predecessors, Schulman endeavoured to emphasize the Jews' political loyalty, in order to avoid the misleading impression that revolutionary actions could be even partly justifiable. In light of the situation in Russia in the 1870s, with the activities of the nihilists, the opposition groups, the attempts on the life of the tsar, and the aftermath of the 1863 Polish Revolt, this point had to be made clear beyond any doubt. In his introduction to the fourth part Schulman sought to respond to the analogy drawn by antisemitic historians between the Jewish wars at the end of the Second Temple era and the French Revolution. In this interpretation the Zealots and the Jacobins, John of Giscala, Simeon bar Giora, Robespierre, and Danton were all presented as belonging to the same historical category of revolutionary leadership. Schulman, whose earlier writings had denounced Jewish revolts, considered this analogy a complete fabrication and asserted that

the wars of the Jews are as far removed from the French Revolution as the east is from the west. The path of the Zealots and their philosophy is as far from the path and philosophy of the Jacobins as the sky is from the earth, and the superiority of the officers of that war—John of Giscala and Simeon bar Giora—over the officers of Sodom—Robespierre and Danton in that revolution—is as the superiority of light over darkness.[225]

How could one justify the first-century revolt against the Romans, on one hand, while rejecting every revolt and revolution in principle and condemning the French Revolution in particular, on the other hand? Schulman proposed four differences that, in his view, proved that the Jewish Revolt was justified and the French Revolution was not. First, Rome was a 'monstrous animal' that cruelly and unjustly set upon the Jews of Palestine, violating their peace and well-being. Rome's provocative behaviour and the existential danger to the Jews left no room for surrender. In contrast, the revolutionaries in France faced no such provocation or existential danger. Rather, they themselves were the initiators and attackers. Secondly, despite their difficult situation, the Jews did not intend to revolt against the Roman emperor, as the French revolted against Louis XVI. Their sole objective was to replace the evil governors ruling Palestine. Thirdly, only the 'poor people' and 'the young men of heroic strength whose hearts were enraged' initiated the revolt, while the upper classes attempted to restrain them. Only when it became clear that Rome could not be influenced by peaceable means to accept the Jews' demands to replace the governors did the 'Jewish noblemen follow the lead of the warriors in the war of the Almighty'. Finally, the revolt against the Romans was a war of monotheists against cruel pagans who had attacked what was sacred to the Jews, and, from this point of view, their struggle must be seen as an exalted vision and a

[224] Schulman, *Divrei yemei olam*, iv. 13–19.   [225] Ibid. 9–13.

holy war that had a just and worthy aim. Perhaps, Schulman wrote, if the revolutionary camp had not been split into factions, the 'flag of Zion' might have flown from the roof of the Capitol in Rome. The French Revolution, on the other hand, did not have a just aim. Quite the contrary: the insurgents fought against religious belief and not for it, wielding their weapons against a righteous king. Morally speaking, this was an unworthy, illegitimate revolution.[226]

In this apologia Schulman cleansed the Jewish past of the 'stain' left by the revolt against Rome. It also appears that he was frightened by his own audacity in endorsing 'the French insurrection' in so far as the achievement of 'Jewish liberty' was concerned, and since *Divrei yemei olam* was, to a great extent, a government-sponsored book, he was forced to emphasize the importance of Russia as a superior model to France. Improvement of the Jews' situation, Schulman claimed, was by no means contingent upon political revolution or changing forms of government. He reiterated the idealization of Russian Jewish history and the view that the Russian monarchs had always been benevolent kings who did not persecute the Jews, and that 'all men remained calm and quiet, [and] none were fearful'. The Romanovs' rise to power had brought with it an even more benevolent attitude towards the Jews, and during the reign of Alexander II 'Judah is redeemed and Israel shall dwell in tranquillity.'[227] Hence there was no need for revolution in Russia. The enlightened absolutist government, which demonstrated religious tolerance and encouraged education, could bring about the same conditions that had developed in western Europe as a result of the emancipation. The Jews' integration into the economic and cultural life of Russia, which Schulman depicted from his vantage-point in 1870, would, in his view, gradually bring about emancipation in Russia as well. 'Before much time has passed,' he believed, 'the Jews living in Russia will become equal to all the citizens of the land in all civil laws and all offices and ordinances of the country.'[228]

After completing the first four parts of *Divrei yemei olam*, Schulman planned to translate a history of Russia that would include the history of the Jews in that country. This decision was reinforced by his visit to St Petersburg in 1867, but, as noted above, the Society for the Promotion of Enlightenment among the Jews rejected his request, and assigned the task to the student Solomon Mandelkern. Nevertheless, the society's secretary, Leon Rosenthal, helped Schulman publish the book *Kiryat melekh rav* (The City of the Great King, 1869), in which, brimming over with enthusiasm and Russian patriotism, he described 'the history of Petersburg the capital, from the day of its foundation until the present, a description of its houses, its palaces and castles, the wonders of its fine buildings, the richness of its treasures, and all its power and splendour'.[229] The book surveyed 'the new Rome', maintaining a laudatory attitude towards the rulers, and legitimizing enlightened Russian absolutism from Peter the Great to Alexander II.

[226] Ibid. 11–12.   [227] Ibid. 20–1.   [228] Ibid. 22.
[229] Schulman, Letter to Gurland, 'Mikhtavim', 410.

Rosenthal also funded the printing of a geography book in Hebrew, *Meḥkarei erets rusiyah* (Studies of Russia, 1869), in which Schulman included an abridged history of Russia supplemented by maps of Russia in Hebrew. *Meḥkarei erets rusiyah* described 'the greatest, the mightiest, the most prodigious of all the nations of the world, our homeland; and we eat of her fruit and are satisfied by her bounty and by the benevolence of her rulers, the benevolent kings. It was the first of a series of geography books written by Schulman, and was followed by the ten parts of *Sefer mosdei arets: teḥunot kol artsei tevel vetoledot yoshveihen* (The Foundation of the World: The Features of All Countries and the History of their Inhabitants), once again funded by Rosenthal. Schulman saw these works as an essential supplement to *Divrei yemei olam*.

In 1871 Schulman completed an additional series of books, *Toledot ḥakhmei yisra'el* (Biographies of Jewish Sages), which from the start was intended to be incorporated into the larger work *Divrei yemei olam*.[230] The four volumes of this work were printed in Vilna two years later, and included biographies of figures from the eleventh to the sixteenth centuries. This work echoed Levinsohn's maskilic apologia and the eighteenth-century *Hame'asef*, attempting to prove that even in the Middle Ages Jewish history had maintained a succession 'of illustrious figures who dispelled the darkness from the inhabitants of the earth'.[231] The biographies of these writers, poets, philosophers, diplomats, rabbis, and scholars were also meant to encourage respect for the Jewish people, and this project was a clear continuation of Schulman's book on antiquity.

Schulman's introduction pointed out that the first part of *Toledot ḥakhmei yisra'el* was based on the writing of 'the glorious wise rabbi, Professor Rabbi Tsevi Hirsch Graetz, may God bless him with long life, who sanctified the name of Israel in his magnificent book on the history of the Jews'.[232] However, a comparison between Schulman's book and Graetz's *Geschichte der Juden* reveals that the former was actually an almost literal translation of the sixth and eighth parts of Graetz's work—a fact Schulman did not trouble to disclose to his readers. In these volumes, which encompass the history of medieval Spanish Jewry from the time of Samuel Hanagid to the time of Maimonides, Graetz had included a series of biographies, which perfectly suited Schulman's needs.

In the 1860s and 1870s Graetz's books became the primary source of Jewish history for German-reading maskilim in Russia, displacing Jost's works. Anyone who wished to investigate historical issues could no longer disregard his *Geschichte der Juden*. Once again, as with Jost, the question arises as to how Graetz was received by the Russian maskilim. I shall attempt to address this, in the context of the discussion of Kalman Schulman, and then return, in the next chapter, to the subject of the reception of Graetz's work.

---

[230] A single chapter was printed in 1868 in *Hakarmel*, 7 (1868), 71–2, 78–9, 88–9, 95. Schulman noted there that this was a chapter from part 2 of *Divrei yemei olam* which had not yet been published.

[231] Schulman, *Toledot ḥakhmei yisra'el*, i. 4–5.   [232] Ibid. 11.

Graetz was perceived as the greatest and most important chronicler of Jewish history, whose like had never been known before and would never be known again. The newspaper articles announcing the publication of the various volumes of his book, until the project was completed with the eleventh volume in 1870, lauded his knowledge of details and his ability to recognize 'the internal, unifying causes of events that appear to have no order to them'.[233] Very few people dared find weaknesses in Graetz's work. One critic was an anonymous writer in *Hamagid* who alluded to 'his fanciful suppositions'. Another was Ephraim Deinard, who protested at the inadequate representation of Russian Jewry in Graetz's book. Deinard, insulted and bursting with Russian Jewish pride, reprimanded Graetz: 'He had no right to cross the boundary of Russia to see the ways of the Jewish people and their deeds in that country, in order to pass judgement on what he saw there; and every man of knowledge will agree with me that one can judge our brothers in Russia differently, and perhaps find among them sages as wise as those of Germany, and even wiser.'[234] Perez Smolenskin (1842–85) levelled even harsher criticism against Graetz's pro-German approach and his neglect of the Jewish sages of Russia. In order to compensate for this, in 1877 Smolenskin proposed to Benjamin Mandelstamm (1805–86) that he write a history of the Jews in Russia:

And in Germany, those Jewish scholars and historians will believe that only they merit the title of men, and that the history of the Jewish people in Germany is the history of the entire people, for there is not even a single mention in Graetz's books of the history of the scholars of Russia, or the wonderful things that were done there for fifty years. We cannot accuse Graetz of being sparing with his words; on the contrary, we are awed by the great indulgence shown in his books, which led him occasionally to write pages instead of one word, but nevertheless he abridged his discussion of the Jewish scholars of Russia.[235]

Graetz was the sole source of information on many historical subjects. The partial translations into Hebrew that appeared intermittently in the Hebrew press included chapters on Moses Almosnino, Solomon Ibn Gabirol, and the Reuchlin–Pfefferkorn dispute.[236] This last chapter, from the ninth volume of *Geschichte der Juden*, was part of the first attempt to translate Graetz's books into Hebrew. It was made by Joseph Hertzberg (1802–70) from Mohilev, who had subscribed to Levinsohn's *Te'udah beyisra'el* in the 1820s, translated several of Mendelssohn's philosophical works in the 1840s and 1850s, and had also worked on a Hebrew translation of Kant's *Critique of Pure Reason*. According to his son-in-law, Hertzberg completed his translation of the eighth and ninth volumes of *Geschichte der Juden* in 1868, and the unpublished manuscript remained in his son-in-law's possession after his death. A letter Hertzberg wrote to Samuel Fuenn and appended

---

233 Anon., 'Besorat sefarim', *Hamagid*, 15 (1871), 31–2 (book notes).

234 Ibid.; Deinard, *Sefer masa kerim*, 63–4.

235 Mandelstamm, *Hazon lamo'ed*, 5 (editor's note).

236 J. L. Frankel, 'Rabi moshe almosnino'; Blumenfeld, 'Rabi shelomoh ibn gevirol'; Hertzberg, 'Maḥloket reukhlin vefeferkorn'.

to the three chapters of the translation published that year in *Hakarmel* indicated
that he planned to translate the entire book. Hertzberg asked Fuenn to help him
print the book and to assist him financially by addressing the readers of *Hakarmel*
and enlisting subscribers for the book in advance. Alternatively, Hertzberg
suggested that Fuenn publish the translation at his own expense. In his efforts to
persuade Fuenn to accept his proposal, Hertzberg claimed that the enterprise
would be very profitable and that the book would be much in demand. He was
prepared to take only a few copies of the book as payment for authorship. In any
case, the plan was never carried out, and the fate of the manuscript of the translated
sections is unknown.[237]

The second attempt to translate Graetz into Hebrew was made at the initiative
of the booksellers and publishers Winter Brothers of Vienna, who obtained translation rights from Graetz. They chose Abraham Cohen Kaplan, a maskil from
Kovno then living in Vienna, to take on the job. Kaplan began with a translation
of the third part, which covers the years from the height of the Hasmonean period
and the death of Judah Maccabee to the destruction of the Second Temple.[238]
Kaplan apparently tried to postpone the translation of the first parts, which dealt
with the period of antiquity, to a later stage; perhaps he feared that Graetz's historical analysis might appear too daring in the eyes of the traditional Hebrew
reader in eastern Europe. Kaplan also attempted to render the translation suitable
for the Jewish reader, by changing the Christian date of the destruction of the
Temple and omitting Graetz's scholarly notes. 'Not for students of history', Kaplan
wrote in his introduction, 'but for ordinary readers are we publishing these works
in Hebrew, and these readers, when they learn that the writer has presented proof
of his words in his book in the German language, will believe the translation and
will not enquire any further.'[239] The average reader would trust Graetz's credibility, and, in Kaplan's opinion, needed neither references nor scholarly, critical discussions; the maskilim would have no need at all for a Hebrew translation, since
they could read the original German.

Kaplan's translation of the third part appeared serially, in ten pamphlets, during
1875. For some reason, however, the translation was halted at this early stage.
The Winter Brothers looked for another translator, and Gurland, who was then
editor of the literary column 'Book News' in *Hatsefirah* and was in contact with
the publishers in Vienna, recommended Kalman Schulman as a suitable candidate.[240] In 1876 Schulman undertook the task, and his first three pamphlets
appeared the same year, including Graetz's introduction to the first part and his

[237] On Joseph Hertzberg and his attempt to translate Graetz's *Geschichte der Juden*, see Gottlober,
'Hagizrah vehabeniyah', 76–81; Hertzberg, 'Mikhtav lefin'.

[238] A. Kaplan, *Divrei yemei hayehudim*. Avraham Zuckerman of Warsaw was appointed by the
publishers as the sole distributor of this translation (see *Hatsefirah*, 2 (1875), 184). See also Zitron,
The Makers, ii. 160–1.   [239] Kaplan, *Divrei yemei hayehudim*, 9.

[240] Gurland, 'Hadashot sifriyot', 183.

description of the period from the conquest of Palestine to Saul's kingship.[241] Schulman's translation was also halted at this initial stage, when less than 200 pages, covering only the first five chapters of the first part, had been written. The criticism levelled at Schulman from various directions, his own disappointment at problems with the printers in Vienna, and Winter Brothers' dissatisfaction apparently led to the translation's termination. Biographies of Schulman suggest that Graetz himself informed the Winter Brothers that he was withdrawing his consent to having the book translated because of the changes Schulman had introduced into it. Another source indicates that it was a financial crisis at the printing-house, rather than problems with the translation itself, that prevented the continuation of Schulman's translation.[242]

When the first pamphlet, containing a translation of the introduction, appeared, Gurland praised Schulman, emphasizing in particular the quality of the translation as compared to Kaplan's, which he considered most defective. He advised Schulman to improve the translation even more by abridging or eliminating the author's notes so as to facilitate reading.[243] Essentially, Schulman's attitude towards Graetz was a mixture of admiration and reserve. He considered him a great historian but he rejected what he called Graetz's unrestrained criticism, especially the freedom he allowed himself to slight the honour of the great men of the nation—an ambivalent attitude which resembled Rapoport's confrontation with the German Jewish historian Jost in the previous generation. 'Many times', Schulman claimed, 'he swerved from his path, passed a distorted judgement, defiled men of repute, desecrated holy men, brought shame upon their honour, and cast aspersions on the memory of their holiness.'[244] Graetz's radical critical approach was unacceptable to the moderate maskil, for whom the Jewish past was a collection of 'sacred memories' of the nation. Schulman received complaints from Orthodox Jews, who believed that such a book should not be translated at all, for it contained sharply critical views and was not written from the vantage-point of religious faith. Schulman, most of whose books had found a place on the bookshelves of non-maskilic homes, was very sensitive to his reputation in the eyes of the Orthodox and responded quickly in order to allay their doubts. In an open letter printed in *Hatsefirah* he declared that such fears were unfounded; he intended to adapt Graetz's books to suit the tastes of the Orthodox reader as well, and would express his own personal rejection of 'free criticism'. Nonetheless, Schulman defended Graetz, justifying him and affirming his veracity, for he had never been one of the religious reformers and had always remained faithful 'to God and all that is sacred'. *Die Geschichte der Juden* was of supreme importance and its writer should therefore not be scorned. Nonetheless, Schulman promised

---

[241] Schulman, *Divrei yemei hayehudim*.

[242] Zitron, *The Makers*, ii. 160–1; J. Klausner, *History of Modern Hebrew Literature*, iii. 373–4; Schulman, *Luah ahiasaf*, 7 (1899), 322–4 (autobiographical note).

[243] Gurland, 'Hadashot sifriyot', 183.   [244] Zitron, *The Makers*, ii. 160.

to be careful in his translation and admitted that he intended to translate select-
ively: 'Heaven forbid that I should clothe the offspring of gentiles and deceitful
sons in the holy language . . . and in my translation as well, I have chosen the path
of faith, and have omitted all things based on the spirit of free criticism.'[245]

A comparison between the translation of Graetz's introduction to the first part
and the original reveals that Schulman produced a maskilic–traditional adaptation, with departures from the original and his own additions. In the introduction
to the first volume, which appeared only two years before Schulman's translation, Graetz grappled with the secret of the Jewish people's survival throughout
history, underscored the unique nature of Jewish history, and explained the Jews'
universal mission to disseminate monotheism, spirituality, and morality.[246] This
perception of history by no means contradicted Schulman's maskilic perception
and he could easily embrace it. He therefore translated the entire introduction,
but his revisions indicate that he attempted to add the religious significance of
history to Graetz's original. An example of this appears in the opening sentence, in
which Graetz presented the unique phenomenon of continuous Jewish existence
for 3,000 years. Schulman added: 'A people whose strength lies in its God will arise
and be inspired from the beginning of history and up to the present generation.'[247]
Whereas Graetz wrote about Jewish ideals and values, such as the idea of equality,
Schulman attributed these to God's teachings; and where Graetz described the
superiority of ancient Hebrew poetry, which celebrated sanctity rather than heroism, tragedies, and comedies, Schulman added that the purpose of Jewish poetry
was to express 'the exalted and holy spirit of God, to teach people to know the
Almighty'.[248] Graetz depicted the Jewish religion as spiritual, moral, and rational,
a faith that not only taught the principles of abstract faith but also inculcated
moral behaviour. This did not suffice for Schulman, who added the recognition
of God and the observance of His commandments as fundamental components of
religion. The Jews' mission, according to Schulman, included not only fulfilling
the prophets' vision but also knowing 'what God demands of them', according to
'the vision of the Torah'.[249] At the end of the introduction, too, Schulman added
his own conclusion to that of Graetz, who had asserted the antiquity of the Jewish
people and the continuity of its history; Schulman claimed that the secret of Jewish
survival lay in the preservation of the Torah: 'The Jewish people still maintain
their belief and faith in their God, and the trumpet call of His Torah, as in the
days of antiquity'.[250] Schulman could not reconcile himself to what he considered
the abandonment of Providence and the role of the Torah and the commandments in Jewish history, and he attempted to rectify this wrong. In Graetz's view,

[245] Schulman, 'Mikhtav galuy', 262–3.
[246] H. Graetz, *Geschichte der Juden*, vol. i, pp. xix–xxxv (this introduction was not translated into
Hebrew in the Rabinowitz edition). Cf. Schulman's introduction, *Divrei yemei hayehudim*, 3–26.
[247] H. Graetz, *Geschichte der Juden*, vol. i, p. xix; Schulman, *Divrei yemei hayehudim*, 3.
[248] Schulman, *Divrei yemei hayehudim*, p. xvii.   [249] Ibid., p. xx.   [250] Ibid., p. xxvi.

the Jewish religion expressed a divine idea and bore socio-legal significance. Schulman, on the other hand, continued to see religion first and foremost as the relationship between the Jew and his Creator, manifested primarily in the observance of the commandments. This difference in views had an enormous impact on the way in which Schulman translated Graetz.

Schulman's assertion that he chose to translate Graetz 'through faith' and the fact that he allowed himself to omit the radical conclusions derived from 'free criticism' incurred the wrath of Moses Leib Lilienblum (1848–1910). In an article Lilienblum wrote for *Hatsefirah* in 1876 he called upon the Winter Brothers to compel Schulman to translate all of Graetz.[251] Lilienblum praised the publishers for having initiated the translation; it was inconceivable that Jewish history should be available only in a language that most Jews could not read, and the translation would right this wrong to some extent. Lilienblum levelled severe criticism against Kaplan's translation, censuring his omission of the scholarly notes. In Russia there were surely many learned men more capable of investigating Graetz's sources than the German scholars. 'By what right', Lilienblum asked, 'did these publishers decide on their own to rob those learned in the Talmud of the possibility of investigating Graetz's words at their source and judging them?'[252] Furthermore, Lilienblum attacked Schulman's moderate translation, bluntly calling it nothing but a falsification:

Who granted him the right to omit those things he did not like? If he had had the ability to write a history book himself, as did the consummate scholars Rabbi Nahman Krochmal and Samuel Fuenn, and had omitted certain things in it, then he could have justified himself by saying that since he was of the Jewish faith, he was doing what he thought was right, for he was the one to decide what his book would contain; but he is translating, and who gave him the power to falsify his translation? . . . Or does this distinguished translator think that this translation was made only for Jewish children, like his books *Harel*, *Halikhot kedem*, and others, which he took care to write in a style acceptable to yeshiva students?[253]

This was the most aggressive challenge yet to Schulman's tendency to popularize. Lilienblum, a radical maskil, could not accept what he believed was dilettantism, an attempt to appeal to the Orthodox reader, and a frivolous approach to scientific Jewish historiography. In his article he requested that Graetz forbid Schulman from continuing his lies and his distortion of the German historian's book; and he suggested to Schulman that if he was truly concerned about the faith of the yeshiva

[251] Lilienblum, 'Al devar ha'atakat grets', 303, 312; id., *Complete Works*, ii. 117–18. Cf. a later review by Gordon of Schulman's translation of *Antiquities*, in which he accused Schulman of having introduced corrections into Josephus' text which rendered the translation fit for pious Jews but not for scholars of ancient history; J. L. Gordon, 'Bikoret sefarim'.

[252] Lilienblum, *Complete Works*, ii. 117. Lilienblum also protested about the high price of the book, which, at 2 roubles and 80 kopeks, was one of the most expensive on the list of books offered by Zuckerman.   [253] Ibid. 118.

students, he would do better to leave the work of translating Graetz's book to a more accurate translator. The Hebrew reader in eastern Europe deserved an undoctored version of this scientific study.

In contrast to Lilienblum, the young Nahum Sokolow (1859–1936) published an article supporting Schulman's right as a translator to adapt the book as he saw fit. A historian, Sokolow believed, is indeed obligated to recount what has occurred without advocacy or moralizing, but to fulfil this obligation is impossible. One cannot cut oneself off from world-views, and this fact also explains why history books vary. As long as he does not alter the facts, the translator is entitled to draw conclusions different from those of the writer. Graetz was a most important historian, but his weakness was his inability to control his bias and the integration of his opinions into his writings. Schulman, as his translator, would therefore do no wrong by eliminating Graetz's views, thereby saving his readers from radical opinions and also increasing their numbers, for some of them might have refrained entirely from purchasing the book in its original form.[254]

Even before this criticism was published, Schulman regretted having undertaken the translation. He found it particularly difficult to work with a printing-house so far away in Vienna. 'If I had known at the outset', Schulman wrote, 'that so many egregious errors would be made at the printing-house, I would not have gone near this burdensome work.'[255] Sokolow, looking back in 1884, placed the blame for the failure of Graetz's first translators on the immensity of the task, and proposed forming a group, 'a company of writers', that would prepare a Jewish history book in Hebrew. A single translator, Sokolow believed, could not bear the entire burden. This time, he proposed, Graetz's work should not be translated, but rather an original book, based on new research, should be written by a group of scholars in Russia.[256] Sokolow's proposal was never carried out, and a complete and accurate Hebrew translation of Graetz did not appear until fourteen years after Schulman's effort. This was by Saul Pinhas Rabinowitz (1845–1910), and began to appear in 1890, nine years before Schulman's death.[257]

The thousands of pages Kalman Schulman wrote represented the peak of the intensive literary activity that promulgated maskilic history on different levels

[254] Sokolow, 'Lamenatse'ah al shigayon'; Kressel's introd. to Sokolow, *Ketavim*, iii. 22. In 1905 Sokolow himself tried to translate Graetz's entire work, but he only published one part, entitled 'Toledot hayehudim'.   [255] Schulman 'Mikhtav galuy', 262–3.

[256] Sokolow, 'Kol mevaser', in id., *Ketavim*, iii. 573–81.

[257] Other unsuccessful attempts at translation included J. L. Kantor, 'Ben-Ami', in the monthly supplement to *Hayom* 1887 (Kantor received Graetz's permission to translate pt. 8 of his book in instalments in this supplement, but even this partial translation was never completed); A. D. Finkel (Warsaw, 1894) (the work was published in a series of pamphlets; all in all, pts. 4–5 of Graetz's book appeared). The translator claimed that he already had the complete translation in his possession, and that, unlike Rabinowitz, he had neither added nor omitted anything from the original. See Kressel, 'Saul Pinhas Rabinowitz'. An adaptation of Graetz's work in Yiddish by J. H. Lerner was published in Warsaw in 1897–8 (on Lerner, see Werses, *Haskalah and Shabbateanism*, 184).

among various social classes. By the early 1880s bookshops and bookshelves were filled with original historical studies in Hebrew, translations, textbooks, historical novels, and popular historical stories translated into Hebrew and Yiddish, written at a low level so that women and girls could acquire some historical information. New horizons were opened to the Jewish reader, helping him to fathom the complexities of international political events in contemporary Europe. He was exposed to information that enabled him to become acquainted with the national struggles in Italy and Germany, to become aware of European colonialism in Asia and Africa, to learn about the American Civil War, and to understand the historical background of the *Kulturkampf* taking place in Bismarck's Germany. As far as Jewish history was concerned, the maskilim attempted to convey to their readers their entire world-view, particularly their awareness of the crucial transition that had begun in the modern era and the critical role of enlightened absolutism; consciousness of the historical continuity and legitimacy of the Haskalah; and a condemnation of injustice, religious fanaticism, prejudice, and superstition. These messages were embedded in practically every historical work, whether it was a scholarly study, a translation, or a Yiddish story. While traditional history was content to print and reprint Josippon and the old chronicles or hagiographic stories of well-known rabbis, the maskilim gave a new look to the history shelves in Jewish libraries. It is true that the overwhelming majority of the books they contributed were not original but drew on German Jewish historiography and historical novels. However, from this time onwards a new corpus of historical works took its place alongside the traditional historical literature. Most of these new works were written in a flowing style that was very different from the discursive style of the traditional chronology and hagiography, and they lacked the traditional theological interpretation. A collection of secular historical information was created, even though it was often written from a religious point of view, as in Schulman's works. This was a detailed, usually factual, and occasionally dramatic history that could successfully compete with traditional chronicles and gradually alter conventional attitudes towards the past.

The picture sketched in this chapter, however, is far from complete. At the same time as maskilic history was being disseminated through the channels described here, an increasing number of voices in the maskilic camp itself were challenging the basic assumption of the Haskalah in general and of maskilic history in particular. Lilienblum's trenchant criticism of Schulman's mediocre and popular translation of Graetz was only one manifestation of the new mood of the Haskalah movement in Russia, and of the new approaches to history, which will be reconstructed in the next chapter.

FIVE

Maskilic History in Crisis

THE RADICAL HASKALAH: A LOSS OF OPTIMISM

THE intellectual world of Russian maskilim in the 1860s and 1870s was marked by internal change and revisionism that led them to question the basic premisses of the maskilic sense of the past. There was struggle and strife, not only between the traditional camp and the maskilic élite but also within the ranks of the standard-bearers of modernity in Jewish society. Rifts were evident among the maskilim, leading to the formation of distinct groups. The Haskalah's diversification during this period resulted from the emergence of a new generation of young maskilim, some of whom were sharply opposed to the older generation, including both its Orthodox members and the founding fathers of the Haskalah. These developments also occurred against the background of other changes during the reign of Alexander II in Russia: the government's policy of Russification, growing Russian cultural influence on Jewish intellectuals through the schools and the universities, and the penetration of concepts and ideals espoused by the radical Russian intelligentsia into the maskilic consciousness. Some of the maskilim had also begun to have second thoughts about the entire maskilic ideology, largely as a result of their frustration and disillusionment about an imminent solution to the 'Jewish question' in Russia and their scepticism about the chances of the Haskalah's overwhelming success within the general Jewish community.

The maskilim began to re-examine the fundamental concepts of the Haskalah and to ponder the role of the Hebrew language. Was there any need to continue to encourage it? What attitude should be adopted towards the Russian government? Had the time come to press their demands on the rabbis and to call for a new, updated *Shulḥan arukh*? Should they continue their extreme anti-hasidic approach? Ought they to continue to follow the tradition of the Berlin Haskalah? These and other questions became the focus of public debate in the 1860s and 1870s, leading the maskilim to the recognition that the very concept of the Haskalah was far from self-evident and monolithic. 'The word Haskalah', Moses Lilienblum wrote in 1872, 'has not yet been sufficiently defined.'[1]

In the 1860s the radical maskilim burst onto the stage of the Haskalah in Russia, provoking a protest from within the maskilic camp. They were young self-educated

---

[1] Lilienblum's letter to J. L. Gordon (1872), in Lilienblum, *Letters*, 133.

men in their twenties and thirties, natives of Lithuania and Belarus, employed in teaching and clerical positions. The most prominent members of this group were Abraham Uri Kovner (1842–1909), Abraham Jacob Paperna (1840–1919), Shalom Abramowitz (Mendele Mokher Seforim), Moses Lilienblum, Judah Leib Levin (1844–1925), Isaac Kaminer (1834–1901), Joseph Judah Lerner, Morris Vinchevsky (Benzion Novakhovichi, 1856–1932), and Aaron Samuel Liebermann (1845–80). The radical maskilim were not an organized group that worked together or co-ordinated their activities; in fact, they were not all active at the same time. When Liebermann, for example, began to organize a Jewish socialist group in the 1870s, Kovner and Paperna were no longer engaged in literary criticism. Nor was it an ideologically homogeneous group: Paperna, for instance, hardly ever digressed from his line of moderate and positivist literary criticism, while Kovner, Abramowitz, and Lilienblum developed a strongly positivist approach to all spheres of Jewish life. Levin, Vinchevsky, and Liebermann, on the other hand, combined their positivism with a socialist ideology and concepts borrowed from the doctrine of historical materialism. Nonetheless, these young men had enough in common to justify regarding them as a sub-group within the wider circle of maskilim.[2] They were all Hebrew writers who lived and worked within their Jewish environment. This fact, in addition to their being self-educated and hence 'an intelligentsia without diplomas', like the moderate maskilim and the members of the older generation, set the radical maskilim apart from the Russian Jewish intelligentsia that was emerging at the same time.[3] They all followed a similar path from the traditional world through the moderate Haskalah until they were exposed, generally in large cities such as Kiev or Odessa, to the fashionable intellectual circles of Russia. Levin, for example underwent a radical transformation after reading the works of Dimitri Pisarev (1840–68), an influential literary critic, in Kiev in 1872. He then went on to read literary criticism by Belinsky (1811–48) and to learn about economics and sociology from the writings of Karl Marx, Adam Smith, Charles Darwin, Herbert Spencer, and the positivist British historian Henry Thomas Buckle.[4] Pisarev's radical criticism also influenced the young Abramowitz, and like Levin, Lilienblum also moved from a time of bitter crisis, when he became disillusioned with the Haskalah, to a phase of belief in the new radicalism, under the influence of the book *What is to be Done?*, by Nikolai Chernyshevski (1828–89). Kovner had been exposed to similar Russian literature in the early 1860s, when he stayed in Kiev with his brother Saul, then a medical student at the university.[5]

---

[2] Bartal, 'Radical Enlightenment', 328–39. J. Frankel, *Prophecy and Politics*, 28–48.

[3] Tcherikower, *Jews in Time of Revolution*, 189. On the radical stream, see J. Klausner, *History of Modern Hebrew Literature*, iv. 139–89.

[4] J. L. Levin, *Zikhronot vehegyonot*, 53–67. Cf. the autobiography of E. Ben-Yehuda, *A Dream Come True*, 60–4.

[5] J. Klausner, *History of Modern Hebrew Literature*, iii. 378–9; iv. 16; Lilienblum, *Autobiographical Writings*, i. 26–39 (introd. by Breiman); id., 'Ḥatot ne'urim' (1876), ibid. ii. 72–3; id., *Letters*, 129–30.

The fact that these young maskilim were regarded by moderate maskilim as nihilists, arrogant youths advocating a destructive ideology, religious apostasy, social anarchy, and political revolution, was another reason they were lumped together as a cohesive group and seen by their opponents as likely to bring chaos into the world.[6]

This radical stream began by criticizing the literature of the Haskalah. Among the first to do so were Abramowitz, who in 1860 attacked Eliezer Zweifel, a classic representative of the moderate Haskalah, with the aim of shattering the complacency of the 'old generation', and Abraham Uri Kovner, an even harsher critic, who claimed that the works of the Haskalah authors were cut off from the spirit of the time and the real problems of the people.[7] The yardstick Kovner used in judging the writers of his generation was whether their work truly benefited Jewish life; he reached the conclusion that most of them failed to meet this criterion and were tainted with idealism and vacuity. 'Don't look heavenward,' Kovner insisted, 'for we are here on the earth; let them write things that concern the earthly life of the Jews.'[8] The mission of the Haskalah, the radicals argued, was to inject vitality into Jewish life, acting as a counterweight to the traditional leadership that was suffocating it. Another flaw of Hebrew literature, in Kovner's view, was that it revered authoritative sources from the past. Each generation had to confront the problems of its time and solve them in its own way; dependence on 'authorities' enslaved all thought and degraded creativity: 'If we are too respectful of documents and authorities and fear to inveigh against them publicly in the city square, then we will never take so much as one step forward.'[9] Man must be guided by free will—the fundamental idea of Russian radicalism. In Levin's words, 'Happy is the man with a strong free will; it will not give way and he will live according to it. The light of life is sown for him in full.'[10] The radicals believed that Jewish culture was permeated with an excess of spirituality, which they wished to replace with the natural sciences. The education of a youngster pursuing 'true enlightenment' should concentrate on the natural sciences, the handmaiden of real life.[11] The nineteenth-century ideal of science and the realism and positivism they learned from Russian radicalism made these young maskilim aware of the centrality of social and economic issues, and they tended to identify with the downtrodden Jewish masses. Their impassioned cry was: 'Give the people bread! Let them breathe

---

[6] Gottlober, *Igeret tsa'ar ba'alei ḥayim*; id., '13 mikhtavim', 419–22; editorial in *Hamagid*, 19 (1875), no. 37; editorial in *Hakarmel haḥodshi*, 3 (1876), 393–6; Liebermann, *Katavot uma'amarim*, 147–54.

[7] Abramowitz, *Mishpat shalom*, 9–46; id., Reshimot letoldotai', 4; A. U. Kovner, 'Ḥeker davar'. Cf. Miron, *From Romance to the Novel*, 246–8.

[8] A. U. Kovner, 'Ḥeker davar', 45; id., 'Ruaḥ ḥayim', 183–6.

[9] A. U. Kovner, 'Ḥeker davar', 37; Abramowitz, *Ein mishpat*, 7–10. The quotation is from one of the protagonists in Braudes' novel *Hadat vehaḥatim*, i. 229, 280–1. Cf. Paperna, *Collected Writings*, 415.   [10] J. L. Levin, 'Torat haḥayim', 626–9.

[11] Lilienblum, 'Mahi haskalah', 116; Abramowitz, *Toledot hateva*.

the air of life! Soothe the emotions of our brothers and sisters!',[12] and they fervently demanded new objectives and a new agenda for the Haskalah.

As far as the moderate maskilim were concerned, radicalism posed a dangerous threat and was a total departure from the Haskalah. The exposure of Jewish socialists in Vilna and the threats levelled by the regime against the revolutionaries also convinced the moderate maskilim that this 'dreadful nihilism' was far more dangerous than the 'fanaticism' of the enemies of the Haskalah.[13] 'Enlightenment without faith and the fear of God bears the seeds of death. Keep these destructive maskilim away from your homes lest they inject their venom into the spirit of your offspring', warned the editor of *Hamagid* in 1875, even explicitly naming Kovner and Lilienblum as the men responsible for disseminating harmful ideas.[14] However, while the radicals did challenge the moderate Haskalah and discarded some of the basic principles that it had formulated at the end of the eighteenth century, they still remained maskilim, even when their criticism was at its harshest. One of their aims was to move the Haskalah in Russia onto new tracks which would be more appropriate to the spirit of the time, as well as to 'save' it from what they viewed as its certain demise, thus enabling it to exist for another generation. This is the spirit in which Kovner's despairing call can be understood: 'Autodidacts and teachers, if you want to gain the love of the younger generation and of your pupils, walk together with them in the spirit of the time; do not attempt to fetter that spirit, which will cleave mountains and shatter rocks, for your efforts will be in vain.'[15]

One of the major areas in which the radical maskilim proposed an alternative to the moderate Haskalah was historical consciousness. At first glance, the radical Haskalah might appear to be a anti-historical stream, whose representatives vigorously attacked the traditional maskilic preoccupation with history and the entire range of Jewish studies.[16] One of the sharpest of these attacks was that levelled by Kovner against Luzzatto, whom he denounced as a supremely negative example of a sterile and ineffectual scholar. Kovner's positivist concepts and his reverence for science led him to conclude that natural scientists and economists stood on the highest rung of science, for their research made a direct and concrete contribution to human life. Only they were capable of providing man with the tools

[12] Vinchevsky, 'Panim ḥadashot', 25–6. The poetry of the physician and maskil Dr Isaac Kaminer, written during the 1860s and 1870s, dealt almost exclusively with social and economic themes: see Kaminer, *Shirei yitsḥak kaminer*; on Kaminer, see J. Klausner, *History of Modern Hebrew Literature*, vi. 208–42). See also Lilienblum, 'Tikun medini', 372–3.

[13] Nihilism in Russia has been defined as 'An intellectual movement which flourished in Russia in the 1860s, and which expressed itself in a revulsion against tyranny of authority, a rejection of the obligations of traditional morality and questioning of every general principle and ideal value, all in the name of the sovereign individual' (*Encyclopaedia of the Social Sciences*, ed. D. Sills, xi. 337–78). See also Pipes, *Russia under the Old Regime*.

[14] *Hamagid*, 19 (1875), no. 37. See also *Hakarmel haḥodshi*, 3 (1876), 393–6.

[15] A. U. Kovner, *Ketavim*, 214.

[16] See Werses, 'The Relationship between Belletristic Literature and Jewish Wissenschaft', 593–8.

to conquer nature and subjugate it for his own benefit; and only they were capable of bringing about the utopia in which Kovner believed: universal peace and happiness, to be achieved by the triumph of science. In a classification of various types of scholar according to these criteria, the 'researchers of antiquity' were assigned a relatively low status. Nonetheless, Kovner did not entirely negate the value of study of the past and acknowledged the importance of exposing the secret pages of history, as well as the need to use philology as an effective tool in understanding the past. However, he stipulated that the historian and the philologist must know how to endow their scholarship with the breath of life and to ensure that it would be of some real benefit. He described those archaeologists and philologists engaged in research for its own sake as 'circus acrobats', misleading the masses and conducting studies that had no purpose or benefit. In his opinion, Luzzatto was at a midpoint: he had not yet descended to the lowest stage, that of a philologist–acrobat, but neither had he made proper use of his talents. With the exception of several important and useful projects, such as his translation of the Bible into Italian, Kovner did not find any 'breath of life' in Luzzatto's work.[17]

In the 1870s the radical maskilim adopted an even more extreme attitude towards historical research than had Kovner. The most outspoken was Lilienblum, who almost totally repudiated historical–philological studies, particularly those conducted by Jews. Contrasting research with the real, everyday needs of Jewish society, he insisted that the maskilim must—at least temporarily—turn all their energies to an attempt to solve earthly problems:

Is this the time for writers to engage in such scholarly pursuits as will advance erudition and history in general, when the majority of our people lives in the heavens and it is up to us to bring them down to earth, to reawaken them, and to revive their feelings? Most Jews need bread, a sense of life, a knowledge of the necessities—while most of our writers forget these wretched folk and are concerned only with science and history, and with lofty and abstract literature.[18]

Lilienblum regarded a preoccupation with history as a luxury that the Jews in their present state could ill afford. The nations of Europe could lavish vast funds on archaeological excavations and historical research, but the Jews of Russia urgently needed profound improvements in their daily lives. Before attention was paid to academic pursuits that were of no use in daily life, the economic existence of the people should be addressed. 'The British have the right', Lilienblum said, 'to study antiquity, because the British people have a true knowledge of life and have many authors who engage in all spheres of science, crafts, and medicine, not only poetry and romances.' It was reasonable to find thirty historians among a hundred writers, but the Haskalah presented an anomaly in which nearly all the writers were engaged in studying ancient history. Only when times were better

[17] A. U. Kovner, 'Ruaḥ mishpat', 167–76.
[18] Lilienblum, 'Al ḥakirat kadmoniyot', 110–12.

could the maskilim turn to the past, but here and now history sounded like an uplifting melody being played to men hungry for bread. He compared maskilim engaged
in the study of history to crabs walking backwards, indifferent to the present.[19]

Levin pursued Lilienblum's more radical line, also contrasting the study of
antiquity and real life. 'You, the enlightened, be of some benefit!', he cried, demanding that the maskilim write 'books of life' that would teach the Jews how to
live and earn their livelihood, rather than books of history.[20] In a satirical vein,
Abramowitz, in his novel *Susati* (My Mare) mocked the study of history, which
was required for students preparing for the admission examinations to the Russian gymnasium: a history replete with 'nonsense, the quarrels and wars that men
wage against one another, wounding and killing each other from the earliest times
to the present, and the need to remember the dates and places where all of this
occurred'. And 'such things', he wrote scornfully, 'they call history'.[21] Kaminer
scoffed at the 'new maskil', whose entire knowledge of history added up to little
more than juicy gossip, such as 'the empty chatter about famous women, whom
they really loved and whom they were just deceiving. The many mistresses of
Louis XIV, all the modest or brazen beauties, the unmarried and the married . . .
and he is privy to all their secrets.'[22]

The radical maskilim's low opinion of what they regarded as an excessive preoccupation with history was also linked to their demand that the maskilim cut
themselves off from the authority of the past and grapple with the present and its
problems. 'Why have they wandered so far into past times, where they seek meaning, rather than turning their attention to present-day life?', Kovner asked, for life
in the present was rich enough for them to find material for literature and poetry
without having to 'take flight to the days of yore'.[23] The radicals argued that the
young generation was entitled to cast off the burden of the past and to break out
of its stagnation. It was their destiny to be the 'harbingers of times to come' and to
build 'the future upon the ruins of the past'.[24] Needless to say, for the radical
socialist maskilim, led by Aaron Liebermann, belief in a break between the present and the past was a fundamental plank in their ideology, as is evident from
Liebermann's manifesto *El shelomei baḥurei yisra'el* (For the Welfare of the Young
Men of Israel): 'Cast off the entire past and forge a link with the working people and
those who love them; only they will inherit the future.'[25]

[19] Lilienblum, 'Kahal refa'im', 442–3. When in 1868 the maskilim of Kovno suggested to Lilienblum, who had run away from Wilkomir, that he read oriental studies at the university, he declined
their offer, stating that philosophy could not provide him with spiritual or material sustenance and
he ought rather to engage in science (Lilienblum, 'Ḥatot ne'urim', in *Collected Writings*, ii. 170).

[20] J. L. Levin, 'Eshmerah lepi maḥsom', 136.

[21] Abramowitz, *Susati*, 307–49 (the first version in Yiddish: *Di kliatzhe* (Vilna, 1872)).

[22] Kaminer, 'Dror yikra', 29–39.

[23] A. U. Kovner, 'Shenei nevi'im mitnabim besignon eḥad', 227.

[24] Lerner, *Doresh el hametim*, 5–6.

[25] Liebermann, *El shelomei baḥurei yisra'el*. See also J. Klausner, *History of Modern Hebrew Literature*,
vi. 254–6.

Those maskilim who did not identify with the radical stream were aware of this amalgam of criticism of the study of history and of the anti-historical view that characterized the radicals. The topic came up, for example, in a mini-polemic conducted in the pages of *Hakarmel* between Judah Leib Kantor and the acting editor, Hayim Leib Markon (1848–1909), over how much space should be allotted to 're-search into antiquity' in the Hebrew press. Kantor stated that, while he opposed too intensive a preoccupation with history, particularly since readers sought more interesting material, he did not hold historians in low esteem, for, in his view, they were no less important than scholars in the natural sciences. 'Anyone desiring to gain knowledge in the present and the future must know and understand the past', Kantor wrote, expressing his antipathy to the anti-historical stream:

Do not believe, sir, that I speak here in the name of those yelling at the top of their voices, 'Bring us clear information, bring us the knowledge of nature, bring us physics and chemistry, technology, physiology, geology, economics; leave the past and look only at the present; the past is dead and gone from the land and we have naught to do with it; our faces are turned only to the present and the future.[26]

Kantor believed the radical stream was a passing fad, although he felt the radical maskilim were correct on one point: there were many studies that contributed nothing to the overall knowledge of universal history and amounted to no more than 'historical sermons'. Markon replied at length to this point, arguing that owing to the special character of Jewish history—its length, its geographical dispersion, and its insubstantial historiography—Jewish studies ought not to omit a single detail.[27]

Was the radical Haskalah really an anti-historical trend that negated the past and its study and utterly rejected 'history'? A careful perusal of their writing shows this was not the case. They did indeed reject any history, philology, and archaeology that had an antiquarian orientation in dealing with the past; they had no interest in mythological exploits and political and military events; they scoffed at anecdotes and were opposed to conciliatory maskilic history of the type written by Kalman Schulman.[28] However, the radicals formulated their own historical concepts and constructed a new picture of the past, inspired by contemporary positivist and materialist trends in historiography and European historical thought. Having challenged maskilic history, the radicals attempted to offer their own alternative.

The scientific ideal, which promised the demystification of the world and the possibility of explaining every phenomenon scientifically, also had an impact on nineteenth-century historiography, and empirical, positivist, and deterministic explanations of history were common. Intense economic activity, industrialization,

[26] Kantor, 'Mikhtav el ha'ozer beharedaktsion', 66–70.

[27] Markon, 'Ma'aneh lekantor', 224–32.

[28] See Liebermann's letter from St Petersburg (1870): 'Schulman's book and his literary style are not at all pleasing to me, in particular in *Divrei hayamim*, in which he hardly knew his left hand from his right' (in Karol, *The First Centenary of Aaron Liebermann*, 17).

and the growing influence of the masses also led to a search for economic factors in history, and greater attention than in the past was paid to the role of the proletariat in history. The renowned positivist philosopher Auguste Comte (1798– 1857) believed that history was moving towards the positivist age, in which a scientific élite would organize human life according to empirically formulated laws, and that every historical event must be examined according to general scientific laws.[29] The radical maskilim in Russia drew their positivist concepts not directly from Comte but from Henry Thomas Buckle, a British historian who was among his followers. Both parts of Buckle's book *History of Civilization in England* (1856, 1861) were translated into Russian, German, and other languages, and became very popular along the Russian intelligentsia and the maskilim.[30] History, according to Buckle, was subject to universal laws. It was scientific, had no metaphysical dimension, expressed free will, and was devoid of any theology. Statistics determined the laws of society, and enabled the prediction of its future development. Buckle held that the purpose of scientific historical writing was to examine the interaction between nature and man, and to determine physical and mental laws. He asserted that history must be studied using methods similar to those of the natural sciences, in order to reveal its statistical constancy. Scientific laws, not Providence, moved the wheels of history. Using his reason, man was capable of attaining so high a degree of control over nature that he could become increasingly independent of it. Moreover, the accumulation of scientific knowledge and understanding was the basis for human progress.[31]

Positivist history also led to the idea of history being governed by physiological and biological laws and to materialist history. John William Draper (1811–82), a British scientist who was also a historian, attempted to prove in his book *A History of the Intellectual Development of Europe* (1861) that there was a physiological explanation for every historical event, and that the human intellect was also subject to this natural law. Draper, who was strongly influenced by Darwin, explained the theory of historical stages not only as a speculative historical–philosophical periodization but as a scientific biological method. Every nation and every religion, he asserted, must be examined according to its biological age and the degree of its biological development. He made no effort to conceal the conflict between religion and science, and held that the rise of the age of science would inevitably lead to the decline of religion. From now on, he claimed, it would be science that would provide all the answers, explanations, and truths, and faith would have no place in the scheme of things. Other scientist–historians, the most popular of whom in Russia were J. Moleschott of Heidelberg and Ludwig Büchner (1824–99) of Tübingen, also proposed materialist, atheist, and Darwinist concepts of history, which asserted that all the processes of life and society could be explained according

---

[29] Breisach, *Historiography*, 269–75; Chadwick, *The Secularization of the European Mind*, chs. 7–8.
[30] See Y. Shavit, 'The Works of H. T. Buckle', 401–12.
[31] Gardiner, *Theories of History*, 109–15.

to the laws of chemistry and physics. Draper's book was one of the works that influenced Judah Leib Levin and helped him to construct his concept of history as a radical maskil. Levin was also the first to try his hand at translating Marx's *Das Kapital* into Hebrew. Marx's historical materialism, which placed economic activity at the centre of historical dynamics, also had an effect on the radical maskilim's consciousness of the past. Aaron Liebermann, the radical maskil and socialist, translated the *Communist Manifesto* into Hebrew.[32]

During the reign of Alexander II the Russian intelligentsia took a sharp turn from idealism to positivism and realism, and began to ask 'What is to be done?'— the very phrase Chernyshevski had used as a title for his book. Russian intellectuals read Moleschott's and Büchner's books, and were inspired by them to formulate materialistic world-views. Ludwig Feuerbach (1809–72) explained that the idea of God was nothing more than a projection of human desires, Buckle provided a key to an understanding of society and history, and the materialists depicted a world composed solely of matter. The literary critics Pisarev and Nikolai Dobrolyubov (1836–61) assigned primacy to the material manifestations of life and nature and derided artistic aesthetics. In their opinion, art played merely a social role. Pisarev, who wrote popular articles on the natural sciences, famously claimed that a pair of shoes had greater value than all of Shakespeare's plays. The Russian populists embraced the notion that the class war was dominant in history, and revolutionary democrats of all types believed that Russia's future was not predetermined, but that it could take its destiny into its own hands and overcome its backwardness. The model that radical Russian authors presented as a challenge to enlightened Russian youth was that of a radical, rationalist young person, a utilitarian, an atheist, and a realist, who believed in science and was not restrained by social and family authority, but was solely concerned with issues of present-day life and totally committed to act for the benefit of the common people.[33]

It was in this context that the radical maskilic trend emerged. The radicals pressed for true history, not in the sense of the fruit of archaeological or philological research but in the positivist sense of scientific fact and concrete reality. Lilienblum, who had inveighed against the excessive interest in history, under the influence of Buckle, Pisarev, and others, believed that it was possible to write history that merited inclusion in the body of 'absolute knowledge' that was of practical benefit. This 'absolute knowledge', he wrote in his autobiography *Ḥatot ne'urim* (Sins of Youth), is 'nothing other than a knowledge of nature and reality and the events of history with all their causes, which gave rise in turn to the events that occurred after them'.[34] This true and realistic approach would reveal a starkly terrible past: a succession of horrendous atrocities, religious fanaticism, senseless bloodshed, the cruelty of the Inquisition, slavery, the pursuit of power, the miscarriage of justice, and mendacity.[35]

[32] J. L. Levin, *Zikhronot vehegyonot*, 53–67; Weinryb, 'A. S. Lieberman', 317–48.

[33] Walicki, *A History of Russian Thought*, 183–221; I. Berlin, *Russian Thinkers*.

[34] Lilienblum, 'Ḥatot ne'urim', in *Collected Writings*, ii. 111.   [35] Id., 'Olam hatohu', 49–109.

Here this radical maskil, in his pessimistic view of the past, departed from mask-ilic history, which, although it had not ignored the dark moments in history and had vigorously denounced them, had nonetheless tried to emphasize the struggle of the 'forces of light' in each and every historical stage, in the optimistic belief that reason would triumph.

The radical maskilim saw the course of history as a sequence of revolutions: the rebellion of the new generation against the old, casting out the old to make room for the new. But not every revolt brought progress in its wake. The radicals thought that only momentous changes in the natural sciences were progressive, while they viewed changes in other fields as merely the substitution of 'one folly for another'.[36] They also continued to view the modern era as a very significant historical turning-point and believed in contemporary human progress. However, they saw the great good of the 'modern era' only in the scientific and technological discoveries of the time. The period was gauged in positivist, rather than political, moral, or philo-sophical terms. The historical heroes who figured in their historical past were no longer benevolent kings, or philosophers and writers, but rather natural scientists, explorers, and inventors. Civilization would not have evolved without Newton, Copernicus, and Columbus, men who had dared to rebel against past authority, to invent new methods, and open unknown horizons, argued Abraham Paperna.[37] Inspired by Buckle's historical analysis, the radicals believed that, unlike the earliest generations, when man was timid and powerless in the face of nature, contempor-ary man was acquiring the ability to control nature through science.[38]

Kovner, undoubtedly the leading figure among the radicals in the 1860s, grappled with the world-view, contemporary reality, and past of traditional Jewish society and tried to comprehend why its members were finding it so difficult to accept the 'modern era' as a historical turning-point. Of course, he reasoned, anyone who had been brought up to disdain real life and to improve only his spirit and his soul could not find any meaning or benefit in the discovery of America, in Copernicus' astronomical method, in Newton's law of gravity, in Gutenberg's printing press, or in the invention of the railway, the telegraph, the hot-air balloon, or machines. For such a person, *tsadikim* concerned with eternal life carried greater significance than either Shakespeare or Buckle.[39] The need to introduce an awareness of the positive features of the 'modern era' thus became an element common to the ideolo-gies of both the moderate and the radical maskilim. However, while the moderates characterized the modern era as a time of political, religious, and ideological changes, the radicals measured it by scientific progress that provided material benefit.

The world-view of the radical Haskalah was also expressed in historical explana-tions of a new type. Rationalistic and moralistic explanations, based on man's free choice of truth and good, gave way to the determinism of natural laws. In 1869

[36] Paperna, 'Kankan hadash male yashan' (1867), 9–10.   [37] Ibid. 83–4.
[38] Bazilevski, *Divrei binah o ha'emunah*, vol. ii; Abramowitz, 'Mah anu', 464–85, 526–34.
[39] A. U. Kovner, 'Ru'ah hayim', 186.

Moses Bazilevski of Kiev translated into Hebrew the chapter from Buckle's book dealing with the laws of history, as an illustration of his principal claim that there was no contradiction between the new scientific theories and the Jewish faith.[40] Bazilevski regarded Buckle's *History of Civilization in England* as the most important book written in his generation and wanted to clear Buckle of the charge of materialism. In his opinion, Buckle had taken a moderate position in the dispute between those advocating free will and those favouring determinism and natural laws. Man, according to Buckle, was not a passive pawn in the hands of materialistic factors but was subject to the laws of statistics: 'Statistical facts utterly contradict the materialists and clearly demonstrate the existence of a spiritual dimension which governs man and limits him.' However, he did admit that with regard to man as a part of society, his behaviour was determined, and was subject to the state of his society and the natural conditions of his location. In any event, whether historical laws were spiritual or materialistic, in the final analysis, laws and scientific formulations were the determining factors.[41]

Most of the radical maskilim adhered, either entirely or partly, to concepts of historical determinism and materialist natural laws. Kovner, accepting the premiss that the action of nature was 'the keystone of everything that happens to every nation, in all generations', held that climate determined the cultural level of each nation. Hence, the Enlightenment, which developed primarily in temperate climates, fared particularly well in England—another notion he derived directly from Buckle.[42] Lilienblum, who also adopted these notions, believed that the characteristic traits of nations were shaped by nature and circumstances. The propensity for imaginativeness, for example, which he believed characterized the Jews, could be explained by the natural landscape of Asia, which aroused the imagination.[43] Thus the true and absolute knowledge that he called for had to emphasize the laws of history:

The laws of history that govern the lives of human beings have the very same importance as the laws of nature acting upon the various bodies, or in other words: the laws of history for humans who are not savages like prehistoric man are like the laws of physics operating on animals, which we say are governed by the laws of nature. Thus we must say that the laws of history constitute the nature governing man and that part of his essence in which he surpasses the simple forms of life.[44]

Lilienblum was not arguing that the laws of history are necessarily physical laws (as Draper had claimed, for example), but he did distinguish between the natural laws of physics, that govern man's animal side, and the natural laws of history, that govern his human side. He did not expand on this issue, nor did he specify to which laws of history he was referring.

[40] Bazilevski, *Divrei binah o ha'emunah*.

[41] Ibid. vi. 141–64: 'Review of the Great Scholar Buckle's Study of the Laws and Processes of the History of Mankind' (Heb.).   [42] A. U. Kovner, 'Heker davar', 57–72.

[43] Lilienblum, 'Olam hatohu', 49–109.   [44] Lilienblum, *Autobiographical Writings*, ii. 172.

For the socialist Vinchevsky, the issue was far simpler. He accepted the deterministic concept in its entirety, as well as its Darwinist aspect. In his view, the law
of inevitability governed all of creation, and men actually had no freedom of
choice at all. Man's imagined freedom was the result of his innate tendencies and
the 'course of blood and brain' that predetermined everything.[45] Abramowitz cited
a natural historical law that justified the European imperialism and colonialism of
the time: while the basic trait of wild and ignorant peoples was an absence of movement, enlightened peoples were characterized by constant movement. Hence 'every
nation which, through its intellectual movement, has attained a highly esteemed
level of perfection will go far from its own land, or will send from within its midst
many of its own members to the ends of the earth to establish colonies'. Having
accepted this historical law, Abramowitz viewed colonialism as a decree of nature
and the expression of a universal law which linked internal, mental dynamics to external, political dynamics. He explained that only the intervention of enlightened
peoples among the ignorant, whether by means of wars or trade relations, would
enable the latter to develop. In his view, the Jewish exile, which followed the completion of the Jews' perfection through their monotheistic faith, exemplified the
same historical law.[46]

Radical maskilic history explored new directions, presenting a pantheon of
heroes of a new type and formulating historical schemas that had not previously
been a part of the maskilic sense of the past. Kovner added a scientific essay entitled 'For how many Years has Man Existed on the Earth?' to his 'Ḥeker davar'
(An Inquiry, 1865). Here, for the first time, he looked far back into the past to the
prehistoric era. Unless we are aware of that era, he argued, we will be incapable of
comprehending our true place in the universe and in time. The essay stated that
geological and archaeological research had shown that humans had lived on the
earth for more than 100,000 years. The biblically based date of Creation thus did
not meet the test of scientific research. Humans had lived on the earth for a very
long time before the Flood and had developed gradually from a savage to an
enlightened state. Kovner wished to inform Hebrew readers about the ice age, the
evolutionary changes that animals had undergone, and the warming of the outer
crust of the earth, and to provide them with evidence of the existence of the world
and man for hundreds and thousands of years.[47]

The radicals searched through history to find heroes who would exemplify the
ideals of the radical Haskalah. For example, Vinchevsky's greatest hero was Ludwig
Börne (1786–1837), the champion of liberalism, whom he regarded as one of the
'pioneers' of history, in the vanguard of his generation: 'deeply concerned, daunt-
less men, fighting vigorously against all those who love the old and the obsolete'.[48]
The talmudic sage Elisha ben Avuyah, as Lilienblum depicted him, was also seen

[45] Vinchevsky, 'Al ha'ovna'im', 307–8, 324.   [46] Abramowitz, 'Mah anu'.
[47] Kovner, 'Ḥeker davar'. Criticism of Kovner's new geological theory was voiced by Habavly,
Ma'amar shoresh davar, 9–10.   [48] Vinchevsky, 'Toledot ludvig barnea', 47, 72–5, 92–5.

as a radical maskil in every sense, sensitive to social issues and steadfastly rebelling against authority and tradition. Elisha became a heretic because he dared to live according to new, true views, and Lilienblum credited him with social and economic convictions close to those of socialist dogma.[49] Liebermann published 'Toledot dr. yonah ya'akobi umife'alotav' (The Biography of Dr Johann Jacoby and his Wondrous Deeds), depicting a new heroic figure: a Jew from Königsberg who was active in the 1848 revolutions, advocated social reform, combined German social-democratic politics and a universal Jewish identity in his own life, and for whom 'the entire human species was his people and the whole earth his country'. This was a man who, in Lilienblum's eyes, was worthy of admiration and emulation.[50]

Liebermann stood out among the radicals thanks to his solid materialistic concept of history and his acceptance of Marx's historical theories as well as of clearly Darwinist ideas. 'The question of the knife and the fork', as he called it, meaning the problem of providing the masses with food, was for him the fundamental issue in the life of every society. The 'question of a livelihood' was 'the key to a solution of all life's riddles', and, in his view, a knowledge of the economic mechanism that covertly drives the overt 'course of the world' should provide an explanation for history as well as the path taken by society in the present.[51] In the war of survival waged throughout history, the strong enslaved those weaker than them, and 'wealth and poverty are the pivot around which all social life revolves'.[52] Following in Liebermann's footsteps, Vinchevsky espoused a historical theory based on that of Marx. All historians who had tried to explain global events by citing ideological causes were totally mistaken; it was not these ideas that drove history, Vinchevsky argued, but only 'the question of the workers, only the desire for life inborn in the heart of every man . . . only they move the wheels of history'. As examples, he cited the revolts of slaves in ancient times, the civil war in Rome, and the Peasants' Revolt in sixteenth-century Germany, all of which were caused by economic and class conflicts, the exploitation of labour, and economic enslavement.[53]

In a series of articles which Liebermann published in his short-lived Hebrew socialist periodical Ha'emet (The Truth), he attempted to formulate his historical theory in an orderly manner, in particular to find some basis for its roots and to point to harbingers of the socialist idea. Once again, Liebermann described 'the universal struggle for survival' as the 'law governing all of history, from inanimate objects and plant life to animate objects and humans', and regarded the 'economic question' as the supreme historical factor. However, he went on to say, man, unlike other creatures in nature, had understood that his existence within nature could

---

[49] Lilienblum, 'Mishnat elishah ben avuyah', 76, 96–9, 108–13, 125.
[50] Liebermann, 'Toledot dr. yonah ya'akobi', 9–12.
[51] Id., 'Petiḥah leshe'elat hasakin vehamazleg', 33–40.
[52] Id., 'Mikhtavim vereshimot', 80, 92.   [53] Vinchevsky, 'She'elat hapo'alim', 3–7.

only be assured if he maintained a social order in which brotherhood and friendship prevailed. This was the strategy of man's struggle for survival, and in order to ensure it, men had fought throughout history for the sake of ideals aimed at establishing universal brotherhood. Unfortunately, history portrayed a sorry picture of fierce struggles for lofty ideals which were waged in vain. Religious wars, colonialism and the enslavement of the blacks, the Inquisition, and the witch trials were among the examples Liebermann cited to demonstrate events on the bloody and agonizing stage of history. The French Revolution and the 1848 revolutions had brought certain reforms and more freedom and equality, but man was still far from achieving happiness. As long as the problem of poverty remained unsolved, as long as there were economic problems, the barrier to the attainment of human brotherhood would not be torn down, nor would the hardships of the battle of survival come to an end.[54]

Liebermann and Vinchevsky, with their socialist approach and their closeness to Marx and materialism, were relatively isolated among the radical maskilim. This is evident, for example, from Lilienblum's criticism at the end of the 1870s. He took pains to emphasize his objection to materialism: 'I have never read the works of Marx and Ferdinand Lassalle [1825–64], and I certainly would not follow in their footsteps', Lilienblum declared. As a radical maskil, he made sure that there was a clear boundary separating him, as a 'realist', from the socialists and materialists. He also took them to task for their utopian–messianic ideas: in aspiring to reach the seventh millennium, when all men would be virtuous and united and no social classes nor tyranny would remain, they were forgetting the sixth millennium, the actual present whose urgent problems needed to be addressed today. The socialists, in his opinion, stood outside their own time, remote from their own generation; their theories were unrealistic and hence of no use in everyday life: 'It is not for the members of our generation; hence, I whose range of vision is but short . . . will not look towards the seventh millennium but at the time in which I live.'[55]

The radical maskilim had a different view of their own times. In the 1870s, even before the pogroms in Russia in the 1880s, the optimistic concept of the 'modern era', which had been a basic element in the ideology and consciousness of the Haskalah for nearly a century, from its origins in Germany to the time of Kalman Schulman and his colleagues in Russia,[56] was already fading from the thoughts of the radical maskilim. The worsening economic situation of Russian Jewry, especially in Lithuania, from the end of the 1860s onwards, the Odessa pogroms of 1871, and a growing sensitivity to social problems all undermined the maskilic image of the present as an advanced stage in a progressive process. By the mid-1860 Kovner

[54] Liebermann, 'Milḥemet hayekum', 17–21. See also id., 'Hitpatḥut ḥayei haḥevrah', 25–31; id., 'Shitat makiaveli', 46–50; id. 'Letoledot ha'utopiyot', 1–36.

[55] Lilienblum, 'Teshuvah meshuleshet', 305–6; id., 'Al ḥet', 385; id., *Autobiographical Writings*, iii. 198–200.   [56] Zipperstein, *The Jews of Odessa*, 114–19, 139–50.

had already questioned the maskilim's belief that Russia had 'adopted the virtues of justice, and would henceforth rule with fairness and probity', and that within Russia 'wisdom had raised its head and expelled all injustice'. Kovner decried this belief not only as a reflection of naïvety and false idealization but also as historical ignorance.[57]

The radical maskilim who were closest to socialist tenets in their beliefs were also the harshest critics of the century in which they lived. In 'Shir hayiḥud lamatbe'a' (In Adulation of the Coin), Kaminer expressed serious doubts about the rosy image of the present: as long as economic problems, class differences, the suffering of the poor, unfair competition, oppression, and wars still existed, 'the age of knowledge has not yet come, not yet come!'[58] Another socialist poem, by Vinchevsky, called into question the image of the present that had appeared, for example, in Gordon's 'Hakitsah ami'. Had the morning really dawned and the night ended? For only when the people awoke from its sleep and acquired a class consciousness, and the legions of the enslaved, with the help of men of knowledge and talent, broke the bonds that fettered them, only then would the age of true light, reserved for the future socialist revolution, shine forth.[59]

The radicals' criticism of the Haskalah and its literature and their disillusionment with what they called 'the empty chaos that our writers give the name of Haskalah',[60] led them to re-evaluate their own age. Judah Leib Levin's poem 'She'elot hazeman' (Questions of the Time, 1876) was perhaps the most incisive challenge by the radicals to the image of the nineteenth century as an enlightened epoch. Levin soberly took stock of the nineteenth century from the standpoint of the beginning of its last quarter:

> I ask myself—why consider this century blessed,
> Numbered in the ranks of glory and success?
> Has it in truth ascended to the very height,
> So thoroughly permeated by wisdom and its light,
> Its leaders and sages superior men
> So enlightened in wisdom and moral ken?
> Or is it but an illusion, a bit of unreality—
> The glitter of rotting wood, a flash of foam on the sea![61]

Levin's conclusion was that the nineteenth century showed a negative balance of achievements which by no means justified optimism. The difficult, unresolved questions of the time: primarily, 'the women's question'—the oppression of and discrimination against women; 'the workers' question'—the labourers' enslavement to their masters; and the 'Jewish question', which in Russia was far from finding an emancipatory solution, all testified to the fact that the 'modern age' had

[57] A. U. Kovner, 'Ḥeker davar', 13.

[58] Kaminer, 'Shir hayiḥud', 42.   [59] Vinchevsky, 'Shomer mah milailah', 26–7.

[60] Lilienblum, *Autobiographical Writings*, ii. 129.   [61] J. L. Levin, 'She'elot hazeman', 140–3.

a long way to go before religious tolerance and true social equality were realized. If such questions were still being asked, Levin wrote in his poem, the nineteenth century was not an 'enlightened epoch' but, like all its predecessors, 'an epoch of force, of the oppressing fist'.[62]

Since the radical maskilim were conscious of social and economic issues and identified with elements of socialist thought and its slogans, championing liberation of the workers, the poor, and women, they disavowed maskilic optimism, which, as described above, had hitherto been a staple of maskilic propaganda, as well as providing the perspective for their view of the past and the future. In this sense, the radicals' pessimistic view of the period marked the first stage in the decline of the Haskalah as a general outlook and world-view, a trend that spread to the moderate wing of the Haskalah after the pogroms of the 1880s. For example, Paperna, a radical maskil in the 1860s and a member of Hibat Zion in the 1880s and 1890s, sharply satirized the basic concepts of the Haskalah and its values in a poem: 'enlightenment, progress, civilization, nineteenth century, emancipation— only the mute will not keep these words upon their lips; they are names with magical qualities, as if they would bring redemption, light, and life; but where is this life, light, and happiness? When shall we see equality, freedom, justice, and honesty? . . . We shall eat straw in Europe, just as we did in Egypt.'[63]

How was the historical Jewish question viewed in terms of the positivist and socialist concepts of radical maskilic history? The radicals, who were opposed to the philological approach to the study of Jewish history, proposed an alternative: a history that would be of use to the Jews and would teach them, for example, how Judaism had strayed from its original path, or how the Jews had contributed to universal history in the various sciences.[64] However, their rejection of the optimistic image of the 'modern age' also wrought a change in their perspective on Jewish history. They developed a sceptical attitude towards the 'benevolent rule' that supposedly benefited the Jews, and became increasingly sensitive to antisemitic manifestations in contemporary Russian public opinion as well as in the past. Levin regarded the hostile attitude towards Jewish rights of the Russian representative at the 1878 Berlin Congress, for example, as a sign that should dispel the maskilim's sympathetic attitude towards the regime.[65] In Abramowitz's writings the transition was more obvious. While the accepted maskilic historical schema of suffering and persecution in the Middle Ages in contrast to the advent of the glorious modern era still played a role in his novel *Ha'avot vehabanim* (Fathers

---

[62] Ibid. 143. On the discussion of the 'women's issue' in Russia in the second half of the 19th c., see Feiner, 'The Modern Jewish Woman', 470–99.

[63] Paperna, 'Sihot hayim ve'ofot', 344–64. The quotation is from p. 352. See also Y. Shavit, *Athens in Jerusalem*, 180–1.

[64] A. U. Kovner, 'Ru'ah mishpat', 167–76; Kaminer, *Kinot misiduram*, 18, 27; Lilienblum, 'Kehal refa'im', 442–3.

[65] J. L. Levin, 'Mikhtavo ley. l. gordon'; A. U. Kovner, 'Tseror perahim', 80, 125–6; J. L. Levin, *Zikhronot vehegyonot*, 61–2.

and Sons), 1868),[66] the Odessa pogrom in 1871 induced him to write *Susati*, which bore no vestige of his former optimism. In this allegorical narrative the Jewish people had once again become the 'the world's mare' in the modern age, destined to wander endlessly carrying heavy burdens, as horsemen mount and ride it, its hide covered with scars that tell the tale of its wretched life. The difference between the nineteenth century and the one that preceded it could be summed up by the fact that in the present more efficient tools were used to slaughter 'beasts' than in the past.[67] In effect, the point Abramowitz was making in this story was that as long as the Jewish question still persisted, one could not speak of an enlightened generation. This was the true criterion by which to judge the validity of the Haskalah's concepts and the benevolent rule and humanism of the nineteenth century.

The radicals also directed their critical barbs at the reformist policy of the Russian government, in which most of the moderates still discerned positive and vital steps leading to the enlightenment and reform of Jewish society. Why should the decree of compulsory education, asked Abramowitz, be directed only at the Jews in Russia? Moreover, the government was erring in assigning priority to education, when there was a more urgent need to reform the economy, to ensure the Jews a livelihood, and to grant them civil rights; only then should education have its turn. In this criticism, Abramowitz overturned the accepted maskilic formula: education was not the prerequisite for the improved status of the Jews in Russia, but rather civil rights were a prerequisite for education. Unless the most elemental needs of life were provided, he argued, enlightenment was a luxury.

The demands the government was making on the Jews, calling on them to undergo a drastic transformation, a rapid process of all-embracing reform, and the abandonment of all the 'abominations of the past', were, in Lilienblum's eyes, unfeasible and totally contradictory to the laws of history. Anyone taking a sober look at universal history, from its inception to the nineteenth century, 'so highly lauded by all heartless men', would realize that the 'abominations' in history had not vanished easily or completely. No 'abomination' disappeared until it was replaced by another. Lilienblum's pessimistic view of history was attended by scepticism about the possibility of combating superstition and ignorance. These, he believed, were integral components of human history. As support for this view, he cited the example of France: with rivers of blood and enlightened philosophy, the French had carried out a revolution, but today, a century after Voltaire, they were again entering into an alliance with the Pope. If the forces of reaction could once again prevail in an enlightened country like France, and if the revolution there was incomplete even after a hundred years, then one could hardly single out the Jews as a conservative and stagnant people.[68]

Liebermann, who approached history from the vantage-point of materialism,

[66] Abramowitz, *Ha'avot vehabanim*, 13, 46–7.

[67] Id., *Susati*, 312–14, 328–9, 331–3. See also Bartal, 'Radical Enlightenment', 17–20; id., 'Gentiles and Gentile Society', 90–5.   [68] Lilienblum, 'Ḥatot ne'urim', 212–13.

also applied this concept to the Jewish question. He believed that scientific, free-thinking historical criticism would prove that the conflict between Jews and their environment was based on economic rather than on political or national issues, which outwardly seemed to be the crucial causes of the conflict. His statement of the law of history was that 'The question of the pocket, or the economic issue, is in fact the sole motive for all the pageants of life, in every place and at all times, but it always takes a different form, depending on the level of the development of peoples in each particular place and time.' In ancient times the economic question appeared in the guise of racial hatred, in the Middle Ages of religious fanaticism, and now it was antagonism between nations. Once the Jewish question was cor-rectly diagnosed as an economic question, its solution would be evident: economic changes in Russia and within Jewish society, the blurring of national differences, closer ties with the surrounding cultures, and recognition of the supra-national class interests of the proletariat would, in Liebermann's opinion, lead to a resolu-tion of the Jewish question. This question, he believed, was now a part of the 'question of the entire human species', and a solution of the universal question would inevitably bring about a solution to the Jewish question.[69]

Other radical maskilim followed the same line. Vinchevsky explained that the ordeals suffered by the Jews in the Diaspora were not the result of religious fan-aticism but rather stemmed from economic competition for sources of livelihood and a war of survival; Levin regarded hatred of the Jews as 'competitive hatred', and the socialist poet Kaminer placed an emphasis on the class struggles within Jewish society. He regarded the struggle between the rich and the poor as the cause of the rifts in Jewish history, with the rich acting against the interests of the general populace, and the poor acting as the saviours of the Jews: Moses, Ezra, and Judah Maccabee came from the ranks of the poor; the rich Jews in the Second Temple period were those who were attracted to Greek and Roman culture; and Josephus, who betrayed his brethren, was a member of the wealthy élite.[70]

Unlike Kaminer, Liebermann, Lilienblum, and Levin, Abramowitz did not use socio-economic terminology, and in explaining the Jewish question he still adhered to the idealistic concepts of the Haskalah. In an article published in serial form in *Hamagid* in 1875, he continued the same line he had begun in his novel *Susati*, levelling forceful—although of course covert—criticism against the policies of the Russian government.[71] Abandoning the maskilic concept of the reign of Nicholas I, Abramowitz argued that he could explain the failure of the various initiatives for reforming the Jews as well as the Jews' objection to them. The government's great error, and that of the maskilim who supported it, lay in the coercive method, which damaged the self-respect of the Jews and took no account of the historical

[69] Liebermann, 'She'elat hayehudim', 1–5.

[70] Vinchevsky, 'Ḥezyonot ish haruaḥ', *Asefat ḥakhamim*, 135–6; J. L. Levin, 'She'elat hayehudim', 162, 177, 191–3, 226; Kaminer, *Kinot misiduram*, 4–6; Kaminer, 'Akhan ben zeraḥ', in id., *Shirei yitsḥak kaminer*, 109–13.   [71] Abramowitz, 'Hagoy lo nikhsaf'.

laws that operated within Jewish history. What were these historical laws which Abramowitz uncovered and with which he explained the reaction of the Jews to the government's reformist policies? Here Abramowitz came up with an exceptional explanation which combined accepted maskilic historical thinking, the idealism formulated by Krochmal, and scientific positivism.

The historical fate of the Jews was astonishing. Their continued existence, which resembled the survival of some prehistoric animals, and their extraordinary historical situation had given rise to popular satanic images that inspired the restriction, expulsion, and isolation of the Jews. Not only religious hatred was at play here, but the historical mechanism of folly versus reason—a mechanism familiar from eighteenth-century theories as one of the elements in the historical concepts of the European and the Jewish Enlightenment: 'When folly has the upper hand in religion and morals and in the spirit of the people, then the Jews are at the bottom of the heap. The vicious fanatics mistreat them with malicious fury, and spreaders of lies and calumny come and accuse them of strangeness.' On the other hand, when 'the force of folly is weakened at some place and at some time and is pushed aside by human intellect—the angel that redeems men from ignorance and hypocrisy—then at once, by virtue of this redemption and change, the Jews are saved together with all mankind'. From an inverse perspective, the situation of the Jews was 'a yardstick by which to trace the rise and decline of the spiritual freedom and level of knowledge of all peoples at every moment in time'.[72] The Jews' internal history too, explained Abramowitz, was closely linked to processes of change along the axis from folly to reason: the creative power of the nation was weakened in an age of folly and reawakened in an age of reason. There was nothing new about these ideas, but he also tried to fit his maskilic sense of the past into the more rigid framework of natural historical laws. Influenced by his deep interest in 'natural history', Abramowitz applied scientific terminology from the animal world to the historical world. In his formulation, the reaction of the Jewish organism to external distress was defined as a 'frozen slumber', when 'the arteries of the body of Jewry are constricted and can have no sensation of external events'. The system of folly and reason, insularity and openness, cultural decline and cultural florescence, became for Abramowitz a biological mechanism whose precise functioning was also defined by two biological-historical laws which, in his view, were peculiar to Jewish history. The first of these was defined as:

Constriction and separation from the external world when painful and malevolent events injure them from without. As a result they are saved from self-destruction and their lives are preserved. Accordingly, when all sensation is weakened, the body of Judaism will no longer be in danger of becoming decomposed by external events and evil forces threatening to disperse it, like the other nations, which fall apart and are mixed into the body of another nation that overcomes them with its strength. This historical law is consonant with the natural law, unique to some animals, which is the deep sleep of hibernation and

[72] Abramowitz, 'Hagoy lo nikhsaf', 172.

the feebleness of sensation during the winter, when they lie like corpses, feel no cold nor anything else that happens to them, and awaken to the warmth of the sun.[73]

This 'historical law' explained the insularity of the Jews as a biological tactic in the nation's war of survival and as a natural reaction to external dangers. This was also how Abramowitz explained the insularity and suspicion of traditional Jewish society in relation to the government's reformist policy—reactions which were understandable in the light of the historical law as a natural response to an external threat to the Jewish organism. From Krochmal he learned the explanation for the unbroken continuity of the Jewish people throughout the cycles of history, and that it stemmed from their 'eternal spirituality'. However, in Abramowitz's version, this purely idealistic concept underwent a process of 'biologicalization', which gave scientific-empirical weight to Krochmal's original concept and was formulated in Abramowitz's second historical law of reproduction, which was unique to the Jews:

The immortality of the spiritual and its changing forms as the conditions of the Jews change through the ages leads to a constant revival . . . and a renewal during each era of perfection, rising to the heights of enlightenment. A parallel to this law for the Jews is the natural law of reproduction, which is unique to some species of animals, which through a vital internal force always regenerate amputated limbs.[74]

It is remarkable that Abramowitz formulated historical laws unique to the Jewish people despite the fact that other radical maskilim pointed to a universal socio-economic law. Abramowitz explained this difference too in biological terms, based on his conception of the human species as an organism whose limbs were formed by the various peoples. The Jews, like all the other limbs in the body, had functions and features that differed from the others; only when all the peoples functioned in accordance with the special natural laws did natural harmony reign and 'the histories of all the private nations are intertwined and complement one another'. This led Abramowitz to his last conclusion, which directly concerned the Russian Jewry of his own time. The policy of the Russian government, which adopted coercive measures and thought 'it could change by force the nature that the Almighty had stamped on the nation', was tantamount to a gross interference with the historical law. It was thus no wonder that the reformist policy had not been successful and that the Jews instinctively reacted to it by 'constricting'; and isolating themselves, contrary to the government's intentions. Russia, in Abramowitz's view, was pursuing the same mistaken policy towards the Jews as had Antiochus, Trajan, Hadrian, Ferdinand and Isabella, and other 'hegemons and rulers', all of whom 'in their own times forcibly tried to bring the Jews closer to them, but instead of moving them even slightly towards them, only managed to drive them further away, and their aggressive ways gave rise to acts of resistance and much opposition among the Jews'.[75]

[73] Ibid. 183.   [74] Ibid.   [75] Ibid. 190.

Abramowitz's basic assumptions and his natural historical laws—the law of 'hibernation' in adverse conditions and the law of 'reproduction'—emphasized the unique historical and national character of the Jews as a historical as well as an immutable biological fact. However, other radicals, in particular the socialists like Vinchevsky, rejected this concept as anachronistic. Vinchevsky held that the era of science was working towards the complete unification of all peoples, and that the Jews were also subject to universal laws. 'The telegraph, the railways, the telephone, steamships, and the like', he wrote in 1878, 'have done more to further enlightenment than all of your poems and other nonsense . . . the unification of the Jews with all other peoples is imminent'.[76] Time, which was marching forward, would leave behind Hebrew literature, which was nearing its end. Vinchevsky placed in the mouth of the protagonist of his story 'Panim ḥadashot' (New Faces, 1878) a historical schema that foresaw the liquidation of the Jews as a people: the persecutions of the Middle Ages, the era of the Inquisition, and the Crusades were all in the realm of the past, and the physical destruction of the Jewish people was no longer a real danger. The 'modern age' was drawing the Jews, who had hitherto been isolated, in the direction of inevitable assimilation with their neighbours. The Hebrew language and its literature would become library exhibits at best. The radical maskil hero of the story argued that what was involved was not just an aspiration or an ideology but actually a historical inevitability. Technology and science were uniting the world; life and the struggle for survival were far stronger than any opinions or ideas. The liquidation of the Jewish nation was no longer the product of a cruel plot devised by fanatical enemies but the deterministic result of supra-personal historical forces: 'It is not a few people who have tried to destroy our unique national spirit, but all of history and most of its recent offspring.'[77] This historical course, which would lead to the disappearance of the Jews as a people with its own identity, was thus conceived in positivist and materialist terms as an irreversible process.

In their adoption of patterns of positivist and materialistic historical thinking, in their scepticism about the very existence of a positive historical transition in the modern era, in moving the focus from education, literature, and culture to social and economic problems that were seen as the focus and the force driving historical dynamics, and in their vision of the future disappearance of the Jewish people the radical maskilim veered sharply away from the path of the moderate Haskalah, shattering the basic assumptions of its concept of history and picture of the past. Basic elements in historical thought were replaced by others: religious fanaticism gave way to economic competition, the historical transition embodied by benevolent rulers and enlightenment was replaced by the new technology and the innovations of modern science, and the idealistic laws of history, subordinate to the 'spirit of the time' and the 'spirit of the nation', were rejected in favour of bio-

---

[76] Vinchevsky, 'Ḥezyonot ish haruaḥ'.   [77] Id., 'Panim ḥadashot', 100–2, 113–17.

logical and deterministic laws. The radical maskil became increasingly pessimistic and disillusioned with the Enlightenment and all its fine ideas that were never realized. He turned his attention to new issues, such as the inferior status of women and workers, and placed his trust in science, in the hope that it would provide him with a secular, precise, true, and certain explanation and would foretell the inevitable events of the future. The fairly small group that introduced this direction in the Haskalah strayed very far from its path, although it shared the general maskilic aim: the reform of Jewish society. Moreover, the trend set by this radical camp did much to discredit the concepts of 'maskilic history' at the close of the 1870s.

THE ANTICLERICAL STRUGGLE

'Maskilic history' was stretched to its limits when it was enlisted in the anticlerical cultural struggle waged by Lilienblum and Gordon. The religious reform controversy in Russia lasted only four years, from 1868 to 1871, but as will be seen later, Gordon carried it on throughout his lifetime. Relations between traditional society and the maskilim had not been so tense since the time of the polemic surrounding the government-sponsored Haskalah in the 1840s, and the vituperative and slanderous articles written during the controversy bear witness to the ferocity of the conflict. More than at any time in the past there were maskilim in Russia who dared to advocate religious radicalism, to attack the traditional rabbinic leadership, and to call for a new *Shulḥan arukh* (halakhic code). In the face of these attacks, a more cohesive Orthodox society emerged, reacting with propaganda in the form of handbills and newspapers as well as personal attacks, aimed at blocking the Haskalah in general and religious radicalism in particular.[78]

Even before the 1860s there had been elements of moderate religious reform in the Russian Haskalah in the form of aesthetic changes in the synagogue, but no real public debate had arisen until this later period. Throughout the controversy the maskilim constantly reiterated their objection to movements for religious reform like the one in Germany, followed a more moderate line than that adopted, for example, by Joshua Heschel Schorr in Galicia, and rejected all attempts by their opponents to point to a link between their demand for reform and the conferences of reformers in Germany held during those years. In general, few challenged the basic principles of the halakah. Rather, the controversy reflected the courage of some maskilim, who had become more self-confident during the reign of Alexander II, and their growing sensitivity to social issues. It is not surprising to find that radical maskilim like Abraham Uri Kovner, his brother Isaac Itsik Kovner,

[78] Zinberg, *A History of Jewish Literature*, vii. 147–61; Katzanelson, *The Literary War*; J. Klausner, *History of Modern Hebrew Literature*, vi. 198–226; Meyer, 'The German Model', 67–91; id., *Response to Modernity*, 197–200.

and of course Lilienblum were among the first to call for religious reform, since their demands for reform were fuelled primarily by the economic hardships of Russian Jewry at the end of the 1860s, and not necessarily by religious and historical–philosophical concepts and the emancipatory aspiration for integration into non-Jewish society that motivated the proponents of reform in Germany.

The concept of life which underpinned Lilienblum's radical approach also moved him to urge that the halakhic code of the *Shulḥan arukh* be updated by a special assembly of rabbis. In making this demand, he was aware of the status of the Talmud and of the rabbis, but wanted to prevent a contradiction between life and religion at all costs.[79] The historicization of the halakhah—placing it in its historical context—played a very minor role in justifying the reforms. The major points in the maskilim's argument were an appeal to humane feelings, a stress on social evils and the suffering of the poor, and an emphasis on the economic aspect of halakhic rulings. By pressing these points, the maskilim tried to convince the rabbis to accede to their requests. Another striking fact is that the leading participants in the polemic on religious reforms in Russia were not men of Wissenschaft des Judentums, engaged in historical–philological study of the sources, like Geiger and Schorr, but publicists, novelists, and poets.

Lilienblum both opened the polemic and played a key role in it in the eyes of both the maskilim and the Orthodox. In his case, the controversy went beyond the literary domain, adversely affecting his own life. In his native town of Wilkomir, in Lithuania, Lilienblum was persecuted, threatened, and vilified until he was forced to flee, and took refuge in Odessa, with the support of the Kovno maskilim, in 1869.[80] In 'Orḥot hatalmud' (The Ways of the Talmud, 1868) and in another article entitled 'Nosafot le'orḥot hatalmud' (Additions to The Ways of the Talmud) Lilienblum argued that throughout its history, from the days of Ezra to the talmudic period, halakhic tradition had constantly undergone change and reform, and that the 'spirit of the time' was the criterion to be applied in reforming religion, because it expressed the 'spirit of life' of the period and the society.[81] In his opinion, the Talmud was created in extraordinary circumstances after the destruction of the Temple and reflected the Sages' desire to provide their people with succour, to console them, and to lay down clear rules and guidelines for continued Jewish existence. With the exception of several rulings that were *halakhot lemoshe misinai* (laws given to Moses at Mount Sinai), most of the Talmud was made up of later rulings, regulations, and decrees that 'the sages of each and every generation were entitled to change as needed'. As long as the Jews lived under a harsh, oppressive rule, the existing halakhah was valid and justified, but in the modern age of freedom there was a need to ease and liberalize its restrictions, before the tendency to

---

[79] On Lilienblum's role in the polemic, see Lilienblum, 'Ḥatot ne'urim', in *Collected Writings*, i/1, and the editor's introd., ibid. 14–20. Lilienblum's writings on religious reform have been collected in the first volume of his *Collected Writings*.   [80] Id., 'Ḥatot ne'urim', 158–65.

[81] Id., 'Orḥot hatalmud', 7–31; id., 'Nosafot le'orḥot hatalmud', 32–52.

abandon the Jewish religion became dominant. As a radical maskil, Lilienblum thought that it was the dangers of the modern age that ought to motivate the rabbis to introduce religious reforms.

Hayim Joseph Sicular of Mohilev, another participant in the polemic and a friend of Lilienblum's, asserted that the obstinacy of the 'shepherds of Israel' would work to their disadvantage: just as the kingdom of Rehoboam was divided because he refused to listen to the advice of the elders and just as the Christian religion was split in 1517 and, in the seventeenth century, was dragged into the grim Thirty Years War because the priests paid no heed to reformist criticism, so the obstruction of religious reforms in Judaism would surely lead to the abandonment of all restraint.[82] Lilienblum stated explicitly that the Talmud, in his view, was a human creation, 'a product of its time and [contemporary] life; not from heaven did it come down to us, but life on earth gave birth to it.'[83] Real life, in his opinion, was the basis for and source of halakhah and the criterion for evaluating its validity. Lilienblum concentrated in particular on the halakhic rulings of the *Shulḥan arukh* and concluded that this halakhic work was even more seriously flawed than the Talmud. While the talmudic Sages were still endowed with a considerable measure of 'life spirit' and were familiar with the 'human spirit', the *Shulḥan arukh* was totally opposed to life. There was no other choice, then, but to write a new halakhic work, which he described as a 'pure and amended *Shulḥan arukh*', that would solve the problem of the intolerable gap between an 'Asiatic' halakhah and 'European' Jewish life in the modern age.[84]

At this stage the Orthodox camp began to react, and Lilienblum, who was conscious of the ferment that his two articles had aroused, was compelled to take an apologetic position. Again and again he reiterated that his demand for religious reform was in no way associated with the German Reform movement. Unlike Schorr, for example, he did not employ the method of philological criticism of the Talmud, and unlike the reformers in Germany, he did not speak about any reform in the Jewish faith and its principles, nor about the idea of mission or any change in synagogue ritual. He had never advocated radical reforms such as the nullification of the commandment of circumcision, and in principle he was not convinced that 'we can cancel religion in the name of the nineteenth century . . . not everything done or thought in the nineteenth century is based on the spirit of enlightenment and knowledge. And not all of ancient tradition is linked to the sanctity of religion.' He believed that the reforms made in the Jewish religion in the past proved it was possible to introduce change without taking a radical, destructive approach.[85]

In a long article Moses Eiseman, who supported Lilienblum's demands, tried to

[82] Sicular, 'El ro'ei yisra'el'.

[83] Lilienblum, 'Midrash soferim', *Collected Writings*, i. 53; id., 'Orḥot hatalmud', 32. On the circumstances surrounding the writing of the article, see a letter from Lilienblum to J. L. Gordon (1871), in Lilienblum, *Letters*, 129.   [84] Id., 'Nosafot le'orḥot hatalmud', 49–52.

[85] Id., 'Al devar hatikunim badat' (1870), 94, 99, 100, 119, 126–7.

expand the historical scope of the polemic on religious reform and to set it within
the context of the historical rivalry between religion and monarchy. According to
the historical law he formulated, the material, spiritual, and moral well-being of a
state was contingent on harmony between 'religion and monarchy'. As long as the
two fulfilled their roles, harmony prevailed, but when religion and the Church
gained control over the monarchy, the state immediately declined into an era of
confusion and licentiousness. From the reign of King Solomon to the destruction
of the First Temple, for example, the monarchy was stronger than the religious
establishment, as it was also in Herod's time. The reversal of power after Herod
was catastrophic and led to the destruction of the Second Temple. The controversy
in Russia in his own time seemed to Eiseman yet another campaign in the historic
war now being waged between religion and the rabbis on one side and Jewish
society on the other. He contended that all religions underwent constant change
consistent with the spirit of the people, the spirit of enlightenment, and climatic
conditions, and that throughout Jewish history time had also left its imprint on the
religion; therefore, he argued, the rabbis were obligated to reform the religion so
that it would no longer contradict the new 'sense of life' of the present generation.[86]

In 1870 Lilienblum decided to withdraw from the polemic on religious reforms.
His decision was not motivated by his opponents but rather by the cataclysmic
effect of his realization that he no longer believed that the Torah was given at
Sinai. An apostate who no longer believes in the divine validity of the Torah, he
wrote in his autobiography, cannot conduct a campaign for religious reform. From
that moment, he confessed, 'I became a non-believer.'[87] The stronger his radical
positivist views became, the more he regretted having engaged in a foolish attempt
to link religion with life. At the very most, he was prepared to help Gordon, who
had been influenced by Lilienblum and to a great extent continued in his path,
while warning him that someone with no faith in his heart could not build, but
only destroy.[88]

From 1869 to 1870 Gordon joined in the fight for religious reforms, supported
Lilienblum, and immediately became the target of attacks by the Orthodox.[89] His
major contribution to the struggle was his fiercely anti-rabbinical poetry.[90]

It is somewhat misleading to describe Gordon as Lilienblum's supporter in the
struggle for religious reform. Lilienblum did in fact call upon the heads of the
rabbinate to make vital and urgent halakhic changes, and to a great extent maintained the maskilic belief that the ills of Jewish society could be cured through a
reform of the rabbinate based on the emergence of a new type of rabbi who would
be part of a reformed leadership. He did his utmost to prove to the rabbis of his
time that if they would only formulate a new *Shulḥan arukh*, purged of many rules

---

[86] Eiseman, 'Harabanut'.   [87] Lilienblum, 'Ḥatot ne'urim', 49–51.
[88] Lilienblum, *Autobiographical Writings*, iii. 159–60, 166, 172–3.
[89] On J. L. Gordon, see Stanislawski, *'For Whom Do I Toil?'*
[90] Frozer, 'Letters to J. L. Gordon', 132–5, 145–59; J. L. Gordon, *Letters*, i. 143–8.

which were no longer valid and were an obstacle to life, they would succeed in maintaining a living, dynamic relationship between Jewish society and religion and religious customs, as their predecessors had in the distant past. In the spirit of the Russian Haskalah from the days of Levinsohn onwards, Lilienblum argued that this would not necessitate a radical revolution, since precedents for change existed within Jewish tradition. In contrast, Gordon, who also called for religious reforms, believed the core of the problem was the rabbis' domination and their unchallenged authority. Changes in the Jewish religion were not Gordon's first priority. A liberal anticlerical Jew of contemporary western and central Europe, who had closely followed and been influenced by the course of the *Kulturkampf* in Europe, Gordon waged a Jewish equivalent. Its purpose was to denounce the grave damage caused to the Jews in the past and the present by the rule of the rabbis—the 'Jewish Church'—and to weaken their authority and remove their influence from areas which he defined as none of their business.

When in 1866 Gordon published his well-known and highly influential poem 'Hakitsah ami' in Fuenn's *Hakarmel*, he had not yet strayed from the maskilic mainstream of the time or given any thought to a cultural struggle. Like Levinsohn before him, he had urged Jewish society at large to take part in Russian life as productive, useful, and loyal citizens, basing his argument on the optimistic maskilic belief that 'the night is over, the day is breaking! . . . Arise and see changes wherever you turn your face; yet others will come in our time and place.' And in prose he wrote, 'It is not fitting for a European man to adhere rigidly to the customs of Asiatics.'[91] Gordon was so carried away that he described Tsar Alexander II as a modern-day Cyrus. Fuenn proudly presented 'Hakitsah ami' to the readers of *Hakarmel* on the opening page of the first issue of the new year.

By 1868, when Gordon published the poem 'Bein shinei arayot' (Between the Lions' Teeth), the historical rabbinic leadership was the target of his criticism. As recorded above, there was a long maskilic tradition behind the demand that the rabbis assume social responsibility and provide leadership in tune with the needs of the time; however, Gordon made a more outspoken attack than any other maskil on what he regarded as the rabbis' grievous shortcomings. In Gordon's poem a young Jewish couple, victims of the fate of their people during the revolt against the Romans, were described as victims first and foremost of the rabbinic leadership, which had neglected the practical, political, and military needs of the nation, choosing instead to withdraw into the *beit midrash* and enclosing themselves within the four walls of the halakah. Gordon left his readers in no doubt that he was not referring solely to that tragic chapter in past history, regarding it as the manifestation of a terrible flaw that had persisted to the present day: 'For hundreds of years teachers led you and built houses of study, and what did they teach you? . . . to walk against life . . . to be dead on the earth, to live in the skies . . . they displayed you to the generations as a mummy.'[92]

[91] J. L. Gordon, 'Hakitsah ami', 17.   [92] Id., 'Bein shinei arayot', 103.

The poem aroused much attention immediately upon its publication, and the controversy surrounding it coincided with the severe economic crisis that beset Lithuanian Jewry in 1868–9. A. Ehrlich remarked from Germany that the defeat of the Jews in the revolt had been inevitable; far larger and stronger states had fallen at the hands of the Roman empire. But he too understood that in his poem Gordon had made no pretensions of being a historian and that his sole purpose was to lash out at the rabbis. Other critics who rushed to defend the honour of the sages and inveighed against Gordon's interpretation argued that one could not infer from the fact that the sages were preoccupied with halakhah that the study of war had been neglected, for there had been Jewish heroes who had fought valiantly in fierce battles. Others argued that on the eve of the destruction of the Temple, the sages had followed the tactics of Rabbi Yohanan ben Zakai; anticipating the loss of the state, they had invested their efforts in building the walls of the Talmud to serve as a substitute for national unity. According to this claim, their behaviour was in fact justified and realistic, and had proved itself over time.[93]

From a different vantage-point, Jehiel Michael Pines (1843–1912), a moderate opponent of religious reforms, attacked Gordon's depiction of the last days of the Second Temple period, rejecting Gordon's contrast between religion and 'real life'. In contrast to Gordon, Pines claimed that the sages had gathered together during the revolt not only to form a circle for the study of the halakhah and a forum for enacting halakhic decrees, but also to meet as an assembly to consider how the success of the political struggle could be achieved. In his view, the regulations they passed bore a national and political character, and were intended to strengthen the barrier between Jews and non-Jews 'in the spirit of the piety that had revived the national spirit of Israel'. Gordon's depiction of the Second Temple sages as dim-witted infants, occupied with insignificant matters at a time of great danger, was a false version of historical reality. The Pharisees also concerned themselves with national life; the disciples of Rabbi Akiva, for example, were men of war and freedom fighters, and Josephus himself, who came from a family of priests and disciples of the Pharisees, knew how to build fortifications and command legions. If Gordon had demonstrated a better knowledge of history, Pines argued, he would never have reached his mistaken conclusion, and would also have understood that there was absolutely no basis for expecting the Jews to have spent a long period of time preparing themselves for a revolt and adapting themselves to Roman military tactics.[94]

Gordon responded to his critics in 1871 in the pages of *Hamagid*. He argued that he had never claimed to have written a historically accurate poem; his purpose was to depict the state of the nation in the crucial period of the revolt and the destruction. From this standpoint, he argued, the historical picture that emerged in 'Bein shinei arayot' was actually very reliable. Gordon insisted that no meeting

[93] Ehrlich, 'Al hasefarim', 247; Elkenitzki, 'Lo zeh haderekh', 204.
[94] Pines, *Yaldei ruḥi*, i. 86–96 n.

of the military leadership like that of the rabbis had taken place, that the military preparations for the rebellion were inadequate, and that the leaders were concerned with *halakhot* which were of no practical use. He agreed that the heroism of the fighters was undeniable and that Josephus' writings supported that, but claimed that they were clearly not well versed in the advanced methods of war of their time, and were therefore defeated. Why did the sages not adopt the method followed by Rabbi Akiva, who aspired to political freedom during the Bar Kokhba revolt? And why did they fail to take full advantage of the years between the death of Agrippa and the beginning of the revolt, when they could have spent the time making the proper preparations?[95]

As related above, Lilienblum abandoned the cause, and Gordon remained nearly alone, while in the meantime the cultural struggle in Europe was intensifying and the Catholic Church, headed by Pope Pius IX, was trying to fight back by means of stern anti-liberal encyclicals. The Jewish reader was kept constantly informed of the details of this confrontation. Zederbaum, the editor of *Hamelits*, reported in his column 'Halikhot olam' (The Ways of the World) what he interpreted as the defeat of Catholicism: pious Christians were casting off all restraint, and the bonds that the Church and the Jesuits had placed on them were loosening. The old élite of the Church, which had maintained control over knowledge and education for centuries, was giving way to the new élite of the liberal enlightenment. Could the rabbis in our midst survive as the last clerical leaders on earth, asked the editor, adding: Did our rabbis not realize that their rejection of the demand for religious reforms was imbued with the spirit of the unyielding 'Syllabus of Errors' that guided the Catholic Church?[96]

In 1869, when Gordon composed his satire 'Bizekhutan shel rabanim' (By the Merit of Rabbis), he had already come to the conclusion that the moment was ripe for an all-out battle against the rabbinate. Appealing to his readers, he asked each of them to report on the evil deeds and injustices perpetrated by the rabbis.[97] In 1870 the *Kulturkampf* in Europe spread even further afield. The armies of Italy entered Rome and deprived Pius IX of his political power, and he retorted with his dogma of papal infallibility. 'The reign of Catholicism in the land has come to an end!', *Hamelits* declared, and the maskilim, including Gordon, who felt threatened by the counter-attacks against him in *Halevanon*, drew an analogy between Jewish Orthodoxy and Catholicism. More and more, the polemic over religious reform was viewed within the broader framework of the rivalry between religion and monarchy.[98]

The events of the cultural struggle in Europe enabled the maskilim to interpret their war in an overall historical context and also bolstered their confidence in the

[95] J. L. Gordon, 'Venikeiti mipesha rav', 125.

[96] Zederbaum, editorials, *Hamelits*, 8 (1868), 211–12, 218–20, 304, 342; id., editorials, *Hamelits*, 9 (1869), 171, 179, 241.　　　　　　　　[97] J. L. Gordon, 'Bizekhutan shel rabanim', 328–9.

[98] Zederbaum, editorials, *Hamelits*, 10 (1870), 315, 322.

justice of their cause. The Orthodox of *Halevanon* were of course the fanatical 'Jesuits', the rabbis were represented as Catholic priests, and the maskilim saw themselves as anticlerical warriors with the 'spirit of the time' on their side. This world-view was lucidly demonstrated in Gordon's long article 'Binah leto'ei ruah' (Wisdom for the Misled), published in 1870. In a militant vein, despairing of any possibility of reforming the rabbinate, he wrote, 'The rabbis are but Jesuits for whom the desired end justifies all means.' While the entire human species had already risen above the days of the Crusades, the tortures of the Inquisition, and the auto-da-fés of the Jesuits, the rabbis had remained behind. He believed the rabbis had missed the opportunity presented in the 1840s. If they had supported Nicholas I's reformist policies, they might have earned the respect of the Jewish public at large, but instead they preferred to cry out like the Pope 'Non possumus', and 'still wish to govern all spirits and souls, now when the Pope . . . who had fallen from his high position, must allow freedom to all spirits'. What was urgently needed now was not only reform in the religion—changes in the *Shulḥan arukh* in keeping with Lilienblum's demands, for example—but first of all reform of the rabbinate, the 'Jewish Church'. If the rabbinate fell at the hands of the maskilim and was replaced by 'men who knew the Torah' and would be eminently capable of introducing reforms in the religion, then Jewish society would be saved from complete ruin. If the rabbinate should fall on its own, as it were, then the Jews of Russia would become like the Jews of Germany, who had no knowledge of the Torah and whose sons had completely abandoned Judaism.[99]

The polarization between the religious guidance of the Church and secular political interests in Catholic Europe induced Gordon to denounce the rabbinate, imagining what the situation would be like if the days of the Messiah arrived while the rabbinate was in its present deplorable state. He had no doubt that if a Jewish state were to be established, the rabbis would not be fit to serve as its leaders. They could not function in a state that required the existence of military men, ministers of the treasury, engineers, diplomats, physicians, tradesmen, and intellectuals. And if they insisted nonetheless on preserving their position of authority and introducing a halakhic regime, then 'the following day all the nations around us would arise to wipe us off the face of the earth, for it is impossible for civilization to exist in this manner'.[100]

When these hard words were printed in *Hashaḥar* in 1871, the focus of the *Kulturkampf* was then in Germany. Bismarck, the 'iron chancellor' of the unified state, declared war on the Church's centres of economic, political, and educational power. *Hamagid*, printed in Lyck in eastern Prussia, kept its readers in Russia informed of these events. Its editor, David Gordon, reported on the preparations for the passage of the anti-Catholic 'May laws' in 1873 and observed that the new

[99] Letter to Yehoshua Sirkin (6 July 1870), in J. L. Gordon, *Letters*, i. 158.
[100] J. L. Gordon, 'Hashmatah', 154–6.

dogma of the Pope's infallibility was a source of concern for many European countries. After all, 'the days are past when people feared the Pope and shook at his admonition; now he is laughed at by all honest men'. The Catholics were in distress and Gordon was glad, seeing their crisis as some kind of historical retribution for the Church's persecution of the Jews in the past.[101]

In 1876 Gordon visited Germany for the first time and witnessed at first hand both the *Kulturkampf* and the struggle in the Jewish community over the Law of Secession (*Austrittsgesetz*), a Jewish supplement to the general cultural struggle.[102] After the passage of this law in 1876—against the objections of the non-Orthodox —Jews were permitted to leave the united congregation and to establish a separate framework. It was this situation that inspired Gordon's most vehemently anticlerical poem, 'Kotso shel yod' (The Point of a *Yod*). One of the central characters in the poem is Rav Vafsi, who has all the traits of a Catholic priest: 'He knew not the ways of peace; compassion was foreign to him; he knew only how to destroy and ostracize, to prohibit and forbid.' His ruling was final and unchallengeable, and in the poet's eyes he was one of the 'priests of power' who in the name of the Almighty had 'lit bonfires and sacrificed hundreds of thousands'.[103] Gordon returned to St Petersburg, feeling increasingly threatened by the criticism and denunciation of the Orthodox. He expressed his sense of being a 'fighter for light' in another poem, 'Shenei yosef ben shimon' (Two Josephs son of Simon), in which he described the nightmare of a young man who wanted to be both a physician and a rabbi who would revoke halakhic prohibitions, but who knew subconsciously that he would surely fail and end up joining the historical pantheon of the ostracized: 'The land opens wide its mouth, and the iniquitous of Israel of all times, those who have mocked the words of the sages, are condemned to the flames of destruction.' Marching in the procession of deviants in his dream were Elisha ben Avuyah (second century AD), Uriel da Costa, and Baruch Spinoza, followed by maskilim from the time of Mendelssohn to Schorr, Levinsohn, Adam Hakohen, Erter, and Mapu. They were all tied to the stake, burned, and sacrificed. 'Happy are those who are persecuted for their thoughts!', Gordon cried, with the sense of being a maskilic martyr, prepared to sacrifice his life on the altar of liberalism as the last link in a chain of historical martyrs.[104]

At that very time, in 1879, Gordon suffered the harshest blow of all when he was imprisoned and banished after being falsely accused of subversive political activity. This experience left an indelible mark on him. In 1880, after his return to St Petersburg, he saw himself as a nineteenth-century Uriel da Costa, a victim of Jewish fanaticism. 'That same famous incident took place not in Amsterdam in the seventeenth century but here before our very eyes,' Gordon wrote, 'with only one difference: instead of the old weapon of excommunication, now they have

---

[101] Anon., 'Al hamedinot bo ye'amer', 57–8, 69–70, 79–80.
[102] J. L. Gordon, 'Al nehar kevar', 285–90. See also Stanislawski, *'For Whom Do I Toil?'*, 226–7.
[103] J. L. Gordon, 'Kotso shel yod', 129–40.   [104] Ibid. 148–66.

recourse to political slander and acts of deception and deceit.'[105] From this point onwards Gordon's historical perspective broadened. In 'Tsidkiyahu beveit hape-kudot' (Zedekiah in Prison) his picture of the past reflected not only the struggle between fanatical rabbis and wayward liberals and the fight for freedom of thought, but also a sequence of historical struggles between the Kingdom of Heaven and the kingdom of earth, between religion and monarchy: 'Yea, from this day forward, there is a quarrel between the adherents of the Torah and the government. The visionaries and prophets have always wished to see the kings submit to them.'[106]

The poem focused on King Zedekiah's attempt to settle accounts with the prophet Jeremiah. The king represents political, military, pragmatic, and national considerations, while the prophet represents the rabbinate, which is alienated from real life. Gordon tried not only to arouse the reader's sympathy for the tragic fate of the imprisoned king but also to rehabilitate Zedekiah's historical image, for he believed the Bible had not given him the respect he deserved. It is possible, Gordon argued, that Zedekiah's rebellion against the neighbouring powers had no chance of succeeding, but at least it was motivated by justified national and political aims. His war was waged for freedom and he was right in refusing to accede to Jeremiah's demands. After all, who was the historical Jeremiah? A 'soft-hearted man with a submissive soul, who advised us to choose shame, slavery, and obedience'. Jeremiah was depicted as a prototype of contemporary rabbis, a priest who even when the kingdom was about to fall devoted all his attention to ritual and commandments and the imposition of prohibitions. Like the sages during the revolt against Rome, the prophet valued religion over the interests of the state, spiritual over real life, and thus actually precipitated the downfall of the kingdom. The conflict between priesthood and monarchy which Jeremiah and Zedekiah represented in the First Temple era was, in Gordon's view, only a single stage in a series of campaigns in the historical struggle being waged between *malkhuta de'ara*, the temporal kingdom, and *malkhuta derakia*, the celestial kingdom:

The controversy between Zedekiah and Jeremiah is an age-old controversy that began at the dawn of history and continues to the end of all generations—between the temporal kingdom and the celestial kingdom, which recurs from time to time to this very day wherever these two authorities stand on their own (like the controversy in our own time in Germany between the government and the Pope, which is known by the name *Kulturkampf*). It is the controversy that existed before the days of Zedekiah, between Saul and Samuel, and after him, in the days of the Second Temple, between the Sadducees and the Pharisees, and it resounds to this very day within our own people between the maskilim and the ultra-Orthodox.[107]

The spokesman of Orthodoxy often levelled personal attacks against Lilien-blum, Gordon, and others,[108] but they also attempted to rebuff the maskilim's

---

[105] Ginsburg, *Historical Writings*.
[106] J. L. Gordon, 'Tsidkiyahu beveit hapekudot', 98–101.
[107] Ibid. 341–8 n.
[108] See Lipschitz, *Zikhron ya'akov*, ii. 65–8, 77–81.

demand for religious reforms by refuting their basic historical assumptions. In an anonymous pamphlet entitled *Milḥamah beshalom* (A War against Peace), printed in Vilna in 1870, members of the militant circle of Orthodoxy rejected the concept of the spirit of the time: 'This period of time has no greater demands than all other times in the past', the pamphlet claimed; if the spirit of the time had any unique traits at all, they were negative: 'an arrogant spirit, a spirit of envy, a spirit of mendacity, impiety, falsehood, and deceit'. In such a period it was actually those who succeeded in resisting the spirit of the time who deserved praise. What prevailed today was not progress, reason, or morality but rather reaction, moral deterioration, and the ruin of religion—an inverse definition of the maskilic spirit of the time.[109] Pines, too, although he accepted some of the maskilic demands in the areas of education, economics, and reforms in religious institutions and did not hesitate to criticize the old order, identified with the Orthodox position on this matter. He rejected the portrayal of the history of the Jewish religion as a series of reforms, claiming that religion embodied an eternal idea, expressed not only in faith but also in the practical commandments. In principle, no changes should be introduced into the religion. The changes made in previous generations were indeed in response to the changing spirit of the time, but were a totally dissimilar process: first, the practical religious norm was established and spread throughout the Jewish people, and only afterwards was the halakhic reform introduced.[110]

At the end of the 1880s the controversy about religious reforms was recorded in the form of a novel written from the standpoint of the maskilim's failure to induce the rabbis to take the initiative in introducing reforms. The young Reuben Braudes had already conceived the idea of writing a novel based on the polemic during his first meeting with Lilienblum in Zhitomir in 1869, when the latter was on his way to Odessa. But the book itself, *Hadat vehaḥayim* (Religion and Life), was only written and published in instalments in *Haboker or*, edited by Gottlober, between 1876 and 1879.[111] Braudes undertook to supply future historians with a first-hand description of the events of 1868–9 in Lithuania in order to prevent the historical picture from being distorted. Future historians were otherwise liable to wander aimlessly 'among heaps of faded pages in the libraries and lose their way'. The 'Three Year War', as Braudes dubbed the controversy, was apt to be erroneously interpreted, and he regarded it as his duty to ensure that in the future, too, all would understand that the maskilim were the justified party in the dispute. At the beginning of the third part of the book the author himself bursts into the novel, prefacing it with what amounts to a historical essay. Braudes attempted to understand the controversy over religious reforms in terms of the familiar historical mechanism of the struggle between the forces of progress and the forces of conservatism. History proved, he asserted, that attempts to block progressive forces

---

[109] Anon., *Milḥamah beshalom*, 10–13.
[110] Y. M. Pines, 'Ḥalifat mikhtavim'; id., *Yaldei ruḥi*, ii. 35–41.
[111] Braudes, *Hadat vehaḥayim*; Feingold, 'The Works of R. S. Braudes'.

only caused them to become more extreme. Human beings could not endure pressure, oppression, and intolerance, and the more they were tortured, the more freedom would they demand. During the controversy the rabbis in Russia had acted contrary to the laws of history and had learned nothing from the lessons of the past (e.g. the quarrel between the sects during the Second Temple period, the secession of the Karaites in the eighth century, the messianic radicalism of Shabbetai Tsevi, the conflict between hasidim and mitnagedim). He believed that seceding and radical groups in Jewish history were successful because of the strong opposition they encountered. The rabbinic leadership was responsible for a long series of fateful historical errors, and the 'Three Year War' in Russia was but one more stage in its 'procession of follies'.[112]

Although there was probably nothing in this historical schema to encourage those maskilim who advocated reforms, it did enable them to view the controversy as a historically significant episode, of the same magnitude as previous key events in Jewish history.

THE HISTORICAL VINDICATION OF HASIDISM

Challenges to the Haskalah's fundamental principles and concepts of the past also came from within the moderate Haskalah itself, which was far removed from both socialist and positivist radicalism and anticlerical radicalism. One outstanding example of this position can be found in the attempt by Eliezer Zweifel to re-evaluate the hasidic movement from a positive historical viewpoint. His book *Shalom al yisra'el* (Peace upon Israel), published in 1868 in Zhitomir, where he taught in the rabbinic seminary, met with severe criticism from his friends and colleagues in the Haskalah.[113] They regarded it as reflecting a new stance, amounting to a complete departure from the anti-hasidic maskilic consensus that had existed for decades. Nearly everyone denounced Zweifel's deviant position, which at the time was so revolutionary that the maskilim found it impossible to comprehend 'what had induced him to shock the world of literature at this time with views so incompatible with the spirit of the Haskalah'.[114] An examination of Zweifel's outlook and his consciousness of his place in the maskilic camp in the 1860s shows that his 'deviation' actually stemmed from his attempts to come to terms with the changes of the time as a moderate maskil.

In the struggles waged by the new generation Zweifel was one of the first targets of the radical Haskalah's criticism. In fact, Abramowitz's criticism of Zweifel's collection of poetry *Minim ve'ugav* (Flute and Strings) can be regarded as the

---

[112] Braudes, *Hadat vehahayim*, i. 229, 280–4, 286, 363; ii. 13–43.

[113] Following the controversy about his book, Zweifel added new volumes: ii (Zhitomir, 1869); iii, pt. 1 (Zhitomir, 1870); iii, pt. 2 (Vilna, 1873); iv (Zhitomir, 1873). On Zweifel's life and his book, see his brief autobiography, id., 'Toledot eli'ezer tsevi tsveifel', 274–6; see also Rubinstein, introd. to *Shalom al yisra'el*, 7–34; Feiner, 'The Turning-Point', 167–210.

[114] Slonimski, editorial, *Hamelits*, 8 (1868), 274.

opening shot in the battle between 'sons and fathers'. Appearing in the young Abramowitz's first book, *Mishpat shalom* (The Judgement of Peace), this critique, by his own testimony, was intended to shatter the peace of mind of the writers of the old generation. He asserted that these writers, including Zweifel, were basking with self-satisfaction in the 'garden of literature'. They believed that 'human reason was in such retreat and the critics so weakened that they could not disturb their peace of mind or rob them of their honour and glory, and every book they wrote was sacred in their own eyes'.[115] Abramowitz wanted to challenge the notion of a literary 'authority', to instigate a debate, and to present demands typical of the radical Haskalah; like Kovner, he depicted Zweifel as a representative of the writers of outmoded, useless literature, divorced from real life.[116]

The controversies sparked off by Abramowitz's *Mishpat shalom* and Kovner's acrid articles made the maskilim of the old generation retreat to a defensive position. They reacted by trying to enhance their self-image as 'survivors' and as the 'elders' who were guarding the flame of the 'true Haskalah', in the face of the younger generation's destructive trends and 'insolent criticism'. The maskilim who had recently been the 'trailblazers' in Jewish society now had to defend themselves against those who were even more daring.

The 'old writers, survivors of the old generation', had shaped their world-view by grappling with the extremes in Jewish society, and regarded themselves as 'middle-of-the-road maskilim', adopting a synthetic and harmonious approach to questions of religion and society. 'He is one in a thousand,' Mattityahu Strashun (1819–85) wrote about Zweifel, 'who has summoned all his remaining strength, religion, and faith on his right hand, and profound observation and free enquiry on his left.' He was an exceptional man in a generation in which 'on one side are the young people . . . [who have] lost their faith . . . and on the other, the ignorant, who consecrate and sanctify everything that is old and musty'.[117] The maskilim of the old generation 'did not swallow the Haskalah whole nor were they choked by it', but preserved a 'middle-of-the-road' position, in keeping with Zacharias Frankel's moderate attitude towards halakhic reform, rejecting both Orthodoxy and radical reform. Zweifel identified with this 'positivist-historical' school of thought, founded by Frankel in Germany, and thought it the most suitable for his contemporaries in the circle of moderate maskilim in Russia. There he found a maskilic identity for himself, a group of like-minded thinkers, and a secure place on the map of contemporary ideological streams.[118]

---

[115] Abramowitz, *Mishpat shalom*, 9–46. He attacked maskilim like Zweifel for their hypocrisy and their vacillation between the two camps: 'In truth they have neither anything of hasidism nor of the Haskalah in them, and they fall between two stools' (ibid. 14–16). In retrospect, Abramowitz spoke about his motives for criticizing Zweifel's *Minim ve'ugav* in his short autobiography, 'Reshimot letoledotai', 4.   [116] A. U. Kovner, 'Ḥeker davar', 34–5, 68.

[117] Strashun, approbation to Zweifel's *Sanegor*, 5 (the approbation was signed in 1875).

[118] Zweifel, *Shalom al yisra'el*, vol. iii, pt. 2, 117–19; iv. 50–2.

Zweifel, very much like Fuenn, regarded himself as a historian; his writing is eclectic, making free use of the terminology and ideas of contemporaneous historical thought. He saw himself as continuing in the path of Levinsohn, Rapoport, Krochmal, and Frankel in historical writing, and represented his *Shalom al yisra'el* as a work of the same sort as theirs. However, his concept of history was neither coherent nor systematic in structure, but rather an amalgam of various concepts and ideological elements prevalent in his time. It was particularly marked by the influence of Krochmal's *Moreh nevukhei hazeman* and the use of Hegelian terminology typical of the period. Zweifel aspired to write a historical study that would nullify all contradictory views. He adopted dialectical historical dynamics, understanding dialectical development as the highway of history and as an expression of God's plan and desire: 'The Almighty always places the opposites and the extremes precisely one against the other, in order to pave the way for the mid-point and to maintain and strengthen it.' Thus controversies were 'inevitable in the course of events, and the truth only becomes clear through arguments and contradictory claims'. At every moment history could be seen to be moving towards the mid-point—compromise, synthesis, and harmony, which were objectives fixed by the Almighty. Zweifel interpreted the concept of 'peace' as an embodiment of harmony, and used it to explain why he had chosen to call his book *Peace upon Israel*. In his opinion, 'peace' denoted a situation in which there was absolute compatibility and agreement, while any other situation was tantamount to dissension and disharmony.[119]

Zweifel asserted that historical events must be seen in the context of their time and place, and that in particular the spirit of the time must be regarded as the supra-personal Hegelian factor that moved the wheels of history. His basic assumptions, which included the need to seek the historical roots of events in order to understand them, the dialectical dynamic of historical development as a vital prerequisite for the achievement of harmony, and a search for causal laws, a sequence of events and a spirit of the time in history, led Zweifel to conclude that every event in Jewish history was inevitable and legitimate and fulfilled a historical function. Hence every historical phenomenon should be tolerated, including those which might appear to be aberrations. Incidents of secession and departure from the main historical current also called for detailed historical study.

However, it was not only Zweifel's sense of tolerance and leniency, based on historicist principles, that led him to assert that the various streams of Judaism should be granted legitimization. He was also affected by trends of schism and ideological and social polarization among the Jews, and his growing anxiety at this state of affairs led him to rethink his position, as had Rapoport in Galicia earlier in the century. The growing divisiveness and assimilation in nineteenth-century central and western Europe and the 'growth of a new generation of radical followers

---

[119] Zweifel, *Shalom al yisra'el*, i. 16–23; vol. iii, pt. 1, 47–8. See also Zweifel, 'Tsidkat hashem'.

of the Haskalah' in Russia spurred Zweifel to redeem the 'honour of the ancient nation'. He regarded himself and the 'survivors' close to him and his views as the 'lovers of their people', the only ones capable of recognizing the most urgent objective: the preservation of 'our nationhood'.[120] Zweifel feared that the bonds of national unity were in danger of being severed entirely unless a serious effort was made to mend the breaches. His analysis of modern Jewish life led him to conclude that the growing weakness of 'talmudic Judaism', split between Torah scholars, kabbalists, and hasidim, on one hand, and the growing strength of the Haskalah, on the other, was liable to jeopardize national cohesiveness.

In *Shalom al yisra'el*, Zweifel presented a detailed exposition of the world-view of the harmonious Haskalah, with its trends of national unity, historicist basic assumptions, and 'middle-of-the-road' position. As a moderate maskil he aspired to 'correct distortions' and to grant legitimization to all three social-ideological streams: hasidism, the mitnagedim, and the Haskalah. In his book he examined these streams according to the criteria of the harmonious Haskalah. He saw this as a mission that a moderate maskil, a survivor of the old generation, must undertake 'to mediate peace between sects quarrelling without cause', although it was a thankless and unpopular task. His purpose was not just to vindicate hasidism but also to apply the scalpel of 'study, criticism, and enlightenment' to hasidism, the mitnagedim, and the Haskalah, in order to prove that it was possible to overcome the contradictions between the three and lead them to a state of harmony. 'I am the first to accept this justification [and] this responsibility', he declared.[121]

It has already been noted that in the maskilim's struggle against the hasidim, particularly in Galicia in the first half of the nineteenth century, 'hasidism' and 'science' were regarded as two clear-cut alternatives battling for the hearts and minds of young Jews. The opposition between hasidism and the Haskalah was accompanied by a historical picture of the past that supported this maskilic belief. Zweifel, in contrast, armed with dialectical and dynamic concepts, was capable of breaking new ground and viewing hasidism as an integral part of Jewish history that had evolved within the framework of divine law: the revival of hasidism by the Ba'al Shem Tov stemmed from and was part of the tradition of a personal Providence. Indeed, *Shalom al yisra'el* was mainly devoted to an attempt to trace the historical dynamic by which hasidism legitimately, and perhaps even inevitably, became an integral part—and certainly not a deviant stream—of Jewish history. Zweifel's revolutionary conclusion was that the prevailing understanding of the relationship between the streams should be replaced by a new view: it should no longer be seen as a dichotomous set of contradictory streams but as a harmonious system.

In his opinion, the spirit of the time, which ruled the conduct of men without

[120] Zweifel, *Sanegor*, 15, 20, 27; id., *Shalom al yisra'el*, ii. 7.
[121] Ibid., vol. ii, title-page, 5–9, 26–7.

their knowledge, had underpinned the emergence of hasidism, which came into the Jewish world in response to a spiritual crisis and by way of divine leadership:

Whenever the Almighty sees that men's faith in Him and in His ability and wisdom begins to falter and is about to totter, He puts in that very place or in another place men of Torah and piety, imbued with the Holy Spirit, who reinstate faith, reinforcing and bolstering it on every side, in every corner, until there is no rent or defect in it. And it is no wonder that, for this purpose, the Almighty sometimes makes use of persons who exaggerate and go to great extremes in their piety.[122]

Hasidism was the fourth and last stage in Zweifel's historical schema. The Oral Torah had come into being in response to the crisis of exile, to strengthen national bonds. Later the rationalistic and mystical approaches to the Torah had served a similar purpose. Yet in the final analysis, 'every new thing grows old and time leaves its mark'. As a response to recent spiritual frailty, expressed in Shabbateanism and other phenomena, hasidim came onto the scene.[123]

The theory of a harmony in which hasidim, mitnagedim, and maskilim could maintain peaceful relations was presented as the 'three shepherds' theory, which Zweifel found evident in Fuenn's writings. It first appeared in the latter's *Kiryah ne'emanah*, its assumptions partly based on the Krochmalian philosophy of history. The theory depicted hasidism as a religious revival movement and pointed to the fact that two other 'shepherds' appeared at the same time as the Ba'al Shem Tov, the founder of hasidism. These were Elijah ben Solomon Zalman, the Vilna Gaon, and Moses Mendelssohn. According to the theory of dialectic opposites, God's purpose was to bring about a spiritual and religious revival among the Jews after a low ebb in their history; hence, the 'three shepherds' stood at the threshold of a new historical era:

For He will use every artifice to bring into the world diverse and contrary views at the same time and to place great men at their head, men who will fight one another valiantly with their minds and courageous hearts, to exalt their own way of thinking and to overcome their opponents. And the purpose of these battles and quarrels is in the design of the Almighty: to revive the spirit of religion among His people, to renew their strength and rejuvenate them, to inject them with new life, courage, and resoluteness, so they will not be ruled by time, which destroys everything.[124]

The fundamentals of Judaism were Torah study, faith, and education, but the essential balance between the three was not always maintained. For this reason, Fuenn believed that the Ba'al Shem Tov, the Vilna Gaon, and Mendelssohn should be seen as the 'emissaries of Providence', and that the struggles between hasidim, mitnagedim, and maskilim were legitimate and essential, as well as being divinely authorized:

[122] Zweifel, *Shalom al yisra'el*, i. 16–28.   [123] Ibid. 46–8.
[124] Fuenn, *Kiryah ne'emanah*, 141–3.

God saw . . . and He raised up for us three shepherds in different places to support the three pillars . . . the Almighty called upon Rabbi Elijah in Lithuania to safeguard the Torah, to purify its Talmud, and to oversee its logic and its diligent study. He called upon the head of the hasidim in Volhynia to marshal devotion and to fan the embers of feeling. He found the great sage of our people Moses ben Menachem in Germany, and called him to place the candle of enlightenment in the lamp of religion.[125]

By including hasidism in a general historical schema as one of the three social-ideological streams in Judaism, on one hand, and by equating the contribution of their 'founding fathers', each of whom merited an unshakeable authoritative status, on the other hand, Zweifel supported his conclusion that processes of reconciliation and cross-fertilization must develop in the future. From this point onwards, the way was open to rapprochement and a re-evaluation of the hasidic movement. But Zweifel aspired even higher, and in order to persuade his opponents that there was a firm basis for his demand that hasidism be accepted into the bosom of the Jewish people, he tried to prove its legitimacy in other ways too.

Zweifel believed that a meticulous analysis of the teachings of hasidism and the figure of the hasidic *tsadik*, as well as their comparison with talmudic and kabbalistic beliefs and views, would prove that hasidism was really an offshoot of the religious mainstream of Judaism. He summoned scores of quotations and citations as precedents to prove that, in principle, there was nothing new or innovative in hasidism, and that all its ideas had always existed in Judaism. To substantiate his claim, Zweifel cited testimonies from various sources praising the Ba'al Shem Tov and his approach, quoting them at length, particularly in the case of the Lurianic kabbalah, to demonstrate the element of continuity in hasidism. He rejected all claims that the Ba'al Shem Tov was a backward man of no learning and depicted him as a kabbalist of the same stature as Luria, the Vilna Gaon, and others, a man who during his lifetime had already achieved fame as a great and honoured rabbi. This defensive tactic was primarily intended to create a bridge between mitnagedim and hasidism, for Zweifel himself believed that kabbalist literature contained many deplorable elements, damaging to morality, reason, and propriety. However, these arguments were intended to undermine the position of the mitnagedic camp, for he believed that they ought to understand that all criticism and denunciation levelled at hasidism really amounted to a criticism of kabbalah in general.[126]

In Zweifel's view, not only could hasidism be depicted as a normative system of ideas, which made it imperative to blur the artificial differences between hasid and mitnaged, but one could also find positive elements in it from a maskilic perspective. By pointing out modern ideas inherent in the teachings of hasidism, Zweifel argued that hasidism was not a routine and unbroken continuation of Lurianic kabbalah but a modern stage of its development. In the Ba'al Shem Tov's teachings Lurianic concepts had undergone a transformation, moving the arena

---

[125] Ibid.; Zweifel, *Shalom al yisra'el*, i. 20–2. Cf. Pinsker, *Likutei kadmoniyot*, 2–3.
[126] Zweifel, *Shalom al yisra'el*, i. 39–50; ii. 14–15, 27, 61, 66, 99, 111, 124.

of spiritual events from the theosophical realm to the human psyche. He endowed the Ba'al Shem Tov with a rationalist image, stating that he had never used holy names or amulets as professional miracle-workers did. The Ba'al Shem Tov had uncovered a new aspect of kabbalah: 'We have nothing at all to do, he said, with those *sefirot*, *orot* (lights), and *partsufim* (divine configurations) that float high in the air or up in the seven heavens, but rather with those same *sefirot*, *midot* (attributes), and *orot* that are in the heart of man.'[127] The proclamations and utterances he heard from the heavens were nothing other than 'voices of repentance and sublime thoughts', and he employed the concept of *ha'alat hanitsotsot* ('the uplifting of the holy sparks') in order to 'separate the spirituality and vitality of things from their corporeality, to perceive the subtleties of the sources from which they emanate, and to find joy in the pleasantness of the spiritual and the beauty of the abstract'.[128] Ostensibly, then, hasidism had removed foreign and miraculous elements from its teaching and hasidic *tsadikim* had not accepted the Lurianic theory literally but had psychologized it.

To demonstrate the profundity of hasidic theory, Zweifel also compared it to Neoplatonism and to Spinoza's teaching. He saw a parallel between the philosophical method of the Neoplatonists and 'the major element that the Ba'al Shem Tov infused into hasidic doctrine, namely the notion that all lower things are examples of higher ones; for example, all instances of beauty that the eye perceives below are but miniatures of the ideal all-embracing beauty of the upper world'.[129] Zweifel devoted an entire portion of his book to his claim that the Ba'al Shem Tov's teaching was identical to Spinoza's pantheistic theory, basing this on the hasidic premiss 'There is no place devoid of Him'. Anyone accepting this analogy must concede that hasidism was in fact a profound, elaborate system of ideas that could not be lightly dismissed: 'the pure teachings of the Ba'al Shem Tov, which were suspect and thought by many to be merely superstition and foolishness, or an errant fantasy that only the poorest of minds could accept, and the pure theory of Spinoza . . . in themselves and in their source are one and the same . . . and that source is the true inner communion with God'.[130]

Zweifel resorted to another defensive tactic, suggesting that hasidism had greater potential than other elements in Jewish society for absorbing the path and values of the Haskalah. Hasidism had emerged as a response to 'the mental stagnation of the old rabbis' and as a protest against 'the moral state of the talmudic scholars, resulting from an absence of life and a lack of proper feeling'. The hasidim found no peace for their souls in the barren *pilpul* of the Talmud and the study of fine points of halakhah, and yearned for new spiritual nourishment. Hence, since hasidism was actually a challenge to the modes of talmudic study and the pedantry of the commandments, Zweifel reasoned, the hasidim actually stood shoulder to shoulder with the maskilim in the forefront of the struggle for reform

---

[127] Zweifel, *Shalom al yisra'el*, vol. iii, pt. 1, p. 31; ii. 20.   [128] Ibid. i. 59–60.

[129] Ibid. i. 56, 93–4.   [130] Ibid., vol. iii, pt. 2, pp. 63–4.

in traditional society. The Ba'al Shem Tov's theory of *avodah begashmiut* (earthly worship of God) had opened the way for *tsadikim* and hasidim to worship God through physical, external acts, based on the idea that 'by the consecration of faith, material pleasure becomes spiritual too'. This concept also explained the lavish courts of the *tsadikim*, their objection to asceticism, and the many luxuries they enjoyed.[131]

In Zweifel's view, the espousal of worldly pleasures was an important, progressive element introduced by hasidism into Jewish society, which had previously been characterized by the denial of such pleasures and had not given any thought to aesthetics or beauty. Moreover, the fact that hasidism preached moral virtues, modesty, and humility and was opposed to greed, frivolity, and mendacity showed that it had a fitting and healthy approach to life that conformed to the values of the maskilim. The freshness and vitality of hasidism were clearly manifested in social encounters in the courts of the *tsadikim*: 'All there become brothers, the sons of one father; no one sets himself higher than another, the rich are not disdainful of the poor, no rabbi elevates himself by degrading the common man.' Brotherhood and joy prevailed in the hasidic community, and this experience of communion released the hasid from his concerns and torments, enhanced his confidence, and provided him with solace.[132] Zweifel based these observations on the works of the German Jewish proto-Zionist Moses Hess (1812–75), who referred to hasidism as a regenerative movement rather than as a deviant or regressive phenomenon. In his opinion, the lifestyle of the hasidic community could be described as socialist, and its mode of religion as 'emphasizing the inner essence of the religion more than the external performance of its precepts'. Hess valued hasidism highly as a movement of renewal, and called for a recognition of its historical importance as a positive transitional phenomenon: 'Hasidism . . . serves as a natural transition, within the living spirit of a Judaism (which has been influenced more instinctively than consciously by the spirit of modern times), and thus forms a transition from medieval Judaism, which should still be conceived as undergoing development.'[133]

In the regenerative elements of hasidism Hess found the potential for a national Jewish movement and perhaps also for religious reform, while Zweifel saw it as the potential for the triumph of the Haskalah in Jewish society. Hitherto the maskilim had seen their mission as the dissemination of the values of Haskalah within the camp of mitnagedim, and had regarded the hasidim as enemies lightyears away from the Haskalah; now Zweifel painted a completely different picture. He thought it more likely that hasidism would be the first to draw close to the Haskalah rather than the reverse, since it already embodied maskilic elements that could provide a common ground, and was so open to life.

The maskilim, who disputed Zweifel's views and rejected his defence of hasidism, called upon him to take account not only of the founders of the movement

---

[131] Ibid., vol. iii, pt. 1, pp. 26–8; ii. 30–5.   [132] Ibid., vol. iii, pt. 1, pp. 17–28.

[133] Hess, *Rome and Jerusalem*, 145–8.

but also of its later stages. This forced Zweifel to draw a distinction between the original, authentic, and pure hasidic movement and what seemed to be its decline and corruption in the course of the nineteenth century. He admitted that the early hasidim could hardly have imagined what their disciples would do and how far they would stray from their path and teachings, interpreting them in an incorrect and distorted manner. Indeed, he observed, 'the devil has begun to dominate the deeds of hasidism and to dance between the rays of its light'.[134]

The re-evaluation of hasidism, first coherently expressed in Zweifel's *Shalom al yisra'el*, was thus linked to Zweifel's world-view and his standing in maskilic circles in Russia in the 1860s and 1870s. In making this shift, Zweifel did not cross any lines. During the controversy many did claim that Zweifel was mentally un-balanced, and that after having been a member of the maskilic élite for years he had become a turncoat, an out-and-out hasid. But the truth is that he remained a maskil throughout, in every sense, from the standpoint of his social circle, his sys-tem of values, and his thought and self-awareness. Although some of the hostility towards *Shalom al yisra'el* was reminiscent of the voices of disillusionment and astonishment heard in the 1820s and 1830s among Galician maskilim in reaction to rumours of their friend Samuel Bick's defection to hasidism, Zweifel, unlike Bick, was not a maskil who had taken up hasidism and moved to the opposite camp. Bick expressed great dissatisfaction with the values of the Haskalah and its rationalist approach, and found in hasidism a stress on emotion, love of the Jewish people, and a great degree of social sensitivity, but Zweifel, in contrast, invested considerable intellectual effort in proving hasidism to be one of several legitimate ideological streams in Judaism in the eighteenth and nineteenth centuries. His point of departure was, and remained, the maskilic position, and his legitimization of hasidism was basically the fruit of rationalist maskilic thinking. In his world-view, hasidism was an integral part of a crystallized system, which represented the har-monious stream in the Haskalah. He arrived at his favourable evaluation of hasid-ism on the basis of a historical outlook and historicist concepts and his desire to reinvigorate the crumbling sense of national unity. Zweifel believed that the true, authentic approach of the Haskalah—the harmonious maskilic view—demanded the acceptance of hasidism into the bosom of the Jewish people. He held to this conviction despite the fact that even within the camp of moderate maskilim, to which he belonged, his position was regarded as deviant and as an audacious breach of maskilic conventions. In Zweifel's view, it was precisely the 'middle-of-the-road' maskil who was more capable than any other of observing hasidism object-ively without being biased in either direction.

Zweifel provided much important raw material for modern research on hasid-ism. By including in his book a wide and diverse selection of historical sources for the history and teachings of hasidism, he also introduced the fundamental assump-

---

[134] Zweifel, *Shalom al yisra'el*, i. 27–8; ii. 21–2. See also id., 'Zikaron livenei yisra'el o asham ḥasidim', 127–35.

tion that the phenomenon of hasidism was a subject that deserved historical research, based on its own sources. His interpretation of hasidism also gradually
permeated general attitudes towards the movement, and despite the acrimonious
debate, it had already begun to have an effect by the 1870s. However, the negative
hasidic stereotype did not disappear, nor did the literary struggle by the Haskalah
against hasidism draw to a close. The publication of the eleventh volume of Graetz's
Geschichte der Juden in 1870 actually reinforced the prevalent maskilic view of
hasidism. Moreover, it gave it the stamp of approval of an authoritative historian,
held in high esteem by Russian maskilim. Graetz contrasted hasidism and the
Haskalah, in terms of absolute opposites—ignorance versus reason, darkness
versus light—and denounced hasidism as replete with fantasy, superstition, de-
generacy, and acts of madness, motivated by the 'false kabbalah'. Furthermore, as
a result of his consideration of the historical dimension as well as the ideological
aspect of hasidism, he regarded it as a negative phenomenon, typical of its time
and place, in accordance with his general attitude towards east European Jewry:
'There are persons, times, and places in which the line of demarcation between
trickery and self-delusion cannot be distinguished.' There was really nothing surprising about this phenomenon, for in Poland Christians and Jews, Jesuits and
kabbalists lived together in a state of 'primitive barbarism'. While the major role
in the 'rejuvenation of the Jewish race' was played by Mendelssohn and the Berlin
Haskalah, Graetz believed that paradoxically and dialectically the hasidim also
had a share in the historical transition of the mid-eighteenth century. Hasidism
came into being in reaction to 'rabbinism', which was marked by 'the dryness and
fossilized character of talmudic study'. Hence, Graetz stated, continuing the idea
raised by Solomon Maimon eighty years earlier, it embodied a certain element of
reform, even if the main players were unaware of their role. Graetz asserted that
the hasidim had almost totally abandoned talmudic study and concluded that they
had a part in the destruction of talmudic Judaism, a process that he regarded as
one of the hallmarks of the modern age in Jewish history: 'Reason and unreason
seem to have entered into a covenant to shatter the gigantic structure of talmudic
Judaism . . . Mendelssohn and Israel Ba'al Shem, what contrasts! Yet both uncon-
sciously undermined the basis of talmudic Judaism.'[135]

Gottlober, Zweifel's friend but also his opponent on the subject of *Shalom al*
yisra'el, was greatly influenced in his attitude towards hasidism by Graetz's book,
but apparently Zweifel's ideas also had an impact on him. He believed that hasidism had diverted the kabbalistic stream from the dangerous messianic Shabbatean
and Frankist route to a modern moderate anti-messianic path. Hasidism stood
firmly on 'the ground of Judaism' and should not be regarded as an aberration like
the deviant messianic movements. In the spirit of Graetz's views, and perhaps
also somewhat in line with Zweifel's outlook, Gottlober saw a new and reformist
method in hasidism: 'The new method, introduced by the Ba'al Shem Tov into

---

[135] H. Graetz, *Geschichte der Juden*, xi. 93–115.

the world of Judaism, brought a breath of new life into it and roused it from the slumber in which it had languished for many years in the bosom of the talmudic rabbinate.'[136] But this was only true when hasidism was judged in comparison to rabbinic Judaism, which, in his view, was formalistic and moribund. When compared to the Haskalah, however, it could only be evaluated in negative terms, since there was no room in it for 'the sciences and the knowledge so essential to mankind', and in hasidic writings one could find a great deal of nonsense and delirium. From the outset, the ability of hasidism to function within Jewish society as a reforming movement was extremely limited.[137]

Gottlober did find a positive aspect in the battles between hasidism and mitnagedim, since in the final analysis they helped to strengthen the Haskalah. The mitnagedim's negative representation of the *tsadikim* and the hasidim and the hasidim's assault on the rabbis helped to weaken the authoritative and sanctified image of the traditional leadership and of normative values, thus opening the way for an alternative, in the form of the Haskalah: 'They unwittingly did us a good turn by opposing the rabbis, for they opened the eyes of many to see that both the rabbis and the hasidim were wide of the mark, and they began to seek a different path, a search that led them to the path of science and knowledge, and this was the profit that was gained thereby.'[138]

In Gottlober's opinion, a greater potential for real reform lay in the approach of the Vilna Gaon. However, unlike the Ba'al Shem Tov, the Vilna Gaon was completely oblivious to the needs of Jewry, and hence it never occurred to him that reforms were necessary. He thus never assumed the mantle of leadership, although potential for real reform was inherent in his personality and teachings; while the Ba'al Shem Tov did take on the role of a leader, his kabbalistic education and his delusions prevented him from bringing about salvation. The light had to shine forth far from Poland, in Prussia. However, once the Haskalah finally arrived in Poland in the early nineteenth century, it did spread with ease to the hasidic districts. Although a large centre of maskilim developed in Lithuania, Gottlober asserted that from the standpoint of its 'qualitative spread', the Haskalah made its greatest gains in the area of Volhynia because there the hasidim had already made 'a wider breach in the lofty wall of the *Shulḥan arukh* than in those places where the mitnagedim had fortified that wall and built higher and more fortified walls atop it'.[139]

The maskilim's opposition and hostility to hasidism did not dissipate, but Zweifel's *Shalom al yisra'el* did shatter one of the hitherto unchallenged dogmas of the Haskalah: the delegitimization of hasidism. At the same time, it also undermined some concepts of 'maskilic history'. From then on, it became much harder to accept simplistic historical outlines that portrayed history as an arena of battles between the 'good' and the 'bad', men of reason and fools, the progressive and the

---

[136] Gottlober, 'Hagizrah vehabeniyah', 49–52. Cf. id., *Toledot hakabalah*.
[137] Id., 'Hagizrah vehabeniyah', 68–9.   [138] Ibid. 119–21.   [139] Ibid. 121.

reactionary, or to adhere to the historical model that mapped out the legitimate high road, from which deviant side roads diverged—two of the prominent features of the maskilic picture of the past, formulated under the influence of the struggle against the hasidic enemy. Nineteenth-century historicism, as adopted by Zweifel, demanded that all historical phenomena should be described objectively.

FROM 'MASKILIC HISTORY' TO 'NATIONAL HISTORY'

While the radical Haskalah was rejecting maskilic idealism and proposing positivist history and Zweifel was challenging the anti-hasidic aspect of the maskilic picture of the past, 'national history' was emerging, with Perez Smolenskin at its helm. In his attempt to destroy the historical image of Mendelssohn, he almost totally obliterated maskilic history.

In the late 1860s Smolenskin began to examine Jewish society in eastern Europe from an unusual vantage-point which had a great impact on his analyses and conclusions. He was a typical Russian maskil: his early life in Belarus, his studies in the Shklov yeshiva, his attempts to find direction for his life first in hasidism and then as a young self-educated maskil were all stages that characterized the lives of most young men of his generation.[140] After five years (1862–7) in Odessa, however, Smolenskin wandered westwards, ultimately settling in Vienna. There, in 1868, he began to publish a Hebrew journal, Hashaḥar (The Dawn), which became a forum for the Haskalah movement in eastern Europe. As a Russian Jewish maskil living in the cosmopolitan capital of the Austrian empire, Smolenskin's situation was a far cry from that of his counterparts in Russia. He was exposed to political and social events, principally the national ferment in central and western Europe; he was knowledgeable in modern European history; and he was closely and directly acquainted with central European Jews and the political and religious problems of the emancipation era with which they were grappling. He maintained a continuous correspondence with the maskilim in Russia and Galicia, distributed Hashaḥar through a network of agents in eastern Europe, and provided east European maskilim with a Hebrew platform for their journalistic and literary writings, as well as for their articles on Jewish studies. Hashaḥar also published trenchant maskilic articles, whether critical of the religious leadership or supportive of radical and socialist trends, which could not be published in Russia. In terms of Smolenskin's social-ideological link with the world of the eastern European Haskalah, national borders were irrelevant, but in terms of his personal experience, intellectual world, and contact with Western Jewry, his Viennese background was highly significant.[141]

As a result of this, Smolenskin anticipated maskilim in Russia in changing his priorities with regard to the aims of the maskilic struggle. I have already mentioned

---

[140] On Smolenskin, see J. Klausner, History of Modern Hebrew Literature, v. 15–268; Freundlich, Peretz Smolenskin.

[141] Wistrich, The Jews in Vienna, 350–5; id., 'The Modernization of Viennese Jewry', 55–7.

the heavy criticism levelled by the maskilim not only against the enemies of the Haskalah but also against assimilationists, pseudo-maskilim, and acculturated Jews. Smolenskin was more disturbed by the problem constituted by the latter group, since he was living in a Western Jewish community. He reacted to the events of Jewish life in both eastern and western Europe. In his criticism of religious reform, for example, he took into account not only the writings of Lilienblum and Gordon but particularly those of the German reformists. The contents of *Hashaḥar* must therefore be read with the utmost care in order to discern the fundamental change Smolenskin demanded of the maskilim.

'Not like the former days are these days', he wrote in his introduction to *Hashaḥar* (1868). Twenty or thirty years ago the brunt of the war was internal: 'The benighted, sanctimonious obscurantists and their entire army waged war on those who sought to spread precious light on the paths of their brethren.' Not even a single maskil of the previous generation could have imagined a day when the war would be renewed, this time between the maskilim and those who opposed the Hebrew language (and, in fact, those who opposed all maskilic values). This new war, Smolenskin argued, was far more difficult and more dangerous than its predecessor. As long as the maskilim were engaged in a struggle against the 'sanctimonious', there was still hope that the acquisition of knowledge would rid them of their folly. Now, however, this was not merely a war of folly versus reason but a war against a multitude who were crying, 'The Hebrew tongue is nothing to us, nor is the legacy of the Jewish way.' 'All men who love their people will be horrified to hear such words', Smolenskin wrote, expressing his extreme dismay as well as his genuine doubt that the Haskalah could offer a way to reform these 'arrogant hypocrites'.[142]

Smolenskin's *Hashaḥar* demanded that the struggle against 'the benighted' be postponed, and that the Haskalah's first priority be the struggle against the 'pseudo-Haskalah', which he considered not only a distortion of the Haskalah but also an undesirable anti-nationalist trend that endangered national Jewish existence more than the 'benighted' endangered Jewish culture and society. This idea, which informed Smolenskin's philosophy from the late 1860s onwards, was the hallmark of what may be termed the 'national Haskalah'—Haskalah combined with criticism of anti-nationalist trends and the reinforcement of national consciousness. His familiarity with Western Jewry led Smolenskin to the conclusion that the nationalist Haskalah would achieve its goals if Western anti-nationalistic tendencies were halted before they could penetrate eastern Europe.

Smolenskin's avowed nationalist view was formulated in his long articles published in the 1870s 'Am olam' (The Eternal People, 1872) and 'Et lata'at (A Time to Plant, 1875–7). A striking and interesting feature of this perspective was the transformation of traditional and maskilic concepts, which acquired nationalistic

---

[142] Smolenskin, 'Petaḥ davar', pp. iv–v; Feiner, 'Smolenskin's Haskalah Heresy', 9–31.

significance through their secularization. Smolenskin's principal aim was to prove that the Jews had been a people in the past and were a people in the present, and to reject attempts to define the Jews in the modern era, perhaps even from the time of the destruction of their independent state, as merely a religious community. He believed that although the Jews did not possess the standard appurtenances of a nation, such as territory, political government, and a uniform language, these had been replaced by different national possessions. For him, Hebrew was not simply the holy tongue or the language of the pure, classical Jewish Haskalah but rather the language that 'will bestow honour and glory upon us, and will bind us to the joys of bearing the name Israel'.[143] The Hebrew language was the only relic that had survived among the ruins of the ancient glory and the Temple, and those who betrayed it were traitors to their people and their religion.[144] The terms 'faith', 'Torah', and '*mitsvah*' were also transformed and secularized in Smolenskin's philosophy, becoming the cornerstone of the nation. Torah and *mitsvot* were perceived not as a system of practical laws but rather as a spiritual system. Customs, in and of themselves, were nothing more than 'corpses . . . [and] dead carcasses', subject to the vicissitudes of time; but Torah was a spiritual essence, the 'glue' that united the nation: 'God, as King, and the Torah, as the tie that binds the nation, give us life today, and only through them shall we know what our lives are; and knowing that, we shall also know what we were, for we are one people, and not merely believers in the same creed or religion.'[145]

Smolenskin's national approach tended towards cultural–spiritual nationalism. 'We are a people', he declared, and our unity 'will come into being only when it is based upon a feeling of brotherhood, a national feeling'.[146] Influenced by Krochmal, Smolenskin's national view was underpinned by the idea of 'the distinctiveness of the spirit of Israel', coupled with a romantic nationalistic feeling and a feeling of brotherhood, which together created national and spiritual unity.[147] He believed that the Bible constituted an immense national treasure as a repository of memories that preserved Jewish historical roots, a picture of the past that revealed national unity, and a series of religious commands. It was nothing less than 'the amalgamation that would unite and unify the hearts of the Jewish people wherever they live'.[148] Smolenskin, who perceived religion as the main substitute for a land, a country, and a language, therefore opposed religious reforms of the kind being instituted in Germany. While it was true that the halakhah must be updated and revised, he felt that those who made such revisions arbitrarily would ultimately violate brotherhood, endanger unity, and place the existence of their people at risk.

Jewish history played a key role in this process of transforming traditional terms and concepts, of secularizing, spiritualizing, and nationalizing 'Hebrew',

---

[143] Smolenskin, 'Even yisra'el', no. 3, pp. 5–6. Cf. Bartal, 'From Traditional Bilingualism', 141–50.
[144] Smolenskin, 'Even yisra'el', no. 3, pp. 5–6; see also Smolenskin, 'Et la'asot', 170–8.
[145] Id., 'Et lata'at', 20.   [146] Ibid. 28–9. Cf. Y. Kaufmann, *Exile and Foreign Land*, ii. 289–99.
[147] Smolenskin, 'Et lata'at', 17–19.   [148] Id., 'Am olam', 33.

'Torah', 'religion', and 'commandments', which were appropriated and enshrined in the repertoire of national assets. Smolenskin considered history to be perhaps more crucial than any other element in achieving the two goals of the national Haskalah: to shape a national consciousness and to censure anti-nationalists.

Like most maskilim, Smolenskin was not a historian who wrote original studies but rather a thinker whose outlook was historical in nature. As a nationalist-maskilic propagandist, Smolenskin demanded that the approach to writing Jewish history be revised; he wanted a new Jewish historiography that would conform to his views. He introduced the guidelines of this type of historiography in 'Even yisra'el' (The Rock of Israel), a long article published in serial form in *Hashahar* during 1868–9. This was a critique of *Der jüdische Stamm* (The Jewish Tribe), an ethnographic study written by Adolf Jellinek (1820–93), the well-known Viennese Jewish preacher and scholar. At the heart of Jellinek's study was an attempt to prove the universality of Judaism and the Jewish people.[149] In his critique Smolenskin proposed a distinction between 'universal history' and 'national history'. In universal history the historian intended to present the general history of peoples, relating to them as if they were a single organism and consciously ignoring their individual nature. Each people was examined only according to the function it fulfilled as part of the whole organism. Continuing this characteristic maskilic line of thought, Smolenskin believed that universal history enabled us 'to understand the last on the basis of the first, and to judge the first on the basis of the last'.[150] In other words, universal history provided historians with the ability to prophesy the future, as well as with the knowledge of how to evaluate historical changes correctly. In contrast, national history concentrated on one people, which it viewed as a complete organism, disregarding its internal contradictions, disputes, and divisions. It sketched the lines of national history, emphasizing the common, unifying elements of the people whose history it recounted. National history, however, also fulfilled a maskilic–didactic function, passing judgement on a particular people by comparing it to others.

How was it possible, Smolenskin enquired, that non-Jewish historians describing Jewish history held such disparate views of it while their opinion of other peoples, such as the French or Germans, for example, was unanimous? Why did some historians condemn and others glorify the Jewish people? It was apparently not the historians who were to blame, nor their research methodology and writing, but rather the unique nature of Jewish history. Standard historiography recounted the history of peoples possessed of territory, government, and a living language, and was based on the belief that the attributes of a people and its natural, ecological environment were interdependent. This type of historiography was incapable of fully and accurately explaining the history of a people lacking the usual characteristics of a nation. The singularity of Jewish history therefore required a singular historiography.

[149] On Adolf Jellinek and his book, see Wistrich, *The Jews in Vienna*, 50–6.
[150] Smolenskin, 'Even yisra'el', no. 3, p. 6.

Smolenskin believed that the ideal chronicler of Jewish history should himself be Jewish, able to draw on resources such as a knowledge of the Hebrew language, Jewish sources, and the social milieu. He should be bold, for his task would lead him along paths that other historians had yet to tread, and he would have to resolve the difficult questions he would undoubtedly come up against during his writing of Jewish history: what was the mysterious force that had endowed the Jewish people, throughout their history and all their wanderings, with national unity? What tools should be used in analysing the history of national unity, when geography, governments, legal systems, and educational and economic conditions varied so greatly among all the Jewish communities? Since the earlier historians differed from one another, which of them should be used as sources? How could a historian cover the entire period of 4,000 years? And must the chronicler of Jewish history depart from the view that the course of history is progressive, an approach that had always underpinned written histories of other peoples, moving from the early generations of savages and pagans to the later, enlightened generations? Was the process the Jewish people underwent actually a reverse, regressive one? How, then, should the historian navigate between the traditional approach glorifying the ancients and the view that sharply opposed them?

Smolenskin did not respond to these questions in a structured manner, although it is clear from them that he expected that the future historian would believe in the uniqueness of Jewish history. The historian's main task was ultimately to portray and prove the national unity and historical continuity of Jewish history. Methodologically, Smolenskin suggested that the historian should combine the method of universal history with that of national history: just as the universal historian described the development of all peoples, so the Jewish historian must describe the Jews as a single organic people, focusing on the overall, unifying character of all Jewish communities, and obscuring local individuality, while, as a national historian, he must explain how the Jews differed from other peoples. Smolenskin formulated this combined methodology, which in his opinion suited the needs of the national historiography of the Jews, in the following words: 'Look to the nation and show only the paths and ideas followed by all the Jews, by all their factions in all the countries of their dispersion, if only they, and not other peoples, followed these paths and held these ideas.'[151]

The ideal historiography, in Smolenskin's view, would become a major national asset and an endless source of national self-respect, like the Hebrew language: 'For our history will be like a land and a country, the tie that binds together those exiled among the nations of their dispersion, making them a single people.' History would provide the eternal proof to all those who were unconvinced 'that we are a people', for it would serve not only as a repository of information but also as an 'advocate'.[152]

---

[151] Ibid., no. 6, p. 7.   [152] Smolenskin, book review, *Hashaḥar*, 5 (1874), 78–9.

Smolenskin himself never created the ideal national historiography he preached, although he did sketch several of its guidelines and described sections of pictures from the past he believed it should paint. All this was done in the hope that historians would soon emerge who would adopt his views and write the hoped-for historical study. In terms of the development of the maskilic picture of the past, the version formulated by Smolenskin in *Hashaḥar* in the 1870s embodied first and foremost the transition from 'maskilic history' to 'national history'.

In April 1871 Smolenskin received the first news of the pogroms perpetrated against the Jews of Odessa, and published his initial response immediately on the back cover of *Hashaḥar*. The Odessa pogroms caused him to re-evaluate the maskilic perception of 'the modern era':

Do not believe what is spoken in this era of the knowledge and love of man, do not listen to the words of those who glorify this time as a time of human justice and honest opinion; it is a lie! For at the time of the crusaders and the blood-soaked government of Isabella in Spain, murderers aspired to blood vengeance, and so it is in this time.[153]

This emotional response by Smolenskin resembles those written ten years later by the maskilim in reaction to the 1881–2 pogroms. The encounter with antisemitism in its most brutal form was sufficient to eradicate from the maskilic consciousness the favourable conception of the 'modern era' that they had so warmly defended and cultivated for almost a century. As discussed above, the radical maskilim had linked their protest against the nineteenth century to social and universal matters (such as the plight of the workers and of women), while, for Smolenskin, the national issue was of dominant importance. He believed that antisemitism as a constant historical phenomenon in the history of the Jews grew out of the tension between national power and national weakness, and not out of religious or economic antagonism. This analysis led him to conclude that the solution to the 'Jewish question' entailed strengthening Jewish national consciousness and increasing the ability of the Jews to engage in organized political activity. He made no mention at all of amassing national power in physical terms, and, in the wake of the Odessa pogroms, explained that his call 'Teach the sons of Judah warfare!' was intended only to arouse a change of consciousness, and to urge political lobbying.[154] In any event, in the early 1870s Smolenskin inveighed against those who believed that 'the modern era' was superior to its predecessors: wars had not ceased, blood continued to be spilled, and religious fanaticism had not disappeared.

It took only a year for Smolenskin to temper his scathing view of the 'modern era'. In his articles 'Am olam' and 'Et lata'at' he returned to his self-awareness as a maskil who admitted the advantages of the modern era, but this time he based his views on a different and more complex interpretation than before. In 1871 his response had been spontaneous and emotional, a contradiction of fundamental maskilic optimism; but when the emotional turmoil had abated somewhat, Smolen-

---

[153] Smolenskin, 'Lelamed livenei yehudah keshet!', 361–3.   [154] Ibid.

skin came to a more balanced view of the modern era. He had no doubt that in universal history it symbolized a shift for the better, as compared to the past: man's mastery of nature, scientific thought, human liberty, the transfer of religious faith from the public domain and the state into the heart and conscience of the individual, progress, release from the yoke of the Church, the defeat of the Jesuits and the Inquisition—all these were the hallmarks of the period as seen by a confirmed Jewish liberal like Smolenskin.[155] In his picture of the past, both universal and, as will be seen, Jewish, Smolenskin judged history by a twofold standard: first, the national unity of a people versus their tendencies towards dissolution and division; and secondly, the preservation of 'the spirit of freedom' versus oppression, coercion, and clericalism. In this picture of the past the processes occurring in the modern era were not necessarily revolutionary and progressive, but rather involved a conflict of opinions, regression, 'cohesive forces', and 'disruptive forces'.[156] Martin Luther's historical image was, on one hand, that of the modern father of liberty and, on the other, a lamentable example of renewed oppression. From his reading of the historical literature on Luther, Smolenskin came to the conclusion that he had not created something *ex nihilo* but had continued a gradual process that had already begun to develop during the fourteenth and fifteenth centuries. The German anti-scholastic humanists, led by Reuchlin, had laid the groundwork for undermining the Pope's status. Luther, who came after them, was endowed with a revolutionary spirit; he did not pursue their moderate, balanced path but demanded that his views and new faith be granted the same validity and sacred authority demanded by the Pope, against whom he was rebelling. And what did Luther gain?, asked Smolenskin. He broke the old fetters only to replace them with new, stronger ones. Paradoxically, claimed Smolenskin, it was the Catholics who continued to struggle for liberty, enlightenment, and tolerance, while the Protestants, who believed they had already achieved liberty, had, in truth, become enslaved to new dogmas.[157]

Smolenskin acknowledged Luther's positive impact on the dissemination of sacred writings in a language the people could understand, 'like an angel sent to open the eyes of the blind who had wandered in darkness for hundreds of years'. Nor did he ignore the unintentional contribution of his struggle against the Church to a positive change in attitudes towards the Jews in Protestant countries.[158] However, he did not gloss over Luther's anti-Jewish views and held him up as an undesirable example of a radical revolutionary. In his view a historical figure must function as 'a mediator', wise enough to understand which elements of the past and of tradition should be preserved and which should be rejected. He saw no justification in a sudden innovation that was neither based on nor drew from the historical past, and he also doubted that the historical importance of a single

[155] Smolenskin, 'Am olam', 8–10, 127–35; 'Et lata'at', 48.   [156] Smolenskin, 'Am olam', 5–11.
[157] Ibid. 11–13.   [158] Smolenskin, 'Et lata'at', 45–8.

individual could be compared to the crucial impact of the masses on historical changes.[159]

Smolenskin also employed this rationale in his rejection of the trend towards religious reform in Germany and Russia. Like Pines, he argued that rash and radical changes should not be made without taking into account tradition and history. He wrote in 'Am olam' that there was some justification for the Reformation in Germany, since the Germans had to throw off the yoke of the Jesuits and the Pope. Such, however, was not the case for Jewish society, and the rabbis did not possess the kind of coercive power that the Catholic clergy had. Smolenskin accused the German Jewish Reform movement of being a perfunctory and spurious emulation of the German Reformation.[160] He used the same argument to reject Jewish social- ist radicalism, because of its severance of its links to the past, and he criticized the Haskalah for not understanding that the spirit of a people that had existed for 4,000 years could not be so precipitously altered.[161]

Smolenskin's censure of Luther was yet another aspect of his anti-Germanism. What role had Germany played in the transition from the old to the modern era? Undoubtedly, Smolenskin replied, this transition did begin on German soil, with the German humanism of the late Middle Ages and its continuation in the Re- formation. However, the Germans, who created the idea of humanism, were spirit- ually barren and never implemented that exalted notion. German impotence, he believed, was rooted in universalism, an abstract, illusory idea completely di- vorced from reality. He believed that the primary links between a man and his family and people could not be replaced by an abstract slogan calling for 'the love of all people', thus, in effect, attacking yet another central maskilic concept. The Germans had a propensity for theoretical thinking, and the concepts of liberty, religious tolerance, and humanism that had developed in Germany were adopted by other countries. France used them in a political revolution, and the French re- volt against a tyrannical government was, in effect, a revolt against a government of priests.[162]

As a liberal, Smolenskin justified the French Revolution, believing it to be legit- imate and even necessary, for 'The force of necessity compelled those oppressed by the heavy yoke to strike out against their masters.'[163] 'War pits lovers of freedom against those who preach religion', and since the men of religion were responsible for the oppression, the revolution was directed first of all against 'the black ravens that gathered to suck the blood of the masses'. Later it became a political struggle against rulers whose power was based on their collaboration with the priests. With the fall of the priests and rulers, the oppressed, including the Jews, were lib- erated. In Smolenskin's opinion, 'men of freedom' seeking allies for their cause

---

[159] Smolenskin, 'Toledot harav'.   [160] Smolenskin, 'Am olam', 26, 127–35.
[161] Smolenskin, book review, Hashahar, 8 (1877), 470–2; Smolenskin, 'Et lata'at', 93–5.
[162] Id., 'Am olam', 14–15, 127–9; id., 'Et lata'at', 45–7.
[163] Id., 'Am olam', 19–23; id., 'Et lata'at', 47–8.

realized that the Jews could never be suspected of love for the clergy and nobility, and were therefore natural partners in their struggle for liberty.[164] He did, however, have one strong criticism of the French Revolution, which he employed as a weapon in his war against Jewish religious reformers and radical maskilim who believed that the Jewish people could be changed in one fell swoop, with total disregard for their historical legacy: this was the revolutionary dynamic that transformed the revolutionaries into oppressors, which Smolenskin considered as a parallel to the Lutheran Reformation. The principle of liberty was not preserved in a revolution, 'and those who initially aided the people in their fight for freedom and liberty were the very ones who placed a yoke upon the people and, with unheard-of malice and cruelty, spilled blood as if it were water'.[165] The revolutionary command that prohibited religious ritual oppressed and enslaved the people as much as had the priests against whom they were rebelling. The fact that the principle of national unity was not preserved was an even more grievous flaw. Disagreement among the revolutionaries, the multiplicity of parties, and their divisiveness caused those with vested interests to subvert 'any spirit of unity in the heart of the people. Each group thought only of its own desires, and was never concerned with the people as a whole and the laws of the land . . . Thus they weakened the strength of the land, which was torn to pieces and became a scene of plunder.'[166]

Strongly influenced by Henry Buckle's *History of Civilization in England*, Smolenskin's view of revolution also served him well in his attempt to destroy the German model of the Haskalah. He learned from Buckle that revolution against a government that interferes in and damages the lives and rights of its citizens is inevitable, and moreover, that the English historical model was superior to those of France and Germany. The French model was preferable to the German model, demonstrating greater liberalism, pragmatism, and activism. France, however, took second place to England, whose political system and economic achievements Smolenskin enthusiastically admired. From Buckle he learned that England had developed the ideology that led to revolution, and that the French philosophers had had to study the work of English thinkers before they could formulate their own ideas. The seventeenth-century Glorious Revolution in England had preceded the French Revolution, and the English therefore had seniority over the French in the positive transition from the old era to the new age of liberty: 'The land of Britain was the first to begin to fight for freedom and liberty. In the war for freedom fought in America, these ideas expanded and become stronger, and, from America, they reached France, which had always been oppressed by fierce rulers who did the bidding of the Pope in Rome.'[167] Only in England, Smolenskin

---

[164] Id., 'Am olam', 131–2.   [165] Ibid. 13.   [166] Ibid. 41.

[167] The quotation is from Smolenskin, 'Am olam', 131. See also ibid. 40–1, 131–43; id., 'Et lata'at', 60–1, 195–200. On the French Revolution, see Buckle, *History of Civilization in England*, 213–60, 323–424.

continued, could one find the proper combination of liberalism, a government of political parties that accepted the majority view, and national unity—a combination that did not exist in the French Revolution.[168]

Smolenskin's picture of the European past was constructed primarily to include the history of the Jewish people, 'a small world' within universal history. The two major trends he considered crucial in European history were those he singled out in his analysis of Jewish history: first, the ideological and religious conflicts between the seekers of liberty and those who withheld it; and secondly, the struggle between nationalists, on one hand, and assimilationists and cosmopolitans, on the other—between national unity and divisiveness and dissolution. The first trend, of course, had dominated the maskilic consciousness of the past, but the second had already become apparent in the Galician Haskalah of the first half of the nineteenth century. Smolenskin's innovation was his clear preference for surveying and evaluating history according to the second trend, as well as his attack on the Haskalah for strengthening the anti-national tendency of the modern era.

Smolenskin's 'national history' reflected a dichotomous picture of the past that included a series of conflicts based on ties or lack of ties to the nation. During the First Temple period it was the prophets of Ba'al who led the people to ruin; and the members of the élite, consisting of the leaders and priests, were traitors who, in their desire to live in security like all non-Jews, denied Jewish national identity.[169] In contrast to Gordon, whose poem 'Tsidkiyahu beveit hapekudot', accused Jeremiah of attempting to impose the authority of the rabbis on the secular, monarchical government, Smolenskin justified the prophet. Smolenskin regarded his demand to refrain from fighting and his stand against the prophets of Ba'al as ensuring the survival of the Jews for all generations to come. During the Second Temple period the war was waged between the Hellenists and the patriots, faithful to their homeland, who fought for their independence. Smolenskin portrayed the Hellenists, who were traitors to their Jewish nationality, as the prototype of the anti-national Jews of the eighteenth and nineteenth centuries.[170] Those who wished to adopt Hellenism were condemned as destroyers of Jewish brotherhood who rent the tissue of unity, drew upon a foreign culture, and ignored the contradiction between the Jewish and the Greek spirits. The conflict between the Sadducees and the Pharisees was also interpreted according to this model. The position of the Sadducees, who, in Smolenskin's opinion, had renounced the hope of redemption, manifested an anti-national tendency, whereas the Pharisees preserved the elements of Jewish nationalism.

Like Luzzatto before him, Smolenskin exposed the foreign components of the 'Jewish spirit' in the Jewish philosophy of the Middle Ages and also heaped criticism on the venerated image of Maimonides. He believed that Maimonides was a totally contradictory figure who was burdened by a deep inner conflict between his

[168] Smolenskin, 'Am olam', 39–41.   [169] Ibid. 100–6; id., 'Et lata'at', 36–40.
[170] Smolenskin, 'Am olam', 88, 100–6; id., 'Et lata'at', 171.

identity as a scholar and a believer and as a philosopher and talmudist. In Smolenskin's view, in order to avoid being accused of having excessively liberal ideas, Maimonides was forced to balance his philosophical *Moreh nevukhim* with the *Mishneh torah*, a strict, rigid halakhic code. In the final analysis, Smolenskin argued, Maimonides did not make an important contribution to the national future of the Jewish people, and he should not be absolved of the charge of having taken 'the path of the Greeks'. Smolenskin went so far as to draw an analogy between what he considered Maimonides' attempt 'to unite the sons of Israel and the sons of Greece' and the aspirations of the nineteenth-century religious reformers to adapt 'the Torah of their forefathers' to the ways of other nations.[171]

During the modern era the Haskalah had championed the anti-national trend. It was no accident, Smolenskin claimed, that the Haskalah flourished particularly in Germany, in the humanistic, cosmopolitan climate of German culture—which, it should be remembered, he scathingly criticized. The Haskalah's attempt to emulate this humanism, which was nothing more than yet another version of 'the Greek spirit', constituted a threat to the foundation of the nation's faith. Smolenskin facilely allowed himself to look back and see eighteenth-century Berlin Jews as the Hellenists of Jerusalem 2,000 years earlier.[172] He even questioned the image of the Habsburg Emperor Joseph II as a benevolent, enlightened ruler and reformer, the harbinger of change in the state's attitude towards the Jews, and a figure who had been admired by the maskilim for almost a century. Sceptical about the intentions of the government in the 1870s, Smolenskin pointed out that Joseph had been a Catholic emperor who had actually still harboured the traditional Catholic view of the Jews, and would happily have handed over a million converted Jews to his priests.[173]

In his attitude to the struggle between the maskilim and the hasidim, too, Smolenskin crossed the boundary line of maskilic concepts and images and, from the standpoint of his national approach, appeared to join Zweifel. The conflict seemed to him totally unnecessary because it damaged national unity, and he believed that hasidism, 'the Jewish homeland', was preferable to the Haskalah, which was 'a foreign land'. He openly expressed his worst heresy, in terms of the east European Haskalah, in the wish 'Would that all Israel were hasidim and not immoral maskilim, who hate their people and seek to destroy all its memories, its Torah, and its name.'[174] However, it is clear that this was a position taken for rhetorical and polemical purposes only, and did not represent Smolenskin's true beliefs, as it did Zweifel's.

Smolenskin's awareness of the national past was encapsulated in his denunciation of Mendelssohn's historical image.[175] Smolenskin's opponents viewed his anti-Mendelssohnian proclivities as a drastic and unpardonable breach of the

[171] Id., 'Am olam', 125; id., 'Et la'asot', 173; id., 'Et lata'at', 40–3.
[172] Id., 'Et lata'at', 171 n., 197–200.   [173] Ibid. 251.   [174] Ibid. 93, 229, 257.
[175] Shohet, *Changing Eras*, 242–6; Barzilay, 'Smolenskin's Polemic against Mendelssohn', 11–48.

Haskalah's boundaries. He stubbornly asserted that he had intended not to attack Mendelssohn on a personal basis but rather to expose and condemn his erroneous views, which had led the Jews along dangerous paths towards national extermination for almost a century, but in fact, he was uncompromisingly settling accounts with this historical figure. His primary goal was to shatter Mendelssohn's illustrious and authoritative image:

For this man, Moses ben Menahem, was to the maskilim what Moses, our lawgiver, was for God-fearing men. They look towards him, observe him, and every word he spoke or did not speak, but was spoken by others in his name, was considered sacrosanct. And any man who dared to judge the ways of ben Menahem and his teachings, and who denied the teachings of Moses, was stoned by the maskilim, just as the believers stone those who publicly disavow the Torah of Moses.[176]

Smolenskin himself was aware that he was challenging the hitherto unquestioned maskilic dogma that also served as the criterion or pledge of allegiance of the loyal maskil: 'I believe with perfect faith that ben Menahem was the greatest of the sages and the father of the maskilim; his teachings are the true teachings which will never change, and his path is the holy path from which we must not stray.' Smolenskin believed that by sanctifying Mendelssohn the maskilim had become the fanatical 'hasidim' of the Mendelssohnian Haskalah, raising their master to the status of a *tsadik* without critically examining his views. Smolenskin considered himself a maskil loyal to the Haskalah, the only one who showed the courage and independence of thought to free himself from prejudice, even if the prejudice was that of the Haskalah itself. He did not fear impugning the sanctity of the fathers of the Haskalah if his criticism of their actions would rid the Haskalah of its prejudice, he declared. 'What did ben Menahem possess that made him our teacher and rabbi, the star that illuminated the entire nation?' This was the fundamental question that, until the 1870s, had been answered by the maskilim only with laudatory words for 'the founding father' of the Haskalah.

The first accusations against Mendelssohn, voiced in 'Am olam' in 1872, were related to Smolenskin's changing assessment of the modern era in the wake of the bloody events in Odessa. The blatant violence of antisemitic trends made him see the eighteenth-century Haskalah's cosmopolitan ideas and perception of religious tolerance in a new light. He believed that Lessing, Mirabeau, and those close to them in Mendelssohn's generation who shared their beliefs were merely isolated examples, unrepresentative of their generation. All the others persisted in their hatred of the Jews and denied them rights and liberty, which could only be bought at the price of religious conversion. According to Smolenskin, the conversion to Christianity of many of Mendelssohn's descendants and disciples constituted the strongest proof of the fact that the ideas of the European Enlightenment had not become rooted in German society and culture. He summarily rejected the excuses

[176] Smolenskin, 'Et lata'at', 10.

that attempted to draw a line separating Mendelssohn from the proselytes (such as the claims that his disciples did not fully understand their rabbi and therefore strayed from his path). For Smolenskin, conversion to Christianity was the criterion by which Mendelssohn and his message should be judged:

Moses ben Menahem taught the love of all men, and the members of his family and those who heard his message followed his teaching. And what became of them? Almost all of them converted; his entire family and his associates who listened to his teachings about man did not wait until one faith had been given to all people, for by leaving the customs of their religion they sought to adopt the dominant faith. And that was the result of the teachings of their mentor ben Menahem.[177]

For Smolenskin, conversion was unmistakable proof of the failure of the maskilim's cosmopolitan approach and belief in a 'modern era' that heralded a favourable transition towards religious tolerance. The power of the 'dominant faith' did not diminish; not a single member of Lessing's family, for example, converted to Judaism. He also considered Mendelssohn's translation of the Bible to be part of the destructive trend in terms of Jewish religious and national identity. Translation of the Torah into German lowered it to the status of a 'slave to the German language', and it became a tool for teaching German to Jewish youth.[178] The *Biur*, which the maskilim believed was the first impressive chapter in the revival of the Hebrew language and its literature, seemed to Smolenskin to be yet another way of degrading the Torah, of forsaking the national language of Hebrew.

Smolenskin's attack on Mendelssohn and the Berlin Haskalah was trenchantly expressed in his long article 'Et lata'at', which appeared in *Hashahar* between 1875 and 1877. The fundamental question posed by the article, 'What are we, the house of Israel: one people or merely believers in the same creed?', was highly significant, especially in the central and western Europe of the emancipation era, and the fact that Smolenskin was living in Vienna heightened his sensitivity to this issue. The government's tendency towards Russification, as well as Jewish acculturation during the reign of Alexander II, made this matter relevant to Russian Jews as well. Smolenskin's answer to this crucial question, as already noted, was indubitably on the side of national identification, and his aim was therefore to refute the conception that the Jews were merely a religious sect, a notion he believed underpinned the identity of the modern Jews of his time. He stubbornly claimed that this basic idea had been inculcated by Mendelssohn.

In Smolenskin's indictment Mendelssohn was depicted as having been responsible for defining Judaism solely as the observance of commandments. Smolenskin also accused him of having emptied these commandments of their national content, which Smolenskin considered crucial: the Hebrew language, Jewish history, Torah in its broader meaning, and the expectation of future redemption. Smolenskin's challenge to Mendelssohn's perception of Judaism was combined with an

[177] Id., 'Am olam', 141.   [178] Id., 'Et la'asot', 197.

attempt to shatter his venerated image: should the ideas of a mediocre person possessed of a divided personality and a weak character be accepted? Mendelssohn
was not an original thinker, claimed Smolenskin; he did not possess the attributes
of a leader and reformer, and was inclined towards complacency and timorous-
ness. Like Maimonides, his identity was divided between that of the scholar and
the strict observer of the commandments—'A free mind and a slave's life'—an
internal contradiction that Smolenskin believed was highly problematic. At most,
Mendelssohn was 'a man of knowledge', a figure capable of improving his generation and expressing the spirit of its age, but not a 'man of the spirit', able to rise
above his generation and foresee the future. Mendelssohn was only caught up in
the heart of historical events by accident, and 'in his time [history] seized him by
the hair of his head and hurled him to a place he had never before known, to be
the head of a movement in Israel'. Mendelssohn had never put aside his own personal affairs, as leaders must, in order to devote himself to his people. In his
obsequiousness to Frederick the Great he shrank from debates on sensitive issues
and displayed no particular sensitivity to the pain of his people. Despite this, or
perhaps because of it, Mendelssohn was eminently suited to the needs of his generation and embodied their aspirations for assimilation into the German nation.
In Smolenskin's opinion, non-Jews accorded him great respect and held him in
high esteem—an important element in the maskilic image of Mendelssohn—
solely because he was such a rare and amazing phenomenon: a Jew who was neither
a pedlar nor a talmudist, but who 'wrote and spoke in the lucid language of a writer
of the country'. Moreover, it appeared that Mendelssohn was exploited by anti-
semites for the very purpose of attacking through him the other members of Jewish
society, whose virtues were far inferior to his.[179]

Mendelssohn not only led a negative, destructive movement towards modernization and adopted the German universal humanism so antithetical to Judaism,
but, in Smolenskin's view, he also halted the positive movement towards modernization; thus, basing an understanding of the historical process of the modern era
entirely on Mendelssohn was a grievous error. To establish this claim, Smolenskin sketched an alternative maskilic path which did not include Mendelssohn or
necessarily pass through Berlin. It was not Mendelssohn who had aroused the Jews
from their historical slumber in the Middle Ages; there were, in fact, no sudden
and precipitous revolutions in history. Many years before Mendelssohn, influenced
by the European spirit of the time, Jews had studied science and languages. This
was a natural, gradual, and developmental process that should have continued and
expanded to encompass Jewish communities everywhere. Unfortunately, however,
the activities of the Berlin maskilim, with Mendelssohn foremost among them,
particularly in his German translation of the Torah, forestalled this natural historical development. The Berlin Haskalah was provocative in nature and stirred

[179] Smolenskin, 'Et lata'at', 10–17, 32–6, 68–104.

the anger of traditional Jewish society and its rabbis. It was the reaction to the Haskalah and the conflicts and struggles that followed in its wake that divided Jewish society from that time onwards into the 'God-fearing' and the 'seekers of knowledge'. It was Mendelssohn, and particularly his apostate disciples, whom the God-fearing held up as warning signs of the inherent danger of the Haskalah. If it had not been for Mendelssohn, claimed Smolenskin, 'The spirit of the Jewish people would have become one that sought knowledge', and now there was no chance that this would happen: 'If it had not been for ben Menahem and his translation, who knows if all our sons would not have become seekers of science and believers in the faith as they once were.'[180] This would have been especially true if the Haskalah had taken the east European path, which, Smolenskin believed, had begun with the Vilna Gaon. Mendelssohn's appearance on the scene thwarted the possibility that the maskilic trends of the Gaon and his followers would continue. Mendelssohn did not understand the spirit of the age, and acted in an anti-historical manner, leading, among other things, to the formation of a militant Orthodoxy.[181]

As far as both the Haskalah and the Jewish people in the nineteenth century were concerned, the image of Mendelssohn was an obstacle, embodying almost existential danger. Smolenskin demanded a halt to the influence of the leader of the Berlin Haskalah, the maskil who preached assimilation and led his people to religious conversion, denied the historical roots of the Jews, and undermined their national identity. The time had come to repair the damage Mendelssohn had caused, 'to rejuvenate the Jewish people if they wish to survive'.[182] Deposing Mendelssohn from his lofty position in the pantheon of maskilic heroes was a national mission of the greatest urgency for Smolenskin.

He even proposed that Mendelssohn be replaced in the pantheon by another exemplary, more 'national' figure: Manasseh ben Israel. The choice of Manasseh (who had long been a hero of the Haskalah) as an alternative historical figure to Mendelssohn represented a twofold change in the maskilic picture of the past: pushing the processes of the modern era, especially religious tolerance, back from the eighteenth to the seventeenth century; and shifting the focus westwards from Germany to the Netherlands and England—the ideal liberal country in Smolenskin's eyes, and a counterbalance to cosmopolitan Germany. He spared no superlatives in describing the image of Manasseh ben Israel:

A man greater than his brothers in those times, a man pure of heart and great of spirit who, for the sake of his people, neither rested nor yielded, and sacrificed himself on the altar of his love . . . there have not been many people like him in Israel. He rose as a saviour and a rabbi, a redeemer and a liberator, and his only wish, the only desire of his heart, was to help his people improve their lot. And if this man had not made a great contribution to

[180] Ibid., ii. 77–8.
[181] Ibid. 72–8, 193–200, 268. Cf. various assessments of the Vilna Gaon's image and his historical role: Etkes, 'The Vilna Gaon and the Haskalah', 192–217.   [182] Smolenskin, 'Et lata'at', 133.

wisdom, and if he had not been among the upholders of the Jewish faith, even then, it would be our obligation and our duty to sanctify his name as one of the visionaries and prophets and warriors whose blood was spilled for their people.[183]

Smolenskin portrayed Manasseh's lobbying for the Jews' return to England as the exemplary nationalist activity of a national figure, in contrast to Mendelssohn, and noted that England was a model that should be emulated by other countries. 'We could almost state', Smolenskin claimed, 'that all the good that the Jewish people enjoyed was thanks to Manasseh ben Israel. He was chosen to be the guardian of Israel, to redeem it from its afflictions.'[184] Manasseh, as opposed to Mendelssohn, was a Jewish sage renowned throughout the non-Jewish world who did not abandon his national pride and commitment. Unfortunately, however, his was not the dominant path in modern Jewish history; once again it was German Jewry that chose a different and destructive path. In Smolenskin's analogy between the alternative hero, Manasseh ben Israel, and Mendelssohn the former was compared to Oliver Cromwell and the latter to Napoleon Bonaparte. Cromwell, who 'rose to deliver his people and his country', was honest, loved the people, was a patriot, and drew his ideals from the Scriptures. Smolenskin found similar qualities in Manasseh, a contemporary of Cromwell, and considered them to be the major figures of a new era, one in European history and the other in Jewish history. Mendelssohn, in contrast, was compared to the negative historical figure of Napoleon, egotistical and ambitious, 'who rose to the heights by force of arms . . . he fought wars for his own sake, not for the sake of his country; and when he seized the sceptre of rule, he forgot his origins and became a tyrant like all the Roman tyrants in their time'.[185] Napoleon lacked all honesty and faith, pursued honour, oppressed his people, and led them to the abyss. Consequently, history has judged him to be the person who ended the era that began in Cromwell's time. According to this analogy, Mendelssohn's historical position was at the bleak close of the period that had opened with Manasseh ben Israel, and had promised so much. Indeed, the reversal of the picture of the past was illustrated here in all its severity; not only was Mendelssohn unworthy of being hailed as the dominant figure of the modern era, but he also instigated a negative reaction and forestalled positive trends through his intervention.

Smolenskin's efforts to demolish Mendelssohn's historical image were completely at odds with the veneration Mendelssohn had enjoyed in the Haskalah until Smolenskin's time, for since the 1860s and 1870s there had been a marked tendency towards even greater adulation of his august image. 'Mendelssohnian literature' had reached the height of its success at the very time that Smolenskin so trenchantly attacked it. It is no wonder, then, that Mendelssohn's image served as the focus of such a strident controversy among Russian maskilim. In 1860 a new edition of Euchel's biography of Mendelssohn was published in Lvov, in Michal

---

[183] Smolenskin, 'Et lata'at', 49.   [184] Ibid.   [185] Ibid. 85–8.

Wolf's series *Zemirot yisra'el* (Songs of Israel).[186] Gottlober, who was staying in Lvov at the time, added his own homage to Mendelssohn to the book. The same year Mendelssohn's introduction to Manasseh ben Israel's *Teshuat yisra'el* was translated for the Russian supplement to *Hakarmel*. In 1862 the eighteenth-century Hebrew translation of Mendelssohn's *Phaedon* by Isaiah Beer-Bing of Metz was republished. It was decided to bring out a new edition of the book because it was out of print and because of the great importance of 'the illustrious man, our rabbi, Moses ben Menahem', who 'like the ancient Moses ascended to the summit of the mount of reason to bring down the sacred idea . . . and who for his people has been the sun of justice and has sheltered them under his wings until this very day'.[187] Four years later a Hebrew edition of *Abhandlung über die Evidenz in metaphysischen Wissenschaften* was published in Warsaw, and from 1867 onwards the Hebrew reader was able to learn about Mendelssohn's concept of Judaism from Gottlober's translation of *Jerusalem*.[188] Back in the 1850s Gottlober had planned to translate Lessing's *Nathan der Weise* into Hebrew, partly because it contributed to Mendelssohn's historical image. In 1872 he finally completed this project, and the book appeared in Vienna in 1874.[189]

In addition to the republication of these works, there was a flurry of interest in Mendelssohn and in the Berlin Haskalah. For example, *Hakarmel* reported on the memorial days held for Mendelssohn by members of Hevrat Dorshei Tovbat Am Yisra'el Begermaniyah (The Society for the Welfare of the Jews in Germany), as well as on the plan to purchase the house in which Mendelssohn had been born in Dessau. The editor even encouraged the Jews of Russia to contribute to this important cause, for there, in Dessau, the great light was born from whose rays they too derived benefit.[190] In the debates between radical and moderate maskilim there was one point on which both sides agreed: that 'Mendelssohn's time' had ushered in a new era in Hebrew literature.[191] The only remaining question was whether that era had ended, as the radicals claimed, or was still continuing in the last third of the nineteenth century. Clearly, then, Smolenskin's iconoclastic assault on Mendelssohn struck at the very heart of a maskilic consensus that had endured for many years.

In their literary discussion of Mendelssohn's image the maskilim based their positions on three main works: Euchel's biography, Kayserling's German biography of 1862, and the chapters which Graetz had devoted to Mendelssohn in the eleventh part of *Geschichte der Juden*. Apparently it was the publication of Graetz's book in

[186] Euchel, *Toledot harav*.   [187] Mendelssohn, *Phaedon* (Lyck, 1862).
[188] Zhitomir, 1867. Another translation of *Jerusalem* was made by Gruenbaum Fiodorov (Vienna, 1876).
[189] Gottlober also planned to print and distribute pictures of Mendelssohn and Lessing (see Gottlober, 'Kol kore', *Hashahar*, 4 (1873), 393–4). See also Müller, 'Toledot natan', 9–53.
[190] Fuenn, editorials, *Hakarmel*, 3 (1863), 247, 334, 381.
[191] A. U. Kovner, *Ketavim*, 32–5, 210; Gottlober, *Igeret tsa'ar ba'alei hayim*, 15, 21.

1870 that first spurred Smolenskin to turn his attention to Mendelssohn, and his criticism of Graetz in this context was probably not just one more factor in the 'Mendelssohn controversy' but one of its principal causes. It should not be overlooked that Smolenskin had already begun to express his nationalist ideas in 1870, and it was only later that Mendelssohn became his chief target. Graetz was a staunch admirer of Mendelssohn, and in volume xi of his *Geschichte der Juden* he presented him not only as a man who opened a new period but as the historical Jewish embodiment of the entire modern age. According to Graetz, it was Mendelssohn who gave new life to the Jews, promoted the emancipation, and with great courage faced the rabbis who opposed him.[192] Graetz canonized the historical image of the Haskalah and endowed Mendelssohn's maskilic image with a historiographical–scientific stamp of approval in the same way as he had totally condemned and stigmatized hasidism.

Smolenskin threw down the gauntlet to Graetz. As early as 1872 he had criticized Graetz's research on the Song of Songs, and rejected his conclusion that it dated from the third century BC. Guided by his nationalist approach, Smolenskin also included the Song of Songs in the repertoire of national assets, as a poem sacred to all lovers of their nation and a memorial to the glorious days of the Jewish people. In his opinion, such poetry was appropriate only to the period of stability and peace that typified the days of King Solomon; Graetz had greatly erred in his dating of the book and in attempting to show Greek influence in its lines.[193] In 'Et lata'at' Smolenskin incisively inveighed against Graetz's idealization of Mendelssohn. How was it possible that such a talented and renowned historian, who had written the history of the Jews with laudable objectivity and had never hesitated to challenge cherished conventions, had halted before the figure of Mendelssohn and failed to apply critical criteria to him? 'How did it come about that a man like him would choose one person in his generation, ben Menahem, and judge him as little less than a god?'[194] Graetz had misled his readers, Smolenskin asserted, for anyone unversed in Jewish history was likely to get the impression that no greater hero than Mendelssohn had ever graced it: 'A man who has done all this is not a man but a god, a god great in his wisdom, heroism, and eternal glory and all the other illustrious attributes.'[195] How, for example, was it possible to exalt Mendelssohn while simultaneously denouncing his disciples as 'sinners, malicious, empty-headed, and rash men, who shame their people because such apostates have emerged from their midst'? Did not the repudiation of his disciples bear testimony to some fault on the part of their great teacher? Smolenskin believed there could be only one explanation for this one-sided, distorted position: the Germanocentric bias that contemptuously ignored east European Jewry. From his youth onwards Graetz had always given preference to German Jewry over the Jews of other lands, and

[192] H. Graetz, *Geschichte der Juden*, xi. 1–92.
[193] Smolenskin, 'Mishpat haruts', 257–70, 313–30.
[194] Smolenskin, 'Et lata'at', 10–13.   [195] Ibid.

'in the land of Ashkenaz, the Jew began to regard himself as a man only from the days of ben Menahem'.[196]

From this point onwards the battle between Smolenskin and Graetz began to take shape as a conflict between the east European maskil and the German Jew, who in Smolenskin's eyes was no more than a direct heir of Mendelssohn. This was the basis for Smolenskin's conclusion that Graetz had not written real history but a fictional historical novel. Following the publication of 'Et lata'at', Smolenskin predicted, it would be necessary to rewrite the history of the modern era; he also predicted that within five years at the most the historiographic revision that he called for would indeed be carried out, and that historians would base their writings on his national concept. He did not feel that he was ready to undertake this awesome task himself, but he did believe he had succeeded in providing the guidelines for a historiography that would be an alternative to Graetz's work, and that this new historiography would be underpinned by nationalist maskilic principles. However, Smolenskin was moved to call for this alternative historiography not only because of his national and anti-Mendelssohnian views, but also because he was so annoyed by the takeover of Wissenschaft des Judentums by German scholars. He believed that the German language in which the Wissenschaft's works were written was an obstacle to Hebrew readers in eastern Europe. Only when a large corpus of Wissenschaft literature was accessible in Hebrew would it be possible to judge whether the conclusions of the German Jewish historians had passed the test of criticism, and only then would the monopoly of German scholars on Jewish history be broken.[197] He was also troubled by the discriminatory attitude towards Jewish history in eastern Europe and the scant weight assigned it in German Jewish historiography. Smolenskin's supporter Pesah Ruderman, for example, claimed that Graetz could make amends for his sin as a historian only by adding a twelfth part to his book, dedicated to the history of Russian Jewry in the nineteenth century. With a sharp sense of injustice Ruderman asked, 'Were there not also scholars among us striving to better the situation of their people in rain and wind? Did we not also know the name of the Rambeman [Mendelssohn]? Could Mendelssohn have inspired our spirit had we not had among us sages who loved their people?'[198] For the Russian maskilim, Levinsohn was the founding father of the Haskalah in their country, and Graetz's neglect of him was very offensive to them. The time had come to balance the historiographic picture presented by Graetz's book; it could no longer be believed 'that only in the land of Ashkenaz were there great good men, Jewish sages and authors, and that among the Russian Jews who number five times as many as the Jews of Ashkenaz, there is not one man of knowledge and great deeds in whom his people can take great pride'.[199]

Smolenskin's opponents in the 'Mendelssohn controversy' based their arguments on his scathing criticism of Graetz, claiming it was his hatred of Graetz

[196] Ibid. 14.   [197] Ibid. 235–6.

[198] Ruderman, 'Ha'emunah vehasifrut', 176–83.   [199] Smolenskin, 'Hosafah letoledot', 23–4.

that had unhinged his mind and provoked his attack on Mendelssohn. Gottlober, for example, stated that Smolenskin's sole aim was to compete with the great Jewish historian from Germany and to prove his own superiority. He found no justification for Smolenskin's critique of Graetz, and asserted that Mendelssohn's image was not at all dependent on either historiography or historians: the belief that Mendelssohn was the 'head of the maskilim' spread throughout the Jewish world not because of Graetz's *Geschichte der Juden*, but because of the testimony of history itself. History produced its own evidence, without the mediation of a historian, and it was history that had constructed Mendelssohn's revered image, making it the province of the Jewish public at large. In his opinion, anyone who asked how Mendelssohn became an authority was asking an ahistorical question: 'Why did it happen thus rather than otherwise? What actually has happened is ample evidence, and no other testimony is needed. This is one of the truths of events throughout the generations which even the most obstinate will not deny, unless he is deranged.'[200]

Gottlober was Mendelssohn's principal defender in the controversy. It will be recalled that this moderate maskil of the old generation had left the traditional hasidic world to join the world of the Haskalah under the influence of Mendelssohn's writings, history, and outlook, and was the translator of *Jerusalem*. He was shocked by Smolenskin's 'Et lata'at' and was one of the first to hasten to defend the honour of the 'father of the Haskalah'. Gottlober also saw the need to counteract Smolenskin's publicist forum. In order to do so, he founded his own periodical in Lvov in 1876, called *Haboker or* (The Morning Light), which was in the front line of the opposition to *Hashaḥar* in the 'Mendelssohn controversy'. In the leading article in the first edition of his new periodical Gottlober entered the fray against Smolenskin.[201] 'Perez, weeds will grow from your cheeks but ben Menahem will not be disgraced as you dream of!', Gottlober proclaimed.[202] In his defence of Mendelssohn, Gottlober noted that Jewish public opinion over the years and the writers of the Haskalah were all in agreement about Mendelssohn's importance for all generations. It was unjust to censure Mendelssohn because his disciples had strayed from the straight and narrow, nor was it correct to assert that his *Biur* had paved the way for assimilation. On the contrary, he was influential in preventing the abandonment of the Hebrew language.[203] Gottlober also rejected Smolenskin's key claim that Mendelssohn's approach was anti-national, and in his reply stated that Mendelssohn's method actually contributed to national cohesiveness since it viewed the religious laws as linking individual Jews to the nation. As a counterweight to Smolenskin's denunciatory words, Gottlober attempted to exalt Mendelssohn's virtues still further, raising his historical image to new heights. His words in defence of Mendelssohn overflowed with adulation for the great 'reformer', who was responsible for 'all the good reforms made in Jewish life from

---

[200] Gottlober, 'Et la'akor natua', 6–13.   [201] Ibid. 4–17, 77–86, 225–33.
[202] Ibid. 11.   [203] Ibid. 13, 77–8, 80–5, 232.

that time to this very day', and he ended with a declaration of renewed faith which was tantamount to a reaffirmation of the 'maskilic covenant':

Were it not for Mendelssohn, the Rambeman of blessed memory . . . were it not for that grand and noble personality, who was rightly honoured, endowed with a unique title in his time . . . neither you nor I would be what we are . . . and who knows what would have been after our time had the Almighty not sent him to us . . . the Rambeman is truly the man whom his followers named as the third in Jewish history after Moses ben Amram and Moses ben Maimon . . . Moses ben Amram received the Torah from heaven: Moses ben Maimon breathed the spirit of life into it; and Moses ben Menahem made for us a temple in [his book] Jerusalem.[204]

The contest between Gottlober and Smolenskin lasted from 1876 to 1877 and was waged as a public duel, accompanied by personal invective, on the pages of *Hashahar* and *Haboker or*. Other maskilim joined in the fray.[205] Fuenn, for example, enlisted *Hakarmel* in Mendelssohn's defence, and in an article entitled 'Rabbi Moses ben Menahem Mendelssohn: The Heights of his Wisdom, the Qualities of his Spirit and his Actions for the Good of his People', he described Mendelssohn as a figure totally consistent with the ideal of the moderate Haskalah: a moderate, cautious reformer, whose method was one of civility, explanation, and learning; a maskil who recognized the dangers of the radical approach and was concerned about a schism within his people; a devoted Jew who in his person combined knowledge and faith; and a leader who acted for the sake of the Jews in the non-Jewish environment.[206] That year two more articles in support of Mendelssohn were published, although these were somewhat less exuberant in their admiration of him and not totally devoid of criticism. Ruderman, a graduate of the rabbinic seminary in Zhitomir, who was then a student at the rabbinic seminary in Breslau, blamed Mendelssohn for not having offered positive directions for the future to replace what he had tried to destroy. Mendelssohn, in his words, had 'uprooted and pulled down, but had not planted', and was in fact responsible for assimilation in Germany. Nonetheless, there was no denying his epochal role, nor could one overlook the fact that he was the first to break away from tradition. In this sense, Ruderman stated, Mendelssohn resembled Luther as well as the Ba'al Shem Tov. 'Just as Luther liberated his brethren from the yoke of the holy fathers, so the Rambeman and the Ba'al Shem Tov liberated us from the yoke of *pilpul* and fault-finding sermons, from the burden of the *geonim*, the rabbis, the sermonizers, and thousands of other such scoundrels.'[207] Eleazar Schulmann of Kovno (1837–1904) suggested a more balanced view: on one hand, it could not be denied that

---

[204] Ibid. 232–3.

[205] Smolenskin, 'Le'ohavei *Hashahar*', 261–8; Gottlober, 'El mol *Hashahar*', 37–40; Smolenskin, 'Atah aromem, atah anaseh!', 128–34; Gottlober, 'Peresh al penei perets', 148–51.

[206] Fuenn, 'Harav mosheh ben menahem mendelson', 261–8, 299–308; id., 'Lezekher kevod mendelson', 399.   [207] Ruderman, 'Lema'an yedu', 65–80.

Mendelssohn was the 'father of the Haskalah', but on the other hand, the fact that
he did not lead the Jews towards a 'national Haskalah' did have destructive implications. Despite all Mendelssohn's great virtues, Schulmann admitted, he did lack
'true love for the ancient faith of his people and a recognition of the value of its
nationalism, and that was a great obstacle and stumbling-block for us'.[208]

Gottlober invited his supporters in the battle against Smolenskin to air their
views on the pages of *Haboker or*, and the first to take advantage of the opportunity was Aharon Zupnik of Galicia. His words reveal how profoundly Smolenskin
had offended Mendelssohn's admirers. They expressed the pain and anger of a
maskil confronted by the fragments of his shattered idol, wondering how anyone
could dare to violate the honour 'of Moses who dwells in the shelter of the Most
High'. You are guilty of a 'criminal injustice', he said, addressing Smolenskin; 'you
have committed a sin against the Rambeman, the light of our eyes, you have sinned
against Jewish literature, sinned against the Jewish public, sinned against our holy
tongue'.[209] Another admirer, Jehiel Mendelson of Lublin, deplored the unjust action
of Smolenskin, who 'had wounded with his great, powerful sword our beloved
teacher, removing from him the mantle of his glory and stripping him of the rabbi's
robe, dishonouring and demeaning him in the public eye'.[210] He believed that
Smolenskin would surely fail in his attempt because he could not succeed in overturning the widely held popular historical view; the people knew who deserved
esteem, and hence no one could weaken their feeling for their 'guide' and 'redeeming angel'.[211]

Mendelssohn's defenders did not in fact argue with Smolenskin's national premisses, and they certainly did not represent anti-national positions. Their only
aim was to convince maskilic public opinion that Smolenskin had erred in choosing Mendelssohn, of all people, as an anti-national model. Beyond their attempts
to shore up Mendelssohn's historical image, Smolenskin's opponents also spoke
in the name of history, asserting that neither the historian nor the publicist was
entitled to change the collective and popular historical consciousness or to deny
what in their view had been 'proved' by history itself. This was the claim, for example, that lay behind Jehiel Mendelson's statement that the people alone could
decide which heroes would figure in their pantheon and that it was totally unjustified to dictate to them who was and who was not worthy of being appointed to it.
Lilienblum espoused a similar view. He felt the entire controversy was unwar-
ranted and absurd, not only because it did not touch on the true issues of Jewish
life, but also because he believed Mendelssohn had fulfilled an essential historical
role. On the basis of his deterministic concept of history, Lilienblum maintained
that the 'spirit of the generation' had called on Mendelssohn to appear on the stage

---

[208] Schulmann, 'Mimekor yisra'el'. The quotation is from pp. 34–48.

[209] Zupnik, 'Setirat zekenim binyan', 217–20, 291–3; M. Hacohen, 'Dor holekh', 7–12, 62–70,
121–31, 177–83.

[210] J. Mendelson, 'Moshe veyisra'el'. The quotation is from p. 592.   [211] Ibid. 592–607.

of history, and that if he had not done so, then undoubtedly another man would
have emerged to fill a similar role. Mendelssohn, Lilienblum stated, 'was an
inevitable product of historical development'. Even conversion to Christianity in
the post-Mendelssohn generation was an inevitable result of historical circumstances (in particular the fact that the Haskalah had preceded legal emancipation),
and 'was by no means a result of Mendelssohn's halakhic rulings'.[212]

The steadfast veneration of Mendelssohn's image by maskilim like Fuenn,
Zweifel, Gottlober, Kalman Schulman, and others of the 'old generation' was in
fact an expression of their continued loyalty to the German model adopted by the
Haskalah in eastern Europe from its inception onwards. The fact that the maskilic
world of the members of this generation was largely shaped by the heritage of the
Berlin Haskalah probably also explains their turbulent emotional response to any
affront to the 'sacred figures of the Haskalah'. Mendelssohn's defenders accused
Smolenskin and his supporters, most of whom were young maskilim in their
twenties, of identifying with the radical and nihilistic stream of Haskalah. The
struggle thus took on the nature of a conflict between the young and the old
(although there were young men among Mendelssohn's admirers), like the controversy about Abraham Uri Kovner's radical criticism at the end of the 1860s.
The maskilim who supported Mendelssohn understood Smolenskin's 'heresy' as a
challenge directed against the moderate Haskalah. Gottlober, whom Smolenskin
frequently called the 'old man' during the controversy, retorted that he was by no
means ashamed to be a member of the 'camp of the old' since his generation was
superior to the new generation to which Smolenskin belonged. Gottlober never
doubted that Smolenskin had attacked Mendelssohn because he could not reconcile himself to the fact that he was deemed an authority in the Haskalah movement:
'Because Mendelssohn had become an authority, Smolenskin permitted himself,
or regarded it as his duty, to slander him so that he might blacken his name and
misconstrue and pervert his words, all in order to observe the commandment:
thou shalt nullify all authority, which is the first of the ten commandments of the
nihilists.'[213] Smolenskin and his supporters were aware that they were leading
iconoclastic trends and attacking the basic premises of the Haskalah,[214] nor is
there any doubt that the 'Mendelssohn controversy' was but one episode in a series
of manifestations of ferment and rethinking among Russian maskilim during the
reign of Alexander II. However, Smolenskin's call for a revision in the fundamental
consciousness of the Haskalah by no means meant that he adhered to the positivist
views that underpinned the radical Haskalah.

The Mendelssohn controversy marked the final stage in the series of dramatic
changes undergone by 'maskilic history'. It was important because it suggested a
new picture of the past, a deliberate replacement of the 'maskilic history' that

---

[212] Lilienblum, 'Tsorkhei amenu veda'at soferav', 164–6. See also Lilienblum's derisive response
to the article 'Et lata'at' in his letter to Levin in 1875, in *Reshumot*, 4 (1926), 379.

[213] Gottlober, 'El mol *Hashaḥar*', 37–40.   [214] Schulmann, 'Mimekor yisra'el', 10.

Smolenskin had censured as harmful. Smolenskin constructed his national picture of the past at the expense of Mendelssohn and Graetz. It was revolutionary in the sense that it denied the role of the German model in the process of the Jewish people's rejuvenation in the modern era; it reassessed the accomplishments of the Haskalah and the tidings of the modern era; and it stressed that the mechanism of nationalism versus anti-nationalism had accompanied Jewish history from ancient times. This picture of the past, which Smolenskin constructed on the ruins of Mendelssohn's historical image, hitherto one of the pillars of 'maskilic history', inevitably had to clash with the accepted maskilic consciousness of the past. It undermined maskilic optimism about both the past and the future, and tried to marginalize the importance of the maskilic historical mechanism of folly versus reason. It changed the accepted periodization, decried the excessive integration of non-Jewish elements, assigned greater weight to east European Jewry, reshuffled the pantheon of historical heroes, and also attributed greater significance to popular historical consciousness.

Smolenskin's sense of the past and the Mendelssohn controversy form a fitting final destination in a journey that has followed the course of 'maskilic history' from its origins in the 1780s in Königsberg and Berlin. With the undermining of 'maskilic history', even though this was not yet universally accepted, the demise of the maskilic sense of the past was unavoidable. While at the end of the eighteenth century the maskilim in Germany engendered a transformation in the traditional sense of the past, leading to its replacement by a maskilic historical consciousness, a century later it was the nationalist maskilim in eastern Europe who voiced the need to nurture a national historical consciousness. Neither the destruction of Mendelssohn's image nor the devaluation of Graetz's historiography were vital prerequisites for the formation of a national view of the past. But Smolenskin was the first to signal the shift in the nineteenth century by demanding a historical alternative, 'national history' that would match the national consciousness taking shape among Russian maskilim in the 1870s and 1880s.[215]

[215] Breiman, 'The Change in Public Jewish Thought', 83–227.

CONCLUSION

New Directions

A T THE END of the eighteenth century the maskilim firmly believed that a favourable historical shift was taking place which promised an ideal future for all humankind, including the Jews. This belief gave rise to a new sense of the past that no longer matched the traditional concept of history. The maskilim in Germany, the first consciously modern Jews, were the bearers of this new sense of the past. These young men fervently believed they had a mission to transform and regenerate Jewish society and culture in order to adapt it to the modern age and its challenges. In their opinion, the hallmarks of this new era were a modern state with an enlightened absolutist government; an open bourgeois society; rational thought; the culture and values of the Enlightenment; religious tolerance; and man's growing scientific achievements.

The new historical consciousness had emerged even before Zunz and the members of the Verein für Kultur und Wissenschaft des Judentums had laid the foundations of modern Jewish historiography and the methodical, scientific study of Jewish history and sources. It also preceded the appearance of modern Jewish historians (Zunz, Jost, Geiger, Graetz, and others) in nineteenth-century Germany. At first maskilic awareness of the past was not expressed in original historiographic works but in somewhat less prestigious forms of writing about the past: journalism, translations and adaptations, biographies, satire, and comments about the value and role of history. The maskilic historical consciousness differed from that of Wissenschaft des Judentums. It had little relationship to the idea of science, and was neither academic nor professional. The maskilim employed their new sense of the past in their efforts to persuade traditional Jewish society that changes in various spheres of Jewish life were imperative. They used the past during the transitional stage of German Jewry, when much criticism was levelled against obsolescent concepts and social, cultural, and religious patterns that were regarded as irrational. At the same time an alternative to tradition was proposed in the form of the Haskalah—an ideology opposed not only to traditional society and its values but also to uncontrolled acculturation and assimilation with no intellectual basis.

The maskilim's endeavour to shape a past that could serve the aims of the Haskalah, their need to construct a new identity, and their acceptance of historical approaches that characterized the new attitude of the Enlightenment to history led them to cast aside the traditional sense of the past. New answers were given to the question of the legitimacy of the study of history. The fundamental concept of history as didactic and exemplary remained valid, nor was its religious benefit dismissed, but emphasis was now placed on the educational and moral value of universal and Jewish history for the young maskil. According to this approach, then, the study of history could be helpful in training the ideal Jew, who would also be a loyal citizen, for it would endow him with rationalist thought, moral criteria, useful knowledge, and a better understanding of the Jewish sources. In the historical explanations provided by the maskilim, Providence continued to play a role, though now only as a meta-explanation, while most of their efforts were directed at uncovering the earthly, human, moralistic, and contextual causality immanent in historical phenomena. History was increasingly conceived as an arena of human actions, exemplifying its secularization. The consciousness of a historical turning-point and the concept of the 'modern age' gave rise to a new periodization and a progressive approach to the course of historical time. These paved the way for the maskilic vision of the future, the aspiration to cast off past authorities, and the idea that the 'last' and the modern were superior to the 'first' and the ancient. The reason or folly, virtue or immorality, of historical events and personalities were the criteria for judging whether they were good or bad. The maskilim used the historical biographies of Maimonides, Abrabanel, Mendelssohn, and others as examples to project their vision of the future into the past. These historical figures were depicted as modern maskilim in every sense, men who could endow eighteenth-century maskilim with legitimization and a distinguished lineage. The exemplary historical figure was depicted as a militant personality, advancing against the stream, obstinately struggling for the sake of the truth, and standing firm in the face of the refusal of 'ignorant fools' to accept the light of the Haskalah. The values attributed to these historical personalities were modern: they were exponents of productivization, who combined the 'teaching of God' and the 'teaching of man', encouraged the study and use of foreign languages, and advocated programmes for educational reform. Their moral level was very high, their approach rationalistic, and through their encounters with the non-Jewish world they legitimized such contacts for generations to come and served as examples of good Jewish leadership. The historical biography was, in fact, an encapsulation of the new picture of the past. It was underpinned by the clear demand that the present be examined in the light of ideal past examples and that history should be rethought.

Thus a new Jewish consciousness of the past emerged and followed two separate paths. One was that of the maskilim; the other was that of the scholars of Wissenschaft des Judentums and of those Jews who had largely already left the ghetto. In the light of the profound difference between these two trends, the maskilim cannot be regarded as the founders of the Wissenschaft, and in fact the latter was openly opposed to the path of the Haskalah. The Haskalah in Germany declined and drew to a close at the turn of the century, but the maskilic sense of the past continued to function and to serve the maskilim of eastern Europe in the nineteenth century as well, in an era when historical approaches and historiography in Europe were changing drastically. This is not at all surprising. In eastern Europe the new sense of the past was promulgated by maskilim who resembled their predecessors in eighteenth-century Germany, despite the distance in time and place. They were intellectuals who had received a traditional education but were later exposed to European culture (at first German, and at the end of the period, Russian too), and who engaged in the writing of history without having had any formal academic training. Among the east European maskilim there were hardly any real historians, and they therefore turned to popular German historiography (by writers such as Pölitz, Bredow, and Weber), studying, adapting, and translating it into Hebrew. In these German books they also found enlightened approaches to history which lasted into the nineteenth century. These works contained relatively simple historical narratives, suited to the intellectual level of many of the maskilim and their readership among yeshiva students and the Jewish bourgeoisie. The maskilic sense of the past also continued to function in the east European Haskalah movement because it promoted objectives similar to those of the eighteenth-century German maskilim. The maskilim shaped 'maskilic history' and employed it in their struggles to introduce dramatic changes in traditional society, as well as in their battles with opponents of the Haskalah, at a time when the Haskalah was perceived by many Jews as both innovative and opposed to the accepted norms.

The east European maskilim were primarily Hebrew writers, and their great interest in both universal and Jewish history enriched Hebrew literature with many historical works. In these they attempted to clarify various issues in Jewish history, drawing upon the 'science of Judaism' even as they criticized it. Translations of books of universal and Russian history, popular historical tales, historical works in Yiddish, and historical novels created an alternative body of literature for the Jewish reader, competing with the traditional historical literature (Josippon, *Seder hadorot, She'erit yisra'el*, and the like), which was constantly reprinted throughout the nineteenth century.

However, this book goes far beyond a survey of maskilic historical writing. From the outset 'history' for the maskilim was more a sphere of knowledge that could be exploited for various purposes than a field of scientific research. The ideal model, exemplified by Maimonides, for example, was first shaped in the German Haskalah, and east European maskilim continued to make use of it. The same was true of Mendelssohn's historical image as the 'father of the Haskalah' and a historical hero who marked the transition to the modern age. An emphasis on the historical antagonism between reason and folly served the Galician maskilim well in their struggle against hasidism. Levinsohn justified the path of the Haskalah and gave it authoritative support by reconstructing the 'chain of Haskalah', thus providing deep roots for nineteenth-century maskilim. Russian maskilim during the reign of Nicholas I enlisted history in their propaganda struggle to convince Jewry that a political transformation was in fact taking place; Krochmal and Fuenn examined the role of Jews in universal history to clarify their historical uniqueness. 'Maskilic history' was still perceived as a guide and the maskilim regarded the past as a useful quarry of the basic material for building the new Jewish society of which they dreamed. They used the past in propaganda advocating modern education, freedom of opinion, a change in traditional dress, religious reforms, Russian patriotism, and political loyalty to the government. However, they also employed it in attacking assimilation and in strengthening the Jews' sense of unity and a shared destiny. When cultural and social ferment increased and processes of modernization were accelerated during the reign of Alexander II, the maskilic camp diversified. A new generation of maskilim emerged, introducing a radical stream of Haskalah. The moderates contended with the radicals, the maskilim were exposed to Russian positivism and nihilism, and a national trend developed within the Haskalah. All these developments undermined the maskilic sense of the past and introduced new historical concepts. The optimistic idea of the 'modern age' began to crumble; positivist and materialist historical concepts emerged; an attempt was made to incorporate hasidism into Jewish history as a legitimate phenomenon; and in Smolenskin's *Hashaḥar* a vigorous campaign was launched to destroy Mendelssohn's venerated historical image in the name of a nationalist approach.

'Maskilic history' too actually included many elements which Smolenskin could have interpreted in retrospect as 'nationalist', had he wanted to. They included pride in the Jewish historical heritage, recognition of the continuity of Jewish history, the importance accorded to unity, pride in the survival of the Jewish people, and love of the nation. Nonetheless, the maskilim made use of 'history' principally for the purpose of achieving the internal reform of Jewish society and preparing it for the transition from the 'old' to the 'new', and to a lesser extent for strengthening Jewish national consciousness. This latter topic was generally one that the maskilim took for granted, and they directed most of their efforts to broadening universal horizons. Only when national consciousness and identity seemed to be waning did the maskilim denounce the assimilationists. At such times they also enlisted history for this purpose. Galician maskilim, for example, accused the hasidim of disrupting national unity, and the moderate Russian maskilim used historical tales translated from German to reinforce and preserve national identity. Smolenskin regarded himself as living in a different reality, in which the strengthening of national consciousness was no longer taken for granted but had become an overriding aim, while the maskilic struggle against tradition and the traditional was relegated to second place. For this purpose, he tried to shatter the image of the Berlin Haskalah, which to his mind represented an anti-national ideology, and in his endeavour to achieve national unity and nurture Jewish national identity he began to forge a national sense of the past.

At a time when 'history' was harnessed primarily to achieve national goals—a process that began with Smolenskin and continued in the 1880s and 1890s in the Hibat Zion movement—it was already possible to speak of 'national history', which, while it may have included some maskilic elements, signalled the end of the maskilic sense of the past. In the initial spontaneous reactions of Russian maskilim to the shock of the 1881–2 pogroms, there was absolutely no reference to the 'modern age', and the cornerstone of the maskilic sense of the past seemed to have been uprooted. 'It is thousands of years since we were dispersed', wrote J. L. Gordon in October 1881, as he rhapsodized about the shared destiny, the common origin, and other traits that bound the Jews into one nation. His historical perspective seemed to be reverting to the traditional view: 'we have seen evil times; we will also see the good, we will yet live in the land where we dwelt before'.[1] The consciousness of a turning-point had moved Gordon in 1863 to write his poem 'Hakitsah ami' out of his belief in profound historical change ('Great changes have come and gone, and other events are still taking place'), but it later gave way to a sense of the continuity and perpetuation of exile. In March 1881 Lilienblum wrote, in response to rumours about the expected pogroms, 'Why do they persist in vain in bringing back their beloved Middle Ages, for they will never return!' By May 1881 he was already tormenting himself after having experienced the horror of the pogroms in Odessa: 'I am glad I suffered, for at least once in my lifetime I had the opportunity to feel what my forefathers felt throughout all the days of their lives . . . for after all, I am their child, their torments are dear to me, and I would profess to partake of their honour.'[2] The return of the Middle Ages, which brutally burst into the maskilic consciousness, completely changed the basic concepts underlying the maskilic sense of the past. The age that had been described as bitter and harsh but never to return was suddenly present in the modern era too. It was no longer possible to portray the contrast between the modern age and the Middle Ages as the basis of maskilic ideology. From then on, a new historical interpretation was given to Jewish fate and hatred of the Jews, regarding the national foreignness of the Jews as a fundamental factor in Jewish history ('Semites are we in the midst of . . . Aryans').[3] European civilization, the benevolent kings, hopes for emancipation, and liberal ideas no longer functioned as the mainstay of maskilic optimism. In the Hibat Zion movement in the 1880s and 1890s the foundations were laid for a national and Zionist sense of the past.

'Zionism', wrote Shmuel Almog, 'blends an aspiration for national liberation with a trend of national reconstruction, and it requires the official stamp of history.'[4] The aims assigned to 'history' at the inception of Zionism included the glorification of the past for the purpose of reinstating Jewish honour; provision

---

[1] J. L. Gordon, 'Bena'areinu uvizkeneinu nelekh', 30–1.

[2] Lilienblum, 'Derekh teshuvah', 188–9.

[3] Ibid. 196–8; Breiman, 'The Change in Public Jewish Thought'.

[4] Almog, *Zionism and History*, 11.

of proof for the historical continuity of the Jewish people; and an emphasis on active self-expression in relation to the non-Jewish world. In the Hibat Zion movement the period of the return to Zion, an era which had not figured greatly in the Haskalah's picture of the past, became a historical model from which Hovevei Zion societies drew names and symbols, and which they used in making analogies and searching for precedents for their present activities.[5] The revolt of the Hasmoneans in the second century BC became a quintessential Zionist symbol and provided an activist myth which contained a national victory, physical heroism, and a struggle against assimilationists.[6] In the textbook written by Eliezer Ben-Yehuda in Jerusalem in the year 'one thousand, eight hundred and twenty-two of our exile', with the title *An Abridged History of the Children of Israel Settled on their Land*, he placed emphasis on the existence of the Jewish people 'as a political people, in the days when it lived a full life, loved freedom, and gave its life up for it'. The various rebels—the Hasmoneans, the Zealots, and Bar Kokhba— were depicted by Ben-Yehuda as freedom fighters in national secular wars. It is little wonder, then, that he denounced Josephus as 'a coward, a hypocrite, base in nature, seeking only to benefit himself, a faithful lover of the Romans and a traitor to his people'.[7] In discussions held by teachers in Palestine on the teaching of history, everyone agreed that the past should be taught from a national standpoint, in order to inculcate a love of the land and the Hebrew language.[8]

While the Haskalah movement searched the Jewish past for events and persons that exemplified reason and virtue, modern nationalism gathered a roster of 'national assets'. Jewish history was perceived as one of the most important. 'The days of the Haskalah are behind us', wrote Micha Joseph Berdiczewski (1865–1921) in 1897, and 'we must bear in mind that we are all nationalists and that all the forces that have acted upon us are equally sacred'.[9] He used this argument in appraising hasidism as a positive phenomenon, a significant historical expression of the 'national soul' and a product of the 'spirit of the people'. 'We, the young,' Berdiczewski went on to say, 'have stopped hating hasidism and jesting about it . . . we want to get to know the forces that were active in our development.'[10] In this neo-romantic and nationalist atmosphere the view of the Jewish past changed, and with it the criteria by which social forces and works of spiritual creation were judged. Berdiczewski, in his post-maskilic nationalist stance, arrived at a favourable view of hasidism, but not with the same goal in mind as Zweifel: to achieve national unity and to open new paths for the triumph of the Haskalah. Rather, he

---

[5] Shohet, 'Symbols and Folklore', 228–50; Y. Shavit, 'The Return to Zion', 359–72.

[6] Luz, 'On the Myth of Revival', 44–52; Almog, *Zionism and History*.

[7] Ben-Yehuda, *Kitsur divrei hayamim livenei yisra'el*, 135.

[8] Minutes of the first teachers' meetings in Palestine, in Druyanow (ed.), *Writings on the History of Hibat Zion*, 992–1002. See also Elboim-Dror, *Hebrew Education*, vol. i, ch. 3.

[9] Berdyczewski, 'Al devar haḥasidut', 264; id., 'Olam ha'atsilut', 8–9. See also Werses, *Story and Source*, 104–18, 'Hasidism in Berdyczewski's World'.

[10] Berdyczewski, 'Al devar haḥasidut', 264.

was eager to enlist hasidism as a 'national asset'. The belletristic history became
one of the means of developing a popular national historical consciousness. A
second edition of Schulman's *Harisot beitar* was printed in 1884, and this time it
was read in a historical period vastly different from that of the 1850s. Now it served
trends of national activism, despite assertions of political loyalty to the ruling
power, of which Schulman never tired.[11] In the 1880s and 1890s Mapu's *Ahavat
tsiyon* too was read from a different perspective, not only as a novel bearing
anti-traditional maskilic messages, but as a consummate expression of romantic
nationalism: 'It was this story that aroused in the hearts of many of our fellow Jews
a yearning for life in village and field, for work on the land in general and love of
Zion and our ancient memories in particular.'[12]

In the 1880s in Russia the idea of the 'chronicles of our people' as a national
asset and a key source of nationalist consciousness prompted the need for a book
of Jewish history, written in Hebrew, with a distinct national orientation. It is in
this light that one can understand Nahum Sokolow's plan to establish a group of
scholars and historians who would publish a Hebrew alternative to Graetz's
dominant work.[13] Sokolow believed it was very important to write an original
work that was not a translation from the German and whose authors empathized
with the history of the Jews and could closely identify with their fate. Anyone
who did not know the history of the Jewish people, Sokolow wrote in the plan
for his historiographic project, did not live the 'collective life', nor could he live
'as a man who is one of his people, as an inherent part of the collective'.[14] In the
end, however, Graetz's work did become the history book of the Hibat Zion movement, after it was converted into a 'national history' by its adapter and translator
into Hebrew Saul Pinhas Rabinowitz in the early 1890s. Graetz himself, in a letter
from Breslau in 1888, commended the translator's initiative and noted how important it was that the Hebrew reader know 'the deeds of our forefathers'. But he
also reiterated the clear-cut emancipatory orientation that underpinned his work:
since the persecutions and tribulations of the Jews had ended for those segments
of the people who 'had been given freedom and the right to be like any citizen of
the land', thus 'there is hope for the remainder of their brethren who are still
under the iron yoke that they too will be redeemed'.[15] Rabinowitz, in contrast,
attributed nationalist intentions to Graetz ('to strengthen the foundations of the
nation and the love of the people's virtues'), and appended a Zionist message to
his *Geschichte der Juden*:

When the Jews have greater knowledge of themselves, the assets of their spirit, their grace,
and their fine qualities, our youth will know and recognize that in the thousands of years of

[11] Schulman, *Harisot beitar*, introd. to the 2nd edn.
[12] See Werses, *Yiddish Translations of 'Ahavat Tsiyon'*, 23–30.
[13] Sokolow, 'Kol mevaser', 573–81.   [14] Ibid. 577–8.
[15] H. Graetz, *Sefer divrei yemei yisra'el*, preface, 1; for Rabinowitz's announcement of the printing
of Graetz's book, see *Keneset yisra'el*, 3 (1884), 645. Cf. Avineri, *Varieties of Zionist Thought*, 36–48.

our wandering the eye of Jacob has remained undimmed . . . and they will also come to know that in days to come Jacob will take root in the land of his fathers and the bud of an eternal people will blossom in the place which has been its source from time immemorial.[16]

In the 1890s Ahad Ha'am was certain that the break with the Haskalah was complete. The controversy over Mendelssohn's historical role, for example, seemed to him emotional and motivated by interests that had become irrelevant. Only now, he wrote in *Hashiloaḥ* in 1896, when the Berlin Haskalah was no longer influential, could Mendelssohn be seen as nothing more than an 'imaginary hero', rather than as either a towering saint or a destructive anti-nationalist villain. The time had come, Ahad Ha'am declared, to regard the Berlin Haskalah as 'a historical vision that is alien to us, that can and must be objectively clarified, without [Mendelssohn's] memory impelling our hearts towards either love or hate, which obscures our judgement'.[17] In fact, maskilic concepts, principles, and outlooks continued to influence the nationalist and Zionist stream in eastern Europe, and the maskilic sense of the past resonated in the Zionist historical awareness. This was particularly true in regard to the Zionists' critical attitude towards Jewish life in the Diaspora. There was also a similarity between the Haskalah and Zionism in their models of the role played by the past: both movements made selective use of the past in order to build their identity, find legitimization, and educate Jewish society. However, while Zionism attempted to construct a new national Judaism, the Haskalah hoped to use the past to build a new, regenerated, and transformed Jewish society and culture, free of all its old flaws and fit for normal life in the modern age. In this sense, maskilic history—the fruit of the maskilim's collective sense of the past over a century—did indeed serve the transformative ideology of the Haskalah of bringing the Jewish people out of the old world into the new.

[16] H. Graetz, *Sefer divrei yemei yisra'el*, Rabinowitz's words on the second title-page (unnumbered), and on p. iii. In *Hamelits* praises were heaped on Graetz on his seventieth birthday: 'A people who has no history book is not a people, and Graetz, who produced a history book for us, has established us as a people and elevated us among the languages' (1887, issue 192). See also H. Graetz, 'Mikhtav galuy', 71–2, 259–61.

[17] Ahad Ha'am, 'Yalkut katan', 279–80 (in a review of Bernfeld's book *Dor tahapukhot*).

Glossary

aggadah   Story; non-halakhic material in the Talmud.

amora (pl. *amora'im*)   An authority from the time of the Talmud.

ba'al shem   'Master of the Divine Name'; title given from the Middle Ages onwards to one who possessed the secret knowledge of the Tetragrammaton and other holy names, and who knew how to work miracles by the power of these names.

Ba'al Shem Tov   Popular title of Israel ben Eliezer (*c*.1700–60), the charismatic founder of hasidism (q.v.) in eastern Europe.

beit midrash (lit. house of study)   Place where Jewish men gather to study in the traditional Jewish way.

derekh erets   Proper behaviour.

Edict of Tolerance   Edict issued by Emperor Joseph II in 1782 for the Jews of Vienna and Lower Austria. It was one of a series of patents granted to the major non-Catholic denominations of Austria, guaranteeing existing rights and obligations and laying down additional ones.

Essenes   A religious communalistic Jewish sect or brotherhood in the latter half of the Second Temple period, from the second century BC to the end of the first century AD.

etrog (pl. *etrogim*)   A species of citrus fruit used in the ritual on Sukot (q.v.).

Frankists   Followers of Jacob Frank (1726–91), the head of a mystical antinomian sect among Polish Jews.

gaon (pl. *geonim*)   'Excellency', title of the heads of the great colleges that flourished in Babylonia from the seventh to the eleventh centuries; later, title of any distinguished rabbi and talmudist.

halakhah   The legal or prescriptive part of Jewish tradition which defines the norms of behaviour and religious observance. Based on the legislation in the Bible, it was developed in the Talmud and later in a varied body of literature, including codes, commentaries, and responsa. (*halakhot*, individual rulings)

hasidism   A mystically inclined movement of religious revival consisting of distinct groups with charismatic leadership. It arose in the borderlands of the Polish–Lithuanian Commonwealth in the second half of the eighteenth century and quickly spread through eastern Europe. The hasidim emphasized joy in the service of God, whose presence they sought everywhere. Though their opponents the mitnagedim (q.v.) pronounced a series of bans against them beginning in 1772.

ḥeder   Colloquial name for a traditional Jewish elementary school.

ḥokhmah   Wisdom. In the Pentateuch and Prophets all wisdom is seen to be of divine origin; a group of later books (Job, Ecclesiastes, Proverbs, Song of Songs) was known as the wisdom literature. Rabbinic and medieval literature debated whether *ḥokhmah* encompassed only Jewish sources and knowledge or external ones as well. The Haskalah generally advocated a broad definition of the term to incorporate secular knowledge such as languages, science, and mathematics, but there was disagreement over whether it should include such a controversial subject as philosophy.

kabbalah   Trend in Jewish mysticism from the twelfth century onwards, deriving from the Zohar (q.v.) and having profound impact on hasidism (q.v.) and other forms of Jewish Orthodoxy.

Karaism   Schismatic movement in Judaism (from the ninth century) which rejected rabbinic authority.

kloyz (Yiddish)   Private *beit midrash* (q.v.).

magid   Preacher.

me'asfim   Hebrew writers associated with the journal of the Berlin Haskalah, *Hame'asef* (The Gatherer) (1784–1811).

melamed   Teacher in a *ḥeder* (q.v.).

Midrash   Body of rabbinic literature from the mishnaic and talmudic periods, containing homiletical expositions of biblical texts, sermons, and halakhic analyses of biblical texts; 'midrash' can by extension be used to mean the rabbinic interpretation rather than the plain meaning of a biblical text.

minhag   Custom.

Mishnah   First and most authoritative codification of halakhah (q.v.) found in the Oral Law (q.v.), dating from the early third century.

mitnagedim   The rabbinic opponents of hasidism (q.v.).

mitsvah (pl. *mitsvot*)   Commandment(s); colloquially, 'good deeds'.

Oral Law   The authoritative interpretation of the Written Law (Pentateuch), regarded as given to Moses on Sinai, and therefore coexistent with the Written Law.

peshat   The plain or literal meaning of Scripture.

Pharisees   Immediate ancestors of the *tana'im* (q.v.); forebears of all contemporary versions of Judaism; contrasted with Sadducees (q.v.).

pilpul   Casuistic discussion of the Talmud; by derivation it can also mean a form of hair-splitting argument.

Sadducees   First-century movement in Judaism which, among other things, denied retribution after death and rejected the authority of contemporary (Pharisaic) rabbis.

Sages   Collective term used of the rabbis of the talmudic period.

Shabbateanism   Seventeenth- to nineteenth-century messianic movement named after Shabbetai Tsevi (1626–76), the largest and most influential such movement in Jewish history.

Shekhinah   The Divine Presence of God.

Shulḥan arukh   The authoritative code of Jewish law compiled by Joseph Karo in the sixteenth century, with glosses by Moses Isserles (1525/30–1572).

Sukot   Feast of Tabernacles, observed for eight days in the month of Tishrei (autumn).

talmid ḥakham   Talmudic scholar.

tana (pl. *tana'im*)   An authority from the time of the Mishnah (q.v.).

torat ha'adam   'The law of man'; a phrase used by the maskilim to signify the humanistic ethics they espoused.

torat hashem   'The law of God'; contrasted with *torat ha'adam* (q.v.).

tsadik (pl. *tsadikim*)   The leader of a hasidic group, often credited with miraculous powers by his followers.

yeshiva   The highest institution in the traditional Jewish system of education.

Zohar   Key text of that trend in medieval Jewish mysticism known as kabbalah (q.v.); traditionally ascribed to the second-century *tana* (q.v.) Rabbi Simeon bar Yohai.

Bibliography

ABRAMOWITZ, SHALOM JACOB (MENDELE MOKHER SEFORIM), *Collected Writings* (Heb.) (Tel Aviv, 1958).

——*Divrei hayamim livenei harusim* [History of the Russians] (Odessa, 1868).

——*Ein mishpat* [A Critical Eye] (Zhitomir, 1867).

——*Ha'avot vehabanim* [Fathers and Sons] (Odessa, 1868); repr. in id., *Collected Writings*, 7–52.

——'Hagoy lo nikhsaf' [Shameless Nation], *Hamagid*, 19 (1875), 164–5, 172–3, 183, 190, 198–9.

——'Lekhu hezu mife'alot hashem' [Gaze on the Wonders of God], *Hamelits*, 1 (1861), nos. 16, 18, 20.

——'Mah anu' [What Are We?], *Hashahar*, 6 (1875), 464–85, 526–34.

——*Mishpat shalom* [A Prudent Critique] (Vilna, 1860).

——'Reshimot letoldotai' [Autobiographical Notes], in id., *Collected Writings*, 1–6.

——*Sefer hakabtsanim* [Book of Beggars], ed. D. Miron (Tel Aviv, 1988).

——*Susati* [My Mare] (Yiddish version, *Di kliatshe*, Vilna, 1873); repr. in id., *Collected Writings*, 307–47.

——*Toledot hateva* [Natural History] (Leipzig, 1862).

ADAMS, H., *History of the Jews from the Destruction of Jerusalem to the Nineteenth Century* (Boston, 1812).

AHAD HA'AM, *Complete Works* (Heb.) (Tel Aviv, 1947).

——'Moses', in id., *Complete Works* (Heb.) (Tel Aviv, 1947), 342–7.

——*Pirkei zikhronot ve'igerot* [Memories and Letters] (Tel Aviv, 1931), 45.

——'Yalkut katan' [Small Pouch], *Hashilo'ah*, 2 (1897), 278–80.

Allgemeine Deutsche Biographie, 56 vols. (Leipzig, 1875–1912).

ALMANZI, JOSEPH, 'Toledot r. mosheh hayim luzato' [Biography of R. Moshe Hayim Luzzatto], *Kerem hemed*, 2 (1836), 54–67.

ALMOG, SHMUEL, *Zionism and History* (Heb.) (Jerusalem, 1982).

ALTER, M. HALEVI, 'Sihah be'erets hahayim' [Conversation in the Land of the Living], *Bikurei ha'itim*, 6 (1825), 6–24.

ALTMANN, ALEXANDER, *Moses Mendelssohn: A Biographical Study* (London, 1973).

——'A New Evaluation of Moses Mendelssohn's *Jerusalem* in the Light of Biographical Data' (Heb.), *Zion*, 33 (1968), 47–58.

AMADIS DE GAULA, *Alilot ha'abir amadish de ga'ulah*, Hebrew trans. by the physician Jacob di Algaba (Constantinople, *c.*1541), critical edn., introd. Tsevi Malakhi (Tel Aviv, 1981).

AMELANDER, M., *She'erit yisra'el hashalem* [The Remnant of Israel] (Jerusalem, 1964).

ANON., 'Al hamedinot bo ye'amer' [Of the Nations it is Decreed], *Hamagid*, 18 (1873), 57–80.

ANON., 'Hamelukhah veharabanut beportugal' [The Monarchy and the Rabbinate in Portugal], *Hakarmel*, 5 (1865), 138–40.

ANON., 'Hatsofeh' [The Watcher], *Hamagid*, 2 (1858), 34–5, 50–1.

ANON., 'A Letter from a Polish Sage on the Critique' (Heb.), *Zion*, 1 (1841), 188–92.

ANON., *Milhamah beshalom* [War against Peace] (Vilna, 1870), 10–13.

ANON., 'Tefilah lesokrates' [Prayer to Socrates], *Hame'asef*, 4 (1788), 166.

ANON., 'Toledot harav don yitshak abravanel' [Biography of R. Don Isaac Abrabanel], *Hame'asef*, 1 (1784), 38–42, 57–61.

ANON., 'Toledot hazeman' [Contemporary History], *Hame'asef*, 5 (1789), 365–7.

ANON., 'Toledot hehakham shimshon blokh' [Biography of Samson Bloch], *Kokhavei yitshak*, 7 (1846), 40–5.

ANON., 'Toledot rabenu shmuel hanagid' [Biography of Samuel Hanagid], *Hamagid*, 1 (1857), 105–6; 4 (1860), 33–4, 37–8, 41.

ARIELI, YEHOSHUA, 'The Modern Age and the Problem of Secularization: A Historiographical Study', in Y. Gafni and Y. Motzkin (eds.), *Kingship and Monarchy: Relations between Religion and the State among Jews and Non-Jews* (Heb.) (Jerusalem, 1987), 165–216.

——'New Horizons in the Historiography of the Eighteenth and the Nineteenth Centuries', in M. Zimmerman *et al.* (eds.), *Studies in Historiography: Selected Essays* (Heb.) (Jerusalem, 1987), 145–68.

ASCHER, SHAUL, *Leviathan, oder über Religion in Rücksicht des Judentums* (Berlin, 1792).

AVINERI, SHLOMO, 'The Fossil and Phoenix: Hegel and Krochmal on the Jewish Volksgeist', in Robert L. Perkins (ed.), *History and System, Hegel's Philosophy of History* (Albany, NY, 1984), 47–72.

——*Moses Hess: Prophet of Communism and Zionism* (New York, 1985).

——*Varieties of Zionist Thought* (Heb.) (Tel Aviv, 1980).

AVSHALOM (pseud.), 'El tiferet yisra'el, hahoker hagadol ha'elohi rabenu moshe mendelson' [To the Glory of Israel, the Great Scholar, Moses Mendelssohn], *Bikurei ha'itim*, 7 (1826), 97.

BADER, GERSHOM, *Medinah vehakhameiha* [Galician Rabbis and Scholars] (Vienna, 1934).

BAER, F. YITZHAK, *Galut* [Exile], trans. R. Warshow (Lanham, Md., 1988).

BAHARAV, G. (Bugrov), *Ma'asim shehayu* [Tales from the Past], trans. from Russian by J. Grasovsky (Warsaw, 1899).

BARAN, JOSEPH, 'Divrei hayamim la'i sitsiliyah' [The History of Sicily], *Hame'asef*, 5 (1789), 199–221.

——'Divrei hayamim le'artsot yavan' [History of the Lands of Greece], *Hame'asef*, 6 (1790), 195–201, 230–42, 293–300, 328–33.

——'Divrei hayamim lemalkhei ashur vemedai' [The History of the Kings of Assyria and Media], *Hame'asef*, 5 (1789), 66–78, 101–24.

——'Divrei hayamim lemamlakhot ha'aratsot: takhlit hadevarim ha'eleh veto'aletam' [The History of Kingdoms of the World], *Hame'asef*, 4 (1788), 368–85.

——'Divrei hayamim vehakorot leha'ir kartago' [History of the City of Carthage], *Hame'asef*, 5 (1789), 344–8; 6 (1790), 12–24.

BARASH, MOSHE, 'Vasari' (Heb.), *Zemanim*, 13 (1983), 24–38.

BARAZ, SHIMON, *Ma'arakhei lev* [Heartfelt Sentiments] (Königsberg, 1785).

——'Toledot rabenu mosheh ben maimon' [Biography of Maimonides], *Hame'asef*, 3 (1786), 19–27, 35–47.

BAR HIYAH, ABRAHAM, *Sefer megilat hamegaleh* [The Book of the Scroll of the Revealer] (Jerusalem, 1968).

BAR-ILAN, MEIR, 'Books from Cochin' (Heb.), *Pe'amim*, 52 (1992), 74–100.

BARON, S., *History and Jewish Historians* (Philadelphia, 1964).

——'Samuel David Luzzatto and the Revolution in 1848–1849', in M. D. Cassutto, J. Klausner, and Y. Gutman (eds.), *The Book of Asaf* (Heb.) (Jerusalem, 1953), 40–63.

BARTAL, ISRAEL, 'The East European Haskalah and the Karaites: Image and Reality' (Heb.), in *Proceedings of the Eleventh World Congress of Jewish Studies*, division 2, vol. ii (Jerusalem, 1994), 15–22.

——'From Traditional Bilingualism to National Monolingualism', in Lewis Glinert (ed.), *Hebrew in Ashkenaz: A Language in Exile* (New York and Oxford, 1993), 141–50.

——'Gentiles and Gentile Society in Hebrew and Yiddish Literature in Eastern Europe, 1856–1914' (Heb.) (Ph.D. diss., Hebrew University of Jerusalem, 1980).

——'The Heavenly City of Germany and Absolution, à la Mode d'Autriche: The Rise of the Haskalah in Galicia', in J. Katz (ed.), *Toward Modernity* (New Brunswick, NJ and Oxford, 1987), 33–42.

——*Jews in the Age of Changes* (Heb.), Open University of Israel 10 (Tel Aviv, 1978).

——'Mordechai Aaron Guenzburg: A Lithuanian Maskil Faces Modernity', in Frances Malino and David Sorkin (eds.), *From East and West: Jews in a Changing Europe 1750–1870* (Oxford, 1990), 126–47.

——'Radical Enlightenment and Jewish Socialism', in Imanuel Etkes (ed.), *Religion and Life: The East European Jewish Enlightenment* (Heb.) (Jerusalem, 1993), 328–39.

——'Zikhron Ya'akov: Orthodox Historiography?' (Heb.), *Milet*, 2 (1985), 409–14.

BARZILAY, I., 'The Ideology of the Berlin Haskalah', *Proceedings of the American Academy for Jewish Research*, 25 (1956), 1–37.

——'The Italian and the Berlin Haskalah', *Proceedings of the American Academy for Jewish Research*, 29 (1960–1), 17–54.

——*Menashe of Ilya: Precursor of Modernity among the Jews of Eastern Europe* (Jerusalem, 1999).

BARZILAY, I., 'National and Anti-National Trends in the Berlin Haskalah', *Jewish Social Studies*, 21 (1959), 165–92.

——*Shlomo Yehuda Rapoport (Shir)* (Ramat Gan, 1969).

——'Smolenskin's Polemic against Mendelssohn in Historical Perspective', *Proceedings of the American Academy for Jewish Research*, 53 (1986), 11–48.

BAT-YEHUDAH, G., 'R. Nachman Krochmal and his National Perception' (Heb.), *Areshet* (Jerusalem, 1944), 419–30.

BAUMINGER, ARYEH, BUSAK, MEIR, and GELBER, NATAN MICHAEL (eds.), *Sefer kraka* [The Book of Krakow] (Jerusalem, 1959).

BAZILEVSKI, MOSES, *Divrei binah o ha'emunah vehokhmat hateva* [On the Natural Sciences] (Zhitomir, 1870).

BECKER, CARL L., *The Heavenly City of the Eighteenth Century Philosophers* (New Haven, 1993).

BECKER, K., *Weltgeschichte für Kinder und Kinderlehrer* (Berlin, 1801–5).

BEER, I., 'Was hielten die griechischen und früheren römischen Philosophen und Geschichtschreiber von den Juden', *Bikurei ha'itim*, 5 (1824), 30–40.

BEER, PETER, 'Chassidäer', in J. S. Ersch and J. G. Gruber (eds.), *Allgemeine Encyclopädie der Wissenschaften und Künste*, vol. xvi (Leipzig, 1827), 192–6.

——*Geschichte, Lehren und Meinungen aller Bestandenen und noch bestehenden religiösen Sekten der Juden*, 2 vols. (Brünn, 1822–3).

——*Sefer toledot yisra'el* [The History of Israel], 2 vols. (i: Prague, 1796; ii: Vienna, 1808).

BEILINSON, MOSES ELIEZER, *Alei hadas* [A Myrtle Leaf] (Odessa, 1865).

——*Galut sefarad* [The Exile from Spain] (Vilna, 1860).

BEN-AMI, 'Kalman Schulman' (Heb.), *Reshumot*, 6 (1930), 114–24.

BEN-ARI, NITSA, *Romance with the Past* (Heb.) (Tel Aviv, 1997).

BENDAVID, LAZARUS, *Etwas zur Charakteristick der Juden* (Leipzig, 1793).

BEN-ISRAEL, HEDVA, *English Historians on the French Revolution* (Cambridge, 1968).

BEN JONES, R., *Napoleon: Man and Myth* (New York, 1977).

BEN-SASSON, HAYIM HILLEL, *Continuity and Variety* (Heb.) (Tel Aviv, 1984).

BEN-YEHUDA, ELIEZER, *A Dream Come True*, trans. from Hebrew T. Muraoka, ed. G. Mandel (Boulder, Colo., 1993).

——*Kitsur divrei hayamim livenei yisra'el, beshivtam al admatam* [Abridged History of the Jews Living in their Land] (Jerusalem, 1892).

——'She'elah nikhbadah' [A Weighty Question], in id., *Hahalom veshivro* [Dream and Awakening: A Selection of Letters on Language Issues], ed. R. Sivan, 2nd edn. (Jerusalem, 1986).

BEN ZE'EV, JUDAH LEIB, *Mavo el mikra'ei kodesh* [Introduction to the Holy Scriptures] (Vienna, 1810).

——*Mesilat halimud* [The Path of Learning] (Vienna, 1802).

——*Otsar hashorashim* [A Compilation of Roots], 3 vols. (Vienna, 1807–8; 1834).

——*Yesodei hadat* [The Foundations of Religion] (Vienna, 1811).

——(ed.), *Hokhmat yehoshua ben sirah* [The Wisdom of Joshua ben Sira] (Breslau, 1798; Vienna, 1814).

——(ed.), *Megilat yehudit* [The Scroll of Judith] (1799; Vienna, 1819).

BERDYCZEWSKI (BIN-GORION), MICHA JOSEPH, 'Al devar hahasidut' [On Hasidism], *Hamagid leyisra'el*, 33 (1897), 264.

——'Olam ha'atsilut' [The World of Emanation] (1888), in Immanuel Bin-Gorion (ed.), *Pirkei volozhin* (Holon, 1984), 7–37.

BERLIN, ISAIAH, 'Fathers and Children: Turgenev and the Liberal Predicament', text of the Romanes Lecture, 1970, repr. in Ivan Turgenev, *Fathers and Sons* (Harmondsworth, 1986), 7–61.

——*The Hedgehog and the Fox: An Essay on Tolstoy's View of History* (London, 1978).

——*Russian Thinkers* (London, 1978).

——*Vico and Herder* (London, 1976).

BERLIN, SAUL BEN TSEVI HIRSCH LEVIN, *Besamim rosh* [Perfumes] (Berlin, 1793).

——*Ketav yosher* [A Certificate of Integrity] (Berlin, 1794), repr. in Yehuda Friedlander, *Studies in Hebrew Satire*, vol. i (Heb.) (Tel Aviv, 1979), 91–112.

BERMAN, I., 'Mipi olalim' [From the Mouths of Babes], *Hashahar*, 2 (1871), 13–16.

BERNEY, ARNOLD, 'The Historical and Political Conceptions of Moses Mendelssohn' (Heb.), *Zion*, 5 (1940), 99–111, 248–70.

BERNFELD, SIMON, 'Dorshei reshumot' [On Jewish Historiography], *Hashilo'ah*, 2 (1897), 97–110, 193–208, 394–407, 508–19.

——*Dor tahapukhot* [A Generation of Changes] (Warsaw, 1897).

——*Toledot shir* [Biography of Shir (Solomon Judah Leib Rapoport)] (Berlin, 1899).

BICK, JACOB SAMUEL, 'El maskilei benei ami!' [To the Maskilim of My People]!, *Hatsefirah* (Zolkiew, 1824), 71–4.

——'Mikhtav 22' [Letter no. 22], *Kerem hemed*, 1 (1833), 81–2.

——'Mikhtav leshir' [A Letter to Rapoport], *Otsar hasifrut*, 3 (1889), 25–6; 4 (1892), 267.

Bikurei ha'itim hahadashim, ed. I. S. Reggio and I. Bush (Vienna, 1845).

BLOCH, SAMSON HALEVI, Letter to the editors, *Yerushalayim*, vol. ii (Lvov, 1845), 12.

——'Mikhtav leyehudah vorman miyeroslav' [A Letter to Yehudah Worman of Jaroslaw], *Kerem hemed*, 2 (1836), 81–5.

——*Shevilei olam* [Ways of the World], 3 vols. (Zolkiew and Lvov, 1822–55); vol. iii written and published by A. M. M. Mohr.

——*Teshuat yisra'el* [Israel's Salvation] (Vienna, 1814).

——*Toledot rashi* [Biography of Rashi] (Lvov, 1840).

BLUMENFELD, M. M., 'Rabi shelomoh ibn gavirol' [R. Solomon Ibn Gabirol], adapted from H. Graetz, *Hamagid*, 10 (1866), 141.

BODEK, JACOB, 'Mikhtav le'avraham mendel mor' [Letter to Avraham Mendel Mohr], *Yerushalayim*, 3 (1845), 14–15.

——'Toledot uriel da kosta' [Biography of Uriel Da Costa], *Tsefirat tifarah*, 7–9 (Vienna, 1850), 26–9.

BONFIL, REUVEN, 'How Golden was the Age of Renaissance in Jewish Historiography?', *History and Theory*, 27 (1988), 78–102.

——'Some Reflections on the Place of Azariah de Rossi's Meor Enayim in the Cultural Milieu of Italian Renaissance Jewry', in Isidor Twersky (ed.), *Jewish Thought in the Sixteenth Century* (Cambridge and London, 1983), 23–48.

——(ed.), *The Writings of Azariah de' Rossi* (Heb.) (Jerusalem, 1991).

BOSSUET, J., *Discourse on Universal History*, trans. E. Forster (Chicago, 1976).

BRAUDES, REUBEN ASHER, *Hadat vehaḥayim* [Religion and Life], 2 vols. (Lvov, 1877).

BRAVER, M., *The Biography of Rabbi Zevi Hirsch of Zidichov* (Heb.) (n.p., 1972).

BREDOW, GOTTFRIED GABRIEL, *Umständlichere Erzählung der merkwürdigen Begebenheiten aus der allgemeinen Weltgeschichte* (Reutlingen, 1812).

BREIMAN, S., 'The Change in Public Jewish Thought at the Beginnings of the 1880s' (Heb.), *Shivat tsiyon*, 2–3 (1951–2), 83–227.

BREISACH, E., *Historiography* (Chicago, 1983).

'Briefe aus Galizien', *Kalender und Jahrbuch für Israeliten auf das Jahr 1847* (Vienna, 1846), 197–202.

BRILL, JOEL, *Be'ur lesefer tehilim* [Commentary on the Book of Psalms] (1791; Prague, 1835).

BROOK, ABRAHAM, 'Ginzei nistarot' [From the Archives], *Hamagid*, 3 (1859), 169–170, 175.

BUBER, MARTIN, 'A People and its God' (Heb.), *Knesset*, 6 (1941), 287–95.

BUCKLE, HENRY THOMAS, *History of Civilization in England*, 2 vols. (London, 1856, 1861; 2nd edn. London, 1908).

BURCKHARDT, JACOB, *The Civilization of the Renaissance in Italy*, trans. S. G. C. Middlemore, with a new introd. by P. Burke and notes by P. Murray (Harmondsworth, 1990).

BURKE, PETER, *The Renaissance Sense of the Past* (New York, 1970).

BURY, J. B., *The Idea of Progress* (New York, 1970).

BUSAK, MEIR, 'The Jews of Krakow in the Second Half of the Nineteenth Century', in A. Bauminger *et al.* (eds.), *Sefer kraka* [The Book of Krakow] (Jerusalem, 1959), 89–125.

BUTTERFIELD, H., *Man on his Past* (Cambridge, 1955).

CAPSALI, ELIJAH, *Seder eliyahu zuta* [A History of the Ottoman Empire] (Jerusalem, 1979).

CARDOZO, ISAAC, *Las Excelencias de los Hebreos* (Amsterdam, 1679); Hebrew trans. with introd. and notes by J. Kaplan (Jerusalem, 1971).

CARLYLE, THOMAS, *On Heroes, Hero-Worship and the Heroic in History* (1840; London, 1907).

CARO, DAVID, *Sefer tekhunat harabanim* [The Character of the Rabbis] (Vienna, 1824).

CASSIRER, ERNST, *The Philosophy of the Enlightenment* (Boston, 1966).

CHADWICK, OWEN, *The Secularization of the European Mind in the Nineteenth Century* (Cambridge, 1975).

CHAJES, TSEVI (HAYOT), 'Imrei binah' [Words of Wisdom], in id., *Kol sifrei tsevi hirsh ḥayot*, ii. 869–972.

——*Kol sifrei tsevi hirsh ḥayot* [The Complete Works of Tsevi Hirsch Chajes], 2 vols. (Jerusalem, 1958).

——'Minḥat kana'ut', in id., *Kol sifrei tsevi hirsh ḥayot*, ii. 973–1031.

——'Tiferet lemosheh', in id., *Kol sifrei tsevi hirsh ḥayot*, i. 395–433.

COHEN, SOLOMON, *Podeh umatsil* [Ransomer and Saviour] (Warsaw, 1886).

COHEN, TOVA, *From Dream to Reality: Descriptions of Eretz Yisrael in Haskalah Literature* (Heb.) (Ramat Gan, 1992).

——*Solomon Loewisohn's* Melitsat yeshurun: *The Author and his Work* (Heb.) (Ramat Gan, 1989).

CONDORCET, A. M., 'Sketch for a Historical Picture of the Progress of the Human Mind', in P. Gardiner, *Theories of History* (New York, 1959), 51–8.

CONFINO, MICHAEL, 'Peter the Great: Legend and Reality' (Heb.), in *The Great Man and his Age: Lectures Delivered at the Eighth Convention of the Historical Society of Israel* (Jerusalem, 1963), 135–56.

D'ALEMBERT, J., *Preliminary Discourse to the Encyclopedia of Diderot*, trans. R. Schwab (Indianapolis and New York, 1963).

DAN, JOSEPH, 'The Beginnings of Hebrew Hagiographic Literature' (Heb.), *Jerusalem Studies in Jewish Folklore*, 1 (1981), 82–100.

——*The Hebrew Story in the Middle Ages* (Heb.) (Jerusalem, 1974).

DARNTON, ROBERT, 'In Search of the Enlightenment: Recent Attempts to Create a Social History of Ideas', *Journal of Modern History*, 43 (1971), 113–32.

DAVID, ABRAHAM, 'The Historiographical Work of Gedalya Ibn Yahya' (Heb.) (Ph.D. diss., Hebrew University of Jerusalem, 1976).

DE' ROSSI, AZARIAH, *Meor einayim* [Enlightenment of the Eyes] (Mantua, 1574; repr. Vilna, 1866).

DEGANI, BEN ZION, 'The Structure of World History and the Redemption of Israel in R. David Gans' *Tsemaḥ david*' (Heb.), *Zion*, 45 (1980), 173–200.

DEINARD, EPHRAIM, *Sefer masa kerim* [The Crimean Journey] (Warsaw, 1878).

——*Sefer milchemet kerim* [The Crimean War] (Warsaw, 1879).

DICK, ISAAC MEIR, *Alte yidishe sagen* [Old Jewish Sayings] (Vilna, 1876).

——*Der aroysgetribener un bald tsurikgerufener yoysef* [Joseph—Expelled and Immediately Called to Return] (Vilna, 1877).

——*Der vunderlekhe geshikhte fun der ershter hatoke vos unzere toyre hekdoyshe iz netak gevorn* [The Wondrous Tale of the First Translation of our Holy Torah], in id., *Hadrat zekenim.*

——*Di blut hokhtsayt fun pariz* [Bloody Midnight in Paris] (Vilna, 1870).

——*Di shreklekhe geshikhte fun shabse tsvi* [The Terrible Tale of Shabbetai Tsevi] (Vilna, 1864).

——*Hadrat zekenim* [The Dignity of the Aged] (Vilna, 1864).

——*Haore'ah* [The Guest] (Vilna, 1846).

——'Mikhtav le ḥ. y. gurland' [A Letter to Gurland], *Reshumot*, 2 (1922), 408.

——*R. shemayah mevarekh hamo'adot vedivrei sipur aherim* [R. Shemayah, Blesser of Festivals and Other Stories], ed. D. Sadan (Jerusalem, 1967).

DINUR, BENZION, *At the Turn of the Generations* (Heb.) (Jerusalem, 1955).

——'The Awareness of the Past in the National Jewish Consciousness and its Problems' (Heb.), in *Awareness of the Past in General History and in Jewish History: Lectures Delivered at the Thirteenth Convention of the Historical Society in Israel* (Jerusalem, 1969), 9–24.

——'The Great Man and his Age in General History and in Jewish History' (Heb.), in *The Great Man and his Age: Lectures Delivered at the Eighth Convention of the Historical Society of Israel* (Jerusalem, 1963), 9–13.

——*Historical Writings* (Heb.), vol. iv (Jerusalem, 1978).

DOHM, CHRISTIAN WILHELM VON, *Über die bürgerliche Verbesserung der Juden* (Berlin, 1781).

DORMAN, MENAHEM, *The Spinoza Dispute in Jewish Thought* (Heb.) (Tel Aviv, 1990).

DRAPER, JOHN WILLIAM, *A History of the Intellectual Development of Europe* (1861; London and New York, 1896).

DRUYANOW, ALTER (ed.), *Writings on the History of Hibat Zion and the Settlement of Palestine* (Heb.), vol. iii (Tel Aviv, 1931).

DUBNOW, SIMON, *History of the Jews in Russia and Poland*, 2 vols., trans. from Russian by I. Friedlander (Philadelphia, 1946).

——'Nahpesah venahkorah' [We Should Look and Seek], *Pardes*, 1 (1892), 221–41.

——*Sefer hahayim* [Book of Life], trans. M. Ben-Eliezer (Tel Aviv, 1936).

DUCKLES, V., 'Johann Nicolaus Forkel and the Beginning of Music Historiography', *Eighteenth Century Studies*, 1 (1968), 277–88.

EHRLICH, A., 'Al hasefarim bo ye'amer' [On Books], *Hamagid*, 12 (1868), 247.

EICHHORN, JACOB, *Sefer adat ya'akov* [The Community of Jacob] (Breslau, 1844).

EINHORN, I., 'Rabenu gershom meor hagolah' [Rabbenu Gershom, Light of the Exile], *Hakarmel*, 2 (1862), 77–8, 149–50, 185–6.

EISEMAN, MOSES, 'Harabanut' [The Rabbinate], *Hamelits*, 10 (1870), nos. 7–8, 10–11, 14, 17, 21–4, 28.

ELBAUM, JACOB, *Openness and Insularity: Late Sixteenth-Century Jewish Literature in Poland and Germany* (Heb.) (Jerusalem, 1990).

ELBOIM-DROR, RACHEL, *Hebrew Education in Erets-Yisra'el* (Heb.), vol. i (Jerusalem, 1986).

ELIAV, MORDECHAI, *Jewish Education in Germany during the Haskalah and Emancipation* (Heb.) (Jerusalem, 1960).

ELKENITZKI, S. P., 'Lo zeh haderekh' [This is Not the Way], *Hakarmel*, 8 (1870–1), 195–6, 203–4.

ELKOSHI, GEDALIAH, 'The Hebrew Press in Vilna in the Nineteenth Century' (Heb.), *He'avar*, 13 (1966), 59–97; 14 (1967), 105–52.

EMDEN, JACOB, *Megilat sefer* [An Autobiography], ed. A. Bick (Jerusalem, 1979).

Mitpaḥat sefarim [A Scroll Wrapper] (Altona, 1768; repr. Jerusalem, 1970).

——*Mor uketsiah* [Myrrh and Cassia] (Altona, 1761).

EPSTEIN, JOSEPH, *Divrei hayamim lemalkhei rusiyah* [History of the Kings of Russia] (Vilna, 1873).

——*Miryam hahashemona'it* [Miriam the Hasmonean] (Vilna, 1873).

——'Toledot menasheh ben yisra'el' [Biography of Menashe ben Yisrael], *Hakarmel*, 3 (1862), 62–3, 69–72.

——'Toledot yost' [Biography of Jost], *Hakarmel*, 3 (1863), 125–6.

ERIK, MAX, *The History of Yiddish Literature* (Yid.) (Warsaw, 1928).

ERTER, ISAAC, 'Gilgul hanefesh' [Reincarnation], in id., *Hatsofeh leveit yisra'el*, ed. Friedlander, 124–70.

——'Ḥasidut vehokhmah' [Hasidism and Wisdom], *Kerem ḥemed*, 2 (1836), 138–47; repr. in id., *Hatsofeh leveit yisra'el*, ed. Friedlander.

——*Hatsofeh leveit yisra'el* [The Watchman of the House of Israel], ed. M. Letteris (Vienna, 1864); ed. Y. Friedlander (Jerusalem, 1996).

——'Mikhtav lesaks' [Letter to Sachs] (14 Feb. 1851), *He'avar*, 1 (1918), 157–8.

——'Moznei mishkal' [Scales], *Bikurei ha'itim*, 3 (1822), 166–9.

——'Toledot *Heḥaluts*' [The History of *Heḥaluts*], with supplement by J. H. Schorr, *Heḥaluts*, 1 (1852), 3–19; repr. in id., *Hatsofeh leveit yisra'el*, ed. Letteris, 6–14.

ETKES, IMANUEL, 'Between Change and Tradition' (Heb.), introd. to Isaac Baer Levinsohn, *Te'udah beyisra'el* (Jerusalem, 1977).

——'"Compulsory Enlightenment" as a Crossroads in the History of the Haskalah Movement in Russia' (Heb.), *Zion*, 43 (1979), 264–313.

——'The Question of the Forerunners of the Haskalah in Eastern Europe' (Heb.), *Tarbiz*, 57 (Oct.–Dec. 1987), 95–114.

——'The Vilna Gaon and the Haskalah: Image and Reality', in id. and Joseph Salmon (eds.), *Chapters in the History of Jewish Society in the Middle Ages and the Modern Period: Essays in Honour of Jacob Katz* (Heb.) (Jerusalem, 1980), 192–217.

ETKES, IMANUEL (ed.), *Religion and Life: The Jewish Enlightenment in Eastern Europe* (Heb.) (Jerusalem, 1993).

ETTINGER, SHMUEL, 'The 1804 Regulation' (Heb.), *He'avar*, 22 (1977), 87–110.

——*History and Historians* (Heb.) (Jerusalem, 1992).

——'Jews and Judaism as seen by English Deists of the Eighteenth Century' (Heb.), *Zion*, 24 (1964), 182–207.

——'Jews in the Enlightenment' (Heb.), *Zemanim*, 3 (1980), 48–61.

——'Principles and Trends Shaping the Policy of the Russian Regime' (Heb.), *He'avar*, 19 (1972), 20–34.

EUCHEL, ISAAC, 'Davar el hakore mito'elet divrei hayamim hakadmonim' [On the Benefits of History], *Hame'asef*, 1 (1784), 9–14, 25–30.

——'Igerot meshulam ben uriyah ha'eshtemoi' [Letters of Meshulam, son of Uriah of Eshtemoa; series of pseudepigraphic letters], *Hame'asef*, 6 (1790), 38–50, 80–5, 171–6, 245–9; repr. in Y. Friedlander (ed.), *Studies in Hebrew Satire: Hebrew Satire in Germany*, vol. i (Heb.) (Tel Aviv, 1979).

——*Toledot harav hehakham hahoker elohi rabenu moshe ben menahem* [Biography of Moses ben Menaham Mendelssohn] (Berlin, 1788; Vienna, 1814; Lvov, 1860).

FAHN, REUVEN, *Selected Essays on the Haskalah* (Heb.), vol. ii (Stanislav, 1937).

FEIGENSOHN, S., 'The History of the Romm Printing House', in Dov Lipetz, *Lithuanian Jewry*, vol. i (Heb.) (Tel Aviv, 1959), 268–96.

FEINER, SHMUEL, 'Did the French Revolution Influence the Development of the "Berlin Enlightenment"?' (Heb.), *Zion*, 57 (1991), 89–92.

——'Isaac Euchel: Entrepreneur of the Haskalah Movement in Germany' (Heb.), *Zion*, 52 (1987), 427–69.

——'Jewish Society, Literature, and Haskalah in Russia as Represented in the Radical Criticism of I. E. Kovner' (Heb.; English abstract), *Zion*, 55 (1990), 283–316.

——'Mendelssohn and Mendelssohn's Disciples: A Re-examination', *Leo Baeck Institute Yearbook*, 40 (1995), 133–67.

——'The Modern Jewish Woman: A Test-Case in the Relationship between the Haskalah and Modernity' (Heb.; English abstract), *Zion*, 58 (1993), 453–99.

——'"The Rebellion of the French and the Freedom of the Jews": The French Revolution in the Image of the Past of the East European Jewish Enlightenment', in Richard Cohen (ed.), *The French Revolution and its Historiography* (Heb.) (Jerusalem, 1991), 215–47.

——'R. Y. B. Levinsohn and the Year 5600' (Heb.), *Cathedra*, 34 (1985), 179–80.

——'Smolenskin's Haskalah Heresy and the Roots of Jewish National Historiography' (Heb.), *Hatsiyonut*, 16 (1992), 19–31.

——'Sola Fide! The Polemic of Rabbi Nathan of Nemirov against Atheism and Haskalah', in D. Assaf, J. Dan, and I. Etkes (eds.), *Studies in Hasidism* (Heb.) (Jerusalem, 1999), 65–88.

——'The Turning-Point in the Evaluation of Hasidism: Eliezer Zweifel and the Moderate Haskalah in Russia' (Heb.), *Zion*, 51 (1986), 167–210.

FEINGOLD, BEN-AMI, 'Haskalah Literature Discovers America', in Michal Oron (ed.), *Between History and Literature* (Heb.) (Tel Aviv, 1983), 91–104.

——'The Works of R. S. Braudes' (Heb.) (Ph.D. diss., Hebrew University of Jerusalem, 1977).

FISCHER, MEIR (MARCUS), *Historische Taschenbuch* (Prague, 1814).

——*Korot shenot kedem* [Ancient History] (Prague, 1812).

——*Toledot yeshurun taḥat memshelet mahadi ve'imam aderis* [Jewish History under the Rule of the Mahdi and Imam Aderis] (Prague, 1817).

FISHMAN, DAVID E., *Russia's First Modern Jews: The Jews of Shklov* (New York, 1995).

——'Science, Enlightenment and Rabbinic Culture in Belorussian Jewry: 1772–1804' (Ph.D. diss., Harvard University, 1985).

FLECKELES, ELEAZAR, *Olat tsibur* [Public Offering] (Prague, 1786).

FLEKOVITCH, I., *Avinadav* (Odessa, 1868).

FLESCH, JOSEPH, *Ḥayei moshe ve'aseret hadibrot* [Life of Moses and the Ten Command-ments] (Prague, 1838).

——*Hayoresh divrei elohim* [Heir to the Words of God] (Vienna, 1830).

——*Ḥizayon bein habetarim* [Vision of the Covenant] (Prague, 1830).

——*Reshimat anshei mofet* [List of Exemplary Men] (Prague, 1838).

FOIST, AARON, 'Katalog hasefarim' [Catalogue of Books], *Hamagid*, 20–1 (1876–7), 397.

FRANK, YA'AKOV ELIYAHU, 'Tazkir' [Memorandum], *He'avar*, 19 (1972), 81–2.

FRANKEL, J. L., 'Rabbi Moses Almosnino' (Heb.), *Hamagid*, 10 (1866), 5–6, 14, 21–2, 29, 37, 45, 53.

FRANKEL, JONATHAN, *Prophecy and Politics: Socialism, Nationalism and the Russian Jews, 1862–1917* (Cambridge, 1988).

FRANKEL, YIRMIYAHU, *Interpretation of 'Susati'* (Heb.) (Tel Aviv, 1946).

FREUNDLICH, C., *Peretz Smolenskin* (New York, 1965).

FRIEDBERG, ABRAHAM SHALOM, *Emek ha'arazim: sipur mirashei ha'inkvizitsiyah besfarad* [Vale of Cedars: A Story of the Spanish Inquisition], 2 vols., Beit Ha'otsar 2 (Warsaw, 1875–6).

——*Sefer hazikhronot* [Book of Memoirs] (Warsaw, 1899).

FRIEDBERG, CHAIM, *Bibliographical Lexicon* (Heb.), vols. i–iv (Tel Aviv, 1949–51).

FRIEDLÄNDER, DAVID, 'Brief zu Meir Igger' (Apr. 1799), *Zeitschrift für die Geschichte der Juden in Deutschland*, 2 (1888), 269–71.

FRIEDLÄNDER, DAVID, *Igeret lehod ma'alato ha'adon teler* [Letters to Teller] (1799), trans. M. Di-Nur, introd. Richard Cohen (Jerusalem, 1976).

[——] *Sendschreiben an seine Hochwürden . . . Probst Teller zu Berlin, von einigen Hausvätern Jüdischer Religion* (Berlin, 1799).

FRIEDLANDER, YEHUDA, *Hebrew Satire in Europe in the Nineteenth Century* (Heb.), 3 vols. (Ramat Gan, 1984, 1989, 1994).

——*Studies in Hebrew Satire*, i: *Hebrew Satire in Germany* (Heb.) (Tel Aviv, 1979).

FRIEDMAN, A., *Sefer hazikhronot* [Book of Memoirs] (Tel Aviv, 1926).

FRIEDMANN, F., *Die galizischen Juden in Kämpfe um ihre Gleichberechtigung (1848–1868)* (Frankfurt am Main, 1929).

FROZER, M. (trans.), *Emek ha'arazim* [Valley of Cedars], by Grace Aguilar, 2 vols. (Warsaw, 1875–6).

——'Letters to J. L. Gordon' (Heb.), *He'avar*, 11 (1964), 145–59.

FUENN, SAMUEL JOSEPH, 'Bustenai: sipur miyemei hageonim' [Bustenai: A Story from the Time of the Geonim], *Hakarmel*, 8 (1897), 207–8, 211–12, 223–4, 237–8, 247–8, 287–8.

——*Divrei hayamim livenei yisra'el* [History of the Jews], 2 vols. (Vilna, 1871, 1877; 2nd edn. Vilna, 1894).

——'Dor vedorshav' [A Generation and its Investigators; autobiography], *Hakarmel hahodshi*, 4 (1879), 9–15, 73–80, 193–201, 259–66, 331–9, 461–71.

——*From Militant to Conservative Maskil: A Selection of S. J. Fuenn's Writings* (Heb.), ed. Shmuel Feiner (Jerusalem, 1993).

——*Hahiluf* [The Exchange] (Vilna, 1873; 2nd edn. 1881).

——*Hakadish lifnei kol nidrei beveit hakeneset hayeshanah-hadashah befrag* [Kaddish before Kol Nidrei in the Old-New Synagogue of Prague] (Vilna, 1876).

——'Harav mosheh ben menahem mendelson' [R. Moses Mendelssohn], *Hakarmel hahodshi*, 3 (1876), 261–8, 299–308.

——'Have'adim' [The Committees], *Hakarmel*, 7 (1868–9), 161–2, 389–90.

——*Keneset yisra'el* [The Congregation of Israel] (Warsaw, 1887).

——*Kiryah ne'emanah* [Faithful City] (Vilna, 1860).

——'Kol kore' [A Voice Calls], *Hakarmel*, 8 (1870), 217.

——'Lezekher kevod mendelson beyamav be'enei gedolei doro' [In Memory of Mendelssohn in the Eyes of the Great Men of his Generation], *Hakarmel*, 7 (1868–9), 399.

——'Mahberet rishumim shel fuen' [Fuenn's Notebook], MS 4098, Manuscripts Department, National and University Library, Jerusalem.

——'Mikhtav lebetsalel stern' (1840) [A Letter to Betzalel Stern], *Hapardes*, 3 (1897), 150–1.

——*Nidhei yisra'el* [Outcast of Israel], vol. i, pt. 1 (Vilna, 1851).

——'Perek 5 shel hakerekh hashelishi shel *Divrei hayamim livenei yisra'el*' [=*Divrei hayamim livenei yisra'el*, vol. iii, ch. 5], *Ha'asif*, 5 (1889), 180–204.

——*Safah lane'emanim* [Language for the Faithful] (Vilna, 1881).

——*Shenot dor vador* [History of the Generations] (Königsberg, 1847).

——*Ya'akov tirado: Sipur korot yesod hama'alah leyishuv hayehudim hasefaradim beholand* [Jacob Tirado and the Establishment of the Sephardi Jewish Community in Holland] (Vilna, 1874).

——'Yisra'el ba'amim' [Israel among the Nations], *Hakarmel*, 7 (1868), 41–2, 49–50.

FUNKENSTEIN, AMOS, 'Continuity and Renewal in the Nineteenth Century' (Heb.), *Proceedings of the National Israeli Academy of Sciences*, 6 (1981), 105–31.

——'Maimonides: Political Theory and Realistic Messianism', *Miscellanea Medievalia*, 2 (1977), 81–103.

——'Nahmanides' Typological Reading of History' (Heb.), *Zion*, 45 (1980), 35–59.

——*Perceptions of Jewish History* (Berkeley, 1993).

GANS, DAVID BEN SOLOMON, *Tsemah david* [Offspring of David] (Warsaw, 1871; Jerusalem, 1983).

GARDINER, P. (ed.), *Theories of History* (New York, 1959).

GAY, PETER, *The Enlightenment: An Interpretation*, 2 vols. (New York, 1966–9).

GEIGER, ABRAHAM, 'Rabbi Levi bar Abraham bar Hayim', *Hehaluts*, 2 (1853), 12–27.

——'Eleh shivrei luhot munahin ba'aron' [These are the Fragments of the Tablets which were Placed in the Ark], *Hehaluts*, 4 (1859), 50–2.

GELBER, NATAN MICHAEL, 'The Haskalah Movement', in id. (ed.), *Encyclopaedia of the Jewish Diaspora* (Heb.), vol. iv (Jerusalem and Tel Aviv, 1956), 215–64.

——'The Jews in the Krakowian Republic 1815–16', in Aryeh Bauminger, Meir Busak, and Natan Michael Gelber (eds.), *Sefer kraka* [Book of Krakow] (Jerusalem, 1959), 39–88.

——'The Jews in Stanislav', in *Arim ve'imahot beyisra'el* [Prominent Jewish Communities], vol. v (Jerusalem, 1952), 27–37.

——*The Jews of Brody* (Heb.) (Jerusalem, 1955).

——'The Jews of Tarnopol' (Heb.), in P. Korengreen (ed.), *Encyclopedia of the Jewish Diaspora*, vol. iii (Jerusalem, 1955), 46–103.

——'Mendel Lefin of Satanow's Proposals for the Improvement of Jewish Community Life Presented to the Great Polish Sejm (1788–1992)' (Heb.), in *The Abraham Weiss Jubilee Book* (New York, 1964), 275–305.

GERMAISA, JUDAH LEIB, 'Ibn Ezra' (Heb.), *Hamagid*, 11 (1867), 181–2.

——*Toledot rusiyah* [History of Russia] (Sedalikow, 1836).

GERONDI, M. S., 'Al devar toledot hagaon r. mosheh hayim luzato' [Biography of Moses Hayim Luzzatto], *Kerem hemed*, 2 (1836), 53–4.

GEYL, P., *Napoleon: For and Against* (London, 1949).

GIBBON, EDWARD, *The Decline and Fall of the Roman Empire* (1776–88; repr. New York, 1955).

GILBOA, MENUCHA, *Hebrew Periodicals in the Eighteenth and Nineteenth Centuries* (Heb.) (Jerusalem, 1992).

GILON, MEIR, 'Hebrew Satire in the Age of Haskalah in Germany: A Rejoinder' (Heb.), *Zion*, 52 (1987), 524–30.

GINSBURG, SAUL, *Historical Writings* (Heb.) (Tel Aviv, 1944), 96–113.

GLATZER, NAHUM, 'The Beginnings of Modern Jewish Studies', in A. Altmann (ed.), *Studies in Nineteenth-Century Jewish Intellectual History* (Cambridge, 1964), 135–49.

GOLDBERG, ABRAHAM, *Masa tsafon im ma'aseh roke'ah* [Prophecy to the North and the Rokeach Affair] (Lvov, 1848).

GOLDBERG, BERISH, *Sefer ohel yosef* [Book of Joseph's Tent] (Lvov, 1866).

GOLDMAN, Y., *Shanim kadmoniyot* [Ancient Times] (Vilna, 1879).

GOLDSHTOF, FEIVEL, 'Hatelunot al sifri korot ha'olam' [Criticism of my Book *Korot ha'olam*], *Hamagid*, 7 (1863), 31–2.

——*Korot ha'olam* [General History], 2 vols. (i: Vienna, 1858; ii: Lvov, 1860).

——*Leket ma'amarim* [Collection of Essays] (Krakow, 1869).

——'Napoleon al i hasela mekonen bemar nafsho' [Napoleon on the Rocky Isle Bewailing his Bitter Fate], *Kokhavei yitshak*, 23 (1857), 55–7.

GÖLTER, G., 'Die Geschichtsauffassung Friedrich Christoph Schlossers' (Ph.D. diss., University of Munich, 1966).

GOOCH, G. P., *History and Historians in the Nineteenth Century* (London, 1952).

GORDON, DAVID, 'Al devar haye'ud hale'umi shel ha'umah hayisra'elit' [On the National Objective of the Jewish People], *Hamagid*, 13 (1869), 230.

——'Beshuvah vanahat tivashe'un' [In Peace and Tranquillity Shall You Be Redeemed], *Hamagid*, 7 (1863), 121, 129–30.

——'Besorat sefarim' [Book Announcements], *Hamagid*, 20 (1876), 87.

GORDON, JUDAH LEIB, 'Al nehar kevar' [On the River Kevar], in id., *Collected Works: Prose*, 285–90.

——'Bein shinei arayot' [Between the Lions' Teeth], in id., *Collected Works: Poetry*, 103.

——'Bikoret sefarim' [Literary Criticism], *Hamelits*, 23 (1887), no. 42.

——'Binah leto'ei ruah' [Wisdom for the Misled], *Hamelits*, 10 (1870), nos. 30–3, 35–6, 39–43.

——'Bina'areinu uvizkeneinu nelekh' [We Shall Go, Young and Old], in id., *Collected Works: Poetry*, 30–1.

——'Bizekhutan shel rabanim' [By the Merit of Rabbis], *Hamelits*, 9 (1869), 328–9.

——*Collected Works of J. L. Gordon: Poetry* (Heb.), 3rd edn. (Tel Aviv, 1956).

——*Collected Works of J. L. Gordon: Prose* (Heb.) (Tel Aviv, 1960).

——'Erets bavel ha'atikah vehakhameiha' [Ancient Babylonia and its Sages], *Hashahar*, 2 (1871), 241–60.

——'Hakitsah ami' [Awake, my People], in id., *Collected Works: Poetry*, 17.

——'Hashmatah' [Omission], *Hashaḥar*, 2 (1871), 154–6.

——'Kotso shel yod' [The Point of a *Yod*], in id., *Collected Works: Prose*, 129–40.

——*Letters*, 2 vols., ed. Y. Y. Weisberg (Warsaw, 1894–5).

——'Pirkei zikhronot' [Autobiographical Chapters], in id., *Collected Works: Prose*, 309–14.

'Tsidkiyahu beveit hapekudot' [Zedekiah in Prison], in id., *Collected Works: Poetry*, 98–101.

——'Venikeiti mipesha rav' [I Shall Be Innocent], *Hamagid*, 15 (1871), 101–2, 109–10, 117–18, 125–6.

GORDON, MIKHEL, *Di geshikhte fun rusland* [The History of Russia] (Zhitomir, 1869).

GOREN, JACOB, 'The Image of Jews and Judaism in Protestant Old Testament Criticism from the Mid-Eighteenth Century to the 1830s' (Heb.) (Ph.D. diss., Hebrew University of Jerusalem, 1975).

GOTTLOBER, ABRAHAM BAER, '13 mikhtavim me'et gotlober' [Thirteen Letters by Gottlober], *Reshumot*, 2 (1922), 414–42.

——*Bikoret letoledot hakara'im* [A Critique of Karaite History] (Vilna, 1864).

——'El mol Hashaḥar' [To the Publisher of *Hashaḥar*], *Haboker or*, 2 (1877), 37–40.

——'Et la'akor natua' [A Time to Uproot], *Haboker or*, 2 (1876), 4–17, 77–86, 225–33.

——'Et lata'at' [A Time to Plant], *Hamelits*, 5 (1865), no. 12.

——'Hagizrah vehabeniyah: korot hitpathut hahaskalah biyisra'el be'erets rusiyah vepolin' [History of the Development of the Haskalah in Russia and Poland], in id., *Zikhronot umasaot*, vol. ii (Jerusalem, 1976), 25–149.

——*Hanitsanim* [The Buds] (Vilna, 1850).

——*Igeret tsa'ar ba'alei ḥayim* [A Letter on the Prevention of Cruelty to Animals] (Zhitomir, 1868).

——'Kirot libi homeh' [My Heart Bewails the Walls], in id., *Hanitsanim*, ii. 215–16.

——'Kol kore' [A Voice Calls], *Hashaḥar*, 4 (1873), 393–9.

——*Kol shirei mahalalel* [Collected Poetry of Mahalalel (= Gottlober)], vol. i (Warsaw, 1891).

——'Mashal shalosh hataba'ot' [The Story of the Three Rings], in id., *Hanitsanim*, 7–65, 88–90.

——'Peresh al penei perets' [Against Peretz (Smolenskin)], *Haboker or*, 2 (1877), 148–51.

——*Pirḥei ha'aviv* [Spring Flowers] (Jozefow, 1837).

——'Semel hakinah' [Symbol of Fanaticism], *Hashaḥar*, 4 (1873), 496–507.

——*Toledot hakabalah vehaḥasidut* [History of Kabbalah and Hasidism] (Zhitomir, 1869).

——*Zikhronot umasaot* [Memoirs and Journeys], ed. R. Goldberg, 2 vols. (Jerusalem, 1976).

GRAETZ, HEINRICH, *Die Construction der jüdischen Geschichte* (1846), trans. into Hebrew by Y. Tolkes, introd. S. Ettinger (Jerusalem, 1969).

GRAETZ, HEINRICH, *Die Geschichte der Juden*, 11 vols. (1853–75; Leipzig, 1900).

——'Mikhtav' [Letter], *Keneset yisra'el*, 3 (1888), 260–1.

——'Mikhtav galuy' [An Open Letter], *Keneset yisra'el*, 3 (1888), 71–2.

——*Sefer divrei yemei yisra'el*, Hebrew trans. of *Die Geschichte der Juden*, with notes, by Saul Pinhas Rabinowitz, vol. i (Warsaw, 1891).

——*The Structure of Jewish History and other Essays*, trans. and ed. I. Schorsch (New York, 1975).

GRAETZ, MICHAEL, 'The Formation of the New "Jewish Consciousness" in the Time of Mendelssohn's Disciples: Shaul Asher' (Heb.), *Studies in the History of the Jewish People and the Land of Israel*, 4 (1976), 219–37.

——*The Jews in Nineteenth Century France: From the French Revolution to the Alliance Israélite Universelle*, trans. J. M. Todd (Stanford, Calif., 1996).

——'On the Return of Moses Hess to Judaism: The Background to *Rome and Jerusalem*' (Heb.), *Zion*, 45 (1980), 133–53.

GRANOWITZ, A. M., 'Toledot kopernikus' [Biography of Copernicus], *Hamagid*, 17 (1873), 100.

Great Soviet Encyclopaedia, 31 vols. (New York, 1973–82).

GREENBERG, LOUIS, *The Jews in Russia*, 2 vols. (New York, 1944, 1951).

GUENZBURG, MORDECAI AARON, 'Al devar habegadim' [On Clothing], in *A Collection of Essays in a Supplement to 'Hamelits'* (St Petersburg, 1899), 90–1.

——*Avi'ezer* [Avi'ezer; autobiography] (Vilna, 1864).

——*Devir* [anthology of letters and essays], 2 vols. (Vilna, 1855, 1862; 2nd edn. Warsaw, 1883).

——*Gelot ha'arets hahadashah* [Discovery of the New World] (Vilna, 1823).

——*Hamat damesek* [The Damascus Affair] (Königsberg, 1860).

——*Hamoriyah* [Mount Moriah] (Warsaw, 1878).

——*Hatsarfatim berusiyah: divrei yemei 1812–1813* [The French in Russia 1812–1813] (Vilna, 1842).

——*Itotei rusiyah mi'et heyotam legoy ad hayom hazeh* [The Chronicles of Russia, from Early Times to the Present] (Vilna, 1839).

——'Kikayon deyonah' [Jonah's Gourd], in id., *Hamoriyah*, 38–48.

——*Kiryat sefer* [City of the Book] (Vilna, 1847).

——'Melekh asur berahatim' [A King Caught in the Tresses], in id., *Devir*, i. 52–65.

——'Mikhtav' [Letter (Vilna, 1837)], in S. Loewisohn, *Erets kedumim hu sefer mehkarei erets* (Vilna, 1839), pp. xvii–xxvi.

——*Pi haherut: milhemet ha'ashkenazim veharusim betsarfat beshenot 1813–1815 ad galut kaisar napoleon me'al admato* [The Advent of Freedom: The War by Germany and Russia against France 1813–1815 up to the Exile of Napoleon] (Vilna, 1845).

——*Sefer yemei hador* [History of the Generation] (Vilna, 1860).

——*Toledot benei ha'adam: divrei hayamim kolel korot kol benei ha'adam miyom bo'am lekelal hayishuv ad yemei hador hazeh*, pt. 1: *Makif korot kol yemei hakedem mireshit yemei hatoledah ad ḥurban roma* [The History of Mankind to the Present Day, pt. 1: From Ancient Times to the Destruction of Rome] (Vilna, 1835).

——'Toledot napoleon bonaparte', in id., *Hamoriyah*, 9–37.

GURLAND, H. J., 'Ḥadashot sifriyot' [Literary News], *Hatsefirah*, 3 (1876), 183.

GUTMANN, Y., The Foundations of R. Nachman Krochmal's Thought' (Heb.), *Kneset*, 6 (1941), 259–86.

HABAVLY, T. D., *Ma'amar shoresh davar* [On the Root of the Matter] (Vilna, 1866).

HACOHEN, ADAM (Abraham Dov Lebensohn), 'El bozei haḥokhmah' [To Those who Despise Wisdom], in id., *Shirei sefat kodesh*, ii. 154–61.

——'Haḥemlah' [Pity], in id., *Shirei sefat kodesh: mivḥar*, 114–49.

——*Kinat soferim* [Lamentation of Writers] (Vilna, 1847).

——'Kol na'akat bat yehudah' [The Weeping of the Daughter of Judah], in id., *Shirei sefat kodesh: mivḥar*, 101–13.

——*Shirei sefat kodesh* [Poems in the Holy Tongue], 3 vols. (i: Leipzig, 1842; ii: Vilna, 1856; iii: Vilna, 1870).

——*Shirei sefat kodesh: mivḥar* [A Selection of Poems in the Holy Tongue], ed. Y. Friedlander and M. Gilboa (Jerusalem, 1986).

——and Lebensohn, Micha Joseph (Mikhal), *Kol shirei adam umikhal* [The Poems of Adam and Mikhal], vol. i (Vilna, 1895).

HACOHEN, JOSEPH, *Emek habakhah* [Vale of Tears] (Krakow, 1895).

HACOHEN, MORDECAI BEN HILLEL, 'Dor holekh vedor ba' [Generations Come, Generations Go], *Hashaḥar*, 9 (1878), 7–12, 62–70, 121–31, 177–83.

HACOHEN, SHALOM, 'Divrei hayamim lebavel' [The History of Babylonia], *Hame'asef* (1810), 23–30, 35–9.

——'Gerush hayehudim misefarad' [The Expulsion of the Jews from Spain], *Hame'asef* (1810), 20–48, 72–80.

——'Ḥeshek shelomoh' [Solomon's Desire], *Kerem ḥemed*, 4 (1839), 253–6.

——*Ketav yosher* [Certificate of Integrity] (Vienna, 1820).

——*Kore hadorot* [Caller of the Generations] (Warsaw, 1838).

——*Mata'ei kedem al admat tsafon* [Eastern Plants on Northern Soil] (Frankfurt, 1818).

——'Toledot heḥakham don yitsḥak abravanel' [Biography of Don Isaac Abrabanel], *Bikurei ha'itim*, 1 (1820), 14–19.

HA'EFRATI, JOSEPH, *Alon bakhut* [The Oak of Weeping] (Vienna, 1793).

HALEVI, A., *The Historical-Biographical Tale* (Heb.) (Tel Aviv, 1975).

HALEVI, N., 'Malkhei haro'im hiksas' [The Kings of the Hyksos Shepherds], *Hamagid*, 4 (1860), suppl. to no. 49.

HALKIN, SIMON, *Modern Hebrew Literature from the Enlightenment to the Birth of the State of Israel: Trends and Values* (New York, 1970).

HALPERN, ISRAEL, 'Traces of the Division of Poland in the Historical Doctrines of Nachman Krochmal' (Heb.), *Zion*, 8 (1942), 201–2.

HAMPSON, NORMAN, *The Enlightenment* (London, 1987).

HARKAVY, ABRAHAM ELIYAHU, 'Derishot vehakirot benoge'a lekorot yisra'el be'erets rusiyah' [Investigations and Inquiries on the History of the Jews in Russia], *Hakarmel*, 4 (1864), 258–9, 358–60; 5 (1865), 14–15, 22–4, 83–4, 239–40.

——'Rusiyah besifrut hayehudim' [Russia in Hebrew Literature], *Hakarmel hahodshi*, 3 (1875), 27–34, 91–100.

——and Halberstam, C., *Zikaron larishonim* [A Memorial to the First], 2 vols. (Vilna, 1881).

HARKAVY, TSEVI, 'Abraham Harkavy' (Heb.), in S. Mirsky (ed.), *Personalities and Figures in Jewish Studies in Eastern Europe* (New York and Tel Aviv, 1959), 112–25.

HARMELIN, M. L., *Sefer haholets* [Against Schorr's *Hehaluts*] (Lvov, 1861).

HARRIS, JAY W., *Nachman Krochmal: Guiding the Perplexed of the Modern Age* (New York and London, 1991).

HAY, D., *Annalists and Historians* (London, 1977).

HAYOT. See Chajes, Tsevi

HEERN, A., *Handbuch der Geschichte des europäischen Staatensystems* (1809; repr. Göttingen, 1830).

HEGEL, GEORG WILHELM FRIEDRICH, *The Philosophy of History*, trans. J. Sibree (New York, 1956).

HEILPRIN, JEHIEL, *Seder hadorot* [Order of the Generations] (Warsaw, 1877–82; Jerusalem, 1956).

HENDEL, M., 'Maskilim and Haskalah in Bolechow in the Nineteenth Century', in *Memorial Book of Bolechow* (Heb.) (Haifa, 1956), 35–40.

HERR, MOSHE D., 'The Conception of History among the Sages' (Heb.), *Proceedings of the Sixth World Congress of Jewish Studies*, vol. iii (Jerusalem, 1977), 129–42.

HERTZBERG, JOSEPH (trans.), 'Mahloket reukhlin vefeferkorn' [The Controversy between Reuchlin and Pfefferkorn], *Hakarmel*, 7 (1868–9), 117–18.

——'Mikhtav lefin' [Letter to Fuenn] (Summer 1868), Schwadron Collection, Manuscript and Archives Department, National and University Library, Jerusalem.

——(trans.), *Mo'adei shahar* [M. Mendelssohn's *Morgenstunden*] (Königsberg, 1845).

HERZFELD, LEVI, *Geschichte des Volkes Israel*, 3 vols. (Brunswick, 1847, 1855, 1857).

HESS, MOSES, *Rome and Jerusalem* (New York, 1945).

Hevrat Dorshei Leshon Ever, 'Nahal habesor', *Hame'asef*, 1 (1784), 1–15.

HOFFMAN, C., *Juden und Judentum im Werk deutscher Althistoriker des 19. und 20. Jahrhunderts* (Leiden, 1988).

HOLBERG, L., *Jüdische Geschichte von Erschaffung der Welt bis auf Gegenwärtige Zeiten*, 2 vols. (Altona, 1747).

HOLISH, L., 'Mikhtav leshir' [A Letter to Rapoport], *Kerem ḥemed*, 2 (1836), letter no. 21 (pp. 133–8).

HOROWITZ, HEIKAL, *Tsofnat pa'ane'aḥ* [Zaphnath-paaneach (Gen. 41: 45)] (Berdichev, 1817).

HORWITZ, RIVKA, 'Rationalistic and Anti-Rationalistic Motifs in S. D. Luzzatto' (Heb.), *Eshel be'er-sheva*, 2 (1980), 287–310.

——*Zacharias Frankel and the Beginnings of Positive-Historical Judaism* (Heb.) (Jerusalem, 1984).

HUME, DAVID, *The Natural History of Religion* (1757; Oxford, 1976).

HURWITZ, ELIEZER, and FUENN, S. Y. (eds.), *Pirḥei tsafon* [Flowers of the North], 2 vols. (Vilna, 1841; 1844).

IBN VERGA, SOLOMON, *Shevet yehudah* [The Staff of Judah] (1554; Jerusalem, 1974).

'Igerot' [Letters], *Reshumot*, 4 (1926), 361–84.

IGGERS, G., *The German Conception of History* (Middletown, NY, 1983).

——*New Directions in European Historiography* (London, 1984).

ISRAEL, JONATHAN, *European Jewry in the Age of Mercantilism 1550–1750* (Oxford, 1985).

JACOB, MARGARET C., *Living the Enlightenment* (New York and Oxford, 1991).

JEITELES, BARUCH, *Ma'arakhei lev* [Heartfelt Sentiments] (Prague, 1789).

JEITELES, JUDAH LOEB, 'Reshit bikurim' [Preface], *Bikurei ha'itim*, 11 (1830), 23–6.

——'Siḥot ḥakhmei amim' [Conversations between Sages], *Bikurei ha'itim*, 11 (1830), 147–8.

JOELSON, *Toledot ha'avot* [The History of our Forefathers] (n.p., 1820).

JOST, MARCUS, *Geschichte der Israeliten*, 9 vols. (Berlin, 1820–8).

——'Megilat mordekhai' [The Scroll of Mordechai], *Zion*, 1 (1841), 10–14, 27–32, 41–6.

KAMINER, ISAAC, 'Akhan ben Zerah', in id., *Shirei yitsḥak kaminer*, 109–13.

——'Deror yikra' [A Call to Freedom], *Haboker or*, 2 (1877), 29–39.

——*Kinot misiduram shel benei dan* [Lamentations from the Prayer-Books of Dan] (Vienna, 1878).

——*Shirei yitsḥak kaminer* [Poetry of Isaac Kaminer] (Odessa, 1906).

——'Shir hayiḥud lamatbe'a' [In Adulation of the Coin], *Ha'emet* (1877), 42.

KAMPF, ISADORE, 'B. V. Spinosas Theologisch-Politischer Tractat', *Literaturblatt des Orients*, 3 (1842), 524–31.

KANEL, S., 'Lekorot gerush hayehudim misefarad' [On the Expulsion of the Jews from Spain], *Hamagid*, 22 (1878), 419–21.

KANT, IMMANUEL, *The Critique of Pure Reason* (Chicago, 1956).

——'The Idea of a Universal History from a Cosmopolitan Point of View', in P. Gardiner (ed.), *Theories of History* (New York, 1959), 22–34.

KANT, IMMANUEL, *On History*, trans. L. W. Beck (New York and London, 1986).

——'Physische Geographie', in *Kants Werke. Akademie Textausgabe*, vol. ix (Berlin, 1968), 156–65.

KANTOR, Y. L., 'Mikhtav el ha'ozer beharedaktsion' [Letter to the Editor's Assistant], *Hakarmel*, 4 (1879), 65–72.

KAPLAN, ABRAHAM (trans.), *Divrei yemei hayehudim*, vol. iii (Vienna, 1875).

——*Ḥayei mapu* [Biography of Mapu] (Vienna, 1870).

KAPLAN, YOSEF, *From Christianity to Judaism: The Story of Isaac Orobio de Castro*, trans. R. Loewe (Oxford, 1989).

KAROL, TSEVI, *The First Centenary of Aaron Liebermann* (Heb.) (Merchavya, 1945).

KATZ, JACOB, *From Prejudice to Destruction: Anti-Semitism, 1700–1933* (Cambridge, 1980).

——*Out of the Ghetto* (Cambridge, Mass., 1973).

——'To whom was Mendelssohn Replying in *Jerusalem?*', *Scripta Hierosolymitana*, 23 (1972), 214–43.

——*Tradition and Crisis: Jewish Society at the End of the Middle Ages*, 2nd edn., trans. B. D. Cooperman (New York, 1993).

KATZ, SIMCHA, 'Letters of Maskilim on the Disgrace of Hasidim' (Heb.), *Mozna'im*, 10 (1940), 266–76.

KATZANELBOGEN, A. M., *Sipurei ḥakhmei yavan* [Tales of the Greek Sages] (Vilna, 1864).

KATZANELBOIGEN, HAYIM LEIB, 'Avodat hakeramim behiyot benei yisra'el al admatam' [Work in the Vineyards when the Jews Lived in their Land], *Hakarmel*, 1 (1860), 13–15.

KATZANELSON, GIDEON, *The Literary War between the Orthodox and the Enlightened Jews* (Heb.) (Tel Aviv, 1954).

KAUFMANN, DALIA, 'Hebrew and Yiddish Drama Translations from the Late Eighteenth Century up to 1883: A Comparative Study' (Heb.) (Ph.D. diss., Hebrew University of Jerusalem, 1983).

KAUFMANN, YEHEZKEL, *Exile and Foreign Land* (Heb.), vol. ii (Tel Aviv, 1930).

KELLY, D., *Foundations of Modern History Scholarship* (New York and London, 1970).

KERA, JOSEPH, 'Toledot rabi naftali' [Biography of Rabbi Naphtali], *Hamagid*, 1 (1857), 101–2, 202–3.

Kerem ḥemed, ed. Shmuel Goldenberg and Solomon Rapoport (Vienna, 1833–6; Prague, 1838–43).

KESTENBERG-GLADSTEIN, RUTH, *Neuere Geschichte der Juden in den böhmischen Ländern*, i: *Das Zeitalter des Aufklärung 1780–1830* (Tübingen, 1969).

——'On the History of the Jews in the Czech Lands' (Heb.), *Gesher*, 56–60 (1970), 35–48.

——'A Voice from the Prague Enlightenment', *Leo Baeck Yearbook*, 6 (1964), 295–304.

KIEVAL, H., 'Caution's Progress: The Modernization of Jewish Life in Prague 1780–1830', in Jacob Katz (ed.), *Toward Modernity: The European Jewish Model* (New Brunswick, NJ, 1987), 71–105.

KLAUSNER, ISRAEL, 'The Decree on Jewish Dress, 1844–1850' (Heb.), *Gal-ed*, 6 (1982), 11–26.

——*Vilna, 'Jerusalem of Lithuania': Generations from 1881 to 1939* (Heb.) (Tel Aviv, 1983).

KLAUSNER, JOSEPH, *Creators and Builders* (Heb.), vol. i (Tel Aviv, 1944).

——*History of Modern Hebrew Literature* (Heb.), 6 vols. (Tel Aviv, 1952–8).

KLEINMAN, MOSES, *Figures and Ages* (Heb.) (Paris, 1928).

KLUGER, I., *Toledot shelomoh* [Biography of Solomon] (Lvov, 1888).

KOCHAN, LIONEL, *The Jew and his History* (Plymouth, 1977).

KOCKA, JÜRGEN, *Geschichte und Aufklärung* (Göttingen, 1989).

KOHN, P., 'Romm's Printing House in Vilna' (Heb.), *Kiryat sefer*, 12 (1935), 109–14.

KOIFMANN, AARON, 'Mikhtav al devar haḥinukh' [A Letter about Education], *Pirḥei tsafon*, 1 (Vilna, 1841), 55–6.

Kokhavei yitsḥak, ed. Mendel Stern (Vienna, 1845–69).

KOPITZSCH, FRANKLIN, *Aufklärung, Absolutismus und Bürgertum in Deutschland* (Munich, 1976).

KOVNER, ABRAHAM URI, 'Ḥeker davar' [An Investigation], in id., *Ketavim*, 5–45.

——*Ketavim* [Writings] (Tel Aviv, 1947).

——'Ruaḥ ḥayim' [Spirit of Life], in id., *Ketavim*, 177–8.

——'Ruaḥ mishpat' [Spirit of Judgement], in id., *Ketavim*, 167–76.

——'Shenei nevi'im mitnabim besignon eḥad' [Two Prophets Prophesy in the Same Style], in id., *Ketavim*, 224–33.

——'Tseror peraḥim' [A Nosegay], in id., *Ketavim*, 49–199.

KOVNER, ISAAC, *Sefer hamatsref: An Unknown Maskilic Critique of Jewish Society in Russia in the Nineteenth Century* (Heb.), ed. Shmuel Feiner (Jerusalem, 1998).

KRESSEL, GETSEL, 'A Chapter in Jewish Culture in the West', in *On Hebrew and Jewish Booklore* (Heb.) (Studies and Essays) (n.p., n.d.).

——'Saul Pinhas Rabinowitz' (Heb.), *Me'asef*, 2 (1961), 599–601.

KROCHMAL, ABRAHAM, 'Even haroshah' [Foundation Stone], special supplement to *Hashaḥar*, 2 (1871).

——*Iyun tefilah* [A Study of Prayer] (Lvov, 1885).

——'Toledot rabi yehudah hanasi' [Biography of R. Judah Hanasi], *Heḥaluts*, 2 (1853), 62–93; 'Bi nesiah' [Continuation] *Heḥaluts*, 3 (1857), 118–40.

——'Toledot shemuel yarḥinai' [Biography of Samuel Yarhina'ah], *Heḥaluts*, 1 (1852), 66–89.

KROCHMAL, NAHMAN, *Collected Writings* (Heb.), ed. Simon Rawidowicz (London, 1961).

——'Mikhtav leze'ev shif' [Letter to Ze'ev Schiff], in id., *Collected Writings*, 413–16.

——'Mikhtav lishmuel goldenberg' [Letter to Shmuel Goldenberg], *Kerem ḥemed*, 4 (1839), 260–74.

——*Moreh nevukhei hazeman*, in id., *Collected Writings*, 1–334.

KUNITZ, MOSES, *Beit rabi* [The Rabbi's House] (Vienna, 1805).

——*Ben yoḥai* (Vienna, 1817).

——*Sefer hamatsref* [Book of the Forge], 2 vols. (i: Vienna, 1820; ii: Prague, 1857).

KUPFER, EPHRAIM, 'Jacob Samuel Bick in the Light of New Documents' (Heb.), *Gal-ed*, 4–5 (Tel Aviv, 1978), 353–547.

LAHOVER, P., *Between Old and New* (Heb.) (Tel Aviv, 1951).

——*History of Modern Hebrew Literature* (Heb.), 4 vols. (Tel Aviv, 1966).

——*Researches and Experiments* (Heb.) (Warsaw, 1925).

——'Visible and Hidden in Krochmal's Doctrine' (Heb.), *Kneset*, 6 (1941), 296–332.

LANDAU, YEHEZKEL, *Derushei hazelah* [Rabbi Landau's Sermons] (Warsaw, 1886).

LANGBANK, A. HALEVI, 'Toledot rabi mordekhai ben rabi herts' [Biography of Markus Herz], *Hamagid*, 4 (1860), 81, 83, 97.

LEBENSOHN, ABRAHAM DOV. *See* HACOHEN, ADAM

LEBENSOHN, MICHA JOSEPH. *See* MIKHAL

LEDERHENDLER, ELI, *The Road to Modern Jewish Politics* (New York, 1989).

LEHMANN, J. H., 'Maimonides, Mendelssohn and the Measfim: Philosophy and the Biographical Imagination in the Early Haskalah', *Leo Baeck Yearbook*, 20 (1975), 87–108.

Leksikon fun der nayer yidisher literatur [Biographical Dictionary of Modern Yiddish Literature], ed. S. Nieger and J. Shatzky, 8 vols. (New York, 1956).

LERNER, JOSEPH JUDAH, *Doresh el hametim* [Questioning the Dead] (Odessa, 1868).

——*Hakuzarim* [The Kuzaris] (Odessa, 1867).

LESSING, GOTTHOLD EPHRAIM, *Die Erziehung des Menschengeschlechts* (Berlin, 1780, 1785).

——*Die Juden* (1749), Hebrew trans. Shlomo Hacohen (Warsaw, 1872).

——*Nathan der Weise*, Hebrew trans. A. B. Gottlober (Vienna, 1873).

LETTERIS, MEIR, 'Davar el hakore' [A Word to the Reader], *Hatsefirah* (Zolkiew, 1824).

——'Masa i hasela' [Prophecy from the Rocky Isle], in I. S. Reggio and I. Bush (eds.), *Bikurei ha'itim haḥadashim*, (Vienna, 1845), 19.

——*Migdal oz leramḥal* [The *Migdal oz* of M. H. Luzzatto] (Leipzig, 1837).

——*Mikhtavei ivrit* [Hebrew Letters] (Vienna, 1856).

——*Mikhtavim* [Letters] (Lvov, 1827).

——*Sefer mikhtavei benei kedem* [Letters of the Ancients] (Vienna, 1866).

——*Toledot avi hayakar . . . gershon halevi leteris* [Biography of My Beloved Father, Gershon Halevi Letteris] (Vienna, 1864).

——'Toledot hamehaber' [Biography of the Author], introduction to Isaac Erter, *Hatsofeh leveit yisra'el*, 2nd edn. (Warsaw, 1883).

——'Toledot hehakham hahoker barukh di spinoza' [Biography of Spinoza], in I. S. Reggio and I. Bush (eds.), *Bikurei ha'itim hahadashim* (Vienna, 1845), 27–33.

——'Toledot r. nahman krokhmal' [Biography of Nahman Krochmal], in id. (ed.), *Hame'asef lashanah harishonah*, 93–114.

——*Zikaron basefer* [Memoirs] (Vienna, 1869).

——(ed.), *Hame'asef leshanah harishonah* [The First Year of *Hame'asef*], annotated and enlarged edn. (Vienna, 1862).

LEVIN, JOSHUA HESCHEL, *Aliyot eliyahu* [The Ascents of Elijah; biography of the Vilna Gaon] (Vilna, 1856).

LEVIN, JUDAH LEID, 'Eshmerah lepi mahsom' [I Shall Keep a Guard on my Tongue], in id., *Zikhronot vehegyonot*, 135–7.

——'Mikhtavo ley. l. gordon' [His Letter to Y. L. Gordon] (Oct. 1872), *He'avar*, 1 (1918), 194–7.

——'She'elat hayehudim' [On the Jewish Question], *Hakol*, 4 (1879), 65–70.

——'She'elot hazeman' [Questions of the Time], in id., *Zikhronot vehegyonot*, 140–3.

——'Torat hahayim' [Theory of Life], *Hashahar*, 10 (1880), 626–9.

——*Zikhronot vehegyonot* [Memoirs and Pensées], ed. Y. Slutsky (Jerusalem, 1968).

LEVIN, MENDEL, *Alon moreh* [On Maimonides' *Guide*], suppl. to *Hamelits* (Odessa, 1867).

——*Masaot hayam* [Sea Journeys] (Zolochev, 1818; Lvov, 1859).

LEVIN, MORDECHAI (MARCUS), *Social and Economic Values: The Idea of Professional Modernization in the Ideology of the Haskalah Movement* (Heb.) (Jerusalem, 1975).

LEVINE, HILLEL, 'Dwarf on the Shoulders of Giants: A Case Study in the Impact of Modernization on the Social Epistemology of Judaism', *Jewish Social Studies*, 40 (1978), 63–72.

——'Menahem Mendel Lefin: A Case Study of Judaism and Modernization' (Ph.D. diss., Harvard University, 1974).

LEVINSOHN, ISAAC BAER, *Ahiyah hashiloni* [Ahijah the Shilonite] (Leipzig, 1863).

——'Beit ha'otsar' [The Treasury], ii (1826), in *Shorshei halevanon* (Vilna, 1841).

——*Beit yehudah* [The House of Judah], 2 vols. (Vilna 1839, 1858).

——*Bikurei rival* [Collected Writings] (Warsaw, 1888).

——'Divrei tsadikim' [Words of *Tsadikim*] (1830), in id., *Yalkut rival*, 140–9.

——*Efes damim* [No Blood; on the blood libel] (Vilna, 1837; repr. Warsaw, 1879).

——'Emek refa'im' [Valley of Ghosts] (1821), in id., *Yalkut rival*, 118–39.

LEVINSOHN, ISAAC BAER, *Eshkol hasofer* [Collected Works] (Warsaw, 1891).

——*Pituḥei ḥotam* [Engravings of a Signet] (Warsaw, 1903).

——'Ta'ar hasofer' [The Author's Razor], in id., *Bikurei rival*, 167–94.

——*Te'udah beyisra'el* [A Testimony in Israel] (Vilna, 1828).

——*Yalkut rival* [Anthology of Writings] (Warsaw, 1878).

——*Yemin tsidki* [In Support of My Justification] (1837; repr. Warsaw, 1881).

LEVINSOHN, YEHOSHUA, *Erets rusiyah umelo'ah* [The Land of Russia] (Vilna, 1869).

——'Hayehudi harishon bitseva ḥeil ostrikh' [The First Jew in the Austrian Army], *Hakarmel*, 4 (1863), 32, 39–40.

——'Korot ḥokhmat hatekhunah' [The History of Astronomy], *Hakarmel*, 4 (1864), 336.

——'Od hapa'am mendelson' [Mendelssohn, Once Again], *Hamagid*, 17 (1873), 37–45.

——'R. akiva iger' [Rabbi Akiva Eiger], *Hakarmel*, 8 (1870), 45–6, 61, 78–9.

——'Rapha'el milodelah' [Raphael of Lodela], *Hamagid*, 12 (1868), 45.

——'Shenot ra'inu ra'ah' [The Evil Years We Have Seen], *Hakarmel*, 8 (1870), 118–19, 134–46.

LEWIN, L., 'Aus dem jüdischen Kulturkampf', *Jahrbuch der jüdisch-literarischen Gesellschaft*, 12 (1918), 163–94.

LIBERLES, ROBERT, 'Dohm's Treatise on the Jews: A Defense of the Enlightenment', *Leo Baeck Yearbook*, 33 (1988), 29–42.

LIEBEN, K., *Sefer galed* [A Memorial Book] (Prague, 1856).

LIEBERMANN, A. D., *El shelomei baḥurei yisra'el* [For the Welfare of the Young Men of Israel] (London, 1876).

——'Hitpatḥut ḥayei haḥevrah bishenot habenayim' [Development of Social Life in the Middle Ages], *Ha'emet* (1877), 25–31.

——*Katavot uma'amarim bevpered 1875–1876* [Liebermann's Writings in *Vpered* 1875–1876], ed. M. Mishkinsky (Tel Aviv, 1977).

——'Letoledot ha'utopiyot' [The History of Utopias], in id., *Writings*, 1–36.

——'Megaleh sod' [Revealer of a Secret], *Asefat ḥakhamim*, 1 (1878), 13–15.

——'Mikhtavim vereshimot shenimtse'u beginzei ma'arekhet *Ha'emet*' [Letters and Notes Found in the Archives of the Editorial Board of *Ha'emet*], in id., *Writings*, 80–92.

——'Milḥemet hayekum be'ad kiyumo beyaḥas el ḥayei haḥevrah' [The Battle for Survival in Relation to Social Life], *Ha'emet* (1877), 17–21.

——'Petiḥah leshe'elat hasakin vehamazleg' [An Introduction to the Question of the Knife and Fork], *Ha'emet* (1877), 30–40.

——'She'elat hayehudim' [The Jewish Question], *Ha'emet* (1877), 1–5.

——'Shitat makiaveli' [The Method of Machiavelli], *Ha'emet* (1877), 46–50.

——'Toledot dr. yonah ya'akobi umifalotav' [Biography of Dr Johann Jacoby and his Works], *Ha'emet* (1877), 9–12.

——*Writings* (Heb.) (Tel Aviv, 1928).

LIEBESCHÜTZ, H., 'Mendelssohn und Lessing in ihrer Stellung zur Geschichte', in Siegfried Stein and Raphael Loewe (eds.), *Studies in Jewish Religion and Intellectual History Presented to A. Altmann* (Tuscaloosa, Ala., 1979), 167–79.

LILIENBLUM, MOSES LEIB, 'Al devar ha'atakat grets' [On the Translation of Graetz], *Hatsefirah*, 3 (1876), 303, 312.

——'Al devar hatikunim badat' [On Religious Reform], in id., *Complete Works*, i. 91–131.

——'Al hakirat kadmoniyot', in id., *Complete Works*, ii. 110–12.

——'Al het shelo hatanu' [A Sin We Did Not Commit], *Hakol*, 3 (1878), 385.

——*Autobiographical Writings* (Heb.), ed. S. Breiman, 3 vols. (Jerusalem, 1970).

——*Complete Works* (Heb.), 4 vols. (Odessa and Krakow, 1910–13).

——'Derekh teshuvah' [The Way of Repentance], in id., *Autobiographical Writings*, ii. 143–201.

——'Hatot ne'urim' [Sins of Youth]: published in id., *Complete Works* and in id., *Autobiographical Writings*.

——'Kehal refa'im' [Company of Ghosts], in id., *Complete Works*, ii. 413–60.

——*Letters of M. L. Lilienblum to J. L. Gordon* (Heb.), ed. S. Breiman (Jerusalem, 1968).

——'Mahi haskalah?' [What is the Haskalah?], in id., *Complete Works*, ii. 113–16.

——'Midrash soferim' [The Scribes' Midrash], in id., *Complete Works*, i. 53–9.

——'Mishnat elishah ben avuyah' [The Doctrine of Elisha ben Avuyah], *Asefat hakhamim*, 1 (1878), 76, 97–9, 108–13, 125.

——'Nosafot le'orhot hatalmud' [Additions to The Ways of the Talmud], in id., *Complete Works*, i. 32–52.

——'Olam hatohu' [World of Chaos], in id., *Complete Works*, ii. 49–109.

——'Orhot hatalmud' [The Ways of the Talmud], in id., *Complete Works*, i. 7–31.

——'Teshuvah meshuleshet' [A Threefold Reply], *Hakol*, 4 (1879), 305–6.

——'Tikun medini vetikun sifruti' [Political Reform and Literary Reform], *Hashahar*, 2 (1871), 372–3.

——'Tsorkhei amenu veda'at soferav' [The Needs of our People and the Opinion of its Writers], in id., *Complete Works*, ii. 161–76.

LILIENTHAL, MAX, Letter to his father (1842), *Publication of the American Jewish Historical Society*, 35 (1939), 45–9.

LIPETZ, DOV, 'The Karaite in Lithuania', in id. (ed.), *Lithuanian Jewry* (Heb.), vol. i (Tel Aviv, 1959), 138–50.

LIPSCHITZ, JACOB, 'Lahat haherev hamithapekhet' [The Fiery Blade of the Two-Edged Sword], *Halevanon*, 9 (1873), 275–6.

——*Zikhron ya'akov* [Memoirs: History of the Jews of Russia and Poland], 3 vols. (Kovno and Slobodka, 1924–30).

LOEWISOHN, SOLOMON, *Erets kedumim hu sefer mehkarei erets* [An Adaptation of *Mehkarei erets* by Ya'akov Kaplan] (Vilna, 1839).

LOEWISOHN, SOLOMON, *Meḥkarei erets* [A Biblical Geography] (Vienna, 1819).

——*Melitsat yeshurun* [The Poesy of Jeshurun] (Vienna, 1816; repr. Tel Aviv, 1954).

——*Mivḥar ketavav* [Selected Writings] (Jerusalem, 1984).

——*Vorlesungen über die neuere Geschichte der Juden*, vol. i (Vienna, 1820).

LOWENSTEIN, STEVEN M., *The Berlin Jewish Community: Enlightenment, Family and Crisis, 1770–1830* (Oxford, 1994).

——'The Yiddish Written Word in Nineteenth-Century Germany', *Leo Baeck Yearbook*, 24 (1980), 179–92.

LÖWITH, K., *Meaning in History* (London, 1976).

LUZ, EHUD, 'On the Myth of Revival of the Maccabees' (Heb.), *Ha'umah*, 56 (1978), 44–52.

——*Parallels Meet: Religion and Nationalism in the Early Zionist Movement, 1882–1904*, trans. L. J. Schramm (Philadelphia, 1988).

LUZZATTO, SAMUEL DAVID, *Avnei zikaron* [Memorial Stones] (Prague, 1856).

——*Igerot shadal be'ivrit* [Luzzatto's Hebrew Letters], ed. S. E. Graber, 9 vols. (Przemysl and Krakow, 1882–94).

——*Ketavim* [Writings], 2 vols. (Jerusalem, 1976).

——*Meḥkarei hayahadut* [Studies in Judaism] (Warsaw, 1873).

——'Toledot shadal' [Autobiography], *Hamagid*, 2 (1858), 66–7.

MAGID, DAVID, 'List of Articles and Books by Abraham Harkavy', *Memorial Book to Abraham Harkavy* (Heb.) (St Petersburg, 1909).

MAHLER, RAPHAEL, *Hasidism and the Jewish Enlightenment: Their Confrontation in Galicia and Poland in the First Half of the Nineteenth Century*, trans. E. Orenstein, A. Klein, and J. Machlowitz (Philadelphia, 1985).

——*History of the Jewish People in Modern Times* (Heb.), 7 vols. (Tel Aviv, 1960–80).

——'The Sociological and Political Roots of the Haskalah' (Heb.), *Orlogin*, 2 (1951), 61–77.

——'Tolerance and Freedom of Thought in Israel' (Heb.), *Orlogin*, 1 (1950), 85–94.

MAIMON, SOLOMON, *The Autobiography of Solomon Maimon*, trans. J. C. Murray (London, 1954).

——*Givat hamoreh* [The Hill of the Guide], new edn. by S. H. Bergman and Nathan Rotenstreich (Jerusalem, 1965).

——*Lebensgeschichte*, 2 vols. (Berlin, 1792–3).

——*Mafteaḥ korot hafilosofiyah* [The Key to the History of Philosophy] (Berlin, 1791).

MALACHI, A. R., 'Joseph Judah Lerner' (Heb.), *Hado'ar*, 14 (1935), nos. 10, 11.

MALLER, YEHIEL, 'El ir moladeti stanislav!' [To my Native City, Stanislav!], *Kokhavei yitshak*, 13 (1850), 34–7; 7 (1846), 40–5.

——'Yedid hanetraliyut' [The Friend of Neutrality], *Kokhavei yitshak*, 12 (1848), 58–74.

MANDELKERN, SOLOMON, *Ezra hasofer* [Ezra the Scribe] (Vilna, 1866).

——*Sefer divrei yemei rusiyah* [Book of Russian History], 3 vols. (Warsaw, 1877).

MANDELSTAMM, B., *Hazon lamo'ed* [Vision for an Appointed Time], vol. ii (Vienna, 1877).

MAOR, I., 'Historians of Russian Jewry: Ilya Orshansky and the Historiography of Russian Jewry' (Heb.), *He'avar*, 20 (1973), 49–61.

MAPU, ABRAHAM, *Ahavat tsiyon* [The Love of Zion] (Vilna, 1853).

——*Ashmat shomron* [The Guilt of Samaria] (Vilna, 1865–6).

——*Ayit tsavua* [Hypocrisy] (Vilna, 1858, 1861, 1864; 2nd edn. 1869).

——*Collected Works* (Heb.) (Tel Aviv, 1939).

——'Hozei hezyonot' [The Visionaries], in id., *Collected Works*, 453–73.

——'Igeret le'ahiv' [A Letter to his Brother] (1857), Yadin Collection, Manuscripts and Archives Department, National and University Library, Jerusalem (no. 253).

   Mikhtavei avraham mapu [Abraham Mapu's Letters], ed. Ben-Zion Dinur (Jerusalem, 1970).

——'Mikhtavim le'avraham kaplan' [Letters to Abraham Kaplan], *Kiryat sefer*, 6 (1929–30), 571–7.

MARGOLIES, B. M., *Samuel David Luzzato: Traditionalist Scholar* (New York, 1979).

MARKAL-MOSESOHN, MIRIAM, *Hayehudim be'angliyah* [The Jews in England], 2 vols. (Warsaw, 1869, 1895).

MARKON, HAYIM LEIB, 'Ma'aneh lekantor vere'av' [A Reply to H. Kantor and his Friends], *Hakarmel hahodshi*, 4 (1879), 224–32.

MARKUS, R. A., *Saeculum: History and Society in the Theology of St. Augustine* (Cambridge, 1970).

Memorial Book of Mosty-Wielkie (Heb.) (Tel Aviv, 1975).

MENDELE MOKHER SEFORIM. See ABRAMOWITZ, SHALOM JACOB

MENDELSON, JEHIEL, 'Mosheh veyisra'el' [Moses and Israel], *Haboker or*, 3 (1878), 590–614, 648–53.

MENDELSON, MOSES (HAMBURG), *Metsiat ha'arets hahadashah* [The Discovery of the New World] (Altona, 1807).

MENDELSSOHN, MOSES, *Abhandlung über die Evidenz in metaphysischen Wissenschaften* (1763), Hebrew trans. R. Fürstenthal, *Ma'amar haberur hafilosofi* (Warsaw, 1866).

——*Gesammelte Schriften Jubiläumsausgabe*, 24 vols., ed. F. Bamberger *et al.* (Berlin, 1929–38); repr. and continued under the editorship of Alexander Altmann (Stuttgart, 1971–98).

——*Jerusalem*, in id., *Gesammelte Schriften*, viii. 99–204; Heb. trans. A. B. Gottlober (Zhitomir, 1867); Heb. trans. Abraham Gruenbaum Fiodorov (Vienna, 1876).

——*Jerusalem and Other Jewish Writings*, trans. and ed. A. Jospe (New York, 1969).

——*Phaedon* (Berlin, 1767); Heb. trans. I. Beer-Bing (1786–7; Lyck, 1862; Warsaw, 1885).

MENDES, DAVID FRANCO, 'Toledot harav yosef mikandiyah' [Biography of R. Joseph of Crete], *Hame'asef*, 1 (1784), 124–7.

——'Toledot heḥakham hamefo'ar orobiyo' [On the Great Sage, Orobio de Castro], *Hame'asef*, 4 (1788), 219–23.

——'Toledot heḥakham mosheh rafa'el daguilar' [Biography of Moshe Raphael D'Aguilar], *Hame'asef*, 2 (1785), 16–17, 26–7.

MENDES-FLOHR, PAUL R. (ed.), *Modern Jewish Studies: Historical and Philosophical Perspectives* (Heb.) (Jerusalem, 1979).

MEYER, MICHAEL, 'Abraham Geiger's Historical Judaism', in J. Petuchowski (ed.), *New Perspectives on Abraham Geiger: An HUC–JIR Symposium* (Cincinnati, 1975), 3–16.

——'The Emergence of Modern Jewish Historiography: Motives and Motifs', in Ada Rapoport-Albert (ed.), *Essays in Jewish Historiography* (Atlanta, 1991), 160–75.

——'The German Model of Religious Reform and Russian Jewry', in I. Twersky (ed.), *Danzig, between East and West* (Cambridge, Mass., 1985), 67–91.

——*The Origins of the Modern Jew, Jewish Identity and European Culture in Germany, 1749–1824* (Detroit, 1979).

——*Response to Modernity: A History of the Reform Movement in Judaism* (New York and Oxford, 1988).

——(ed.), *The German Rabbinical Conferences, 1844–1846* (Heb.) (Jerusalem, 1986).

MEZAH, JOSHUA (ed.), *Gan peraḥim* [A Garden of Flowers] (Warsaw, 1891).

MICHAEL, REUVEN, 'The Contribution of *Sulamith* to Modern Jewish Historiography' (Heb.), *Zion*, 39 (1974), 86–113.

——'Did the Triumph of the Ideas of "The Enlightenment" at the Start of the French Revolution Cause the Demise of the "Berlin Enlightenment"?' (Heb.), *Zion*, 56 (1991), 275–98.

——*I. M. Jost: Founder of Modern Jewish Historiography* (Heb.) (Jerusalem, 1983).

——*Jewish Historiography from the Renaissance to Modern Times* (Heb.) (Jerusalem, 1993).

——'Peter Beer (1758–1838): Author of the First Monograph on Jewish Sects' (Heb.), in *Proceedings of the Ninth World Congress of Jewish Studies*, division B, vol. ii (Jerusalem, 1986), 1–8.

——'The Renewal of Interest in the History of the Jewish People at the Beginning of the Nineteenth Century' (Heb.) (Ph.D. diss., Hebrew University of Jerusalem, 1975).

——'R. Israel Loebel's German Booklet' (Heb.), *Kiryat sefer*, 51 (1976), 315–23.

——'Solomon Lewinsohn: His Approach to Jewish History', in S. Ettinger (ed.), *Nation and History*, vol. ii (Heb.) (Jerusalem, 1984), 147–62.

MIESES, JUDAH LEIB, 'Al devar sibat he'ader haḥokhmot ha'enoshiyot bivenei amenu' [Why Science is Lacking among our People], *Hatsefirah* (Zolkiew, 1824), 54–69.

——*Kinat ha'emet* [The Zeal for Truth] (Vienna, 1828); repr. in Y. Friedlander, *Hebrew Satire in Europe*, vol. iii (Ramat Gan, 1994).

——'Mikhtav 2' [Letter no. 2], *Kerem ḥemed*, 1 (1833), 129–34.

——'Mikhtavim' [Letters], *Bikurei ha'itim*, 11 (1830), 131–42.

MIKHAL (Micha Joseph Lebensohn), 'Shirei bat tsiyon' [Songs of a Daughter of Zion], in A. D. Lebensohn and id., *Kol shirei adam umikhal* [The Poems of Adam and Mikhal], vol. ii (Vilna, 1895).

MINOR, Z., 'Toledot yemei kedem' [Ancient History], in Israel Wohlmann (ed.), *Hakokhavim* (Vilna, 1865), 118–20.

MINTZ, ALAN, 'Guenzburg, Lilienblum and the Shape of Haskalah Autobiography', *American Jewish Studies Review*, 4 (1979), 71–110.

MIRON, DAN, *From Romance to the Novel: Studies in the Emergence of the Hebrew and Yiddish Novel in the Nineteenth Century* (Heb.) (Jerusalem, 1979).

——*The Traveler Disguised* (New York, 1973).

——*When Loners Come Together: A Portrait of Hebrew Literature at the Turn of the Twentieth Century* (Heb.) (Tel Aviv, 1987).

MIRSKY, SAMUEL K., *Personalities and Figures in Jewish Studies in Eastern Europe* (Heb.) (New York and Tel Aviv, 1959).

M.N., 'Letoledot harav hagaon' [Biography of Rapoport], *Hayahadut*, 1 (1885), 46–7, 83.

MODENA, LEONE (Judah Aryeh), *Leket ketavim* [Selected Writings] (Jerusalem, 1968).

MOHR, ABRAHAM MENAHEM MENDEL, *Dagul merevavah* [One in a Thousand: On Napoleon I] (Czernowitz, 1855).

——*Gibor milḥamah* [A War Hero] (Lvov, 1856).

——*Ḥut hameshulash* [A Triple Thread: On Napoleon III] (Lvov, 1853).

——*Kolombus: hu sefer metsiat erets amerikah* [Columbus: The Discovery of America] (Lvov, 1846).

——*Mikveh yisra'el* [Hope of Israel] (Lvov, 1847).

MÖLLER, H., 'Aufklärung, Judenemanzipation und Staat. Ursprung und Wirkung von Dohms Schrift über die bürgliche Verbesserung der Juden', in W. Grab (ed.), *Deutsche Aufklärung und Emanzipation* (Tel Aviv, 1980), 119–49.

——*Vernunft und Kritik. Deutsche Aufklärung im 17. und 18. Jahrhundert* (Frankfurt am Main, 1986).

MONDSCHEIN, ZELIG, *Imrei yosher* [Just Statements] (Lvov, 1862).

——'Mishpat emet' [A Just Sentence], *Kokhavei yitsḥak*, 10 (1846), 21–32.

MONTESQUIEU, C., *Considerations on the Causes of the Greatness of the Romans and their Decline*, trans. O. Lowenthal (New York, 1965).

——*The Spirit of the Laws*, trans. T. Nugent (New York and London, 1949).

MORPURGO, RACHEL, 'Korot hazeman' [Events of the Time], *Kokhavei yitsḥak*, 14 (1850), 35.

MÜLLER, D., 'Toledot natan heḥakham' [Biography of Nathan the Wise], *Hashaḥar*, 4 (1873), 9–53.

MULLER, SHELOMOH, *Ḥeshek shelomoh* [Solomon's Desire] (Vienna, 1826).

MURHARD, F., 'Früheste Geschichte des Menschengeschlechtes', *Sulamith*, 3 (1811), 152–70.

MYERS, DAVID N., *Re-inventing the Jewish Past* (New York and Oxford, 1995).

NADEL, G., 'Periodization', in *The International Encyclopedia of the Social Sciences*, ed. D. Sills, vol. xi (New York, 1968), 581–4.

——'Philosophy of History before Historicism', *History and Theory*, 3 (1964), 292–315.

NARDI, TSEVIYAH, 'The National Doctrine of Peretz Smolenskin' (Heb.) (Ph.D. diss., Hebrew University of Jerusalem, 1976).

——'Transformations in the Enlightenment Movement in Russia', in Immanuel Etkes (ed.), *Religion and Life: The Jewish Enlightenment in Eastern Europe* (Heb.) (Jerusalem, 1993), 300–27.

NATHANSON, BERNHARD (DOV BAER), *Be'er yitshak* [On I. B. Levinsohn] (Warsaw, 1899).

——*Sefer hazikhronot* [Biography of I. B. Levinsohn] (Warsaw, 1878).

NATHANSON, NATHAN, *Sefat emet: kolel hayei hehaham vehatalmudi mordekhai felungiyan* [The Language of Truth: Including the Life of the Talmudic Scholar, Rabbi Mordechai Plungian] (Warsaw, 1887).

NEANDER, A., *Genetische Entwicklung des vornehmstem gnostischen System* (Berlin, 1818).

NEVAKHOVICH, JUDAH LEIB, *Kol shavat bat yehudah* [The Daughter of Judah Cries Out] (Shklov, 1804), repr. in *He'avar*, 2 (1918), appendix, 1–34.

NISANBOIM, I., *In my Lifetime* (Heb.) (Jerusalem, 1961).

N.K. (pseud.), 'Devarim ahadim mitoledot shelomoh maimon' [Some Words about Solomon Maimon's Life], *Hamagid*, 8 (1864), 29–61.

OFEK, URIEL, *Hebrew Children's Literature: The Beginnings* (Heb.) (Tel Aviv, 1979).

ORENSTEIN, MORDECAI, 'Toledot goyei yemei kedem' [The History of Ancient Peoples], suppl. to *Hashahar*, 10 (1880).

Otsar hasifrut, 5 vols., ed. Shealtiel Graber (Krakow, 1887–96).

PAPERNA, ABRAHAM JACOB, *Collected Writings* (Heb.), ed. Y. Zmora (Tel Aviv, 1952).

——'Kankan hadash male yashan' [A New Vessel Full of Vintage Wine], in id., *Collected Writings*, 7–130.

——'Sihot hayim ve'ofot' [Conversation of Animals and Birds], in id., *Collected Writings*, 344–64.

PATTERSON, DAVID, *Abraham Mapu* (London, 1964).

PELLI, MOSHE, *The Age of Haskalah: Studies in Hebrew Literature of the Enlightenment in Germany* (Leiden, 1979).

——'The Image of Moses Mendelssohn in the Hebrew Haskalah Literature of Germany' (Heb.), *Proceedings of the Fifth World Congress of Jewish Studies (1963)*, vol. iii (Jerusalem, 1972), 182–269.

——*Moses Mendelssohn: Bonds of Tradition* (Heb.) (Tel Aviv, 1972).

PERL, JOSEPH, *Bohen tsadik* [Who Tries the Righteous] (Prague, 1838).

——'Katit lamaor' [Oil for the Lamp], *Kerem hemed*, 2 (1836), 16–39.

——*Luaḥ lishenat 1816* [Calendar for 1816] (Tarnopol, 1816).

——*Megaleh temirin* [Revealer of Secrets] (Vienna, 1819).

——*Über das Wesen der Sekte Chassidim* [On the Essence of Hasidism], vol. i, ed. A. Rubinstein (Jerusalem, 1977).

PERLES, N., 'Al devar to'elet yediat hatoledah' [The Benefit of Historical Knowledge], *Hamagid*, 3 (1859), suppl. to no. 6.

PHILIPPSON, LUDWIG, 'Aufforderung an alle deutsch-lesenden Israeliten zur Gründung einer Israelitischen Literatur-Geselsschaft', *Allgemeine Zeitung des Judentums*, 19 (1855), 87–9.

——'Baruch Spinosa (eine Skizze)', *Sulamith*, 7 (1832), 327–36.

——*Gesammelte Schriften*, 4 vols. (Breslau, 1891).

PHILIPSON, D., *Max Lilienthal: Life and Writing* (New York, 1951).

PIEKARZ, MENDEL, 'The *Uman* Period in the Life of R. Nahman of Bratslav, and its Importance in the Development of Bratslav Hasidic Thought' (Heb.), *Zion*, 36 (1971), 61–87.

PINES, JEHIEL MICHAEL, 'Ḥalifat mikhtavim al devar hanosafot le'orḥot hatalmud' [Concerning the Supplements to 'The Ways of the Talmud'], *Halevanon*, 6 (1869), nos. 21–2.

——*Yaldei ruḥi* [My Spiritual Children], 2 vols. (1872; vol. i repr. Jerusalem, 1934).

PINES, MEIR, *Histoire de la littérature judeo-allemande* (Paris, 1911).

PINSKER, SIMHAH, *Likutei kadmoniyot* [History of Karaism and Karaite Literature] (Vienna, 1860).

PIPES, RICHARD, *Russia under the Old Regime* (Harmondsworth, 1984).

PITLIK, S., 'S. L. Rapoport's Historical Method', *Jewish Quarterly Review*, 31 (1940–1), 123–39.

PLUNGIAN, M., *Sefer ben-porat* [biography of R. Manasseh b. Joseph of Ilya] (Vilna, 1858).

POCOCK, J. G. A., 'Gibbon's *Decline and Fall* and the World View of Late Enlightenment', *Eighteenth Century Studies*, 10 (1977), 287–303.

PÖLITZ, K. H. L., *Die Weltgeschichte für gebildete Leser und Studierende*, 4 vols. (1804; 4th edn. Leipzig, 1824).

PORTER, ROY, *The Enlightenment* (London, 1990).

POSNER, A. T., 'Rabbi Kalman Schulman' (Heb.), *Hatsefirah*, 26 (1899), nos. 23–6, 30–4.

RABINOWITZ, I., *Ben onesh, o maḥazeh korot yamim avaru* [The Punished, or A History Book] (Odessa, 1865).

——*Hamenorah, o yerushah yekarah, maḥazeh korot avaru* [The Lamp, or A Precious Heritage: A History Book] (Odessa, 1866).

RABINOWITZ, T. M., 'The Attitude of the Kabbalah and Hasidism to Maimonides', in J. Fishmann (ed.), *Maimonides* (Heb.) (Jerusalem, 1935), 279–87.

RAEFF, M., *Russian Intellectual History: An Anthology* (New York, 1966).

RAKOWSKI, A. A., *Ḥoter migeza yishai o david elroi* [A Descendant of Jesse: David Elroi] (Warsaw, 1883).

—— *Nidḥei yisra'el* [The Exiled of Israel], Beit Ha'otsar 1 (Warsaw, 1875).

RAPOPORT, SOLOMON JUDAH LEIB (SHIR), 'Al devar yehudim ḥofshi'im hanimtsa'im be'erets arav uve'erets kush ad hayom' [On Jews Living in Arab and African Lands], *Bikurei ha'itim*, 5 (1823), 83.

——'Al mot harav heḥakham hafilosof rabi naḥman krokhmal' [On the Death of the Learned Rabbi and Philosopher R. Nahman Krochmal], *Kerem ḥemed*, 6 (1841), 41–9.

——'Bikoret' [A Review], *Bikurei ha'itim*, 12 (1831), 175–6.

——'El re'a yakar' [To a Dear Friend], *Kerem ḥemed*, 1 (1833), 75–7.

——*Erekh milin* [Talmudic Encyclopedia] (Prague, 1852).

——'Hatselaḥat habayit' [Success of the House], *Bikurei ha'itim*, 1 (1820), 110–13.

——*Igerot shir* [Letters] (Przemysl, 1886).

——Letters to Zunz, *Allgemeine Zeitung des Judentums*, 59 (1895), 236–7.

——'Mikhtav' [Letter], *Bikurei ha'itim*, 7 (1827), 8–24.

——'Mikhtav' [Letter], *Kerem ḥemed*, 4 (1839), 245–7.

——'Mikhtav 3' [Letter no. 3], *Kerem ḥemed*, 3 (1838), 38–53.

——'Mikhtav 3' [Letter no. 3], *Kerem ḥemed*, 6 (1841), 41–9.

——'Mikhtav 5' [Letter no. 5], *Kerem ḥemed*, 7 (1843), 150.

——'Mikhtav 23' [Letter no. 23], *Kerem ḥemed*, 1 (1833), 83–7.

——'Mikhtav larabanim' [A Letter to the Rabbis], *Yeshurun*, 1 (1856), 40–6.

——'Mikhtav lebik' [A Letter to Bick] (Nov. 1830), *Hashaḥar*, 4 (1873), 486.

——'Mikhtav lem. a.' [Letter to M.A.], *Bikurei ha'itim*, 8 (1827), 8–24.

——'Ner mitsvah' [Lamp of the Commandment] (1815), in *Naḥalat yehudah* [The Inheritance of Judah] (Krakow, 1868), 1–26.

[——] Review of Joseph Perl, *Boḥen tsadik*, *Kerem ḥemed*, 4 (1839), 45–57.

——Review of Joseph Perl, *Megaleh temirin*, *Bikurei ha'itim*, 12 (1831), 163–7.

——'She'erit yehudah' [Remnant of Judah], *Bikurei ha'itim*, 8 (1827), 171–254.

[——] *Tekhunat ha'ir paris veha'i elba* [A Description of Paris and the Isle of Elba] (Lvov, 1814).

——*Tokheḥah megulah* [An Open Reproach] (Frankfurt, 1846).

——'Toledot rabenu ḥai gaon' [Biography of Rabbenu Hai Gaon], *Bikurei ha'itim*, 10 (1829), 79–95.

——'Toledot rabenu ḥananel' [Biography of Rabbenu Hananel], *Bikurei ha'itim*, 12 (1831), 1–83.

——'Toledot rabenu natan ba'al he'arukh' [Biography of R. Nathan, Author of the *Arukh*], *Bikurei ha'itim*, 10 (1829), 7–79.

——'Toledot rabenu se'adyah vekorot sefarav' [Biography of R. Sa'adiah and his Books], *Bikurei ha'itim*, 9 (1828), 20–37.

——'Zeman umekom r. ele'azar hakalir' [The Time and Place of R. Eleazar Hakallir], *Bikurei ha'itim*, 10 (1829), 95–123.

RAPOPORT-ALBERT, ADA (ed.), *Essays in Jewish Historiography* (Atlanta, 1991).

RAWIDOWICZ, S., 'R. Nachman Krochmal and his Attitude to Hasidism, Enlightenment and Nationalism' (Heb.), *Hatoren*, 11 (1925), 155–74.

REGGIO, ISAAC SAMUEL, 'Al te'udat zera avraham vetakhlit emunotav' [Testimony to the Descendants of Abraham], *Otsar neḥmad*, 3 (1860), 51–4.

——*Beḥinat hakabalah* [An Examination of the Kabbalah] (Gorizia, 1852).

——'El haḥokerim bekadmoniyot yeshurun' [To Students of Jewish History], *Kerem ḥemed*, 2 (1836), 39–52.

——*Hatorah vahafilosofiyah* [The Torah and Philosophy] (Vienna, 1827).

'Introduction', *Bikurei ha'itim*, 9 (1828), 3.

——'Shenei ḥakhamim gedolim bilti mefursamim' [Two Great Unrenowned Sages], *Bikurei ha'itim*, 11 (1830), 12–14.

——'Toledot heḥakham haḥoker barukh di spinoza' [Biography of Baruch de Spinoza], in *Bikurei ha'itim haḥadashim*, ed. id. and I. Bush (Vienna, 1845), 27–32.

REICHNEU, JOSEL, 'Toledot hazeman' [News], *Hame'asef*, 7 (1794), 68–74.

REIFMANN, JACOB, 'Te'udat harabanim' [A Testimony to the Rabbis], in Israel Wohlmann (ed.), *Hakokhavim* (Vilna, 1865), 60–78.

REILL, P. H., *The German Enlightenment and the Rise of Historicism* (Berkeley, 1975).

——'History and Hermeneutics in the Aufklärung: The Thought of J. C. Gatterer', *Journal of Modern History*, 45 (1973), 24–51.

REISEN, Z., *Lexicon of Yiddish Literature* (Yid.), vol. i (Vilna, 1929).

'Report of the Society for the Promotion of Enlightenment among Jews for 1865' (Heb.), *Hakarmel*, 6 (1866), 49–50.

RESSER, SAMUEL, *Eine kurtze allgemeine Weltgeschichte* [A Short General History of the World] (Vilna, 1863).

——*Koroys yisroel: di alte geshikhte funem folk yisroel* [Jewish History] (Vilna, 1869).

——*Rabah* (Yid.) (Warsaw, 1876).

ROSENTHAL, J., 'Voltaire's Philosophy of History', *Journal of the History of Ideas*, 16 (1955), 166–7.

ROSENTHAL, LEON, *Toledot ḥevrat marbei haskalah beyisra'el be'erets rusiyah* [History of the Society for the Promotion of Enlightenment among the Jews in Russia], 2 vols. (St Petersburg, 1886–90).

ROSKIES, DAVID, 'Isaac Meir Dick: The Artist as a False Magid' (Heb.), *Ḥuliyot*, 1 (1993), 7–47.

——'Isaac Meyer Dik and the Rise of Yiddish Popular Literature' (Ph.D. diss., Brandeis University, 1974).

ROSMAN, MOSHE, 'The History of a Historical Source: On the Editing of *Shivḥei habesht*' (Heb.), *Zion*, 58 (1993), 175–214.

ROSS, I., 'Maimonides and Progress: The Historical View of Maimonides' (Heb.), in Yehezkel Cohen (ed.), *Society and History* (Jerusalem, 1980), 529–48.

ROSTOVSKY-HALPERN, S., *History of Hebrew Literature* (Heb.) (Tel Aviv, 1954).

ROTENSTREICH, NATHAN, *Jewish Existence in the Present Age* (Heb.) (Merhavya and Tel Aviv, 1972).

——*Jewish Philosophy in the Modern Era* (Heb.) (Tel Aviv, 1966).

ROUSSEAU, JEAN-JACQUES, *Confessions*, trans. J. Cohen (London, 1953).

ROZENBERG, SHALOM, 'Getting Back to Heaven: Notes Concerning the Restorative *Ge'ulah* in the Jewish Philosophy of the Middle Ages' (Heb.), in *The Messianic Idea in Israel* (Jerusalem, 1982), 37–86.

RUBIN, SOLOMON, 'Avnei miluim' [Precious Stones], *Hashaḥar*, 7 (1876), 49–55.

——'Ma'aseh bereshit shel hakena'ani sanḥoniton' [On the Caananite Sanchoniton], suppl. to *Hashaḥar*, 3 (1872).

——'Menaḥem habavli hu meni haparsi' [Menahem the Babylonian is Meni the Persian], suppl. to *Hashaḥar*, 4 (1873).

——'Mikhtav mishelomoh rubin' [A Letter from Solomon Rubin], *Kokhavei yitsḥak*, 25 (1860), 103–307.

——*Moreh nevukhim heḥadash* [The New Guide of the Perplexed] (Vienna, 1856).

——*Teshuvah nitsaḥat* [A Crushing Reply] (Lvov, 1859).

——*Uriel Acosta* (Vienna, 1857).

RUBINSTEIN, ABRAHAM, 'The Booklet *Katit lamaor* by Joseph Perl' (Heb.), *Alei sefer*, 3 (1976), 140–57.

RUDERMAN, PESAH, 'Ha'emunah vehasifrut' [Faith and Literature], *Haboker or*, 2 (1877), 176–83.

——'Lema'an yedu' [So They May Know], *Hashaḥar*, 7 (1876), 65–80.

RUPIN, ARTHUR, *The Sociology of the Jews*, i: *The Social Structure of the Jews* (Heb.) (Berlin and Tel Aviv, 1930).

SACHS, SENIOR, 'Kol kore' [A Voice Calls], *Kerem ḥemed*, 8 (1854), 213–20.

SADAN, DOV, introd. to I. M. Dick, *R. shemayah mevarekh hamo'adot vedivrei sipur aḥerim*, ed. D. Sadan (Jerusalem, 1967), 7–15.

SALMON, JOSEPH, 'David Gordon and the Periodical *Hamagid*' (Heb.), *Zion*, 47 (1982), 145–64.

SAMET, MOSHE S., 'M. Mendelssohn, N. H. Wessely, and the Rabbis of their Generation', in A. Gilboa, B. Mevorach, *et al.* (eds.), *Research into the History of the Jewish People and the Land of Israel* (Heb.), vol. i (Haifa, 1970), 233–57.

SANDLER, PEREZ, *Mendelssohn's Edition of the Pentateuch* (Heb.) (Jerusalem, 1984).

SCHENK, H. G., *The Mind of the European Romantics* (Oxford, 1979).

SCHIFFER, FEIVEL, *Devar gevurot* [Heroism] (Warsaw, 1845).

—— *Toledot napoleon* [Biography of Napoleon] (Warsaw, 1849).

SCHLESINGER, ISSACHAR BAER, *Hahashmona'im* [The Hasmoneans] (Prague, 1817).

—— 'Pitagoras ehad mishivah hakhmei yavan' [Pythagoras, One of Greece's Seven Sages], *Bikurei ha'itim*, 12 (1831), 84–101.

SCHOLEM, GERSHOM, 'The First Two Testimonies on the Relation between Hasidic Groups and the Ba'al Shem Tov' (Heb.), *Tarbiz*, 20 (1949), 228–40.

—— 'From Philosopher to Kabbalist (A Legend of the Kabbalists about Maimonides)' (Heb.), in *The Maimonides Book of Tarbiz* (Jerusalem, 1935), 90–8.

—— *Sabbatai Zevi*, trans. R. J. Z. Werblowsky (London, 1973).

SCHORR, JOSHUA HESCHEL, 'Bikoret ma'amar *Magen vetsinah* shel modinah bemahadurat geiger' [A Critique of Geiger's Edition of Modena's *Magen vetsinah*], *Hehaluts*, 3 (1857), 146–8.

[——] 'Carakterıstik der jüdischen Sekten in Galizien', *Allgemeine Zeitung des Judentums*, 2 (1838), 283–4.

—— 'Davar be'ito' [Everything in its Time], *Hehaluts*, 1 (1852), 47–50; 2 (1853), 37–58.

—— 'Masa rabanim' [The Rabbis' Vision], *Hehaluts*, 1 (1852), 36–46; 3 (1857), 47–68.

—— 'Mikhtav lehaver' [Letter to a Friend], *Hehaluts*, 1 (1852), 91–116.

—— 'Odot maskilim tse'irim be'arei mitsar' [On Young Maskilim in Provincial Towns], *Hehaluts*, 3 (1857), 67–8.

—— 'Peshatei dikara' [Meaning of Scripture], *Hehaluts*, 1 (1852), 95–7.

—— 'Rabi aharon el-rabi' [Rabbi Aaron El-Rabi], *Zion*, 1 (1841), 166–8, 193–6.

—— 'Rabi yitshak elbalag' [Rabbi Isaac Elbalag], *Hehaluts*, 4 (1859), 83–94.

—— 'Shenat taryad' [The Year 1854], *Hehaluts*, 3 (1857), 1–19.

—— 'Shenat taryag' [The Year 1853], *Hehaluts*, 2 (1853), 1–12.

—— 'Shivrei luhot' [Broken Tablets], *Hehaluts*, 4 (1859), 53–65.

—— 'Simat ayin al hamishnah vehagemara' [A Look at the Mishnah and the Gemara], *Hehaluts*, 1 (1852), 50–65.

[——] 'Streit zwischen Autorität und Kritik', *Israelitische Annalen*, 1 (1840), 169–72.

SCHORSCH, ISMAR, 'Breakthrough into the Past: The *Verein für Cultur und Wissenschaft der Juden*', *Leo Baeck Yearbook*, 33 (1988), 3–28.

—— 'The Emergence of Historical Consciousness in Modern Judaism', *Leo Baeck Yearbook*, 27 (1983), 413–37.

—— 'Ideology and History in the Age of Emancipation', in H. Graetz (ed.), *The Structure of Jewish History, and Other Essays* (New York, 1975), 1–62.

—— 'The Myth of Sephardic Supremacy', *Leo Baeck Yearbook*, 34 (1989), 47–66.

—— 'The Production of a Classic: Zunz as Krochmal's Editor', *Leo Baeck Yearbook*, 31 (1986), 281–315.

SCHULMAN, KALMAN, 'Arba'ah mikhtavim mi'et shulman' [Four Letters by Schulman], *Reshumot*, 2 (1922), 410–13.

——*Divrei yemei hayehudim* [History of the Jews] (Vienna, 1876); Heb. trans. of pt. 1 of Heinrich Graetz, *Geschichte der Juden*.

——*Divrei yemei olam* [World History], 9 vols. (Vilna, 1867–84).

——*Halikhot kedem* [Ancient Customs] (Vilna, 1854).

——'Hamasa la'ir hamelukhah peterburg' [Journey to St Petersburg], *Hakarmel*, 6 (1867), 273–4.

——*Harel* [Mountain of God] (Vilna, 1866).

——*Harisot beitar* [The Ruins of Betar: On Bar Kokhba's Heroism] (Vilna, 1858; 1884).

——*Kadmoniyot hayehudim* [Jewish Antiquities] (Vilna, 1864).

——*Kiryat melekh rav: toledot peterburg habirah* [City of the Great King: The History of St Petersburg] (Vilna, 1869).

——*Mehkarei erets rusiyah* [Studies of Russia] (Vilna, 1869).

——'Mikhtav galuy' [Open Letter], *Hatsefirah*, 3 (1876), 262–3.

——'Mikhtavim' [Letters], *Reshumot*, 2 (1922), 410–12.

——*Milhamot hayehudim*, 2 vols. (Vilna, 1862–3); Heb. trans. of Josephus Flavius, *The Jewish Wars*.

——*Mosadei erets: tehunot kol artsei tevel vetoledot yoshveihen* [The Foundations of the World: The Features of All Countries and the History of their Inhabitants], 10 vols. (Vilna, 1871–7).

——*Sefer ariel* [The Book of Ariel] (Vilna, 1856).

——*Shevilei erets hakedoshah* [Paths of the Holy Land] (Vilna, 1870).

——*Shulamit* (Vilna, 1855).

——'Toledot harav naftali herts veseli' [Biography of R. Naphtali Herz Wessely], introd. to Naphtali Herz Wessely, *Divrei shalom ve'emet* (Warsaw, 1886).

——*Toledot hakhmei yisra'el*, 4 vols. [Biographies of Jewish Sages] (Vilna, 1873; 1879).

——*Toledot yosef* [Biography of Josephus Flavius] (Vilna, 1859).

——'Toledot yosef ben matitiyah hakohen hamashuah hamekhuneh flavius yosefus' [Biography of Josephus], *Hakarmel*, 1 (1860), 79–80, 87, 95–6.

——'Tseror igerot ley. l. gordon' [Collection of Letters to J. L. Gordon], *Me'asef*, 1 (Jerusalem, 1960), 536–53.

SCHULMANN, ELEAZAR, 'Mimekor yisra'el' [Of Jewish Origin], *Hashahar*, 7 (1876), suppl.

SCHWEID, ELIEZER, *Jewish Thought in the Twentieth Century*, trans. from Hebrew by A. Hadary (Atlanta, 1992).

SCOTT, H. M. (ed.), *Enlightened Absolutism, Reform and Reformers in Later Eighteenth Century Europe* (London, 1990).

SEDINOVA, J., 'The Hebrew Historiography in Moravia in the Eighteenth Century: Abraham Treibitsch', *Judaica Bohemiae*, 10 (1974), 51–61.

SEMLER, J. S., *Übersetzung der Allgemeine Welthistorie*, vol. xxviii (Halle, 1765).

SFORNO, OBADIAH, *Be'ur al hatorah* [Commentary on the Pentateuch] (Jerusalem, 1992).

SHA'ANAN, ABRAHAM, *The New Hebrew Literature* (Heb.) (Tel Aviv, 1967).

SHAPIRA, TUVIAH PESAH, *Sipurim* [Stories], Beit Ha'otsar 3 (Warsaw, 1876).

——'Toledot hehakham r. shabatai meshorer bas' [Biography of the Scholar R. Shabbetai Meshorer Bass], *Hakarmel hahodshi*, 2 (1873), 111–24.

SHATZKY, JACOB, *Kultur geshikhte fun der haskalah in vilna* [Cultural History of the Haskalah in Vilna] (Buenos Aires, 1950).

SHAVIT, YA'AKOV, *Athens in Jerusalem*, trans. C. Naor and N. Werner (London, 1997).

——'King Herod: A Historical Personality Looking for a Writer' (Heb.), *Idan*, 5 (1985), 166–80.

——'The Return to Zion in Hibat Zion' (Heb.), *Hatsiyonut*, 9 (1984), 359–72.

——'Truth shall Spring out of the Earth: The Development of Jewish Popular Interest in Archaeology in Erets Israel' (Heb.), *Cathedra*, 44 (1987), 27–54.

——'Window on the World' (Heb.), *Kesher*, 4 (Nov. 1988), 3–10.

——'The Works of H. T. Buckle and their Application by the Maskilim of Eastern Europe' (Heb.), *Zion*, 49 (1984), 401–12.

SHAVIT, ZOHAR, 'Literary Interference between German and Jewish Hebrew Children's Literature during the Enlightenment: The Case of Campe', *Poetics Today*, 13 (1992), 41–61.

SHELLY, HAYIM, *The Study of the Bible in the Literature of the Haskalah* (Heb.) (Jerusalem, 1942).

SHENFELD, BARUCH, 'Ha'adam' [On Man], *Bikurei ha'itim*, 6 (1825), 83–5.

——'Hithavut haserarah' [On the Formation of Government], *Bikurei ha'itim*, 9 (1828), 158–67.

——'Ma'amar hahanhagah' [On Leadership], *Bikurei ha'itim*, 7 (1826), 34–44.

——'Mikhtav mito'elet derishat korot kedem' [On the Benefit of the Study of History], *Bikurei ha'itim*, 10 (1829), 71–4.

——'Orhot kedem' [On History], *Bikurei ha'itim*, 10 (1829), 60–70.

——'To'elet derishat korot hayamim' [The Benefit of Studying History], *Hamagid*, 1 (1857), 125.

SHENFELD, RUTH, 'The Hebrew Historical Novel in the Twentieth Century' (Heb.) (Ph.D. diss., Hebrew University of Jerusalem, 1981).

SHMERUK, CHONE, 'Authentic and Imaginative Elements in Joseph Perl's *Megaleh Temirin*' (Heb.), *Zion*, 21 (1956), 92–9.

——*Yiddish Literature: Chapters in its History* (Heb.) (Tel Aviv, 1978).

SHOHAM, HAYIM, *'Nathan Der Weise' among his Own* (Heb.) (Tel Aviv, 1981).

SHOHET, AZRIEL, *Changing Eras: The Beginning of the Haskalah among German Jewry* (Heb.) (Jerusalem, 1960).

SHOHET, AZRIEL, *The Crown Rabbinate in Russia: A Chapter in the Cultural Struggle between Jews and Maskilim* (Heb.) (Haifa, 1975).

——'Symbols and Folklore in Hibat Zion' (Heb.), *Shivat tsiyon*, 2–3 (1951–2), 228–50.

SICULAR, HAYIM JOSEPH, 'El ro'ei yisra'el' [To the Shepherds of Israel], *Hamelits*, 8 (1868), nos. 39, 41, 43.

SIEDEFELD, GABRIEL, 'Hashivui' [Equality], *Bikurei ha'itim*, 7 (1826), 82–4.

SILBER, MICHAEL K., 'The Historical Experience of German Jewry and its Impact on Haskalah and Reform in Hungary', in Jacob Katz (ed.), *Toward Modernity* (New Brunswick, NJ, and Oxford, 1987), 107–57.

——'Roots of the Schism in Hungarian Jewry' (Heb.) (Ph.D. diss., Hebrew University of Jerusalem, 1985).

SINKOFF, NANCY B., 'Tradition and Transition: Mendel Lefin of Satanow and the Beginning of the Jewish Enlightenment in Eastern Europe 1749–1826' (Ph.D. diss., Columbia University, 1996).

SLUTSKY, YEHUDA, 'The Emergence of a Russo-Jewish Intelligentsia' (Heb.), *Zion*, 25 (1960), 212–37.

——*The Haskalah Movement among the Jews of Russia* (Heb.) (Jerusalem, 1977).

——*The Russian Jewish Press in the Nineteenth Century* (Heb.) (Jerusalem, 1970).

SMOLENSKIN, PEREZ, 'Am olam' [Eternal People], in id., *Ma'amarim*, i. 1–163.

——'Atah aromem, atah anaseh!' [Now I Will Praise!], *Hashahar*, 8 (1877), 128–34.

——'Et la'asot' [A Time to Act], in id., *Ma'amarim*, i. 170–8.

——'Et lata'at' [A Time to Plant], in id., *Ma'amarim*, ii. 290–3.

——'Even yisra'el' [The Rock of Israel], *Hashahar*, 1 (1869), no. 3, pp. 5–8; no. 4, pp. 3–8; no. 6, pp. 2–7; no. 11, pp. 73–91.

——'Hosafah letoledot [yosef rabinovits] me'et hamotsi la'or' [Supplement to the Biography of Joseph Rabinowicz by the Publisher], *Hashahar*, 6 (1875), 23–5.

——*Kevurat hamor* [A Donkey's Burial] (1874), ed. D. Weinfeld (Jerusalem, 1969).

——'Lelamed livenei yehudah keshet!' [Teach the Children of Judah to Shoot!], *Hashahar*, 2 (1871), 361–3.

——'Le'ohavei *Hashahar*' [To the Friends of *Hashahar*], *Hashahar*, 7 (1876), 261–8.

——*Ma'amarim* [Articles], 3 vols. (Jerusalem, 1925).

——'Mishpat haruts' [A Firm Decision], *Hashahar*, 3 (1872), 257–70, 313–30.

——'Petah devar' [Preface], *Hashahar*, 1 (1869), pp. iii–vi.

——'Toledot harav eli'ezer halevi horovits' [Biography of Rabbi Eliezer Halevi Horowitz], *Hashahar*, 1 (1869), appendix.

SOBEL, ZALMAN, *Sefer dorot olamim* [Book of Past Generations] (Warsaw, 1865).

SOKOLOW, NAHUM, *Baruch Spinoza and his Time* (Heb.) (Paris, 1928).

——'David Frishmann' (Heb.) (1923), in *Personalities* (Jerusalem, 1958), 281–3.

——'Hayehudi vahafilosof' [The Jew and the Philosopher], *Hatsefirah*, 3 (1876), 151–2, 159, 167–8, 175.

——*Ketavim* [Writings], iii: *Hatsofeh leveit yisra'el* (Jerusalem, 1961).

——'Kol mevaser' [A Voice Announces], in id., *Ketavim*, iii. 573–81.

——'Lamenatse'ah al shigayon' [To the Choirmaster], *Hatsefirah*, 3 (1877), 399.

——*Toledot hayehudim*, vol. i, adapted from S. Graetz, *Geschichte der Juden* (Warsaw, 1905).

SORKIN, DAVID, *The Berlin Haskalah and German Religious Thought* (London and Portland, Oreg., 2000).

——'From Context to Comparison: The German Haskalah and Reform Catholicism', *Tel Aviver Jahrbuch für deutsche Geschichte*, 20 (1991), 23–58.

——'The Impact of Emancipation on German Jewry: A Reconsideration', in J. Frankel and S. J. Zipperstein (eds.), *Assimilation and Community: The Jews in Nineteenth-Century Europe* (Cambridge, 1992).

——*Moses Mendelssohn and the Religious Enlightenment* (London, 1996).

——*The Transformation of German Jewry, 1780–1840* (Oxford, 1987).

SPICEHANDLER, E., 'J. H. Schorr, Maskil and Reformist', *Hebrew Union College Annual*, 31 (1960), 122–81; 40–1 (1970–1), 503–28.

SPITZ, I. T., 'Toledot rabi avraham ben ezra' [Biography of Rabbi Abraham ben Ezra], *Bikurei ha'itim*, 7 (1826), 49–55.

STANFORD, M., *The Nature of Historical Knowledge* (Oxford, 1987).

STANISLAWSKI, MICHAEL, *'For Whom Do I Toil?' Judah Leib Gordon and the Crisis of Russian Jewry* (New York, 1988).

——*Tsar Nicholas I and the Jews: The Transformation of Jewish Society in Russia, 1825–1855* (Philadelphia, 1983).

STANISLAWSKI, S., 'Toledot yisra'el balashon harusit' [Jewish History in the Russian Language], *Hashilo'ah*, 2 (1897), 359–64.

STEINBERG, BERNARD, 'Nahman Krochmal and Hermann Cohen, and the Influence of Maimonides on their Thought' (Heb.) (Ph.D. diss., Hebrew University of Jerusalem, 1985).

STEINBERG, JOSHUA, *Or layesharim* [A Light to the Righteous] (Vilna, 1866).

[STERNHARZ, NATAN, OF NEMIROV], *Sefer makhnia zedim* [Subduing the Evildoers] (Jerusalem, 1982).

STRASSBURGER, B., *Geschichte der Erziehung und des Unterrichts bei den Israeliten* (Stuttgart, 1885).

STRELISKER, MORDECAI, 'Al devar hato'elet misipurei korot shenot dor vador' [On the Value of History], *Bikurei ha'itim*, 6 (1830), 142–6.

STROMBERG, R. N., 'History in the Eighteenth Century', *Journal of the History of Ideas*, 12 (1951), 294–303.

TAL, URIEL, *Christians and Jews in Germany: Religion, Politics and Ideology in the Second Reich (1870–1914)*, trans. N. J. Jacobs (Ithaca, NY, 1975).

TALMON, JACOB, *The Origins of Totalitarian Democracy* (New York, 1960).

——*Political Messianism: The Romantic Phase* (Boulder, Colo., 1985).

TARNOPOL, JOACHIM, 'Hashpa'at hamamlakhot haneorot veruah hazeman al mahalakh hishtalmut ha'ivrim umatsavam hamedini' [Influence of the Enlightened Lands and the *Zeitgeist* on the Progress and Political Situation of the Jews], *Hamagid*, 3 (1895), 87–8, 96, 103–4, 107–8, 110–11, 115–16.

TAUBES, J., 'Nachman Krochmal and Modern Historicism', *Judaism*, 12 (1963), 150–64.

TCHERIKOWER, ELIAHU, 'The Jewish Masses, the Maskilim, and the Government during the Reign of Nicholas I' (Heb.), *Zion*, 4 (1939), 150–69.

——*Jews in Time of Revolution* (Heb.) (Tel Aviv, 1958).

TELEKS, I., 'Abraham Goldberg' (Heb.), *Gazit*, 11–12, no. 6 (1944), 43–4.

THOMPSON, J. W., *A History of Historical Writing*, 2 vols. (New York, 1942).

TOLSTOY, LEO, *War and Peace*, trans. L. and A. Maude (Chicago, 1952).

TOPOVER, JACOB, 'Kol haderor' [The Voice of Freedom], *Kokhavei yitshak*, 15 (1851), 64–7.

TOURY, Y., *Between Revolution, Reaction, and Emancipation: A Social and Political History of the Jews in Germany in 1841–1871* (Heb.) (Tel Aviv, 1978).

——*Die jüdische Presse im österreichischen Kaiserreich 1802–1918* (Tübingen, 1983).

TRIEBESCH, ABRAHAM, *Korot ha'itim* [A History] (Brienne, 1801); ed. Jacob Bodek (Lvov, 1851).

TSAMRIYON, TSEMAH, *Hame'asef: The First Modern Periodical in Hebrew* (Heb.) (Tel Aviv, 1988).

——'The Promotion of Culture and Education in *Hame'asef*' (Heb.), *Studies in Education*, 28 (1981), 5–50.

TURGENEV, IVAN, *Fathers and Sons*, trans. Rosemary Edmonds (Harmondsworth, 1986).

TWERSKY, ISADOR, *Introduction to the Code of Maimonides* (New York, 1980).

URBACH, EPHRAIM E., 'Halakhah and History', in Jacob Neusner (ed.), *Jews, Greeks and Christians: Religious Cultures in Late Antiquity*, Studies in Judaism in Late Antiquity 21 (Leiden, 1976), 112–28.

VINCHEVSKY, MORRIS (BENZION NOVAKHOVICH), 'Al ha'ovna'im' [On the Potter's Wheel], *Hakol*, 4 (1879), 307–8, 324.

——'Hezyonot ish haruah' [Visions of an Intellectual], *Asefat hakhamim*, 1 (1878), 105–8, 119, 135–6.

——'Panim hadashot' [New Faces], *Asefat hakhamim*, 1 (1878), 25–6.

——'She'elat hapo'alim be'artsot haberit' [The Question of the Workers in the United States], *Asefat hakhamim*, 1 (1878), 3–7.

——'Shomer mah milailah' [Watchman, What of the Night?], *Asefat hakhamim*, 1 (1878), 26–7.

——'Toledot ludvig barnea' [Biography of Ludwig Börne], *Asefat hakhamim*, 1 (1878), 47, 72–5, 92–5.

VOLTAIRE, *The Age of Louis XIV and Other Selected Writings*, trans. J. H. Brumfitt (New York, 1963).

——*Philosophical Dictionary* (1764), trans. T. Bestermant (New York, 1971).

——*The Philosophy of History* (London, 1766; New York, 1965).

VYVERBERG, H., *Historical Pessimism in the French Enlightenment* (Cambridge, 1958).

WACHLER, L., *Lehrbuch der Literaturgeschichte* (Leipzig, 1827).

WALICKI, A., *A History of Russian Thought* (Stanford, Calif., 1979).

WARSHAVSKY, ISAAC, *Sefer toledot yisra'el* [A Book of Jewish History] (Odessa, 1867).

WEBER, G., *Allgemeine Weltgeschichte*, 15 vols. (Leipzig, 1857–81, 1882).

——*Lehrbuch der Weltgeschichte* (1846; Leipzig, 1888).

WEINRYB, DOV, 'A. S. Lieberman: The Development of his Convictions' (Heb.), *Zion*, 4 (1939), 317–48.

——'On the Biography of R. Isaac Baer Levinsohn' (Heb.), *Tarbiz*, 5 (1934), 199–207.

WERSES, SHMUEL, 'Autobiography in the Haskalah' (Heb.), *Gilyonot*, 17 (1945), 175–83.

——'Between Two Worlds: Jacob Samuel Bick between Haskalah and Hasidism: A New Scrutiny' (Heb.), *Gal-ed*, 9 (1986), 27–76.

——'Echoes of Lucian's Satire in Hebrew Enlightenment Literature' (Heb.), *Criticism and Interpretation*, 11–12 (1978), 84–119.

——'The Expulsion from Spain as Reflected in Haskalah Literature' (Heb.), *Pe'amim*, 57 (1993), 48–81.

——'The French Revolution as Reflected in Hebrew Literature' (Heb.), *Tarbiz*, 58 (1989), 483–521.

——'Hasidism and Haskalah Literature' (Heb.), *Molad*, 18 (1960), 379–91.

——*Haskalah and Shabbateanism: The Story of a Controversy* (Heb.) (Jerusalem, 1988).

——'Highways and Byways in the Study of Haskalah Literature' (Heb.), *Jerusalem Studies in Hebrew Literature*, 12 (1992), 7–28.

——'Legends about the Ten Tribes and the Sambatyon in Modern Hebrew Literature' (Heb.), *Jerusalem Studies in Jewish Folklore*, 9 (1986), 38–66.

——'Mordechai Plungian: Portrait of a Typical Vilna Maskil', in Stanley Nash (ed.), *Between History and Literature: A Jubilee Book in Honour of Yitshak Barzilay* (Heb.) (Tel Aviv, 1997), 149–60.

——'On the Track of the Lost Book *Mahkimat Peti*' (Heb.), *Kiryat sefer*, 55 (1980), 379–7.

——'The Relationship between Belletristic Literature and Jewish Wissenschaft in the Haskalah Period' (Heb.), *Tarbiz*, 55 (1986), 567–602.

——'Samuel David Luzzato in his Own Eyes' (Heb.), *Me'asef*, 5–6 (1965), 703–15.

——*Story and Source: Studies in the Development of Hebrew Prose* (Heb.) (Ramat Gan, 1971).

——'The Unknown Original Version of Samuel Jacob Bick's Letter to Tobias Feder' (Heb.), *Kiryat sefer*, 58 (1983), 170–87.

WERSES, SHMUEL, 'An Unknown Satirical Work by Joseph Perl: The Periodical *Kerem hemed* and its Contributors as Seen by a Hasid' (Heb.), *Hasifrut*, 1 (1968), 206–17.

——*The Yiddish Translations of 'Ahavat tsiyon' by Abraham Mapu* (Heb.) (Jerusalem, 1989).

——(ed.), *Trends and Forms in Haskalah Literature* (Heb.) (Jerusalem, 1990).

WESSELY, NAPHTALI HERZ, *Divrei shalom ve'emet* [Words of Peace and Truth], 4 vols. (Berlin, 1782–5; 2nd edn. Vienna, 1826).

——'Magid hadashot' [The Teller of News], *Hame'asef*, 6 (1790), 129–60, 257–76.

——*Shirei tiferet* [Songs of Glory] (Berlin and Prague, 1789–1811; Warsaw, 1858).

WIDOVER, HALEVI HAYIM GERSHON, 'Hayehudim uleshonot eiropah' [The Jews and European Languages], *Hamagid*, 3, (1859), 37, 41, 49, 53–4, 61, 65, 69.

——'Mifalot hakhmei dorenu' [The Wonders of our Generation's Sages], *Hamagid*, 2 (1858), 69, 73–4.

WIENER, MAX, *Jüdische Religion im Zeitalter der Emanzipation*, trans. into Heb. from German by Leah Zagagi (Jerusalem, 1974).

WILENSKY, MORDECAI, *Hasidism and Mitnagedim: A Study of the Controversy between them in 1772–1815* (Heb.) (Jerusalem, 1970).

WISTRICH, ROBERT, *The Jews in Vienna in the Age of Franz Joseph* (Oxford, 1990).

——'The Modernization of Viennese Jewry: The Impact of German Culture in a Multi-Ethnic State', in Jacob Katz (ed.), *Toward Modernity* (New Brunswick, NJ and Oxford, 1987), 43–70.

WOLF, IMMANUEL, 'Über den Begriff einer Wissenschaft des Judentums', *Zeitschrift für Wissenschaft des Judentums*, 1 (1822–3), 1–24.

WOLFSOHN-HALLE, AARON, *Avtalyon* [Bible Stories for Schoolchildren] (Berlin, 1806).

——*Mavo lebe'ur lemegilat rut* [Introduction to Commentary on the Book of Ruth] (Berlin, 1788).

——'Sihah be'erets hahayim' [Conversation in the Land of the Living], *Hame'asef*, 7 (1794–7), 54–67, 120–53, 203–28, 279–98; repr. in Y. Friedlander (ed.), *Studies in Hebrew Satire*, i: *Hebrew Satire in Germany* (Heb.) (Tel Aviv, 1979).

Yerushalayim, 3 vols., ed. Jacob Bodek, Nahman Fishman, and Abraham Mendel Mohr (Zolkiew, 1844; Lvov, 1845; Prague, 1845).

YERUSHALMI, YOSEF HAYIM, *Zakhor: Jewish History and Jewish Memory* (Seattle, 1982).

YOVEL, YIRMIYAHU, *Kant and the Philosophy of History* (Heb.) (Jerusalem, 1988).

Y. SH. P. A., 'Yitshak ba'er levinson mikremnits' [I. B. Levinsohn of Kremnitz], *Hamagid*, 7 (1863), 357, 373, 381, 389, 397–8.

ZACUTO, ABRAHAM, *Sefer yuhasin hashalem* [Book of Genealogy] (London and Edinburgh, 1857).

ZALKIN, MORDECHAI, 'The Jewish Enlightenment in Russia 1800–1860' (Heb.) (Ph.D. diss., Hebrew University of Jerusalem, 1996).

——'The Vilna Haskalah (1835–1860)' (Heb.) (MA diss., Hebrew University of Jerusalem, 1992).

ZALKIND, S. Z., 'Korot yediat toledot hateva' [A History of the Natural Sciences], *Hakarmel*, 1 (1861), 106–7, 230–1, 237–8.

ZAMOSC, DAVID, *Nahar me'eden* [River from Eden: A Jewish History] (Breslau, 1837).

ZEDERBAUM, A., *Leket ma'amarim* [Collection of Articles] (St Petersburg, 1889).

ZIEZLING, B. Z., 'Gevul olam' [Boundary of the World], *Hakarmel hahodshi*, 1 (1872), 471.

ZINBERG, ISRAEL, *A History of Jewish Literature*, 12 vols., trans. B. Martin (New York, 1972–8).

ZIPPERSTEIN, STEVEN, 'Haskalah, Cultural Change, and Nineteenth Century Russian Jewry: A Reassessment', *Journal of Jewish Studies*, 35 (1983), 191–207.

——*The Jews of Odessa: A Cultural History* (Stanford, Calif., 1985).

——'Transforming the Heder: Maskilic Politics in Imperial Russia', in Ada Rapoport-Albert and id. (eds.), *Jewish History: Essays in Honour of C. Abramsky* (London, 1988), 87–109.

ZITRON, SAMUEL LEIB, 'The Dynastic Struggle in the Volozhin Yeshiva' (Heb.), *Reshumot*, 1 (1925), 123–35.

——*The Makers of the New Hebrew Literature* (Heb.) (Vilna, 1922).

ZOHAR, NAOMI, *Olelot mibatsir: Haskalah, Hasidism and Mitnagedim in Neglected Literary Works* (Heb.) (Jerusalem, 1987).

ZUCKERMAN, A., 'Katalog hasefarim' [Catalogue of Books], *Hashahar*, 8 (1877), suppl. to no. 5.

ZUNZ, LEOPOLD, *Die gottesdienstlichen Vorträge der Juden* (Berlin, 1832); trans. M. A. Jack as *Haderashot beyisra'el vehishtalshelutan hahistorit* (Jerusalem, 1954).

——'Toledot r. azariyah de rosi' [Biography of R. Azariah de' Rossi], *Kerem hemed*, 5 (1841), 131–58.

ZUPNIK, AARON, 'Setirat zekenim binyan' [Against the Destruction of Mendelssohn's Image], *Haboker or*, 2 (1877), 217–20, 291–3.

ZWEIFEL, ELIEZER TSEVI HAKOHEN, 'Hakham be'einav ba'al talmud uva'al agadah yahkereinu' [On the Ba'al Shem Tov, the Vilna Gaon, and Mendelssohn], *Hamagid*, 5 (1861), suppl. to no. 10.

——*Heshbono shel olam* [Reckoning of the World] (Warsaw, 1878).

——'Mikhtavo leharkavy mishenat 1880' [Letter of 1880 to A. Harkavy], *Reshumot*, 6 (1930), 512–13.

——*Minim veugav* [Flute and Strings] (Vilna, 1858).

——'Misped' [Eulogy], *Hashahar*, 6 (1876), 188–91.

——*Sanegor* [Defence Counsel] (Warsaw, 1885).

——*Shalom al yisra'el* [Peace upon Israel], 4 vols. (i: Zhitomir, 1868; ii: Zhitomir, 1869; iii, pt. 1: Zhitomir, 1870, pt. 2: Vilna, 1873; iv: Zhitomir, 1873); ed. Abraham Rubinstein (Jerusalem, 1973).

——'Teshuvah lemithasdei uman' [A Reply to the Hasidim of Uman], *Hakarmel*, 1 (1862), 110–11.

ZWEIFEL, ELIEZER TSEVI HAKOHEN, 'Toledot eli'ezer tsevi tseveifel ketuvot biyedei atsmo' [Autobiography], *Otsar hasifrut*, 2 (1888), 274–6.

——'Tsidkat hashem' [The Righteousness of the Almighty], *Hamelits*, 1 (1861), nos. 45–7.

——'Zikaron livenei yisra'el o asham ḥasidim' [A Memorial for the Children of Israel or the Guilt Offering of Hasidim], in id., *Shalom al yisra'el*, iii, pt. 2, appendix, 127–35.

Index